The Kula

New Perspectives on Massim
Exchange

Necklace

Armshell

The Kula

New Perspectives on Massim Exchange

edited by
JERRY W. LEACH
and
EDMUND LEACH

CAMBRIDGE UNIVERSITY PRESS

CAMBRIDGE
LONDON   NEW YORK   NEW ROCHELLE
MELBOURNE   SYDNEY

Published by the Press Syndicate of the University of
Cambridge
The Pitt Building, Trumpington Street, Cambridge CB2 1RP
32 East 57th Street, New York, NY 10022, USA
296 Beaconsfield Parade, Middle Park, Melbourne 3206,
Australia

First Published 1983

Printed in Great Britain at the
University Press, Cambridge

Library of Congress catalogue card number: 82 4142

British Library Cataloguing in Publication data

The Kula: new perspectives on Massim exchange.
1. Economics, Primitive—Papua New Guinea
I. Leach, E.R.   II. Leach, Jerry W.
381'.0995'3   GN671.N5

ISBN 0 521 23202 3

wv

Contents

Contents

Preface

This volume has been developed from the Proceedings of the Kula and Massim Exchange Conference held at King's College, Cambridge in July 1978. Most of the essays presented here are revisions of papers originally prepared for the Conference though others have been written subsequently. It has not been practical to publish the full proceedings of the Conference and the reader will find that occasional oblique cross-reference is made to unpublished items.

The general objective of the Conference was to assemble a comprehensive 'picture' of the *kula* as it is currently practised and to relate this record to earlier accounts both of the kula and of analogous wide ranging exchange systems in the same region. Malinowski's original (1922) description of the kula had a profound influence on the subsequent development of anthropological theory and practise. Modern developments in that theory, together with very recent advances in ethnographic understanding, and major changes in the political and economic organisation of the region made a reassessment of Malinowski's innovative study particularly timely.

Of the twenty-three participants in the Conference, seventeen had had recent fieldwork experience in the Massim area. Seven of these studies had been on islands where the kula had not previously been directly observed. Martha Macintyre prepared *The Kula: a Bibliography* as an adjunct to the project. This is published separately. J. W. Leach was the principal organizer of the Conference and the principal editor of this volume. The identity of surnames of the two co-editors is a coincidence. The editorial Introduction by J. W. Leach and the editorial Conclusion by E. R. Leach are entirely independent productions and neither of us is in any way responsible for the views expressed by the other. J. W. Leach's status is that of an anthropologist with extensive, recent, first hand experience of the kula region; E. R. Leach's status is that of a senior anthropologist who was at one time a pupil of Malinowski.

Preface

We acknowledge with gratitude the financial and other support provided by the (British) Social Science Research Council, the King's College Research Centre and the Esperanza Trust for Anthropological Research. Many of the participants received generous financial support from their home institutions.

E.R.L.

J.W.L.

Massim name-locator map. 1:1,000,000

This map includes almost all of the Milne Bay Province.
Based on Woodlark Island (3095), fourth edition, produced by Australian
Division of National Mapping, 1973.

ISLAND INDEX
(local term in capitals if known)

1. ANAGUSA, Bentley
2. BAGAMAN
3. BASILAKI, Moresby
4. BUDADAN, Budelun, Budibud, Nada, Naal, Nadili
5. DADAHAI, Dedehai
6. DOBU, Goulvain, Edugaura
7. DUGUMENU, Digumenu
8. Fergusson, Bwaiowa, Moratau
9. GAWA, Lougaw, Guawag
10. Goodenough, Morata
11. GUMAWANA, Gumasila, Gumasi, Urasi
12. HEMENAHA, Flat
13. IWA, Jouveney, Iw
14. KAILEUNA, Kayleula
15. KAWA
16. KIMUTA
17. KIRIWINA, Trobriands, Boyowa, Kilivila
18. KITAI
19. KITAVA, Jurien, Nowau
20. KOYAGAUGAU, Dawson, Kainawari, Ole, Gaboyin
21. KUANAK, Gigila
22. KUYAWA, Kuia, Kuiao
23. KWALAIWA, Watts, Kwaraywa, Kolaiwa
24. KWATOITA, Wawiwa
25. KWEAWATA, Kweiwata
26. MISIMA, St Aignan, Masima, Malek
27. MNUWATA, Munuwata, Manata
28. MOTURINA, Motorina
29. MUWA, Muwo
30. MUYUW, Woodlark, Murua, Myuwa, Muluwa
31. MWADAU, Madau
32. NABWAGETA, Nabogeta, Tuboa
33. NALUWALUWALI, Skelton, Naramarawai
34. NASIKWABU, Alcester, Tokuna, Tokona
35. NIGAHAU, Nigaho
36. NIMOWA, Nimoa
37. NIVANI
38. Normanby, Duau, Duaua
39. NUAKATA
40. NUAMATA, Nuama
41. NURATU
42. PANABARLI, Panabari
43. PANABUSUNA
44. PANAEATI, Deboyne, Panniet
45. PANAMAN
46. PANAPOMPOM
47. PANATINANI, Joannet
48. PANAUMARA, Palakelu, Pananumara
49. PANAWINA
50. ROGEIA, Rogea, Logea
51. SABARL, Sabara, Owen Stanley
52. SAMARAI
53. SANAROA, Welle, Magaru
54. SIMSIM
55. TEWARA, Tewala, Tauwara
56. TEWATEWA, Hummock
57. TUBETUBE, Slade, Kainawari
58. TUMA, Lotuma, Tum
59. UTIAN, Brooker
60. UWAMA, Vama
61. VAKUTA, Lagrandiere
62. VANATINAI, Sudest, Tagula, Taguna, Yamba
63. WAGIFA
64. WAMEA
65. WANIM, Grass
66. WARAMATA, East
67. WARE, Teste, Wari, Chas, Tchas
68. WAVIAY, Vaviai
69. YANABA, Yalab, Yarabu, Yanabw
70. YEGUMA, Egum, Yemgwa, Albatross, Panamoti
71. YEINA, Piron
72. YELA, Rossel

ix

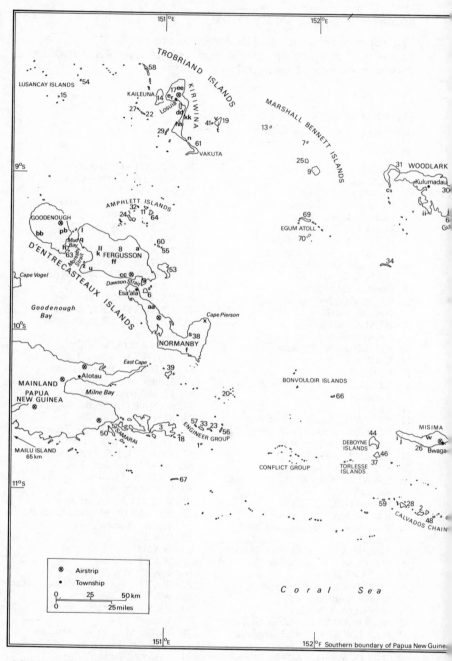

Massim name-locator map

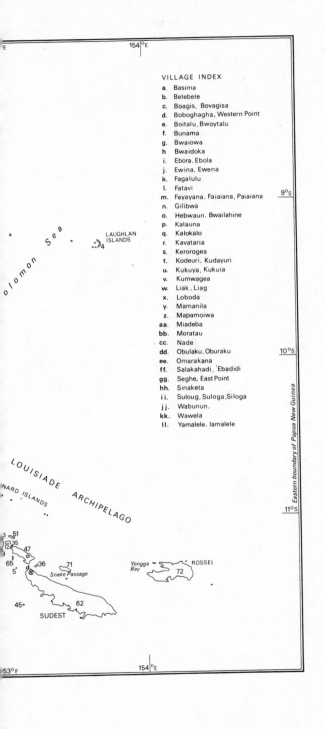

154°E

VILLAGE INDEX

a. Basima
b. Belebele
c. Boagis, Bovagisa
d. Boboghagha, Western Point
e. Boitalu, Bwoytalu
f. Bunama
g. Bwaiowa
h   Bwaidoka
i. Ebora, Ebola
j. Ewina, Ewena
k. Fagalulu
l. Fatavi
m. Fayayana, Faiaiana, Paiaiana
n. Gilibwa
o. Hebwaun, Bwailahine
p. Kalauna
q. Kalokalo
r. Kavataria
s. Kerorogea
t. Kodeuri, Kudayuri
u. Kukuya, Kukuia
v. Kumwagea
w. Liak, Liag
x. Loboda
y. Mamanila
z. Mapamoiwa
aa. Miadeba
bb. Moratau
cc. Nade
dd. Obulaku, Oburaku
ee. Omarakana
ff. Salakahadi, Ebadidi
gg. Seghe, East Point
hh. Sinaketa
ii. Suloug, Suloga, Siloga
jj. Wabunun,
kk. Wawela
ll. Yamalele, Iamalele

9°S

10°S

11°S

Eastern boundary of Papua New Guinea

Solomon Sea

LAUGHLAN
ISLANDS
4

LOUISIADE ARCHIPELAGO

WARD ISLANDS

3 51
35
47
65 36 71
5 Snake Passage
45 62
SUDEST

Yongga
Bay ROSSEI
72

153°F

154°E

Introduction

JERRY W. LEACH

Bronislaw Malinowski's *Argonauts of the Western Pacific* (1922) has had a greater influence on the development of social anthropology than any other single ethnographic monograph. In form, it is a description, given in unprecedented detail, of a system of ceremonial exchange called the *kula* which is practised by the inhabitants of a cluster of islands lying off the extreme eastern tip of the sub-continent of New Guinea.

Malinowski's book was a work of over 500 pages which freely acknowledged a large number of puzzles being left to future ethnographers and theorists. Malinowski also provided his readers with a much reduced model of the kula which, in still further reduced form, is now a standard feature of anthropological textbooks. According to the model, the 'essence' of the kula is the clockwise circulation of necklace valuables (*veguwa* or *bagi*; Malinowski's *soulava*) around a 'ring' of islands; the necklaces are handed on from individual to individual in exchange for armshells (*mwali*) which circulate anti-clockwise around the same 'ring'.

The purpose of this present volume is to bring Malinowski's *Argonauts* up to date, firstly by reporting what is happening in the kula sixty years after Malinowski's original observations, secondly by filling in major gaps in the accounts left by Malinowski and later anthropologists, and thirdly by reconsidering, in light of this new evidence, just how far the theoretical issues posed by the system have been satisfactorily answered by past investigators or can be answered now.

Students of these matters have repeatedly returned to two overarching questions of kula analysis: (1) how does the kula work, and (2) why do men kula at all? Malinowski evidently felt he understood the answer to the 'how' question, though, if modern practice is a guide, he in fact missed a good deal, but he left the 'why' question more open. His final chapter of *Argonauts* entitled 'The Meaning of the Kula' reveals uncertainty and is contradicted in some of his later publications. Numerous anthropologists have made contributions on both these themes. The next

1

Jerry W. Leach

two sections of this Introduction summarize this earlier work. Received Model of the Kula provides a schematization of what has been seen as the fundamental structure and logic of kula exchanges. Basic Interpretive Themes is a compressed distillation of the key ideas which theorists have put forward to explain the *raison d'être*, the 'why', of the total system.

Received Model of the Kula

Malinowski worked in the Massim, the cultural region encompassing islands east of mainland New Guinea, in 1915–16 and 1917–18. He first came in contact with kula exchanging in 1915 on Woodlark Island while making a reconnaissance tour of the area (1922:477; 1967:94). He went on to do intensive fieldwork for two years on Kiriwina Island of the Trobriand Group. His kula research was concentrated in the 1917–18 period.

From his Trobriand vantage point, Malinowski gathered first-hand information on, geographically speaking, about one-quarter of the total kula area. He lived (see Map 1 [p. 20]) in north and south Kiriwina and visited Vakuta, the Amphletts, Tewara, Sanaroa, and Bwaiowa, the southeastern peninsula of Fergusson – roughly the northwestern sector of the kula region. He filled in his information on parts of the system which he did not know personally with informant interviews in the district centre Samarai and with Europeans who knew the Massim (1922:494–508; 1967:118). An intellectual legacy of the inherent biases in Malinowski's access to kula information has been that the 'Trobriand kula' has come to be 'the kula' for subsequent scholars.

Malinowski was not the 'discoverer' or first publicist of the kula as is popularly believed (see pp. 8 ff.). What he did do was to dwarf what had been written before him with systematic analysis and detail, laying stress on evidence for what then appeared to be a nearly unique human institution. He, therefore, gave salience to almost all the basic information which, in skeletal abstract, is called here the Received Model of the Kula. Its fundamental points are:

(1) the kula is a system of socio-economic exchange centred on two kinds of valuables, armshells and necklaces, with other minor valuables of secondary use;

(2) the two valuables must circulate against each other – the opposite-flow rule (author's term, not Malinowski's) – armshells being exchanged for necklaces or vice-versa, but never armshells for armshells or necklaces for necklaces;

(3) viewed from above, the armshells move counter-clockwise and the necklaces

2

clockwise around a giant circle of islands and communities (see Map 1);

(4) the valuables are system-communal property and can not be owned privately or kept in one's possession for very long;

(5) the valuables derive their principal social value and meaning from being the objects of kula exchange, having few other uses in the social lives of the transactors or in their pursuit of an economic livelihood;

(6) shells accumulate value as they circulate among partners around the ring;

(7) armshells are ranked in value against each other as are necklaces inter-ranked amongst each other, the highest of each type being named and having shell-histories;

(8) the valuables are exchanged according to the principle of reciprocity, like value for like value;

(9) the reciprocation of valuables must be delayed, not simultaneous, transactor A going to B to seek a prestation shell x, B returning later to A for a reciprocating shell y, C coming to A to seek shell x, and later A going to C to get a reciprocating shell z;

(10) actual exchanging takes place only between individuals, though these individuals often move *en bloc* as 'kula communities' from one island or area to another;

(11) kula exchanges occur between kula partners, individuals who are, unless serious breaches take place, in fixed lifelong relationships with each other (*pace* Fortune 1932:214);

(12) with rare exceptions, only men can be kula participants;

(13) a man is brought into the kula at adulthood by a kinsman, usually a father or mother's brother;

(14) a man may have a minimum of two partners, one on either geographical side, or multiple sets of partners up to large numbers such as 100 or more as in the case of local leaders;

(15) a man's partners normally come from the kula communities to his proximate geographical left and right, though they sometimes come from within his own kula community;

(16) partnerships are linked in chains around the ring, but a man exchanges only with partners to his proximate left and right, not with everyone around the entire chain of which he is one link;

(17) kula participants solicit particular shells from their partners with preliminary gifts of valued items, which should be themselves ultimately reciprocated;

(18) transactors do not haggle with their partners over relative values in exchanges (*pace* Fortune 1932:208);

(19) men gain considerable prestige from participating in the kula;

(20) a large amount of utilitarian trade in essential and luxury resources takes

3

place on kula expeditions, though this kind of exchanging is conceptually and behaviourally separate from kula exchange to the participants;

(21) kula partners do not trade or barter in a utilitarian sense with each other (*pace* Fortune 1932:208);

(22) except in minor details, the transactional rules of kula exchange are the same all around the ring.

This compressed account of the kula-as-it-has come-to-be-known highlights some of the key problems observers have puzzled over in trying to understand the mechanics of the exchange system:

(A) are the kula valuables a kind of money or a medium of circulation? (Malinowski 1921; Mauss 1925; Herskovits 1940; Einzig 1949; Firth 1957; Dalton 1965)

(B) how are the relative values of the valuables determined? (Mauss 1925; Fortune 1932; Lee 1949; Firth 1957; Belshaw 1965; and in this volume Campbell, Damon, Firth, Gregory, Munn)

(C) how separate is kula exchange from other forms of exchange within and between communities? (Rivers 1926; Fortune 1932; Belshaw 1955; Firth 1957; Harris 1969; Weiner 1976; Damon 1978; E. Leach 1978; and in this volume Campbell, Damon, Macintyre, Munn, Scoditti, Thune)

(D) what are the intra-societal uses of kula shells around the island system and how do these affect the meaning and value of the kula in different places? (Roheim 1950; Uberoi 1962; Weiner 1976; Munn 1977; Damon 1978; J. Leach 1978; and in this volume Campbell, Damon, Leach, Macintyre, Munn, Scoditti, Tambiah, Thune)

(E) what are the sanctions underlying kula reciprocity? (Mauss 1925; Warnotte 1927; Fortune 1932; Firth 1957; Uberoi 1962; Weiner 1976; Damon 1978; and in this volume Campbell, Damon, Munn, Scoditti, Strathern)

(F) how does one gain (or lose) prestige in the kula and what good is it once acquired? (Mauss 1925; Fortune 1932; Austen 1945; Uberoi 1962; Powell 1969; Brunton 1975; Weiner 1976; Damon 1978; J. Leach 1978; and in this volume Campbell, Damon, Munn, Scoditti, Thune)

(G) how does a person expand his place in the kula, i.e. move from a single set of partners to multiple sets, increasing the flow of shells through his position in the system, when exchanges are seemingly one-for-one, balanced, and constantly reciprocal? (Fortune 1932; Uberoi 1962: Weiner 1976; Damon 1978; and in this volume Campbell, Damon, Gregory, Munn, Macintyre, Strathern, Thune)

(H) how is continuing debt between partners sustained when $A \rightleftharpoons B$ equivalence exchange, even if delayed, seemingly cancels debt by the rule of reciprocity? (Mauss 1925; Sahlins 1965; Sahlins 1972; Damon 1978; and in this volume Campbell, Damon, Gregory, Munn, Strathern)

(I) does (or did) the kula prevent war between small stateless societies, thereby allowing the circulation of differentially distributed resources among them? (Mauss 1925; Fortune 1932; Malinowski 1935; Powell 1960; Uberoi 1962; Brookfield 1971; J. Leach 1978; and in this volume Irwin, Macintyre, Scoditti, Thune)

(J)   is the whole kula like the Trobriand kula? (Fortune 1932; Roheim 1950; Firth 1957; Uberoi 1962; Brunton 1975; Hage 1977; Munn 1977; Damon 1978; and in this volume *passim*)

(K)   how has the kula changed over time? (Austen 1945; Belshaw 1955; Powell 1956; Firth 1957; Lauer 1970; Brunton 1975; Damon 1978; E. Leach 1978; J. Leach 1978; and in this volume Firth, Gregory, Irwin, Damon, Macintyre, Scoditti, Thune)

Discussion, from new theoretical and ethnographic perspectives, of many of the propositions of the Received Model and of the common questions which it generates motivates much of this volume.

Basic Interpretive Themes

Even if one has an omniscient understanding of the rules and patterns of the transactional complex called kula, the question of the motive force underlying it all remains. What do people get out of the kula that moves them to devote their time, energy, resources, and reputations to it? How and why did it come into being? Why does it continue?

Attempts over the years to find the underlying *raison d'être* of the system may be synthesized into three main interpretive themes:

> Theme R – recirculation of material resources
> Theme P – prestige competition
> Theme S – social communication.

It is an interesting feature of the intellectual history of kula analysis that few theorists have ever advanced only one of these interpretations without at least elements from one or the other of the remaining two. Most commonly, one finds an interdigitation of two or all three themes put forward with differing relative weightings of their significance, one being more fundamental than the other(s). For reasons of space, neither the minor explanations of the kula, e.g. the psychoanalytic, nor the internal variations and nuances within particular interpretive rubrics, e.g. among old-school Marxists, structural Marxists, cultural materialists, and formalist economists in relation to interpretation R, can be highlighted here. The short syntheses that follow aim to put central ideas in sharp relief but inevitably are overly homogeneous in relation to the varied vocabularies, underlying assumptions, and elaborations on particular themes.

The argument of interpretation R – recirculation of material resources

Jerry W. Leach

– is that the exchange of kula valuables is an elaborate constantly self-renewing treaty-like contract which sustains peace between otherwise hostile local groups that lack centralized authorities, allowing them the security to trade valued resources which are differentially distributed throughout quite varied island ecologies (Rivers 1926; Warnotte 1927; Fortune 1932; Malinowski 1935: 456; Uberoi 1962; Harris 1969; Lauer 1970a; 1970b; Brookfield 1971; Hage 1977).

The strengths of this interpretation have been that the islands are quite varied in their resources, some with stone and some without, many lacking clay for pots or proper shells and feathers for ornamentation, others having inappropriate trees or lashing-vines for canoes and a few being deficient in certain foods. In commonly available goods, the volume densities per capita in coconuts, pigs, pandanus, betelnut, bananas, and various woods are obviously quite different around the network of islands. Localized work specializations in pottery, canoes, ornaments, stone, carving, basketry, and special skirts are also differentially placed around the system. On many of the smaller islands population density is high in relation to the area of potentially cultivatable land and weather patterns are sufficiently irregular to produce a drought of several months duration every 4–5 years. There has been, too, a long-preservation crop, the yam, at the subsistence base of almost all the voyaging communities and, in the past, a democratic distribution of weaponry – spear, club, and shield – among the kula peoples, most of whom, in any case, lived at some distance from their linked exchange communities and were not therefore immediately-juxtaposed potential enemies.

The major weakness of interpretation R is that it does not explain the emic model of the kula, the participants' central concern with the 'useless' armshells and necklaces. Nor does it allow for the regular occurrence of non-kula trade between communities within the system or between kula and neighbouring non-kula peoples. This interpretation does not provide any explanation for the presence of the opposite-flow rule, which in any case works quite differently in northern and southern kula areas. Furthermore, interpretation R leads one to expect an exchange of labour between neighbouring kula communities, for which there is little evidence. Neither does R account for the presence in the system of some islands rich in indigenous resources with little need to engage in overseas trade at all.

The argument of interpretation P – prestige competition – is that the kula is a process through which the members of small local descent groups, who would find openly aggressive face-to-face competition intolerably disruptive, are able to compete against one another as individuals by seeking prestige in an external field of action, the theatrical trading of kula shells (Mauss 1925; Uberoi 1962; Belshaw 1965; Ekeh 1974; Weiner 1976).

The strengths of interpretation P are several. The kula does seem to be about prestige or 'name' everywhere, though in varying degrees and with differing cultural purposes from community to community. The argument fits with the participants' concentration on the shells and with kula when and where it is practised with little or no solicitory giving or exchange of goods. It also fits well with the tendency in kula communities for leaders to be participants in the system, handling more shells with more partners than their confrères. The interpretation makes exclusive male participation somewhat more understandable as the kula becomes similar to male competitive systems for the acquisition of wealth, power, and prestige elsewhere in the world. Interpretation P suggests an explanation for the complex inter-ranking of shells and for the problem of why men tend to enter the kula with low-ranking valuables and move up the rank hierarchy over time. Finally, the interpretation fits tolerably well with the common Melanesian egalitarian social premise that each man is formally as powerful as every other man.

The main weaknesses of interpretation P are that it does not explain why there are several distinct types of kula valuables, why there is an opposite-flow rule, why there is delayed exchange with continuous-debt partnerships, and why there is an ideal of reciprocal equivalence in kula transactions. All these key elements of the kula would seem to hinder the maximum pursuit of prestige, slowing down the velocity of status-acquiring transactions considerably. Interpretation P has not so far shown how kula transactors expand their place in the system, their number of partnerships, or the flow of valuables through their hands. It is also somewhat problematical, given this line of argument, that many men are content to practice a non-expansionary, steady-state mode of exchange over long periods, even their entire kula careers. Interpretation P presupposes that kula prestige stands at the apex of all modes of prestige acquisition in the entire kula region. Yet this is only assertion, not established fact, and there is disagreement on the point among first-hand observers. Moreover, interpretation P should be able to show why alliances among partners geographically distant is a more efficient mechanism for generating competitive prestige than alliances with external groups closer at hand, which might be expected to produce more support, more resources, and more valuables faster than alliances with remote partners.

The argument of interpretation S – social communication – is Durkheimian. It suggests that the exchange of kula valuables is an externalized concrete expression of an abstraction, the valued network of person-to-person relationships which constitutes the social order. The prestations exhibit an ongoing dialectic: on the one hand the oppositions Ego and Alter, We and They, Value-givers and Value-receivers, Living and Dead; on the other the temporary mediation of these oppositions through the assertion of mutual relationship. Following this line of argument, manifested exchanges of 'useless' but symbolic objects help to hold society together, make the social world safer, and allow the accomplishment of a wider range of human ends than would otherwise be possible, especially in the absence of centralized structures of authority (Malinowski 1922; Lenoir 1924; Mauss 1925; Fortune 1932; Evans-Pritchard 1951; Labouret 1953; Firth 1957; Polanyi 1957; Uberoi 1962; Blau 1964; Ekeh 1974; Weiner 1976).

The strengths of interpretation S are that it accords with the high social value given to the shells by the transactors, makes more understandable the constant-circulation attribute of the kula, and makes sense of low-prestige and low-resource-circulation kula. This line of argument initiates explanation (and prediction) of a wide range of internal social-exchange uses of kula valuables, principally at marriage and death, within varied kula communities. It also suggests a strong tendency towards conservatism of the exchange objects, their 'message-bearing' load being so heavy as to make substitutes unacceptable. It is congruent with the system-communal level of shell possession relations and suggests that the compulsory opposite-flow rule in some way represents the unavoidable complementariness of on-going social relationships.

The weaknesses of interpretation S are that it runs counter to seeing the kula as a mode of prestige acquisition, making expansionary transactions, chicanery, competitiveness, and sorcery seem a 'deviant' activity, even though these aspects of kula are salient to participants and not at all infrequent. Furthermore, interpretation S has so far provided no explanation for the ranking of the shells or for the fact that neighbouring non-kula peoples, as well as almost all women and indeed many men who live in the kula area, do not participate as transactors in the system at all.

In short, none of the existing interpretations offer more than a partial explanation for the kula and the academic debate badly needs rekindling with fresh evidence and insight.

Unfolding of published kula

The kula entered Western writing over 125 years ago through observations about its valuables. The earliest missionary residents of the area noted the exchange of boar's tusks for 'coral' necklaces between Muyuwans and islanders to the southwest, calling the objects 'the money and jewellery of the country' (Thomassin 1853:294). They also commented on the extensive flow of yams, coconuts, various woods, feathers, betelnut, and stone axeblades among islands, whether resource-rich or deficient (Thomassin 1853:293–4; Salerio 1862:343).

The German academic Finsch sensed deep socio-economic significance in the strings of Spondylus (*sic*), *Conus* armshells, and round tusks circulating as 'barter' (*Tauschmittel*) in southeastern British New Guinea, without seeing structural patterns in the exchanges (1888b:215). He provided early photographs and drawings of some kula valuables with details of their manufacture (1887:157 and plate VI; 1888a:293–340 and plates XV and XX). Finsch's reference to 'Kulala' (a grammatical possession form) as a place in the northern Massim from which various objects came is possibly the first published use of the term 'kula' (1888b:282).

In the early 1900s, the missionaries Gilmour of the Trobriands and Bromilow of Dobu were prompted to report on 'periodical trading expeditions' (Moreton 1905:33) by the Administrator of the colony F. R. Barton, who had himself written up the *hiri* exchange system of the south coast of Papua (1903:18–20; 1910:96–120). Gilmour indicated inter-island exchange of two types in his limited area: 'pure trading expeditions' and voyages 'principally concerned in the exchange of the circulating articles of native wealth, the mwale (arm shells), and solava and Bagidou-bagi (shell-money), in which trade was only a secondary consideration' (in Moreton 1905:70–1; cf. Malinowski 1922:500–1). He gave a detailed list of imports and exports to and from Kiriwina, superior, incidentally, to that later given by Malinowski in the *Argonauts*. Bromilow's paper, nowhere fully published, was excerpted in Moreton (1905:33) and Seligmann (1910:530 and 539). It describes the circulation of the armshells and necklaces among most of the islands of the northern Massim, including the D'Entrecasteaux and the islands south of Normanby, calling the system of exchange a 'reciprocal agency' (1910:539) among participants (*gumagi*). Bromilow probably deserves credit for being first among observers in conceptualizing the kula as a kind of ring. He was also most likely to have been the first European kula transactor (1929:128–9).

Seligmann added considerable ethnographic detail about trade routes in the east and south of the kula area, on the stone quarries of Muyuw, and on the economic values of the valuables (1906:235–42 and 347–69; 1910:226–40 and plates LIX–LXIV), but his data-collection period was pre-1905 and he could not personally confirm the existence of Bromilow's exchange patterns in the northern Massim and the D'Entrecasteaux. Malinowski himself made a pre-*Argonauts* contribution to the unfolding of the kula through his fieldwork on Mailu Island, documenting trade into and out of the southern kula area (1915:620–46) and the manufac-

Jerry W. Leach

ture of armshells (1915:643–4). However, there is no mention of a kula exchange system as such in his Mailu publication.

Prior to Malinowski's fieldwork in the Trobriands, the kula had been 'discovered' by outside observers but led an obscure published existence. Malinowski first came in contact with the system in 1915 on Woodlark in his pre-Trobriand tour but had little sense of the significance of what he encountered (1922:477; 1967:94). His interest in the subject was aroused on Kiriwina in 1915–16 and he researched it intensively in 1917–18 when his language command was very good. The kula was probably his major intellectual reason for a second period of Trobiand fieldwork.

From his kula-related data, he wrote two preliminary articles (1920: 97–105; 1921:1–16), the first of which contains a rather different map of the kula than the one later published in the *Argonauts* (cf. 1920:98; 1922: 82). His full-length manuscript was finished on the Canary Islands in 1921 and rejected by six publishers (H. Wayne 1978: personal communication) before its release in 1922. About one-third of the 250,000-word monograph is directly about transactional aspects of the kula, the rest being relevant contextual ethnography on magic, leadership, canoe-making, sailing, mythology, and the like. In his later career, Malinowski largely ignored the kula using only snippets of information in his concentrated texts on internal Trobriand organization (1926; 1932; 1935). The book went on to several reprintings and translation into French in 1963, Italian in 1973, and German in 1979 (Macintyre 1983).

Subsequent to Malinowski, Fortune next documented the kula of 1927–8 from the Dobuan perspective (1932:200–34 and *passim*), emphasizing the peace-sustaining function of ceremonial exchange, the south-to-north redistribution of pottery, the entrance and overload of new shell valuables at certain points in the ring, the exchange of material utilities done, entirely without barter, the impermanence of many kula partnerships, and the element of chicanery (*wabuwabu*) and the sanction of sorcery in exchanges. The Hungarian psychoanalyst Roheim developed a partial theory of the kula (1950a:151–243) based on fieldwork on northeastern Normanby in the early 1930s. Austen, government officer in the Trobriands in 1932–4, discussed the indigenous concept of 'valuable' (veguwa or Malinowski's *vaygu'a*) and reported on then current kula practice (1945:22–7). Powell, based on Trobriand fieldwork 1950–1, noted the expansion of the kula since early colonial times, its vital significance to small islands in the Massim, and its role in local leadership and alliance formation (1956:529–35). Uberoi, from library sources, provided in *Politics of the Kula Ring* (1962) a valuable synthesis and re-interpretation of theoretical ideas which had built up over the forty years since the *Argonauts*.

10

Fink (now Latukefu) documented a modern function of the kula, electioneering (1965:285–300), later confirmed by J. Leach (1976:469–91) and amplified to include being a medium for the testing of political strength by rival social movements in the Trobriands of the 1970s (1978: 193–208). Lauer provided new kula-area information with intensive studies of pottery in the Amphletts and the D'Entrecasteaux as well as quantitative details on inter-island trade patterns in the late 1960s (1970a; 1970b; 1971; 1974; 1976) Egloff, through excavations, formed the intriguing hypothesis that the isolation of Goodenough Island and the mainland from the kula-area must date back about 500 years (1978:429–35). Weiner set the kula, as a search for male valuables and renown, in the context of her re-interpretation of Trobriand male–female relations and intra-societal transactions, also introducing the concept of *kitom*, privately-owned or person-tied kula shells (1976: 129,180–1). The concept took on expanded meaning as a conversionary category throughout different levels of symbolic and exchange value in Munn's research on Gawa (1977:39–53). Scoditti semiotically analysed kula canoe prow-boards on Kitava (1977:198–232) and Damon (1978) has written up, from a neo-Marxist perspective, the first intensive full-length field research done directly on the kula, though on Woodlark, since Malinowski's.

Trobriand Reaction to the *Argonauts*

Leach and Campbell sought Trobriand opinion of Malinowski's book. On Kiriwina, Kitava, and Kaileuna, the work was little known away from mission and educational sites. On Vakuta, probably the most schooled island of the Trobriands, knowledge of the existence, but not the contents, of the book was common. Neither researcher found any resident Trobriander who owned a copy of the book nor any evidence that the book had ever been sold in the islands.

Sexual Life of Savages is locally the most popular of the works by *Misikambati* (Mr. Malinowski), sometimes also called *Kisimbati*, despite consternation over its title. *Argonauts* probably ranks second, with a title which, when explained, captures Trobriand imaginations. The photographs are most evocative. It creates amazement when Trobrianders discover that the book stimulates discussion of kula shells, myths, magic, and the behaviour of famous transactors in universities and schools in America, Japan, England, Australia, and Africa. It is a marvellous revelation that the book, perfectly in keeping with what kula is all about, carries name and fame for transactors beyond their islands into the citadels of more powerful outsiders. Some people termed the text a 'new myth' (*livau*).

11

Jerry W. Leach

Probably less than twenty-five Trobrianders had read *Argonauts* through by the mid-1970s. In their critique, they said the locus of competition seemed misplaced. Kula partners, it was argued, compete with the transactors of their home area, or other nearby areas with equal access to external partners, for the favours of those partners. Men must avoid the appearance of competing with their own partners abroad. In soliciting shells, Malinowski is said to have overemphasized the role of magic in moving partners' minds and underemphasized the element of verbal manipulation and rhetorical skill, as well as the elements of charm and beauty. The techniques of political intelligence gathering prior to an expedition, as well as the problems of timing group and shell movements, are said to be necessary, but almost absent, to the text. A religious level to the kula, that men whose names are preserved by the system break out of the cycle of reincarnation through Tuma, to live above ground forever, is also said to be missing. Despite these points, Trobrianders are proud of the existence of the book.

Kula of the 1970s: overview

Antiquity

The history of the kula has always been a major academic unknown. The paucity of written records from the nineteenth century, coupled with the slight amount of archaeological work in the Massim, has left us very much with a 'twentieth-century' view of the institution. Egloff has presented the first hint of possible age parameters for the kula with his observation that trade between the Goodenough-mainland zone and the kula area attentuated sometime after 1500 A.D. (1978:434). In the five centuries prior to that time, the Trobriands had received a steady flow of mainland pottery while Woodlark produced its own wares, which it has not done for the last 150 years at least, or was largely supplied from the southern islands of the Massim (Egloff 1978:435). Irwin, from Mailu excavations, states that kula-type armshells and necklaces have an antiquity in the Massim of nearly 2,000 years (below p. 71). Mackay (1971) recorded a kula armshell with the full cone intact, a lengthwise slit, and exterior engravings – quite unlike any other shell in the system – which was recently discovered buried on Nuratu Island next to Kitava but is now in circulation (See Plate 6 at p. 428f).

Colonial Influences

The Massim area entered Western records with Torres' contact of Sudest

12

and Sideia Islands in 1606, followed by D'Entrecasteaux's voyage through the region in 1793. During the first half of the nineteenth century, there was sporadic contact between local populations and European whalers and traders coming into the area in search of food and fresh water. This stimulated the spread of epidemic diseases, especially venereal disease, and the introduction of metal, principally as tools.

European settlement began in the second half of the century with the shortlived establishment of French and Italian Catholic mission stations on Woodlark between 1848 and 1856. Traders and prospectors established outposts around the Massim in the 1870s and 1880s. The stone quarrying of hornfels[1] on Woodlark, previously a major item in ritual exchange and tool-making in the Massim, came to an end at about this time. There are indications of a sharp decline in population in some parts of the region during this period, namely on Woodlark (Damon 1978:21), Sudest, and Misima (Nelson 1976:18–74), associated mainly with gold rushes in the 1890s.

At this time Europeans introduced significant amounts of beads, tobacco, rope, and other small-scale items of trade, some of which became incorporated into the kula. More valuable items such as knives, axe-blades, metal rods for digging sticks, and metal pieces for adze blades tended to remain in the locality where they were first acquired. Large quantities of kula-type shells were acquired by Europeans at this period either as curios or for trade with local populations. Several thousand such objects have ended up in ethnographic museums throughout the world. The vast majority of these objects are armshells, most of which are, by kula criteria, from amongst the low-ranking categories of shells (Macintyre 1983:77–8). Some of these shells may have been made specially for trading to Europeans who were known to have employed Kiriwinans, Muyuwans, and Yelans in the manufacture of imitation 'valuables' which were intended for subsequent use as objects of exchange. We do not know what effect these activities had upon the system as a whole, but 'counterfeit' valuables of this type have often been rejected if extraneous or unfamiliar materials had been used in their manufacture.

Apparently no Europeans participated in kula exchanges during this period, but individuals and groups from local populations were sometimes carried between islands on European vessels, rather than their own canoes, for kula purposes.

A colonial government presence was established at Samarai in 1886 with later stations on Sudest, Misima, and Woodlark. Patrols and punitive expeditions from these government stations more or less ended local warfare in the kula area between 1890 and 1920. At the beginning of this period, most warfare in the region seems to have been intra-island rather than inter-island.

Blackbirders from Queensland took labourers from the Louisiades and probably the D'Entrecasteaux Islands and Woodlark between 1883 and 1885, but this activity was stopped and many of the islanders made their way home. Blackbirding did not have a long-term effect on the region.

Effective missionization began in 1891 with the arrival of European and Polynesian Methodists on Dobu. Further mission stations were quickly set up on Panaeati, Kiriwina, and Tubetube. Within two decades the mission had satellite stations throughout much of the Massim. The use of Dobuan, the *lingua franca* of the church, facilitated kula expeditions in the northwestern and southern parts of the kula area (see Map 1). Missionaries were tolerant of or ignored the kula during that early period. From 1920–60, however, official Methodist policy was to oppose the kula on the grounds that it encouraged sexual immorality and deceit, contrary to the Ten Commandments, wastefulness of time and resources, and the continued use of magic. This policy resulted in the exit from the system of one kula village on Kaileuna (Montague 1978), the public disavowal (yet continued private use) of magic in kula activities on Kitava, Vakuta, and possibly Dobu, and the need for surreptious participation in kula by some local church leaders and indigenous missionaries. The policy was liberalized through changes of personnel around 1960, but many of its effects still remain.

European-owned coconut plantations were first established in the Laughlans in the 1880s. They became widespread between 1900 and 1920 during the period that the colonial government actively encouraged European settlement. In recent times, participation in plantation labour has often delayed or interrupted the development of an individual's kula career. It has also, on occasion, provided the basis for later kula partnerships.

Along with the establishment of missions, plantations, pearling stations, and government posts came trade stores and the regular supply of introduced foodstuffs and commodities. European money then came to be sought for transactions in this luxury sphere. It was acquired through plantation labour, the sale of pearls and local artefacts, and work for Europeans. Money began to be a minor item in kula solicitation soon after the establishing of trade stores in the 1880s. It also became a source of kula disputes, especially when valuables were sold to Europeans which should have been passing along traditional kula paths. In recent decades, people in 'modern' occupations, such as schoolteachers, policemen, medical orderlies, and civil servants, who have no traditional channel for getting into the kula, have sometimes tried to buy their way in by making large cash payments for initial shells, often to be disappointed as their first exchanges went unreciprocated due to the perceived illegitimacy of their 'entrance' into the system.

The existence of trade stores and the reserves of food which become available through European and now national sources in an emergency have greatly reduced the significance of the kula as a social mechanism which gives access to resources of other islands.

European and government activities have led to the establishment of regular trawler services throughout the area. Kula participants can now move from island to island on most, but not all, links in the inter-island ring. Motor launches rented for the purpose are often used in the southern kula area. Launch or trawler kula has nowhere replaced canoe voyaging, except possibly on Dobu, but is almost everywhere in the region an alternative form of movement. Overuse of trawlers, however, is a point of inter-community criticism as an 'untraditional' or 'uncourageous' or 'unknowledgable' mode of kula movement. Regularized transportation has also come to serve as a sometime source of reconnaissance information. Crewmen, passengers, and advance kula scouts pass messages around the system on the whereabouts and movements of renowned shells. In recent years, letters and even telegrams have been used for this purpose, as have schoolchildren away on other islands.

Kula went into implicit suspension in 1942–5 during the allied occupation of the area. People were warned against inter-island sailing due to the possibility of aerial bombardment. After the war came an intensive period of gardening needed to rebuild seed supplies. This was followed by an efflorescence of kula in the late 1940s. The use of money in kula transactions probably reached a peak in this period as a consequence of the surplus of cash acquired during the occupation. The amount of cash in circulation later declined but increased again when tourism and government spending created renewed access to funds in the 1960s and 1970s.

Population increased in the post-war years due to malaria eradication and widespread access to rural health services, which were major government priorities throughout the period. The population of the kula region was roughly 50% higher in the 1970s than it was at the time of Malinowski's research (1915–18).

Local government councils were introduced throughout the area from 1958 onwards. In 1967 the Trobriand council debated a proposal that it should exercise control over competitive kula expeditions, especially their timing, and over sorcery and 'trickery' in kula transactions. The members of the council eventually decided that, as they were a 'modern' institution, they had no role in regulating the kula. Individual coucillors have sometimes attempted to settle kula disputes over broken paths and

Jerry W. Leach

bad transactions. This was a role which colonial officials had formerly tried to avoid but had often had thrust upon them. Their avoidance, when possible, was partly because of the complexities involved and partly because of their mistaken belief that such matters were essentially trivial.

In modern democratic elections in 1960s and 1970s it seems to have been a minor advantage to council candidates that they have a sound kula reputation but of major importance for national candidates in parliamentary elections (Fink 1965; Gostin *et al.* 1971; J. Leach 1976). The Trobriand M.P. during 1964–72 gave great prominence to his position in the kula. The national electorate for the northern Massim and the Louisiades from 1968–75 was called the Kula Open. In the mid-1970s, kula acquisitions were one test of the relative strength of rival social movements in the Trobriands (J. Leach 1978:193–208).

More significant than these political adaptations of the kula was the continuing decline of material-resource transfer associated with the system. The existence of regular shipping services meant that yams, betelnut, sago, bananas, pigs, chickens, feathers, various woods, and minor amounts of handicrafted ware wanted elsewhere could be more frequently and conveniently moved by modern transport (cf. Brookfield with Hart 1971:324–7). Most Amphlett pottery, formerly a key item in kula trade (Malinowski 1922:282–8) but never exclusively moved by kula means alone, is now moved without reference to kula links (Lauer 1970:172). Most kula expeditions of the 1970s set out with resources intended as personal (hardly ever sufficient) provisions for participants plus minor amounts of solicitation items such as tobacco, betelnut, exotic foodstuffs, money, matches, betel pepper, and the like. The vigorous pursuit of kula shells seems undiminished despite its relative detachment from inter-island resource transfer.

Participation

If one characterizes the kula area as the region where the opposite-flow rule (armshell-against-necklace) pertains, and this notion works better conceptually in northern sectors than in the south, then the geographical extent of the kula has remained fairly stable, but not fixed, over the last century. Kula-type valuables, including armshells and necklaces, circulate all over the Massim and up the Papuan coast, but without reference to the opposite-flow rule or its equivalent.

Montague (1978) reported the exit from kula participation of the men of Kaduwaga village on Kaileuna Island in the Trobriands about 1960. The decision appears to have been motivated by a progressive new leader who has wanted modernization for his village and the closest possible

16

affiliation to the church and the government. Participation, however, remained unchanged in two other kula villages of Kaileuna (Lauer 1970a: 170). Leach (below pp. 142f.) reports a probable diminution of inter-mediary–transactor participation in northwestern Kiriwina, especially along the lagoon coast (*Kulumata*), due to intensive mission influence and mod-ernization pressure arising from a growing sector of non-traditional occ-upations. Northeastern and southeastern Kiriwina, where modernization and mission pressures have been less, sustain a rate of kula participation roughly on par with that of Malinowski's period of research. Campbell (personal communication, 1978) reports that Vakuta, where mission affiliation and aspirations for modernization are strong, has remained an island of undiminished kula enthusiasm, with nearly all adult men partici-pating, despite the public disavowal of magic, if not its private discontin-uance. Scoditti (below p. 257) reports a similar phenomenon for one of the three kula communities on Kitava.

In the northeastern kula area, there are apparently no major changes in the geographical extent of kula participation, though the Woodlark–Laughlans link is now very nearly inactive (Damon 1979: personal communication).

In the southern kula area, Macintyre (below p. 373) reports what must be reduced participation and interest in kula. Thune (below pp. 352, 354), however, records the existence of a new kula community on the southeast coast of Normanby. These are former mountain-dwellers who have moved to the littoral in recent decades and felt it useful to join the system. North of them are the people of Duau, a long-standing kula community for whom the system is a minor preoccupation, so much so that they are often circumvented by communities to their south and west (Dobu and Bwaiowa) who prefer direct exchanges. The major known change in Dobuan kula participation in recent decades is the considerable involve-ment of women as transactors in lieu of their absent menfolk or in their own right (Lithgow 1978). The southern kula area apparently uses more modern transportation than the north, with the Dobu area being the most intensive of all – a factor which facilitates female participation. Chowning (below p. 425) recounts Dobuan attempts in recent decades to draw the peoples of south Fergusson into the kula, some reacting positively to this avenue for new status and others negatively to the potential loss of freedom over the dispensation of their valuables.

Malinowski made no estimate of the number of kula transactors in the system of his day nor has one been attempted since. The following table is an estimate for the 1970s, incorporating a revised identification of kula communities (cf. Malinowski 1922:80, 103, 470–7). Kula participant means in the table 'shell transactor by the opposite-flow rule' and does

17

Kula Demography 1970s (e = estimate)			
Kula Community	Population	Census	Participants
1. KAILEUNA	1,246	1971	135e
(Kaileuna Island)	(953)		(60e)
(Mnuwata Island)	(125)		(35e)
(Kuyawa Island)	(168)		(40e)
2. KILIVILA (N.E. Kiriwina)	2,937	1971/1973	400e
3. KULATANAWA (N.W. Kiriwina)	9,576	1971/1973	60e
4. SINAKETA (S.E. Kiriwina)	737	1971/1973	100e
5. VAKUTA	513	1971/1973	110e
6. OKABULULA (No. Kitava)	590	1971/1973	80
7. KUMWAGEA (S.W. Kitava)	302	1971/1973	37
8. LALELA (S.E. Kitava)	480	1971/1973	65
9. IWA	590	1980	120e
10. KWEAWATA	252	1980	40e
11. GAWA	532	1979	118
12. NAYEM (Madau & N.W. Wdlk)	502	1980	110e
13. WAMWAN (Central Woodlark)	528	1980	110e
14. MUYUW (S.E. Woodlark)	700e	1975	150e
15. BUDIBUD	168	1971/1975	5
16. YANABA	100e	1977/1975	40e
17. YEGUMA	100e	1977/1975	30e
18. NASIKWABU	80e	1977/1975	30e
19. BWANABWANA	834e	1977/1979	23
(Koyagaugau)	(54)		(5)
(Tubetube)	(140)		(6)
(Naluwaluwali)	(100)		(2)
(Kwalaiwa)	(200e)		(3)
(Tewatewa)	(110e)		(4)
(Kitai)	(110e)		(1)
(Anagusa)	(120e)		(2)
20. S.E. NORMANBY	1,300e	1977	200e
21. DUAU	750e	1977	200e
22. DOBU	400e	1977	150e
23. BWAIOWA	950e	1977	350e
24. SANAROA	60e	1977	25e
25. TEWARA	12	1972	7
26. BASIMA	275e	1977	100e
27. KWATOITA	50e	1969	15e
28. N. AMPHLETTS	180e	1969	70e
(Nabwageta)	(100e)		(40e)
(Gumawana)	(65e)		(30e)
(Wamea)	(15e)		(1e)

not encompass the many other forms of supportive, feeder, or derivative relationships that could be called participation in a wider sense.

Roughly speaking, there were about 3,000 (± 20%) kula transactors in the system during the 1970s. This is probably more than in the period of Malinowski's research, the increase being due to an approximate 50% expansion of regional population since that time and some geographical expansion of the system as well. It is impossible to estimate whether the rate of participation is higher or lower. One generalization that does emerge, however, is that smaller islands tend to full adult male participation while larger ones (Woodlark excepted) tend to partial participation. Other evidence suggests that smaller islands tend to produce more dynamic transactors.

Except for Yela (Rossel), all the languages of the Massim are Austronesian and there is a considerable sharing of basic terms as well as other vocabulary around the region (Lithgow 1976). Grammatical structures are very similar across the northern Massim but shift substantially when compared with the D'Entrecasteaux and the southern islands (Capell 1969:126–9). The best available evidence to date (Lithgow 1976) on the mutual intelligibility or otherwise (ignoring the controversy over how to organise the languages into family-type groupings) of the languages of the islands of the Massim indicates five kula-area languages.

Kula transactions, recognized since Malinowski's research to be verbally elaborate (1922:95–9, 472–5), normally take place around the system between speakers of minor dialectal variants of the same language. When larger linguistic differences are encountered, an inter-language patois is used. This often consists of each group speaking its own language to their counterparts, using simplified vocabulary and grammar and appropriate foreign borrowings for the occasion. Dobuan, the common language of the Church in an earlier era, is an aid in inter-language situations. English, though now more important than Dobuan as a lingua franca, is still spoken by few and avoided as inappropriate, except for loan words, in kula speech. Language differences tend to magnify as transactors move further from home. This may be a factor in explaining why participants exchange in roughly adjacent sectors of the total ring.

Shells

Malinowski gave no aggregate estimate of the kula shells in circulation in his time. Firth (below pp. 94–6) by compilation and inference from Malinowski's data estimates there were roughly 3,000 armshell pairs and 3,000 necklaces in circulation sixty years ago. There are still no firm aggregate figures even for the 1970s. Estimates indicate that the numbers

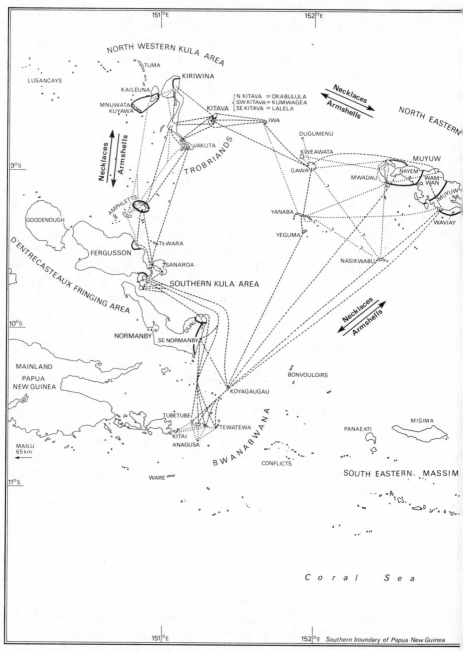

Map 1. Kula in the 1970s. This map includes almost all of the Milne
Bay Province of Papua New Guinea. Based on Woodlark Island (3095)
fourth edition, produced by Australian Division of National Mapping,
1973.

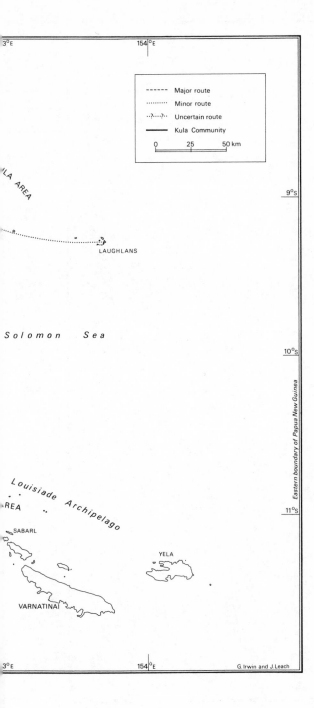

22

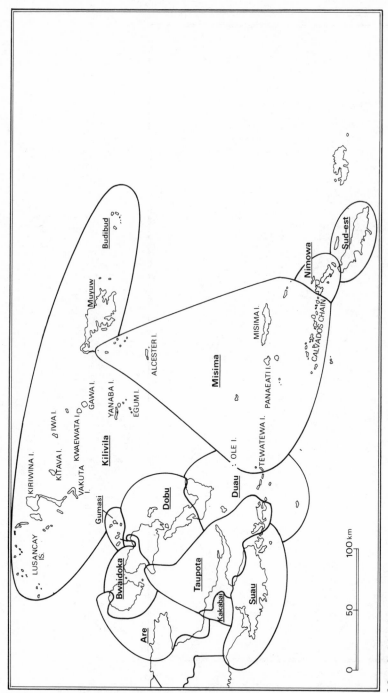

Map 2. Massim language groupings.

LUSANCAY IS.

KIRIWINA I.

KITAVA I.

IWA I.

VAKUTA I.

KWAEWATA I.

GAWA I.

Muyuw

Budibud

Gumasi

Kilivila

YANABA I.

EGUMI I.

ALCESTER I.

Dobu

Bwaidoka

Are

Taupota

Kakaban

Suau

Duau

OLE I.

TEWATEWA I.

PANAEATI I.

Misima

MISIMA I.

Nimowa

Sud-est

CALVADOS CHAIN

0   50   100 km

are in the low thousands. Transactors and observers indicate that the volumes are not, however, roughly balanced. The volume of armshells is clearly greater than that of necklaces. Armshells of the 1970s circulate as single, not paired, objects, except for a small number of large high-ranking ones which are linked in sets with one or two small non-equivalent shells. The reasons for the unpairing of the armshells are unclear. Conceivably it occurred through pressure of increased demand as the numbers of participants grew, possibly coupled with diminution of the rate of manufacture compared with the rate of outflow to non-kula areas and to artefact buyers. Necklaces, as well, have been altered by shortening. Very few of the double-armspan type (Malinowski 1922: Plate LXI and 87) remain. Some long-string necklaces may have become two short-string ones, but more likely sections have been removed for the adorning of young people (Malinowski 1922:87) or for use in non-kula exchanges. People of the Massim have been much less willing to sell or trade out necklaces rather than armshells as is shown by the vast imbalances between the two in the world's museum collections (Macintyre 1983:78).

Armshell and necklace imbalances vary according to the rank of the valuable (this volume 236ff; 302ff.). At the lowest level of rank classification the imbalance is greatest. At the uppermost level, pre-eminent armshells and pre-eminent necklaces are approximately equal in number. There is uncertainty over the imbalance in the intermediate levels. Armshells are still made in Woodlark but their rate of in-flow into the system there is unknown (Damon 1978:89–90). The rate of Trobriand production has probably fallen over the last three decades, due to the ending of manufacture in one major village on Kaileuna (Montague 1978: cf. Lauer 1970a:170) and in the village of Kavataria on the lagoon coast (cf. Malinowski 1922:502). Necklaces still come into the system from the Calvados Chain from Rossel and Sudest (cf. papers by Liep, Lepowsky, and Battaglia). The Papuan coast source (cf. Malinowski 1922:506–7) is now believed to be insignificant. The in-flow of new valuables into the system continues but is probably reduced compared with Malinowski's period.

Liep (1983:85–6) reports that kula necklaces are made from *Chama* shell, especially *Chama (pacifica) imbricata* (Broderip), not *Spondylus* as Malinowski assumed. Armshells probably come from several species of *Conus* shell. *Conus leopardus* (Roding) is now more commonly used than Malinowski's identification *Conus millepunctatus* (Lamarck). *Leopardus* is probably the source of large armshells and *Conus literatus* the smaller ones (Liep 1983:86). Shell decoration has not been immutable over time. Extensive pearling in the Massim between 1870–1920 may have begun the conversion of pendants on necklaces from helmet shell (Malinowski 1922: Plate XVIII–photograph from early collections in the British Museum) to gold-lipped oyster shell (below p. 234), though other constituent items have remained the same (Malinowski 1922:86–7). Armshells have been more variable in ornamentation, accepting wide varieties of cowrie pendants, beads, trinkets, and rope (cf. Malinowski 1922: Plates XVI, XVII, LX; below pp. 231 f.). Despite these changes, the heart of what is valued, the smooth string of *Chama* and the half-*Conus*, have remained constant in design over the last century.

Malinowski stated that, in terms of shell symbolism, armshells were conceived of as 'female' in contrast to 'male' necklaces, suggesting that more had to be given to acquire the armshells (1922:356). Leach (1981: 56) and Weiner (1976) found the reverse symbolic identifications among kula participants on Kiriwina in the 1970s. Leach's informants stated that armshells like men move around the most and seek out their more sedentary opposites. However, among non-participants in northern Kiriwina, the Malinowskian version still remains. Observers report intriguing transformations in the contrastive male–female symbolism of the shells around the system of the 1970s. Shells are said to 'marry', 'divorce', and 'give birth' in various ways as they move against each other. A fascinating problem remains in interpreting these meanings against the variations in marriage and matrilineality, the volume and velocity of contemporary shell movements, and the transactional strategies of equivalence and gain around the ring.

A major deficiency of Malinowskian kula analysis has been the absence of the concept of the private or person-tied kula shell (kitom or cognates). Over the years this has impeded understanding how participants expand their place in the system and how shells function in domains of exchange other than kula, especially intra-community transactions. A major theme of this volume, pursued in the papers by Strathern, Gregory, Weiner, Campbell, Munn, Damon, Thune, and Macintyre, is how kitoms variously work in the societies around the ring. The matter is highly complex. Roughly speaking, a kitom shell is one not moving by or obligated under the opposite-flow rule. It may be newly acquired prior to being put first into kula. It may have been in circulation but reached a point in which all reciprocal claims against it have been met, being thus momentarily freed of obligation. It may be temporarily outside kula, moving from person to person as an affinal gift, then a mortuary prestation, later a land prestation, before being exchanged again in a kula partnership. At these points and many others, individuals have a great deal more control of the valuables which can be said to be private to them. The puzzles come in unravelling how shells can be said to be the kitom of some specific person, of several different people, and of nobody (i.e. system-communal) simultaneously, but from different perspectives. There is probably not a homogeneous kitom concept, or concept-set, around the ring, but rather cognate co-variation of attributes.

Malinowski nowhere made explicit use of the concept of a kula 'path' (*keda* or cognates) though some aspects of this polysemic concept are found implicitly within his analysis of partnerships (1922:91–4, 274–81). Austen mentioned the notion first in a single sentence (1945:26), but it waited until Weiner (1976) and especially Damon (1978) to be developed. The concept is crucial in the papers of Gregory, Munn, Damon, Thune, Weiner, and particularly Campbell, in tackling such questions as how participants gain or expand the flow through themselves of more and larger shells over time, how they maintain obligation between themselves in the face of potential completion through reciprocation, how they build kula careers, and how they conceptualize the system of which they are a part. Briefly put, paths are viewed as (linear or circular) chains of ideally trustworthy, but actually calculating partners, routes along which shells move, linkages between kula communities, channels of resource transfer and reserve food supply, and avenues for name-formation. Kula path is a key summarizing concept which draws participants' and observers' models of the system closer together, further integrating knowledge of how and why the system works the way it does.

Comparison

This volume opens out kula analysis from its former preoccupations with Kiriwina, Malinowski's fieldwork base, to the examination of parts of every sector of the sytem and fringing areas beyond. The authors herein, in their individual ways, tend to focus on the role of valuables within and between their local or neighbouring social systems. Their local systems are, and have been, cognate with each other, sharing overlapping but not identical patterns of organization, belief, and exchange. The kula too shares this characteristic. An analogy is the game of bridge which now internationally has a small core of common rules everywhere but wide variations from nation to nation in point counting, bidding, signalling, and even reasons for playing. The object of kula-area comparison is to find the common features and place them within the fuller cultural context of each cognate social system.

Another question is whether or not Malinowski's kula can be compared with the kula of the 1970s. One-half the participants in this project have had first-hand experience of the system, while three-quarters were

Jerry W. Leach

personally familiar with the Massim. Their collective opinion is that the kula has been, on balance, a conservative institution. By factoring in known, but not massive, changes in the colonial period, one may still observe in the cultures of the region much of what Malinowski described. In particular, it is possible to concentrate on the fundamental mechanics of kula exchange, using Malinowski as a point of departure, and to advance the understanding of how the kula worked and works, both in his day and in the 1970s. Less confident, however, are opinions about the underlying *raison(s) d'être* of the system. Reasons for continuation may be substantially different from those of origination or institutionalization in earlier periods.

Note

1 I am indebted to Dr. William G. Melson and Dr. Adrienne Kaeppler of the Smithsonian Institution for the identification of the stone from the Suloga quarry on Woodlark as 'dark green hornfelsed tuff or meta-rhyolite'. This stone has been identified in previous publications as andesite, jade, jadite, ignimbrite, rhyolite, or simply greenstone. J.W.L.

PART: I

Kula area – general

1 Chieftainship, kula and trade in Massim prehistory

GEOFFREY J. IRWIN

Introduction

This paper has three parts. The first describes a spatial analysis of ethnographic data from the Trobriand Islands and advances another theory on the origins of chieftainship. The second part investigates locational factors within the wider *kula* network, in order to throw light on aspects of its development. The third considers the emergence of the kula within the more general context of the development of trade and economic specialisation in the Massim.

These questions are approached in two ways. The first is by taking a broadly anthropological perspective of archaeology. In its widest sense, archaeology is concerned with the relationship between material culture and human behaviour (Reid, Schiffer and Rathje 1975). Both of these occur in the present and the past, which accounts for the existence of many kinds of archaeology including prehistoric, historic and ethnographic branches. In Melanesia there is a direct and recent relationship between prehistory and history. Culturally and ecologically there is a large measure of continuity between them. Study of the ethnographic situation sometimes provides insights for the interpretation of earlier ones, for in many cases what people are doing at present is the current state of a cultural development which can be traced back for a thousand years.

Not very much archaeology has been done as yet in or near the Massim. However, given the local situation, it is no surprise to find that what has been done is generally ethnographic in approach (e.g. Lauer 1974; Egloff 1971). Within the kula area itself, there are no excavation reports of substance. To try to get around this paucity of primary prehistoric data, the second approach to the questions listed above, is from the perspective of Mailu.

At the close of prehistory, this small island some 25 km from the

29

western boundary of the southern Massim was the location of a large and influential community described as the 'metropolis' of its area (Saville 1926:19). It was a centre of specialised manufacture and trade. It provided the communications link between the Massim and communities up to 250 km to the west (Malinowski 1915; Saville 1926). Archaeological evidence shows that some 2,000 years ago the Mailu area was settled by people with an agricultural and fishing economy who lived in coastal villages which were functionally unspecialised. Through time, the settlement on Mailu Island diverged from the others at an increasing rate. It became more central in terms of the pattern of regional communication. It acquired a monopoly of pottery making. As the economic context of pottery production changed from local, low-volume and domestic to centralised, high-volume and specialist, the pottery itself became transformed into a highly standardised trade ware and elements of the manufacturing technology became particularly sophisticated. Mailu's population grew much larger than any other local community and was also perhaps starting to show signs of social stratification. The various factors which caused this pattern of cultural change have been studied in detail (Irwin 1974, 1977). Much of what is known of the Mailu case will be shown to have direct relevance for aspects of Massim prehistory, despite the fact that archaeological evidence from the latter remains fragmentary.

Part one: the development of Trobriand chieftainship

Political leadership in the Trobriand Islands has been a matter of particular interest because it was unusual for Melanesia. It is clear that Trobriand society was egalitarian in comparison to stratified societies in many parts of the world and therefore that Trobriand chiefs were chiefs in a strictly limited sense. However, the political system was distinct from the 'big-man' system in that a local Trobriand subclan or *dala* had only one recognised leader, not any number. Further, the many subclans and their respective leaders had different ascribed ranks (Brunton 1975:544).

One aspect of the ethnographic evidence that has not been exploited in analysis is that the system of rank was spatially variable. Evidently individual villages enjoyed considerable autonomy although a number of clusters of contiguous villages had corporate identity. If more than one dala occupied a village, only one was recognised as its 'owners' and supplied the village leader. Subclans were either of recognised rank (*guyau*) or commoners. Powell believes that all those which supplied cluster leaders were guyau (1960:124). By extrapolating from Powell's maps (1960:122–3) to the villages shown on Malinowski's (1922:50), it would seem that approximately one third of villages were of guyau status in the early years of this century. Among these only the Tabalu subclan was regarded everywhere as pre-eminent. Ultimately rank came from possession of special powers. The Toliwaga, main political rivals of the Tabalu in the contact period had potent war magic, but this was reckoned to be less powerful in the long run than the Tabalu magic of weather and prosperity (Powell 1960:128–9).

In each of several of the districts identified by Malinowski (1922:66–70) – namely Kiriwina, Tilataula, Kuboma and Luba – one chief enjoyed recognised senior status, although between the districts their relative ranks were not the same. Chieftainship of this kind was not found in the districts of Kulumata and Kaybwagina, nor on Vakuta and Kayleuna (Malinowski 1922:68–9).

It is clear also from descriptions that these districts were readily distinguishable in economic terms. Their respective specialities are well known (Malinowski 1935:12–22). In the north, Kiriwina had good soils and was renowned for agriculture, although some casual fishing was done by villages along the north coastal strip. Tilataula, and most of Kuboma were cut off from the sea by swamp and their maritime activities were minimal. In Tilataula axe-grinding and gardening were important. The villages of Kuboma had a number of things in common besides their famous craft specialists and their infamous status. They lay inland and were also somewhat separated from other areas of dense settlement. They had stonier garden land than in the north, except, interestingly, around the highest-ranking village Gumilababa. Their pattern of specialisation and separateness fit their situation. Geographically the villages of Kulumata lay along the southern boundary of Kuboma and provided the hinterland with marine resources and coastal access. Further, it comes as no surprise to find that the relative speciality of the villages around the lagoon was fishing. In the south, the district of Kaybwagina had some extensive barren areas. The large community of Sinaketa depended partly on fishing, specialised manufacture and trade as did certain other villages in similar circumstances elsewhere. Malinowski pointed out that ecological factors were not a sufficient explanation for the geographical distribution of economic activities (1935:9, 21–2). However, we can at least note that ecological and cultural patterns were compatible.

Clearly there was spatial variability in Trobriand ecology and economic activity. There was also a spatial aspect to variation in leadership in that there were people of different rank living in different places. This raises the possibility that there could be some correspondence between the respective patterns.

31

Geoffrey Irwin

Rank and centrality in the Trobriands

One of the many factors which leads to the differentiation of settlements and their inhabitants is the advantage of central location. If centrality can be quantified, it allows other factors such as ecology to be evaluated more precisely. In the Mailu case it was found that the emerging specialisation and political influence of the island coincided with an increasing locational advantage among contemporary villages. This suggests the possibility that there could be a locational component to the origin of Trobriand leadership.

Malinowski's map of villages and districts (1922:50) is the basis for the map shown in Map 1, which shows the same information in addition to a reconstructed communications network linking the villages together. (The names of the villages are given in Table 1 below). The network is based in part on information on particular land and sea routes given by Malinowski (1922:164–5; 1935:Fig. 13).However, beyond this and for the most part, it is hypothetical. Briefly, each village has been joined to its three nearest neighbours. Some likely additional links have been added between pairs of villages, together with a small number of paths which are regarded as being of more intermittent usage. The basic assumption is simply that pairs of villages close together enjoyed more interaction than ones further apart. This is essentially a commonsense proposition of demonstrated merit as applied to other cases (e.g. Irwin 1974; Terrell 1976). Such networks while admittedly probabilistic have the virtue of treating all sites alike. Results obtained from them can be compared also with those from maps of actual paths (see below).

Connectivity analysis is a method for quantifying the relative centrality of interacting sites (Pitts 1965; Carter 1969) and was used in the Mailu study (Irwin 1974, 1977). Briefly, each site is compared with all others in terms of how central it is with respect to the network. There are two major methods of calculation (Haggett 1967:635–8). The first of these is known as 'short path' connectivity. Sites are compared in terms of the shortest path linking each one to all of the others. This method is clearly applicable to cases where the movement of people or goods is being considered, which involves the energy costs of transport. However, not all communication follows the most direct routes, or even single routes. The second method, which has been called 'connection array' connectivity compares individual sites not just in terms of the shortest paths but in terms of many alternate paths of given length. This model is perhaps more appropriate to the study of how information and ideas actually flow around within a network and are continuously reinforced by face-to-face communication. Normally a link between any pair of sites is given the

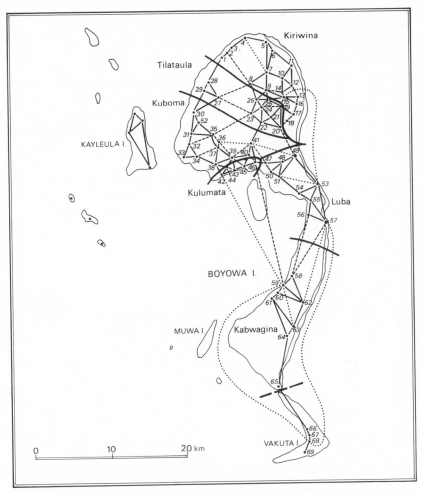

Map 1. Network of communications based on Malinowski.

same numerical value as any other link. However it is possible to weight them differentially to allow for the fact that paths vary in both their social and spatial significance. Such weighting enables the construction of more realistic models. Between them, the various methods of analysis can cover a range of cultural situations. The following independent analyses were carried out to investigate spatial patterning in Trobriand leadership, using the B6700 computer at the University of Auckland.

Geoffrey Irwin

Solution 1

This consisted of a short-path analysis by district; i.e., each site was compared with every other in terms of its centrality within the district. All links were given equal weight and those shown as intermittent in Map 1 were not included. The results are shown on the map in Map 2. It was found (1) that in Kiriwina, Omarakana, the village of the most senior Tabalu line, ranked third in centrality. (2) In Tilataula district, Kabwaku, the dominant village, proved to be the best-connected site. (3) In Kubo-

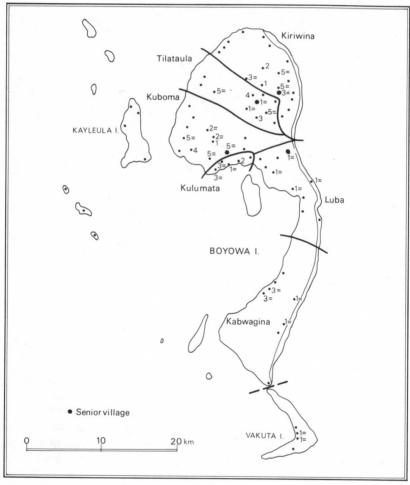

Map 2. Connectivity by district (solution 1).

34

ma, Gumilababa, the village of the highest chief, was not most central but was situated next-door to the village that was. (4) In Luba four villages ranked first equal, one of which was Olivilevi, the home of the district representatives of the Tabalu. (5) Results for the other districts are shown. These results were generally confirmed by others based on the unweighted connection-array method.

Solution 2

Analysis by single district was artificial owing to the small number of sites in some districts and especially because of the certainty of contact between them. Interaction of various kinds is documented across boundaries, as for instance in *urigubu* payments. In Map 3 the districts of Kuboma and Kulumata are shown combined. It can be seen that in terms of the short-path solution Gumilababa shifts to second place while in terms of connection array analysis (not shown) it actually ranks first. It is evident that some kind of relationship between the pattern of communication between sites and the relative political status of their leaders, is beginning to emerge. The chance of this arising at random is remote.

Analysis of the districts of Luba and Kaybwagina in combination, directs attention to the village of Wawela described by Malinowski as important for astronomical knowledge, the calendar and association with the flying witches. Of greater importance though, is the fact that in addition to its specialisation, it was formerly a very big village (Malinowski 1922:68). Its position in this analysis may be taken as a reflection of the significance of the interaction between these two districts.

Solution 3

This analysis is of little importance. Briefly, the three central districts of Kuboma, Kulumata and Luba were analysed in combination by the short path method. It is interesting to note that Kuboma's village Gumilababa ranks as the best-connected.

Solution 4

This analysis is regarded as the most realistic and successful of all. It is based on the whole of Boyowa Island (Map 4). Each village is compared with every other in terms of its relative centrality in the whole island. Moreover the method used was weighted connection-array connectivity. The weights, which were those shown in Map 1 fare briefly as follows: (1) a value of 1.0 was given to links between all three nearest neighbours in the

Geoffrey Irwin

same district; (2) 0.8 was given to links between three nearest neighbours which crossed a district boundary; (3) 0.6 was given to likely additional links within districts; (4) 0.3 was assigned to those which crossed district boundaries; (5) 0.2 was given to those links which were the same as the previous category except that they involved sea transport; (6) a value of 0.2 was also given for links deemed likely intermittent ones, within a district; (7) 0.1 was assigned to those which passed between districts. Thus while the analysis was designed to include patterns of centrality within the whole island, the weighting emphasised paths thought to have

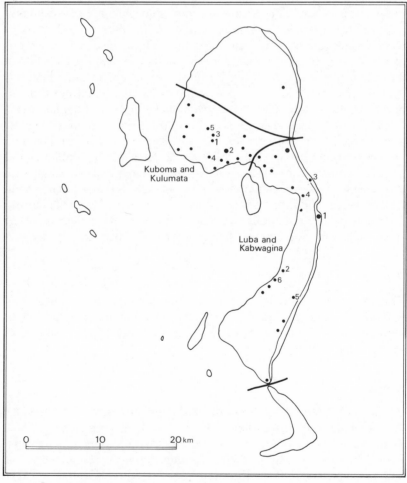

Map 3. Connectivity by pairs of districts (solution 2).

36

been used most frequently and also gave greater weight to within-district interaction than to that passing between districts.

In Map 4 sites are ranked by district, in terms of their centrality scores. It can be seen that there is a perfect correlation with the political ranking of villages in Kiriwina, Tilataula, Kuboma and Luba. Table 1 lists the connectivity scores of each village, together with its rank order of centrality. It can be seen that Omarakana, Kabwaku, Gumilababa and to some extent Olivilevi, are markedly more central in their districts than nearly all of the other villages. Neither Kulumata nor Kaybwagina were single

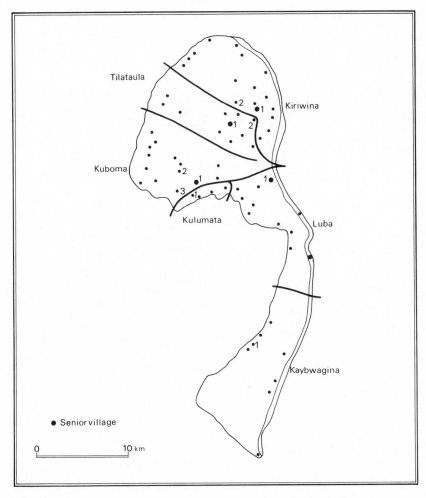

Map 4. Connectivity in the whole island (by district) (solution 4).

political units under the sway of a single leader like the others. It can be seen that neither the villages of Kavataria nor Sinaketa, which were prominent settlements in their respective districts, ranked as most centrally located in them. However, it can be seen in Table 1 that connectivity scores were generally low among these villages and that Sinaketa was not far behind the most central place in its district.

Map 5 shows the results of the same analysis in the form of a contour map. Each contour shows the percentage connectivity that each included village has of the whole island. A number of observations may be made.

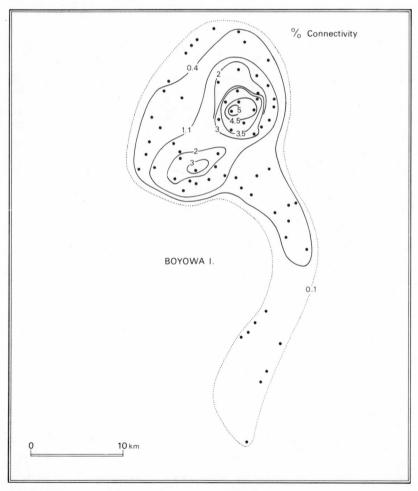

Map 5. Connectivity in the whole island (solution 4).

1. The northern districts have the highest connectivity values. The village of Kabwaku of greatest military fame, is shown to be the most central site in the whole island, higher even than Omarakana, although its value for centrality was very high too.
2. There is a fall-off in values for connectivity as one moves south.
3. Compared to other villages of district chiefs, Olivilevi in Luba has a relatively low value. It is interesting to note that this village became a Tabalu location only relatively recently.
4. The decrease in centrality values towards the south parallels the decreasing power and influence of village leaders.
5. The cluster of high value sites in the northeast coincides with a major agricultural area and in addition, it includes only one of the three prominent axe-grinding villages mentioned by Malinowski (1935:14).
6. The industrial villages of Kuboma form the nucleus of another cluster to the mid-west. At the southern side of this lie the coastal villages of Kulumata which provide entry ports to the area.
7. It can also be seen that the fishing and other villages of Luba fall together in value, as do those in the south in Kaybwagina.

Overall, this analysis has produced a coherent and plausible result. One of the most important conclusions is that the location of district chiefs apparently is predictable. However it is interesting to note that the precise locations of lesser guyau do not appear to be predictable. In Table 1 other villages reported to be guyau around 1950 (Powell 1960: maps 1 and 2, pp. 122–3) were generally not very central, at least in the communications system of Malinowski's time.

Solution 5

This analysis is of a different network to those described above. It stems from an attempt to improve, or at least to test, the quality of the data that has been used already. Map 6 is based upon village locations and communications routes shown by Powell (1960: maps 1 and 2, pp. 122–3). It depicts more accurately the shape of the Trobriands and also shows the distribution of areas of swamp and high ground. Only the villages listed by Malinowski have been extracted from Powell's maps, but their locations are shown as they were around 1950. The network of intervillage links is based on the Trobriand paths drawn by Powell while roads specified as European have been excluded almost entirely. Powell's pattern of routes was not a precise one and therefore the network in Map 6 is no more than a good approximation of it. The other source of error which cannot be controlled at present is any movement in village locations and routes between 1915 and 1950. In spite of the limitations, this

Table 1. *Connectivity of Trobriand villages ca. 1910: Solutions 4, 5 and 6*

Site No.	Village		Solution 4			Solution 5			Solution 6
			Connectivity %	Rank by district	Rank by island	Connectivity %	Rank by district	Rank by island	Rank by island
1.	LABAI		0.167	18	62	0.557	18	40	33
2.	KAIBOLA		0.404	15	52	2.084	12	17	14
3.	LUEBILA		0.177	17	60	1.356	14	25	23
4.	IDALEAKA		0.345	16	55	2.628	10	14	10
5.	KAPWANI		0.835	14	40	1.340	15	27	24
6.	YUWADA		0.952	13	37	1.999	13	20	17
7.	KUDOKABILIA		2.251	4	15	3.261	8	11	7
8.	DIAGILA		2.315	3	13	3.705	6	8	2
9.	KABULULA		3.889	2	8	5.509	2	2	4
10.	LILUTA	*	1.608	10	27	0.871	16	32	28
11.	M'TAWA	*	0.955	12	36	0.642	17	39	36
12.	KWAYBWAGA		1.488	11	29	5.419	3	3	1
13.	TILAKAIWA		1.633	9	26	3.698	7	10	12
14.	KASANAI		2.168	5	17	4.832	4	4	5
15.	OMARAKANA	+	3.915	1	7	7.090	1	1	3
16.	YOLAWOTU		1.661	8	25	4.136	5	7	11
17.	KAULAGU		1.683	7	24	3.225	9	12	13
18.	YALUMUGWA	*	1.865	6	18	2.368	11	16	18
19.	WAKAILUA		4.818	2	2	4.571	1	5	6
20.	MOLIGILAGI		3.325	8	10	1.789	6	21	25
21.	OBOWADA		3.977	6	6	3.701	3	9	8
22.	OBWELIA		4.040	5	5	2.552	5	15	16
23.	OKAIKODA	×	3.350	7	9	1.750	7	22	22

24.	KABWAKU	×	5.278	1	1	3.009	4	13	15
25.	WAKAISA		4.693	3	3	4.156	2	6	9
26.	OKAIBOBWA		4.185	4	4	1.486	8	24	27
27.	BOYTAWAYA		0.975	9	34	0.341	10	48	43
28.	TUBOWADA	×	0.377	11	53	1.242	9	29	21
29.	KAULIKWAU	×	0.471	10	50	0.276	11	51	46
30.	KULUVITU		0.760	12	41	0.355	9	47	45
52.	OLIESI	*	0.888	11	38	0.020	12	63	63
31.	LOBUA	* *	1.078	9	33	0.080	11	61	59
32.	SIVIYAGILA	*	0.967	10	35	0.321	10	49	48
33.	BAU		0.544	13	47	0.004	13	65	65
34.	BOYTALU		1.259	8	32	0.496	7	42	39
35.	IALAKA		1.794	5	21	0.798	5	34	32
36.	BUDUWAYLAKA	*	1.541	7	28	2.009	2	19	20
37.	LUYA		2.336	2	12	0.763	6	36	34
38.	WABUTIMA		2.274	3	14	0.484	8	43	44
39.	GUMILABABA	+	3.290	1	11	0.806	4	33	30
40.	KAPWAPU	*	1.685	6	23	2.032	1	18	19
41.	KUDUWEKELA		2.178	4	16	1.498	3	23	26
42.	KAVATARIA	+	1.323	4	30	0.547	3	41	37
43.	OYUVEYOVA		1.807	2	20	0.735	2	37	31
44.	OSAYSUYA		1.829	1	19	0.461	4	44	38
45.	TEYAVA		1.710	3	22	0.357	5	46	47
46.	TUKWAUKWA	+	1.309	5	31	0.791	1	35	35
47.	OKOPUKOPU		0.742	3	43	1.336	2	28	29
48.	OKAIBOMA		0.734	4	44	1.037	3	30	40
49.	OLIVILEVI	+ *	0.851	1	39	1.340	1	26	41
50.	ILALIMA		0.563	6	46	0.938	4	31	42
51.	OSAPOLA		0.727	5	45	0.444	6	45	50

Table 1 – *cont.*

Site No.	Village		Solution 4			Solution 5			Solution 6
			Connectivity %	Rank by district	Rank by island	Connectivity %	Rank by district	Rank by island	Rank by island
53.	DUBWAGA		0.743	2	42	0.724	5	38	49
54.	KAITUVI		0.526	8	49	0.161	8	57	60
55.	KWAYGULA		0.529	7	48	0.234	7	53	57
56.	OBULAKU	*	0.279	10	56	0.095	10	60	61
57.	WAWEKA	*	0.438	9	51	0.148	9	58	56
58.	KAULASI		0.203	4	59	0.228	3	54	53
59.	SINAKETA	+	0.227	3	58	0.201	4	55	54
60.	BWADELA		0.288	1	54	0.237	2	52	52
61.	LOUYA		0.164	6	63	0.176	5	56	55
62.	KUMILABWEGA	*	0.268	2	57	0.293	1	50	51
63.	BWAGA		0.173	5	61	0.134	6	59	58
64.	OKAYEULO	*	0.110	7	64	0.038	7	62	62
65.	GILIBWA		0.033	8	65	0.010	8	64	64

+ Tabalu *guyau*
× Toliwaga ,,
* other ,,

NB Powell (1960) differs from Malinowski (1922) by locating 1 Labai in Tilataula not Kiriwina, 19 Wakailua in Kiriwina not Tilataula and 44 Osaysuya in Kuboma not Kulumata.

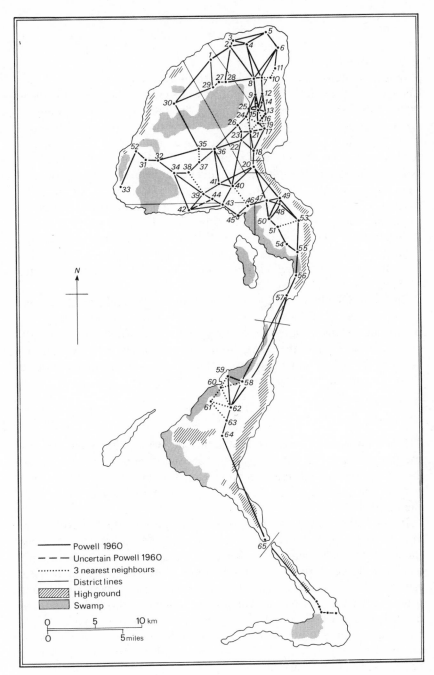

Map 6. Network of communications, based on Powell.

revised network does offer the opportunity to duplicate the results obtained using a map which in some respects at least, is more accurate than the one based on Malinowski.

Solution 5 was a weighted version of the network shown in Map 6. Links between pairs of sites within districts were given a value of 1.0; those which crossed district boundaries were given 0.9. The percentage connectivity of each site within the whole island is shown in Table 1 together with their centrality ranks both by district and island. The results of this analysis are substantially similar to those of Solution 4 which used the network based on Malinowski. The level of agreement between the two rank orders was calculated by the Spearman Rank Correlation Coefficient, $R = 0.659$; $t = 6.959$ which is significant beyond the 0.001 level.

Inspection of the results supports the following observations.

1. Whereas in Solution 4, Kabwaku, the most military prominent village in the Trobriands was the most central place, in Solution 5, the most central by a wide margin is Omarakana, home of the highest-ranking chief.
2. In Luba, Olivilevi is still most central, but in Tilataula and Kuboma, the villages of Kabwaku and Gumilababa both rank only fourth.
3. It is interesting to note that of the six villages on Boyowa Island with residential Tabalu, the ranks within the five districts where they occur are 1, 1, 1, 3, 4, and 4. However, there is no evidence that any other guyau subclan had any tendency to be central.

Solution 6

This was an experimental re-run of Solution 5, which did not employ any weighting of links. In other words, there was no bias in the network. The 2 results shown an extremely high level of agreement, $R = 0.975$ (on a scale where $1.0 =$ identity); $t = 35.225$, which is highly significant beyond the 0.001 level.

It was found in every district except Kiriwina, that the 3 most central villages were the same in Solution 6 as in Solution 5, although sometimes their relative orders changed. In Kiriwina, the 3 most central in Solution 5 were found among the first 4 in Solution 6. However, this final analysis failed to find precise locations of the highest-ranking chiefs in districts where they occurred. It is concluded that to achieve this final step in an analysis of the whole island, some degree of weighting is necessary of communication within districts as against interaction between them. Given the ethnographic, ecological and locational situations, such as procedure is entirely justifiable.

Before proceeding to the interpretation of these results, two observations may be made. Firstly, this analysis has been able to show that the pattern of Trobriand leadership described ethnographically earlier this century, had a material expression in the distribution of contemporary village sites. Just as it is possible to distinguish the economic districts on ecological grounds, it would be possible to suggest on archaeological grounds alone, which villages in them could have been of importance politically. In this case the chronological context is an ethnohistoric one. However it provides a baseline from which one can proceed into the past to attempt to trace the emergence of Trobriand leadership. In general it is implied that archaeological analysis can be used to test independently some patterns revealed in ethnography and that in some cases, study of this kind may be freed from dependence on oral testimony.

The second observation concerns the kind of assumptions upon which this analysis was based. They are neither elaborate nor especially theoretical. The network analysis was based on the idea that there is a tendency that people will interact more if they live closer together. Similarly, living within easy reach of other people and of resources may be generally more advantageous than being more remote from them. These are essentially commonsense propositions. In some way they are implicated in the origins of Trobriand chieftainship. This comes as no surprise because it is established that they were one effective variable in the case of Mailu (Irwin 1974, 1977). Moreover there are other parallel cases. Locational factors have been implicated in the fortunes of big-men in the Torrecelli Mountains of New Guinea (B. Allen pers. comm.) and in the Siwai area of southern Bougainville (Callen 1976).

The implications for Trobriand chieftainship

Spatial analysis can be used to appraise theories on why leadership developed in the Trobriands as it did. The situation is that one variable – relative centrality – has been quantified, which enables an assessment to be made of the relative importance of other variables which have been suggested. It is reasonable to expect that several causal factors were involved, as in the case of the emergence of Mailu as a large and specialised community (Irwin 1977). If so, one could not justify a case for locational determinism. The spatial analysis merely corroborates what Malinowski had to say about the whereabouts of high-ranking individuals and their villages. It is now clear that there is a spatial dimension to the same pattern. However, the cultural process which produced the pattern remains to be inferred.

According to the ethnographies, there are four clans made up of a large number of subclans or dala. Subclan membership conferred status.

According to Trobrianders, dala, with a set of associated ranks, were created fully formed. Their ancestors were autochthonous and emerged through holes in the ground near to where their descendants still live (Malinowski 1922:70) as village 'owners' (Powell 1960:121). According to the centrality analysis, it would seem that high-ranking ones were very judicious in the holes they chose.

However, the exception to the rule was that the highest-ranking dala, the Tabalu, emerged near the village of Labai in the northwest of Kiriwina, but are found in several important centres throughout the Trobriands, as described above. How do we account for this distribution? Did Tabalu ancestors migrate to villages which coincidentially happened to have locational advantages or were important otherwise for specialised manufacture, trade or Kula? Or did the owners in important villages become Tabalu on the spot, as Uberoi believes (1962:39)?

There is evidence that both processes may have occurred. Malinowski reports that the prominence in Luba of the chief of Olivilevi is the result of a younger line of Omarakana having branched off 'some three genera-tions ago' (1922:68). Similarly, a branch of Tabalu came down to Vakuta and settled 'perhaps four to six generations ago' (1922:69). On the other hand there is the possibility that there was sufficient flexibility for sub-clans to change their affiliation. Brunton reports that the village of Suviyagila in Kuboma acquired guyau status between the time of Malinowski and that of Powell (Brunton 1975:552). Further, Vilaylima in Luba, once a commoner village, reportedly became a Tabalu location for two generations, but returned to its original owners when the only remaining Tabalu woman died childless (Malinowski 1935:365–6). Neither of these villages shows out as being central according to analysis or otherwise important, which may explain the failure to consolidate guyau status. What is significant is that the two instances suggest the possibility for local dala rank to change (although they do not necessarily illustrate it). However, this does not carry explanation very far. There is still the problem of explaining rank differences within the Tabalu, from place to place.

Dala status and the district economy

Several people have related rank to the strength of a district's economy. Malinowski did, and Powell too invoked associated demographic factors (1969:601). Uberoi argued a very specific case (1962:43). He held that the rank of a dala was the result of: (1) economic advantage especially in terms of garden land and fisheries; (2) the extent to which its village was a centre integrating the economic activities of its neighbours; (3) its position in the network of overseas alliances. Essentially, the first of these points invokes ecological factors, while the remaining two are concerned with inter-site spatial relationships distinguished according to distance. Brunton has criticised the scheme (1975:551). He notes, for instance, in terms of Uberoi's third point, that Vakuta is more important in the kula than Omarakana, yet in Vakuta rank is inoperative despite the presence of the Tabalu. Brunton argues as if this invalidates Uberoi's scheme. In fact it merely indicates that one factor is ineffective in this case. The other two factors still can account for the rank difference between Omarakana and Vakuta. Malinowski described the district economy of Kiriwina as the most pronounced (1935:369) while Omarakana scored very much higher than Vakuta in terms of connectivity analysis.

It is clear that centrality and ecology affect dala status. It has been found within districts, that the most central villages were the places where the highest-ranking individuals were found. It is not difficult to suggest why this should be. Chiefs managed unusually large quantities of resources and it is agreed that the basis of such wealth was polygamy. Rank was quite directly expressed in the number of wives. The chief of Omarakana had 16 wives in Malinowski's time, while his predecessor Enamakala had 19 in 1893 (Annual Report 1893–4:19). In 1950 despite long-established missionary activity, there were still 13 (Powell 1960: 136). In traditional Trobriand society it seems that all leaders of village clusters of guyau status became polygamists. An emerging leader might also expect to be given wives by traditional allies outside the cluster while he might demand them from traditional rivals of subordinate subclans (Powell 1960:136). Powell also claims (1960:136), giving some idea of scale, that in Kiriwina in 'olden times' the leader of Kwaybwaga cluster might have had about 9 wives while the leader of the Omarakana cluster might accumulate 40 in a successful political career.

Under the system of urigubu (to oversimplify the case), the bulk of one's annual harvest went to fill the yam house of one's sister's husband. The basis of chiefly power was the increased quantity of such tribute (Powell 1960:134), for while most people's income and outgoings were about the same, polygamists received more than they gave away (Powell 1969:584). The respective ranks of giver and receiver affected the size of urigubu gifts. Values given by Powell (1969:583) and Malinowski (1935: Appendices II, III and IV) show that rank differentiation among Trobriand village and cluster leaders was reflected in very great variation in the number and size of the gifts they received. It is also clear that some leaders of high status commanded very considerable resources indeed. The receipt of multiple gifts was simultaneously a consequence and cause of a leader's pre-eminence (Powell 1969:591). The status of chiefs lay not only in the resources at their command, but under this system, potential political rivals were deprived of the opportunity to accumulate comparable quantities of the resources.

Villages have been described as predominantly 'urigubu endogamous' and village clusters even more so (Powell 1969:591). Only a leader maintained a significant amount of contact beyond these limits. Figures supplied by Powell (1960:125) for 1950 show that male household heads within the Omarakana cluster of villages gave 55% of urigubu gifts within their own village from which thay also gained 56% of their receipts. Within the village cluster the comparable figures are 80% and 75%. By contrast, the chief Mitikata gave only 3 gifts, all to men of his own village, whereas of the 76 gifts he received, 10% came from within his village, a further 15% from other villages within the cluster and the remaining 75% from beyond it (Powell 1960:125). If this situation was characteristic of traditional society then it can be seen that most urigubu payments were in respect of marriages within or near the village and were locally integrative. However, payments to leaders of guyau status reflect their importance in the external relationships of the cluster; mainly within the district but sometimes even beyond it.

Thus ranking chiefs received far more than other people both in terms of frequency and volume of payments. In addition, many of their contacts were external. The obvious inference is that at harvest time there were a lot of yams on Trobriand roads, travelling especially to chiefs, often over fair distances. It is known that the villages of the highest-ranking chiefs were centrally located within their districts, which was ideal given their role as both collection and redistributive centres for goods. For not only did they accumulate wealth, subsequently thay also disbursed it. Much of the urigubu they received went to support the corporate activities of their subclans and villages, to underwrite capital works such as canoe building, to contribute to distributions such as at mortuary rites and especially feasts of merit (Powell 1969:584). Needless to say, whenever yams were left to rot in chiefly yam houses, this effectively removed them from circulation and from the control of other individuals, thereby reinforcing chiefly power (see Rathje 1978).

It can be noted that Brunton argued recently (1975:551) that a dala is more likely to be a centre for economic exchange as a consequence of its high-rank, not as a cause. The evidence presented above suggests that the case is much more likely to be the other way around.

There is a further general point to be made about rank and the district economy. From north to south the economic strength of districts generally diminishes. The amount of good gardening land tends to reduce, although not in a regular way and the number of villages gets smaller too. Vakuta is said to have better gardens than Sinaketa (Mali-nowski 1935:291), but there were only a handful of villages there. Over-all, one's impression is that the 'demographic horsepower' of districts reduces towards the south. Certainly the absolute agricultural productiv-ity does. Similarly it has been shown that values by village for centrality within the island fall off markedly towards the south, a pattern, of course, which corresponds to the decreasing rank of Tabalu leaders; they are no longer chiefs, but just headmen.

These various factors presumably are related. Ecological and demo-graphic factors are evident in village density and distribution which in turn affect the pattern of centrality as well as the quantities of agricultural wealth available for collection and control at central places by 'central' (very high-ranking) people. The development in Sinaketa and Vakuta (and to an extent Kayleuna and Kavataria), of centres of specialised manufacture, trade and kula is entirely consistent with local ecology, but according to this analysis, their emergence was independent of rank, the size of the district economy, and the patterns of centrality within it. Whether their emergence was affected by their centrality in relation to overseas kula will be discussed below.

Rank and the kula

The argument so far implies that the origin of rank differentiation in the Trobriands can be explained satisfactorily without recourse to the kula as another effective variable. However one recent theory has included it very explicitly. Brunton has argued that participation in the kula became the basis of social differentiation, with political success based largely on success in the kula (Brunton 1975:553). He observes that formerly, kula routes could have passed through Vakuta and Sinaketa *en route* between Dobu and Kitava (1975:548). It would be quite possible to short-circuit the network and leave out Kiriwina, whose position is rather precarious. Powell (1978) notes that Kiriwina could expect more adverse winds on the sea-leg to Kitava than the other Trobriand communities to the south. Brunton also argues that Kiriwina plugged into the kula circuit at a late stage (1975:553). This view is very plausible and is corroborated by the fact that myths of the kula refer only to the southern parts of the Trobriands (Malinowski 1922:306–7). The question is how part of the north succeeded in getting in.

The view of this writer is simply that political differentiation developed in the north as described above. The power of the chiefs of Omarakana did not stem from kula participation; rather they became important in it simply because they were influential anyway, for independent reasons. In other words, political power at home was a pre-requisite for a Kiriwina man's prominence in the kula, not the consequence.

Brunton's theory is the reverse of this and the process of change he envisages is more elaborate. Initially he believes some men in the north – the Tabalu – supplied women to a kula community to the south in the manner reported by Malinowski (1935:290–1). In return for their urigubu payments they subsequently received *vaygu'a* valuables which they used as kula (Brunton 1975:553). These men then allegedly became the link for further aspirants who sent their sisters south too. What was critical to their success, it is alleged, was that they were able to exploit an environmental situation to 'close off the exchange system and erect barriers to the convertibility of Kula items' (Brunton 1975:553). Stringent control of this kind was not possible in other areas, but in the north, where valuables were scarce, keeping participation in sufficiently few hands resulted in the development of stratification. In Kiriwina, the argument continues, the only local economic specialisation was gardening, which meant that individuals could not undermine the locally closed system by engaging in other side-trade of significance. Once prominent leaders began to emerge they were able to consolidate their positions by establishing control of pigs, and other resources (Brunton 1975:553–4).

The theory is ingenious but gives rise to certain objections: (1) it does not specify precisely how the northern region was geographically 'closed'. The ethnographies, which report numerous contacts with other parts of Kiriwina Island, Kayleuna, Kitava and perhaps the Lusancays, suggest a much more 'leaky' system than Wogeo, which Brunton uses as a model (Brunton 1975:555). (2) It is arguable that kula participation was kept in a few hands although it is likely that the bulk of it was. (3) In stating that there was no alternative to kula exchange in the north to exploit as the means of increasing status, Brunton has overlooked the axe blanks imported from the Suloga quarry on Woodlark and the subsequent grinding and polishing to produce finished implements, that was carried out in Tilataula and Kiriwina. The widespread distribution in Papua of these axes, as documented archaeologically, testifies to the importance of the industry. E. Leach (1978) has suggested that the power of the chiefs, depended upon their monopolistic control of the stone axes. However to suggest that the way to political power was to establish a corner in the axe trade begs the question of how certain individuals were able to gain an advantage in the first place. Rather than invoke random causation or speculate at the level of individual personalities, one can argue that the relative locational advantages enjoyed by certain villages – as demonstrated above for the settlement pattern of the early 1900s by connectivity analysis – contributed initially to the emergence of higher rank which was associated with particular localities. This could have been the initial advantage which set other developments going. Changing patterns of centrality and the antiquity of the axe trade are questions that can be pursued archaeologically. Identification of the prehistoric social context of the exchange of valuables might be rather more difficult. However, it is clear that theories of the origins of stratification in the Trobriands are capable of expression as hypotheses to be subjected to archaeological scrutiny.

Warfare

Because nothing succeeds like success, it is likely that in Trobriand prehistory, emerging political power, whatever its initial causes or cause, was able to consolidate and enhance itself by other additional means. One obvious factor that has been discussed is warfare. Powell has argued that rank is advantageous in 'so small and densely populated an island' (1969:601). Certainly demographic and ecological factors would seem to increase the likelihood of warfare, given a population of approximately 130 people per cultivable square mile on an island subject occasionally to drought, during which villages and districts might be forced to compete with one another (Powell 1960:119). Moreover, in social terms, village clusters which were not allied under one leader may have had the tendency to be competitive (Powell 1960:139).

Powell has suggested (1978) that northerners may have aided and abetted the build-up of their leaders so that they became strong enough to dominate the south militarily if needs be, so that they (the northerners) could participate in the kula. This theory can be regarded as unnecessary now that it has been established that the northern leaders had an independent basis for their power.

In the contact period the political history of the Trobriands was dominated by rivalry between Omarakana Tabalu and the Toliwaga of Tilataula district (Seligmann 1910:663–8; Malinowski 1922:66). Around 1885 Enamakala laid waste many villages of Tilataula, allegedly because the chief of Kabwaku had refused him a wife (Powell 1960:141–2). In 1889 when Enamakala had lost some local support and after some of his allies had changed sides, he was driven south into exile. Apparently no attempt was made by either party to occupy the lands or villages of the other during their period of defeat nor to oppose directly their return to power.

It is risky to generalise on a single case and it must be borne in mind also that Europeans were on the scene and probably influencing events at this time. However one might wonder whether the normal outcome of

51

war was the eventual re-establishment of the former political situation (perhaps as some system of checks and balances against the over-aggrandisement of either party), or whether the former situation would not necessarily be restored. For instance one might speculate that the Toliwaga faction might have established permanent supremacy over the Tabalu had not history interrupted prehistory. Subsequently perhaps, the Toliwaga might have tried to legitimise their new situation either by becoming Tabalu themselves, or by altering somehow the accepted relative status of the respective dala. There is no reason to suppose Trobriand culture was incapable of such accommodation. However, to speculate on what was happening in prehistoric politics is fruitless until archaeological data which bears on the question is collected.

Conclusions

The emergence of rank differentiation in Trobriand Island prehistory probably was multi-causal. This section of the paper has attempted to quantify just one of the factors involved. This in turn allows evaluation of the effect of other factors, on a more realistic basis than if none of them has been controlled with any precision.

It is suggested that certain people in central places enjoyed an initial advantage that they were able to consolidate by gaining control over a range of economic resources. By the contact period the relative power of chiefs corresponded quite closely to the patterns of centrality among the spatial distribution of contemporary villages. Variations in rank were also related to the relative strength of the district economies, as these affected the amount of agricultural wealth available for collection and management by 'central people' at central places, largely through the institutions of polygamy and urigubu. Thus there was a complex interplay of ecological, demographic, locational and social factors within a system which has been emerging through time. Moreover, it seems that it is possible to explain Trobriand chieftainship such as it was, without recourse to the kula. It is relevant to note that Powell too, has argued that kula is a relatively unimportant institution; in Kiriwina at least, being secondary to kinship and marriage. The way to power he believes, is by urigubu not kula, although the latter can be used to sustain competition between individuals living too far apart to compete by more normal means (Powell 1965:48; 1969:601).

However, this theory of the emergence of chieftainship does not explain all that is characteristic of the Tabalu, just as the concept of centrality does not include all kinds of relative locational advantage that can apply to sites. In the four districts where we can say district chiefs occurred, the Tabalu monopolised the positions except in Tilataula. However, Tabalu occurred elsewhere in other villages, having the status of ordinary village leaders. It is notable that all such villages, while not central to internal communications, were otherwise very strategic in a locational and ecological sense. In Vakuta and Sinaketa Tabalu were present in villages which were specialist centres of manufacture, trade and kula. The economic orientation of these villages was entirely compatible with, although not necessarily the result of, the pattern of locally available resources. Much the same can be said of Kayleuna where Tabalu occurred also. Kavataria, a specialised centre with an estimated 1,000 inhabitants at contact (Seligmann 1910:662), conformed to the pattern too. Finally, Tabalu recently settled in the village of Tukwaukwa in Kulumata (Malinowski 1935:366) which lay strategically on one of the major routes inland to northern areas of the main island. Therefore we can say generally that all residential Tabalu groups enjoyed locational advantages. The more chiefly groups were working within a system where internal agricultural production was of greatest importance. The others were operating in places with more specialised economic roles, located at important points of articulation with the overseas communications system. One might even wonder whether there was any advantage in the very absence of chieftainship in communities practising such an economy.

Among dala of guyau rank, the Tabalu appear to be different in kind as well as degree. According to the results of this analysis, of all guyau groups, it is only the Tabalu who consistently occur in places which are central or otherwise strategic. There is no increased probability of this for other dala (except perhaps the Toliwaga who, as well as their situation in Tilataula, evidently were found also in a village in Vakuta). The Tabalu also differed in being the only group acknowleged to be spatially mobile. All others were autochthonous.

One final point relates to how static or dynamic Trobriand society was at the end of prehistory. Because the incoming of the Government froze a political situation (Seligmann 1910:694), there seems to have been a tendency in subsequent ethnography to see the system as one simply oscillating between the ultimate and penultimate recorded states, rather than shifting from one state to an entirely new one. For instance, European intervention may have caught the Tabalu at their moment of ascendancy before declining and being superseded. Alternatively if there was a capacity, as discussed above, for village ownership to change dala affiliation, then Tabalu might have been the category describing whichever group that happened to be established currently on top.

Geoffrey Irwin

Part two: sense and centrality in the kula ring

This part of the paper extends the discussion of centrality from the Trobriands to the wider kula ring. Three similar studies have been made of the kula, using connectivity analysis. Map 7 depicts this writer's version of the network. Each circle on the map encloses a kula community and the lines between them are the exchange links reported by Malinowski (1922) and Fortune (1932). As a further comment on locational factors in the Trobriands it can be seen that in general, the regions that are most accessible to an external kula community, are themselves communities. Kitava has links with Kiriwina in the north, Vakuta to the south and reportedly a trickle passed through the centre. The southern communities of Sinaketa and Vakuta had links to the south. Tilataula and Kuboma faced away from the kula and evidently played no part in overseas exchanges. Even Kayleuna, occupying a maritime situation in the west operated most of its overseas trade outside the kula. Again it is evident that locational factors accord with spatial variability in behaviour.

The first analysis of the whole kula was by Brookfield who used the short-path method (Brookfield with Hart 1971:325). He found that Tubetube was the most central place, which correlates with an economy based on middleman trade and the specialised manufacture of pottery and nose ornaments (Brookfield with Hart 1971:327). The results of a study by Hage (1977) agree closely with Brookfield's. Hage applied the Mailu model (Irwin 1974) to the kula and argued that Tubetube was like Mailu in being: (1) the most central place in its network; (2) too small to support its own population; (3) a settlement of economic specialists. Detailed results of the various analyses are presented in Table 2. Even though different kula networks were used in each case, it can be seen that the short-path solutions of Brookfield and Hage agree quite closely with one another and with that presented by the writer. In addition, the solution using unweighted connection-array connectivity is identical in its first three places with the short-path one.

The economic and ecological similarity of Mailu and Tubetube is obvious. One can readily think of other examples of societies of industrial and maritime specialists who are located on small islands. In Melanesia there are the Siassi traders of the Vitiaz Straits (Harding 1967) and closer to hand, the Amphlett Island potters. It is tempting to explain their economies in ecological terms. The impoverishment of local resources could be seen as the primary incentive to trade. However this theory cannot accommodate the fact that a great many very small islands with meagre resources are either unoccupied or only sparsely occupied. To be a successful trader, one needs to have potential customers nearby. It is

54

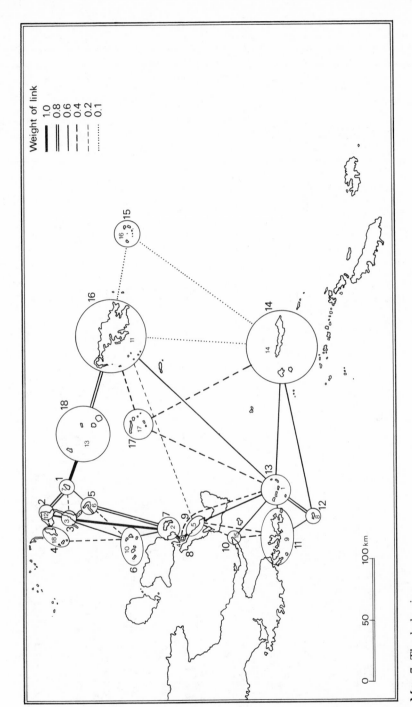

Map 7. The kula ring.

Table 2. Centrality of kula communities

	Site No.	Weighted connection-array connectivity		Connection-array connectivity		Short-path connectivity	Hage Short-path connectivity	Brookfield Short-path connectivity
		Rank	%	Rank	%	Rank	Rank	Rank
KITAVA	1	7	9.7	15	3.5	6=	6=	5=
KIRIWINA	2	12	9.5	17	2.2	12	9	5=
SINAKETA	3	3	8.0	11	4.1	8	8=	5=
KAYLEULA	4	18	7.9	18	1.4	13	11	5=
VAKUTA	5	6	6.7	14	3.6	7	6=	4=
AMPHLETTS	6	10	5.8	16	3.2	9=	8=	4=
N.W. DOBU	7	2	5.7	12	3.9	5	3=	2=
DOBU	8	4	5.5	9	5.3	2=	2	2=
S.E. DOBU	9	5	5.4	3	8.4	3	5	3
EAST CAPE	10	15	5.3	7	5.8	9=	8=	5=
EAST END ISLANDS	11	9	5.3	6	6.8	10	7=	5=
WARI	12	8	5.2	8	5.7	9=	7=	5=
TUBETUBE	13	1	4.8	1	12.2	1	1	1
MISIMA	14	14	4.6	4	8.2	6=	6	5=
LAUGHLAN	15	16	4.2	13	3.7	11	10	–
WOODLARK	16	11	4.1	2	9.4	2=	3=	4=
ALCESTERS	17	17	3.9	5	7.3	4=	3=	5=
MARSHALL BENNETTS	18	13	1.2	10	4.4	4=	4	–

suggested that there is a locational component to the development of these specialised communities too. The application of ecology in this way can be something of a red herring as an explanation. In the Mailu case, it was found that the pattern of local resources was merely compatible with the island's economic and political function. It did not explain for instance, why such a community was not situated in any one of a number of other equally-endowed locations (Irwin 1978b).

In the kula area at least two such local systems have developed during prehistory (see below), rather as is known to have happened on Mailu. Tubetube is the most striking parallel; the Amphletts may be a rather different case. The latter were located between the resource-rich volcanic islands of the D'Entrecasteaux and the low coralline Trobriands which lacked important industrial materials such as obsidian, available to the south. Trade between these areas makes good sense and it can be seen that the Amphletts were conveniently located to act as stepping-stones between them. The importance of such a role has recently been argued by Kaplan (1976) in the case of Nissan Island which lies between the Bismarck Archipelago and the Solomon Islands. Moreover, the Amphletts are small, with meagre local resources. At the end of prehistory the island women were specialist potters with a virtual monopoly of supply to the Trobriands, Marshall Bennetts and northwestern Dobu. Further south their pottery was found together with ware from other sources as it was on Woodlark (Malinowski 1922:282; Fortune 1932:207). One apparent anomaly of the network analysis is that the Amphletts consistently rank relatively lowly with respect to the network as a whole. However inspection of a map of the kula shows that they are well enough located with respect to the area of distribution of their pottery market in the northeast, which adequately explains their specialisation. Their lack of centrality in the wider network fits the absence in the Amphletts of a developed maritime middleman trader role as in Tubetube.

The case of the industrial specialisation of Kuboma represents another kind of development. Like the Amphletts and Tubetube the district of Kuboma was a net importer of food (Malinowski 1922:88; Brookfield with Hart 1971:327). However unlike them, it was cut off from the sea in a part of the kula with very low centrality. The absence of overseas traders in Kuboma is in keeping with this. Coastal neighbours of Kuboma were middlemen in the overseas trade of its goods.

While network analysis has thrown some light on a few parts of the kula network, most others remain largely in the dark. As well as this, the network analysis has some additional serious drawbacks. Firstly, Malinowski knew the Trobriand situation well and was able to identify a number of kula communities there. Consequently, it takes more steps in

Geoffrey Irwin

a network to pass through the Trobriands, than say Woodlark Island which is shown as a single community, even though very likely it was not. Uneven information of this kind introduces bias into analysis against the Trobriands. Secondly, there is considerable uncertainty about the precise configuration of the network. For example: (1) Malinowski was in doubt as to whether East Cape was included or not (1922:498). (2) There is doubt about the link between the Laughlans and Misima (1922:495). (3) Malinowski (1922:80) showed Yeguma and the Alcesters as a node and Hage (1977:28) follows him, whereas Brookfield with Hart (1971:325) do not. (4) On the other hand Malinowski (and Hage) did not show the direct link between southeast Dobu and Woodlark Island (nodes 9 and 16 in Map 7) referred to by Fortune (1932:202) and shown by Brookfield with Hart. (5) Finally, even the established links probably varied a lot in terms of the volume of traffic along them. One known instance is the relatively low frequently of communication between Kitava and Sinaketa *via* Wawela and other villages of Kaybwagina. Another is the link between Woodlark and the Laughlans.

To take account of these problems, a further analysis was done employing the weightings shown in Map 7. The results are shown in Table 2. This solution is partly successful in that: (1) it gives parts of the Trobriands and the Amphletts rather more centrality in the system; (2) it reduces the significance of some nodes connected by intermittent links, such as the Alcesters (node 17). (3) Tubetube remains most central. However, there is no real control of what is happening to the other places.

A further problem is that Malinowski (1922) described overseas kula rather in isolation from the wider context of interaction between local communities both within the Massim and further afield. He saw it essentially as a closed circuit of exchange of valuables, although he was aware of regular inputs to the system from outside – armshells from parts of Murua and the Trobriands and necklaces from the central Papuan coast and Rossel Island which entered from the south. He was also aware of the regular leakage of armshells from the system through the Mailu trading network (Malinowski 1915:622–3). These external links and the interal equilibrium of the kula ring itself must have been interrelated in a systematic way. To study centrality in the kula without taking note of the pattern of associated communication is not very realistic.

Proximal-point model

A simpler method of studying the kula is the network shown in Fig. 1. It was constructed in a similar way to the networks for analysis of internal

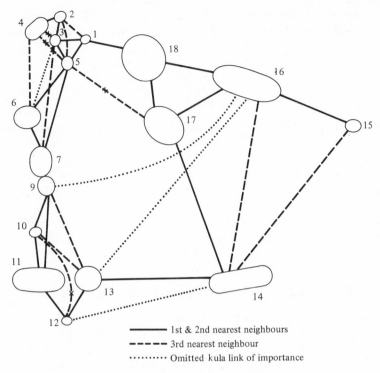

1st & 2nd nearest neighbours
----- 3rd nearest neighbour
.... Omitted kula link of importance

Figure 1. Proximal point network of kula communities.

communications in the Trobriands (above), and also to one of the Solomon Islands used successfully by Terrell (1976). Briefly, this map shows the locations of the various Kula communities (with the exception of Dobu Island which was omitted for simplicity). Next, it joins each community, or node, to its three nearest neighbours, showing third-nearest neighbour links as dashed lines. Certain links which were not reported to be part of the kula have been marked with crosses. On the other hand certain important kula links which were not already included have been added and shown as dotted lines to distinguish them.

Inspection of Fig. 1 supports a number of observations.
1. It can be seen that the proximal-point pattern constructed is very similar to the actual kula network, especially in the west.
2. Some of the kula links about which there was uncertainty, as between nodes 14–15 and 14–16, are only dashed lines.
3. The functional specialisation of the skilled sailors and traders of Tubetube is apparent in the pattern of dotted lines. They sailed further afield than other communities.

59

This model does not contribute to the question of why some places in the Massim were part of the kula while others were not. It simply takes the information on the location of communities as given. However, its basic conclusion is that direction, and sheer distance to be sailed, may have had some influence on the pattern of inter-community links. If one were considering the question of why the kula was in the form of a ring, at least part of the answer might be because that is how the islands are distributed geographically. Such an answer of course, would not explain why the kula was a double ring (i.e. having articles moving in both directions).

This conclusion implies that a gravity model is as appropriate to the configuration of the network as a centrality model or an ecology one. It is clear that no single explanatory model is sufficient to explain the ethnographic evidence. The development of the kula in prehistory is likely to have been multi-causal and complex. The various models can be considered in the light of the archaeological evidence.

Part three: economic specialisation and trade in Massim prehistory

This section of the paper investigates aspects of Massim prehistory and in particular, the development of patterns of specialised manufacture and trade which created the inter-island communication upon which the kula came to be based. The difficulty is that the archaeological data which bears on the question is fragmentary. Published information from within the kula area itself is still restricted to surface collections. To make the best of this information, it can be considered in a wider context. Excavations at both Collingwood Bay (Egloff 1971) and Mailu (Irwin 1977) can provide some time control for kula prehistory, although conclusions reached at this stage are necessarily tentative.

From Mailu pottery to Massim prehistory

In addition, the study of prehistoric and modern pottery of Mailu is helpful for interpreting comparable material from the Massim. Briefly, it has been established that through time the potters of Mailu acquired a monopoly of manufacture and supply in their area. As the economic context of production changed from a domestic craft to a centralised and specialised one, there were associated changes in the pots themselves, in ceramic technology and also in the size and characteristics of the market. Thus in the form and style of prehistoric pots themselves, as well as in their spatial distribution, there are clues about the context of production which can support theories about manufacture and trade in Massim prehistory. These theories can be tested against archaeological evidence as it comes to hand and also in the light of aspects of modern ceramic technology in the same areas. The argument necessitates a digression into Mailu data. However this will be brief and selective; fuller accounts are available elsewhere (Irwin 1977). 'Pottery is the biggest industry on Mailu Island. Only women and girls engage in it. The food supply of the community largely depends upon it. The Mailu-speaking people generally, and their nearer neighbours, prefer boiled food. Their own way of expressing it is: "We like gravy"' (Saville 1926:143).

Pottery has been made on Mailu Island for the last 2,000 years. The modern industry is the current expression of an unbroken stylistic tradition which goes back half of that time. Pots are made by the coil technique and the clay comes from deposits on Mailu itself. It is always worked with salt water, not fresh and no temper is added. Tests by Rye (1976) have shown that, technologically, this produces the most satisfactory results in terms of the characteristics of the clay. It is significant that in the beginning of pottery making on Mailu, beach-shell temper was added to the local clay, but this practice was soon (and advantageously) abandoned (Irwin 1977:225–6).

A study of the work of nine potters in 1973 showed that the technology is extremely standardised. In terms of firing technique, the whole industry could be, in statistical terms, the work of a single potter. Control of firing temperatures was found to be very sophisticated. Fig. 2 plots the temperature curve of a pot made by the potter Rigo and illustrates the phases of the firing process. It can be seen that during the first minutes temperatures remained low. During this time the inverted pot was resting on three stones set among the embers of the previous fire and dry sago-palm midrib fuel was arranged around it. In this test it can be seen that temperature was monitored at the exterior base of the inverted pot. Heat from the remnant embers was absorbed slowly, which protected the pot against thermal shock during the stage of dramatic temperature rise which follows ignition. In the fourth minute the fuel was ignited by torches of dried sago-palm leaves. Each black arrow in the graph indicates one torch and four were used. These were placed on the windward side of the fire so that the flames were quickly fanned downwind on to the fuel. In this firing and others, temperature climbed at a high, normally steady rate. The graph indicates a straight line relationship between time and temperature and a rate of climb of around 100 degrees centigrade per minute. The peak exceeded 1,000 degrees. However, some small deviations from the rate can be seen. Whenever temperature failed to rise, or fell slightly, for a period as long as approximately thirty seconds, the potter intervened. In two instances a single torch was applied to a

61

Geoffrey Irwin

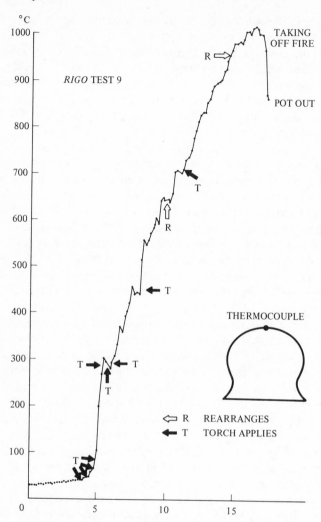

Figure 2. Temperature curve in Mailu pottery firing.

particular part of the fire. In one instance three torches were used one after another. In a fourth instance, rearrangement of fuel was performed apparently as an alternative to use of a torch. In all cases the rate of temperature-climb was quickly reestablished. The graph also reveals that several lesser deviations did not provoke remedial action.

Over seventeen firing tests it was found that there was a very high correlation between temperature deviations and potter's intervention. It indicates a remarkable awareness of firing conditions on the part of the

62

potters and an equally high degree of control. It would also be fair to say that the sensitivity of the potters to changing conditions of firing was at least equal to that of the sophisticated pyrometer used to monitor it. How they were able to do it remains largely unexplained. However, this is just one of many examples of how simple tools may be associated with complex technology.

Fig. 3 illustrates another characteristic feature of firing on Mailu. When temperature was monitored at more than one location, it can be seen that the curves followed independent trajectories. However, in all of the firing tests, at the precise point of temperature-curve intersection, or very close to it in time, the pots were removed from the fire. This is interpreted as follows: in order to produce a clear coloured unsmudged surface, pots must be removed from the fire while still at high temperature, which involves thermal shock. If all parts of a pot are at the same temperature, including inner and outer wall surfaces at the same place (Fig. 3) this minimises stress in the fabric of the vessel and reduces the chance of breakage. If pottery is one's bread and butter as it was on Mailu, this is a sensible way to behave. In several months on the island in 1973, the writer failed to record a single breakage.

As part of the Mailu pottery study in 1973 a 'census' of all pots in the village was taken. It was found that in form, decoration and distribution the pottery was entirely homogeneous; in short it was a standardised trade ware, just as it was at the end of prehistory. Fig 4a illustrates for instance, that two dimensions (orifice diameter and vessel height) which together give a good idea of overall proportions, are related in a simple linear way. As one increases so does the other. Evidently the Mailu make only the one kind of pot which comes in different sizes. However it can also be seen that the range of size of pots made for trade is more restricted than those made for home consumption. Similarly, Fig. 4b illustrates the extremes of the range of vessel shape. It can be seen that even they are virtually identical. Finally, a study of the distribution of pottery decoration technique and motif failed to find any variation which corresponded to any kinship or residence group on Mailu.

The situation was not always like this in prehistory. It has been possible to divide the last 800 years into two ceramic periods, one developing into the other. The two separated by a process of standardisation some 400 years ago. The earlier material was stylistically diverse, the later material was uniform. On the basis of this it was predicted that there could have been a change in the economic context of production and distribution too (Irwin 1974). The model in brief, was that if pottery making is a widespread domestic craft carried out intermittently, there is a tendency for the technology to be homogeneous and perhaps rather crude, while at the

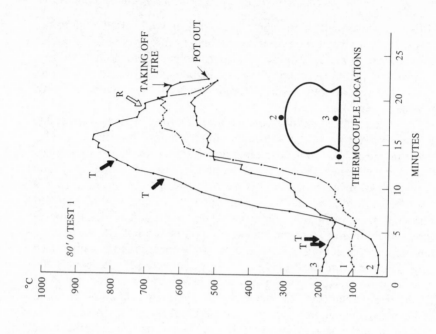

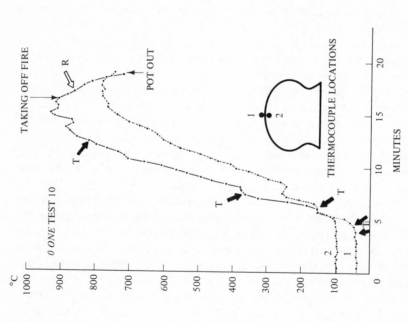

Figure 3. Temperature curves in Mailu pottery firing.

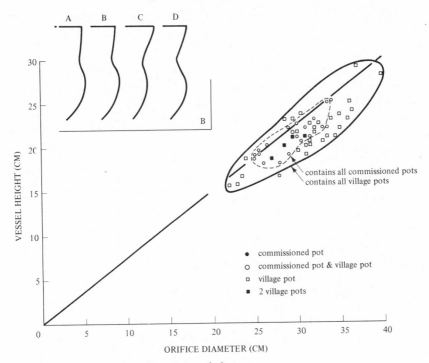

Figure 4. Mailu pots in 1973: size and shape.

same time there will be a great variety in the detail and finish of pots as each potter expresses her own individuality. Specialists have an opposing formula, a firm unity. They display more standardised and improved production methods while shapes, sizes and decoration of pots become very uniform. Thus from the pottery evidence alone one can predict that prior to the emergence of the trade ware, pottery making was a widespread skill. Independent evidence (based on chemical analysis of potsherds and clay sources) shows this to be the case (Irwin 1978a). Mailu acquired her proprietary specialisation during prehistory. Fig. 5 shows that as this happened the pottery also became finer, through a series of excavated layers on the island. From the Mailu point of view as specialists there were advantages to be had, although one can only speculate as to how they were perceived. (1) Firstly, thinner vessel walls means more economical use of clay. (2) It also means faster drying of vessels before firing and hence more rapid manufacture. (3) Thinner-walled vessels boil faster in use and were sometimes preferred (Lauer 1974:190). (4) There is an indication that there was a reduced chance of breakage in manufacture. (5) Finally, there is the possibility currently under investigation,

65

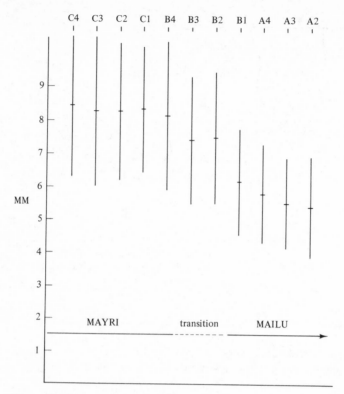

Figure 5. Mean vessel thickness, ca. 1200 A.D. to present.

that finer vessels were no more able to withstand mechanical shock in use than thicker ones. If in fact they were weaker, this too would be in the interests of the island community. An inbuilt obsolescence may have been developing.

Allied to these changes was a gradual expansion in the area of distribution of pots deriving from the Mailu Island clay source. There was a progressive expansion of Mailu pottery along the coasts and a deeper penetration inland into the Owen Stanley Range. As the island's population was growing, so was the size of its pottery market.

Modern pottery in the Massim

The Mailu case has obvious implications for the Massim. The professional appearance of Amphlett pottery is stressed. According to Lauer's description (1974) it is clear that it is highly standardised and the various modern vessel types can be identified readily in archaeological surface collections. Moreover, Amphlett pottery is as fine or perhaps even finer than Mailu ware. There are interesting parallels in firing technique as well. For example, large Amphlett pots are fired singly and the fires are built over smouldering coconut husks which preheat the vessel and may protect it from thermal shock, according to the Mailu principle. Lauer recorded a temperature of 918 degrees centigrade at the rim of one inverted pot, which implies that maximum temperature at the base could exceed even those of Mailu, although Lauer did not measure this. Further, it is evident that just as in Mailu, Amphlett pots seldom break in firing. Given the knowledge of Mailu prehistory, one can predict a considerable time depth of the specialised Amphlett industry.

As an aside, there is an interesting implication here for the antiquity of the Hiri, the system of long distance trade between the Port Moresby area and the Gulf of Papua. Important items in this trade were the large quantities of Motu pots which were traded for sago. Apparently when the Hiri was drawing close and the Motu potters hard-pressed, the losses in firing sometimes became very high indeed (Groves 1960). One could argue from this that Hiri voyages on the scale described, began relatively recently because the pottery industry had not had sufficient time to adapt technologically to the new economic situation. Again by analogy with the Mailu case, the fact that Motu pottery has become markedly more plain in surface finish in recent prehistory (Bulmer, pers. comm.), suggests that large-scale production is a comparably recent development. Some linguistic evidence supports this theory. Dutton has found that the Hiri trade language is extremely homogeneous throughout the area where it is spoken. This may be an indication of shallow time-depth. Certaintly one possible interpretation of the evidence is that the language has not had time to diversify (Dutton 1978).

Lauer believes that there is a general level of technological similarity between Amphlett pottery and the three industries of northwestern Goodenough Island indicating some as yet unknown prehistoric relationship between them. However the differences are significant. On Goodenough Island pottery making is not an economic necessity as in the Amphletts. It merely provided some additional food. It was made for local consumption rather than overseas trade. A number of other characteristics conform to the model presented here. (1) Typologically the ware was less standardised than Mailu and Amphlett ware. Lauer reports that the three ethnographic types are not distinguishable archaeologically. (2) Reported maximum temperatures in firing are lower and management operations were less sophisticated than the Mailu. (3) In locational terms Goodenough Island has less ecological inducement to

Geoffrey Irwin

trade and is less strategically situated with respect to potential markets than the Amphletts.

The pottery industries in the northwest of the Massim as a group are thought to be distinct from another general group in the south. There are considerable similarities between the industries of Tubetube, Wari, Paneati and perhaps even to some extent with Mailu. These industries have not yet been studied in detail, but it is clear at least that in terms of the level of standardisation and sophistication, they bear greater similarity to Amphlett ware than Goodenough, which accords also with the relative levels of economic specialisation on the islands concerned. Lauer has reported from the study of surface collections that since European contact, the southern pottery industry has made inroads into what was formerly mainly the Amphletts' sphere of influence. There is evidence of this in the Trobriands and southeast Fergusson Island (Lauer 1974).

Prehistoric pottery in the Massim

The archaeological situation is far from clear, but on the basis of research by Egloff and Lauer, it is possible to distinguish: (1) pottery made before approximately 1000 A.D.; (2) pottery made after 1000 A.D.; (3) the pottery that was being made at the end of the prehistoric and on into the modern periods. Pre-1000 A.D. material is found in a number of locations. It occurs in surface collections in Collingwood Bay but failed to appear (except at the base) in Egloff's excavated sequence, which establishes its minimum age. It is also widely distributed in surface sites on Goodenough Island, where among the sherds illustrated by Lauer (1974: Plates 58–65) there are some very similar to sherds excavated on Mailu from deposits dated to the first millennium A.D. Again, comparable pottery is widely distributed in the Trobriands in abandoned village sites and also in association with megaliths, which indicates their early age. None has been found in Trobriand burial caves.

Among prehistoric pottery post-dating 1000 A.D., there are at least three different groups. Firstly there is pottery of the kind excavated at Wanigela (Egloff's 'expansion phase'). It is found around Collingwood Bay and is widely distributed in the Trobriands on surface sites. It was also used to contain bones in burial caves. Chemical tests by Key (1968) on some of this ware from the Trobriands, show it to be identical mineralogically to Wanigela ware and it is thought to have been traded from the mainland (Egloff 1978:429). To complicate the situation, the same general kind of pottery also occurs on Goodenough Island and tests on samples collected on Nuamata, indicate that at least some of it was made from Goodenough clays (Egloff 1971:134; 1978:430, 33–4). The inference is that this ware was made within a large cultural province and distributed even more widely. Egloff is unable to see direct continuity between this and the recent and modern Wanigela industry.

A second kind of post-1000 A.D. pottery is evidently ancestral to modern Amphlett ware. Not surprisingly, it is known to occur in the Amphletts and also in Nuamata, eastern Fergusson Island and the Trobriands. In the Trobriands, in the period soon after 1000 A.D., it co-existed with pottery made around Wanigela, but then gradually it began to replace it. The Trobriand take-over by Amphlett ware was evidently complete approximately 5–600 years ago (Egloff 1971:132). Amphlett ware was dominant also among surface collections of this age from eastern Fergusson (Lauer 1971:203).

Finally, in this post-1000 A.D. prehistoric period, a third rather enigmatic class has been identified in the Nuamata funerary collection. It has some affinity with Amphlett ware, but as well as this, it could also be the forerunner of the modern Wanigela industry (Egloff 1971:133).

Hypotheses on Massim prehistory, the emergence of specialised trade and the origins of the kula

Some 2,000 years ago, a number of village communities with related pottery appeared along the south coast of Papua. They are currently known from the Mailu area in the east to the Papuan Gulf. Their radiocarbon ages are statistically alike, so in archaeological terms, if not actual ones, this episode was instantaneous (Irwin 1977:421–2). The evidence – such as it is – suggests that pottery making was introduced from the Massim. It can be supposed that following this time pottery styles diverged in the Massim just as they did along the south coast, according to the relative isolation of communities (Irwin 1977:309). However, it is evident too that certain lines of communication were open. For example obsidian from west Fergusson Island continued to reach Mailu although in diminishing amounts throughout the first millennium A.D. (W. Ambrose, pers. comm.; Irwin 1977:304). Only minute quantities reached Port Moresby sites of comparable age. The only documented trade of this period therefore, shows marked characteristics of distance-decay. At this time in the Massim the general picture is of widespread settlement, currently documented for the mainland coast, the D'Entrecasteaux, the Amphletts and the Trobriands where there were both open settlements and stone structures. Neither on the Papuan south coast, where there is good archaeological control, nor in the Massim, where there is not, is there any evidence for the presence of communities of specialist manufacturers and traders such as were known in later periods.

Geoffrey Irwin

The Wanigela excavated sequence began some 1000 years ago. At that time pottery was being made in Collingwood Bay and was distributed in the Trobriands in village sites and burial caves. Similar ware was found on Goodenough Island and some was even made there too. It is at this time that pottery ancestral to Amphlett ware becomes visible archaeologically. Not only is it found in the Amphletts but it is abundant in the Trobriands where its probable age is established by its association with mainland material. It progressively replaced, and perhaps displaced, the mainland ware, until by approximately 600 years ago an Amphlett monopoly of supply to the Trobriands was virtually complete. Although the evidence is less certain, the probability is that parts of the D'Entrecasteaux and especially the Dobu region, were within the Amphlett sphere also. The Amphlett Islands, small and impoverished in local resources, but strategically located with respect to overseas territories, evidently had developed into proprietary specialists. Further it is hypothesised that, as in the Mailu case, the ceramic standardisation and sophistication described ethnographically, was associated with this process.

Malinowski (1922:46–8, 288) described the Amphletts as culturally intermediate between the Trobriands and the Dobu and this may be interpreted as the product of their pattern of interaction in prehistory. It is predicated that trade extended beyond the Trobriands in the north, to Kitava, the Marshall Bennetts and perhaps to Woodlark. These islands are described as being culturally similar, which supports a theory of maintained communication in the past. Ecologically the Trobriands are similar to their nearer eastern neighbours and there was no impedance to movement.

Although the archaeological evidence is slight, it is likely that similar developments occurred in the south. Tubetube had ecological inducements to trade and it was very centrally located at contact. It is predicated that Tubetube emerged like Mailu, or the Siassi for that matter, into a central place, 'central' both in function and in location. The general similarity of the pottery industries of Tubetube, Wari and Paneati implies time depth to the information flow between them. The Amphletts which were relatively more specialised as potters than Tubetube, but less as middleman traders in the ethnographic situation, had emerged 600 years ago. The Mailu were locally dominant at least 400 years ago and it has been suggested that the Hiri was even more recent. Tubetube probably evolved in the same general time scale.

The evidence suggests the emergence of fields of increased interaction centred on a small number of key locations in the Massim. Two further developments are implied. (1) This provided a context of communication within which the kula could develop. Thus even though armshells and necklace units are known to have an antiquity of nearly 2,000 years in the region, the kula as such probably developed only in the last 500 years. (2) The expanding interaction system enabled further economic specialisation to develop in other places. Items such as canoes, armshells, necklaces and axes were made in particular places in the Massim at the end of prehistory. There is also the case of the industrial villages of Kuboma, whose wares moved through a wide area. Archaeological examples of such trade include the axes of Suloga hornfels found at late prehistoric Papuan sites, while earlier, when Wanigela on the mainland was supplying pots to areas now within the kula, it was itself receiving obsidian from Fergusson Island (Egloff 1978:433).

Brookfield has made the suggestion that the exchange of kula valuables was the vehicle that carried trade around parts of the ring, where without them, there would be little incentive for regular transfer. Such places were between islands that were ecologically similar or had no proprietary specialisation. Thus kula provided continuity for the long distance trade which supported the specialisation found in particular parts of the ring (Brookfield with Hart 1971:327). This theory which is essentially functional, is very plausible in its ethnographic setting. However it cannot easily be applied to prehistory. There are two major problems. Firstly, there is still the question of how the system of exchange of valuables itself got started. Secondly, while the ceremonial exchange of kula valuables was described by Malinowski (1922) as being quite distinct from *gimwali*, or barter of utilitarian trade goods which took place concurrently, one can not assume this for prehistory.

In this regard, one final comparison with Mailu has implications for the kula. The climax of the annual long-distance trading came when the Mailu sailed to Aroma in the west. The most important items to be traded were armshells made by themselves or obtained from the Massim, for pigs, which were consumed at an important festival on the return to Mailu. Shortly before reaching Aroma, the fleet would stop at the small island of Coutance which lies offshore in the barrier reef. There the men blackened themselves, performed magic over the armshells and ritually washed them. The intention was to make the armshells so attractive that the Mailu's Aroma trade-partners would accept them feverishly, with a minimum of haggling. However, usually haggling did take place over the armshells and whatever else the Mailu brought with them (Saville 1926: 158–60). The similarity with magic carried out on kula voyages, as at the beach of Sarubwoyna, is apparent. However the differences are striking too. In the Mailu case the context in which valuables were exchanged was very like gimwali. Given that the Mailu trade network articulated at several points in the east with the Massim, the similarity between the cases is unlikely to be coincidental, but the result of some historical relationship. The separation between the two cases is spatial. However it could be conjectured that had the separation been temporal, then it would be easy to see something akin to the Mailu–Aroma trade being the predecessor of the kula. Currently there is no way of knowing whether this suggestion has any merit at all, but it can be concluded that kula-like activities probably have been variable in their content as well as their distribution. More specific conclusions must await the collection of further archaeological information.

2   The kula in comparative perspective

ANDREW STRATHERN

Introduction

Since Malinowski's time we have been accustomed to speak of Melanesia as an area in which the principle of reciprocity, enshrined within elaborate and enduring forms of ceremonial exchange, is the major guiding force in local societies. Explicit comparisons of exchange systems in different parts of the region have, however, not often been undertaken. Such comparisons readily suggest themselves in ethnographic terms: the 'trading' aspects of the *kula* are reminiscent of Vitiaz Straits trade, as described by Harding (1967), and its 'ceremonial' aspects at once call for reference to Highlands New Guinea exchange festivals. Analytical comparisons, of course, must be based on limited sets of analytical themes. In this paper, then, I look at the basic rules in a set of exchange systems; at how those rules are manipulated in strategies; at the resultant meaning of exchanges; and finally at their material basis and likely trajectory of development. The geographical areas I am concerned with are: the kula area itself; the Highlands area, particularly Melpa (Mount Hagen) and Enga; trading systems of the Northern New Guinea coast, that is, the Vitiaz Straits and Huon Gulf; and the Tolai area of East New Britain, with brief reference also to links in shell trade between Malaita and the North Solomons Province of Papua New Guinea. None of the systems in these areas exactly duplicates any other, and my aim in choosing them is not primarily topological. It is rather that they appear worthwhile to consider in the light of the questions I wish to ask, i.e.:

1. What are the basic forms of 'advantage' envisaged or prescribed by the rules of exchange?
2. In what ways are these advantages in practice realised?
3. Is there a significant link between exchange practices and symbolism?
4. In contexts of manifold introduced changes, especially the introduction of money and capitalist enterprise, how have these systems altered internally?

Andrew Strathern

Each of these questions is prompted by field materials on the Melpa in the first instance; however, they are sufficiently general to be widely applicable. It is difficult to consider each question separately, so I combine discussion of them in what follows.

'Profit' in the Melpa 'moka'

The most striking and obvious feature of the Melpa *moka* exchange system is that it prescribes a form of 'profit-making'. This 'profit' does not have the same meaning as it does in a capitalist economy, for it is encompassed within a wider rule of reciprocity. However, the rule that 'profit' (just to continue for a moment to use this term, in a provocative and metaphorical manner) not only can but should be made, is of primary significance in the dynamics of exchange practices themselves. The form in which the rule appears is relative: that at each stage more should be given than was received last time. Moka is, properly speaking, the part that is 'more'. The rest is just paying debts. The quantity of the 'more' is variable, and it is here that possibilities of manipulation and variation enter, giving rise to a range of outcomes, from over-gifting as a means of humiliating a recipient to under-gifting as a means of sabotaging his plans or simply as an involuntary result of one's own bad luck. The volatile nature of empirical outcomes is well recognised in the Melpa notion of luck (*kil køi*), of spells used in the past to attract wealth to one's men's house, and in the professions of anxiety and tension which always accompany the period of building-up resources or expectations towards a particular festival. The basis for the rule itself which people give is simply that without it moka would indeed not be different from 'trade' or 'barter', that is, from an exact exchange of perceived equivalents (*mel rop roromen, rarop roromen*, phrases also used nowadays for purchases with cash in stores and contemptuously applied in moka to those who do not give extra amounts on top of their debts). The further implication of the rule is that without giving 'more' a man cannot achieve status as a big-man: he does not make 'increase', as he should. But this picture of lopsidedness in any given sequence of vice-versa movement of objects, essential as it is to the ethic of status, vanishes when one looks at the longer-term context. While in principle a transactional sequence can break off after only one pair of moves of initiatory gift followed by main gift, partnerships are such that a reversal of the sequence is implied. In this case, the apparent 'profit' occasioned by the 'generous' main gift is annulled. Each profits in turn. Further, the difference from capitalist profit-making is apparent even in the fact that in a given sequence the donor of the main gift who makes a loss in material terms achieves a corresponding gain in political prestige. This is hardly so in the process of extraction of surplus and profit-making in capitalism (cf. Steiner, 1954). The real locus of extraction occurs at the domestic level, rather than in the exchange partnerships between domestic and political units. In the exchange partnerships, what is being manipulated is time and its productive capacities. The items of wealth include pigs, which breed; shells (up to the end of the 1960s), which were exchanged at the rate of two shells+one pig for eight or ten shells in moka: and cash, which can be earned by selling crops, stock, or labour. In order to gain, from initial investments, a set of returns, and then convert these into final prestige by making moka, timing is all: hence the prevalence of struggles over the timing of specific prestations in which the men of a group must be seen to co-ordinate their activities (A. J. Strathern 1971).

The Tolai and Siassi

To what extent are similar rules found elsewhere? In the Tolai system it appears that 'profits' could be made in two different ways: first by the mechanism known as *vuvue*, a festival at which men repaid gifts made to them earlier, apparently with some 'interest'; and second by sponsoring *matamatam* or *tubun* rituals, at which an outlay in paying for dances and food was more than recompensed by novices' fees and gifts from spectators (A. J. Strathern 1975:366–7). Here there does seem to be a way of collecting a surplus of shell currency (*tambu*) from ceremonies without thereby immediately incurring equivalent obligations to repay. However, this has to be seen in the context of a wider situation, in which tambu is actually accumulated, to be stored in large coils and eventually redistributed to meet debts and obligations to kin and friends, at a person's funeral. This tendency to accumulate must militate against any speeding up of the process of profit-making and reinvestment, since large quantities of tambu are continually being immobilised in a way which would make no sense in the Melpa moka system. In the moka there is no virtue in hoarding. Moreover, as pigs are so important (whereas they are not in the Tolai case, as far as I know), hoarding presents definite problems of maintenance, given the level of population density and the prevalent mode of subsistence by shifting cultivation. If people do hoard, as for example the Maring seem to do (Rappaport 1967), they set definite ceilings on the size of prestations they can manage (A. J. Strathern 1969).

Tolai profit-making may be compared further to that of the Siassi traders in the Vitiaz Straits. Here we are dealing with trade 'proper', in the sense that the Siassi were middlemen, specialising in canoe travel between a number of islands and mainland places and in the multiple exchange of products between such places. They themselves had the advantage of skill in canoe-building and sailing, and can be seen as classic entrepreneurs, bearing the costs and risks of dangerous travel and thereby extracting various kinds of direct profit by manipulating exchange rates for products. Before 1933, the Siassi also held a monopoly of coconut production, and obtained pots from the mainland Sio people for these. The Sio people in turn traded their pots for taro and tobacco with inland peoples, and the Siassi obtained these. A major part of the Siassi's strategy was to take goods from one area where they were not scarce or not regarded as having high prestige and transport them elsewhere, to places in which they did carry prestige or were vital for life-cycle rituals. Thus they took Sio pots to the West New Britain coast, where they were used for bridewealth and in return received pigs. Their own final aim was to use surpluses of food and pigs generated by trade in feasts to demonstrate big-manship and celebrate the life-cycles of kinsfolk on their own island.

Their success in doing so can be measured against the fact that without trade they would themselves be unable to meet their own subsistence needs; nor did they control any significant craft production (until they had to take over the manufacture of wooden bowls, when the Tami Islanders to their east abandoned making these). These bowls were high-value goods, needed in the conversions of items into pigs. Thus ten Sio pots or one large bowl could be exchanged for one dog, and the dog then exchanged for a pig; or two boar's tusks (recognised as a valuable by the Tami people and also mainlanders) for three bowls and these in turn for two pigs. More strikingly, twenty to forty coconuts could obtain ten pots in Sio, and these were then exchanged for one dog, and finally for a pig in New Britain. By another set of conversions via the island of Umboi, one pig would fetch five to ten packets of processed sago, and these then sold for fifty to a hundred pots in Sio, and those in turn would bring five to ten pigs in New Britain. The productivity of the inland areas for taro-growing, the labour, mostly of women, in pot-manufacture at Sio, the vegetable production of Umboi and the production of pigs in West New Britain were thus all harnessed by the Siassi. The surpluses were then apparently liquidated in internal feasting, used to generate forms of ranking or prestige in Siassi groups themselves. Exactly what rules governed the internal Siassi 'game of prestige' is less clear, because the system was already in decay when Harding studied it, owing to the disruption of Siassi monopolies over the movement of craft goods and production of coconuts (Harding, 1967). There is no strategy of hoarding; the dimensions manipulated are space and knowledge, the latter symbolised in the notion of Siassi control over canoe and weather magic. The system is clearly one of trading, but the final objective of the chief traders is to convert the products of such trade into pigs, which were then slaughtered to obtain political status.

'Conversions' in the kula

In the moka, prior to European influence, such conversions could not directly occur, since the goods appropriate to these exchanges were in a special sphere of exchange. However a transformation occurred when Europeans, entering the Highlands from the 1930s, offered shell valuables directly in return for labour and vegetables. In the kula there has been, since Malinowski's time at least, an arrangement whereby young men gave yams as *pokala* to *dala* (subclan) heads and received valuables of kula type in return. Further, this kind of transaction was replicated with a standard flow of vegetable gifts from wife's to husband's people and *youlo* gifts of valuables in return; and this on a regional basis between Kiriwina and Sinaketa, since the Sinaketans, who were short of vegetable produce but specialised in manufacture of *Spondylus* shell discs used in types of necklaces, married Kiriwina women. In this way they received vegetable foods and gave shell valuables (as a kind of covert bridewealth?) in return. Their headmen's dependence on Kiriwina was broken by the pearling industry introduced by Europeans, whereby Sinaketans became rich and To'uluwa of Omarakana did not benefit at all (Uberoi 1962; 116, 122).

In kula, then, a conversion between vegetables and valuables is recognised, and must be reckoned one of the important means whereby individuals enter the kula exchanges proper, by taking valuables received as youlo and utilising these to set up a partnership. The social context here is no different from Hagen, where wealth derived from affines is also circulated into moka; and since yams at least are regarded as valuables themselves in the same way as pigs (fed on vegetables) are in Hagen, the underlying logic in the two systems is quite similar in fact. What has to be considered further, however, is whether there is any principle of profit in kula. The evidence is hard to interpret.

There is certainly competition to receive kula valuables, and this generates situations and tactics again exactly comparable to those in the moka. Fortune's story of Monitor Lizard (Uberoi 1962:93–4) can be paralleled exactly by Melpa stories of how big-men promise a single pearl shell to many different partners and extract goods from each, subsequently disappointing all but one and asking the others to wait. The same devices were used by practitioners in a cult centered on the ritual acquisition of money in Hagen during 1970–1 (A. J. Strathern 1979–80). But such a manipulation of the rules, while predictable and in moka actually intrinsic, is nevertheless different from a basic rule of 'generous giving' to overwhelm, albeit temporarily, one's recipient partner. This does not seem present in kula exchange, for there is a very rigid rule that armshells circulate one for one against necklaces on a definite grid of partnerships. How definite and circumscribed this grid in practice is proves difficult to tell from Malinowski's accounts. There must clearly be room for switching of partners and for the innovative entry of newcomers into the networks. Such entry is signalised and accepted by the presenting and receiving of solicitory gifts as *vaga*:

> The *vaga*, as the opening gift of the exchange, has to be given spontaneously, that is, there is no enforcement of any duty in giving it. There are means of soliciting it (*wawoyla*), but no pressure can be employed. The *yotile*, however, that is, the valuable which is given in return for the valuable previously received, is given under pressure of a certain obligation. (Malinowski 1922:353)

From this, and Malinowski's discussion on succeeding pages, one gains the impression that gifts are individually paired off in terms of comparability or equivalence. A vaga gift has to be met by a *yotile* of equivalent value, and in the absence of entirely objective standards each partner argues over whether such equivalence has been reached or not. The way these two categories or gifts are co-ordinated in the inter-island kula is such that prospective recipients are the ones who travel overseas. They take neither vaga nor yotile with them. They expect to receive yotile for vaga they gave previously, and that would be when they were themselves visited. In addition they will receive vaga for the next round again, so that the partnership remains in imbalance. This is how I read Malinowski's report that: 'First, the initial gifts (*vaga*) are given, and only after this is over such valuables as have been due of old to their partners and which have to be given as clinching gifts (*yotile*) are handed over.' (Malinowski 1922:491)

In this passage it is the hosts who give both vaga and yotile to their visitors. A different context occurs in the internal Kula, in exchanges between To'uluwa, the Omarakana chief, and his partners from villages to the west. When he brought home 213 pairs of armshells from Kitava, partners brought him necklaces as vaga for these, and he gave them armshells almost at once as yotile. The temporal gap between vaga and yotile is thus closed in inland kula. In all these contexts, however, vaga and yotile are equivalents. Further categories, such as *pari*, *pokala*, *kaributu*, *wawoyla*, and *kwaypolu* need also to be considered, and seem to introduce complications to disturb this straightforward picture of equivalence. To obtain a vaga gift, a partner may give food (pokala) or a minor valuable (kaributu). After this has been done to the partner's satisfaction, he will hand over the vaga. But if the yotile later returned is equivalent to the vaga, this means that the pokala or kaributu gifts are unaccounted for. We should then have to posit either that strict equivalence does not always characterise kula exchanges or that the yotile may be seen as 'worth' less than the vaga, so that we have: pokala+kaributu+yotile=vaga. Malinowski partly answers the problem by stating that the food gifts would be returned later, though without strict equivalence, and the kaributu also, 'in an equivalent form' (p. 355). In practice, there may be ambiguities precisely on these grounds, and this could help to explain why partners are dissatisfied; or differences of rank between partners may act as intervening variables.[1]

In kula with the Dobuans, Trobrianders do carry gifts with them as pari. Not knowing so much about what valuables individual Dobuans have, they make mistakes in soliciting with gifts which are too fine. But that problem, Malinowski notes, is taken care of by the fact that 'if there was an exceptionally valuable gift in the visitor's *pari*, it will have to be returned later on by the Dobuans' (op. cit.:355). Thus, a fine pari gift will bring a separate reward and not simply be counted against a single yotile. Similarly, if a man cannot supply a proper yotile as 'tooth' (*kudu*) to the vaga he received, he will give a *basi* (= 'to pierce') instead, and this basi in turn will be reciprocated for later when he has met his main yotile debt. The implication of these passages is that if an element of imbalance enters into exchanges, it is adjusted subsequently. The same presupposition underlies the structure of partnerships in Hagen, in which the pressure is always in the direction of maintaining exchanges over more than one sequence, and to do this each event must be arranged in such a way that it looks both backwards and forwards in time, as moka speeches reveal. Rather than exact balance, it is imbalance that is actually sought. In kula, pari gifts made at Dobu are in fact returned with good measure in farewell gifts by the Dobuan hosts. These gifts are known as *talo'i*. A particularly fine item from the pari would be reciprocated exactly, as noted above, but overall 'the *talo'i* always exceeds the *pari* in quantity and value, and small presents are also given to the visitors during their stay' (p. 362). Such parting presents seem clearly designed to indicate the wish to continue the partnership by further exchanges later. In the moka, certain pigs may be given as a direct return to meet debts; further pigs as 'profit', i.e. for moka proper; and yet further items added as 'new' ones, to re-stimulate the partnership. There is consequently at times some ambiguity about whether, debts having been cancelled, the recipient partner now should think only of the 'new' items and retain the 'profit' or should reciprocate

79

for the 'profit' and the 'new' items together. What he does will depend on the overall state of good repair in relationships between the partners themselves, and this is where choice enters. Indeed, each stage represents a cumulation of choices, moving towards greater or lesser mutual involvement.

The category of 'profit-making' tends, therefore, to dissolve when considered more closely, into other categories. First, the 'profit' may have to be returned later. Second, it is in any case a by-product of competitive giving, the aim of which is to acquire renown. Third, it may simply represent the wish by the donors to maintain the partnership through the 'diplomacy of trade', as Sahlins so felicitously put it (Sahlins 1965). It is better, therefore, to refer to 'incremental giving' rather than to a 'principle of profit'. However, the degree to which such incremental giving is seen as intrinsic to ceremonial exchange and is also followed out in practice does seem to be important ethnographically. An overall comparison between the two most elaborate exchange systems in the Highlands, the Enga *tee* and Melpa moka, (themselves historically and geographically linked), Tolai tambu exchanges, and the kula suggests that the tendency towards inflation and increase in the size of networks, velocity of circulation, and volume of exchange is greatest in the case of the two Highlands systems; present, but less so, in the Tolai case; and relatively undeveloped in the kula. This is because rates of exchange as established within each transaction in the context of ongoing partnerships tend more towards parity in kula exchanges than in the other cases. There is competition to secure larger numbers of valuables than others; individual valuables may be worth more than other examples; and there must be both re-creation and attrition of individual exchange partnerships in accordance with a partner's performance. Hence there is plenty of room in kula exchanges for the outcomes to affect in some degree the growth and decline of achieved individual status. Nevertheless, it is prescribed that for an armshell, or more accurately it seems a pair of armshells, a necklace should be given. How specifically the perceived value of a particular armshell or pair of shells could be matched with that of a particular necklace is not easy to work out.[2] But the practice of giving individual names to valuables and of remembering their histories of exchange would lend a certain precision, or at least a finer language of argument, to the processes of relative evaluation; and the expressed aim was to match rather than surpass in terms of the main individual items involved in a transactional sequence. The logic of matching here is quite different from the explicit logic of the moka, with its stress on increment in the main gift. The complications in moka stem largely from this requirement of paying an increment and its calculation in numerical

terms. Since each time an initiatory gift is accepted a promise of increment is made, and since the standard way of securing the required
increment is to reinvest, one can quite easily see how networks will
become extended and/or production intensified in moka. This in turn
leads to unstable competition between big-men and to a lack of established status-hierarchies.

The Enga tee

Evidence from the tee is not so clear on this point. The structure of a
sequence in tee, lasting over a period of about four years, is:

2–3 years	Initiatory gifts (small pigs, pork, axes, salt, shells, plumes, money)
6–9 months	Repayment gifts in live pigs, with shells and cassowaries as 'extras'
6–9 months	Gifts of pork, on basis of one 'side' of pork in payment for one pig received.
	Initiatory gifts.

The exact way in which these transactions are seen as balanced or not
balanced is difficult to discern. Meggitt (1974:176–7), writes: 'When men
believe they have made enough initial gifts, each clan in turn notifies the
next group of recipients along the way and demands repayment in pigs.'

The language he uses is that of debtors and creditors, and one cannot
be sure whether there is an ethic of over-gifting or not.[3] An inflation in the
overall volume of the flow of goods can occur whether there is such an
ethic or not, and this certainly appears to have occurred in the years
following European contact, when the items appropriate to initiatory
gifts increased in availability, while those for the repayment gifts did not
increase so markedly, indeed, in the case of pigs were reduced by the
influx of swine anthrax. As pig producers Enga were then hard put to it to
rear pigs to meet the debts incurred from initiatory gifts. Here, then, we
see the relevance of another factor: historical changes in the supply of
items considered suitable for use in exchanges.

Changes in the supply of valuables

If we look at the Tolai tambu exchanges, we can see that the tambu shells
had to be obtained from outside of the Tolai area itself, by journeys to the

Nakanai area, and when the Lakalai people became aware of the value of tambu they raised its price to their Tolai visitors. The total stocks of tambu have thus been controlled. Moreover, tambu is made perpetually scarce by the practice of long-term saving and accumulation: tambu stocks are thus substantially immobilised. In this way, there can neither be severe inflation in the supply of tambu nor can its velocity of circulation be much speeded, since the aim is to save it rather than continuously to disburse it. No such controls operate on the moka or tee, although the definite phase of slaughtering pigs which is a formal part of tee sequences does serve at least to reduce the overall numbers of pigs periodically. Moreover, in the tee it is pigs which are regarded as central, whereas Meggitt quite rightly points out that in the Melpa moka pearl shells were of great significance, and conditions of supply of these changed very markedly from at least 1933 onwards, when Europeans brought them into the Highlands in much larger numbers than had entered the area through indigenous trade routes to the south.

The moka, therefore, is likely to have gone through a phase of volatile expansion from 1933 to 1963 (when shell moka began to drop out of favour) to an even greater extent than the tee. It is here, indeed, that we must locate the reasons for the eventual replacement of pearl shells with introduced forms of money currency in the moka. In the tee, although money quickly began to be used as a category of initiatory gift, it does not appear as though it has replaced pigs as an appropriate kind of main gift. Pigs remain important in the moka too, but moka with money has become very popular, since money is seen as taking the place of the prestigious pearl-shell moka. In the Tolai systems, tambu remains unchallenged as the proper item for funerary distributions, and it has not been driven out by money at all in this regard, perhaps because of its enduring religious and overall symbolic significance, perhaps because it has not been subject to inflation (cf. Connell, 1977:88).

What of the kula? Here is where contemporary evidence would be most valuable and illuminating. Malinowski (e.g. 1922: ch. 15) was quite explicit about the manufacture of the two most important items in the kula exchanges, the necklaces and armshells, and to a lesser extent about the boars' tusks and stone axe blades which were also significant. Thus the Sinaketan people dived for and obtained the *kaloma* discs used in *soulava* manufacture, and they and the Vakutans specialised in the actual drilling and grinding; and Kavataria and Kayleula people held a monopoly over fishing for the Conus shell used in the making of armshells, although these were also made in numbers at Mailu down the Papuan coast and exported both eastwards towards the kula area and west to Port Moresby, where armshells are important in bridewealth payments. *Beku* axe blades were quarried in Woodlark Island, but polished in Kiriwina, and used as kaributu gifts in kula sequences (Malinowski 1922:502–3). *Mwali* were also previously made on Woodlark. The point to notice here is perhaps simply that there is no one-to-one correlation between control over the manufacture of these objects and dominance within the kula ring as a whole. A proper explanation of this is made more difficult by the fact that Malinowski himself was content to ascribe this situation simply to 'the inertia of custom and usage' (loc. cit. p. 502). The precise linkages between villages are, however, obviously significant, and the overall directionality of kula gifts must also be important. It is interesting to note that the clockwise/anti-clockwise 'rules' of exchange mean that Kayleula and Kavataria people, who manufacture armshells, do not pass these on to Kiriwina (Omarakana), but down to the Amphletts and Dobu, and thence the armshells must travel anti-clockwise right round the ring before getting to Kiriwina via Kitava. Nor did Sinaketa and Vakuta go to Kavataria to obtain armshells. Rather, in generating a flow of necklaces to Omarakana and elsewhere, and thus causing the clockwise flow of these, they were dependent on Omarakana and Kitava separately for their supplies of armshells. Their own exports of necklaces would thus, again, travel long distances before returning to them.

It is clear that in a system so arranged, neither stockpiling nor general dispersal, in several directions, of valuables could occur, and in the long travels of the valuables round the total ring they would tend to become strung out rather than moving all together and *en masse* back to their original makers. The length and complexity of the ring would thus tend to counteract any tendency for manufacturers to be able to stockpile or otherwise gain advantages.

My remarks here are perforce sketchy, and much more thought and information is needed on this issue. Perhaps comparisons with the exact form and length of the Enga tee would be worthwhile. Detailed information on the impact of economic changes would also be illuminating. Uberoi quotes Malinowski on the already changing situation between Sinaketa and Kiriwina in 1918, when the Sinaketan headman was paid by Europeans engaged in the pearling industry, was freed from reliance on Kiriwina for foodstuffs in return for kaloma shell, and was also given vaygu'a (valuables) by the Europeans, although the reference does not tell us whether these were kula valuables that were involved (Uberoi 1962:116; Malinowski: 1922:468). Nor do we know whether the Sinaketan headman used these valuables for ceremonial exchanges to improve his position in the kula, directly or indirectly. When one tries to follow through Malinowski's references to the impact of the pearling industry one also finds that it does not appear as an entry in his indexes,

Andrew Strathern

either in *Argonauts* or in *Coral Gardens*. Clearly, the overall significance of the impact of the European administration, missions, and traders or plantation owners needs to be looked at much more closely than we are enabled to do from Malinowski's own account, and for this reason we are hampered in attempting comparisons with the situation in other areas, such as Rabaul or Mount Hagen. We cannot even tell whether the emphasis on kula exchange which Malinowski observed may have been intensified following pacification in the way that has often been observed or hypothesised for ceremonial exchange systems elsewhere. Given the structural–functional re-interpretation of the kula transactions themselves as a ritual surrogate for war and a means of discharging tension between potential enemies, it would seem important to pursue any information available on alterations in practice within kula partnerships following the assumption of administrative control by the British in Papua. One would like to know also to what extent the Kiriwina chiefs in pre-pacification times owed their position to warfare as well as or in addition to their monopoly of kula exchanges, on which Brunton (1975) has quite correctly remarked (cf. also Malinowski 1922:468 on Omarakana as 'the only locality where the Kula is or ever was to the same extent concentrated in the hands of one man').

The symbolism of kula valuables

That before pacification kula expeditions might run into human hazards in addition to risks from the wind and waves is shown clearly by the Trobriand epic poem *Yaulabuta*. This tells the story of the handsome chief Kailaga of Kumwageya village on Kitava Island. His village was accustomed to sailing on kula voyages to Vakuta, but on one occasion Kailaga was persuaded by a false rumour invented by his enemies to sail instead to the east coast of Kiriwina, believing that a chief there, Bugwabwaga, wished to give him an important soulava necklace. Had he succeeded in obtaining the necklace he would have diverted a coveted kula valuable from its usual circulation. But his enemies from another Kitava village were waiting for him to prevent this, and attacked and killed him. The symbolism which then appears in the verses is highly significant. He is trussed on the boom of his own canoe and then burnt like a pig over a fire. His boar's tusk necklace (*doga*) is cut from his chest and his killers wear it. His captors also break down the wall of their own chief's house in triumph, an act known as *yolawada* and performed when men bring back an important armshell for their chief. They burst into his house through the wall, and he cannot be angry because they have performed such a service for him. The translators comment: 'Here Kailaga's captors perform *yolawada* on their chief's house, as a form of mockery: Kailaga is treated like a rare *mwali* shell, which they have acquired for their chief' (Kasaipwalova and Beier 1978:24.).

The symbolic equivalence between a human victim and an item of wealth is here made explicit. The poem also twice refers to the idea of paying ransom, for a chief captured in war, by means of soulava necklaces (pp. 21, 39).

In the ordinary kula exchanges this grim basis of the value of vaygu'a is not made explicit. It is, however, a basis which is completely shared by the other cultures whose exchange systems we are considering. In Mount Hagen, for example, pigs and pearl shells are pre-eminently items of wealth through which compensation payments for killings can be made. In actual kula, the basic symbolism is shifted slightly. Kula partners are not enemies, but friends, and friendship is expressed in another basic idiom of exchange, sexuality. The partner who is soliciting a valuable, as the 'life' of his friend, makes himself charming and attractive so as to win him over. The giver, and by implication his valuable, appears to be seen as female: the male recipient-to-be tries to attract him so as to secure the valuable. This symbolic locus is cross-cut by the attribution of gender to the valuables themselves. The red soulava are male and the white mwali armshells female.[4] The armshells are usually made into pairs, the right hand one being larger and finer than the left (one wonders if this correlates with another male/female dichotomy). In the Kailaga story, the chief Kailaga, from Kitava which is a source of armshells for Kiriwina, is captured and likened by his killers to an armshell itself; perhaps they are also saying that he is as helpless as a woman ensnared by love magic. In any case, one can see how, in the terms of its own symbolism, the kula appears indeed to replace warfare with exchange, hostility with friendship, antagonism between males with a model of reciprocal benefit summed up in a sexual metaphor: when armshell and necklace meet, it is a kind of marriage. In Hagen also, established exchange relationships, which are mediated through affinal links consequent upon intermarriage, can be expressed in similar metaphors, as when partners say 'I will sleep with you as we have slept together before', or, with more aggressiveness, 'Let us copulate with them so hard that blood flows from our pulled-back foreskins' (i.e. let us make a big moka gift to our partners).

One further aspect of symbolism appears to fit here. Annette Weiner (1976:183, 192, 231), in the course of an elaborate argument on spheres of power exercised by the sexes on Trobriand society, argues that valuables, including shells and stone axe blades, represent for men an avenue to limited individual immortality, as well as a 'cultural manifestation of reproduction' and 'a symbolic element of male regenerative capacity' (pp. 192–3). Thus, she suggests: 'Individual male identity seems more singularly encapsulated in male objects of wealth. These are the only objects which carry a man's name outside dala (subclan) control and circulate beyond his lifetime' (p. 232).

She adds perceptively that even this process is risky. Men 'abduct' valuables from their proper course of circulation (as Kailaga hoped to do in the epic cited earlier); they compete to obliterate each other's names. The naming of actual valuables (Malinowski 1922:503–4) facilitates the accretion of stories of individual owners around them and also the tracking of their progress through a number of different hands, just as was the case with pearl shells in Hagen before Europeans inflated their supply. The investment of a measure of individual identity in valuables would also help to explain why, according again to Weiner, men try to keep track of valuables they once 'owned' (pp. 182–3, with an example of the reclaiming of a beku stone axe blade over a period of seven years). Finally, the whole notion of the kula *ring* as such, in which ideally a valuable returns to the same person after passing through several hands, makes symbolic sense in this context; though one can also easily see the latent contradictions which are involved, since valuables must in fact be 'identified' with more than one individual, and as Uberoi hints at the end of his re-analysis of the kula, they must in fact be identified with the opposite of individual ownership; with, that is, the kula ring itself.

The role of money

Weiner's remarks here are thus extremely interesting, for they raise further questions. How important is the symbolism of individual 'immortality' or supra-local fame to men? Are shells still manufactured, purchased, or exchanged partly because of this symbolism? What would happen if the manufacturers of kaloma shells (used for soulava) or of mwali were diverted from production? An interesting parallel is to be found in trading relations between Malaita and Southern Bougainville (Connell 1977). Connell notes that in the Siwai area of S. Bougainville (originally studied by Douglas Oliver), demand for shell 'money', obtained in trade from Malaita, has grown rather than declined during the last decade, and trading with the Malaitan manufacturers has been systematised. Women do most of the manufacturing work, though it is men who travel to Bougainville to sell the shells. Prices have risen sharply, and the Langalanga people, who are specialists in the craft, have come to rely more and more on their craft production of shell and less on their gardens. One trader made $A9,000 on a single trip in June 1975. The Bougainvilleans are in fact paying out cash, obtained through sales of cocoa, and investing in shell, much as the Tolai also continue to put a part of their savings into the form of tambu, but in the Siwai case people are utilising the shell strings for extensive ritual payments at all stages of the life-cycle and also for the purchase of rights over land. They have not, it seems, made the choice of the Hageners; that is, to convert money back into a ceremonial valuable and use it in their exchanges. Instead, they are controlling levels of inflation by themselves deciding how much shell to import from Langalanga. What has happened in the kula? Could money take the place of vaygu'a? Could the production of vaygu'a be stimulated by similar needs for investment and conversion as operate in Siwai? Has production in fact expanded or declined, and what is the corresponding fate of the kula itself? These questions I can only leave to the kula experts themselves, but if the answers are known they will make full analytical sense only in the context of comparisons with the dynamics of change in other Melanesian exchange systems such as I have attempted briefly to outline here.

Conclusions

Malinowski's ethnography was written before the New Guinea Highlands were first discovered by European explorers. Moreover, at first sight the form of the Kula looks remarkably different from that of Highland exchange systems. My comparative survey here shows, however, two ways in which comparisons can usefully be pursued between the kula and the Hagen moka: first, recent studies of kula exchanges indicate that there is a complex process of matching gifts with returned gifts, and of injecting 'new' gifts, not previously solicited for, into 'chains' of partnerships, in ways which are exactly comparable to the workings of moka and indeed of the Enga tee exchanges. These new parallels indicate that the two fundamental aims of demonstrating prestige and at the same time continuing friendly partnerships underlie the forms of transactions in all three cases. The extent to which the principle of reciprocal increment is explicitly developed, however, varies. It is strongest in moka; evident as a tendency in tee; less clear in kula. On the whole, the two Highlands systems are clearly 'inflationary' and potentially, therefore, unstable; whereas, again, the kula is less obviously so.

This point is connected with the second major focus for comparison: the response of exchange systems to altered conditions. Systems which tend towards rapid expansion and inflation are also liable to occasional collapse and abandonment of one medium of exchange in favour of another, a process illustrated by the progressive abandonment of varieties of shell valuables in the Highlands following the artificial in-

Andrew Strathern

crease in their supply brought about by Europeans. Again, this has not happened in kula, partly because supply rates have, it appears, not altered too markedly, and because the valuables require careful manufacture and remain individually prized objects. There has thus been no overwhelming pressure to discard the armshells and necklaces and operate with money instead. Highlands systems are held in check ultimately by conditions for the production of pigs (and now coffee), so that abandonment of the 'pearl shell standard' has not meant a total loss of stability. In the kula, stability is provided only by the valuables, and their exchange paths themselves, and no conversion of these into money would be truly feasible, although it *would* theoretically be possible for men to buy their way into the kula with money. The reasons why this has not, by and large, happened have much to do with the overall state of economic change – or lack of it – in the Milne Bay area by comparison with the Highlands: a topic of first importance, but beyond this paper's scope.

Notes

1 On this whole question see Firth (1957:221), where the problems are first succinctly posed. Shirley Campbell effectively illuminates the issue raised here (e.g. pp. 213–15). This makes it more possible to see how, in effect, continuous imbalances are matched by kula participants against theoretical aims of equivalence in exchanges. The meaning of the term *kitomu* is also importantly involved here.
2 Again, S. Campbell's work has elucidated this point. This volume Chapters 8 and 9.
3 D. K. Fell, in his Ph.D dissertation, *Holders of the Way* (1978a) deals with this topic in detail. Although there is often in practice some incremental giving in the tee, it still does not appear to be so pre-eminently established as in the Melpa moka.
4 This was the situation in Malinowski's time. The gender attribution has now, it appears, been interestingly reversed. The contemporary version of Yaulabuta, as we have seen, identifies the chief Kailaga as a mwali.

3 Magnitudes and values in kula exchange

RAYMOND FIRTH

This is primarily an exercise in historical reconstruction. Much has been written of the social, political and symbolical aspects of *kula*, but we have been short of information on its economic aspects. Malinowski's penetrating sociological analysis of the process of title-transfer of Trobriand *veguwa*[1] (*vaygu'a* in his spelling) did give some basic economic data. But it still left obscure the process of establishing and maintaining relative values among the objects transferred. Mauss's more general contribution, so stimulating despite some ethnographic errors, was so focussed on his concept of patterns of spiritual bonds between things which were to some extent parts of persons, that he developed no enquiry into the notion of 'equivalence' which was so important for Malinowski. Getting people to realise the wider social implications of what they may first think of as simple material transfers is important. But material problems about the transfers are still crucial. What is the general level of the transactions? By what principle are the objects exchanged actually valued and matched?

I have already referred to some of these problems (Firth, 1957:221; 1967:11–16; cf. 1973: ch. 11). For the modern kula many of the answers are now becoming available. But if we wish to understand more about kula magnitudes and values in Malinowski's time considerable inference is needed, and some speculation. Ideally, I would like here to view kula as a set of macro-economic relations involving price-making mechanisms. For in economic terms, if one disregards the conventional monetary criterion of price, and the argument about what is 'money' anyway, every veguwa transferred, if it is regarded as matched in exchange, has its price. The price may vary from one transaction to another, it may be composed of an assorted bundle of goods and services rendered over a period, it may be regarded as inequitable. But in Malinowski's conceptual model, still basically valid in this particular, a veguwa given as *vaga*, opening gift, predicates an ultimate matching item as return. What determines the level of return, or in concrete terms, why is *this* necklace given in return for *that* armshell?

In the price-making mechanism of the kula certain material criteria are very relevant. The objects exchanged are very durable, non-perishable. This is very important, because it means that within broad limits their quality does not deteriorate over time. Unlike food, they can be held indefinitely in their material form, and therefore the bargaining power of the holder does not diminish over time for any physical reason. From this point of view the prescription about rapid turnover of veguwa, with loss of reputation for a holder who delays too long in divesting himself of a valuable, is a counter-mechanism of a social kind to promote exchange. The valuable does not lose physical quality by keeping, nor does it lose exchange quality. It is the possessor who loses value, i.e. reputation quality, by undue retention. How long is 'undue' retention? For overseas kula in the days of sailing craft a periodicity of transfer in exchange was broadly set by seasonal wind movement. Was 'undue' retention in former times the omission to present the veguwa to the first overseas visitors, or was a lapse of one or two seasons permissible without much criticism, especially for a highly prized object? (Now that mechanical transport has facilitated kula relations, what has happened to the accepted retention period?)

Set off against the general durability of veguwa is their specific variability. Unlike many standardised western products, the quality of which is expected to be the same for every transaction, difference in quality of individual items has traditionally been built into the system of veguwa exchange. As compared with many Oceanic exchange transactions, kula transfers involve a high focus on the individual armshell[2] or necklace transferred, and not – as with Tikopia pandanus mats or barkcloth, for instance – primarily on the fact that *an* armshell or *a* necklace changes hands. Tikopia matching in exchange is primarily by quantity, Trobriand matching of veguwa is primarily by quality. (Such is the impression from Malinowski's account of the major exchanges, reinforced by Fortune's sketch. But the exchange of low-value veguwa may always have been simpler, on a more generalised one-to-one basis.) Moreover variation of the quality of an item in the process of exchange has been difficult. Over time, separation of individual armshells of a pair seems definitely to have occurred. And shell discs may well have been added to or subtracted from a necklace before passing it on. But nominally there seems not to have been a Trobriand parallel to Australian *merbok* customs described by Stanner, whereby items such as red ochre might be regularly 'milked' as they passed along the exchange route (Stanner, 1933:169). Malinowski gave casual references to possible accretions to supply of valuables, but none to cheapening of quality, which could have been risky with the publicity attaching to high-ranking valuables.

A most important criterion of price-making in the kula is that most transactions are not to be taken as single one-off events, but as part of a *flow* which can go on through the lifetime of the participants and even be inherited. Not all transactions have been of this type: ties have been terminated for non-fulfilment of obligation, or freshly undertaken when opportunity allowed. But position of any transfer in the flow means that price need not be subsumed exclusively by reciprocal transfer immediately, necklace against armshell. Past performance and future expectation may have to be taken into consideration in any judgement of 'equivalence' of the two items exchanged.

This also relates to the general classification of kula transactions. These fall broadly under the head of what has been termed 'exchange by private treaty' (Cassady, 1974). Overtly, the system is not a negotiated pricing arrangement. The decision to make an initial transfer of a veguwa is not accompanied by any bargaining, nor in Malinowski's model is a return transfer the clear result of a specific demand for any particular item. But the practice of solicitary and intermediate gifts described by Malinowski (1922:353) from widely known specific stock served as tacit forces of negotiation. These are given much more meaning as parts of a flow of transactions. The concept of exchange by private treaty, with or without specific negotiation, is opposed in general economic thinking to the impersonal market forces by which prices are settled by factors of supply and demand – including those of monopoly and oligopoly and their consumer analogues. In empirical western market conditions the impersonal market forces are modified by or come to expression through negotiated pricing far more often than is apt to be realised. But apart from the private treaty aspect of kula exchange I am interested in the more general supply and demand situation of kula valuables, because I think one cannot understand the pricing mechanism, including Malinowski's notion of 'equivalence', without such information at least in outline.

Such an outline would include a series of inventories and distribution lists, to answer questions of the following kind: What stocks of (a) armshells; (b) necklaces are held at given times by (i) men of different social status and command of other resources, and (ii) men of different communities? What amount of a man's stock of veguwa is disbursed, and what retained, when he is confronted by a visiting overseas expedition? How many kula partners does he have, and what at any given point of time is the level and contractual state of his transactions with each? What has been the history of a man's kula transactions – how did he first enter the kula, with what grades of valuables has he been concerned, and what proportion of his time has he spent on kula operations? As regards veguwa, at any given time, what are the whereabouts of all named armshells and necklaces in any one kula sphere, where have they recently come from, and what are thought to be their probable destinations in the next movement of valuables? As relevance of stocks to values must be affected by velocity of circulation, how rapidly have different items moved in the system? In particular, has there been differential movement as between armshells and necklaces? Since both armshells and necklaces are durable goods, what seem to be the rates of accession to or loss from their kula stock?

Since even in modern conditions answers to all these questions may not be available, it is not surprising that they can be found only partially in Malinowski's account. But by inserting some assumptions which I hope are plausible I have tried to interpret Malinowski's data to yield a serious estimate of the magnitude of kula transactions, if not through the whole kula ring at least in the northern and western divisions, in the 1914–18 period. In so doing I am aware that recent research has indicated that the role of Trobrianders is now less central than one might infer from Malinowski's description. This might seem to imply that conclusions about kula magnitudes of sixty years ago based largely on Trobriand evidence could gravely underestimate the total volume of transactions in the kula ring as a whole. But this issue I leave to others to decide. What does emerge from Malinowski's data, gathered with great care for detail and some enthusiasm for counting, is a general notion, however imperfect, of the quantitative level and periodic impact of kula operations overall. The number of kula transactions, even in the Trobriands, must have been incalculable, especially if exchanges of what Malinowski termed 'inland kula' be taken into consideration. But since the valuables of the 'inland kula' were re-gathered and funnelled into the major overseas channels (1922:474–5) some estimate may be attempted of the number of veguwa themselves by building up from canoe numbers, crew numbers, and amounts of veguwa got on overseas expeditions.

Take canoes and men. Malinowski records that about 1918 approximately sixty canoes for kula operations were current in the Trobriand–Kitava section of the kula ring. Because of decay of some villages and loss of canoes by others, this was only about half the number of canoes fifty years earlier. (Then Kiriwina, for example, had about twenty canoes as against only eight in 1918.) In September 1917, Malinowski records, about forty canoes went on a major expedition to Dobu – eight craft from Sinaketa, twenty-four from Vakuta and ten from Amphletts. In March–April 1918 a return expedition from Dobu to Sinaketa consisted of about sixty proper *uvalaku* canoes, plus a dozen from Amphletts and another dozen from Vakuta – these latter apparently coming along for the travel and excitement. In general, each kula canoe carried a total crew of nine or ten men, but of these only about half would be kula-making men (1922:269, 384, 390, 391). So the Sinaketa–Vakuta–Amphletts expedition would have had some 150 to 200 men engaged in kula, getting necklaces from the Dobuans. The Dobuans would have had perhaps 250 to 300 kula men (Malinowski says 250 at the outside) getting armshells from Sinaketa and Vakuta. (An artist residing in the Trobriands not many years after Malinowski mentions seeing thirty or so Dobuan canoes bound on kula traffic for the Amphletts, Vakuta and presumably Sinaketa (Ellis Silas, 1926:211)). Even if the majority of kula operators acquired only a single valuable apiece, several hundred items would have changed hands on each expedition. Malinowski observed that some men might get none at all, but that canoe captains and expedition leaders, with several partners for their transactions (Kouta'uya of Sinaketa had twenty-seven partners in Dobu) could get considerable quantities.

Now consider the actual valuables. By what must have been a fairly close count when the objects were put on public display, Malinowski stated that the Dobuans got 648 pairs of armshells in their early 1918 visit – 304 pairs from Sinaketa and 344 from Vakuta. This meant an average of nearly thirteen armshell pairs for every five men, he stated, or an average of nearly eleven per canoe (1922:386, 391). Starting from this, can one build up a plausible guess as to the total number of armshells in the Kitava–Trobriands–Amphletts–Dobu area? Of the 304 armshell pairs about half (154) came from Kiriwina, as part of the proceeds of 213 pairs which the chief To'uluwa had been instrumental in getting from Kitava towards the end of March 1918; the other 150 had already been held in Sinaketan stock (1922:386, 474–5). But also towards the end of March, a little earlier than To'uluwa, the Vakutans had been in Kitava and they too returned with 'a good haul' of armshells. Malinowski could not tell how many armshells the Vakutans had already in stock. But considering they could muster nearly three times the canoes (twenty-two as against eight in full fleet) as the Kiriwinans, hence a much larger kula personnel, even though they had no chief of the eminence of To'uluwa, it is reasonable to assume they would have got about as many armshells at least, as the Kiriwinans – i.e. about 200. (Using the Dobuan average as an index would give just about the same figure.) So of the 344 pairs of armshells that the Vakutans gave the Dobuans in April 1918 it seems plausible that about 150 pairs came from their stock and about 200 immediately from Kitava. Looked at another way, around that March period the kula men of Kitava would have given to the Vakutans and Kiriwinans a total of 400 or so pairs of armshells.

These armshells were presumably a major part of a distribution ripple from a *so'i* feast held in Yanabwa, Woodlark island, about a couple of months earlier (January–February, 1918) and for which the armshells had been dammed up for some time (1922:492). But all armshells had to pass westwards through Kitava. Considering that the Kitavans had kula ties not only with Kiriwina to their northwest and Vakuta to their southwest but also some villages in southern Boyowa, one may assume it to be unlikely that they would strip themselves completely for their Kiriwina–Vakuta partners in March 1918. However, since the southern Boyowa transactions were small, a figure of about 100 pairs of armshells seems adequate to allow for Kitavan retention to meet such obligations (1922: 476).

What then might have been the overall armshell situation in the north-west sector of the kula around the early part of 1918? In his synoptic statement on the kula, which gives in general a very clear picture of the flow, Fortune wrote that the northern division annually exported *all* (author's italic) its armshells, new, middle-aged and old, and the south-ern division exported *all* its *Spondylus*-shell necklaces, new, middle-aged and old, in return. This statement makes no allowance for any armshells or necklaces used in 'internal kula' in the seasonal gap between overseas expeditions or given in repayment for, say, harvest supply offerings, and so diverted if temporarily from the kula field (1922:278–81). But anyway it is clear that in early 1918 the Dobuans did not clean out the Trobriands. We know from Malinowski's figures that of the 213 pairs of armshells brought by To'uluwa's expedition from Kitava in March 1918, only 154 pairs were secured by the Sinaketans a few days later – approximately sixty pairs remained in Kiriwina. Again, the men of Sinaketa and Vakuta, for prestige reasons, may have given the Dobuans most of what they had. But two factors make it likely that they retained some stock. In Sinaketa the Dobuan leader had as main partner the second-ranking chief. Now we know that the first-ranking chief participated in the kula so presum-ably he had some armshells still unexpended (1922:268, 388). And con-sidering the links of Sinaketa and Vakuta with Kayleula and the Amphletts they may well have reserved some items against these obliga-tions. In the Amphletts–Kayleula area itself there was certainly some stock of armshells. Though the Amphletts may have had few, Kayleula was known to have a good quantity, which the most important Amphletts headman was proposing to go and collect, after he had ended his visit with the Dobuans to Vakuta and Sinaketa (1922:271).

So at a rough estimate, the armshell position in the broad Kitava–

Trobriand sector around the time of the Dobuan visit in early 1918 might have been as follows:

KITAVA	stock after Vakuta–Kiriwina visits	100	pairs
DOBUANS	taken from Sinaketa–Vakuta *	650	,,
KIRIWINA	retained from Kitava expedition *	60	,,
,,	stock in hand earlier	50	,,
SINAKETA	stock retained from Dobu visit	100	,,
VAKUTA	,, ,, ,, ,, ,,	50	,,
SOUTHERN BOYOWA	,, ,,	20	,,
KAYLEULA	stock ready for Amphletts	50	,,
DOBU	stock before return from Trobriands	20	,,
	Estimated total armshells[3]	1,100	,,

Neither Malinowski nor Fortune hazarded any estimate of total stocks of shell valuables, either in the kula ring as a whole or even in the northern sector of it. Malinowski did say that on big overseas expeditions 'a whole lot of valuables, amounting to over a thousand articles at a time' (1922: 103) changed hands. But this very general statement could have included reference to ancillary valuables such as whalebone spatulae or red *Spondylus*-shell belts as well as to armshells and necklaces. Also, it does not consider what stocks if any might have been retained from transfer. But it does suggest, taken with the other evidence, that mobilisation of either armshell pairs or necklaces at one of the major points of the kula circuit would have yielded around 1,000 items, and that therefore estimation of the total stock of kula valuables depends on how many such major points may be thought to be capable of operation at the same time.

In trying to arrive at some idea of the total volume of kula valuables in existence at any period, the concept of velocity of circulation is important. In theory, with a rapid velocity of circulation it might be possible for each major community to handle the same identical valuables once every year – keep them for a month or so then send them on their way round to turn up again in another twelve months' time. One single set of valuables – in two contrasted series moving in opposite directions – could then serve this ideal model. But we know this has not been the case. A man in the kula never kept any article longer than a year or two, wrote Malinowski, and even this was rather long; but even so, articles took as a rule some two to ten years to make the round (1922:94; see also Fortune: 1932, 205). It seems that kula at one major point often awaited the release of valuables from a point further back in the circuit, but that even so seasonal expeditions regularly took place at approximately the same times between various communities in different sectors. That is to say, kula valuables were not concentrated in a single sector at any one time, but were distributed, as it were in nodules, through the network. One can only guess at the situation elsewhere than in the northern sector. But unless some segments of the ring or network ran dry for more than a year or so, a multiple of three times the Kitava–Trobriands–Dobu sector stock is likely to give only a minimal figure of kula valuables for the whole field, i.e. rather more than 3,000 each of armshell pairs and of necklaces, about sixty years ago.

The significance of such figures in themselves is not great, especially since they rest on such a small base of recorded fact.[4] But they have some interest when taken in relation to the operations of individual kula men and the levels of opportunity open to ambitious attempts at concentration of wealth and power. Moreover, to call attention to major types of query only very imperfectly envisaged and answered in the historical material may help to stimulate even more systematic documentation of a quantitative order in contemporary kula studies.

I turn now to problems of evaluation of kula objects. In relative evaluation within each series, armshells and necklaces, size and colour are well-recognised criteria. But they are embedded in a much wider set of characteristics, some of a formal order and able to be arranged in oppositional manner. Armshells are short objects, necklaces are long; armshells are rings, necklaces, though looped, are strings. (Associated probably with these material qualities come the symbolic attributions of armshells as female and necklaces as male.) Armshells are large single pieces of shell, necklaces are composed of small shell-pieces; the larger the one and the smaller the other the more they are esteemed. Armshells historically have gone in pairs, necklaces are single units. But whereas armshells cannot otherwise be augmented by their own substance, necklaces can be enlarged by putting on extra shell discs – though Malinowski did not say specifically that this could be or was done (cf. Belshaw, 1950:173). Other criteria are of more diffuse order. In colour, armshells of all except the lowest class are white, and necklaces a shade of red; Malinowski noted that the latter were prized according to their pinkness, but he did not discuss the grading of armshells by colour and apparently failed to note that a degree of red striation is associated with armshells of highest rank. Apart from these and other physical criteria, age and a history of kula circulation, linked with the individuality of a personal name, have marked the more important valuables.[5]

In considering evaluation one might start with the hypothesis that the relative value of an armshell pair or of a necklace was dependent upon the amount of labour needed to prepare it – including the discovery, fishing up, breaking down of shell, grinding, polishing, boring and attachment of decorative appendages. (Transport costs need not be included since they may be reckoned as met by the other exchanges taking place at the same time as the kula exchanges. But without holding that kula exchange arose from utilitarian exchange, there is a problem of how far the cost of a kula expedition is in fact carried by exchanges of other more utilitarian kind.) But it is clear that sixty years ago, as now, the labour cost was only one set of factors in the total valuing of any particular kula valuable. Apart from the relevance of specific qualities of size and colour Malinowski makes much of the importance of the traditional and historical antecedents of certain items.[6] How far the enhancement of an item was dependent on the transfer of it through the hands of a series of men of rank is uncertain – modern opinion too seems to differ on this point – but it seems clear that whatever could be recalled of the transactional context of a valuable was a matter of public interest.

What is really difficult to see from Malinowski's data is how evaluation of items to be matched in exchange was ultimately arrived at. He gave no series of matching transactions which would allow us to see just which necklaces were regarded as equivalent – or not – to just what armshell pairs. He made great use of the concept of 'equivalence' – 'fair and full value' as he described it in one context – but his 'concrete' examples seem in fact to have been constructed from more general material (1922:92, 96, 98). From Malinowski's and all subsequent accounts it emerges that the concept of equivalence refers not just to an armshell (pair) being matched by a necklace, but to some system of grading within each of the two series. He refers to the 'many sub-classes' of fine long necklaces and cites a few of the most valuable and of the poorer types (1922:309; cf. 358, 507). And though he implied that armshells too had sub-classes and promised 'later on' to enumerate them all, he did not in fact present any such classification. It is easy to see that top items in each series would have to be matched, since the convention was that one must be given for one – a fine armshell must be countered by a fine necklace, and no multiple of lesser grades could substitute. But how many top items were there? Malinowski named a few, but gave no idea of how many there were or what proportion they bore to similar items of lesser grade, in any local area or even in the possession or under the control of any kula man of substance. Yet in overall terms, if the traditional insistence on the one-to-one rule of a transaction of kula is to be met, either there must be equal numbers of each series at every grade, or there must be elements of flexibility in the system which are not apparent at first sight. The latter would seem to have been the case in kula history.

One possible area of flexibility would be some degree of ambiguity in the allocation of specific armshells or necklaces to a generally acknowledged system of grades. This is not an issue discussed by Malinowski, though he may have implied it in pointing out that there was no exact standard of comparison in the exchange of valuables. He went to some pains to emphasise the difficulty of satisfying a man who had given an item of high value, and the contrast between striving to belittle the object about to be given him in exchange, and the wish to boast of it if it was of fine quality (1922:359). And yet a great number of transactions must have proceeded with basic consensus or the system could never have endured. Exchange by private treaty lacks the dimension of an overt price level, but it can still operate within a general tacit price frame. One further possibility of flexibility within the frame would be that for the majority of kula transactions what I may call 'the range of value tolerance' was fairly wide. For items of fine quality, named and with a kula history, a very close match would be sought and obtained. But it could have been that for the bulk of transactions the most important thing was to get a return of roughly comparable value; that while the grading of valuables by named categories was recognised, there could be difference of opinion, arguable but acceptable, as to exactly which grade of necklace was most appropriate to which of armshell. A third possibility for flexibility in evaluation lay in the gap between 'opening gift' and the return for it. Malinowski observed that these two transfers were distinct in time and in performance, and that this inhibited direct assessment of equivalence. So the original donor, in particular, was not able to confront the two items and compare them point by point. Given a 'crude and fundamental human dissatisfaction with the value received' (1922:352–3) his expression of it had to be perforce to some extent histrionic. It could be indeed that the named grades of armshells and necklaces were as much as anything broad standards of reference, to supply mnemonics for categories of return gifts. Unfortunately Malinowski nowhere gave any detailed account of the observations of any Trobriander who was comparing the quality of armshells or necklaces in examining actual specimens. So it is not clear how far a generally recognised set of graded categories was pre-eminent as a guide to an exchange or was secondary to individual judgement of value in the 'fair' return. The relevance of this point is that the more numerous its separate categories, the more difficult the matching process must have been. This is where indication of the relative numbers or proportions of items in the various grades, and the possibility of change in their numbers becomes of major significance.

One possibility only vaguely hinted at by Malinowski but discussed in some detail by at least one modern commentator, Shirley Campbell, is the re-grading of some items over time. Put rather bluntly in economic terms, a scarcity of items in a high-ranking category of either armshells or necklaces might have been met by raising the status of some formerly lower-ranking items. Such process need not require open agreement; the scarcity itself would tend to an upward re-valuation of marginal items, presumably those of some reputation from previous kula travelling.

An element making for considerable flexibility in the matching aspect of the evaluative process was the time-lag in reciprocation of kula presentations. Normally at least a seasonal gap, this time-lag could be extended because of a tough stance by the partner in debt or because of his inability to lay hands on a valuable of the acceptable quality to give in return for the original item. The possible variation of the time-gap had some interesting implications for the exchange system. It meant that differences in speed of repayment could be translated into differences of velocity of circulation of objects of various grades and types, so compensating for differences in the numbers required for matching in due course. For instance, a high-grade armshell pair needing an equally high-grade necklace in reciprocation would, if such necklaces were scarcer, have to wait for long periods unmatched until such necklace, continuing to move, became finally available. So a given number of armshells of a certain grade could be served by fewer necklaces travelling faster round the ring. On this point Malinowski gave no data. But what he did make clear was the compensatory principle built into the system to obviate an undue time-lag in reciprocation. The kula system is theoretically non-incremental in a material sense, that is, an item presented is not expected to be returned 'with interest', but reciprocated by another of equivalent value. The original donor is expected to stand out of his property without material compensation; without control the system would be open to abuse. (*Basi* intermediary gifts are expected to be repaid; they are to keep the situation open, not to give 'interest' on the original transfer.) Control is afforded by the principle of personal reputation, operating conversely to the time-lag: the longer a man defers reciprocation for a kula valuable, the lower his reputation sinks. Donor gains no material asset by the passage of time, but recipient loses in his immaterial asset. The sanction is imprecise, and is to some extent blurred by the ambiguity of being known for 'hardness' in releasing valuables (1922:271, 360, 498). But protracted delay in repayment can lead to grave disturbance of social relationships. What the time factor allows is great possibility of manipulation of transactions with an eye to personal advantage. It gives flexibility in choice of items for reciprocity, and opportunity for reviewing partnership strategy – including possible switching of partner-routes in gift of valuables or visits of expectation, in pursuance of what Malinowski referred to as a 'shunting-station' role (1922:278).

Of cardinal importance in interpreting the evaluative process of the

Raymond Firth

kula, with its notion of matching armshell pairs and necklaces is the question of rate of accretion and rate of leakage of valuables into and out of the kula network. From Malinowski's information it is not possible to get any adequate idea of these rates, though from general data of about that period it seems probable that shell items, in kula or related forms, did move in and out of the system, both within the island communities and along the New Guinea mainland coast. Fortune (1932:206) states plausibly that the extra amount contributed by any one year's shell fishing was little compared with the great stock in circulation, from generations of fishermen. But unless the leakage into the field of, say, personal adornment and marriage payments had been fairly heavy, over many generations the increments of such durable goods must have magnified the stocks very considerably. What is unlikely is that a completely steady relation was preserved between armshell increment (in pairs) and necklace increment. The whole problem of possible surplus or shortfall in one series or the other and in grades of either offers intriguing questions to which only now is modern research beginning to supply answers. One of these questions which demands some historical perspective for satisfactory reply is why armshells, as Malinowski made clear, should have moved generally in pairs whereas necklaces moved singly? This would have been in conformity with their utilitarian function as bodily adornment, with a shell for each upper arm and a loop of several coils for the neck. It would also have fitted the 'right–left' complementarity of armshells mentioned by Malinowski (1922:504). But it might have also been a development to match an increasing evaluation of necklaces. A necklace, unlike an armshell, can be easily enlarged by additional discs. When original stocks were fairly small, did necklaces in kula start off as short loops and become longer with regular production of more discs? But as armshells too increased in number from constant production, did the only simple way of increasing their worth to match the longer necklaces seem to be a doubling of the individual armrings? And still as a problem of numbers, is the reported growth of the practice of using single armshells in modern kula a response to a 'democratisation' of the institution, a marked increase in kula operators; with growing affluence and greater availability of transport, is the demand for valuables for exchange tending to outstrip the supply?

In conclusion I recapitaulate and slightly extend my main argument. Despite the critical feature of kula ideology, the prescription of a one-to-one matching equivalence of armshell (pair) and necklace, which would theoretically demand equal numbers of each series at each parallel grade, it is very unlikely that numbers of armshells and necklaces were ever exactly equal, or if so, that the annual increment of each was exactly the same. Factors of flexibility must have been introduced: by possibility of conversion of kula resources into non-kula goods; by use in kula exchange of items such stone axe-blades as ancillary to armshells and necklaces; and by skilful manipulation of kula items as major and as interim transfers among alternative partners in the light of admissible time delays for reciprocation. From Malinowski's data it is not clear that all these modes of flexibility were in operation sixty years ago, but the last of them, what may be called 'indebtedness engineering', lay certainly at the core of the institution. What is suggested very strongly by the results of modern research is that kula items, at least in the higher grades, were more definitely subject to individual claims of control, and less fixed in value in relation to one another, than Malinowski envisaged. Conventional exchange rates broadly obtained, but it is probable that even more than Malinowski realised, their application consisted in sets of personal estimates which interpreted these conventional rates in the light of individual interest, long-term as well as short-term.

But a note of caution may be timely. It is tempting to project modern findings back into Malinowski's period, and to fill gaps and explain away puzzles of sixty years ago by present-day more sophisticated research. Yet historical perspective requires that note be taken of the great changes within and outside the kula system since Malinowski's day. I mention three features only. One is pearling. Malinowski himself mentions that some Trobriand communities abandoned kula expeditions for pearling and ceased to own canoes, and on the other hand that some shell valuables were imported by pearl traders to pay their divers (1922:468, 500). What was the effect of the stoppage of pearling upon the kula capacity of Trobrianders concerned? More fundamental, probably, have been the effects of changes in transport over the last sixty years. How far has the transition from indigenous sailing craft, largely restricted to seasonal movement, to motor launches and other powered craft of freer movement, owned by both aliens and local people, affected the flow of kula valuables, bearing in mind that any seagoing craft can be a mode of investment and a source of trading income as well as a carrier of kula wealth? Thirdly, with the dramatic development of modern communications, any avenue to public renown becomes of interest to a much wider range of people than those before the electronic age. What has been the relation of achievement in kula to position in modern southeastern New Guinea society, in which politics, the Church, commercial entrepreneurship and administrative bureaucracy all offer means of advancement to ambitious men? (Of women's role in kula at last we are being informed by modern studies such as those of Annette Weiner.) A firmer historical dimension to kula interpretation is now coming to be supplied.

Raymond Firth

But the subtle effects of all such changes upon the evaluation of kula shell goods, both in relation to one another and to non-kula goods, have still to be worked out. Even though Malinowski's model may be no longer adequate for such analysis, his basic formulations still provide a starting-point.

Notes

1 Modern practice seems to equate veguwa and necklace; here I follow Malinowski's usage, to include armshells too.
2 Malinowski sometimes writes of 'armshells' (1922:391) but it is clear that he is really speaking of attached pairs (1922:386). However Uberoi writes of armshells only (1962:112 *et passim*).
3 Items asterisked as noted by Malinowski; others are my guesses from Malinowski's general data. He mentioned at one point (1922, 489) that the Dobuans 'carried about 800 pairs of armshells from Boyowa' on their March–April 1918 expedition. If not a slip, this means that an additional 150 pairs to the 650 cited were got from partners scattered through southern Boyowan villages, but not displayed at the *tanarere* exhibition at Sarubwoyna beach. This would mean that my total estimate should be higher by another 130 pairs.
4 Dr Giancarlo Scoditti has very generously sent me a list he compiled from his field data of 1973–4 and 1976 research in Kumwagea village, Kitava, giving '*kula* men' and the amount of armshells and necklaces they controlled, with location of their partners. A close count for thirty men gave nearly 540 armshells and 520 necklaces controlled. Other kula operators (including one woman 'flying witch') controlled many valuables not precisely counted, so an average of about a score of armshells and of necklaces per operator seems indicated. Close comparability of the data with my estimates from Malinowski's material is not feasible, but a roughly similar order of magnitude is at least suggested.
5 An admirable account of the classification system of kula shell valuables, and of the various indices by which these objects are judged, and of the process of judging, is given by Shirley Campbell in the present volume. From her Trobriand vantage point of Vakuta she has been able to offer significant comparison with Malinowski's material from Kiriwina. (Note that her information reverses the sex identification of shell valuables given by Malinowski.)
6 But while Malinowski wrote of the history and tradition of some named kula objects, especially armshells (1922:89, 504), he gave almost no detail of the transactions in which they had been engaged, and some of them seemed to be of relatively recent manufacture. Some of the names mentioned by Malinowski seem, however, to be still current for certain valuables, at the present day, e.g. as indicated by Shirley Campbell.

4 Kula gift exchange and capitalist commodity exchange: a comparison

CHRIS GREGORY

Acknowledgements

I have learnt much about the Trobriands from informal discussions that I have had with Jerry Leach over the past three years. I am also indebted to the participants of the *kula* conference for many valuable comments on my conference paper. I am particularly grateful to Fred Damon because it was he who introduced me to the bewildering complexity of kula gift exchange in Wabunun village, Woodlark Island, in June 1974. Needless to say, these people should not be blamed for my errors.

The Milne Bay area of Papua New Guinea has been colonised now for almost 100 years. During the early part of this century it was a major centre of mining and plantation development, and many foreign-owned plantations still operate there today. It was also a major administrative centre and a major supplier of indentured labour for plantation and mining capital. The effect of this colonisation process has been to integrate the province's 108,000 people well and truly into the world economy; money circulates freely around the islands and most people have had some experience in handling it either as cash-crop producers, plantation workers, wage labourers, or consumers of imported foodstuffs. An additional effect of this colonisation process has been to provide the conditions for kula to flourish and develop. Kula is very much a modern phenomenon as the recent fieldwork evidence shows: it has not been destroyed by the colonisation process, contrary to what we might have expected.

But how do we explain this?

In order to answer this question we must first come to terms with the distinguishing features of the 'European-type' systems of exchange and 'kula-type' systems of exchange. Are the principles that govern 'kula-type' exchanges the same as those that govern 'European-type' exchanges or different? There seems to be a general consensus of opinion

Chris Gregory

that they are different. However, where the dispute lies is in the formulation of the exact nature of that difference.

The 'formalists' express the difference in terms of a distinction between 'primitive' money and 'modern' money. According to this theory the objects of 'kula-type' exchanges are like money in that they facilitate price formulation and measure profits. Furthermore, it is argued that 'kula-type' transactors are like capitalists in that they aim to accumulate wealth. Thus, according to this theory the only difference between the two systems of exchange is that one is 'modern' whereas the other is 'primitive'. T. S. Epstein is the best known proponent of this approach (1968: Ch. 2).

The substantivists take a slightly different approach. According to Bohannan (1959) the difference is one between a 'unicentric' economy on the one hand and a 'multi-centric' economy on the other. 'Western' money is 'general-purpose' whereas 'kula-type' money is 'limited-purpose' and it is for this reason that we have ranked 'spheres of exchange' in 'kula-type' economies.

It is the aim of this paper to develop a critique of both these approaches by developing the theory of commodities and gifts in the light of the recent evidence of Milne Bay *gift* exchange. The basic argument is that commodity exchange is an exchange of alienable objects between people who are in a state of reciprocal independence that establishes a quantitative relationship between the objects transacted, whereas gift exchange is an exchange of inalienable objects between people who are in a state of reciprocal dependence that establishes a qualitative relationship between the subjects transacting. This argument can be summarised in terms of the following contrasting categories:

commodities	gifts
alienable	inalienable
independence	dependence
quantity	quality
objects	subjects

This argument is a synthesis of the ideas of Marx and Mauss. Their theories of exchange are briefly discussed in the first part of this paper. The remaineder of it is concerned to develop and elaborate the distinction between gifts and commodities that they first developed.

For Adam Smith, commodity exchange was the defining characteristic of people. He argued that it was 'common to all men, and to be found in no other race of animals' (1776:12). It was a natural form of exchange for people to engage in according to Smith.

104

Marx's great advance on Smith was see commodity exchange as a social form and to develop the distinction between commodity exchange and non-commidity exchange. Marx's approach was historical and anthropological and it was his encounter with the nineteenth-century anthropological literature that enabled him to develop this important distinction (see Engel's editorial footnote in Volume III of *Capital* (Marx, 1894:177)). Marx first develops this distinction in Volume I of *Capital* and his perspicacious observation justifies a lengthy quote:

The first step made by an object of utility towards acquiring exchange-value is when it forms a non-use-value for its owner, and that happens when it forms a superfluous portion of some article required for his immediate wants. Objects in themselves are external to man, and consequently alienable by him. In order that this alienation may be reciprocal, it is only necessary for men, by tacit understanding, to treat each other as private owners of those alienable objects, and by implication as independent individuals. But such a state of reciprocal independence has no existence in a primitive society based on property in common, whether such a society takes the form of a patriarchal family, an ancient Indian community, or Peruvian Inca State. The exchange of commodities, therefore, first begins on the boundaries of such communities, at their points of contact with similar communities, or with members of the latter. So soon, however, as products once become commodities in the external relations of a community, they also, by reaction, become so in its internal intercourse. The proportions in which they are exchangeable are at first quite a matter of chance. What makes them exchangeable is the mutual desire of their owners to alienate them. Meantime the need for foreign objects of utility gradually establishes itself. The constant repetition of exchange makes it a normal social act. In the course of time, therefore, some portion at least of the products of labour must be produced with a special view to exchange. From that moment the distinction becomes firmly established between the utility of an object for the purposes of consumption, and its utility for the purposes of exchange. Its use-value becomes distinguished from its exchange-value. On the other hand, the quantitative proportion in which the articles are exchangeable, becomes dependent on their production itself. Custom stamps them as values with definite magnitudes. (Marx, 1867:91).

This passage contains five very important propositions that need to be highlighted: first, commodity exchange begins on the boundaries of 'primitive' communities; secondly, a commodity is an alienable object; thirdly, commodity transactors are in a state of reciprocal independence; fourthly, commodities acquire an exchange-value that appears as a quantitative proportion between the things exchanged; and fifthly, the exchange-value of commodities springs from the methods of production, and in particular from productive labour (as Marx argues elsewhere (1867: Ch. 1, sect. 2)).

The fifth proposition, which was also put forward by Adam Smith, is one of the most controversial in the history of political economy. After

Chris Gregory

1870 it came to be rejected by almost all academic economists. In its place was substituted a theory of prices based upon the proposition that consumers maximise utility subject to constraints. This new theory of value represented a profound break with the past. A different conceptual framework was adopted and all the familiar economic categories, e.g. 'price', acquired a new meaning. 'Scarcity' replaced 'reproduction' as the central organising idea and the search for historically specific theories was replaced with a concern to develop a universal theory. Even the terminology was changed. For example the terms 'use-value' and 'commodity' were replaced by the terms 'utility' and 'goods'. These terminological changes in fact epitomise the whole revolution in economic thought that occurred in the 1870s. The term 'use-value', as it was used by the classical political economists such as Smith and Marx, referred to the physical attributes of a thing. For example, a yam has three use-values in Milne Bay – it is used as a means of production in the form of seed, as an article of consumption when cooked, and as an instrument of gift exchange; a sweet potato, by way of contrasts, only has one use-value – food – because it will not keep longer than a few days after being harvested. The term 'commodity' refers to the social form of use-values and only use-values that can be alienated are commodities for Marx. The term 'goods' has a different meaning. As the word itself suggests, it carries with it a subjective connotation: a thing is a 'good' to an individual if he has a subjective preference for it, and the term 'utility' has been used to describe this 'subjective preference'.

Thus insofar as economic theories are concerned, one is either a 'commodity' theorist or a 'goods' theorist. The formalists and the substantivists belong to the latter school and the distinction they develop between 'kula-type' and non 'kula-type' exchanges is really one between different types of goods. For example Epstein distinguishes between 'primitive' and 'modern' *goods*. However Marx's distinction was between *commodity* exchange and *non-commodity* exchange and the question that his analysis poses is: 'what are the social attributes of a non-commodity?'

The answer is implicit in the five propositions developed above and from these propositions it is possible to develop three positive statements: firstly, non-commodity exchange occurs inside the boundaries of 'primitive' communities; secondly, a non-commodity is an inalienable object; thirdly, non-commodity transactors are in a state of reciprocal dependence.

Marx was not able to develop his theory of the non-commodity form because the anthropological data were simply not available: Papua New Guinea was not colonised until 1883, the year of his death. However the data were available to Mauss and these three propositions are central to his theory. A gift for Mauss is an inalienable object and it is this social property of a thing that is the 'force . . . in the thing given which compels the recipient to make a return' (1925:1). Inalienability creates an 'indissoluble bond of a thing with its owner' (1925:62) and this is a theme that Mauss repeatedly stresses (see 1925:9–10, 11, 18, 24, 31, 42, 46–62, 71). 'We live in a society', he says, 'where there is a marked distinction . . . between real and personal law, between things and persons. This distinction is fundamental; it is the very condition of part of our system of property, alienation and exchange. Yet it is foreign to the customs we have been studying' (1925:46). The implication of inalienability is that gift exchange 'necessarily implies the notion of credit' (1925:35). The implication of the exchange of alienable objects on the other hand is that it necessarily implies the notion of price-formation, i.e., purchase and sale. Such phenomena do not exist with gift exchange as Mauss correctly notes (1925:30).

The goods theorists have failed to grasp these points because in their rejection of Marx's labour theory of value they have thrown the baby out with the bathwater: propositions 1–4 were thrown out along with proposition 5. Thus they see gift exchange as a price-making mechanism and incremental gift-giving as profit-making. For example Firth wants to understand kula transactions as price-making mechanisms above (89); he also wants to apply the equation of commodity exchange, $MV = PT$ where M is the stock of money, V its velocity, P the price of things, and T the transactions. From the Marx/Mauss theoretical perspective kula exchange cannot be understood in this way as I will now try to show. In the process I will attempt to develop some of the theoretical insights of these thinkers.

Let me then summarise the argument so far in terms of a simple example. Suppose A had 3 baskets of yams that he wanted to convert into a canoe, and that B had a canoe that he wanted to convert into 3 baskets of yams. Suppose further that A and B met and that they exchanged these things. This exchange can be represented as follows:

$$A \underset{\text{1 canoe}}{\overset{\text{3 yams}}{\rightleftharpoons}} B$$

This is the general form for the exchange of all things. Suppose now that these things were alienable, i.e. commodities. In such a case a quantitative relationship is established between the objects of the exchange and we get the equation

3 baskets of yams = 1 canoe

Chris Gregory

This equation can be read: 'the price of yams is one-third the price of a canoe'.

Suppose now that these things were inalienable, i.e. gifts. In this case no equation is established. Instead of a quantitative relation between the objects being established, a qualitative relation between the subjects is established and debt is created: A owes B a canoe and B owes A 3 baskets of yams.

Obligations are therefore created and these are only cancelled when the return gift is made. What usually happens, of course, is that the return gift usually exceeds the initial gift. This creates new debt and serves to prolong the relationship. For example, suppose that B gave A 10 yams in exchange for 2 canoes at some later date. The debt situation is now reversed: B owes A 1 canoe and A owes B 7 baskets of yams. Strathern called this principle 'alternating disequilibrium' (1971:222) and coined the phrase to describe the *moka* gift exchange mechanism. Malinowski does not describe a similar phenomenon for the kula that he observed; but it is now very much a part of contemporary kula as the recent evidence shows (see e.g. Damon, 1978: Ch 5). Incremental gift giving raises the question of interest which we will return to below. What we want to establish here is that kula exchange is an exchange of inalienable objects. But how can this be established?

The answer lies in the concept *kitoum*. This was not discussed by Malinowski, which means either that he overlooked it or that it was invented after he left the Trobriands. Whatever the case, kitoum is very much a part of the vocabulary of modern kula and the term is a way of talking about the exchange of inalienable objects. For example, if A has a kitoum that he gives to B as a *vaga* (opening gift), who in turn gives it to C as a vaga, it remains A's object even though C now holds it. This creates a 'road' (*keda*) of debt: C owes B a gift and B owes A a gift. Notice that it is B and C who are in debt because they do not have alienable rights over the instrument of exchange. They have to receive it and give it away as a gift. However A has the option of either selling it to a tourist as a commodity or giving it as a gift because it is his kitoum, i.e., only he has alienable rights over the object. It should be noted that a very high tourist demand for necklaces has developed over the past fifty years and the development of the concept kitoum may be related to this fact. This is only an hypothesis but it is one that needs investigation.

Kula gift exchanges, then, are inalienable conversions of things that create debt. Commodity exchanges on the other hand are alienable conversion of things that create prices. Gift exchanges establish qualitative relations between transactors whereas commodity exchanges establish quantitative relations between the transacted. It follows therefore

108

that things as commodities have an exchange-ratio whereas things as gifts have an exchange-order, a ranking.

It is the exchange-ratio of a thing as a commodity that enables it to form an equation of the type 3 yams = 1 canoe. The exchange-order of a thing as a gift, on the other hand, enables it to establish a qualitative relation with another gift. The quantities involved in the transaction are unimportant. For example if it is established that canoes have a higher rank than yams then it will not affect the exchange-order one bit if thirty yams or 300 are exchanged against the canoe. The exchange-order of gifts is like the rank of cards and like cards the rank is unchanged by an exchange. For example, an ace of hearts will always be worth more than a two of clubs no matter how many times the cards are used. What is determined by the outcome of a gift exchange is not the exchange-order of the objects but the rank of the transactors. In a commodity exchange by way of contrast, the rank of transactors is given and the exchange-ratio of the things is determined. (According to Marx's theory the sphere of commodity exchange establishes one rate – the 'market price' – and the sphere of production establishes another – 'the price of production'. He argues that the latter establishes a 'centre of gravity' around which the former revolves (Marx, 1894: Ch. IX).)

Kula gifts had an exchange-order and from Malinowski's account (1922: Chs III, XIV) it is possible to deduce the following order:

first: big armshells and necklaces
second: small armshells and necklaces
third: whalebone spatulae
fourth: polished axe blades
fifth: pigs, yams, and bananas.

These constituted a ladder of rank up which an aspiring big-man had to climb by the careful manipulation of different gifts. Nowadays the ranking is different. However the shells are still top and their exchange-order is determined in a qualitative way as Campbell's article 'Attaining Rank: Classification of Kula Shell Valuables' (below: 229–48) describes only too well. Size, colour, history, and other personal characteristics are the important determinants of the exchange-order of gifts and not the productive labour time embodied in them. Large instruments require longer to produce; but they last longer too and if allowance is made for this fact then nothing can be said about the relation between exchange-order and productive labour embodied.

However the principal theoretical problem that gift exchange poses is not 'what determines the exchange-order of things as gifts?' The exchange-order of things as gifts relatively stable over time and this can be

Chris Gregory

taken as data for the purposes of synchronic analysis. The theoretical
question can be stated precisely as follows: given the exchange-order of
the objects, what determines the rank of the transactors? The theoretical
question that commodity exchange poses, by way of contrast, is: given
the rank of the transactors, what determines the exchange-ratio of the
objects?

To illustrate this point let us refer once again to the exchange of 3 yams
for 1 canoe between A and B. Suppose that this was a commodity
exchange, i.e., that the objects were alienable, and that A was an agricultural company and B a shipbuilding company. The rank of capitalist
firms is measured by their ratio of capital to labour. For example, if firm
A uses 10 tons of iron and six labourers to produce its annual output and
firm B uses the same amount of iron and only 3 labourers then B can be
said to be more capital intensive. Thus the problem that the classical
political economists posed was: 'Given the capital-labour ratio of the
transactors, what determines the exchange-ratio of the transacted?' (It
should be noted that if one assumes that the capital–labour ratio of
industries is equal, as Marx did in Volumes I and II of *Capital* then
productive labour is a measure of exchange-ratio; but if one assumes that
they are unequal then this rule only holds for the average industry (see
Sraffa, 1960 for a rigorous demonstration of this proposition and for a
discussion of the problems of measuring capital).

Suppose now that the exchange was of gifts and that the canoe was
ranked higher than the yams. Given this data the exchange can be
conceptualised as one where the objects exchange the subjects rather
than the other way round. Thus instead of

$$A \xrightleftharpoons[\text{3 yams}]{\text{1 canoe}} B$$

which describes a commodity exchange, we get

$$\begin{array}{c} \text{1 canoe} \\ A \uparrow \quad \downarrow B \\ \text{3 yams} \end{array}$$

This way of conceptualising gift exchange may be how kula transactors
conceptualise it. They speak of the 'rising' and 'falling' of a man's kula
name (Damon, 1978:44).

The notion that the objects exchange the subjects in a gift exchange
system should be seen in the light of Lévi-Strauss' theory that women are
the 'supreme gift' (1949:65) and that things as gifts are symbolic representations of women. This idea, it seems, was first put forward by

110

Williams who argued 'that the exchange of girls in marriage falls into line with other exchanges. The unmarried girl is, so to speak, the supreme gift' (1936:168). If one accepts this theory, as well as the proposition I have developed here, then gift exchange is a system where women exchange the rank of men! Such a formulation is highly controversial, of course, but it does place the 'sex struggle' at the centre of the problem.

It should be noted that the theoretical question posed here – what determines the rank of gift transactors – does not exist in those societies that practice 'sister exchange', or 'restricted exchange' as Levi-Strauss would call it. In such societies we do not find 'big-men'; nor do we find incremental gift exchange. Instead, such exchanges of things that do exist tend to be non-incremental and that it is elders that dominate and not big-men. Many of the ethnographies from the Sepik District illustrate this point (cf. Gell, 1975: 17–18). However, a consideration of these issues is beyond the scope of this paper.

Let us now examine Bohannan's 'unicentric'/'multicentric' distinction in the light of the previous discussion. At one level of analysis this distinction is correct: it is an implicit recognition of the fact that gifts have an exchange-order and that commodities have an exchange-ratio, i.e. it captures the quality/quantity distinction between gifts and commodities. As an illustration, suppose that a society produces labour, pigs and yams. If this was a commodity economy then these objects would be brought into quantitative relationship with one another and we would get the equation:

x units of labour = y units of pigs = z units of yams

But if this was a gift economy then these objects would be brought into qualitative relationship with one another and we would get a ranking as follows (say):

first: labour
second: pigs
third: yams

Thus it could be said that the commodity economy is 'unicentric' and the gift economy 'multicentric'.

Bohannan then goes on to argue that the impact of 'general purpose money', i.e., an instrument of commodity exchange, is to destroy the 'multicentric' gift economy. He argues that the qualitative ranking of things as gifts is quantified by money thereby converting the multicentric economy into a unicentric one. This argument may or may not be a valid description of what happened in West Africa but it does not describe what is happening in Milne Bay. Here the 'multicentric' gift economy still

111

Chris Gregory

flourishes under the impact of the 'unicentric' commodity economy. It seems that in Milne Bay the gift economy has to some extent qualified the commodity economy rather than the other way around as Bohannan claims.

Part of the reason why Bohannan's 'unicentric'/'multicentric' distinction lacks any explanatory adequacy is that it is wrong when viewed from a slightly different perspective. There is a sense in which the commodity economy too is 'multicentric'. It is possible to dinstinguish three spheres of commodity exchange that are associated with transactors of different 'rank' (or social class to be more precise).

The lowest sphere is that in which the working class operates. They are trapped in a sphere of exchange that can be represented symbolically as C..M..C, where C stands for 'commodity' and M for 'money'. Workers sell their labour-power as a commodity for which they receive money in return. The sale is the C..M phase of the circuit, where C is their labour-power and M their wages. With this money they buy commodites such as food, clothing, and shelter. This purchase is represented by the M..C phase of the circuit. Seen as a whole then the sale and purchase effect an alienable conversion of labour-power into food, clothing and shelter as follows:

$$A \underset{\text{food, etc.}}{\overset{\text{labour-power}}{\rightleftharpoons}} B$$

where A represents the working class and B the capitalist class. This conversion enables the wage labourers to re-sell their labour-power on the market and so the process goes on. This circuit exists in Papua New Guinea. It is most unlike moka or kula gift exchange in that it is non-incremental. The worker who throws away his money into this sphere of exchange receives back an equivalent in food. The workers are well aware of this fact. 'We just eat up our money', they say, 'All our money goes on food and we are fed up' (Strathern, M., 1975:10).

However, the second sphere of exchange, the industrial capitalists sphere, does return an increment to the transactors who participate in it. An industrial capitalist does not sell in order to buy like the worker, he buys in order to sell at a profit. His sphere of exchange can be represented as $M..C..M'$ where $M..C$ represents a purchase, $C..M'$ a sale, and $M'-M$ profit. The most important commodity he buys is labour-power. This commodity alone, according to Marx, produces surplus value, the pure form of profit. This proposition is of course highly controversial but the workers of Papua New Guinea have had little difficulty in grasping it. As M. Strathern notes, 'People nowadays speak of having been tricked by

112

Europeans who "ate" the profits of their labours, putting aside only a minute proportion for wages' (1975:33).

The third sphere of exchange is dominated by the most powerful class of all, the financial capitalist class, the modern-day money-lender. He advances capital in the form of money, M, and receives back, after the lapse of a certain period of time, his original sum plus an increment. This sphere can be represented as M...M', where M is the original sum thrown into the circuits, M' the sum returned to him, and M'−M the increment received. Workers who are able to save can participate in this sphere but their contribution is paltry. One needs a large initial stock of money capital in order to survive in this sphere. For example £100,000 will earn £10,000 if the rate of interest is 10%. This sphere, then, tends to be dominated by the large multinational financial capitalists who lend to the industrial capitalists.

The financial capitalists' sphere is formally identical to a circuit of gift giving. For example, suppose that M = £100, M' = £110, and the price of pigs was £1. In pig equivalents, then, what we have is a situation where 100 pigs are advanced and 110 pigs returned. This is exactly the form of exchange that moka transactions take; it is also the form that lower level kula transactions take. This formal equivalence has misled many anthropologists and economists into thinking that the principle of interest governs gift giving. Boas, for example, maintained that 'the underlying principle [of potlatch] is that of interest-bearing investment of property' (1966:77); a similar argument is at the heart of Epstein's 'primitive capitalism' theory (1968). However this is a profound misconception and it derives from overlooking the fact that gifts are inalienable things whereas commodities are alienable things. If the argument were true it would imply that the link between a gift and a counter gift is the formula $M' = (1+r)^n M$, where r is the rate of interest and n the number of time periods for which the money is lent. But if this formula does not hold then which one does?

For a time period of one, the following formula holds:

$$G'_{t+1} - G_t = G_{t+1,}$$

where G_t is the original gift (vaga), G'_{t+1} the return gift (*kudu*), and G_{t+1} the new gift (vaga).

From Malinowski's account of kula we get the idea that

$$G'_{t+1} - G_t = 0,$$

i.e., that kula was not incremental. This is wrong as the contemporary evidence shows: kula is a form of incremental gift giving.

But what about the 'equivalence' principle, one may well ask. It should

113

be remembered that gifts have an exchange-order which means that if a gift of rank 2 is given the debt so created can only be cancelled by returning a gift of the same rank. It a gift of lower rank is given in return then this merely creates new debt. Suppose that we had an inalienable conversion of the following form

$$A \underset{G3}{\overset{G2}{\rightleftharpoons}} B$$

where G2 is a gift of second rank and G3 a gift of third rank. This could be written G2..G3. However because gifts are inalienable a relationship is established between the transactors and not the transacted; debt is created and the exchange must be reversed if the debt is to be cancelled. Thus in the next period we must get

$$A \underset{G3}{\overset{G2}{\rightleftharpoons}} B$$

Alternatively, this exchange can be written G3'..G2'. Thus the full circuit appears as G2..G3..G2'..G3', which breaks down into two circuits, G2..G2' and G3..G3'. The equivalence condition can therefore be written

$$G2' = G2$$
$$G3' = G3$$

This example illustrates the principle of a *basi*. Consider his example: 'Let us imagine that a Sinaketan man [A] has given a very fine pair of armshells [G2] to his Dobuan partner [B] at their last meeting in Sinaketa. Now, arriving in Dobu, he finds that his partner has not got any necklace equivalent in value to the armshells given. He none the less will expect his partner to give him meanwhile a necklace, even though it be of inferior value [G3]. Such a gift is a *basi*, that is not a return of the highly valuable *vaga*, but a gift given to fill the gap. This *basi* will have to be repaid by a small pair of equivalent armshells [G3'] at a later date' (1922:355–6). Of course what makes Malinowski difficult to read is that he uses the terminology of commodity exchange, in particular the word 'value' (exchange-ratio), to describe the 'rank' (exchange-order) of gifts.

A *basi* has some bearing on the Bohannan's distinction between 'conveyance' and 'conversion' (1968:234–8). A conveyance is an exchange within a sphere and a conversion is an exchange between spheres. Thus a 'conveyance' takes the form G2..G2' and a 'conversion' G2..G3. However, as we have just shown, inalienable conversions are really double conveyances because they create debt that has to be repaid. The only true conversion of gift, it seems, is a 'bridewealth' transaction. Such a transaction is formally identical to the purchase and sale of labour-power, C..M..C, and it can be written G1..G2..G1, where G1 is the 'supreme' gift, female labour. However, whereas the purchase and sale of labour-power facilitates the transformation of labour into things, a bridewealth transfer facilitates the transformation of things into labour. In other words, an alienable conversion involving things and labour is a process of reification whereas an inalienable conversion involving things and labour is an anthropomorphic process. Munn (1977) contains an excellent analysis of the latter process for the Gawa Island case. No attempt will be made to summarise her detailed and complex argument here, suffice it to say that the concept of alienation and anthropomorphism are central themes of her analysis.

So far we have only considered the formula for a gift-giving sequence on the assumption that only one time period is involved. But what formula holds when n time periods is considered? The following:

$$G_{t+n} = G_{t+1} + \sum_{i=2}^{n} (-1)^{i+1} G'_{t+i}, \text{ for } n>1 \text{ and odd.}$$

Thus the operator that links a gift-giving sequence is not the compound interest formula, $(1+r)^n$, but the 'alternating disequilibrium' formula, $(-1)^{i+1}$. This captures the fact that a 'flip-flop' relation of domination and subordination is created between the transactors to a gift-giving sequence over time.

As an illustration, suppose that A and B were involved in the following series of transactions:

t   : B gives A a gift of 10 shells   (i.e. $G_t = 10$)
t+1   : A gives B a gift of 12 shells   (i.e. $G'_{t+1} = 12, G_{t+1} = 2$)
t+2   : B gives A a gift of 8 shells   (i.e. $G'_{t+2} = 8, G_{1+2} = 6$)
t+3   : A gives B a gift of 20 shells   (i.e. $G'_{t+3} = 20, G_{t+3} = 14$)

The first gift (G_t) creates a debt of 10 shells and B is dominant; the return gift (G'_{t+1}) creates a new debt (G_{t+1}) of 2 shells and reverses the relations of domination and subordination; the next return gift reverses the process and so it goes on. In terms of the equation we get

$$G_{t+3} = G_{t+1} - G'_{t+2} + G'_{t+3}$$
$$14 = 2 - 8 + 20$$

Quantitative calculation such as this is only possible within a given sphere where the gifts are homogeneous and where the problem of valuation does not arise. It is not possible to count gifts of a different exchange-order.

Chris Gregory

These equations capture, in a formal way, the temporal dimension of gift-giving and enable us to define the precise difference between inter-temporal incremental gift-giving and intertemporal incremental commodity exchange. But exchange also has a spatial dimension and insofar as commodity exchange is concerned this is captured by the formula,

$$MV = PT,$$

where M is the stock of money, V its velocity, P the price vector, and T the transactions. The value of transactions, PT, in a capitalist commodity economy is always far in excess of the actual stock of money and this situation is brought about because of the high velocity of money the less money is needed and this simple formula captures this relationship.

With gift giving a similar formula exists because the amount of debt is always greater than the stock of instruments of exchange in circulation. However it will not be this equation because gift exchange is not a price-making mechanism; gifts have exchange-order and not exchange-ratio. The general formula for gift exchange is

$$G.V = D,$$

where G the a gift of a given rank, V its velocity, and D the debt created by the gift. If in a given society gifts have ten ranks then ten such equations will exist.

V describes the keda (road) of the gift: the longer the road the greater the debt created. For example, suppose A, B, C, and D were members of a kula keda that was started by A who sent a top-ranking shell (say G2) down the line to D. Suppose further that D sent back a low-ranking shell (say G4) as a basi. This can be represented as follows:

$$
\begin{array}{ccccccc}
& G2 & & G2 & & G2 & \\
A & \rightleftarrows & B & \rightleftarrows & C & \rightleftarrows & D \\
& G4 & & G4 & & G4 &
\end{array}
$$

In this case, then, one G2 creates a debt of $3\times G2$ and one G4 creates a debt of $3\times G4$. In other words, they both have a velocity of 3.

It is debt that keeps a keda alive and this requires that the instruments are inalienable and that they have a high velocity of circulation. In this example this means that the G2 must be A's kitoum and that the G4 must be D's kitoum or someone else's who is not on this particular keda.

Roads such as this exist in moka exchanges too; but there they are called 'ropes' as the title of Strathern's book, *The Rope of Moka*, suggests. It should be noted that his distinction between 'finance' and 'production' (1969) is the distinction between G and V in our formula. A big-man can create debt by production of more G's or by increasing the

116

velocity of circulation of the existing instruments. What distinguishes kula from moka is that kula instruments have direction whereas moka instruments do not. For example, if A gave B a shell in a kula exchange then it could only get back to A via a third partner, C; but in moka B is allowed to return the object directly to A. Thus kula has a tendency to form ring roads whereas moka leads to the formation of straight roads.

Conclusion

Let us now return to the question that was posed at the beginning of this paper: how does one explain the fact that kula has flourished under the impact of colonisation? This question has not been answered. What has been argued is that the problem should be posed in terms of a distinction between commodity exchange and gift exchange and not in terms of a distinction between 'primitive' goods and 'modern' goods. If this argument is accepted then the task is now to link gift exchange and commodity exchange to gift production and commodity production and to examine the interaction of the two at the concrete historical level.

PART II

Northwestern kula area

5 Trobriand territorial categories and the problem of who is not in the kula

⊷⊷

JERRY W. LEACH

Introduction

This paper has basically two purposes. The first is to propose a new ordering of the supra-local territorial categories of Kiriwinan, hopefully adding to, correcting, and making more sense culturally of what has already been published on the subject. The second is to try to shed a little new light on why many Kiriwinan men are not in the *kula*. Kiriwinans, even today, see many virtues in the kula: adventure, vacation, prestige, source of valuables, expanded networks, sexual relations, links to famous men, the maintenance of nautical skills, and the sustaining of cultural tradition.[1] Weiner writes in *Women of Value, Men of Renown*: 'There are two primary roads for valuables: (1) kula and (2) yam exchanges which involve married women' (1976:183). With such manifold benefits, why are approximately 82% of Kiriwinan men not in the system?[2]

Supra-local Territorial Categories[3]

A supra-local territorial category is any term in Kiriwinan that refers to a geographical unit larger than a hamlet, a village, or a modern settlement with their associated garden lands, groves, paths, and wild areas. Such terms are spatial categories of a high order of generality. I restrict this paper to inhabited areas only.

The primary investigators of Trobriand society have to date published twenty-two such territorial categories (cf. maps 1 and 2):[4]

1. Boyowa (Seligmann's Bwaiyor 1910:660; Malinowski 1922:50 and 1932:7 and 146)
2. Kaibwagina (Seligmann's Kaibwagiwa 1910:661; Malinowski's Kaybwagina 1935:290)
3. Kaileuna (Malinowski's Kayleula 1922:50; Montague's Kaileuna 1974: 11; also sometimes heard as Kaileuluwa)

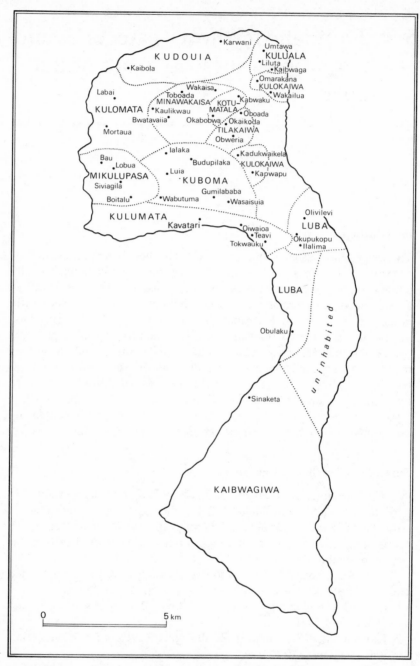

Map 1. Trobriand territorial categories according to Seligmann
(Seligmann 1910, p. 661).

122

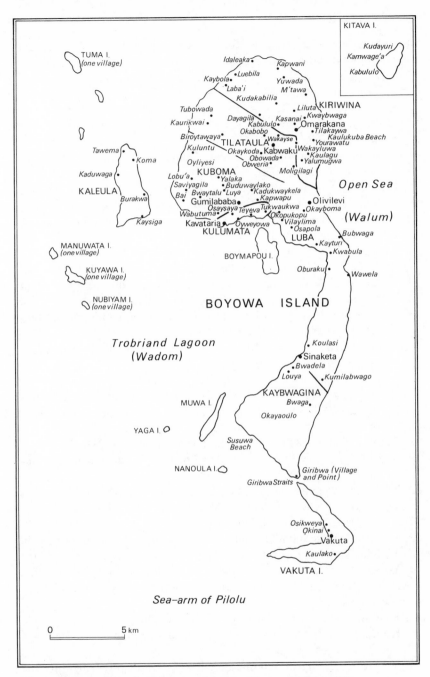

Map 2. Trobriand territorial categories according to Malinowski
(Malinowski 1922, 1961, p. 50).

123

Jerry W. Leach

4. Katumatala (Seligmann's Kotumatala 1910:661; unmentioned in Malinowski and subsequent sources until Lawton, 1968: appendix V)
5. Kawa (Austen, 1945:16; mentioned in Malinowski and others under the introduced name 'Lusancay Islands')
6. Kilivila (unmentioned by this pronunciation in Seligmann or Malinowski; Malinowski's Kiriwana 1922:50 and 1935:54 passim; Weiner's Kilivila 1976:31 passim)
7. Kiriwina (Seligmann, 1910:660–1; Malinowski, 1922:50 and 1935:54 passim; Weiner, 1976:28 passim)
8. Kitava (Seligmann, 1910:670 passim; Malinowski, 1922:50 passim)
9. Kuboma (Seligmann, 1910:661 passim; Malinowski, 1922:50 passim)
10. Kudouya (Seligmann, 1910:661; unmentioned in Malinowski and all subsequent publications)
11. Kulakaiwa (Seligmann's double entry Kulokaiwa 1910:661; Malinowski's Kurokaywa 1935:277; Powell's Kurokayva 1956:32 and 40)
12. Kulila'odila (Malinowski, 1922:205; unmentioned in all subsequent publications; also heard as Kululaodina or Kulilaodina)
13. Kulupasa (Seligmann's Mikulupasa 1910:661; unmentioned in Malinowski and subsequent publications)
14. Kuluwala (Seligmann's Kuluala 1910:661; unmentioned in Malinowski and subsequent publications)
15. Kuyawa (Malinowski, 1922:50; Weiner's Kuia 1976:28)
16. Luba (Seligmann's double entry 1910:666; Malinowski, 1922:50)
17. Mnuwata (Malinowski's Manuwata 1961:50; Weiner's Munuwata 1976:28)
18. Muwo (Malinowski's Muwa 1922:50; Weiner, 1976:28)
19. Simsim (Malinowski, 1935:74; Austen, 1945:16; also heard as Simsimla in Kiriwinan)
20. Tilataula (Seligmann, 1910:666; Seligmann's map erroneously has Tilakaiwa instead of Tilataula; Malinowski,1922:50)
21. Vakuta (Malinowski, 1922:50)
22. Wakaisa (Seligmann's Minawakaisa 1910:661; unmentioned in Malinowski as a supra-local category, only as a name of a village Wakayse 1935:186; Austen, 1945:28; Lawton, 1968: appendix V)

My investigations have produced three additional supra-local territorial categories:
23. Kidodina (synonymous with no. 12 Kulilaodila)
24. Kulitilawa (referring to western Kiriwina, see map 8; also heard as Kulatanawa or Kulitinawa)
25. Yewau (referring to Vakuta and the southern tip of Kiriwina; see map 7; Malinowski's Yayvau 1948(1954):130)

Beyond these, I have found that the names of three local units, norm-

ally understood as the names of villages, are used as the names of
sub-regions and therefore in some contexts as supra-local categories:

26. Sinaketa (a hamlet name used for a large group of coastal hamlets in
    the south in contradistinction to inland areas; Malinowski, 1922:195)
27. Yalumgwa (a village name used more widely to refer to three villages
    as a sub-region; often spelled Ialumugwa; Malinowski, 1935:386
    passim)
28. Kuluvitu (a village name used to refer to all people who live in the
    swamp of northwestern Kiriwina, and hence as a sub-region; Malin-
    owski, 1935:276; also seen as Kuruvitu)

Perusal of the cited sources above will show considerable differences in
the referents of the twenty-two published territorial categories. In my
opinion, the data to date, though partially accurate, suffer from four
weaknesses: (1) being incomplete,[5] (2) conveying the impression that
territorial categories have one level of meaning only, (3) failing to recognize adequately that there are different systems of territorial terms relating to different aspects of Trobriand culture, and (4) conveying the
impression that the categories have unambiguous boundaries. These
weaknesses are understandable in light of the complexity of the systems
and the fact that no investigator has regarded the territorial categories as
anything but a descriptive matter.

My research has led me to interpret the twenty-eight categories as
relating to five aspects of Trobriand culture: topographical separation,
coastal–inland orientation, economic conditions, warfare, and rank and
kula participation. One of the considerable difficulties posed by the
various systems in relation to each other is that the same category may be
used in two or more of the five sets.

Topographical separation

This set quite simply refers to the division into islands. The following 11
categories are involved: Boyowa, Kaileuna, Kawa, Kilivila (indirectly
involved), Kiriwina, Kitava, Kuyawa, Mnuwata, Muwo, Simsim, and
Vakuta.[6] Amongst all investigators, there is the best, though not perfect,
agreement on this set. The problems occur primarily with Boyowa and
Kiriwina, the apparent terms for the main island of the Trobriands.

It is unclear from current evidence if northern Kiriwinans in pre-
colonial times had a name for the entire island on which they lived. My
present opinion is that they did not. Contemporary informants say,
however, that Vakutans called the main island Boyowa but that everybody is now increasingly calling the main island Kiriwina. Apparently
Amphlett Islanders and Dobuans called Kiriwina (contemporary usage)

125

Jerry W. Leach

and sometimes Kiriwina-Vakuta by the term Boyowa. Indeed, Dobuan informants say that the term is from their language, though this statement is hard to evaluate. A further problem is that the people of southern Kiriwina apparently did and still do on occasion call the main island Boyowa, hence Malinowski's use of the term (1922:50; cf. map 2 herein). In addition, southern Kiriwinans sometimes used Boyowa to refer to northern Kiriwina in contradistinction to the south or Kaibwagina. Map 3 roughly shows the Boyowa problem.

A second minor problem occurs with Kiriwina and Kilivila. These are

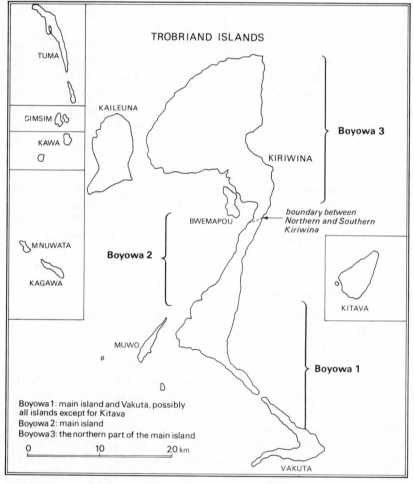

Map 3. Boyowa.

126

dialectical variants of the same term. Surprisingly, despite working in the area, Malinowski never used the second variation Kilivila. In northern Kiriwina today, Kilivila is the pronunciation of the most northern and prestigious economic region (Weiner, 1976: 31, 48, 92, 109). In the Luba area (cf. map 2) and southwards the pronunciation of the same region is Kiriwina. Apparently the prestige of the region led to the generalizing of the name to be the name for the entire island. This was probably done through European influence, especially as Europeans were concentrated around the lagoon where the Kiriwina usage was current. The first missionary to the Trobriands wrote in the late 1890s from his vantage point on the northern lagoon coast: 'Kiriwina is the native name for the Trobriand Group of islands . . .' (S. Fellows, 1973:frame 518). The naming of the new local government council for the Trobriands in 1966 is interesting in light of the problem discussed here. The government officers gave the appellation Kilivila Local Government Council which was established by national ordinance in 1965. When the council convened, the name was criticized as too narrow. Two proposals were put forward: Trobriand and Simla (island). The first was rejected as 'not from our language' and because few people knew the word.[7] The second was ignored and the matter adjourned. The next meeting[8] produced ten proposals:

1. Labai (site of hole of emergence of all Trobrianders)
2. Labai-Kilivila
3. Luluwa-Labai (emergence and peopling of the land)
4. Tosunapula-Labai (people who emerged from Labai)
5. Lavayola Valu (shield of the homeland?)
6. Selavi (bound together)
7. Kiriwina
8. Vasosu (joined or united or tied together)
9. Kivakoni (privileged)
10. Kilivila

Kiriwina carried the day and the name was changed.[9] Interestingly, Boyowa was not proposed.

In closing this section, it is worth noting that topographical terms can be used to denote dialect areas as in *biga Kaileuna* (language of Kaileuna) or *biga Vakuta* (language of Vakuta).

Coastal–inland orientation

The second set of categories will be discussed with reference to Kiriwina only. It involves coast-dwelling as opposed to non-coastal villages, access to the sea, and predominance in fishing. It also relates to the total

127

Jerry W. Leach

problem of the food supply for Kiriwinan society. Map 4 shows the coastal–inland set of categories. Note that the inland term repeats itself in southern and northern Kiriwina.

Kudouya etymologically means 'people who paddle'. Kudouya includes the villages of Labai, Kaibola, Luwebila, Idaleka, Kapwani, and Yuwada (contra Seligmann, 1910:661; cf. map 1 herein). In *Argonauts*, Malinowski shows a vague awareness of such a grouping but does not know its significance: 'Another important omission in the Kula is that of the Northern villages of Laba'i, Kaybola, Lu'ebila, Idaleaka, Kapwani,

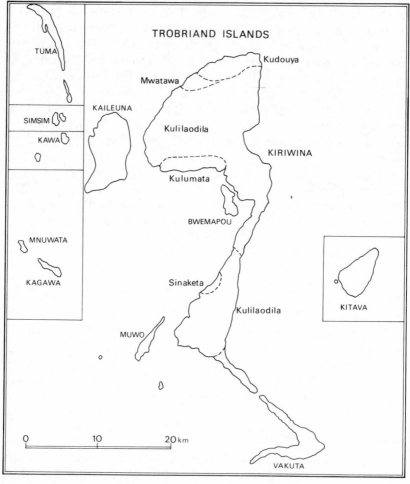

Map 4. The coastal-inland set of categories.

and Yuwada' (1922:476; quote to be referred back to in a later section). Inlanders also sometimes include Mwatawa village in Kudouya (cf. the ambiguous western boundary in map 4), but Kudouyans reject this for reasons given later. Kudouyans are the main fishermen of the north coast (Malinowski, 1918:87–92), especially for mullet and shark, as are the Mwatawans, no doubt causing the ambiguity over the boundary. Kudouyans control most of the northern coastline, except for the Mwatawa area. No inland villages have fishing rights except by permission of the beach-sea owners. Kudouyans have fish/betel-nut exchange relations (*vewoi*) with the villages inland to them.

Kulilaodila etymologically means 'people of the bush'. Kidodina is a synonym. Kulilaodila people do little fishing; some do none at all. They are dependent on their northern and southern coastal relations for the bulk of theiᵣ fish supply. Kulilaodila people on the northeast coast of Kiriwina do very little fishing because the currents are rough and dangerous. Sailing should be done there only in large canoes. People of the northwest coast do some fishing because the water is much calmer. Seligmann's 1910 map (cf. map 1 herein) makes an interesting mistake, calling the northwest swamp-dwellers and Mwatawa and Labai fishermen Kulomata (same as Kulumata) indicating a linkage between sea rights and territorial divisions.

Kulumata etymologically means 'people of the coast'. They are the fishermen (and gardeners) of the northern lagoon coast. Malinowski tried at times to turn them into a political district (1922:50) but in *Argonauts* he also wrote:

The five villages lying on the western coast of the northern half, on the shores of the Lagoon, form the district of Kulumata. They are all fishing villages, differ in their methods, and each has its own fishing grounds and its own methods of exploiting them. The district is much less homogeneous than any of those before mentioned. It possesses no paramount chief, and even in war the villages used not to fight on the same side. But it is impossible to enter here into all these shades and singularities of political organisation (1922:67–8).

Kulumatans control all the lagoon's northern coastline and hence access to the lagoon and to fishing. There is one vital aspect of this control of fishing rights which has not been emphasized in previous publications. Kulumata, though not a strong area for yams, has a constant food supply. The fish supply around Kiriwina, especially in the lagoon, is not greatly affected by weather conditions. The yam- and taro-dependent inland villages face famine every few years due to changing weather conditions (Powell 1956:2). The constant–inconstant food-supply problem has been a source of friction for generations (Fellows, 1973 *passim*

Jerry W. Leach

confirms this point). Malinowski, to my knowledge, drew attention to the problem in only one sentence of his Trobriand corpus:

The local men from the villages of the lagoon, anxious lest their fish supply, which in years of famine is barely sufficient for themselves, should give out, would scour the jungle for the encampments, attack the thin, hunted, and exhausted inlanders, and kill them by the score (1935:162).

In southern Kiriwina, the Kulumata–Kulilaodila situation repeats itself in a minor key (Malinowski, 1922:205). There the term for the village cluster Sinaketa stands as a supra-local category by contrast with Kulilal-odila (Malinowski, 1922:196). Again Sinaketa controls fishing rights and access to the lagoon. Their control is weaker, though, because there is much more exposed coastline and, of course, there is the eastern coast-line of Kiriwina which they do not control. Sinaketa–Kulilaodila as a relationship does not seem to have carried the friction of the homologous relationship in the north.

Economic conditions

The third system of territorial categories, again applying to Kiriwina only, divides the island into five major economic regions as shown in map 5. Two of these regions are divided into sub-regions as will be discussed later.

Kilivila is etymologically uncertain but it may relate to *kili* 'to select, choose, sort out, or change' and *vila* for 'female'. As land is meta-phorically seen as feminine in gender and as Kilivila contains the hole of emergence of Trobriand humanity, could this category be ren-dered 'the transforming or generating female', a Trobriand version of 'mother earth'? Whatever the etymology, Kilivila is well known for its agricultural productivity and abundant yams. It grows excellent long yams (*kuvi*) in or near the coral ridge. Malinowski put this down to the fertility of the soil. This is not exactly the case. Kilivila does have good soil for yams, i.e. not too wet and not too dry, but it is not especially good in taro or bananas. Kilivila's productivity, especially in yams, derives from a land surface largely free of coral waste. In *Coral Gardens and their Magic*, Malinowski himself noted: 'In districts where the ground is very stony, large heaps called *tuwaga* have to be made all over the field. In Kiriwina (i.e. Kilivila) such heaps are almost non-existent (Plates 20, 23, and 26) or scattered far apart (Plates 33 and 43)' (1935:121). In Kilivila around the Omarakana area, about 5% roughly of the cultivated land surface is non-productive because of coral mounds. In the north of Kilivila near the coast, the figure goes up to 10–20%. On the northern lagoon coast, the figure goes up to as high as 50%. Again Malinowski noted this detail without pinpointing its significance: 'But in the western district, in Kuboma, Kulumata, and in the south, the *tuwaga* heaps rise to large conical mounds which stand so close to each other that the fertile, tillable soil runs only in valleys between each stony hillock (see Plate 37)' (1935:121).

Tilataula etymologically means 'people separated from' and, as the region has no coastal boundary, Malinowski's appellation 'landlubber' is apt. Tilataula borders the northwestern swamp (*dumiya*) and therefore

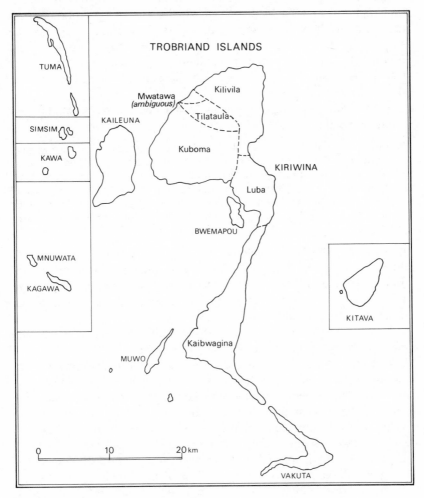

Map 5. The five major economic regions.

has relatively wet soil and no coral ridge. Consequently, the area produces large taro, reasonable small yams (*tetu*), and few long yams (kuvi). It has reasonably good stands of bananas and areca palms.

Kuboma etymologically means 'people of groves of trees'. This area too produces large taro, reasonable small yams, and few long yams. The area is rich in a wide variety of economic trees. The best stand of *Intsia bijuga* (called *meku*) occurs in the area. It is a principal wood for carving. Malinowski called this the 'industrial district' (1922:165) but did not draw attention to the fact that most of its products come from trees.

Luba is etymologically uncertain, but the term in everyday use means 'to wrap'. Luba is the main banana producing area of the Trobriands. As food is basically wrapped in banana leaves on Kiriwina, there may be some connection between the name of the region and the use of its main product. In Luba, yams are not abundant but taro reasonable due to wet soil on the whole. The area has good areca palm groves and has access to the sea and/or the lagoon.

Kaibwagina etymologically means 'area deficient in trees'. Malinowski wrote about the area:

Whole stretches of it – the wide club-shaped expanse in the south of Kaybwagina, the portion north of Kaulasi and south of Wawela – are completely barren, being covered with swamps and coral rocks. But even in the best parts of Kaybwagina, between Sinaketa and Okayaulo, there is but a narrow strip of relatively good soil between the brackish mud of the mangrove swamp and the broad back of the *rayboag* (coral ridge), and then it is much stonier than in the northern district (1935:290)

Kaibwagina grows reasonable taro but is poor in small yams while producing considerable long yams. The area depends a lot on fishing (Malinowski, 1935:290). Malinowski noted that the people of the area had to sail to Kuboma prior to kula voyages in order to obtain manufactured objects for trading purposes (1922:165–6).

Two of the five economic regions have internal sub-regions as shown in map 6. The two regions are Kilivila and Kuboma.

Kudouya is the northern-most sub-region of Kilivila and has been discussed earlier. It is the fishing area, good in yams but poor in bananas and taro. The villages of Kudouya make minor prestations of fish to the chief of Omarakana and contemporaneously to the chief of Omlamwaluva as well. A few of Kudouya's lineages give wives to the Tabalu, so the sub-region is one source of the yams for the yamhouses of those leaders. The ambiguous village Mwatawa within/without Kudouya does not give fish, yams, or wives to the Omarakana Tabalu.

Kuluwala etymologically means 'people in the middle or in between'. It contains the villages of Mtawa, Liluta, Osapola, Kaimwamwala, Kudu-kabilia, Dayagila, Kabulula, and Kwaibwaga. As an excellent yam area, Kuluwalans are also yam and wife providers to the Omarakana–Omlamwaluva Tabalu.

Kulakaiwa etymologically means 'people on high'. Further possible interpretations will be given later. As a sub-region, it includes the villages around Omarakana. The area is excellent in yams, especially long yams which are grown on or near the coral ridge. Prior to European influence, the area was also noted for coconuts.

Yalumgwa is etymologically uncertain but can be rendered as

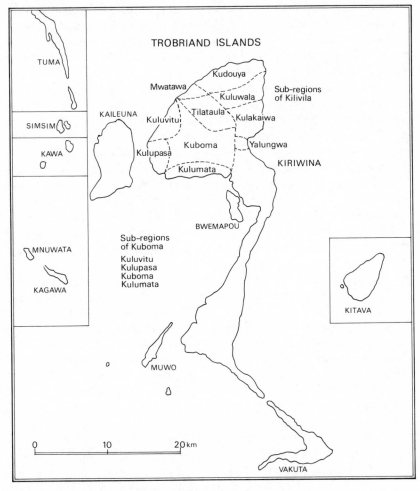

Map 6. Sub-regions of the five major economic regions.

Jerry W. Leach

'linked followers' deriving from *yalu* 'chain, vine-cord, link holding something together' and *lumgwa* 'to follow'. Yalumgwa, usually known as only a village is a sub-region including Mwemwata, Tububuna (usually known as Yalumgwa), and Moligilagi. Malinowski's map of Kiriwina (cf. map 2 herein) at its southeastern boundary is curved in order to include Yalumgwa sub-region, though Malinowski himself was not aware of the sub-region as such. Yalumgwa is strong in both types of yams, but weak in taro and bananas. Yalumgwa as 'linked followers' were the primary wife-providers and yam supporters of the Omarakana Tabalu. Yalumgwa's leader has the privilege (*koni*) of providing the first wife to a new Tabalu chief. The Tabalu leader would initiate this alliance with a presentation of four coconuts to the Yalumgwa leader. Along with Kuluwalans and Kulakaiwans, Yalumgwans are major allies of the Omarakana leaders. However, recently this traditional alliance has not functioned well politically. (J. Leach, in press).

Map 6 shows the major sub-regions of Kuboma. At the northwestern corner of Kuboma is Kuluvitu. Like Sinaketa and Yalumgwa, Kuluvitu is the name of a village which is also used as a supra-local category for the people who live on the dry land next to the coral ridge in the middle of the swamp. Kuluvitu etymologically means 'people of the coral outcrop'. Their garden lands are full of coral waste. Their soil is wet and good for taro. They are weak in small yams but do produce some long yams. Their land area is not great and they must fish as well as garden. There are a considerable number of trees but their area is generally known as 'poor'.

Kulupasa, south of Kuluvitu, etymologically means 'people of the mangrove swamp'. Their area has several inland estuaries with many mangroves (Royal Australian Survey Corps 1966: map SC 56–1). Kulupasans grow reasonable taro and some yams, but their land is poor and full of coral. Their estuaries are a favourite nesting place for stingrays, hence their association with the animal. They mainly kill the ray as its skin is like sandpaper and very useful in carving and because the animal is so dangerous. I understand that rays are mainly eaten in severe famines. Their area is heavily wooded and they were until recently the pre-eminent carvers of the Trobriands (Malinowski 1922:67). The sub-region is largely endogamous so they do not give wives or yams to the chief of Kuboma (Malinowski 1932:420–1).

Kuboma is the central sub-region of the major region of the same name. Kuboma sub-region grows good yams and large taro, but few long yams. The villages of the sub-region formerly gave wives and yams to the chief of Gumilababa until the present holder of the position renounced polygyny. The chief of Gumilababa could formerly amass yam wealth rivalling the Omarakana Tabalu. Kuboma sub-region is noted for the production of combs, baskets, fern armlets, lime gourds, spatulae, and the like (Malinowski 1922:67).

Kulumata, previously discussed, is considered by some to be a sub-region of Kuboma, though people of the area sometimes reject this suggestion. Relations between Kulumata and Kuboma sub-region have economically been those of product exchange. *Vewoi* is the generic term for these exchange relationships, known in Malinowski's writings as *wasi* (1926:22–3) and *vava* (1926:22–3) but also including *kokwava*, bartering for fish with manufactured items and now money.

Warfare[10]

The fourth set of territorial categories deal with warfare regions. There are seven categories encompassing Kiriwina and Vakuta, diagrammed in map 7.

Kulakaiwa, previously noted as the Omarakana-area economic sub-region, is the northeastern war region. Its principal village is Omarakana. Kulakaiwa as a warfare region is roughly coterminous with the economic region Kilivila. Kilivila is more commonly heard and can be used to refer to both types of region. The ambiguous northwestern village Mwatawa, while sometimes is included in Kudouya and (economic) Kilivila, is definitely excluded from Kulakaiwa, as Mwatawans are part of the war region Wakaisa and are allies of the chief of Tubowada.

Wakaisa etymologically is uncertain but it does contain the verb -*kaisa* 'to insult, to antagonize'. This might bear some semantic relationship to the age-old enmity between the chiefs of Wakaisa and Kilivila (Malinowski 1922:66), or as well to the internal friction in Wakaisa due to the fact that it has two rival chiefs from Kabwaku and Tubowada. Wakaisa was formerly known as the most militant of the war regions. In the last major battle fought in Kiriwina in 1899, an alliance of Wakaisan villages were the victors (Fellows, 1973: frames 440–72; Seligmann 1910:664–8). Wakaisans were the last group of Kiriwinans to attack Europeans (Fellows 1973: frames 440–58). When the Kulumata area was raided after the European evacuation of 1943, it was Wakaisans and Katumatalans who were the raiders. The militancy of the Wakaisa region can still be observed in its aggressive style of leadership today. Wakaisa is roughly coterminous with (economic) Tilataula. The latter term is much more frequently heard.

Kuboma is the name for the economic region and the warfare region. The central figure was the chief of Gumilababa. The Kulumata leaders, especially from Mlosaida, Oyuveyova, and Tukwaukwa, were very uncertain, unpredictable allies. In the 1890s the greatest number of actual

Jerry W. Leach

wars (*kabilia*) reported were fought within Kuboma (Fellows 1973: frames 357–481).

Luba, previously discussed, is also the name of a warfare region centred on the chief of Olivilevi. As the region is thinly populated, it was known as 'weak' in warfare. Battles either occurred within the region or regional villages were the supporting allies of villages in other areas, usually in Kulakaiwa–Kilivila.

Katumatala etymologically refers to 'killing'. With the possessive *-la* it can be rendered 'killing place'. This is the most interesting region of all,

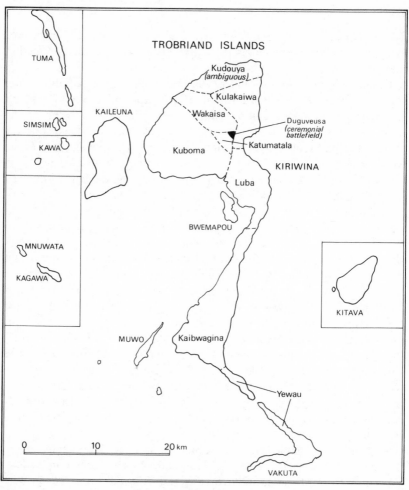

Map 7. The seven categories dealing with war.

136

unmentioned in Malinowski's writings and confused in Seligmann's material where he reverses the positions of Katumatala and Tilakaiwa/Tilataula (1910:661; cf. map 1 herein). Katumatala contains three villages Okaikoda, Wagaluma, and Obweria, and possibly a fourth, Obowada. The northern tip of the Katumatala region contains the traditional ceremonial battlefield Duguveusa. There any set of warring villages could choose to fight. For a payment in ceremonial axeblades, the Katumatalans would clear the field. The highest privilege of the Katumatalans, especially the Okaikodans, was to be able to stop any battle in progress at any point, by plunging a spear into the middle of the battleground and shouting *'Des!'* or 'Finished!' to the accompaniment of the conch shell. Any side that did nʋt desist risked having the Katumatalans, also known as fierce warriors, come in against them. For fighting purposes, Katumatalans were very expensive and unpredictable allies. It is interesting to note the correspondence between contemporary Trobriand cricket (J. Leach, 1975) and the practices of ritualized battle (not raiding): prepared ground, dress, appointed day for fighting, lining up in two long phalanxes of warriors facing each other, and the existence of battle 'umpires'.

Kaibwagina was also a war region and an economic region. As a war region, the area had a southern and island orientation and was seldom involved in northern wars.

Yewau is etymologically uncertain. It means 'substance or substantial' and possibly could be interpreted as 'conveying energy or force, or being the generative force behind human activity', as it usually appears in association with food in my experience. Yewau includes Vakuta and the southern tip of Kiriwina including the village of Gilibwa. Yewau's warfare relations were oriented toward Kaibwagina and the islands of Kuyawa, Mnuwata, and Kaileuna. The fighting between these areas seems to have been in sea battles (*kubilia*) rather than land battles (Malinowski 1922:344).

In closing this section, I must discuss further the meaning of these warfare regions. Firstly, the categories as such are falling into disuse as Kiriwina is now eighty years beyond pacification. Secondly, the terms do not and did not stand for corporate war-making entities. The villages are and were the primary war-making units and in that sense were politically corporate. If not directly involved, villages made decisions on each occasion of impending battle (raid or ritualized war) to fight or not to fight for another village only if solicited by a ceremonial prestation of axeblades (*beku*). Thirdly, warfare was endemic between and within warfare regions, the only difference being that wars across regional boundaries tended to be larger affairs which were harder to stop and had longer-term consequences. Fourthly, villages tended first to go to potential allies in

Jerry W. Leach

their own region for support but could as well seek support in other regions as well. Fifthly, warfare regions are not remembered as having fought *en masse* against each other, each war tending to be a different constellation of allies and enemies. Sixthly, warfare could be fought between neighbouring villages but more commonly, in such a context, dispute led to yam challenges (*buritilaulo*) or fights (*yowai*) without weapons or with only sticks.

Rank and kula participation

The fifth set of territorial categories relate to attributes of rank, one of which is participation in the kula. This set has been largely absent from previous publications, though Seligmann (1910:661; cf. map 1 herein) gives vague evidence of its existence. The set divides either all of Kiriwina or simply northern Kiriwina into two halves. There is no consensus amongst informants over whether southern Kiriwina is a part of this system or not. The two halves are Kulakaiwa and Kulitilawa (or Kulatanawa).

Kulakaiwa has been rendered previously as 'high people' as -*lakaiwa* refers to 'high or on high', usually heard in the term *walakaiwa* 'up high'. A second interpretation is also possible by dividing the term Kulakaiwa into two morphemes *kula* and -*lakaiwa*. By dropping the redundant -*la*, the term can be read out as 'high kula people'. Kulitilawa or Kulatanawa can be rendered as kula (*kuli* is derived from *kula* grammatically) and -*tanawa* meaning 'low, below, down', which is usually heard as *watanawa* meaning 'below or underneath'. Kulatanawa can therefore be read out as 'low kula people'. Kulatanawa is more commonly heard as Kulitilawa. There is a semantic connotation in the changing of the vowels. Changing Kulata- to Kuliti- implies belittlement or mockery. Kulilaodila, discussed previously, also contains the same vowel shift and the resulting mildly derisive connotation.

Map 8 shows one version of the Kulakaiwa and Kulatanawa distinction, the one I believe to be the most common and acceptable. Map 8 also shows the second version, relating only to northern Kiriwina.

The distinction between Kulakaiwa and Kulatanawa seems to connote 'highness' or 'lowness' on three dimensions: (1) chiefly customs relating to height such as in raised houses, raised sitting platforms, high yamhouses, and head height, (2) the growth of long yams, and (3) participation in the kula.

In general, the height of houses, yamhouses, and platforms was and is higher in Kulakaiwa than in Kulatanawa, though Kulatanawa contains several chiefly headmanships of importance. When referring here to

138

Kulakaiwa I am thinking particularly of the villages of Liluta, Omaraka-na, Yalumgwa, Olivilevi, Okupukopu, Ilalima, and Sinaketa. Historical and contemporary evidence indicate that only the Toliwaga chief's house (but not his yamhouse) at Tubowada (in Kulatanawa) and the Tabalu chief's house (but not his yamhouse) at Tukwaukwa were anything comparable to the Kulakaiwa structures, at least for the leading chief's. The Tubowada chief was, of course, a challenger of the Tabalu of Omarakana. Neither he nor the Tukwaukwa chief were in the kula.

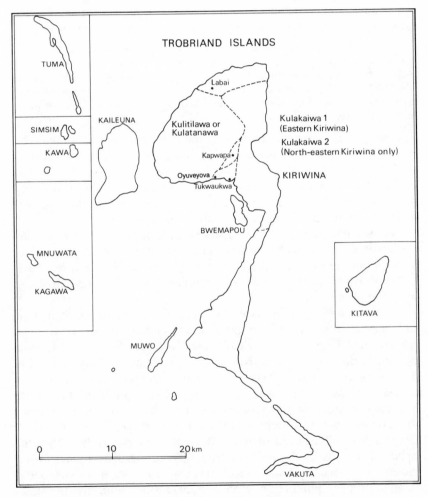

Map 8. Territorial categories related to rank-attributes.

Jerry W. Leach

It is interesting to note that the widest Kulakaiwa boundaries (cf. map 8; Labai-Oyuveyova boundary) includes the following: most of the Tabalu chieftainships of Kiriwina,[11] all of the Kweinama chieftainships,[12] none of the Toliwaga chieftainships, [13] and most of the Kiriwinan kula-transactors. There is a weak expectation that chiefs of Kulakaiwa are more likely to be *giyosola* or chiefly alliance partners with each other than they are with chiefs of Kulatanawa.

The northernmost section of Kulakaiwa is ambiguous and extremely interesting. The coastal group Kudouya is considered a part of Kulakaiwa as a warfare region. Yet using Kulakaiwa as a rank-kula category the very same sub-region is excluded: for warfare Kudouya is in Kulakaiwa, for rank-kula out of Kulakaiwa. Returning to Malinowski's earlier quote:

Another important omission in the Kula is that of the Northern villages of Laba'i, Kaybola, Lu'ebila, Idaleka, Kapwani, and Yuwada. If we remember that Laba'i is the very centre of Kiriwinian mythology, that there lies the very hole out of which the original ancestors of the four clans emerged from underground, that the highest chiefs of Kiriwina trace their descent from Laba'i, this omission appears all the more remarkable and mysterious' (1922:476)

Kudouyans recognize this anomalous state of affairs and are rankled by it. They feel unjustly denied access to the kula, a right which they say they should have. When asked why they are denied access, some say it is because they have no chiefly leaders while the others say their ancestors made a 'mistake' in earlier generations by siding in war with the Tubowada leader of Wakaisa against their 'allies' in Kulakaiwa.

Another ambiguity in the boundary of Kulakaiwa occurs with the inclusion or exclusion of Oyuveyova and Tukwaukwa on the lagoon coast. Though outside the kula, these two villages, especially the latter, have had powerful Tabalu leaders, no doubt generating the ambiguity over inclusion in the first place.

What then is the significance of the Kulakaiwa–Kulatanawa distinction with regard to the kula? I am not precisely sure at this point but there are several telling observations that can be made. First, starting with the northernmost village of Kulakaiwa (excluding Kudouya), we can discover in Malinowski's texts and in the present that every village down the eastern side of the island, i.e. every village within the narrowest boundary of Kulakaiwa, has some kula participants. My records indicate this applies without exception to thirty-five villages from Mtawa to Gilibwa. Secondly, almost all, if not all, village leaders in Kulakaiwa seem to be kula transactors.[14] Thirdly, a crude 1974 census of kula participants indicated 400–500 adult men in Kulakaiwa were in the system, that being of an adult male population of about 1,000 (40%). Fourthly, the same census indicated at least thirteen villages in which all or almost all of the

active adult men were kula transactors.[15] Fifthly, again by joining Malinowskian and contemporary evidence, it seems possible to deduce that
Kulakaiwa transactors all have a right to sail and have overseas partners,
to trade, and to be independent transactors in the sense of opening new
partnerships, breaking off previous partnerships, and expanding their
positions within the system. Sixthly, it seems an attribute of their independent transactor status that Kulakaiwa men transact according to their
rule of delayed exchange, i.e. not giving and receiving shells at the same
meeting of partners. This seems to apply to overseas partners, to north–
south partnerships, and even to transactions with other Kulakaiwa men in
neighbouring villages.

I submit therefore the proposition that all men of Kulakaiwa can by
right be in the kula if they want to be and if they are properly brought
into the system. It is interesting to note that many Kulakaiwa villages
have no pretensions to status other than that they are in the kula, e.g.
Kaimwamwala, Kaulagu, Moligilagi, Okaiboma, Kaituvi, Kaulasi, Loya,
Wawela, Bwadela, Kumilabwaga, Okayaula, and Gilibwa.

If this argument is correct however, we are still left with the same
problem but on a different level: why are not all the men of Kulakaiwa in
the kula? Again I do not pretend to know the full answer but several
observations can be made. First, elderly men often lapse in their kula
activities because the physical demands are too great. Secondly, young
men have a hard time getting into the kula if their father or some affine
does not give them a shell for entrance into the exchanges. Thirdly, some
men's careers are intermittent, in and out of the system, depending on
their other preoccupations, their success in their exchanges, their availability for particular expeditions, their wealth in other valuables used to
solicit kula objects, and their sometime need to convert kula shells out of
the system for internal exchange purposes. Fourthly, some men are
shamed out of the kula by particular expeditions on which they receive
nothing. Fifthly, some men never have sufficient success in internal
exchanges to generate the courage to try riskier ventures. Sixthly, kula is
not all that popular with wives because of the added workload involved
for them, because of the sexual aspect of long-range exchanging, and
because their husbands sometimes waste money and minor valuables in
fruitless pursuit of shells. Hence some men are simply hen-pecked into
non-participation. Seventhly, a few men have inculcated an earlier missionary view that the kula is immoral and a waste of time because it is so
full of lying and deceit, causes many disputes, creates marital dis-
harmony, encourages vanity, and produces – to the Western mind – little
sensible utilitarian outcome.[16]

What then about Kulatanawa? Are they by contrast outside the kula

141

Jerry W. Leach

altogether? I submit that this is not the case but that they are in the kula, if at all, on a very different footing. In Kulatanawa or western Kiriwina there are forty-two villages and thirteen modern settlements, a population of about 1,800 adult men. My 1974 census indicates roughly sixty men in the kula from that area, about 3% of potential transactors. There is in Kulatanawa no village in which most of the adult men are kula participants. There are villages with no one at all in the kula. The numbers of men per village are seldom above one or two and they are usually hamlet managers or village leaders. Why is there such a considerable difference in the rate of participation? Malinowski wrote about the question: 'the district of Western Boyowa carried on exclusively the inland Kula, and that merely in the person of a few headmen of a few villages' (1922:498).

I submit that Kulatanawa men are not of right in the kula but can get in by partnership with Kulakaiwa men. Kulatanawa men in the kula are usually men of high status seeking to reinforce that status by trying to establish ties with men of substance in the Kulakaiwa kula. Nevertheless, Kulatanawa men do not become independent transactors in their own right. They do not sail or go on large expeditions. They conduct their affairs individually and, once established with northern and southern partners, they do not expand their position or readily open new or break old partnerships. They are, in effect, conduits between northern and southern partners who could exchange directly with each other but who, for reasons of expanded networks to important people, choose to do so through reliable middlemen of Kulatanawa. Kulatanawa are not therefore independent transactors as all exchangers are depicted in *Argonauts* but are by contrast 'intermediary transactors'. The key sign of their 'intermediary' status is, in my opinion, that they engage in *simultaneous* exchanges, contrary to the basic rule of delayed exchange obeyed by independent transactors. On 'The Inland Kula' Malinowski wrote:

Next day, several *soulava* (spondylus shell necklaces) were brought to Omarakana by various men from neighbouring villages to the West [i.e. Kulatanawa – JWL], and ceremonially offered to To'uluwa (see Plates LXI, LXII, and Frontispiece). This was in each case a *vaga* (opening gift), for which the giver expected to receive his *yotile* (clinching gift) at once from the store of *mwali* (1922:472).

I return to the initial problem, now on another level: why are so few Kulatanawa men in the kula? Some of the earlier reasons hold here: age, difficulties in getting initial shells, lack of success in internal exchanges, unpopularity with some wives, and shame through loss or denigration by being not reciprocated or being given a grossly inferior shell in return, and inculcation of earlier missionary-inspired attitudes. Nevetheless, this can not be a full answer because the rate of participation is so low.

Going back to the introduction of this paper, I said that the virtues of the kula are seen to be 'adventure, vacation, prestige, source of valuables, expanding networks, sexual relations, links to famous men, the maintenance of nautical skills, and the sustaining of cultural tradition'. Given the intermediary, simultaneous-exchange, non-expansionary status of Kulatanawa transactors, how many of these virtues pertain in their situation? The answer is very few. There is little adventure in it. The vacation, instead of an overseas journey is just a long walk. There is no secondary trade in the relationship and little or no passage of minor valuables in solicitation of shells. The sexual side of the affair is of little significance and, of course, such exchanges have little to do with nautical skills, except for an ordinary canoe trip across the lagoon. Finally, the intermediary does all the travelling to south and north but is not travelled to. What is left? Some prestige and ties to important men. The incentives for kula go down markedly for Kula-tanawa men. What remains is the possibility to reinforce and perhaps extend pre-existing status *vis-à-vis* local rivals. On this basis, one can understand why it is fairly few competitive leaders in Kulatanawa that bother with kula. One must also remember the risks of going into the kula: to go in and do badly is worse than not having gone in at all.[17]

Over the last few pages I have been trying to address the question why some Kiriwinan men are in the kula and some are not. I do not pretend that my answer is complete but a cultural logic of non-involvement does crudely begin to emerge. What seems missing is a mythological basis for the Kulakaiwa–Kulatanawa distinction. Malinowski wrote about kula mythology: 'What I am quite certain of, however, is that the whole of the Trobriands, except for the two points mentioned before (i.e. Wawela and Kasilamaka Passage between Kiriwina and Vakuta, both in the Kasab-waybwayreta myth) lie outside the mythological area of the Kula' (1922: 307). I am not so certain that this will turn out to be the case although I do not have contrary independent evidence in hand at present. In any case, I do feel there is cultural evidence, even in Malinowski's writings, in support of the Kulakaiwa–Kulatanawa distinction. He wrote unknow-ingly about a Kulatanawa village:

An interesting myth localised in Yalaka tells how the inhabitants of that village, prevented by custom from seeing the world on Kula expeditions, attempted to erect a high pillar reaching to heaven, so as to find a field for their adventurers in the skies. Unfortunately, it fell down, and only one man remained above, who is now responsible for thunder and lightning (1922:475).

Jerry W. Leach

This myth-precis fits interestingly with the 'high kula people'–'low kula people' distinction. Custom prevents 'low' people from engaging in kula. They seek to bridge the gap between 'low' and 'high'. The linkage can only be sustained by one man who becomes powerful.

A second piece of cultural evidence supporting the distinction can be found in Malinowski's analysis of shipwreck magic (1922:248–61). There he describes two systems of protective magic or *kaigau*. The first is *giyorokaywa*, used ostensibly to ward off flying witches. The second is *giyotanawa*, used to ward off sharks. These two names contain the classificatory particle *giyo-* referring to chiefs (*guyau*).[18] The final morphemes are *-rokaywa*, a dialectical variation of *-lakaiwa* 'high', and *-tanawa* 'low', which are of course in Kulakaiwa and Kulatanawa. The two magical names can be rendered as 'high chief' and 'low chief'.

Both these systems are to protect a sailor from being 'seen' by flying witches and sharks, but, going further than Malinowski, we can see that they are more than that. The key clue occurs in the name of the systems which is meaningless in Malinowski's account. Both systems are counter-magic against the sorcery of rival chiefs.

The giyorokaywa spells refer repeatedly to the eyes (*mata-*) of various animals, witches, and women of various villages. The 'eyes' stand for 'jealousy, envy, or desire' (Malinowski 1932:141–3). The animals refer to creatures found on the beaches of northeastern and southeastern Kiriwina, in the estuaries of the swampy area between Luba and Kaibwagina, and, if I guess correctly, in Sinaketan–Vakutan waters (i.e. the palolo worm; Malinowski 1935:54). The animals are generally associated with Kulakaiwa and all the villages mentioned are in that region, though Malinowski has unfortunately abbreviated the list (1922:250). The crab especially has a deep association with sorcery in Trobriand mythology, being the original purveyor of the evil (1954:129–30). The women mentioned (1922:250) are the women of the villages left by their menfolk on kula expeditions. The giyorokaywa spells then ward off flying witches, the sorcery of envious 'high' rivals, and the jealousy of women left behind. One of the spells says that explicitly:

I arise, I escape from *bara'u* (sorcery); I arise, I escape from *yoyova* (the corporeal aspect of flying witches); I arise, I escape from *mulukwausi* (the incorporeal aspect of flying witches); I arise, I escape from *bowo'u* (abandoned women?)

and further on

I arise, I escape from the eyes of the *bara'u*; I arise, I escape from the eyes of the *yoyova*, etc. (1922:253).

By contrast, the giyotanawa spells ostensibly are aimed at warding off sharks. They open with references to unmarried persons and go on to

144

refer to the places sharks frequent, being to the west and northwest of Kiriwina and in the lagoon. The spells then confusingly seek to protect the sailor from the parts of his canoe. Malinowski notes the belief that parts of a canoe can 'eat' shipwrecked men (1922:255 and 259) but leaves us without an interpretation. I believe the clues to the interpretation come in the last lines of the spell:

I shut off the skies with mist; I make the sea tremble with mist; I close up your mouth, sharks, *bonubonu* (small worms), *ginukwadewo* (other worms). Go underneath and we shall swim on top (1922:255).

The first two lines refer to counter-magic against sorcery, closing off threats from above and below. About the key concept 'tremble' Malinowski wrote: 'The expression tremble, *maysisi*, refers to a peculiar belief, that when a sorcerer or sorceress approaches the victim, and this man paralyses them with a counter spell, they lose their bearings and stand there trembling' (1922:249–50). I believe Malinowski mistranslates and misunderstands *bonubonu*. He has confused the concept with *bonebona*, the worm-eaten condition of yams. Bonubonu is a type of tree, a light but strong wood which I think is used for making parts of a canoe. It also refers to insects that burrow into the tree, weakening it. Ginukwadewo is also mistranslated in my opinion. A ginukwadewo is a small crab which burrows into the beach. Remembering that much of the best wood comes from Kuboma and that many of the best canoe-builders are from Kulumata (1922:121), I submit that the sailor is trying to block the effects that the sorcery of others, especially others who possibly have provided wood or building skills, might be having in causing the canoe to break up or give way under strain. The danger lies in the sharks and in the potentially ensorceled parts of the canoe. Both of these are dangers from the 'underneath' (1922:255), which at another level refers to the danger from the envy, and hence sorcery, of 'low' rivals.

Conclusion

Previous publications have presented five systems of territorial classification as if they were all of the same order. I have tried to separate and to make more sense of what they mean and how they are used. This task has led onwards to a second one, the problem of why some Kiriwinan men are not in the kula. The answer is incomplete but the question is I think an important one. Why elsewhere around the ring are there people on the fringes of the system who are not in it?

Jerry W. Leach

Notes

1 Some Trobrianders oppose the kula because it was once seen by missionaries to be contrary to the ideal of Christianity. This idea is no longer preached to my knowledge but it is still held by some middle-aged and elderly people.
2 It is very hard to know how many men from Kiriwina were in the kula in Malinowski's day as he was little interested in that kind of quantitative data. As an educated guess, the proportion was then about what it is today.
3 I am grateful to Bernard Mwayubu of Wagaluma village and the University of Papua New Guinea who, in reading the *Argonauts* in 1971, called my attention to some of the inaccuracies in Malinowski's use of territorial categories.
4 I regard the primary investigators as Fellows, Seligmann, Bellamy, Malinowski, Rentoul, Austen, Powell, Julius, Baldwin, Lawton, Weiner, Montague, Scoditti, Campbell, Hutchins, and myself.
5 My own list is also no doubt incomplete as, at a minimum, I know nothing of the territorial divisions on Vakuta, Kaileuna, and Kitava.
6 Tuma is not included because it became uninhabited in 1961.
7 Kilivila Local Government Council Minute No.1 of 26 April 1966.
8 Kilivila Council Minute No.2 of 26 May 1966.
9 The subsequent meeting produced two further proposals: *Vakota* (peace) and *Kilivila Ninatala* (Kilivila of one mind). *Kiriwina* won on 23 June 1966, see Minute No.4. From 1967 the name was the Kiriwina Local Government Council.
10 I am grateful to R. S. Lawton for first calling my attention to the existence of a separate system of terms for warfare regions. My analysis basically complements and extends his.
11 The Tabalau chieftainships in Kulakaiwa are Omlamwaluva, Omarakana, Olivilevi, and Sinaketa. Labai, Oyuveyova, and Tukwaukwa are ambiguously placed. Gumilababa and Mlosaida are the main ones outside.
12 The Kweinama chieftainships are at Liluta and Yalumgwa village.
13 The Toliwaga chieftainships are at Tubowada and Kabwaku.
14 I am not sure if most hamlet managers are as well kula participants. My records do not include that information.
15 The question 'Who in your village is in the kula?' is not unambiguous, as some men may be away working or intermitting in their activities. As well, the question may be interpreted as 'Who is a *real* kula transactor (i.e. has achieved distinction in exchanges)?' I believe the figure of thirteen villages of almost all kula men is, if anything, on the conservative side.
16 This view was propagated by an earlier generation of Methodists. These attitudes were not held by the missionaries of the 1970s.
17 I am uncertain on this point but I believe Malinowski's evidence and mine converge in indicating that Kulatanawa men whom I have labelled 'intermediary transactors' are not partners with each other. More precisely, if A transacts with B who transacts with C, A and C are Kulakaiwa and B may be Kulatanawa. I am arguing that an A – B – C – D set of partners can not have B and C as Kulatanawa. I hope the proposition can be confirmed or denied by others.
18 Malinowski (1921) published forty-two of these classificatory particles. *Giyo-* was not among them. R. Lawton and I have discovered more than 140.

146

6 'A world of made is not a world of born': doing kula in Kiriwina

ANNETTE B. WEINER

Introduction

In *Argonauts of the Western Pacific*, Bronislaw Malinowski devoted much space to explanations of 'economic facts which on the surface are not directly connected with the Kula' (1922:175). Malinowski clarified his reason for this seemingly inappropriate digression by suggesting the importance of understanding Trobrianders' attitudes toward 'wealth and value'. Malinowski emphasized that the *kula* represents the 'highest and most dramatic expression' of the concept of value, and therefore it is imperative to examine 'the psychology that lies at its basis' (p. 176). Thus, kula as it operated in Kiriwina could not be understood apart from the context of internal exchanges. Sixty years later, I proceed from the same point. Kula cannot be analyzed appropriately unless the processes of kula are examined as transformations of the processes underlying internal exchange. Only an understanding of the meaning of wealth and value as such meaning regulates and regenerates relationships between close kin will shed light on the meaning of wealth and value as determined through kula transactions.

From the perspective of the Northern Massim, the strategies and manipulations of kula partners and the complexity of individual kula transactions seem much the same (see e.g., Campbell and Munn, this volume). What, however, appears to emerge as a marked difference in northern Kiriwina is the formalization and elaboration of certain kinds of internal objects of exchange. For example, the organization of control and use rights to land, the distribution of yams and women's wealth (bundles of banana leaves and skirts), and the circulation of stone axe blades (*beku*) represent core cycles of internal exchange. But kula valuables are not directly part of these internal transactions. In other island communities, however, kula valuables are essential to primary internal transactions directly connected to affinal and consanguineal relationships.

147

Annette B. Weiner

In my earlier work, I noted that an armshell or necklace classified as *kitomu* travels on a kula path (*keda*), but throughout its circulation, the valuable is known to belong to one person.[1] When the valuable reaches its destination, the individual to whom it belongs may use it at his own discretion (see Weiner 1976:180–1 for examples). Kitomu operate in similar ways throughout the Massim, but what appears significant from the perspective of a total kula system, are the differences between kula communities in terms of external and internal access to kitomu and the way kitomu may or may not be integrated into internal exchanges.

For example, as Nancy Munn (1977) has shown for Gawa Island and Fred Damon (1978; 1980) for Woodlark Island, kitomu are centrally connected to significant internal transactions. The most detailed account of the internal circulation of kitomu comes from Woodlark where Damon (1978) presents a description of the significance of kitomu (1) in major exchanges at marriage and at the death of a spouse; (2) in serving to symbolically and materially integrate garden work with the procedures of kula activities; and (3) in functioning as routes of access for individual procurement of pigs and canoes. But in northern Kiriwina, kitomu are not essential for marriage transactions (also cf. Munn [1977] on Gawa affinal exchanges which necessitate kitomu payments). Although Malinowski never specifically discussed kitomu, he did describe the importance of kula valuables in mortuary distributions on Kitava (1922:489–93). Whether or not the kula valuables in the Kitava distributions were in fact kitomu, neither kitomu nor kula valuables constitute a formal part of Kiriwina mortuary distributions. As I describe elsewhere (Weiner, 1976), a kitomu may be used in internal exchanges, but the valuable is used as a *substitute* for a stone axe blade, the traditional object of male wealth in the internal system of exchange (also cf. Campbell, this volume, on the problems that occur when kula valuables are needed for internal transactions in Vakuta Island).

Therefore, in sharp contrast to other kula areas, where kitomu are directly integrated into extensive internal exchanges, the activities associated with kula for northern Kiriwina may be diagrammatically represented as an addition to a base of internal exchange enterprises in which every adult participates, and which operate independently both of kula and the individual ownership of kitomu valuables. What appears especially unique in northern Kiriwina is a highly developed *stratification* of objects and resources which supports a more well-defined and operative system of rank than elsewhere in the Massim.[2]

By *stratification* of resources, I mean the formalization of ownership and/or control rights in objects and resources which defines their mode of production and distribution and their loss/or replacement values. These objects and resources operate within specific domains in which they simultaneously encode and act on social and political action. But these domains are not analytical devices circumscribed through a norm of reciprocity within 'spheres' or 'levels' of exchange (cf. Bohannan, 1955; Firth, 1939).

My general approach to exchange theory is that the interplay between human life cycles and the life trajectory of objects of exchange embodies a code, i.e., the reproductive structure, and the production of code, i.e., the symbolization of resources, founded on principles concerned with growth, decay, and death (see also Weiner, 1978; 1979; 1980a). The common denominator of exchange processes is organized around attempts at symbolically regenerating the value embedded in human beings as they move through time from conception to birth, growth, death, and rebirth. In this way, the physical processes of growth and decay are culturally elaborated to the degree that time and resources are used to avert and/or transform the effects of deterioration and death and to facilitate and foster the effects of growth.

Therefore, exchange must be conceptualized as processes of work (encompassing the production and distribution of resources) necessary to reproduce particular values and social relations through time. But the process is not habitual, nor is it automatic. Rather the range of work necessary requires constant attention, effort, and the expenditure of material resources. But such achievement can only be culturally effected via the symbolic elaboration of particular kinds of resources. In the process of elaboration, a resource – 'the gift' – becomes both agent and symbol of the regenerative interests inherent in the reproduction of value through time.

In societies throughout the Pacific, attempts are made to produce both permanent and perishable wealth. The difficulty, however, lies in the frequent physical impossibility of producing a variety of objects of permanent wealth. What we find instead are innumerable solutions. The problem is handled by making perishable, consumable wealth take on some characteristics of permanence at least for a period of time. The essential characteristic of permanent wealth in traditional Pacific societies is that it becomes a possession which takes on an individual identity of its own and a history of its own. Because of its long life trajectory, it may carry a *replacement* value (see Weiner, 1980a) at someone's death and therefore, forms of durable or semi-permanent wealth may create long-term debt which may last beyond the lifetime of an individual. In this way, durable wealth eventually may return to its 'source' – providing new resources out of old ones for new generations.

Therefore, in order to understand the process at work in northern

149

Annette B. Weiner

Kiriwina whereby value and rank are reproduced internally through time, and the articulation between internally and externally defined reproductive sectors, it is essential to diagram the way resources, as symbols of a reproductive code, are ordered, controlled and prevented from dissipation in opposition, or in complement to the basic reproductive structure. In my use of stratification as a means of distinguishing the various reproductive sectors, I am also concerned to establish the kinds of debt that may be regenerated through time,[3] given the life cycles of individuals and the life trajectories of resources as culturally constituted.

In northern Kiriwina, major objects and resources are stratified in such a way that each represents access to a range of the most valued elements, such as the regeneration of *dala* (lineage) blood and land, the reproduction of social relations between close kin, and the reproduction of kula paths. Northern Kiriwina comes closer than other Massim islands in producing permanent debt through at least one generation, with a strong attempt to move such debt into a second and even a third generation. But the production of long-term debt does not come about through kula valuables. Rather, debt is created through the formalization of the circulation of two components of dala: dala property and dala personnel.[4] In the circulation of use rights to these two components, long-term debt is established which generates individual power and control. But because dala property and personnel must finally return to their original source, the replacement costs for the return entail enormous drains on individual wealth accumulations. Therein lies the paradox of the internal system of exchange. Internal exchange cycles permit reproductive expansiveness, but death, as the beginning moment when replacement takes place, operates as a leveling device on individual resource controls. Kula then presents another reality – an opportunity to move into a different kind of system – *where debt becomes detached from death*.

From this perspective, the basic dimensions of the transformation from an internal to an external system involve an internal system founded on 'a world of born' and an external system representing 'a world of made'. The transformation that occurs from the internal system allows kula participants access to a domain *almost* free from the demands that a death makes on their resources – from the demands of women's wealth that continually drain men's wealth – and from a social system structured on principles of blood and land as dala identity and property.

An understanding of the stratification of objects and resources marking the basis for the transformation from internal to exchange reproductive sectors would be incomplete without analyzing the relationship of Kiriwina chiefs to the transformation. In many ways, the reality of the hierarchical position of Kiriwina chiefs is reflected in the processes of

150

doing kula. The position of chiefs is embedded in the internal 'world of born'. Only those men born a member of a particular ranked dala have the inherited right to become a chief.[5] But this same 'world of born' assigns certain prerogatives to *all* individuals, regardless of rank. Unlike Tikopia (Firth, 1936), where a chief controls and even embodies the well-being and fertility of all his clan's lands, a Kiriwina chief controls only his own dala lands in exactly the same way that one man in every dala, regardless of his rank, also controls his own dala land. The position of chief allows for an individual chief's access to increased resources but the position of ranking and chiefs does not alter for anyone, including chiefs, the obligations inherent in internal exchanges.

Rank does not create a differently organized privileged system separate from the system of all. In the final analysis Kiriwina men remain trapped between their 'world of born' – a world regulated by the rights of birth and the exigencies of death – and their 'world of made' – a world containing the shadow of new possibilities. In Kula, 'everything happens as if' men were free agents. But the transformation contains its own range of limitations.

The internal system of exchange: reproductive sector I – dala

Dala is a concept legitimizing rights to individual control of hamlet and garden lands (including areas such as beach and palm groves), as well as other kinds of property such as ancestral names, body and house decorations, magic texts, technical and aesthetic skills. The meaning of dala also legitimizes, through women, an internalized identity of 'same blood' for all individuals born. The regeneration of dala is maintained by the processes of human reproduction and the control of dala property through continuous generations (see Weiner, 1976; 1978; 1980a). But such processes demand continual attention, risk-taking, and the circulation of extensive resources. The reproduction of a human life cycle (encompassing birth, death, and rebirth) and the regeneration of property (pertaining to forms of inheritance, control and use rights) are cultural rather than natural or automatic accomplishments. Thus, they must be worked at continuously, i.e., attended to via exchange, or a dala is lost.

The system of human reproduction accommodates both the regeneration of matriliny and the reproduction of paternal kin relationships. In this way, wealth and value are taken by a man and his sister, members of another dala, and embedded in the man's children who then will contribute throughout their lives to him and to his sister and other members of

Annette B. Weiner

his dala (see Weiner, 1976; esp. 1979). Thus, dala property is being detached and circulated for use by 'others' who are not members of the original dala. The success of the system depends upon the solidarity of the exchange relations nurtured and maintained throughout the life of a man's children (which may extend to a man's children's children), and also upon the ability of members of the man's dala to reclaim and therefore to replace at some later point in time the property he previously detached for his children's use.

The general term for the things a man gives his children is *mapula*, a word Malinowski originally glossed 'equivalence, repayment'. But in trying to understand why 'gifts' given by a man to his wife and children were called 'mapula', yet seemed not to produce any expected return, Malinowski labeled these particular transactions 'pure gifts' (1922:176–7). Although Malinowski (1926) later discarded the classification 'pure gifts' (see Mauss, 1954; Firth, 1951), he never reevaluated the term mapula (see Weiner, 1980a for a critique of mapula and 'pure gifts' as used in Sahlins' (1965) model of 'primitive' reciprocity). Although mapula carries with it a notion of 'repayment' for something previously given, it also carries with it the important principle, replacement (see Weiner, 1980a for a more complete discussion). Certain objects given to others, especially use rights to dala property, at some time must be reclaimed (*sagali*) by members of the original dala. But taking back what was once given as mapula necessitates a *replacement payment*. Therefore, mapula given has long-range spiraling effects. What one individual gives to another not only creates obligations between giver and receiver, but eventually may involve other kin who must use their own resources to reclaim (sagali) what has been given to a non-kin by someone else.

From this perspective mapula transactions necessitate replacement payments that may impinge on the resources of individuals who had nothing to do with the original transaction, but who must bear the burden of reclamation. In one way, the replacement process puts a drain on resources, but at the same time, the process allows for the establishment of long-term debt which in turn continues to regenerate intergenerational social relationships over a long time period. Dala property transacted is not just creating immediate reciprocal obligations between two individuals. Rather, use rights in property may circulate outside the original dala for many years, creating debt that involves the giver (or his heir) and receiver and a range of other connecting relationships (see Weiner, 1976 for other examples of land use and replacement payments for other kinds of dala property). In the process, additional resources, such as yams and women's wealth, are threaded through these relationships, which then may expand into wider networks of social relations and eventually enable greater control over more and more resources.

The system, however, contains risks and hazards. With the passage of time, some property may be lost by the original dala, through, for example, default on reclamation, theft, or compensation payments. But, in general, the system enables some men (i.e., the head of a hamlet) to control resources and to maintain some measure of power over other individuals (members of other dala) via the circulation of use rights in dala property, *without depleting the property* as a potential future resource for others. The creation of permanent or long-term debt in the circulation is highly reproductive for regenerating affinal and paternal relationships through several generations. But enormous attention and the expenditure of great energy are fundamental to the success of any one individual.

From this perspective, the system of rights to land control and/or use in other Massim societies should be of comparative importance. For example, in Dobu, the system seems much more rigidly controlled with less circulation of land to non-members of a lineage. The fact that seed yams may not even be used by individuals who are not members of the owner's *susu* (lineage) (see Fortune, 1932) seems symptomatic of a non-expanding system (see Adams, 1978). On Woodlark Island rights to garden lands and residence are much less formalized and access has not evolved into the tightly controlled organization found in Kiriwina (Damon, personal communication). Without land as a resource that can be converted into power through its controlled circulation as a long-term debt, men have less means to gain formal control over individuals and therefore, less access to additional resources (see Damon, 1978 for examples which seem to indicate situations of less power and control).

Thus, dala as the legitimization of rights to control, creates an approximation of permanent debt, and in so doing creates the potential for individual access to power. The legitimizing rights for chiefs come from the same source – the founders of dala – as do such rights for all other hamlet managers. To oppose the legitimizing rights of a chief, a man without rank would have to allow his own rights to be opposed. In this fundamental way, the relationship between men of rank and men of non-rank remains squared off in that legitimization for both comes from the founders of each – the original source of dala (see Weiner, 1977 for details on the founders of dala).

Death, however, is the moment that allows for the reassemblage of dala property. Following a death, property and even the body and the bones of the deceased are reclaimed (sagali) in the name of dala. The procedures are individually organized and controlled by the hamlet man-

Annette B. Weiner

ager and his most powerful sisters, but the legitimization of such control is vested in the name of dala. Without some 'naturally' recurring moment such as death, to trigger the replacement process, the return of dala property would become subject to individual demand – the kind of demand anathema to the whole system. But although the replacement process is regenerative for dala and reproductive for individuals, it has its own dissipative effect. The replacement value for property and the deceased is wealth items, individually owned.

Thus a price must be paid in order to draw out individual power and control. The end of the debt necessitates an enormous drain on personal wealth (see Weiner, 1976: chaps. 3 and 4 on mortuary transactions). Without such a drain on resources, and with the creation of truly permanent debt free from a replacement value, chiefs might be able to project themselves into a more completely autonomous, hierarchical position. But the need to reclaim one's property, even when rightfully inherited, and to reclaim one's position, even when rightfully marked as 'dala' short-circuits any possible fully separate, privileged position of power. *All* Kiriwina individuals must respond to the exigencies produced by a death. But the responses, even with the constraints of the system, becomes a significant social and political factor as dala property becomes a means of control. In this way, from the very basis of dala, northern Kiriwina seems to surpass other Massim islands in the creation and potential of power and control, not just for chiefs, but for the man in control of each dala.

The process of embedding wealth and value in 'others' may be examined as a primary mode of reproductive expansiveness. In the process, one heightens one's own value while creating potential value in 'others' – because the process depends upon the long-term circulation of possessions from 'others' marked in the name of a dala. But ultimately, dala remains the magnet which attracts the return of all things once given. The periodicity of the attraction depends upon the frequency of death. Not only property such as land, but even the durability of the physical body – human bones – are reclaimed in the name of dala. Such bones are 'carried' for five, ten, as much as twenty years by those 'others' connected to the deceased through paternal and affinal links (see Weiner, 1976 for details of these exchanges). Through bones, now converted into durable wealth, debt is maintained for the living beyond the life of any one person. But even these bones finally are replaced, as traditionally after many years, they were returned to caves marked in the name of a dala.

Thus dala property and persons circulate for many years in the hands of 'others', resembling Mauss' interpretation of the Maori *hau*, 'the spirit of the gift' (see e.g., Sahlins, 1972; Gathercole, 1978 on recent reinterpretations of the hau). Dala returns to its source, but not within the constrictions of a norm of reciprocity.[6] Rather dala property and persons move through time and space, creating the potential for gain (and loss) under the principle of replacement.

The internal system of exchange: reproductive sector II – yams and women's wealth

The temporal dimension to the circulation of dala property and persons may exceed a generation and sometimes even longer and the productive and reproductive value is always determined at some level by the power of dala. Although the replacement process of dala ties individuals to the land and to each other in fundamental ways, it does not create the conditions for more immediate accountability as to the intentions of 'others'. In this respect, the annual circulation of yam harvests encodes the implicit meanings in these relationships in a much more narrow time frame than those circulations marked as dala.

From the beginning of a marriage until the death of a spouse, yams (especially *taytu* [*Dioscorea esculenta*]) encode the state of the reproductive process in social relations – relationships between women and men, and between consanguines, affines, and paternal kin (see Weiner, 1976; 1978 for details). Each year the presentation of yams in name to a married woman by her father or her brother produces wealth in yams for her husband. At the same time, the yams also produce wealth for the woman because her husband must convert his own wealth and labor into accumulations of women's wealth for her every time someone dies in her own or her father's dala.[7] In the course of these transactions, the economic and political strength or weakness of a marriage and of a dala is displayed publicly in the size of the annual yam production. Further, whenever a death occurs in the dala of a woman, the value of her husband may be calculated through her performance in distributing large or small amounts of women's wealth at the women's mortuary ceremony. Finally, when a spouse dies, the full value of the marriage and of the dala of the deceased is made apparent through the amounts of objects exchanged from members of the dala of the deceased to the father and to the spouse of the deceased.

Therefore, the most central relationships (i.e., 'close kin') are continually being evaluated and negotiated in a public arena. In this way the production of yams forces a constant check on the nature and intent of relationships between individuals who, in complementarity to each other, constitute the basis for a range of other relationships (see esp. Weiner, 1979). Yam production provides a public system of checks and balances on the circulation of dala property and social relations between

155

a member of a dala and 'others', by defining the current negotiable status of the parties to the circulation.

Although yams may be described as major wealth objects, which via their circulation keep individuals connected to each other in important ways, and also yams as wealth may be used directly as access to other resources and objects of wealth, the life trajectory of yams is at best less than half a year. Men's wealth in yams dissipates rapidly. Even polygynous chiefs, who may receive enormous quantities of yams (see Weiner, 1976:201–8), are limited in the length of time they have to convert yams into other kinds of resources. In order to maintain the regeneration of new resource potential via relationships, the accumulation of women's wealth, and the circulation of dala property, new yams must be grown year after year. Therefore, while yams exhibit the immediate negotiable value of relationships, the system of investing wealth and value in 'others', from the perspective of yams, contains limitations that inhibit long-term controls over the actions and activities of 'others' (see Weiner, 1976:211–16; n.d.a. for examples). In this respect, yams create neither durable wealth nor permanent debt.

Situations occur, however, where the life trajectory of yams is somewhat extended via the process of rotting. Long *kuvi* yams (*D. alata*), painted and decorated, are hung along the seating platforms of chiefs where the yams publicly display the particular rank and power of chief (as well as the talent and affiliation of the grower). Such yams eventually may be given to 'others', they may be eaten and used for seed, they may be buried with a chief when he dies, or they may be left hanging until they rot (see Weiner, 1976 for examples). The decoration, public display, and the rotting all attest to attempts at circumventing the obvious perishability of a yam, pushing its durability as an object of power beyond its natural state.

On Goodenough Island, through other means, another kind of durability in yams is achieved. According to Michael Young (1971), the largest yams in a competitive display are measured individually 'by means of pandanus "string" tacked with thorns along their greatest length and width'. These 'strings' are then kept in the house of the protagonist 'perhaps for years, until he can pay them back. If he dies without having done so, his heir inherits them and refers to them as his *hiyo* (spear)' (Young, 1971 pp. 195–6). (Martha Macintyre [personal communication] also reports that the storage of yam strings occurs on Tubetube Island.) On Goodenough, the durability of yams through 'strings' creates some form of long-term debt, but the fact that repayment necessitates an equivalent return in yams limits their transactional value as reproductive agent when compared to Kiriwina.

'A world of made is not a world of born': doing kula in Kiriwina

In Kiriwina one part of the circulation of yams transfers long-term debt into another object and another mode of circulation. Because a woman once received yams in name from a man, she remains indebted to distribute her own wealth whenever a member of that man's dala dies. This debt may occur in a woman's own dala (as she received yams from her brother), or in another dala (through a 'fictive' brother who gave her yams), or in her father's dala because following her marriage she first receives yams from her father (see Weiner, 1976, chap. 7 for details of these transactions). The debt incurred through yams may be passed down from mother to daughter to granddaughter. Here again the debt through yams and woman's wealth is retraced to dala. Following a death, women must replace all the social relationships established by the deceased with distributions of women's wealth (see Weiner, 1976: chap. 4). Thus, long-term debt established through women's wealth is being used to assure the proper replacement value at death for dala personnel.

In the process of distributions of women's wealth at a death, a woman's debt becomes a man's debt as well. Kiriwina men (because they received yams from their wives' brothers and fathers) must give up their own wealth and labor in order to procure women's wealth for their wives. Through the past 100 years of Western contact, as men had increasing access to cash and trade-store goods, the economic value of women's wealth has increased (see Weiner, 1980b). In the relationship between men's and women's wealth, the production and distribution of women's wealth has operated as a leveling device for men's wealth – for chiefs as well as other men (see Weiner, 1976; 1980b for details).

But while women's wealth takes away men's wealth, the redistribution of women's wealth at mortuary ceremonies exerts an extremely strong measure of stability in the traditional exchange system. By absorbing fluctuations in economic conditions, especially those resulting from the introduction and continued use of Western cash, women's wealth prevents the internal system of exchange from fragmenting or from shifting into a different kind of system. Further, the nature of the exchange relationships between women and men continually determined through distributions of yams and accumulations and redistributions of women's wealth is constructed in such a way that women and the economic role they play enforce male productivity. Men work for women – both in garden production and in the *valova* transactions where men convert wealth (e.g., pigs, betel, manufactured objects, fish, tobacco and other trade-store commodities) into women's wealth (see Weiner, 1976). *The only objects of wealth, however, that men do not use in this way are stone axe blades* (beku) *and kula or kitomu valuables.*

157

Annette B. Weiner

The internal system of exchange:
reproductive sector III – male valuables

Dala property and persons (including the final form of bones) create forms of debt which provide the very basis of reproductive and productive expansiveness. But these reproductive sectors, so tightly integrated, must eventually turn in upon themselves. Dala must return to dala, and yams must be cooked or returned to seed. Women's wealth not only fades and tears, but newly made bundles as well as old bundles must continually be redistributed at every death. Further, the process of embedding wealth and value in 'others' necessitates waiting for 'others'. Chiefs wait for yams each year, and chiefs at best may only influence rather than directly control the size of the yam production. Men wait for their sons and daughters to grow up and marry, and women wait for their husbands to supply them with additional wealth. Death, too, waits to drain off accumulated resources. Internally created 'close kin' relationships must constantly be 'fed' with yams or the ties diminish, and women's wealth continually subsumes men's wealth.

A more permanent wealth, detached from dala, then holds out the possibilities for the creation of something new – a new basis for relationships and a new form of debt. In Kiriwina stone axe blades (beku) are male valuables.[8] (If beku are unavailable for certain transactions, a man may substitute clay pots, or kitomu [shell valuables] and now Western cash, but some major transactions still require beku.) Unlike the extensive public displays of yams and women's wealth, beku may only be seen briefly during a transaction. At other times, beku are kept hidden, usually buried in the ground under a man's house. Beku are individually owned and inherited by men regardless of rank and dala. When given in particular transactions, beku may be reclaimed by the original owner at a later time (see Weiner, 1976: 180–3 for a description of the circulation of beku). For beku, the replacement must meet the present holder's expectations. Beku are not easy to recapture, and many times they are lost from the original owner's control. Unlike other property, the return of a beku neither contains the sanction of dala, nor is its return triggered by a death. Men say: 'Beku walks very far and a man must walk after it.' The ownership and rights to replacement are independent of other kinds of social relations. To replace his own beku, a man may be forced to walk many miles from his own hamlet and to deal with someone who is neither related to him, nor who was involved in the original transaction. Therefore, the physical circulation of beku is unlike any other resource previously described.

The stone axe blades originally came from Woodlark Island and were

158

polished in Kiriwina. *Kaloma* shells, manufactured in Sinaketa village (located toward the southern end of Kiriwina) were used to purchase the axe blades in Woodlark. Neither the polishing nor the production of kaloma in Kiriwina, nor the purchase of axe blades in Woodlark are on-going concerns today. But beku still continue to be used extensively in Kiriwina exchanges. Prior to colonization, stone axe blades arrived in Kiriwina through kula channels (but not as substitute for an armshell or necklace), or via occasional canoe trips to Woodlark. These routes of access diminished, however, with the advent of colonial trading activities in the early 1900s. Beku were used by traders as payment for labor, especially for divers engaged in the pearling and *bêche de mer* industries. In addition, motor launches between Kiriwina and Woodlark also contributed to easier access for the Woodlark stone blades.

In Kiriwina although stone axe blades are free from the full range of complexity involving relationships organized around the circulation of yams and women's wealth, and free from dala, they play an important role in the initial transactions which involve the beginning of a new reproductive cycle – marriage and children, and a definitive role at the end of a cycle – death. In addition, beku are used for a range of resources, such as payment for purchasing seed yams, performance of magic spells – especially sorcery, the purchase of magic texts, payment for the labor in producing a large yam harvest, payment for gaining allies in war, and compensation payment for 'blood' (killing someone who was a member of another dala). If a man is known to have five beku, he is considered a 'wealthy man', but a man to fear because beku are necessary for sorcery and compensation payments. 'Beku', I was told often, 'are very important but very dangerous things for Kiriwina.'

Beku either cause or reconstitute the loss of property and individuals via the actions of 'others' through time. Thus the main value of beku is as object *par excellence* for securing replacement. Beku act as the primary means for the replacement of dala property, especially land, and for the replacement of individuals through compensation, or even the demise of individuals through sorcery. In marriage and divorce, beku function to replace a child and to replace dala. In mortuary distributions, beku operate as final replacement for the original marriage transaction of valuables (see Weiner, 1976, for examples). But beku, unlike the objects operating in the reproductive sectors previously described, do not reproduce new and continuing relationships through the basic process of embedding wealth and value in 'others'. Beku provide protection against 'others' and the protection is expressed idiomatically as 'fear' rather than as 'love' and 'generosity'.

What makes beku so distinctive, however, from a comparative perspective of the northern Massim is that their use as an exchange object *only occurs in Kiriwina*.[9] In other islands, such as Iwa, Gawa, Woodlark, and even Kitava, kitomu (shell valuables) may fulfill some similar internal exchange functions (cf. Damon, 1980). But unlike beku, kitomu are much more directly integrated into kula activities and therefore kitomu have a different pattern of circulation even in internal transactions (cf. Munn, 1977).

In northern Kiriwina, prior to colonization, kula participation undoubtedly increased an individual's access to beku (as well as clay pots from the Amphletts). Since traditionally only men of rank played the game of kula, access to beku added much to the individual power of chiefs. Beku (and clay pots), however, proliferated the internal exchange sectors for both rank and non-rank persons in their circulation at marriages, harvests, deaths, and as replacements for dala property. Perhaps the use of beku internally, raising kula to a higher order in terms of its tangential connections to internal exchanges was due to historical circumstances. Perhaps at one time, kitomu, as elsewhere, functioned as an integral part of internal exchanges, and with the introduction of beku this essential role was displaced. But unfortunately, I was unable to verify these historical hypotheses.

From the contemporary perspective, beku act on the reproductive sectors through which yams, women's wealth, and dala property flow. Beku have a long life trajectory, outlasting a human life cycle, and as durable wealth, beku both encode and act on the most critical moments in the reproductive structure. Beku, however, are not the means by which long-term debt is initiated in that beku are not reproductive elements such as yams and humans, nor divisible such as dala property may be. Nevertheless, beku in their durability and representation as male valuables secure the kinds of debt generated by these other objects.

From this perspective, as its complement, women's wealth acts on the reproduction structure in a similar way. As beku secure the replacement of dala property and persons, women's wealth secures the replacement of matrilineal identity.[10] Therefore beku, although not explicitly dala property, nevertheless remain primarily attached to the exigencies generated by the reproductive process of embedding wealth and value in others. Only in kula do men achieve a level of reproductiveness without women and without the demands of dala. If kula represents the 'highest and the most dramatic expression' of wealth and value, as Malinowski thought, the processes of kula must bear some resemblance to the basic process of reproductiveness on which internal exchange is based.

The external system of exchange: doing kula in Kiriwina

Transactions in northern Kiriwina surrounding kula events are more complex than originally described by Malinowski, and correlate to a great extent with the kinds of Gawa transactions described by Munn (1977: this volume) and by Campbell (this volume) for Vakuta. But the highest objective in doing kula is to gain a very large valuable, called kitomu, and to secure the exchange of this kitomu (either a *mwali* or a *soulava*) with its opposite [sex] valuable. In Kiriwina, this exchange is called *bivalulu* (to give birth). Munn (1977) describes similar transactions of kitomu on Gawa which she analyzes as being 'reproductive'. But the emphasis she places on the reproductive cycle for Gawans is one that 'perpetually reproduces itself'. In Kiriwina, although the travels of one kitomu allow it to continue to reproduce itself, the ownership of a large kitomu may directly 'give birth' to new kula roads.

In Kiriwina, access to a kitomu is found in Kaleuna Island where armshells are manufactured. Kitomu may be purchased (*gimwali*) with yams, pigs, or large quantities of betel (but yams are the usual commodity).[11] In addition to purchasing kitomu in Kaleuna, it is possible to purchase a kitomu from a kula man or in places outside the kula area such as Port Moresby.

Kitomu is a man's own property. Although he may elect to sell it, or use it for internal exchanges in place of beku, the most reproductive choice is to find another kitomu of similar value and effect that exchange (bivalulu). The kitomu travels through the other areas of the Massim as a kula valuable, but throughout its travels it is known as X.'s kitomu. Therefore, valuables circling on kula paths may have different references to different people at particular places on the path. But to exchange a kitomu for another kitomu does not mean that one's own kitomu is sent off immediately on a kula road. If a man has a large kitomu, he holds it and waits until the message of the availability of his kitomu circulates. The news – a man's name – travels first. The best way to describe the process of bivalulu is to illustrate with a few examples.

Z. of Kwaibwaga village had a very large mwali (armshell) that he purchased with yams from Kaileuna. Z.'s friend in Sinaketa heard about the kitomu and sent Z. a small necklace classified as *vaga*. The following is the way vaga was described to me: 'Vaga is a valuable that is not on your own road [keda]. You give vaga because you love that man very much. He killed a pig for you or brought you yams and fish. So you give him a valuable that is not keda [path]. You give him only because you love him.' The word vaga is opposed to keda (path). A man says, 'Sorry, no vaga, only keda', meaning 'I only have valuables that are part of my kula roads

Annette B. Weiner

– they are already promised to others.' Malinowski described vaga as 'an opening gift' (cf. 1922:353–5), and in some ways, vaga does constitute an 'opening'. But as Campbell (this volume) describes, the primary purpose of vaga is to initiate a new relationship between two men so that later additional shell valuables that will be part of a keda flow between them. According to my informants, vaga is equated with mapula: doing kula for vaga is called mapula; doing kula for kitomu is really kula (kula *wala*).

As I indicated earlier, mapula embodies the concept of replacement – an investment of wealth in 'others' – that later will be reclaimed and replaced. Therefore, vaga as mapula gives a man the opportunity to enter kula by initiating a new road with a vaga. But the vaga itself initially may come from a man not on one's kula path. Prior to giving the initial vaga, men *pokala* (giving objects that will influence the mind of a man) (see Weiner, 1976 on pokala transactions) such as fish, yams, betel, and pig. More significant objects such as beku may also be given (*karibitu* distinguishes these large wealth objects from food as pokala). the idioms for pokala and mapula are 'love' and 'generosity'.

Vaga was described as 'like two friends meeting, but they are not yet sleeping together'. The acceptance of vaga from someone indicates the acceptance of that kula man and his path (keda). Because the path for a large kitomu must be very strong, the choice of a vaga is extremely important, and men work very hard to influence the choice. Prior to choosing a keda, a man with a large kitomu may sit with it for many years. During that time, others will hear of the kitomu and attempt to win it. Men will send small valuables called '*rogita*' (see Damon, 1980 on *logits*). These valuables are meant to be tempting to the kitomu holder, to express without words the fact of one's desire to obtain a vaga and the strength and integrity of one's name and one's ability to work hard in kula. The rogita are another form of pokala, of 'influencing someone's mind' to give a vaga so that a formal set of valuables can begin to flow that will eventually lead to the large kitomu. The rogita will be put on kula paths, but the acceptance of a rogita does not commit the receiver to any further obligation other than the return valuable for the original rogita.

Finally, one man will emerge as the one who will be the strongest and the hardest worker for the chain of valuables that will now begin to flow preceding the kitomu circulation. Once an initial vaga is given, then one particular path is opened. The vaga circulates along the path, but in its circulation it will be classified as *basi* to the other kula partners. In other words, the classification vaga indicates that the valuable can be put on any path, but once accepted by someone and passed along it is then part of a particular path and is classified to others as basi. According to my informants, basi means 'we are already sleeping together, but we are not

162

yet married'. Valuables classified as basi (either armshells or necklaces, depending on the direction they will flow) keep a path alive. The more basi flowing along a path, the more active the kula partners appear to be to others (see Campbell and Munn, this volume).

The return to the kitomu holder Z. for his vaga will be called basi and will be an opposite shell valuable. But the basi will be much smaller than the kitomu. Therefore, the kitomu will continue to sit with its owner and the basi will circulate through the path. A basi will flow from the opposite direction passing through the kitomu holder, and basi will be returned from the opposite direction. Perhaps as many as five or six basi will be exchanged through the kitomu holder. But because the kitomu holder has many basi flowing through him, he may, if he is very clever, divert some of these basi to other paths (see Figure 1).

These basi transactions may be even more complex as often with a large kitomu, the return on the first vaga (i.e., *Basi* A^1) will be another vaga with the basi. In this way, the giving of one valuable produces the return of two valuables. The further return of these two valuables will increase to three, as later another vaga, and two basi are sent back to Z. These increases continue until a kitomu equivalent in size and value to Z.'s kitomu is sent.

During the course of time, another man with a large kitomu will hear about Z.'s kitomu and will begin sending basi to Z., through the path started with the initial vaga. When a large valuable classified as *kudu* is sent, this valuable indicates that the kitomu will follow soon. *Kudu* means 'we are already married' and the situation between us is firmly established. In addition to the kudu, however, another valuable classified as *kunavilevile* is also sent to the original kitomu holder. This valuable is called 'giving birth' (bivalulu) and belongs independently to the kitomu holder. It is his valuable to keep for as long as he wishes, but unlike

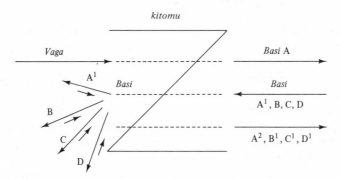

Figure 1. The possibility of basi transactions.

kitomu he cannot sell the valuable or use it in internal exchanges. It is kunavilevile that becomes a vaga and that will at some time begin another kula road. This valuable will attract other men who wish to begin a path with Z. The ability not only to traffic in kitomu, but to gain kunavilevile (i.e., to give birth) gives a man's name renown throughout the kula.

To obtain these increases is indeed difficult and according to my informants, with many new men now playing kula it becomes even more difficult.[12] The great danger in all the plays of strategy is the possibility of diversion – of stealing (see examples from Gawa and Vakuta). A man may delay his partner making him wait another year (see Fortune's 1932:217 example of this) – lying to him that he has no valuable this time. Or a man may give a lesser valuable, keeping a larger one for a new path. If a man is weak, he may lose one or several valuables completely. And finally, the statement made by both Fortune and Malinowski, '. . . many men died for this valuable' indicates the constant danger and threat in playing the kula game. 'To have a large kitomu is every man's desire, but when you have one and marry it to another, then beware, because unless you are a chief, you may die' is a warning I was often told.

The tricks are many, and the only way to succeed is to be strong – to be handsome and to be feared. Seduction through magic and pokala is essential for playing the game well. When men argue with their kula friends, they bring every kind of pressure to bear. In the internal system of exchange, it would be anathema to openly accuse another man of being stingy or of not fulfilling an obligation. But in kula transactions, men argue, reject each other, and threaten in ways that only occur in everyday activities under very unusual circumstances. The only security in kula is a man's name – for in kula a man's name is the only mechanism he has for reclaiming his possessions. A man's name is the measure of his power – his magic – his past performances – his father or his mother's brother – his status within his own society. All these bits of identity are condensed into a name. When men say, 'everyone knows my name', 'my renown spreads', this is the weight and the burden a name must carry (see also Munn, 1977).

Returning again to Malinowski's theme of kula as the 'highest and most dramatic expression' of wealth and value, we find that kula represents a significant transformation from the conceptual frame of dala to the emergence of the individual self – momentarily detached from all the inter-connectedness of internal exchanges. In kula, Kiriwina men finally overcome the boundaries set by the concept of dala and the processes necessary to regenerate these boundaries. In Kiriwina kula valuables add to a man's wealth, but they are not directly essential to internal transactions.[13] Like other objects they do not rot, or fade, or have to be reclaimed with other resources; neither are they drained out of individual control by a death. The process of pokala–mapula–sagali shifts to become pokala–mapula–kula – the reclaiming draining effort of sagali now converted into kula, a reproductive effort that is not defeated by a death.

Kula, therefore, frees men to reproduce without having to reclaim and reorder the products of their reproduction. In kula, wealth and value are embedded in 'others' as in the internal system, but the transformation allows for wealth and value to be compressed into one's own self,[14] rather than into dala. What occurs during kula events has to do with one's own power and ability in direct interaction and confrontation with kula friends and in the indirect renown of one's name without the sanction of dala or the regulatory force of death. Kula for northern Kiriwina is fed by yams (as means to kitomu), but these yams can be removed from the internal system without specific additional repayment in other areas. Therefore, women are removed from the external system of kula – for kula depends upon the reproduction of valuables and one's personal name – and not blood, nor dala, nor the demands of death.

Kula extricates men from the security of dala, the obsessiveness of death, and the interdigitation of affinal obligations. But kula is not a completely new form; it endures as a transformation of an internal form. Kula valuables remain reproductive only within the kula circuit – moving through a trajectory that stands as a metaphor for a human life cycle. But moving through this 'life cycle', is not reproductive in an expansive way. Only very strong men can 'give birth'. And marriage of valuables does not produce marriages of children. Kula as a reproductive cycle can only reproduce and regenerate the wealth and value of the self.

But although men move into the external sector, away from women and *dala*, into a 'world of made', they still are faced with a paradox. Leaving behind a 'world of born', men struggle to create debt through shells and their own names in a world of individual self-aggrandizement. The paradox of kula, as Munn's article (this volume) so skillfully shows, is that each time a kula cycle is completed, the path is closed, and the debt is finished. Thus, enormous energy (i.e., in the circulation of basi) is expended in trying to keep paths open merely to prevent closure. A kula shell, regardless of its size and its reproductive value (i.e., how many other shells will circulate), cannot regenerate permanent debt. Therefore, participation in kula does not lead to the creation of anything new except what is already in the system – more kula valuables and more kula paths. The valuables and paths in producing only short-term debt, cannot be used to transform kula into a different kind of system, nor can these valuables and paths work to transform the internal system in Kiriwina into a more controlling powerful system of chieftainship.

Annette B. Weiner

Kiriwina chiefs, kula, and the Massim

The emergence of a ranking system in Kiriwina with specific coordinates in which power is allocated to a few men as chiefs may be understood as a response to the tightly controlled organization of the reproduction and regeneration of matriliny and paternal kinship continually stabilized via the complementarity between women's wealth and men's wealth. The stratification of this basic organization permits the formalization of the circulation, control, and replacement of dala property which, in producing long-term debt, allows for the development of concentration of power at one level of integration (see Adams (1975) on levels of integration). But even individual allocation of power still remains tied to dala. Kula enhances a chief's power base, and may be the road to increasing stocks of male permanent wealth such as kitomu valuables, or even beku. But kula does not introduce enough power into the internal system so that chiefs themselves become organized into a higher level of integration. (I do not propose my analysis as a timeless model, but until we have more detailed information on internal exchange throughout the Massim it remains difficult to reconstruct changes in kula prior to and immediately following colonialization.)

Although kula seems to hold out the opportunity for new sources of power, the short-term cyclicity of the external system prevents a concentrated integration of power that might emerge into new levels of control. Kula activity neither leads to a shift in the actual working of kula so that a hierarchical inter-island structure develops, nor does the individual concentration of power achieved through kula create a shift in the internal system whereby the highest-ranked chiefs develop a new base for internal control. Thus chiefs in Kiriwina operate within an internal system that has more expansive potential than elsewhere in the Massim, yet both the system of chiefs and doing kula still reflect certain limitations in the allocation of individual power.

In other Massim Islands, the distance between the internal and external sectors of exchange is very close – one feeding into the other. Such dependency on kula for kin obligations necessitates participation in kula by *all* men in a kula area. But in northern Kiriwina, even today when the restriction on kula participation only for men of rank (and their sons) is no longer operative, only some chiefs, and some powerful hamlet managers, and some younger men (who are kin of the above) are active participants in kula. In northern Kiriwina, the distance between the external and internal circulations widens considerably, given the formal stratification of internal objects of exchange. What gives the stratification its power is the meaning that each object encodes as it acts on the reproductive structure. The actual processes of reproduction, however, should not be thought of as mere continuity. For the reproduction of social relations must be interpretated through the *process* of expansion and replacement – that is the process of embedding wealth and value in 'others' outside one's own dala, and the moments when persons and resources must be returned to 'pure' dala. This process demands constant attention and work, with production of wealth that can be drawn on when necessary to prevent the loss at every death of dala persons and property.

In Kiriwina, women's wealth is the object reproducing the core of dala identity, regenerating that identity through time and space. In this way, women's wealth, primary to its economic and social dimensions, contributes to the baseline of the Kiriwina reproductive structure.[15] The various elements that constitute a stratified system in Kiriwina such as dala, yams, stone axe blades, and kula and kitomu valuables may be found in different combinations in most Massim Islands. But although women's skirts play a symbolic role elsewhere in the Massim (see Berde, 1974; Young, 1971), women's skirts do not appear as objects of wealth in any place other than the Trobriands.

The fact that women's wealth secures the replacement of matrilineal identity at each death adds significantly to the power of dala as an element itself in the reproductive process, an element that may be detached and circulated away from its source for the production of long-term debt. It may well be that elsewhere in the Massim, without women's wealth encoding the reproduction of lineage and simultaneously becoming an active agent in the replacement process, the source of power must draw on the external sectors of kitomu and kula, as in Gawa and Woodlark, or remain completely dependent on yams as in Goodenough Island (Young, 1971). In Kiriwina, with the base of women's wealth as both metaphoric code and active agent, stone axe blades provide a further distancing from dependency on kula and kitomu valuables. But when kitomu are essential to internal exchanges, as elsewhere, dependency on external sources becomes significant in that less opportunity exists for individual concentration of power separate from the exigencies of external kula circulation. Therefore, the potential to build up internal loci of power remains extremely limited.

Nevertheless, even in Kiriwina with the potential for power generated through dala, the limitation imposed by death short-circuits any long-term buildup of individual resources. Death also interferes with the operation of kula. When a death occurs in a kula area, all kula activity ceases. These sanctions block valuables in the deceased's village for six months and sometimes longer. Therefore, death in one area simultaneously removes the availability of valuables for a period of time in

Annette B. Weiner

many places throughout the Massim. Just how death affects kitomu and kula valuables in their circulation to other islands and in their integration within internal transactions elsewhere calls for further research.

From the perspective of Kiriwina, given the stratification of objects of exchange, the internal and external sectors of exchange remain reflections of each other in certain basic ways. The process of embedding wealth and value in 'others' in order to develop and maintain one's own present and future value can be seen as a similar process in doing kula. The circulation of kitomu enhances its value as an individual's own kitomu and as a valuable that others will possess as kula. One's self, one's position, and one's potential in both sectors depend upon relations with 'others' because the fundamental process depends upon the circulation of possessions from 'others'. And even in kula where the circulation of possessions finally reproduces the wealth and value of the self, almost free from internal demands, the cycles of exchange are still regulated by cycles of death.

Notes

Acknowledgements

The quotation in the title is taken from the poem, *'pity this busy monster, manukind'* by e. e. cummings.

Over the past 10 years, many institutions have generously contributed to the support of my research on Kiriwina, Trobriand Islands, Papua New Guinea. I am most grateful to the Mary Bullock Workman Travelling Fellowship, Bryn Mawr College; National Institute of Mental Health; National Endowment for the Humanities; American Council of Learned Societies; The University Research Institute, University of Texas at Austin. This paper was revised in 1981 following a return to Kiriwina for which I am indebted to the John Simon Guggenheim Foundation. Revisions were completed while I was a Member of The Institute for Advanced Study, Princeton.

I also thank my Kiriwina friends for their long-term support and commitment to my research, as well as the Milne Bay Provincial Government, the Department of Anthropology and Sociology, University of Papua New Guinea, and the Institute of Papua New Guinea Studies.

1 Damon (1980) presents a critique on kitomu from the perspective of Woodlark (Muyuw), but his interpretation differs in some important respects from my presentation in this essay. [Weiner (1976) has *Kitoma*; Damon (1980 and this volume) *Kitoum*; Leach (this volume) *Kitom* etc.]

2 Although I am interested in analyzing kula as a system, rather than examining the details of kula from the locus of Omarakana or any other specific hamlet, I here base my interpretation both of kula and of chiefs from the perspective of northern Kiriwina.

'A world of made is not a world of born': doing kula in Kiriwina

3 I am indebted to the comments made during the Kula Conference by Maurice Godelier on the significance of permanent debt as the means to create something new in a social system.

4 Dala is not a smaller replica of clan (*kumila*) as originally defined by Malinowski. Therefore, I find the use of 'subclan' inappropriate (see Weiner, 1976:37–60).

5 Controversies over why, and whether or not the Trobrianders have chiefs continue (see e.g., Brunton, 1975; Irwin this volume; Powell, 1960; Uberoi, 1962; Watson, 1956; Weiner, 1976). The position of chief is an inherited one, and therefore I find the category of 'chief' more appropriate than 'leader' (see Powell, 1960) or 'big-man'. Although throughout the article I discuss the power of Kiriwina chiefs, I am not concerned with the power of any specific chiefs such as the Tabalu of Omarakana, but I am accounting for the fact that the power of certain chiefly ranks, including the Tabalu, is much stronger in northern Kiriwina.

6 Mauss (1954) seemed to have had some vision of what I call replacement. He showed that a distinction had to be made between certain kinds of property: '. . . the Kwakiutl and Tsimshian, and perhaps others, make the same distinction between the various types of property as do the Romans, Trobrianders and Samoans. They have the ordinary articles of consumption and distribution . . . They have also the valuable family property – talismans, decorated coppers, skin blankets and embroidered fabrics. This class of articles is transmitted with that solemnity with which women are given in marriage . . . It is wrong to speak here of alienation, for these things are loaned rather than sold and ceded. Basically, they are *sacra* which the family parts with, if at all, only with reluctance' (pp. 41–2).

7 Dried banana leaves constitute the material for the manufacture of women's wealth. All women produce this wealth which consists of beautifully decorated skirts (*doba*), and bundles of strips of dried banana leaves (*nununiga*). This wealth has an economic value, in addition to its social and symbolic significance (see Weiner, 1976:91–120 for details).

8 Kiriwina women do not own beku or kula valuables. If a young child is heir to a kula path, his mother will do kula in his name. In order to kula overseas, however, her husband will take her place.

9 But in the southern Massim, beku play a significant role in internal exchanges. According to Jones (this volume) in Sudest stone axe blades symbolize a range of female and male reproductive qualities. A Kiriwina informant once told me that it was important to understand that beku in Sudest are very different from the way beku are used in Kiriwina.

10 The word nununiga as women's wealth and its connection to dala identity may show some similarity with the concept *nunu, nunuai, niniai* as used in Mota and Aurora. Codrington (1891) gives many examples of these terms referring to images, echoes, shadows, reflections. Thus '. . . a child is the *nunu* of a person deceased'. 'A woman, before her child is born, fancies that a coconut, bread-fruit or some such thing has some original connexion with her infant. When the child is born, it is the *nunu* of the coco-nut, or whatever it may be . . .' (pp. 251–3). Of further comparative interest is a report that traditionally on Aurora, 'women are the mat-makers and mats represent wealth

Annette B. Weiner

[and] the number of a man's wives adds to his prestige, though in some islands mat-makers may be hired to add to the store' (Quiggin [1949–132]). Coote (1883) as cited in Quiggin describes the way in Aurora mats are allowed to rot through a process of slow burning in which black incrustation adheres to the mat and increases its value. 'A fairly old mat is worth as much as a large boar with finely curved tusks' (Quiggin, p. 132).

11 To obtain kitomu with yams involves men on both sides of a yam exchange. For example, if a kula man receives yams from another man, he may take some of them to purchase a kitomu for himself. But if a younger man receives yams from his father-in-law who is a kula man, he may take some of his yams and purchase a kitomu for his father-in-law as payment for making a very large harvest (see Weiner, 1976).

12 Today, older men talk about the misfortunes of young men who return from working elsewhere with cash and want to enter kula. They buy a kitomu and so enter directly. But they soon lose everything because they forget 'that kula takes a lot of work – all the time, you must take care of your friends. These boys do not understand about the work.'

13 Kula men from northern Kiriwina often talk disparagingly about men on Vakuta and Kitava who put their kula valuables into internal exchanges (see also Campbell this volume).

14 From a different perspective, Munn (1977) presented a similar concern with the 'self' in analyzing the symbolism of kula canoes and kitomu: 'The message of this symbolism is that the canoe's "beauty" lies precisely in its capacity to transform the Gawan world outward and to bring back into Gawa the value thus produced – in effect, to refer what is achieved by outward transformation "backward" to the self.'

15 The role of wealth manufactured from fibrous plants and produced by women is not an isolated Trobriand phenomenon. My recent field research in Western Samoa confirms that Samoan fine mats display features similar to those I use in the interpretation of Trobriand women's wealth (see e.g., Weiner, n.d.b).

7   On flying witches and flying canoes: the coding of male and female values

S. J. TAMBIAH

I. The problem

The institution of *kula*, as Malinowski so vividly described it for us, had a conspicuous place in the Trobrianders' – especially the male Trobrianders' – scheme of aspirations and sense of achievement. It was, as is to be expected from Trobriand preoccupation with it, suffused with magical ideas and practices, including those which Malinowski identified as witchcraft and sorcery.

Although Malinowski did not always clearly separate 'witchcraft' from 'sorcery', yet his ethnography portrays a clear distinction between the *bwaga'u* (sorcerer) who is male and the *yoyova* (witch) who is usually female, especially the *mulukwausi* (the flying witch).[1] There are several suggestive differences between their characterizations. Men learn the art of sorcery, transmit it through exchange relations, and practise it intentionally and externally, seeking to achieve effects on other persons or objects. Women's involvement in witchcraft is involuntary, it is transmitted on a hereditary basis, and its characteristic manifestation is as a 'disembodied' internal entity which appropriately attacks the victim's insides.

Our first problem is to seek the logic of this contrastive potency attributed differentially to male and female, and which ramifies with other features of the kula traffic. We shall in this paper focus as our second problem on only one such ramification: the association between female flying witches and the flying canoe celebrated in kula myths and canoe magic. How in terms of Trobriand cosmology can we 'explain' the extraordinary powers attributed to the flying witches, who are on the one hand believed to be deadly dangerous to the kula sailors, and on the other hand provide the positive model of imitation for the kula deep sea canoe (*masawa*)? Aside from the famous Kudayuri myth which treats of flying canoes and witches, canoes are addressed in spells as females and flying

S. J. Tambiah

witches. Indeed canoes are urged to bind their skirts and fly in imitation
of flying witches, who in turn by a symmetrical transfer of attributes are
described as wearing during their flight fluttering pandanus streamers
with which sea going canoes are decorated. Furthermore, just as the
flying witch attacks shipwrecked sailors in order to eat their insides, a
wrecked canoe at sea turns cannibilistic at the moment the *wayugo*
creeper lashings disintegrate.

My discovery procedure is not in 'causal' terms as this is conventionally
understood but in terms of revealing analogical structures that are
embedded in the ethnographic accounts scrutinized, structures that are
related to one another by parallelisms, inversions, oppositions, transposi-
tions etc. I also intend to provide semantic maps of portions of the
Trobriand cosmology that can be inferred from the ethnography examined, and also venture a hypothesis on how Trobriand classificatory
thought generated 'extraordinary' events and persons by 'collapsing'
already separated categories.

II. Male and female attributes in production, reproduction and exchange.

The assembling of the Trobriand cultural code concerning male and
female attributes and their distributional pattern is integral for the solution of the problems we have set ourselves. In attempting to do so, I shall
use Annette Weiner's book *Women of Value, Men of Renown* (1976)
both as a point of reference and a point of departure.

The Female in Trobriand thought is the reproducer of *dala* members,
and the transmitter of dala identity or essence, which she carries *inside*
her as part of her very constitution. This identity is inalienable, timeless
and unchanging, and manifest as the impersonal *baloma* entering her and
becoming incarnated as children. But also note that the baloma permanent essences in being cycled through women are in continuous reincarnating *motion* as well. This double aspect is what we label 'matrilineal
descent', shared by successive generations of brothers and sisters, but
transmitted only through females.

In constrast, the Male is the primary agent who actively establishes and
maintains a *network of interpersonal exchange relations*. The male –
especially the representative of the localized dala as manager/senior male
– is the holder and controller of dala land rights, names, decorations and
spells. Now with regard to such interpersonal relations, a Trobriand male
faces a radical separation between on the one hand his subjection to the
obligatory and invariant intra-dala rule of transmission of privileges and
possessions to his younger brother and sister's son (note here the familiar

172

pokala payment on the claimant's part, which seals the jural right), and on the other hand his freedom to engage in extra-dala voluntary, ambitious, affect-laden acts of aggrandizement and achievement. One instance in the latter domain is the Trobriand man's variable love for his (wife's) children, and his giving free gifts to them. (*Contra* Malinowski who characterized it as extra-normative instinctive behaviour, we should view this orientation of father to son as much an ideological formulation as that of mother's brother to sister's son.) Another instance is the fact that dala possessions and rights are temporarily loanable in the interests of furthering exchange relations (and through them increasing his and his dala's prestige or rank). But note that it is women who then reclaim on behalf of the dala these loaned-out possessions. My reading of the significance of the distribution of women's wealth in mortuary rites is that it is women of a man's dala (as well as his own and his brother's daughters who in this context stand with him) who after that man's death ceremonially sever his affinal ties and exchange relations (with principally his wife and her kin, and his father and his kin), and thereby reclaim the dead man back into his dala in his essential form (i.e. without exchange connections with members of other dala). Women sever these quintessential extra-dala connections by concluding the mourning, especially through the distribution of banana bundles and coloured skirts, and thereby restoring to the deceased's affines their sexuality and enabling the widow to remarry.[2] We should also note that although the leeway given a man to forge voluntaristic networks is a central link in the larger switchboard of political and affinal relations, yet this manipulative possibility, if carried too far to the point of endangering the interests of other dala men and matrilineal heirs, results in counter action by sorcery. Men who commit such excesses invite their murder and/or their supersession.[3]

According to the well-known Trobriand reproduction theory, it is women who 'involuntarily' and 'accidentally' (unless they deliberately expose themselves to the scum, leaves, branches and seaweeds of the shallow waters and creeks) conceive by means of the penetration of baloma spirits, and it is the husband who transfers by periodic sexual activity and nurture his facial and bodily resemblance to the child in the womb, and after its brith leaves his imprint by means of further nurturance and show of affection. The logic of this complementarity is *cross-referenced* in terms of the contrastive roles of father's sister (*tabu*) and mother's brother (*kada*) with regard to their nephew (and niece). The father's sister, with whom joking and teasing with sexual overtones is allowed, is eminently desirable and appropriate as the person who beautifies her brother's son's appearance by the performance of beauty magic and body decoration. Correspondingly, the mother's brother who

S. J. Tambiah

is normally rigidly separated from his sister by the *suvasova* (incest) taboo, can however assist his sister in conceiving a child by bringing her a baler of sea water in which the baloma spirit children are believed to be present, having journeyed from Tuma (Malinowski 1932:150).

The Trobriand relation between brother and sister is as we well know both complex and finely tuned on chords held in high tension. While in the origin myths, brothers and sisters emerge together (a situation which provoked Malinowski to comment on the conspicuous absence of the husband or wife in these myths), yet both myth and social practice insist on the necessity for brothers and sisters to separate. Their emergence together is dictated by their sharing of common dala identity, but their continued co-residence is powerfully suggestive of incest. It is the sister's fate or mission then to be uprooted and to be *mobile* – to be given away to go and live with her husband, to be 'loaned' away by her dala; her sons however are usually reclaimed (in Malinowski's classical description) by her mother's brothers and they return (or have the right to return) to live on dala land. Thus men in contrast to women, once mature stay 'anchored' on their own dala land, cultivate the gardens, and send the best part of the 'children of their gardens', the *taitu* and *kuvi* yams, to their sisters as *urigubu*. Note that the implication and meaning of "anchoring" is crucial in Trobriand ritual: the growing yams are "anchored" in the belly of the garden so that they can grow big and send out shoots (which above ground can branch out in free mobility). Again, the urigubu yams, are 'anchored' in the storehouse by the ritual use of *binabina* stones with magical words, so that the yams will endure and not be consumed quickly.

In line with this brother–sister differential is the baloma-tabu distinction within the category of ancestral spirits. Unlike the impersonal cyclically reincarnating baloma, the tabu are marked, differentiated, individuated and often named ancestors, who emerged from holes in the land (and other sites), and constitute the basis of dala land and rank claims, and dala-linked garden and canoe magic, decorations and taboos. Though theoretically both brothers and sisters because of co-appearance qualify to be tabu, yet virtually males are the stereotype tabu personages by virtue of their residence on dala land and their control of dala possessions while their sisters move away to reside with their husbands. Women of course carry their rank into marriage and observe taboos associated with their rank, and can 'inherit' and learn certain kinds of dala magic. But they cannot practise this magic in their own right, they can only transmit it to their children just as they transmit rank and descent to them.

What I am deliberately leading up to is the proposition that in Tro-

174

briand thought women and men have both stable and volatile capacities in their distinctive ways, that these capacities receive differential stress, and lastly that the dualities of these sexes may be further coordinated in a pattern (as 'the relations between the relations').

Women, the vehicles of cycling dala essence, are invested with the capacities of energy force and motion in their most potent, mobile, and natural (i.e. as an essential accompaniment of femaleness) forms. This stressed attribution has both positive and negative aspects which we shall explore later.

The female who is on the move residentially, mother separated from married daughters, married sisters from each other, finds her anchorage in the marriage relationship. She resides virilocally with her husband and receives the urigubu yams from her brother in recognition of her dala rights, the affinal relation between her husband and her brother, and the conjugal relation between her and her husband. This conjugal and affinal anchorage is in some ways so central a feature of Trobriand social relations that at least one tradition of analysis of kinship terminology, which claims to support and stem from Malinowski's 'extensionist theory', actually flatly distorts a Malinowskian formulation, while quite correctly indicating the critical importance of the husband–wife solidarity unit.[4] From our perspective, the affinal anchorage is dependent on the marital relationship, which in Trobriand terms, is effected as a *sexual relationship* between husband and wife – a voluntaristic exchange relationship (as exemplified by the 'payment' to the woman for sexual favours granted) which separates the *sexuality* of a woman from her involuntary and inhering *procreative* capacity. Thus if a woman disengages from her marital relationship, she is thought to reactivate her propensities for motion and (sexual) aggression, which is exactly what is symbolized, as we shall see later, in the notion of flying witch or the fantasies about sexual attacks by nymphomaniac females.[5] Furthermore, the characterisation of the aggressive power of the detached flying witch as materializing inside her belly is an inversion of a woman's normal conception by baloma intrusion when she is attached in marriage.

Males by contrast to females are in a primary sense regarded as being 'anchored' and stabilized on dala land together with the rights to use and manipulate dala possessions. But hinged to this is the correlated fact that it is men who are the prime activist political actors, who consciously and calculatedly go in search of *butura* (renown) which is a volatile, changing, and mercurial reward won and lost in the channels of exchange networks. And this volatility that carries with it suggestions of being unanchored reaches its pitch of uncertainty and fluidity on the kula seaways, kula exchange being for the Trobrianders a quintessential male activity. The physical state of the canoe on the sea with fluttering pandanus streamers striving after maximum speed is experienced by the men as the most liminal and 'unanchored' state of physical and social existence.

III. Male sorcerer (bwaga'u), female witch (yoyova) flying witch (mulukwausi), and non-human malignant spirits (tauva'u)

We are now ready to grasp the logic of the characterizations of sorcerer and witch. Their mode of operation and their different capacities parallel, indeed are 'projected on', the patterns discussed in the foregoing section.

Sorcerers

Sorcerers, who are always male, engage in concrete acts – they employ words, manipulate substances, have accomplices. According to one description of his technique (Malinowski 1922:74–6), the sorcerer makes his victim take to his bed by use of a spell, then accompanied by accomplices such as 'nightbirds, owls and night-jars' he inserts through the thatch wall of the victim's hut at night a bunch of herbs impregnated with a charm and drops it into the fire. The victim inhales the fumes and is seized by a deadly disease. Should he be foiled in this attack, then he resorts to 'a most fatal rite, that of the pointing bone': a sharp stingaree spine, impregnated with powerful spells and herbs boiled in coconut oil, is pointed at the victim and stabbed at him.

Feared as the black art is, yet the sorcerer produces by his spells and rites only ordinary ailments; he does not produce 'very rapidly fulminating diseases and epidemics' (Malinowski 1948:105). Moreover, a male sorcerer never eats his victim's flesh, and since he is responsible for lingering disease his work can be counteracted (Malinowski 1932–46).

Male sorcery is an 'actual trade' and is transmitted through learning from practitioner to apprentice – who need not be a kinsman – accompanied by the proper gifts and payments. Malinowski reported that there were a number of sorcerers in the district, and in each village one or two men were known to practise. Spells are learned in return for high payment; as in other instances of transmission, a pokala payment by a sister's son ensures the transmission from a mother's brother, while a father may freely teach spells to a son. One of the striking features of sorcery is that it carries no negative evaluation. Every man may aspire to be a powerful sorcerer. True to Trobriand ascription, chiefs and aristocrats (*guyau*) have stronger sorcery and more sorcerers at their side than commoners, and a chief or headman can openly practise sorcery and may publicly boast of its effectiveness as evidence of his special powers. 'Thus sorcery, which is one of the means of carrying on the established order, is in turn strengthened by it' (Malinowski 1922:76 and cf. 64).

How are we to understand the belief that a sorcerer must launch his career as a genuine practitioner by first committing the 'matricidal act' of killing a mother or a sister (i.e. a close female of his own dala) or 'any of his maternal kindred'? This proposition carries at least two concordant meanings: a once and for all extreme act of violence on a (preferably close) female inside the dala ensures the malevolence being practised thereafter outside the dala (i.e. those with whom he has exchange relations), or again an extreme act of violence committed against a close kinswoman emancipates the sorcerer, so to say, from the realm of close affective kin-feelings and catapults him into 'impersonal' violence against others. Either way, the sorcerer's look is 'outward', not involuted or inward after the primal 'internal' act of violence.

The origin stories of sorcery reinforce the significance of its transmission among males in the present time. Sorcery, as all other malevolent phenomena, is believed to have come from the south, in this instance from the D'Entrecasteaux Archipelago. It entered Kiriwina at two points, at Vakuta Island in the south and in the low-status settlements of Ba'u and Bwoytalu. Here are two brief accounts of the first arrival from the south (Malinowski 1948:105–6). (*a*) A crab arrives in Bwoytalu 'emerging out of a hole . . . or else travelling by the air and dropping from above'. The crab, red in color, gives man his magic in return for a pokala payment; the man kills his benefactor and, according to rule, then kills 'a near maternal relative'. Crabs are black in color now because they have lost their powers of sorcery, and they are slow to die for they once were 'the masters of life and of death'. We may take note of these points: man receives sorcery from a non-human animal by means of an exchange relation; the crab, though non-human, emerges from under the ground and has a long life (near-immortality). In this sense crabs are like the baloma ancestral spirits who also live underground and emerge above, and reincarnate themselves by shedding their skin.[6] (*b*) A malicious being of human shape (*tauva'u*) entered a piece of bamboo somewhere on the northern shore of Normanby Island; the bamboo drifted to a promontory on Vakuta, a man pried it open, and the demon taught him the sorcery. Once again we note a twofold idea: the demon this time travels like a baloma spirit from Tuma on water, and teaches man as an act of reciprocity and reward. We shall have more to say about the non-human malignant spirits (tauva'u) in comparison with witches.

S. J. Tambiah

Witches (yoyova) and flying witches (mulukwausi)

Witches move around at night and it is their invisible doubles that do so, wreaking havoc by direct attack. The witch does not practise a trade compounded of spells and rites. The witch 'can fly through the air and appears as a falling star; she assumes at will the shape of a firefly, of a night bird, or of a flying fox, she can hear and smell at enormous distances' (Malinowski 1932:39). The disease which witches cause is incurable and kills rapidly: 'It is inflicted by the removal of the victim's insides, which the woman presently consumes' (*ibid.*:39). Witches have sarcophagous propensities, and feed on corpses. They can also cause a number of minor ailments – such as toothache, certain kinds of tumors, swelling of the testicles and genital discharge (venereal disease?). Witchcraft is involuntarily inherited by a daughter from her mother.

All these characteristics of a female witch that have been listed stand in stark comparison and opposition to the features that constitute a male sorcerer on the axes of: visible/invisible; normal person/invisible double; external practice/internal transformation; ordinary slowly-killing diseases/sudden incurable diseases; voluntary transmission through exchange/involuntary transmission as heritage; non-cannibalistic/cannibalistic; usually, male attack on male/frequently, female attack on male.

A few features from this array may be selected for special mention. The witch involuntarily transforms her 'insides', a propensity so powerful that it is represented as flying (aerial motion) and virulent attack (malignant disease). Clearly the witch and her powers are projected from the procreative powers of women and the notion of baloma reincarnating and cycling through them. But together with parallels go systematic inversions. The involuntary passage of baloma 'inside' a woman is matched by the involuntary hereditary transmission of witchcraft materializing inside her belly; but while the baloma is born as a child from the womb, the witch attacks and consumes the victim's insides. There is also a topographical displacement: while the baloma emerges from under the ground to become incarnate as humans on the ground, a witch already a human on the ground becomes disembodied and takes to the air. Thus *baloma*, *human* and *witch* belong to the three cosmological realms of under the ground, on the ground, and above the ground (sky).

Mulukwausi

We finally come to the mulukwausi, the flying witches, who are the most malignant agents of witchcraft and whose attributes are magnifications of those of ordinary witches. They are actual living women, who have the power to make themselves invisible and to despatch a 'double' (*kakulu-wala*), which can travel vast distances through the air. They are invisible maurauders who 'perch on trees, house-tops, and other high places' and attack from above.[7] They carry their powers inside the 'belly', which is the seat of emotions and understanding, the storehouse of magic and the seat of memory (Tambiah, 1968), and appropriately attack the insides of their victims. They are associated with the smell of carrion, and on land they are feared when death takes place because they swarm and feed on the insides (*lopoulo*=lungs, also insides). At burial, magic is used to ward them off (Malinowski 1948:129).

The mulukwausi come always from the Southern half of the island or from the East, from the islands of Kitawa, Iwa, Gawa or Murua' (1922:76). The places of origin and the pathways of the flying witches thus follow closely the two kula routes that converge on Boyowa – they are associated with the easterners who come to Kiriwina (and to Vakuta and Sinaketa) from Kitava and more easterly places, and with the Dobuans and other southerners from Amphlett Islands who come to Vakuta and Sinaketa. Within Boyowa itself it is the southern parts (including Wawela on the eastern shore) and certain degraded places that are the points of entry.

But whatever the mythic origins of this witchcraft (which like sorcery came from outside on the seaways), current Kiriwinan beliefs clearly portray their own women as capable of being witches. The most salient feature of these beliefs is that Kiriwinan women can gravely endanger the safety of their men at sea on kula voyages by transgressing certain taboos.

Thus a critical theme for this essay is that the mulukwausi are especially dangerous at sea. They look out for prey whenever there is a storm and a canoe is threatened. Men who have been subject to such danger have affirmed that they became conscious of the smell of carrion, a sign of the presence of these evil women.

The mulukwausi conception intersects with the conception of male sorcerer *via* the notions surrounding the tauva'u, the non-human malig-nant spirits which, as we have already seen, are the original transmitters of sorcery knowledge to men.

The flying witches and the tauva'u share the capacity to unleash sudden virulent disease. The flying witches cause sudden diseases, which show no perceptible symptoms and cause quick death (Malinowski 1922:76 and 237–48). Epidemics are attributed to the direct action of tauva'u who too are invisible to human beings and 'walk at night through the villages rattling their limegourds and clanking their wooden sword clubs'. They strike humans with their wooden weapons and make them die on a massive scale of leria and other epidemic diseases. During the severe

179

S. J. Tambiah

dysentery that occurred in 1918 many Kiriwinans reported hearing the tauva'u.

This epidemic (probably influenza?) was seen as the retribution for the killing of a giant lizard by a man of Wawela village – because the tauva'u sometimes change into reptiles and then become visible to human eyes. A reptile of this sort should be placed on a high platform and valuables placed in front of it, an injunction that is similar to that concerning how both chiefs and baloma (when visiting during the *milamala* festival) are to be treated on ceremonial occasions. A final piece of useful information is that 'a number of witches are said to have had intercourse with tauva'u and of one living at present this is positively affirmed' (Malinowski 1948:109).

So, while tauva'u give their sorcery knowledge to men, they copulate with witches; and in their ability to emerge from the ground as reptiles or snakes they are like the baloma – underground creatures who shed skins are also immortal. But while baloma are incarnated through and in women, the tauva'u behave like human husbands towards malevolent women in having sexual intercourse with them.

Malinowski was correct when he observed that Trobriand beliefs towards disease and death 'form an organic whole'. Our description and analysis show that notions surrounding disease, death and danger form an interrelated set and involve an intricate set of contrasts and linkages between *four* conceptions: the male sorcerer, the female witch (and especially the flying witch), the non-human tauva'u malignant spirits, and the human baloma ancestral spirits. Their interrelations already discussed are now summarised in a single diagram (Fig. 1).

The myth of the flying canoe of Kudayuri

Although Malinowski stated that he knew of three versions of the Kudayuri myth, yet he gave the full text of only one, and we for the most part do not know how the versions differed.

The reader of this essay should read the myth text in *Argonauts* (pp. 311–16).

The main sequences of the story are as follows:

Mokatuboda of the Lukuba clan and his younger brother Toweyre'i live in the village of Kudayuri in Kitava with their three sisters (who are later described as yoyova). The whole group had emerged from underground, and are the first possessors of the *ligogu* (adze) and wayugo (creeper) canoe magic.

The men of Kitava plan an overseas kula expedition.
(Kitava is a raised coral island. Its inland part is elevated to a height of about 500 feet. Cf. Scoditti, this volume.)

180

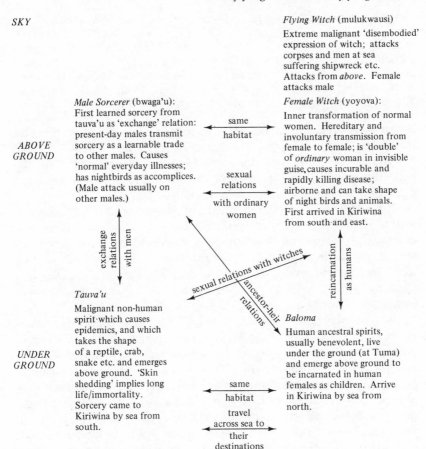

Figure 1

The ordinary Kitava people build their canoes on the beach.

Mokatuboda and his Kudayuri people build their canoe on the hill in the middle of the village.

The ordinary Kitava people launch their canoes in the ordinary way.

The Kudayuri canoe, through Mokatuboda's magic, is launched from the middle of the village and reaches its destination by flying; it starts late but arrives first at each destination.

Later there is a drought in Kitava. The gardens are burnt up and crops fail. Mokatuboda uses his magic to provide a private cloud and a private rainfall which fertilizes his garden exclusively.

Toweyre'i thinking he has learned all Mokatuboda's magic kills him, with the assistance of his subclan brothers and maternal nephews.

Next year another kula expedition is planned and the canoe building proceeds as before with Toweyre'i in charge of the Kudayuri canoe builders. When he uses his magic the canoe fails to fly. The dead Mokatuboda has not passed on the essential magic to Toweyre'i. The three sisters are then angry and fly away as witches, cutting through rocks, and following flight paths analogous to that of the magical canoe, and similar to those that would be taken today by kula fleets starting from Kitava. They eventually become named rocks in named locations.

I shall be primarily concerned with certain implications of the myth integral to the theme of flying witches and flying canoes. The full value of a myth can be established only by relating its internal pattern to the patterns embedded in the other myths of the Trobriand corpus but I cannot undertake such a structuralist analysis here.

My method of interpretation consists of comparing and contrasting the mythic events (the actions of the mythic heroes) with the *social norms* of everyday life incumbent on present-day Trobrianders, and with the patterns of the *canoe magic* that are also practised today and alleged to stem from the Kudayuri myth. In other words, I will attempt to squeeze out meaning by dialectically relating this myth to two other domains, that of extant social norms and that of magical practices.

The first half of the myth is arranged as a repetitive contrastive enumeration of the activities of the Kudayuri group and the other villages of Kitava. These activities range from the sequential procedures of canoe building with emphasis on *parallel* tasks being done in *different* locations (*village* versus *beach*), followed by the kula exchanges at the *same* geographic sites but attended by *differential* success, this difference being dramatically described in terms of the *later departures* of the Kudayuri group but their *earlier arrival* at destinations. It would appear that this repetitive and contrastive arrangement of the events explores the semantic implications of dislocation and displacement of the normal categorical ordering of space and time, and the normal synchronization of ceremonial activities. In the canoe building both groups synchronize their activities, but the Kudayuri group enact them in the *wrong place*. Next, the usual custom in kula expeditions that the canoes depart and arrive as a fleet at the same time (with no doubt precedence in the procession given to chiefs or other leaders) is contravened by the dislocated timing of sailing and arriving[8]. Finally the ordinary expection that the late departer will also thereby arrive later is upset by the flying canoe – which represents a distortion of spatio-temporal, atmospheric and gravitational realities. This method of generating and talking about extraordinary events and propensities through the distortion or dislocation of spatio-temporal order is formalized in Section IV, which deals with the mapping of the categories of land, sea and sky.

There are other ways in which the myth explores the implications of violence and excesses. Mokatuboda of the Lukuba clan and his brother and sisters in being co-resident in the same village present us with a residential anomaly. The co-residence of mature brothers and sisters carries connotations of violating the norm of brother–sister social distance; indeed it smacks of an 'involuted' incestuous relation between brothers and sisters. One could go so far as to say that the ratio of three sisters to two brothers in itself is motivated: it conveys powerfully the measure of the involution in which the sisters outnumber the men!

This involution of the Kudayuri group – associated with the *village* in contrast to the other villages associated with the open *beach* – is reinforced by the abnormal method of building a canoe. Normally the tree is scooped in the village center (*baku*) where also the component parts are made, and the canoe is assembled and lashed together at the beach, the latter being a public event with many helpers joining in. This two-phased procedure from village to beach where the canoe is assembled is all the more necessary in the island of Kitava, a raised atoll, with a sharp decline from the village on the 'plateau' to the beach down below.

Now this extreme isolation of the Kudayuri sibling group is further marked by their pointed refraining from the obligatory ceremonial proceedings on the completion of the canoe, proceedings which emphasize exchange and reciprocity between villages (or settlements/canoe building and owning groups). These festivities are the *tasasoria* (trial run) and the *kabigidoya* (visit of ceremonial presentation) (Malinowski 1922: ch. VI). The launching is accompanied by the *sagali* distribution of food in payment to the canoe expert and helpers. Some days later the new canoe is displayed to friends and relatives, first in the neighbouring villages, and then in other districts, during which valuables and trade goods are collected for the kula expedition.

The myth conveys a strong impression that the 'involuted' nonexchange relations of the Kudayuri group are the basis for its strong ('excessive') magical powers, and that the proper state of affairs is the *dispersion* and *differentiation* of this group (the separation of brothers and sisters), with the converse implication of its becoming open to relations with the outside world. This outcome necessarily also results in a *weakening* (a partial inheritance) of the original magic in its supranormal potent form.

Let us now face the logic of the fratricide. It seems to me that there can be two readings of this act and its consequences which do not so much contradict each other as depict the two sides of the same coin.

One reading would be that the myth states in a fairly straightforward way that, if it had not been for the fratricide, not only would men still know how to build flying canoes but there would be no flying witches to haunt and ravage the real crews of ordinary real canoes. There has to be a younger brother so that he can inherit from his older brother, but he nevertheless inherits imperfectly what is known perfectly by the elder brother on account of his sin of fratricide. Moreover, since the three sisters also know the perfect magic (innately), the younger brother must cause them offence so that they also depart without revealing the secret. It is the offence of fratricide which converts the three sisters into flying witches, and removes them from being residents of Kudayuri village to the top of Botigalea hill.

The second reading tries to answer why the fratricide took place *in the gardens* and why the victim was, killed 'not by the Kitava men, but by his kinsmen', a problem that puzzled Malinowski (1922:319). The puzzle we have to interpret is this: The Kudayuri group with Mokatuboda as the *toliwaga* and his younger brother and 'maternal nephews' (kada) as the crew, triumphantly return from the kula expedition having bested their rival villages by means of Mokatuboda's adze magic which enables the Kudayuri boat to fly. But back in the village, when Mokatuboda practises evil magic (*bulubwalata*) by means of which rain falls only in his garden while drought destroys the gardens of the other men of Kitava, it is his own kin, his younger brother Toweyre'i and his maternal nephews – not the men of other villages – who kill him. In interpreting this event we should first consider the different ethics associated with kula and with *gardening*. Kula activity is *competitive*, the rivals being the other canoe crews in the same expedition, sometimes individuals in the same canoe crew itself. Thus invidious magic and sorcery are alleged to be practised by rivals against each other: it is the order of the day. If you are worsted in a kula transaction you do not kill your successful rival, you practice sorcery against him. But gardening is surrounded by different canons of interpersonal behaviour in the Trobriands (in contrast to Dobu). Gardening is informed by communal and cooperative norms. In theory a whole garden with an enclosure around it (*buyagu*) is assigned to the care of a single garden magician and it is considered to 'belong' to him; within this collective definition an individual works his own plot (*baleko*). The magician right through the gardening cycle practises magic (not evil sorcery) on behalf of the community of gardeners, with individual gardeners subsequently doing their own supplementary rites (Malinowski 1935 vol.2: 85 and 291–2).[9] At the widest and highest level, the chief and his garden magician practise garden magic for the benefit of all in the district. As Malinowski records elsewhere, *waygigi*, the supreme magic of rain and sunshine, is the exclusive privilege of the paramount chiefs of Omarakana (1927:130).

Hence there is good reason why Mokatuboda, the headman, was killed for practising evil rain magic. The fratricide itself is not so much a public delict as an internal affair of the subclan only, very much in the sense that the sin of Cain was adjudged (Schapera 1955:33–43). The Trobriand attitude is illustrated by Malinowski's account of a court case. A blind older brother killed a younger brother for taking his betelnut and was sentenced to twelve months' incarceration by the white resident magistrate. The natives regarded this sentence as an outrageous injustice because: 'The killing of one brother by another is a purely internal matter, certainly a dreadful crime and an awful tragedy, but one with which the outer world is in no way concerned, and it can only stand by and show its horror and pity.'

The fratricide should also be considered in relation to the norms of succession of dala headship in Trobriand matrilineal society: a younger brother succeeds an older, and when the sibling group is exhausted the succession goes one generation down, starting with the oldest son of the oldest sister. Thus the murderers in the myth are the immediate heir and potential heirs. In one sense then the younger brother succeeds his older brother legitimately as succession rules go. And in fact this seems to be the implication in another version of the Kudayuri myth, fragmentarily reported by Malinowski, 'according to which Toweyre'i kills his elder brother in the garden. He then comes back to the village and instructs and admonishes Mokatuboda's children to take the body, to give it the mortuary attentions, and to prepare it for the burial. Then he himself arranges the sagali, the big mortuary distribution of food', as befits the new head (1922:319; 1927:119).

Both readings of the myth converge on the fact that the younger brother's inheritance of the older brother's magic was *incomplete*. Although Toweyre'i had thought he had received the magic of ligogu (adze), of *kunisaleli* (rain magic), of wayugo (lashing creeper), he was mistaken because his elder brother gave him *only part of the magic*, and this partial magic does not enable the canoe to take off from land and fly. 'Thus humanity lost the flying magic forever' (1927:119). There is no doubt that one of the messages of the myth is that the complete canoe magic of the fantastic kind possessed by the first elder, Mokatuboda, of the Kudayuri group, has been irretrievably lost, with a weakened (and more 'realistic') version being actually transmitted to the next head, a younger brother.

At this point let me make a general proposition which is based on a prior analysis of other Trobriand myths. Trobriand myths appear to use the older brother–younger brother and the older sister–younger sister grids to code different messages. For example, like the Kudayuri myth

S. J. Tambiah

the Tudava–Gere'u myth also starts with the older brother as the first hero who in a sense has both very potent – and by that same token 'excessive' and 'unrestrained' – magical powers, and it is the younger brother who practises and transmits the more 'restrained' and more 'realistic' (i.e. more in accord with known human capacities) magic to the descendants. This is an exemplification of how the theme of 'excess and restraint' runs like a thread through many Trobriand myths. The older–younger sister grid codes a quite different message. It is the older sister who is the more orthodox, keeps food taboos, remains at the geographical center of the subclan, and the younger sister who departs to the periphery and breaks food taboos. The result is that an *absolute* distinction of rank is conveyed to their respective descendants, a possibility that is in line with the rule of residence which disperses sisters. By comparison, the older–younger brother does not code permanent rank distinction, and *cannot do so*, because brothers ideally are co-resident, and the younger brother can succeed the older.

We now come to the theme of the flying witches. The drama of the final section of the myth unfolds in this manner. The three sisters became very angry with Toweyre'i for he killed the elder brother and did not learn in full his magic, particularly that which would make the canoe airborne. They themselves had learned the (complete) ligogu and wayugo magic, they had it in their belly (lopoulo), and in fact they were witches (yoyova) and could fly. I would claim that their refusal to share the magic with their younger brother is the counterpart of their own self-propelled take-off. So from the top of Botigalea hill (an elevated above-the-ground position) they departed on their never-to-return flights.

The women's possession of the magic in their belly and of the powers to fly is in line with the male and female propensities already discussed in Section II. While men learn magic and practise it externally upon the world, women inherit and carry sorcery–magic in their belly and internally transform themselves in the same way as they carry and transmit dala identity. This also accords with the ethnographic fact that if the males in a generation are about to die out, a woman could learn men's magic (even magic of gardening and canoe making); but she would not be allowed to practise it herself, her obligation is to teach it to a male heir when she bore him (1932:48).

Finally, let us pay close attention to the flight of the sisters. The piercing through rocks and creating sea passages is a vivid description of the magical potency contained within witches. A recurring Trobriand theme is how these unattached witches (or elsewhere, dynamic kula heroes) representing fantastic speed and motion are finally stabilized as rocks. Rocks are a representation of immobility as well as permanent

186

anchoring (a positive Trobriand valuation). This stabilization of the witches then allows for their becoming agents for granting (restricted) benefits, and their locations appropriately become shrines for propitiation by kula sailors.

The first sister – Na'ukuwakula – flies west, piercing through and leaving a trail from Dikuwa'i to Simsim; the other two travel south, leaving the pierced seaway *via* Giribwa, Tewara, Kadimwatu, Dobu, Saramwa, Straits of Loma (Dawson Straits) and back to Tewara's vicinity. This detailed geographical indexing is actually a mapping of actual sea routes for kula and other expeditions that are in current use (1922: maps on 50 and 82). The mythic routes then code knowledge of actual sailing routes, though the mythic voyages are much longer than those usually undertaken. A final detail is that one sister facing Dobu becomes thereby a cannibal (Dobuans are cannibals) and the other faces Boyowa and is therefore not a cannibal. This may be interpreted as representing the fact that the Dobuans and Boyowans separated by the divide of cannibalism are nevertheless in a reciprocal relationship (as represented by kula exchange), an idea nicely represented by two sisters sharing ties of kinship but standing back-to-back facing opposite directions and representing disjunctive orientations.

Since for the Trobrianders the eye or the tip (*dogina*) of the myth carries the pragmatic punch, what the myth finally leaves us with is the permanent loss of flying canoe magic, but the existence of flying witches as an experiential reality. What the younger brother had and present-day folk have today is a partial canoe magic, but these present-day humans know for a fact that their womanfolk can under certain circumstances turn into witches, flying with fantastic speed, and wielding a potency for aggressive destruction.

The making of a canoe and its associated magic

The *Argonauts* contains together with the text of the myth of the flying canoe a detailed account of the procedures of canoe construction which are followed through in real-life canoe building. Reciprocally, in real life canoe building there are significant cross-references to the myth. This section is concerned with this feedback relationship between mythical charter and magical performance.

Two important facts should be kept in mind when considering this relationship: canoe making is entirely a male activity, and canoes are male property. Moreover, the distancing of women from the artifact is powerfully expressed in the restriction that 'women are not allowed to enter a new *waga* before it sails'. Yet there is the contrapuntal theme that

187

it is desirable that a canoe perform with the speed, aggressiveness and lightness of a 'flying witch', and in this sense the canoe is viewed as a 'woman'.

Although to the European the Trobriand canoe may look like 'an abortive imperfect attempt to tackle the problem of sailing', 'to the native his cumbersome sprawling canoe is a marvellous, almost miraculous achievement, a thing of beauty . . . He has spun a tradition around it, and he adorns it with his best carvings, he colours and decorates it. It is to him a powerful contrivance for the mastery of Nature, which allows him to cross perilous seas to distant places' (1922:106).

On the lightness and buoyancy of the canoe Malinowski wrote: 'It skims the surface, gliding up and down the waves, now hidden by the crests, now riding on top of them. It is a precarious but delightful sensation to sit in the slender body, while the canoe darts on with the float raised, the platform steeply slanting, and water constantly breaking over . . .' (1922:107).

The reader of the ethnography gets a glimpse into why Trobriand canoe magic invokes the butterfly metaphor, and why crew members imagine themselves to be irresistibly attractive to the partners standing on the shore watching their approach: 'When, on a trading expedition or as a visiting party, a fleet of native canoes appears in the offing with their triangular sails like butterfly wings scattered over the water, with the harmonious calls of conch shells blown in unison, the effect is unforgettable. When the canoes then approach, and you see them rocking in the blue water in all the splendour of their fresh white, red and black paint, with their finely designed prowboards, and clanking array of large, white cowrie shells – you understand well the admiring love which results in all this care bestowed by the native on the decoration of his canoe' (1922:108).

There were some three types of canoes in use in the Trobriands, and the *masawa* was the type used in deep sea sailing. Malinowski observed that up to the present not one single masawa had been constructed without the full observance of the magical rites. He went on to assert that for the Trobrianders both magical rites and technical craftmanship were indispensable, and both acted 'independently', the natives understanding 'that magic, however efficient, will not make up for bad workmanship' (1922:108). We may represent Malinowski as striving to say that the technical and magical operations formed an amalgam, one procedure could not work without being in tandem with the other, and in this sense magic 'regulated', 'completed' and lent a creative and anticipatory dimension to the entire activity of canoe making, which was the first link in the chain of kula performances. Indeed the launching of the canoe and especially the formal presentation visit (Kabigidoya) are in one sense the final acts of canoe building and in another sense the preliminaries to the kula voyage.

The construction of the canoe goes through two main phases. The first phase consists in the lengthy and leisurely process (spanning some months of work punctuated by intervals) of preparing the components of the canoe, usually in the village center (baku); this is the business of the canoe builder (expert) and his few helpers; the canoe expert also performs the appropriate magic. The second phase by contrast is brief (a week or two), characterized by intensive work done on a large-scale communal basis; its principal operations are the transport of the dug-out hull of the canoe and its components to the beach, the piecing together of planks and prowboards, the lashing of the outrigger, and the caulking and painting of the canoe. During this second phase are performed certain kinds of kula (*mwasila*) magic, and rites of exorcism, all performed by the owner of the canoe (toliwaga) or his representative.

Examples of magic of the first phase: ethnographic details

(a) The *kaygagabili* spell, which is uttered to make the log lighter for pulling and also to impart to it great speed, employs these words: 'the tree flies; the tree becomes like a breath of wind, the tree becomes like a butterfly . . .' (1922:130).

(b) The canoe expert, when performing the adze magic, makes several recitations which make explicit references to the flying witches of the Kudayuri myth:

(1) The *kapitunena duku* spell, after emphatically stating that other canoes will be 'waved back' so as not to overtake, invokes the 'women of Tokuna, on the top of Si'a Hill', and ends with the onomatopoetic word *saydididi*, in imitation of the sound made by flying witches (1922:130–1).

(2) The next, even more important, magic performed before the special ligogu adze is used for scooping out the felled log, 'stands in close connection to the myth of the flying canoe'. Let me give three excerpts from the spells (1922:132):

(2.1) 'We shall fly like butterflies, like wind; . . . You will pierce the straits of Kadimwatu (between the islands of Tewara and Umama), you will break the promontory of Saramwa (near Dobu), pierce the passage of Loma (in Dawson Straits) . . .'[10]

(2.2) 'Break through your seaweeds. Put on your wreath (of seaweeds), make your bed in the sand.'[11]

(2.3) 'Bind your grass skirt together, O canoe (personal name) fly.'

189

S. J. Tambiah

Examples of magic of the second phase: ethnographic details

The scene now shifts to 'the clean snow-white sand of a coral beach' where the dug-out canoe and its accessories are being assembled, watched in the case of a big chief's canoe by hundreds of natives.

(a) The rite of *katuliliva tabuyo*, belongs to the kula mwasila magic directed at influencing the mind of the kula partner, and is here connected with the inserting of the ornamental prowboards into their grooves at both ends of the canoe. The canoe owner inserts sprigs of mint plant under the board and while hammering them recites a formula which we may interpret as an act by which the owner 'charms' and 'coaxes' the canoe 'as if it were a woman'. We note in this context that the mint plant (*sulumwoya*) plays an important part in the kula mwasila magic as well as in the magic of beauty and in the recitation of love spells. In contexts of 'charming, seducing, or persuading as a rule *sulumwoya* is used' (1922:135).

(b) The body of the canoe, brightened by its three-coloured prowboards, is pushed into the water: 'A handful of leaves, of a shrub called *bobi'u* was charmed by the owner or by the builder, and the body of the canoe is washed in sea water with the leaves. All the men participate in the washing, and this rite is intended to make the canoe fast, by removing the traces of evil influence . . .'[12]

(c) After washing, the canoe is pulled ashore again for the performance of what is considered the most important technical and magical operation in canoe construction – namely, the lashing with the wayugo creeper of the internal framework of some twelve to twenty pairs of ribs, which help to keep in position the gunwale planks that are attached to the sides of the dugout so as to form the deep and wide walls of the canoe. Of the wayugo creeper, Malinowski wrote these significant words (1922:135): 'It is this alone that maintains the cohesion of the various parts, and in rough weather, very much depends on how the lashings will stand the strain . . . Thus the element of danger and uncertainty in a canoe is due mainly to the creeper.'

The wayugo spell clearly contains numerous references to the flying sisters of the Kudayuri myth. Here are two examples:

(1) After suggesting the 'flutter' of pandanus streamers and the 'foaming' of stormy seas the spell continues: 'Before you lies the sea arm of Pilolu. Today, they kindle the festive fire of the Kudayuri, thou, O my boat. . . bind thy skirts together and fly.' Malinowski notes that this allusion to binding the skirt during flying is to Na'ukuwakula, the oldest of the Kudayuri sisters, and that the main part of the spell then goes on to say how 'Na'ukuwakula flew from Kitava through Sinaketa and Kayleula

to Simsim, where she settled down and transmitted the magic to her progeny.[13] The leading words of this *tapwana* part of the spell are *three places* which in sequence are flown to in an aura of mist and smoke and with the force of a wind eddy: Kuyawa (a creek or hillock near Sinaketa), Dikutuwa (a rock near Kayleula), and La'u (a cleft in the sea near Simsim).

(2) In the dogina, the last part of the spell, the magician again urges the canoe to 'fly, break through your sea passage of Kadimwatu, cleave through the promontory of Saramwa, pass through Loma; die away, disappear . . . cut through seaweed, go, put on your wreath of aromatic herbs' (1922:139). The dogina actually refers to the flight details of the younger two sisters, especially their journey in a southernly direction towards Dobu.

A comment on the relations between the Kudayuri myth and the canoe magic explicitly related to it

An unexpected and previously unseen significance (from the analysis of the myth *per se*) reveals itself when we pay attention to the details of the ligogu and wayugo spells.

We note that no mention at all is made in the magic to Mokatuboda, the oldest brother and original headman of Kudayuri village, who knew how to make the canoe fly by reciting spells, and whose murder led to the actual loss of that potent magic. In contrast, the spells *explicitly invoke the three sisters*, and the details of their flight and the places they pierced are meticulously recounted. In addition, the canoe is addressed as a woman.

We have to make the inference from these facts that it is paradoxically the sisters, transforming themselves without divulging the magic, as if the very withholding fuels their self-transformation into flying agents, who have *become the basis of the speed magic*, which men attempt to imitate and impart to the canoes that they make.

Thus we get a new perspective on the myth itself, if we apply to it the tripartite division of *u'ula*, *tapwana*, and *dogina*. The u'ula, the foundation of the canoe magic *via* Mokatuboda, is irretrievably lost; the tapwana is the main story of the myth; and the dogina which Malinowski translated as the 'end' as well as the 'eye' of the spell or myth, is I believe the 'point' of the text, the part that is historically relevant, and that is 'pragmatically' alive today. It concerns the transformation of the sisters into flying witches, and the *continued capacity of women to do so*, while men really cannot make canoes fly. By this route we arrive at the phenomenological truth, which we have suggested in different words before, that the Trobrianders at some level of experience and knowledge

S. J. Tambiah

are aware not only that canoes cannot fly but also that their magic is a culturally constructed technique that attempts to convey to canoes 'performatively' and 'analogously' an innate capacity attributed to women.

A few insights into the manner in which a myth should be read in Trobriand terms are provided by the magic. The concluding portion of the myth deals with the exploits of the *two younger* sisters; it is the flight of the two younger sisters that covers the longest distance, touches the most number of places, and is recorded in greatest detail. It is no accident that the wayugo and ligogu spells are concerned with the exploits of the sisters, and that they again pay most attention to the doings of the two younger sisters. This magical emphasis tells us what part of a Trobriand myth is to be seen as having the greatest relevance *as charter for current practice*. The concluding part is metonymically and indexically closest to the present. If valid, this proposal gives us a new insight into Malinowski's pragmatic charter theory which escaped him.

Let me next raise a problem (without resolving it) concerning the relation between the Kudayuri myth and related canoe magic. The myth (in the only full version that we have) states that the original flying canoe magic practised by the older brother is irretrievably lost, and that the three sisters refused to impart the ligogu and wayugo magic to their surviving brother. This strictly speaking implies that their magical potency was also lost.[14] But the magical practice, which attempts to recapture the transformed flying propensities of the sisters turned witches, is based on the premise that males can recapture the potency which is peculiarly female (and was not gifted to them). Thus myth and rite stand in a dialectical relation: one states the original power was lost and only a weakened form now exists; the other consists of an invocatory formulaic technique combined with manipulation of substances devised by males to activate a potency which is peculiarly female and inaccessible to them.

IV. A semantic mapping of some Trobriand categories: land, sea and sky

What I present now is a recapitulation of the facts already considered in terms of a tripartite scheme consisting of the categories land, sea and sky.

Land

In certain contexts land signifies the value of 'anchoring' and stability; the depths of the land (beneath the surface, the underneath) is the place of

192

habitation of baloma and tabu (as well as the non-human spirits and various forms of reptiles which shed their skin) who are all long-lived and virtually 'immortal'. The *yams* are also anchored in the garden land considered the 'belly'. Yams, baloma, reptiles all emerge from below onto land surface to manifest themselves. Although land is also the point of origin of spirits that can cause havoc, in an overall sense land is positively valued by the Trobrianders as the resource for gardening and as the place of emergence of tabu ancestors and the traditions and possessions they brought with them.

Sea

In this scheme the sea represents motion, turbulence, speed, upward and downward motion, the state of being 'unanchored' as when travelling in a moving canoe. The association of sea with upward motion (1922:107) is aided by the light buoyancy of the craft and the paraphernalia of sailing: pandanus streamers and prowboards. Stability on sea in the sense of being anchored, or lack of motion for lack of wind, is not a desirable condition. But at the same time turbulence of the sea is connected with shipwreck and disaster. Finally, overseas are where the kula valuables and specialized goods and items, not locally available, are acquired – and a kula journey on sea therefore carries all the positive (and negative) associations of speed, competition, renown, failure and disaster. In the tripartite scheme as a whole the sea is the intermediate and liminal zone. It is concordant therefore that the baloma ancestral spirits travel from Tuma to Boyowa on the sea in a journey from the other world to this world.

Sky

The sky and aerial space represents an even more intensified form of the values associated with the sea – as speed, motion, buoyancy, expanse of vision etc. Trobrianders, especially the garden magicians, watch (aside from the sun and moon) the location and movement of certain constellations of stars which are particularly relevant for the calendrical calculations of lunar months and gardening schedules (1922:68 and 221; Austen, 1939). Shooting stars dramatically represent motion in the sky. Of course the flying of birds represents for the Trobriander aerial motion at its best: hence the vast symbolism associated with reef herons (which skim over the surface of the sea at great speed), parrots and parakeets, and various other birds that are carved on the prowboards of Trobriand canoes,[15] and are also invoked in canoe magic and in myths.

S. J. Tambiah

(Interestingly, the night birds – owl, night-jar etc., are considered accomplices of sorcerers, while of course flying witches can also sometimes turn themselves into night birds of prey).

Let me at this point briefly bring into focus (1) the theme of *flying canoes* and *flying witches* and their *necessary* interconnection in Trobriand thought and (2) the theme of *shipwreck* in kula expeditions, because I want to propose a hypothesis as to how both themes represent a certain kind of conjunction in the sea–sky–land categories already outlined.

In Trobriand thought the witch who 'peels off her skin' (*inini wowola*) and transforms herself into a disembodied 'inside' is the epitome of uncanny speed. Trobrianders fantasize their own kula canoes as flying through the air like flying witches.

The mulukwausi as we have seen are 'black' in color, and can take the form of flying foxes, night birds, and falling stars (1922:320 and 412–20).

The canoe urged to fly is actually painted in three colors with black as dominant, and black substances, together with materials light in weight, are used for special effect in the three magical rites of exorcism staged when a canoe is built. And as noted earlier, the adze (ligogu) and creeper (wayugo) magic, which attempt in part to impart the speed of a flying witch to the canoe, do explicitly refer to the Kudayuri myth of the flying canoe and the flying witches.

But there is a certain inversion in the comparison between flying witch and flying canoe. Being women the flying witches cannot build canoes or sail them; but they transform themselves and fly through the air which men cannot do. Thus the man's canoe magic is an exteriorized activity performed on a manufactured object, and this cultural action, so to say, corresponds to the fact that a flying canoe, difficult to create, is a much valued productive enterprise, while a flying witch, not difficult to become in actual life, is a highly feared and disapproved manifestation.

However by another twist in the logic, shipwreck is a point of conjunction where the flying witch at its most malevolent and potent form attacks a 'flying canoe' at its most weak and exposed state of falling apart, its own component parts breaking loose from the lashing creeper which integrates them and themselves turning cannibalistic.

It is clear that, if we study in particular Malinowski's account of shipwreck (1922: ch. X), and place it side by side with his other scattered accounts of sailing and attitudes towards the sea, we could draw a chart representing the different realms spanning sky and sea, the positive and negative features associated with each realm, and the magical 'substances' (and associated spells) used to counter the dangers experienced at sea.

194

Figure 2 plots the dangers and positive features associated with the sky, surface of the sea, and underneath the sea (in a vertical gradient), and the magical operations, especially the substances, used in countering sailing dangers. We may note that *all* three levels on a vertical gradient from above to below – above the sea (sky), surface of the sea, and underneath the sea – are, by the very nature of the sea as an unstable domain, associated in general with motion and speed, and in their negative aspects, with turbulence, instability, danger, violence and disintegration. Of the three levels, the turbulence of the sky of course is taken to be the most dangerous and violent during a storm.

The time of sailing on overseas expeditions is relevant to the actual occurrence of storms. The Trobrianders preferred to do their sailings in the calm periods between the seasons – especially November and December or March and April, or in the time *when the monsoon blows* from the northwest or southwest (usually in the hot summer months from December till March). On the one hand Malinowski correctly noted that much of this sailing was safe: 'Taking the bearing by sight, and helped by the uniformity of winds, the natives have no need of even the most elementary knowledge of navigation' (1922:225). But on the other hand, the very lightness of the masawa canoes and their general fragility combined with poor navigational skills did constitute a real danger when unexpected storms were met with at sea during a monsoon period: a rough sea or a strong wind may drive the canoe into a quarter where there is no landfall to be made. 'Or in stormy weather, it may be smashed on sandbanks, or even be unable to withstand the impact of waves . . . in rough weather, a waterlogged canoe loses its buoyancy and gets broken up . . .' (1922:228). In actual fact accidents were comparatively rare.

A shipwreck in semantic terms is the *unwanted conjunction* of sea and sky at their most turbulent – the meeting point of cosmological and spatial categories previously kept apart: when sky and sea meet so to say, there is also generated in this collapsed space, storm, rain, wind, mist and so on. Similarly, the flying witches also represent the meeting of sky and sea: the flying witches descend from up above on to their helpless victims bobbing on the sea, accompanied by shrieks which are the howling winds. The canoe on the other hand is the victim of the conjunction – when turbulent sea lifts it up to jam it against the collapsing sky crushing it by that conjunction.

There is yet another important conjunction (and paradox). According to both myths and local beliefs a large number of the sea passages, straits between land masses, cleavages in rocky promontories – all important points on the actual kula routes of today – were forced open by flying witches, so powerful and speedy was their motion. Interestingly these

Figure 2. Spatial levels of sea and sky and their attributes

Spatial levels	Negative/dangerous features	Magical substances to counter danger	Positive/helpful features
SKY (Above the sea)	Flying witches, flying foxes, nightbirds, balls of fire, fireflies, shooting stars. Storms, rain, strong winds. (The dangers of the above are worse than the dangers of the below) (1922:246)	Various systems of 'mist magic' (*kayga'u*): bespelled lime from gourd thrown into the air to blind flying witches etc. and to make sailors invisible (*giyorokaywa*)	Moon and constellations such as Orion, Pleiades useful for calendrical calculations; also moon's qualities of whiteness, light, roundness, etc. of positive symbolic value. Small and light sea birds e.g. *manuderi, kidikidi* invoked in spells (1922:253)
SURFACE OF SEA	The falling apart of the mast, ribs and other parts of the canoe, and their becoming eaters of humans	Wild gingers (*leyya*) charmed, chewed and spat to keep danger at bay.	The outriggers lost at shipwreck as floats to hold onto; seaweed as floating substance (associated with baloma)
UNDERNEATH THE SEA	Attackers/eaters of drowning sailors: sharks, poisonous fish (*soka*), stingaree, spiky fish (*baibai*), crabs, seaworms; 'jumping stones' (*vineylida* or *nu'akekepaki* (1922:246) The giant octopus (*kwita*) 'traps' a canoe and holds it fast from moving.	Charmed 'binabina' stones to sink/hold down sharks and sea animals; also mist magic to make the shipwrecked sailors invisible (*giyotanawa*) (The 'mist magic of the underneath' is associated with the dog of the Lukuba clan)	*Iraviyaka* fish (also called *suyusayu*) invoked in *kaytaria* spell to carry the shipwrecked on its back to the shore

196

same stories also recount that witches end their flying careers by becoming the opposite of speed and motion, namely petrified humans i.e. immobile rock outcrops. These rocks represent then the frozen residue of the preceding violent contact between sky (aerial beings), sea and land.

I should like to use the notion of *conjunction* between semantic spaces or categories that are usually kept separate, to add a point or two to the theory of liminal space as developed by Edmund Leach, Claude Lévi-Strauss, and Mary Douglas. The structuralist view is that since the world out there is a flux and in continuous process, man in his cultural garb imposed on this flux a classificatory grid which introduces discontinuities; the intervals or spaces that divide the categories then become ambiguous, sacred and tabooed.

I wish to suggest a classificatory perspective that accords with Trobriand mental dispositions and proclivities; it gives the structuralist formulation a new twist.

It is my sense that Trobriand thought actually operates on and manipulates the classificatory system in such a way that categories already separated are then collapsed or brought into conjunction, so that these meeting points are viewed in themselves, or as sites, for heightened manifestations, extraordinary events, and highly-charged 'excessive' acts. In support of this proposition let me briefly allude to two examples relating to the grid land–sea–sky. The sea is a 'middle' domain between land surface on which humans live and move, and the sky in which they do not normally move. Humans sail on the sea, but sailing is an 'unanchored' and buoyant experience of upward and downward movement, capable of variant expression between the poles of windless calm and fearful storm.

Although land, sea and sky are in ordinary Trobriand experience separate categories and phenomena, yet they clearly also meet:

(a) The meeting point between land and sea is the beach and shallows (and creeks). In ordinary life it is significant that this is the place where women become impregnated by baloma spirits who have come floating from Tuma; this event of procreation is normal and desirable (for married women) and expected as an everday fact.

It is no surprise then that the same site is chosen for the emotionally charged, violent and tabooed copulation of brother and sister described in the Trobriand incest myth (1932:ch. XIV). Three successive copulations take place in shallow sea, beach, and in the grotto located on the coral outcrop between beach and village. Out of this union was produced the most potent form of love magic.

(b) The meeting point between sea and sky in everyday Trobriand experience is either the horizon or the much reduced shapes of the not too distant island of Kitava (seen from the eastern shore of Boyowa), and of some of the Amphlett Islands (seen from Vakuta). In normal times these islands are points reached on kula and other journeys, and where exchange of valuables and goods is effected. But the shipwreck is the violent and catastrophic conjunction that may occur on a kula voyage. At this junction is released the full force of the elements, and the cannibalistic attack of flying witches from 'above' and of creatures from 'below' the sea. It is the site at which men sailors are drowned, dismembered and sucked by the undercurrents of the sea, and where also the victims (and heroes wielding excessive magical powers) become petrified as solid immobile rocks, landmarks for the kula voyagers.

The Trobriand classificatory operations could perhaps be cast in Saussurean language, especially in terms of his distinction between the arbitrary or conventional nature of 'signs' and the motivated nature of 'symbols'. For Saussure the notion of the *value* (*valeur*) of a sign is a function of its position in an associative network, of paradigmatic and contrastive relations existing between all the signs in a set: 'Language is a system of interdependent terms in which the value of each term results solely from the simultaneous presence of the others' (1966:114). Now for Saussure a *symbol* by contrast was motivated in that its signifier-signified relation was deliberately intended to represent, what he called a 'natural' (that is, appropriate in terms of 'content') relation, as for example when a pair of scales is chosen to represent justice. The Trobriand mode of thought employs the motivated 'symbolic' operations of collapsing and bringing into conjunction, of colliding and conflating, differentiated terms or 'signs' in an associative network so as to generate heightened meanings that are considered excessive in terms of the social norms of everyday conduct and/or extra-ordinary in terms of achievements possible in everyday life. This is a Trobriand way of thinking about moral issues, the limits and boundaries of conduct, the circumstances leading to excessive conduct, and the qualities of 'heroic' achievements (together with their nemesis of death or abandonment).

Acknowledgement: I thank Deborah Tooker for drawing my attention to certain details of Malinowski's account of canoe magic.

Notes

1 Although Annette Weiner (1976) mentions that men too can be considered to be witches, it is clear that witches are predominantly, indeed almost always, female.
2 *Contra* Annette Weiner (1976) I prefer to see women's wealth as associated with female 'sexuality', particularly the colored skirts (festively worn by young women) and the banana leaf bundles out of which skirts are made. The plain

natural-colored skirts worn on soot-blacked bodies in the mourning period appropriately signal the depression of sex during that time. So it is appropriate that women's wealth is distributed to the mourners, thus releasing them from further affinal ties and obligations of mourning and restoring them to an active sexual life.

3 This is one of the concerns of many Trobriand myths e.g. those relating to Kudayuri, Kasabwaybwayreta, Tokosikuna, and Tudava.

4 For Malinowski *tama* was in Trobriand terms 'husband of my mother' (1932: 6); he was 'not regarded as of the same bodily substance' but nevertheless stands in a close emotional, legal, and economic relation to the child' (1932: 518). Lounsbury's componential analysis (1965) of Trobriand terms gives 'father' in the genealogical sense as the 'primary meaning' of tama.

E. Leach, in line with Malinowski, glosses tama as 'a domiciled male of my father's sub-clan hamlet' (1958). It is interesting that despite distorting Malinowski at the very beginning of his analysis, Lounsbury makes this sociological assertion as stemming from his linguistic analysis: 'What emerges in the Trobriand case is the clear priority of the husband–wife solidarity unit over that between brother and brother, or between sister and sister, or between mother's brother and sister's son.'

5 I refer here to that description of the flying witch as a woman who leaves her bed by shedding her grass skirt and taking to the air, and the correlated belief that the way to frustrate her is to cover her pubes with her grass skirt.

6 In so far as the crab is described as flying through the air and dropping down, it is being assimilated to the description of a malevolent flying witch, or more accurately, of a baloma-like under-the-ground creature who then has the extraordinary power to fly as well, like a flying witch.

7 Malinowski was not very consistent in his accounts of the relationship between yoyova and mulukwausi, though variant accounts never resulted in flat contradictions. In one place for instance (1922:236) he gave the following gloss: the most dreaded danger for the Trobrianders on an expedition was 'the flying witches, the *yoyova* or *mulukwausi*. The former name means a woman endowed with such powers, whereas *mulukwausi* describes the second self of the woman, as it flies disembodied through the air.' Moreover we note that in moments of great fear, 'the deprecating euphemism – *"vivila"* (woman) would be used' – for fear of attracting the flying witches by sounding their real name.

Although the canonical account says that the mulukwausi sends a double, Malinowski also reports that there are other beliefs which state that the flying witch sometimes 'travels bodily', and sometimes takes the shape of black night birds etc.

8 I mean for example here that the first canoe to touch shore is that of the *toliuvalaku* who receives his ceremonial gift from the partner; thereafter the other canoes can transact with their partners, the toliwaga having precedence over his crew.

9 Rain magic is dala property and is not competitively practised so as to ruin others; and one of the bases of chiefship is that a chief practises rain magic on everyone's behalf. In contrast canoe magic (as opposed to *kula mwasila* magic which is public property and widely accessible) is dala property, and can be competitively practised to outdistance or undo a rival.

199

S. J. Tambiah

10 This is a reference to the actual path travelled by the two younger Kudayuri sisters when they transformed themselves into flying witches.

11 Malinowski's exegesis of this portion of the spell can be improved, by referring to his own ethnography documented in *Argonauts* (pp. 150–1) on human decoration. The natives decorate themselves with large red hibiscus blossoms stuck in their hair and 'wreaths of the white, wonderfully scented *butia* flowers crowned the dense black mops'. The canoe is described similarly as wearing wreaths of seaweed when it is bleached.

In both the ligogu and wayugo spells the canoe is told to 'break through seaweeds, put on wreath and make bed in sand'. The erotic uses of the *butia* wreath are documented in *Sexual Life of Savages* (pp. 254–5). The *butia kayasa* (competitive activity) occurs at the flowering of the *butia* tree which coincides with the milamala festival: this occasion evokes erotic activities and provides opportunities for courtship (*ibid.*, p. 255). Interestingly, butia wreaths are exchanged ceremonially with the blowing of conch shells and these exchanges are called kula; indeed, Malinowski reports that the terminology of kula is used in these exchanges. Here definitely kula exchange between male partners is brought into juxtaposition with courtship and erotic exchange among male and female youth, and the same attribute of beauty and irresistibility is transferred to the kula canoe.

12 The following allusions will I think help us to further understand the symbolism of washing the canoe.

(1) The washing of the canoe reminds us of the importance of body washing and rubbing with leaves in the sea when performing love magic (1932:365fn), or in fresh water when performing beauty magic (1932:351fn); also to be remembered is the final beautification of the kula sailors by washing in seawater with leaves (*silasila*) and by painting themselves at the final halt before meeting their partners (1922:335). These associations convey the idea that the canoe is being 'beautified' by washing.

(2) Secondly, we are reminded of the rites of birth. A new born baby is bathed regularly in warm (fresh) water, with which the mother also washes her own skin, in order to 'keep the skin of the mother and child white'. And most interestingly a witch is believed to wash its new born child *in sea water*, and then to show it to other witches. Thus these associations convey the idea that the canoe is also viewed as being a 'new-born infant', and is washed in sea-water just as a witch does to her infant, and is ceremonially presented to the relevant community.

13 We should note a discrepancy here; according to the myth itself she turned into a stone (1922:315) but in this exegesis Malinowski gives the variant report (1922:138) that she settled down and transmitted the magic to her descendants.

14 Though the myth states that the flying witches were turned to stone, we know that flying witches are believed to exist in the present, and that witches transmit their potency to their daughters on a hereditary basis. Hence the conclusion that the male canoe magic is an attempt to convey to their canoes attributes which they believe are possessed by females.

15 See *Argonauts*, chs. IV and V; Seligmann (1910).

8   Kula in Vakuta: the mechanics of keda

SHIRLEY F. CAMPBELL

In *Argonauts of the Western Pacific*, Bronislaw Malinowski (1922) presents to the anthropologist a picture of an exchange system that is 'simple'
at its operational level, but complex when viewed in association with its
other activities.

> From the concise definition of Kula . . . we see that in its final essence, divested of
> all trappings and accessories, it is a very simple affair . . . After all, it only consists
> of an exchange, interminably repeated, of two articles intended for ornamenta-
> tion . . . Yet this simple action – this passing from hand to hand of two meaning-
> less and quite useless objects – has somehow succeeded in becoming the founda-
> tion of a big inter-tribal institution, in being associated with ever so many other
> activities. Myth, magic and tradition have built up around it definite ritual and
> ceremonial forms, have given it a halo of romance and value in the minds of the
> natives, have indeed created a passion in their hearts for this simple exchange.
> (1922:86)

Malinowski's 'concise definition' portrays kula as exchange of an extensive inter-tribal nature. This fundamental exchange involves two types
of shell valuables which pass in opposing directions around a closed
exchange circuit, never stopping. Men's actions are regulated by a
convention to receive, to hold for a short period, and to pass on.

According to Malinowski, the 'extensive, inter-tribal character' (1922:
81) of kula links men together in networks of partnership that extend
beyond their own social community. 'On every island and in every village
a more or less limited number of men take part in Kula' (1922:81).
Further, Malinowski tells us that '. . . a partnership between two men is a
permanent and life long affair' and that a principle of '. . . once in the
Kula, always in the Kula' (1922:83) is fundamental to the exchange
networks set up. In Malinowski's description of the exchange, when a
transaction has been completed between two partners (i.e., the original
giver receives a 'counter-gift' of equivalent value to the initial 'gift') the
partnership does not terminate. He tells us that partnerships are perma-

nent and men can only kula with their life-long partners, notwithstanding a certain potential for dissolution of the relationship: 'If the article given as a counter-gift is not equivalent, the recipient will be disappointed and angry, but he has no direct means of redress, no means of coercing his partner *or of putting an end to the whole transaction*' (1922:96; my emphasis).

Malinowski does not provide a detailed analysis of kula at the transactional level. He focuses his analysis on myth, magic and tradition and thus directs his monograph to a description of these as they relate to kula. As a result, Malinowski develops certain themes about the nature of kula which in some ways correspond to the ideology of kula as expressed by the Trobriand Islanders, but realised by them as something quite different.

The Kula is not a surreptitious and precarious form of exchange. It is, quite on the contrary, rooted in myth, backed by traditional law, and surrounded with magical rites . . . As to the economic mechanism of the transactions, this is based on a specific form of credit, which implies a high degree of mutual trust and commercial honour . . . Finally, the Kula is not done under stress of any need, since its main aim is to exchange articles which are of no particular use. (1922:85–86)

A half commercial, half ceremonial exchange, it is carried out for its own sake, in fulfilment of a deep desire to possess. (1922:510)

The Kula is thus an extremely big and complex institution, both in its geographical extent, and in the manifoldness of its component pursuits. It welds together a considerable number of tribes, and it embraces a vast complex of activities, inter-connected, and playing into one another, so as to form one organic whole. (1922:83)

During the early part of this century anthropologists were concerned with how 'primitive' societies held together as cohesive entities. Contributing to the pioneering of anthropology, Malinowski concerned himself with putting kula in the context of myth, magic, and tradition in *Argonauts of the Western Pacific*. He stated that kula was basically a 'simple exchange' which was also a means for stimulating and coordinating other socio/cultural activities. This paper, while acknowledging the latter, attempts to look in detail at the operation of the kula transactions, and in so doing presents a somewhat different picture of the 'simple exchange' to that presented by Malinowski in 1922.[1]

Meanings of keda

In this paper I propose to look at inter-community[2] exchange and the operation of *keda*. Keda (road, route, path, or track), is used literally in the context of kula to describe the route along which kula shell valuables are exchanged.[3] However, the word keda is used in other, less literal contexts which give expression to the various 'paths' along which partici- pation in kula leads.

In one sense keda can refer to the linkage between and ultimate network of men involved in kula. On Vakuta it is recognised that every man participates in kula[4] and maintains keda on either side of him, with men of Kitava to the east and men of Gumasila (the Amphletts) and Dobu to the south-west. This is a different state of affairs from the situation on Omarakana as described by Malinowski in 1922, where only a few, high-ranking men participated in kula. On Vakuta people conduct their affairs on a more egalitarian basis than that of Omarakana and other parts of Kiriwina Island. Although the Vakutans recognise someone they call 'chief', this man in fact has few extra advantages over anyone else in the community. This is especially true in the context of kula, where all men have equal opportunity to gain power and influence within the village. In addition, no Vakutan can set up a partnership keda with another Vakutan because to do so would not only endanger the apparent cohesiveness and tranquility of Vakutan society, but also nullify the *raison d'être* of kula. Kula is, I suggest, a highly competitive exchange.[5] But the real competition is not focused at the inter-community level, i.e. Kula communities vying for prestige with each other. Instead, competit- ion is at the intra-community level with Vakutan men setting up keda relationships outside their own communities. The keda can be viewed as an alliance between men from different social environments who work together to accomplish power and influence for each member of the keda within his own social environment.

Inter-community partnerships are not stable and life-long relation- ships; on the contrary, they are highly unstable by virtue of intra- community competition. Men break up partnerships, set up new keda, or reinstate old relationships in response to opportunities for enhancing personal power and influence within their own community. The insta- bility of inter-community partnership, however, will become clearer following a description of the mechanics of kula transactions. My purpose here is to introduce the proposition that an external keda partnership is an alliance that must be understood in terms of intra-community com- petition.

Another use of keda is that it provides a route for trade and external, non-kula relationships. Kula is valued because of the opportunities for setting up trade routes to enable one kula community to procure exotic materials from other kula communities. Although this trade is no longer essential in the Milne Bay, exchange of exotics between communities still occurs to some degree. From Kitava, Vakutans can obtain baskets of a different shape and weave to those made on Vakuta. From the D'Entre-casteaux Islands they procure ochres, wild banana seeds, aromatic leaves, medicines to ward off sorcerers and witches, as well as woven mats made of a high quality pandanus leaf. The kula keda likewise provides an opportunity to establish liaisons with women in other kula communities. According to many male informants on Vakuta, every kula man has relationships with women from Kitava where armshells are obtained, and with Dobuan women from where his necklaces are obtained. While on Kitava in May 1977, I had the opportunity of meeting several of these young girls and women. It is said by Vakutan men that there are many Kitavan and Dobuan babies of these liaisons.

This introduces a further connotation for the word keda that refers to the 'fun and play' aspect of kula. A synonym for kula is *mwasawa*, meaning fun or games. Mwasawa is applied to two aspects of kula. One is the sexual liaisons referred to above; the other is to the outrigger canoe used to carry kula men to their partners' islands. Everything concerning the outrigger canoe; the building, re-lashing, painting, and sailmaking is regarded as 'fun' and carried out in anticipation of the joys of sailing it. It is interesting to note the similarity between the words mwasawa (fun, play), and *masawa* (kula canoe, but not the ordinary fishing canoe).

Keda is further conceptualised as the route to wealth and power. It is through the manipulation of keda at the operational level of kula that men compete for power and influence within their own social milieu. Contrary to Malinowski's impression that shell valuables, as regarded by the natives, 'are supremely good in themselves, and not as *convertible wealth*, or as potential ornaments or even as *instruments of power*' (Malinowski 1922:512; my emphasis), the armshells and necklaces are indeed 'convertible wealth' and used as 'instruments of power'. From the vantage point of Vakuta, it is quite clear that shell valuables can be fed into the internal exchange system[6] as wealth items, thereby securing other wealth in the form of yams, magic, land, and women. The degree to which a man can manipulate his kula keda, and consequently the internal exchange networks through his wealth in the form of shell valuables, determines his status in the power play of local politics.

Finally, kula provides the keda to a man's immortality both within the community and outside it. If in his lifetime a man successfully operates a keda that runs for several complete cycles, not only does he enhance the wealth of the shell and the fame of the partnership through which it passes, but his name becomes associated with the history of the shell for as long as it remains in the kula ring. However, to gain immortality is by no means an easy task, given that other kula men are also manipulating the system to gain similar ends. To maintain a successful keda requires a man's shrewd assessment of the kula environment in the immediate past, present, and future, an understanding of the possibilities for keda manipulation and the inherent dangers that lie therein, as well as a certain degree of luck.

Thus far, I have discussed the various meanings to which Vakutan men apply the word keda; the path of external partnership, trade routes, the route to fun and play, and the path to power, fame, and immortality. In this way, keda is an important concept to the Vakutans for understanding the ramifications of kula. However, keda is also applied to kula in its more literal sense; the route a shell valuable takes as it is exchanged around the 'ring'.

Playing the 'game' of kula involves men in a multitude of choice-situations. Each man who handles a shell in the kula makes choices about relationships with other men, relationships with shells, economic and political relationships, and advantage-situations for a man's individual gain. Kula also involves each man in a gamble, resulting from the potential choices available to other men outside his influence. In the following, some of these choice-situations will be discussed.

The mechanics of keda

There are three separate stages to each keda, which are illustrated by *vaga, basi and kudu*.[7] Vaga refers to a shell which initiates a keda; basi is a shell or shells attracted into a keda periodically between the inception and conclusion of the keda; and kudu refers to the shell that concludes the keda. The three stages of a keda cycle are differentiated in character and intent. The initiating (vaga) and concluding (kudu) stages define and qualify relationships, while the intermediary (basi) stage affirms them. These terms are described in detail below and illustrated in notional form in Figure 7 of the Appendix (p. 221).

The first stage effectively opens a keda with the gradual passage of a shell around the ring, forging a route of partnership alliance. The shell given at the outset of a keda is called vaga. Its purpose is to form a new kula relationship between men so that other shell valuables can pass between them. Vaga theoretically refers to a shell that has had all previous keda relationships completed and is therefore 'free' to initiate new keda exchange obligations. However, this is not always the case.

There are three main ways in which a shell can be acquired for potential use as vaga. First, the payment (kudu) for a pre-existing vaga to the man who started the keda can be recycled into another keda as vaga (Figure 1).

In Figure 1, A has initiated a keda by sending a vaga which links B to D

Shirley F. Campbell

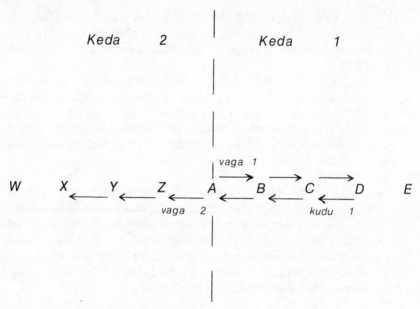

Figure 1. Acquiring vaga through the repayment of a previous vaga.
Note: 1. A. B. C. etc. = individual kula communities
2. *kuda* 1   = *vaga* 2
3. If *keda* 1 is clockwise, then:
    vaga 1   = shell necklace
    kudu 1   = armshell
    vaga 2   = armshell

in a partnership. D receives the vaga and decides to keep it for other purposes. To do so however, he must make an equivalent payment for the vaga and therefore sends a kudu back along the keda. A receives the kudu with which he uses to open another route, by reclassifying it as vaga. This creates a new keda, this time with X, Y, and Z.

A second way in which a man may acquire a shell that he can pass on as a vaga is through the internal exchange system. On Vakuta there are several of these exchange cycles which use shell valuables as one of the wealth items to be exchanged. For example, if a man is to sponsor a *sagali* (distribution of food, skirts, etc.), a wife's brother may contribute by giving his sister's husband a pig; i.e. *dodiga bwala*. The man who has received the pig (ZH) must repay his wife's brother with a shell valuable; i.e. *takola*. Once received, the shell valuable is called by the new owner *kitoum*,[8] which signifies that it can be used either for further internal exchange obligations, or it can be re-admitted to the external exchange cycle as vaga (Figure 2).

206

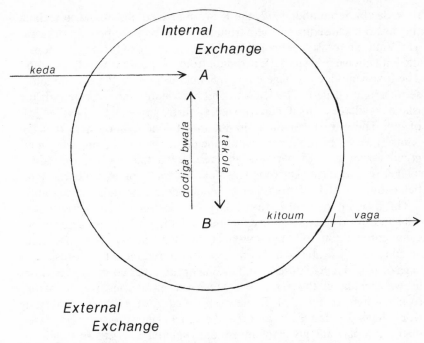

Figure 2. Acquiring vaga through intra-community exchange.

In Figure 2, A receives a pig as dodiga bwala in an internal exchange from B. A receives a shell valuable through his external keda and gives this to B as takola in payment for the pig. B now has a shell valuable which he calls kitoum and decides to use it in external exchange as vaga.

The third way in which a shell valuable can be classified as vaga is when its keda is changed in mid-route (Figure 3). Strictly speaking, shells taken from existing keda should not be called vaga. Vaga refers to a shell whose past exchange commitments have been completed thus enabling it to forge a new keda. Whereas, in the case of a shell redirected in mid-route, its commitments have not been finalised, yet it is being used to create a new keda. A shell that is redirected from an existing keda can cause problems between men because it leaves behind dissatisfaction on either side of the man responsible for the re-direction.

Changing keda is a common practice in kula today, and is said to have been responsible for many deaths by sorcery in the past. Once a shell has been redirected, there is little chance for the previous keda partners to reclaim it. For example, while visiting Kitava Island in May 1977, a Vakutan successfully persuaded (*ririvala* in Vakutan or *wawoyla* in Dobuan) a Kitavan into giving him a *mwari* (armshell),[9] thereby changing

207

Shirley F. Campbell

its keda. In September 1977, the Kitavan arrived on Vakuta to reclaim the mwari because his partners from the old keda were proving difficult. The Vakutan refused to cooperate. On the evening of the first encounter the Kitavan tried to steal the armshell from the house where it was kept. The following day a village court was held to resolve the dispute and a serious fight ensued. The Kitavan and his friends were escorted off the island by village council men who feared further violence or possible loss of life. The mwari remained on Vakuta. Public opinion held that the Kitavan was to blame for the whole incident. He was the one who in his greed forgot his old partners and redirected the mwari to obtain a 'bigger' *vaiguwa* (necklace).[10] The Vakutan was exonerated because his behaviour was that of any other kula man merely trying to attract kula.

This incident introduces one of the prime destructive characteristics of kula and illustrates the ability for individual initiative, and an area not commented upon by Malinowski (Figures 3 and 4). It is not clear whether the Kitavan (D in Figure 3 and 4) had redirected the armshell as vaga or basi. He had described it as one or the other according to whom he was speaking; those through which the mwari had passed before reaching him, or those of the new path (*kedavau*). His own behaviour would have decided the matter if and when a vaiguwa were to be passed up the new path and given to him either as *mapula* basi (Figure 3) or kudu (Figure 4).

Mapula (payment) basi is the return of the basi (see below page 222).

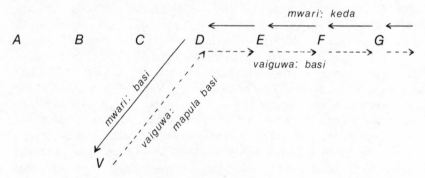

Figure 3. Acquiring basi through manipulation of keda.
Note: 1. ⟵——— = *mwari*
      2. -----▸ = *vaiguwa*
      3. A to G   = intended *keda*
      4. D to V   = new *keda*
      5. D   = Kitavan (re. text)
      6. A, B, and C receive nothing; E, F, and G
         receive payment for their *mwari*.

Were he to treat the shell necklace as mapula basi he would pass it on to the next member of the old path (E, F, and G in Figure 3) from which he received the armshell. D of Kitava should have passed the mwari to C where it would have continued along the correct keda. However, D gave the mwari to V in anticipation of a prize shell necklace. In so doing A, B, and C are severed from the D to G portion of the keda. E, F, and G were worried about losing an armshell and thereby the shell necklace that it would attract back to them. However, D (as illustrated in Figure 3), makes the choice of remaining in a keda relationship with E, F, and G by sending in that direction the shell necklace that he received as mapula basi for the armshell.

An alternative choice for D is to treat the vaiguwa as *kudula*[11] and thus a final payment for the mwari he re-directed in the first instance (Figure 4). The keda of A, B, and C remains disrupted in the same way, as was evidenced in the foregoing example of choices available. However, if D classifies the shell necklace as kudula (of the armshell), E, F, and G are also liable to have their keda disrupted as well as A, B, and C because D declares the vaiguwa his valuable (kitoum) and gives it a new keda by redirecting it along a path as vaga.

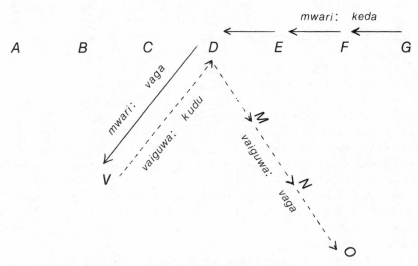

Figure 4. Acquiring vaga through manipulation of keda.
Notes: 1. ⟵——————— = *mwari*
      2. —————-➤ = *vaiguwa*
      3. D   = Kitavan
      4. A to G   = intended *keda*
      5. V, D, M, N, O = new *keda*

In the two examples of choices available to D resulting from his initial decision to change a shell's keda, A, B, and C are severed from any kula relationships with E, F, and G through D., It is unlikely that A, B, and C will kula with D again unless D initiates a keda relationship. Even then it is probable that tension and distrust would remain in their relationship as a result of D's previous behaviour. As concerns E, F, and G, there may be contrasting reactions depending upon which choice D makes. In the first choice D retains the keda relationship with E, F, and G by passing the shell necklace to them in payment for the armshell. However, until D passes a shell necklace to E, the E, F, and G portion of the old keda may have their doubts as to the 'good' intentions of D in upholding their kula. They are aware of the choice available to D of initiating a new keda by sending a shell necklace which he receives in payment for the armshell they gave him (and that he passed to a new man) along a route not including them.

When a vaga is passed on to a new member of the keda, he is told the route by which it has come and what valuable it is trying to attract or 'marry'. He is told where it started and how the original owner acquired it. He may ask, 'Did it come from Gawa?' and the reply may be, 'No, it came from within Iwa', which would tell him that it has passed through an internal exchange and was therefore kitoum. If, on the other hand, he is told it is from Gawa, he works back along the route it has come to determine its point of origin and how it came to be vaga. In this way men of a keda learn the history of a valuable and whether there is any discontent associated with it, or whether all obligations connected with it have been fulfilled, thereby making its handling 'safe'.

A vaga opens up a new route and as it is kula'd links men in its keda. Men linked through a vaga are then in a position to handle the flow of valuables that a vaga attracts to its keda (members); providing the collective interests of all the men in the keda are directed towards its maintenance and stability in response to each individual's desire for local power and influence.

A vaga is sent out to attract a mate and as it is exchanged between communities it forms a route linking men into its keda. As it is passed on, it attracts other valuables into its keda, which are passed back along the route, giving the partners in the keda a flow of wealth while awaiting the final transaction, or kudu. This flow of wealth into and through an operating keda is distinguished as the middle stage of a keda cycle. The transactions that occur during this stage are called basi and mapula basi.[12]

One example of the use of basi is when members of a keda pass valuables back along the route to let those who wait for payment of the vaga know that the keda is still open and that the alliance has not been broken. When the keda is considered 'alive' members will continue to pass intermediary valuables along the route when they are attracted into it as a kind of investment. When it is considered 'dead', because valuables have not been passed back for an extensive period of time, members will begin to set up or feed other keda. In this sense, the basi is described as 'cleaning the way', or cleansing the minds of the members so that they continue to patronize the keda (*biwini* keda, i.e. it will wash the route; *bimigilieu*, i.e. it will be clean and clear).

The other use of basi views it at an angle to the keda. At points along the keda, others outside the partnership may be attracted to a valuable passing along the keda and basi it with the opposite valuable (see Figure 5).

In this Figure, D and F (members of one keda) both hold shell necklaces which are being passed through the keda. X and Y (outside the keda) want the shell necklaces for reasons of enhancing their own keda (thereby their individual prestige), and/or to fulfill external or internal exchange obligations (see pp. 204 and 217). Therefore, X and Y basi D and F by giving the latter armshells. D and F then pass the armshells back along the keda and in so doing, contribute to the stability of their keda (A-G).

The basi puts D and F in one of two possible exchange relationships with X and Y respectively. Firstly, the exchange can be merely reciprocal; i.e. X gives D an armshell and D gets a payment (mapula basi) from C to give to X, thus completing the transaction and the exchange relationship. Secondly, D may break off his keda relationship with E, F, and G (and possibly with A, B, and C) and Kula with X in a new keda relationship (see Figures 3 and 4).

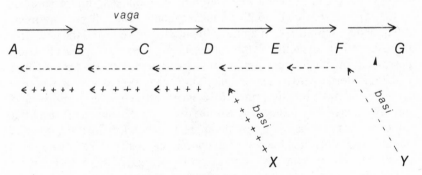

Figure 5. Attracting a shell in another keda through basi.
Note: 1. ———————➤ = *vaiguwa*
      2. ◄ — — — — — — = *mwari*
      3. ◄ + + + + + + = *mwari*
      4. A to G   = *keda*

Men trying to redirect valuables from a keda may be men with whom one already has another keda relationship. For instance, D and X may be members of one keda. X will try to convince D that he should be feeding their joint keda rather than the keda linking D to A–G. D may make a choice between the keda A–G or that which he shares with X according to which one offers him the most success in external and internal exchange.

According to the rules, all basi must be repaid. This is called mapula basi. Accumulating too large a basi debt can be dangerous if one cannot at a particular time manipulate all contacts to fulfill the basi payments. If I, a Vakutan, have a 'big' mwari and a Dobuan gives a vaiguwa to basi it, I would not want to repay the basi with the armshell basi'd because I may have in mind a specific shell necklace I want in return for the 'big' armshell, or a specific keda on which the armshell should pass. However, I want the shell necklace to feed into my keda. Therefore I send the shell necklace to Kitava with a message to find quickly an armshell to mapula basi. If the mapula basi is not quick enough in arriving, I may be obliged to relinquish the 'big' armshell in payment for the basi and as a result upset any other obligations and sound kula planning I may have had. Further, if I were to accumulate several basi debts at once, I may find that I am unable to handle the flood of creditors when they arrive expecting mapula basi, a situation which would jeopardise my kula standing both inter- and intra-communally. Further I may not be able to attract other keda through a proven inability to handle my and others' kula affairs by being unduly greedy.

The middle of a keda cycle is a highly unstable phase for the continuity of the keda. It is the time between the vaga and the closing transaction, when members of the keda wait and depend upon each others' shrewdness and competence in handling kula exchanges. The collective interests are dependent upon each member's loyalty to the keda and the necessity to resist other attractive offers of basi. As the time lapses after the passage of the vaga, members become anxious that the final transaction will not materialise to close the cycle. They may begin to wonder whether they should transfer allegiance to a more attractive proposition and 'break' the keda by redirecting a valuable to another keda. During the middle of a cycle, a keda may dissipate and break before the cycle is closed. Therefore it is necessary to continually feed the keda whenever possible to keep the membership in a positive frame of mind. It should be noted, however, that a keda attracting valuables to it is thereby taking valuables from other keda. A man usually has several keda operating simultaneously and the concomitant option of re-routing valuables from one to another. However, he does this at great risk to his standing in the disrupted keda, his career in kula, and perhaps his life. To be successful in kula, a man has to understand the ground rules for kula, and the full range of possibilities in the exchange. He has to be able at any given time to juggle the intra- and inter-community exchange relationships he is tied to, as very often these are, at any given time, in conflict with each other. Keeping an equilibrium between kula keda and internal exchange is by no means an easy task.

The transaction that closes a keda cycle is called kudu.[13] Kudu is strictly the payment of the vaga. When a kudu reaches the origin of a keda from which the vaga started, any kula belonging to a keda is said to 'die' (*ikariga*) and with it the partnership alliance. The man who issued the vaga has kudula (bite/payment of vaga) with which he can give another keda, feed into an existing keda, basi a valuable from another keda, or use it to fulfill internal exchange obligations. The man who sent the kudu has the vaga for which he can likewise decide its future. Men in between pursue other keda set up through basi exchanges from the now deceased keda, or those other keda that were operating during the lifetime of the now completed keda.

The passing of kudu back along the keda is an ambiguous act in the minds of the keda members. To repay the vaga is in one instance 'good' and desirable, but in another 'bad' and undesirable. The kudu is good in that it relieves the debt that all in the keda sustain while it is 'alive'. However, the principle motivation for men to form keda alliances is to kula, i.e. to hold and pass as many kula valuables as possible during the lifetime of a keda. Kudu signifies the end of this movement of shell valuables through members of a keda and hence the end of a keda partnership. An example of an attempt to keep a keda 'alive' is illustrated in Figure 6 and in the following discussion.

Sawekuku from Gawa received an armshell named Tomadava through an internal exchange. He converted it into vaga and began its keda by giving it to Isaac from Kitava. Isaac gave Tomadava to Kunabu in Vakuta, who gave it to Anton in Dobu, who gave it to Alfred in Duau where it was when I recorded the keda's progression. Alfred (Duau) took the necklace called Gerubara and gave it to Anton (Dobu) as basi, with the implicit message that he wanted the keda to live and not die with only one transaction, providing all other members were agreeable. However, as Gerubara was equivalent in value to Tomadava and thus an appropriate kudu for Tomadava, Alfred (Duau) thought he had better hold on to Tomadava in case Sawekuku (Gawa) and the others of the keda membership decided to take Gerubara as kudu of Tomadava and thus end the kula keda. Anton (Dobu) gave Gerubara to Kunabu (Vakuta), who gave it to Isaac (Kitava), who gave it to Kelabi of Iwa (a new member in the keda), who gave it to Sawekuku (Gawa) where it remained. Sawekuku,

year

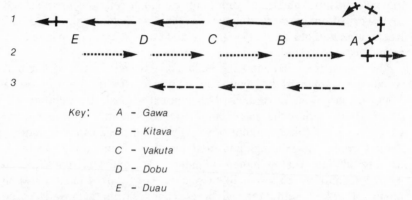

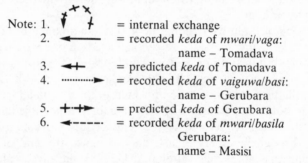

Key:
A – Gawa
B – Kitava
C – Vakuta
D – Dobu
E – Duau

Figure 6. The recorded *keda* of Tomadava.

Note: 1. = internal exchange
2. ◄——— = recorded *keda* of *mwari/vaga*:
name – Tomadava
3. ◄—+— = predicted *keda* of Tomadava
4. ············► = recorded *keda* of *vaiguwa/basi*:
name – Gerubara
5. +··+► = predicted *keda* of Gerubara
6. ◄-----· = recorded *keda* of *mwari/basila*
Gerubara:
name – Masisi

realising that Gerubara could be considered kudu of Tomadava, was somewhat confused by the term basi given to Gerubara by Alfred. He wondered where the kudu for Tomadava was. He held on to Gerubara as potential kudu of Tomadava until he could find out. He did this by sending another armshell called Masisi as mapula basi for Gerubara to let the keda know that he was willing to keep it alive and consider Gerubara a basi instead of kudu. The mwari Masisi was in Vakuta when I recorded its keda. It was subsequently passed on to Anton when he and other Dobuans came to Vakuta in November, 1977 to kula. I was told that once Masisi reaches Duau, Alfred will release Tomadava to continue making its keda and attracting other valuables to its membership, while Gerubara will be released from Gawa to attract basi down the keda.

In the above example, each man in the keda initiated by Tomadava is clearly waiting to see what the intentions of others in the keda are. Sawekuku from Gawa and Alfred from Duau each act with reservation. A rash play could endanger the stability of the keda and hence the

214

potential awards to gain from an extensive flow of wealth along a stable keda. Further, were Sawekuku to send Gerubara on to attract mwari to the keda he started with Tomadava, without waiting to assess the intentions of other keda members, he may find that Alfred of Duau had decided to keep Tomadava to put to other uses of no favourable consequence to the keda through which Tomadava passed. In this case, Sawekuku would clearly have acted foolishly in letting Gerubara go so easily without knowing the full intentions of others, because he would not get another kudu for Tomadava to perhaps invest more profitably in kula.

The kudu marks the end of a keda cycle by relieving the debt contracted by the vaga. However, there is a means by which the keda may be revitalized should a keda membership so desire. This is done in two ways. Firstly, together with the kudu, another shell valuable may be passed back along the keda. This shell will be called vaga. This form of revitalisation reverses the direction of debtor/creditor to the one that existed previously. An alternative means by which a keda is revived is by calling the kudu *kunuireira*, which signifies that the keda lives. Each member expresses his desire to keep the membership together as he passes it one step back along the keda as kunuireira.

When a man receives a shell valuable which is of equal value to the original vaga, he is told that keda members, in the direction from which the shell valuable came, want the keda to remain 'alive' and have thus been calling it kunuireira. It is discussed with the new owner and decided whether he likewise wishes to kula with the men of the keda. When he passes it further along the keda he repeats the message and a further decision is reached. This process continues back along the path until it reaches the origin of the keda. The man who sent the original vaga keeps it as his kitoum but sends another shell down the keda as kunuireira/vaga and the keda is reborn. This method of revitalising a keda does not reverse the vaga/kudu, or creditor/debtor route but maintains the order in which the keda has flowed in the past.

Sending a kudu with a vaga does in effect kill the keda of the shells, but re-opens simultaneously the membership of kula men. Whereas the kunuireira keeps alive the keda of the shells and the partnership alliances.

The three main stages of a keda cycle and the linking process embodied in kunuireira can be described as a reflection of the life cycle as it is perceived by Vakutans. The vaga can be viewed as signifying the inception of a keda, the birth of an alliance between men. The path of the vaga progressively unites men and instills life into a new keda through which men are able to kula. The basi nurtures the growth of the keda, feeding the alliance with shell valuables that preserve the life of the keda and contribute to the accumulation of history to the shells involved. Growth of the keda stimulates a concurrent growth of economic and political power for each individual member of the keda in his own social environment. Growth in a keda is measured by the quantity and quality of shell valuables attracted to the keda as basi. Basi, continually moving through the keda, enable the vaga to complete several cycles around the 'ring', perpetually attracting more basi into its path. The quantity of valuables that pass through a man's hands in a keda also enables him to participate in the internal exchange obligations of his own community, thereby advancing his social standing. Once a shell valuable succeeds in 'biting' a vaga, the death of a keda is imminent. The kudula, or teeth of the vaga, signifies the death of the keda. Kudu is payment for the vaga. Once paid, the debt conceived by the vaga is closed, and with it all movement through the keda gradually ceases as all intermediate debts created by the basi are satisfied.

In Vakutan ideology death is not necessarily final. All yams do not die after each successive yam harvest; some go on to reproduce themselves annually when they are replanted for the following year. Schools of carving do not necessarily cease with the death of a carver, provided that he has passed his *sopi*[14] to an apprentice. The *dala* (subclan) is not destined to become extinct providing there are women to reproduce for that dala. Although biological death occurs to individuals, spiritually they remain alive on the 'spirit' island of Tuma and within the succeeding generations of the dala as their names are recycled into the dala and reborn into new generations. Similarly in kula, the keda may undergo a rebirth through the linking kunuireira (see Appendix, pp. 222–5, and Figures 7 and 8).

The operation of a keda cycle, incorporating vaga, basi, kudu, and kunuireira can be perceived in three ways. These exist not as separate models, but as a continuum between two points dependent upon the degree of idealisation and simplification one incorporates in describing the operation of keda.

According to formal rules governing external exchange, the operation of a keda can be described as an apparently simplistic model. After numerous attempts by Kitavan and Vakutan men to explain how keda operates, I reiterated as simply as possible a model of a keda as I understood it from their explanations. When I had finished I was told I had perceived their descriptions accurately but that these were not entirely representative of true keda operations. This model was a means by which they could simply inform others so as to readily facilitate understanding. It involved the vaga, basi, kudu, and kunuireira regularly moving backwards and forwards in a single keda. A keda is at some point in time conceived through a vaga. As it constructs its path and eventually completes its first cycle around the 'ring', men are locked into its keda. On its future cycles it passes through the same hands[15] and meets shell valuables moving in the opposite direction. Malinowski's dictum 'once in the Kula, always in the Kula' (1922:83) clearly applies to this simple model of an operational keda cycle. Today however, few would accept this as the *modus operandi* of kula. Vakutans say that the simple model of kula would not satisfy the needs of kula men and communities. Continual passage from hand to hand of the same shells on a perpetual keda does not appeal to the imagination of the adventurous 'argonauts of the western Pacific'.

A second model, logically derived from the more formalised rules of keda described above, presents what Vakutans consider to be a more satisfactory framework upon which external exchange should be conducted. The ideal here is to pass as many different shell valuables through the keda for as long as the alliance survives. With respect to the aims of kula, general stability of male alliances is a desirable objective for all concerned. A useful analogy may be derived from the card game bridge where a definite advantage exists for those who play successively with each other over those who continually change partners. The temporal continuity of a bridge partnership fosters easier communication between the members even though the rules of the game only allow an indirect communication. Further, a long-lasting partnership facilitates more indirect communication and understanding of a non-verbal nature. Likewise, relatively stable keda partnerships aid individual members' easier interpretation of the verbal and non-verbal actions of other members. In this way a 'good' keda partnership may gain an advantage over other, less manageable partnerships in the ritualised battle for economic and political power in an individual community.

Although it is desirable for membership of a keda to remain as stable as possible they cannot be content to handle the same set of shell valuables over and over again. 'We want to taste all the famous mwari and vaiguwa.'[16] Again, the aim of kula as perceived by Vakutans is to be understood primarily in a local political and economic context. Access to a quantity of different shell valuables allows greater opportunity for a man to compete in his social milieu while at the same time maintaining a degree of stability in his various keda relationships. If he were to kula perpetually with only one set of unchanging shell valuables, he would be unable to fulfill internal exchange obligations where shell valuables are circulated as wealth items. To do so would severely cripple his and the keda memberships' kula, because the keda could not then attract other shell valuables to it as these would likewise be locked in other keda. A modification of the simple model of keda activity as described above occurs when one factors in the possibility of attracting other shell valuables to a keda from other keda, thus creating a perpetual movement of shell valuables between keda. However, this modification leads us to the opposite point of the continuum to that with which we began and the operational realities of a keda. The third model is derived more from observation than from informants descriptions of the keda and its operation.

Relatively speaking, the acquisition of shell valuables rarely comes from fresh resources; i.e. the sea-bed. Instead men acquire shell valuables from other men; either a keda partner or a man belonging to another keda. Shells passed through keda partners are usually acquired from other men belonging to different keda. On the other hand, men release shells from their keda to another keda. One reason for this is to gain another, possibly 'bigger' shell to feed into your keda so as to keep the partnership alive. The danger then lies, however, in the inability to receive payment for the shell before the keda members in the direction from which the shell came grow impatient. They also have exchange obligations to fulfill. Further, partners on the side to which the shell should have been passed are angry and suspicious of one's intentions. The result is that the keda is in serious danger of breaking and the vaga to go unpaid. This state of affairs was illustrated in Figs 3 and 4 where D forfeited any relationship of trust existing between his keda partners. On either side of D, his partners would, in future exchanges, hesitate or deny him any shell valuables; their actions stimulated by his redirection of a shell valuable to V along a new keda, thus perpetuating a relationship of mistrust between them. A good kula man can manipulate many keda partnerships and redirect shell valuables to different keda because he has been able to develop a relationship of trust between himself and his keda partners.

The successful keda consists of men who are able to maintain relatively stable keda partnerships through good oratorical and manipulative skills, and who operate as a team, interpreting one anothers' movements. Nevertheless, many keda collapse, regularly making it necessary for men to re-align themselves. Some form completely different keda, while the remnants of a broken keda may want to form another keda by drawing in new men. Yet others may never kula again because of their inability to form another keda owing to a reputation for 'bad' kula activity. In reality, the population of shell valuables in any one keda is migratory and the social composition of a keda transitory. A shell's accumulation of history is retarded by continual movement between keda, while men's claims to immortality vanish as shells lose association with these men after being successfully attracted into another keda, thus taking on the identity of its new owners.

Not only can keda be disrupted and alliances broken, but other forces can operate against its smooth operation.

Vakutan society is linked through a variety of exchanges which seemingly permeate every level. A person does not form just one exchange relationship with another, but may in fact have several different exchange responsibilities with one or a number of people. In these relationships each type of exchange underlines quite different feelings towards the relationship and reinforces various social attitudes. Shell valuables acting as the currency of kula are present in many of these internal exchanges and performing the same role. Further, internal and external exchange systems seem to be modelled similarly, in that one wealth category (food – yams, taro, bananas, pig, etc.) moves in one direction while the other wealth category (valuables) moves in the opposite direction.

Men have to participate in internal exchanges. In order to successfully fulfill their obligations, they have also to participate in kula, from which they obtain wealth items for internal exchange. However, the operation of one is disruptive to operation of the other. The disruptive quality of internal exchange is illustrated by the inability of men to put back into the external exchange system that which was taken out for use in the internal exchange system at a given time.

In an example given above, the exchange of pig for a valuable is a one-way activity; pig $\rightleftharpoons$ valuable. The exchange is closed with payment of takola (shell valuable) for the pig. What has happened is that to be able to complete the exchange opened by the pig-giver, the receiver had to take a shell valuable, either passed to him from a keda partner, or acquired through basi, and give it to the pig-giver (WB). With this exchange completed, there is no further transaction between WB/ZH in relation to this particular exchange. In other words, at the time that this internal exchange took place the transaction was opened by giving a pig and closed by repaying with a kula shell valuable. No further transaction is built into this particular internal exchange to enable the pig-receiver (ZH) to obtain a shell valuable and thus replace the one he took out. The ZH's kula is temporarily disrupted until he can obtain another shell valuable either through an internal exchange in which he is the recipient of a shell valuable or from another keda.

According to the rules of external exchange, a shell valuable must be put back into the external circuit if the ZH is to kula again and, by extension, further enable him to participate in internal exchange. A temporary antipathy between the two systems is circular. A man has to participate in one if he wants to participate in the other. However, participation in the internal system temporarily places extra stress on the external system. The debts a man makes by participating in the internal exchange can easily multiply beyond control. By taking a shell out of the external exchange and putting it through the internal system the participant has created a temporary void, in that the wealth he receives from the latter is not transferable to the former. Therefore he will either have to manipulate the internal exchange system so that he receives a shell valuable for other wealth he has given or he will have to take a shell valuable from another keda to repay the source of the lost shell. However, in choosing the latter action he has created another debt in the external exchange system, and so it goes on. Successful participation in both internal and external exchange requires a continual balancing of the two as well as an ability to recognise available choices in the exchanges and manipulative opportunities when they arise.

To Malinowski, the kula which he observed during the second decade of this century appeared as an entertainment to the Trobriand Islanders. The charm of kula resided in the myth, magic and tradition surrounding it; the exchange was only a 'simple affair'.

Instead of being a 'simple exchange', today's kula, as discussed in this paper, is a finely balanced affair. On Vakuta, kula is used as a means by which Vakutan men compete for power and influence in their local political and economic spheres, resulting in the inter-community exchange, kula, being subordinated to the more important intra-community competition.

Appendix

Figure 7. A simplified kula keda [see p. 221].

This figure describes a hypothetical keda, and is intended to illustrate the major details of keda operation as they were discussed in the preceding text and Figures 1 to 6. My intention to illustrate a keda in operation through time and space has necessarily resulted in a certain amount of simplification. For example, a keda does not consequentially elapse in $2\frac{1}{2}$ years following inception; it can be shorter or longer according to particular circumstances. Nor would the depiction of a real keda be as neat as the notional keda illustrated here, because in reality there may be many individuals involved, each acting in accordance with particular life histories.

The format of the diagram is organised along two axes. Firstly, the horizontal axis illustrates a temporal sequence in months, and kula expeditions occurring between different communities and individuals at different times over a $2\frac{1}{2}$ year span. For example, during months 1 and 2 of

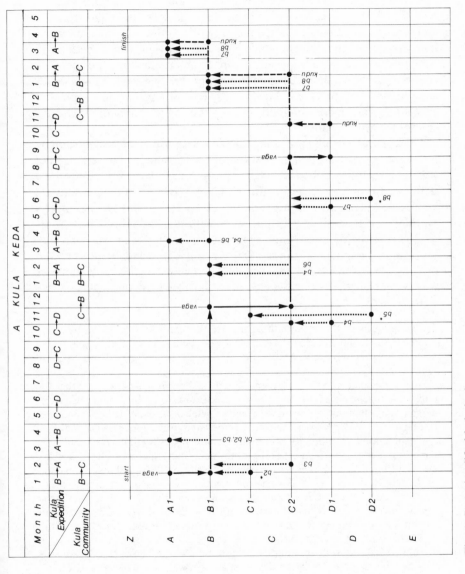

Figure 7. A simplified kula keda.

221

Shirley F. Campbell

the 1st year, individual B1 from community B makes a kula expedition to both communities A and C, resulting in a vaga being elicited from individual A1 and basi from individuals C1 and C2. In the 3rd and 4th month A reciprocates a kula visit to B and elicits not only basi from C1 and C2 but an additional basi from B1 himself, and so on. The timing of a kula expedition generally depends upon wind direction and whether the community to be visited have already made an expedition to the alternate community. For example, community A probably would not Kula with community B until B has kula'd with community C, etc. Typically, expeditions are made annually but can be made more often if other conditions are favourable.

The vertical axis illustrates the spatial relationships between communities involved in a particular kula keda. A, B, C, and D represent distinct kula communities linked through a particular keda. E and Z are kula communities not involved in this keda. A1, B1, C1, C2, D1, and D2 represent kula men within communities A, B, C, and D respectively who are involved directly or indirectly with this keda.

If A to B to C, etc., is anti-clockwise, then the solid line, or vaga, represents the movement of a mwari or armshell, while the dotted and broken lines, basi and kudu respectively, indicate the movement of vaiguwa or shell necklaces. The keda illustrated in this figure is described below.

The keda starts in the 1st month of the 1st year with an expedition by community B to community A. B1 receives a vaga (solid line) from A1 and takes it home to B. At this time community B makes a further expedition to community C.

Two men from community C, men C1 and C2, have heard of the vaga that B1 holds. They each attempt to influence B1's decision as to whom the vaga will go in their shared community by giving B1 vaiguwa (shell necklaces). This is called basi (dotted line). Basi 2 and basi 3 (b2 and b3) are later given to A1 when he makes a kula expedition to community B in months 3 and 4. Basi 1 (b1) is B1's contribution to the keda. Basi 2 and basi 3 are not necessarily the same shells that B1 received from C1 and C2. However, shells of equivalent value should be passed on. In months 10 and 11 of the 1st year community C makes an expedition to community D. C1 and C2 tell men of community D that they have made basi transactions to B1 who holds a vaga, and that they will soon be making an expedition to community B, each with great expectations for the acquisition of the vaga held by B1. In so doing, C1 and C2 each brag of their potential success in an attempt to acquire from community D more basi with which to lure B1 and his vaga. On the diagram we see that D1 gives a basi to C2, and D2 gives a basi to C1 in response to the formers' pointed suggestions, and potential acquisition.

B1 holds on to the vaga for 9 months, until community C goes to community B on a kula expedition. At this time B1 must decide to whom he will give the vaga and thus link into the keda with himself and A1.

Community C visits Community B in months 11 and 12 of the 1st year. B1 gives the vaga to C2.

This transaction presents several situations that require explication.

(1) Firstly, all basi must be repaid. In the case of basi 2 and 3 (b2 and b3), these are passed back along the keda opened by the vaga: i.e. to A1. Although repayment of basi is not shown on this figure, A1 gives mwari to B1 in payment for the basi he received from community C. The fact that C1 did not succeed in the competition with C2 for the vaga, does not interfere with the basi transaction he made to B1 and its return payment. Once made, any outstanding kula relationship between B1 and C1 is finished. Because C2 receives the vaga, he and B1 are linked in a keda relationship. Nevertheless, basi 3 (b3) given to B1 must be returned.

The asterisk alongside of basi 2, basi 5, and basi 8 (b2, b5, and b8) differentiates these from the other basi which were successful in attracting the vaga.

(2) The situation with basi 5 (b5) is somewhat different. C1, thinking that he would get the vaga, convinced D2 to contribute so as to lure the vaga. D1 gave C1 a basi. However, C1 failed to attract the vaga from B1 and therefore basi 5 is never fed into the keda. Instead, C1 will use the basi for another keda or for internal exchange. He repays the basi to D2 through other means outside the keda we are discussing.

In months 1 and 2 of the second year B goes to C and acquires basi 4 and basi 6 (b4, b6); basi 6 being C2's own contribution to the keda.

Months 3 and 4 of the 2nd year see community A visiting community B and receiving basi 4 and basi 6 (b4, and b6) or equivalent shell valuables.

In months 5 and 6 of the 2nd year community C visits community D. Men of D know that C2 has a vaga and so basi it (b7 and b8) in an attempt to attract the vaga.

In months 8 and 9 of the 2nd year community D visits community C. C2 gives the vaga to D1.

D1 decides that he wants the vaga for an alternative obligation and so sends a kudu back along the keda to pay for the vaga and thus end this keda. A vaga is repaid by a kudu of equal value. In months 10 and 11 of the second year community C visits D and C2 receives the kudu from D1.

Months 1 and 2 in the 3rd year of the keda's life sees the kudu with basi 7 and basi 8 (b7, and b8) moving back the keda between communities C and B.

By the 3rd and 4th month of the 3rd year both basi 7 and 8, together with the kudu, find their way to the origin of the keda with community A. Upon receipt of his kudu, A1 is free to use it as a vaga to start a new keda, repay a basi, use as kudu for a different keda, or a multitude of other choices that may present themselves.

Figure 8. The dimensions of keda meaning [see p. 225].

Key: . A, B, C, and D are kula communities

. A1, A2, A3, and A4 are individual men living within community A.

KI
.⟷ = inter-community (island) keda.

Shirley F. Campbell

. A1......$k1$.....B2......$k1$.....C2......$k1$.....D4 = keda 1 between kula men
A1, B2, C2, and D4;

A3......$k2$.....B3......$k2$.....C2......$k2$.....D2 = keda 2 between kula men
A3, B3, C2, and D2; etc.

. A3-----ks-----B3-----ks-----C2-----ks-----D4 = keda of a specific kula
shell between kula men A3, B3, C2, and D4.

This figure illustrates the multi-dimensional character of keda by showing how the 'keda' (path) can refer firstly to the generalised and well known 'kula ring' as illustrated by the link KI between kula communities. Alternatively, keda can be used to describe the links individual kula men have with men in adjacent communities; e.g. kula man C2 has links with kula men B2 and B3 in community B and D2 and D4 in community D, etc. Finally, the 'real' keda of a shell valuable, as it was discussed in the foregoing, is illustrated. The example shows how, if a kula man (e.g. C2) holds more than one keda (e.g. k1, k2), it is possible for a shell's keda to move between individual keda (e.g. ks is redirected by C2 from his k2 keda to his k1 keda).

Notes

1 It may well be that because of time differences between Malinowski's work and my own on the Trobriands, apparent discrepancies concerning kula have resulted in somewhat different interpretations. Another possible cause for disparities may relate to the fact that Malinowski worked primarily from Omarakana on Kiriwina Island, whereas I had the vantage point of Vakuta. Nevertheless, it does appear from his monograph on kula that Malinowski's prime concern was directed to the 'other' activities that kula encompasses, while I involved myself in the actual exchanges and the observable implications arising out of these. The latter, I would suggest, marks the basic division between my own and Malinowski's interpretations of kula.

This paper is based on fieldwork conducted on Vakuta Island during the period September 1976–January 1978. Fieldwork was supported by an Australian National University Scholarship and Research Grant. I gratefully acknowledge Geoffrey Mosuwadoga and the Papua New Guinea Public Museum and Art Gallery for sponsoring my research in Papua New Guinea and offering assistance during my stay there.

My thanks to Professor Anthony Forge, Dr Michael Young and Dr Howard Morphy for invaluable suggestions and advice; and finally to Dr Paul Ratcliffe for editorial comments and the design of Figures 7 and 8.

I am indebted to the kula communities of Vakuta, Kitava, and Dobu, and

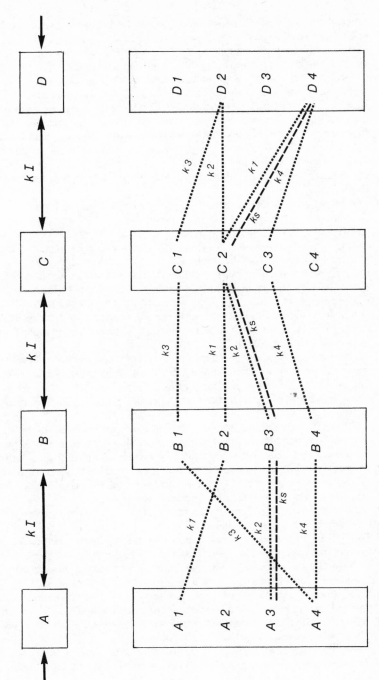

Figure 8. The dimensions of keda meaning.
[For Key see pp. 223–4]

Shirley F. Campbell

especially to Kunabu of Vakuta and Antonio of Kavataria for giving of their
knowledge and insight.

2 My use of 'community' refers to a group of people linked by internal exchange
   systems who kula as a group with other such communities. These communities
   generally correspond to geographical areas, i.e. Vakuta, Kitava, Iwa, Gawa,
   Gumasila, Dobu, etc.

3 As my experience with kula was primarily with the Vakutans, I use them as my
   reference point. However, my brief dealings with the Kitavans and Dobuans
   suggest that ideas held on Vakuta correspond closely to those held in other
   kula communities. Keda certainly seems to be an 'international' construct of
   kula. Throughout this paper I will use only Vakuta as my reference point, but
   this does not necessarily inhibit the extension of these views to other kula
   communities.

4 This I was told is a characteristic of all 'real' kula communities. Every man has
   the opportunity to participate in kula. When I referred to two men who were
   known not to participate in kula, it was pointed out that these men were
   simply 'stupid, rubbish' men. It was emphasised that these two men were not
   married (despite the fact that their ages put them beyond the 'normal' marrying age) because they were unable to attract women as sexual partners,
   except for women socially classified as mentally deranged. To the Vakutans,
   this explained why these two were unable to attract kula partners.

5 Others have suggested that exchange in the Massim appeared to be on a more
   competitive basis than indicated by Malinowski (see Uberoi, 1962; Forge,
   1972; and Brunton, 1975).

6 In this paper I use internal exchange to refer to exchanges occurring within a
   single political/economic community. External exchange is used to refer to
   kula which occurs between communities.

7 These terms are discussed in detail on pages (205), (210), and (213) respectively.

8 A kitoum is a valuable acquired in payment for something given. In this state,
   notions of ownership are invoked in the sense that the valuable 'belongs' to
   the person who receives it in payment; he can therefore do as he likes with the
   valuable. It is interesting to note that although kitoum was not referred to in
   the earlier literature, nearly all recent workers in the Milne Bay Province have
   reported its existence (see other papers in this volume).

9 On Vakuta I learned and spoke their dialect. In this paper the Vakutan rather
   than any of the Kiriwinan dialects is used.

10 Today, the term *soulava* is rarely used when referring to shell necklaces.
   Instead, the word vaiguwa is used. Malinowski glossed vaiguwa (his *vaygu'a*)
   to mean valuables in general. Since I have learned to use vaiguwa in speech on
   Vakuta, I continue to use it here to refer to the kula shell necklaces.

11 Kudu and basi are transactional nouns used in kula. Both can occur in the
   possessive form by adding the 1st degree, 3rd person singular suffix – *la*. In so
   doing, reference is focussed on another shell; the object of kudu or basi.

       vaga → *kudula* (*vaga*) – the teeth of *vaga*

       vaiguwa → *basila* (*vaiguwa*) – its (the *vaiguwa*'s) pierce (*basi*)

   The other possessive form used with kudu and basi is the 3rd degree removed
   possession to refer to a shell belonging to a man:

226

ula kudu – my shell that is the payment of *vaga*

m kudu – your shell that is the payment of *vaga*

12 Mapula means payment, or to pay. Basi means to prick, to pierce, or to sew. The Dobuan word for basi is *rogita*.

13 *Yotile* is another word used with kudu. However, kudu is used to refer to the actual 'bite' of the return payment on vaga, while yotile means payment and refers to a shell as payment for vaga.

14 Sopi literally means water. However, its use in carving terminology refers to distinguishable 'schools' of design used in carving. These 'schools' are passed from a carver to an apprentice who, during his lifetime is entitled to use the designs of his 'sopi' (see Campbell, 1978:1–11).

15 Following the death of a kula man, his keda ideally is inherited by his maternal nephew.

16 I have condensed many statements by Vakutans to this effect into a single sentence which I feel most accurately conveys the intended meaning.

9 Attaining rank: a classification of kula shell valuables

SHIRLEY F. CAMPBELL

Introduction

The exchange of shell valuables in *kula* is the major arena for competition between men of the Massim area in eastern Papua New Guinea. The whole realm of relationships that are defined and differentiated by kula are competitive (see Campbell [Ch. 8, this volume]). This system by which shell valuables are classified and ranked is an index to these relationships and an extension of competition. This paper is intended to contribute further to our understanding of the shell classification system, the criteria by which the shells are placed into categories, the ranking of these categories according to well-defined features, the relative value and relationship between categories, and the means by which certain shells are able to move between categories.[1]

While conducting field research on Vakuta Island (the most southerly island in the Trobriand group), I had the opportunity to travel with and participate in a kula expedition to Kitava Island. I was also able to witness several smaller groups of Kitavans visiting Vakuta for the purpose of amassing shell necklaces (*vaiguwa*)[2] in preparation for a big kula expedition to Iwa, Gawa, Kwaiwata, and Woodlark Island. Towards the end of my stay on Vakuta, a large expedition of Dobuans arrived to kula. During these periods there was ample opportunity to observe and participate in the handling, appraisal, and very visible appreciation of some of the finer kula valuables.

During an encounter between two potential or established kula partners, there are noticeable differences in behaviour and attitude before the shell valuables are openly displayed and immediately afterwards. Before the shells are laid in front of the men their behaviour is jovial. However, when the valuables are presented, the atmosphere changes to one of studied silence. The present owner sits very quietly, suddenly confronted with the reality of his imminent separation from the shell and the accompanying uncertainty as to whether its place will be filled later. He sits quietly, mentally assessing his line of argument concerning the shell and his release of it. The visitor is likewise silent as the kula valuables are laid in front of him. He is also working out a line of argument necessary to acquire the valuable. It is during this period that the shell is critically assessed. The visitor will turn the shell in his hands, noting features which rank the shell in the classification system. If the shell is a *mwari* (armshell),[3] he will hold it for its heaviness. He will turn the shell's back to him and count the number of *buna* (cowrie shells) across its width. He may then place the mwari on his mat with the shell's cut end facing him. He will look at it thus for a long time, taking note of its circumference. When he is satisfied with his assessment of its weight and dimensions, he will look for signs of age, *kala ureri*, or its red striations. If, on the other hand, the visitor is assessing the quality of a vaiguwa (shell necklace) he will hold it along his arm to measure the length of the shell string. He will examine closely the fineness of grinding, the thickness and dimension of each individual shell disc. The vaiguwa is then held at arm's length to assess the colour. Finally, the shell string, held between thumb and forefinger, is run through the hand to determine its most prized quality, the combined smoothness of the ground shell string. If the hand slides along a vaiguwa like oil, or it slips through the hand like a very fine fishing line, it is probably of the highest rank. According to specific qualities of weight, circumference, width, length, and signs of age, Kula shell valuables are thus judged and categorised. In this way, each shell attains rank and is coveted and competitively sought after according to its position within the hierarchy.

The first indication that shells exchanged in kula are classified comes, not surprisingly, from Malinowski. In *Argonauts of the Western Pacific* he states that: 'The necklaces of different length and of different finish have each their own class names, of which there are about a dozen' (1922:199). Although he does not list these 'classes', we do find mention of a few in some of the magic spells related to kula. These are *Bagidou*, *Bagiriku*, and *Bagidudu* (1922:205& 304). None of the mwari classes are named by Malinowski. However, we find that Austen has given an extensive list of mwari classifications:

High-rank mwari:	Muligibagebila
	Mulitaitu
	Tokukua
	Tubatula
	Kaikeketatula
	Kasikeyarakwatola

	Kasikeyaramigumwasila	
	Tupona	
	Tutulu	
Low-rank mwari:	Kauia	(Austen, 1945–6:25)

Apparently, none of these terms correspond to the clasifications I collected, though there may be an explanation for this to which I will return later. Austen's list of vaiguwa classes more closely corresponds to my list, but again there are discrepancies:

High-rank vaiguwa:	Bagiliku	
	Bagidou	
	Bagiyeru	
	Bagisamu	
	Wontia	
	Buduwageru	
	Bagitorobo	
	Taituyanabo	
	Solomoni	
Low-rank vaiguwa:	Rova	(Austen, 1945–6:25)

Main parts of mwari and vaiguwa

Before continuing to enumerate the categorisation and ranking of kula shell valuables, it will be helpful to return to the shells themselves and identify their various parts.

The mwari is produced from shell of the *Conidae* family.[4] It is said to be the male partner[5] in the kula marriage (Figure 1). The rope by which the mwari is suspended and carried is called *kaipwesi*, or more commonly *utunu*. Utunu is a general word for rope. The two *Ovula ovum* shells attached to the kaipwesi are called *lubukaidoga* or rainbow.

The mwari is divided into named parts corresponding to specific features used in classification. Firstly, there is the *dabala* or forehead. This distinguishes the smooth shell area where signs of age can be seen.

Because of its conical shape, the shell has openings of unequal diameter at each end. The greater diameter end is called *pwala*.[6] When manufacturing a mwari, the shell material covering this end is beaten out with a small stone until the full ring is exposed. Small *Ovula ovum* shells are attached to up to one quarter the circumference of the pwala. These shells are called *mwaridoga*. The number of mwaridoga that can be attached help to define the size of the dabala and hence the rank of the mwari.

More *Ovula ovum* shells, known locally as *buna kudula*, are attached

231

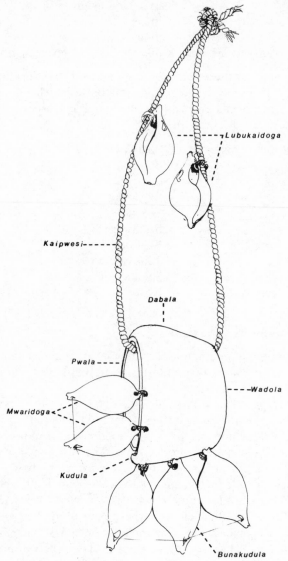

Figure 1. Mwari: named parts.

to the lip of the *Conus* shell. This lip is known as *kudula* (teeth) and can accommodate up to six buna kudula depending on the width of the mwari (or section cut from the *Conus* shell; see Figure 2). A low-ranking shell will accommodate only one or two buna kudula; a middle-ranking shell two to three, and the higher-ranking shells four, five and occasionally six buna kudula. It was explained to me that I should think of mwari in terms of soldiers with insignia (buna kudula) on their uniforms. As the conscientious soldier (mwari) gains more experience and thereby comes to the attention of his superiors, a new stripe or bar is added to his uniform, marking the processual movement upwards in the hierarchy.

Buna kudula and mwaridoga give precise measurement to the mwari, thereby indicating its rank or potentially attainable rank. Men who have never seen a particular mwari will ask how many mwaridoga and how many buna kudula it has. The number will give them a fairly good idea as to the size of the shell and from that an approximation as to its rank.

The last part of the mwari which determines rank and classification is its smaller diameter end. This is made by cutting the *Conus* shell (Figure 2c) leaving a circular opening called the *wadola* or mouth (Figure 2b). The important characteristic of the wadola is its circumference. If the shell is new, and 'white', but the wadola is large, the mwari will eventually climb to a high-ranking position providing all other criteria are filled. However, if the wadola is small, the mwari rarely ever attains high rank, even though it has all the signs of age and other relevant criteria. At this stage it should be noted that the term mwari refers only to the undecorated finished *Conus* shell (Figure 2a). Decoration (or *katububla*) of the shell adds nothing directly to its status and classification. However, the *Ovula ovum* decorations, mwaridoga and buna kudula for example, do not add to, but only indicate status differentials. Decorations using the small *Ovula costellata* shells (buna doga), trade beads, seeds, etc., are used to enhance the general appearance of the mwari and in many cases are used to trick young unknowledgeable men into thinking they have a

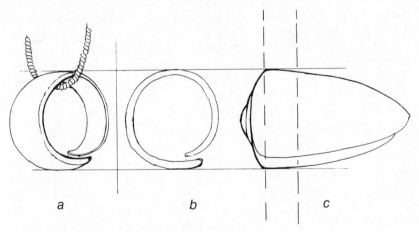

Figure 2. Mwari: sectioned from conus shell.

particularly fine mwari because it is well decorated. Certainly Europeans are easily tricked. It is not unusual to see poorly decorated high-ranking mwari or vaiguwa next to highly decorated low-ranking valuables (see Plate II).

The small shells, *Ovula costellata*, are called *bunadoga*. These are attached to the larger *Ovula ovum* shells and are laced through with trade beads and the black banana seed called *botoboto*. The hanging decorations are called *bwibwi* (or *dauyoyu* in Dobuan). The bwibwi are a fruit from a softwood tree and as seeds are called *sasani*. Besides being decorative, the bwibwi perform another important function, the sound of success; the significance of which will become apparent below.

The terminology for the body parts of the vaiguwa is structured quite differently to that of the mwari. This is not surprising when the physical structure of the two are compared. Whereas the mwari is referred to in terms of a head, with its 'forehead', 'mouth' and 'teeth', the vaiguwa is referred to by using plant terminology, with 'trunk', 'roots', and 'top growth'.[7] The vaiguwa is considered the female partner in kula (see Figure 3).

The end that features the large *Ovula ovum* shell is the *u'una*, corresponding to the base and roots of a plant (an alternative term is *puwala* – male testicles). In accordance with plant terminology, this end should always be held in the lower position opposed to the end where the mother-of-pearl shell is attached. This end is called *dogina*, referring to the top, pliable part of a plant. Alternatively, the dogina end can be called *taigala*, or ear. Both the dogina and u'una are decorations and are irrelevant as indices to classification.

For purposes of classification attention is focused on the middle section containing the string of *Spondylus*[8] shell discs. This section is called the *tapwana*, or in plant terminology, the body/trunk. It is the size, shape, and colour of these shell discs that ranks the necklace. Terms of description or measurement include *kobweyani* (red/high ranking), *kobwaubwau* (black/low ranking), *kokekita* or *kogirigiri* (small or thin/high ranking), *kwaiveka* or *kwaitubwa* (big or fat/low ranking), *komigileu* (clean or smooth/high ranking), and *kopitupitu* (coarse/low ranking).

The hanging assemblages on either end of the tapwana are made up of various types of shells, plastic, money and/or other odd bits and pieces. As indicated earlier, these are mere decorations. However, these assemblages are also called bwibwi like the hanging seeds on the mwari.

It was noted previously that the function of bwibwi is to signify success in a kula exchange through sound. I distinctly remember during all the occasions I was fortunate enough to observe kula, hearing the characteristic sounds of the bwibwi knocking against each other in the darkness.

234

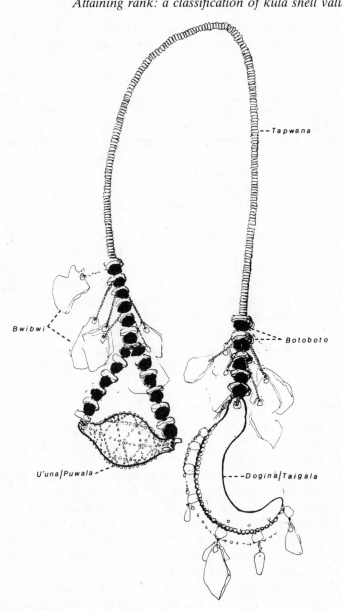

Figure 3. Vaiguwa: named parts.

The bwibwi attached to mwari resemble the sound of bamboo wind chimes while vaiguwa bwibwi recall the tinkling of thin metal wind chimes.

In my experience 'real' kula almost always took place at night.[9] During the day socialising, gaiety, and visiting took place. As it became dark, the kula men got down to serious kula business, in which there was no place for fooling around. It is at night that the vast majority of shells are relinquished and passed one step further along the *keda* (route, path, road). After the battle is over, it is relieving as well as refreshing to hear the gentle chiming of the bwibwi as the shell valuables are carried away in the night. The man who succeeds in winning a kula valuable away from another does not, according to etiquette, carry his own valuable away. Instead, a colleague picks it up and takes it to the beach. As the carrier makes his way to the boats, the sound of bwibwi informs others in the village that someone has succeeded in kula. In response to the sound of bwibwi, villagers will call from the dark to inquire for whom the carrier walks. The success of the man who won a valuable spreads through the darkened village with each step of its carrier. Chiming of the bwibwi triggers off additional conversation around small fires scattered throughout the village about the man's kula, the valuable's keda, how many times it has been around the ring, its dimensions and other related topics that villagers indulge in when kula, undeterred, permeates village life.

Classification of mwari and vaiguwa

Having discussed the various parts of mwari and vaiguwa which arouse admiration and desire, I will now enumerate the various ranking categories told to me by Vakutans.

In the classification of mwari, several criteria come into play. Shells are measured for size, circumference, and width. In higher ranking shells we find the greatest dimensions. In the lower ranking shells, their measurements are smaller. Clearly the dimensions of a shell are limited. *Conidae* do not grow smaller or larger after the animal has left its shell, nor can man interfere significantly in the size of a shell. So shells are, according to size, automatically designated into categories. However, movement does occur between categories as shells are kula'd. Age is another important principle in rank. This is visually determined by colour. It seems that *Conidae*, once they have had the epidermis removed, begin to form red striations, or patina, on the shell surface as it ages through handling. These striations are called ureri. Hence new non-striated shells entering into the classification system are placed into categories at the lower end of the hierarchy. As they age and develop red striations, they are revalued into the upper ranks provided their dimensions equate to higher-ranking criteria.

In the sociology of the classification system only a very few men ever kula with the higher rank of mwari. 'Most men kula for 30 to 60 years and never touch the *mwarikau* class. Only few men ever kula with mwarikau.'[10]

In the classification system, mwari categories are:

High-rank mwari:	Mwarikau
	Mwaributu
	Mwarigidageda
	Tomorimwaiya
Low-rank mwari	Gibwagibwa

Mwarikau refers to the highest rank in the classification of mwari. Shells in this category are said to be '*tommoya kasi mwari*', or the ancestors' mwari. This category is divided into two sub-sections. The upper sub-section is called *bulubula*, or head of the mwari and includes exceptionally famous shells whose histories extend over several generations. Names of bulubula are extensively known throughout all kula communities, and a special note is made when any of them approach a particular kula area. Some of the bulubula presently in circulation include Maikara, Nimoa, Sopi Manuwata, Teburuburu, Rapweyata, Bulivada, Gomani Ikola, and Nanoula. Malinowski made reference in 1922 to Nanoula, Sopi Manuwata and Bulivada (1922:504). Mention of these by Malinowski, who treated them as top ranking at that time, may indicate the general age of bulubula mwari (see Plate IV).

The second, or lower sub-section includes all other Mwarikau mwari which have reached the top class by having all of the necessary qualifications. They are the newcomers, so to speak, to the Mwarikau category. However, all shells in this category have, through time, gradually climbed the hierarchy. They are shells that from the beginning had all of the other prerequisite characteristics, such as at least four buna kudula, and a large mouth or wadola. The only thing they lacked from the beginning was age, history and a concurrent accumulation of mwaridoga. All shells in the Mwarikau category have individual names.

The term Mwarikau has a semantic reference to age in the second half of the word: mwari-kau. *Kau* means blindness and is culturally associated with age. This reference to age is particularly illuminating in view of the prerequisite criterion which distinguishes the Mwarikau category from others.

Mwaributu is the next category of mwari. Its reference is to fame in -*butu*. Mwaributu are described by Vakutans as having made their way

Shirley F. Campbell

Table 1. *Ranking criteria for* mwari *categories*

Mwari category	Main characteristics					
	Personal history	Personal name	Colour	Mwaridoga	Buna kudula	Wadola
Mwarikau	yes	yes	red striations	3–4	4–6	Large
Mwaributu	no	yes	redness	3–4	4–6	Large
Mwarigidageda	no	no	white	2–4	3–6	Medium/ Large
Tomorimwaiya	no	no	white	0–2	0–2	Small/ Medium
Gibwagibwa	no	no	white/ unpolished	0–2	0–2	Small

around the ring enough times to become relatively famous and, most importantly for this category, to have acquired a personal name. A kula shell valuaole can be given names at various times during its career in kula. However, these personal names generally do not remain with the shell until it reaches the higher ranks in the hierarchy. While a shell remains in the middle to lower ranks, it is easily moved between kula relationships or keda (path), because it is of lesser value than high ranking named shells which are more carefully guided along their correct routes. As the shells move between paths, names are forgotten and lost. When shells reach the Mwaributu stage and are more highly valued, men are more concerned with maintaining them on a relatively stable path. This, combined with a gradual accumulation of history, ensures retention of a unique name.

In the Mwaributu category, there are shells that will never reach the Mwarikau stage, because they lack one of the criteria necessary for membership in the first class. However, Mwarikau should have passed through this stage as they age and accumulate history.

Another term used for this category is Mwaridoga which is also the name of shells attached to the pwala to signify rank (see before and Plate I). Strictly speaking, the reference to *Ovula ovum* shells on the pwala is the correct usage of mwaridoga. However, the number of mwaridoga on a shell at this stage in the hierarchy is specifically noticed and used as a measurement of potential in future ranking. As a mwari continues around the ring and up the hierarchy, mwaridoga are added. By the time a shell reaches this category, it should have a number of mwaridoga attached to it. If it does not have sufficient mwaridoga on it, these will be attached in honour of its status. Although Mwaributu is the correct term for this category, it is reasonable that Mwaridoga can be used as an

238

alternative name, because these shells are specific indices to mwari of high status.

The next category down the hierarchy is Mwarigidageda. These mwari are described as 'small' in terms of fame, and 'white', a characteristic of their newness. In fact, some of these shells can show signs of age, becoming slightly reddish, nevertheless they remain white enough to be considered 'new'. New shells can also be placed directly into this category, if they have the requisite size and dimensions for the upper two categories; i.e. able to accommodate at least three buna kudula and have a large enough circumference defining the 'mouth'. It is said that the shells of this category are 'good' mwari and that all men are able to kula with them, whereas, only a few men have access to the upper two categories. Its reference is to *gidageda*, meaning to bite, take hold of, or biting pain. The Vakutans say of this class that one is not afraid to 'throw' it away because it is sufficiently 'big' to 'bite' a replacement. Mwarigidageda have no personal names; they have not yet attracted enough history.

Tomorimwaiya is the term applied to the fourth category of mwari. Tomorimwaiya mwari are described as very small in size and fame. These shells have no names and can accommodate up to two buna kudula.

Gibwagibwa are the lowest ranking class of mwari. They are considered ugly because their 'foreheads' are unpolished and brown. These shells are so small that it is said to be not worth the effort involved in 'cleaning' one. Informants state that no self-respecting kula man would waste his time in soliciting such a specimen. However, young men entering kula relationships take advantage of these. Observations showed that many men do in fact use Gibwagibwa mwari to feed an operating path (see Campbell [Ch. 8, this volume]). While Gibwagibwa is not a mwari keenly sought by 'big' kula men, it does provide the average man with something to kula when higher-ranking shells are scarce. Gibwagibwa can be used in kula discourse as a general derogatory term in reference to mwari which are not necessarily in the Gibwagibwa class.

Gibwagibwa in the Vakutan dialect refers to a small hole scooped out of one of the eyes of a coconut. (*Rowarowa* is the Dobuan term for Gibwagibwa.)

At the beginning of this paper, the mwari terminology documented by Austen in 1945 is listed. It was noted then that his list differed from that given to me by Vakutan informants. Another term that could be added to the kind of list Austen presents is *Sepoulu*, which was used on Vakuta.

Sepoulu are taken from the lagoon around Kaileuna and Kavataria. Its distinguishing feature is an unusually small mouth with respect to the other dimensions it can attain (the mouth is too small to go beyond a man's wrist). Sepoulu, like the terms in Austen's list, refer to Kavatarian names that classify (according to Kavatarian mollusc taxonomy) *Conus* shells as they come from the sea bed. An old Kavatarian informant recognised both systems of classification. He stated that one system classified shells cut and prepared for kula, while the other named specific sizes and shapes of the shell that Kavatarians fish from the lagoon; some of which would later be prepared for kula. Resulting from my puzzlement over Sepoulu, a Vakutan informant assured me that there are many words like Sepoulu, but these do not refer to the kula classification system. Instead, they are 'raw' technical terms found in specific areas where production of kula shell valuables takes place.

Sepoulu, like the mwari terminology given by Austen, are probably technical terms given and known by people directly involved in the fishing and production of shells. Austen's information came from Kavataria, once a major area from which mwari originated.

Like mwari, vaiguwa are ranked in a classification system. Criteria used to classify vaiguwa are age, history, colour and the size of the *Spondylus* discs. Unlike *Conus*, the age of *Spondylus* shell cannot be determined by colour, because this is a natural feature of the shell and does not change with age and use. *Spondylus* shell shows a range of shades between browny-red to a light pinkish-red according to characteristics of the shell. Nevertheless, classification is determined by colour, salmon-red being more highly valued than a browny-red. Age is determined by the shape of the shell string. A high-ranking shell string should look as thin as a fine fishing line and feel like oil because it is old and has been worn with handling. In fact, a shell string goes through stages of grinding and polishing as it travels around the ring to thin it down and make all the shell discs even. A newly entered vaiguwa will not be of the optimum thinness and evenness because of the work involved. It takes a good deal of grinding over a long period of time to reach the appropriate thinness of high-ranking shell strings. The shape of each individual shell disc is also a classification criterion. These should not be thick, nor should there be chips in the discs. Again, the thickness of a shell disc has to be ground out, taking many man-hours. This may be done when temporary owners wish to raise the shell string to a higher rank, have time to do it, and the equipment necessary for such work. Only a few men ever kula with highly-ranked vaiguwa.

In the classification of *vaiguwa*, there are six ranking categories:

High-ranking vaiguwa:	Bagiriku
	Bagidou
	Bagiyeru

	Bagisam
	Taituyanabwa
Low-ranking vaiguwa:	Bagitorobwa

Bagiriku are described as very old and very 'big' in terms of fame. *Riku* means 'earthquake' or 'to shake'. It is said that when men hear the name of a vaiguwa from the Bagiriku category, their bodies shake with desire.

Like Mwarikau, the category Bagiriku is divided into two sub-classes; bulubula, or head, and Bagiriku. The bulubula are the oldest vaiguwa in the ring. Kasanai, Tamagwadi, Tokamrai'isi, Toyaremwa, Subwaigai and Kabwaku are some of the most highly valued shell strings (see Plate V).

The qualities ascribed to Bagiriku are based on a preference for salmon-pink colouration, fineness of individual shell discs, and their overall thinness and uniformity.

The difference between the Bagidou and Bagiriku is in the smoothness and evenness of the shell string. Bagidou are slightly coarser to the touch. The colour of Bagidou should also be the highly valued salmon-pink.

Like Bagiriku, the Bagidou all have personal names. Generally speaking, shell strings acquire names when they fulfill the qualities attributable to Bagidou.

History is another qualification for the Bagidou category. Bagidou are a highly valued class of vaiguwa, and men are, therefore, more careful in keeping their path straight. This allows shell strings to accumulate history more easily than if the paths were continually broken. Bagidou may eventually move into an upper category when, with use and further grinding, they are given the desired tactile quality of smoothness.

Linguistically, Bagidou refers to the act of calling. *Dou* means 'to call' or 'to beckon'. Bagidou are said to 'call' mwari to them, 'not that mwari will come fast and the holder of the Bagidou will not throw it away quickly, it will stay with him for a long time, while it calls many mwari to it!' (informant's comments).

Bagiyeru is the last category of highly valued shell strings. It is described as thin enough to go through a hole in one's nose. Vaiguwa in this category lack the tactile qualities of Bagiriku and likewise are without histories. For these reasons, Bagiyeru do not as a rule have personal names.

Shell strings in the class Bagisam are defined as a mixture of shell discs from other categories. Bagisam shell strings include discs of Bagiyeru, Taituyanabwa, Bagitorobwa, etc. Vakutans say that 'its face is different'. This mixture lacks the uniform quality necessary to the first three categories and thus is not as pleasing to look at or to touch. /

241

Shirley F. Campbell

Table 2. *Ranking criteria for vaiguwa categories*

Vaiguwa category	Main characteristics			
	Personal history	Personal name	Colour	Tactile qualities
Bagiriku	yes	yes	Salmon-pink	Fine/thin
Bagidou	yes	yes	Salmon-pink	Slightly coarse
Bagiyeru	no	no	Salmon-pink	Slightly coarse
Bagisam	no	no	Mixture	Mixture
Taituyanabwa	no	no	Muddy-red	Thick/coarse
Bagitorobwa	no	no	Dark-red	Big/coarse

Taituyanabwa vaiguwa are described as 'black' (*bwaubwau*). The shell discs are in fact a very dark muddy-red. Thickness is also attributed to Taituyanabwa. Individual shell discs are thick and pitted, lacking the desirable smoothness and fineness of their more valued companions. This may be due to a lack of interest and the consequent output of labour in shaping up these shell strings, because by their colour they are doomed to remain in the lower ranks.

Bagitorobwa (or *Wagera* in Dobuan) defines the lowest ranking category of vaiguwa. The shell strings feature very big and coarse discs. To emphasise their polarity from Bagiriku, Bagitorobwa are said to be 'black' and as thick as a finger. It is claimed of Bagitorobwa that they are kula'd by children. According to ideology, like the Gibwagibwa mwari, men would not seek to lower their esteem by possessing these shell strings.

As with mwari, I was informed that there are many other terms for vaiguwa categories, but that these are not strictly related to kula value classification. These other categories refer more to types of vaiguwa from specific geographical areas or to technical stages or types of production processes.

Bagiosi describes shell discs at a certain stage of grinding. They need further evening and polishing. In the kula value classification, these may be classed with Bagiyeru.

Bagimuyuwa or Taitumuyuwa again refers to a type of shell string not strictly encompassed in the value classification system. It seems to be the case that these may be highly valued or not according to criteria operable in the classing of other vaiguwa in a hierarchical structure; i.e. thinness/thickness, smoothness/coarseness. Bagimuyuwa defines *Spondylus* shells from a specific area displaying a particular feature. Muyuwa is a local name for Woodlark Island from which these shell strings are said to

242

originate.[11] The *Spondylus* from this area are white with a very slight pinkish hue. Because of this anomaly, they cannot, strictly speaking, become Bagiriku on the basis of colour. However, according to other criteria of size and dimension, they can be accorded rank within the value system. Therefore, as a category, Bagimuyuwa cannot be described as part of the classification system.

As there are other terms referring to specifically shaped *Spondylus* discs, it may be expedient at this stage to describe these briefly.

Katudababile refers to single large *Spondylus* shells used to decorate the ends of tortoise-shell rings attached to the ear, decoration on a type of grass skirt, and for layering on belts called *wakula*. Katudababile are about the size of a 20-*toya* coin (c. 1⅛ in or 28 mm).

Tumoila refers to a smaller *Spondylus* shell disc about the size of a 10-*toya* coin (c. ¾ in or 22 mm). These are also sewn onto the wakula belts, layered in a single string worn on the forehead or woven into the hair, and used as layered chains in the decoration of a vaiguwa, lime pot, or lime stick.

In this paper, I have defined the criteria by which kula shells are classified, and how they are then arranged into ranking categories. I have also described how shells move between categories and up the hierarchy. From this presentation it would appear that shells enter the system in the lower to middle ranks, and from there move slowly up the hierarchy with an accumulation of features indexing age and history. So there is a tendency towards a gradual revaluation of the shells as they head for the highest rank. But what is to stop the devaluation of the high-ranking shells as more and more shells are revalued into their ranks? Shells are not perishables, and they are certainly not destroyed when they are old to make room for new arrivals. While it is desirable to have new shells moving through the system as a means by which men attach their fame, history, and immortality, it is undesirable to overcrowd the higher ranks and endanger the classification system and the competition derived from it. So what is the 'pressure valve' that allows new shells to enter the system and climb the ranks as they are revalued while safeguarding the highest rank from becoming overcrowded?

Mwari have traditionally been traded outside the kula ring along the Motuan coast to the area around Port Moresby (Malinowski, 1922:506). Today, this movement still persists. In Port Moresby and its environs, mwari are bought for between 50 Kina (USA $70) and 200 Kina (USA $280). These mwari are used in part payment for a bride. The Port Moresby 'market' takes shells from the lower to middle ranks and occasionally removes Mwaributu and Mwarikau mwari from the system.

A safeguard from the possibility of crowding, with the related devalua-

Shirley F. Campbell

tion of the high ranks of vaiguwa, occurs at the village level. Short shell necklaces are used as items of body decoration among the northern Massim people and probably also among the southern Massim. Vaiguwa are dismantled into short lengths and given to wives, children, grandchildren and lovers. Nearly every person on Vakuta, other than kula men, owns a shell necklace (*kuwa*). Vaiguwa which are dismantled usually come from the lower- to middle-ranking categories, and thus provide a 'pressure valve' on the overcrowding of the higher ranks.

While some shells are naturally destined to remain in the lower ranks on account of their physical inability to conform to the ranking criteria, there are a great number of shells fed into the system with potentially high ranking credentials. Most of these must be taken out of the system in order that the classification system does not become meaningless through devaluation of the upper classes. The 'pressure valve' is located outside the system, where mwari and vaiguwu are 'eaten up' by external and unrelated appetites, while the index to competition between men is left unharmed.

Colour symbolism

Colour plays an important role in the classification and ranking of the kula shells. It does seem that certain colour themes are at work in the classification of kula valuables and these will be discussed briefly below.

The undesirability of the white mwari relates specifically to its newness or paucity of age and history. A white mwari is considered clean and uncontaminated. Its clean, shiny forehead shows no record of use and is thus uncontaminated by death. This is a reference to its lack of history. Mwari with history are dangerous in that they cause death through desire and competition. At the social level, symbolic themes ascribed to whiteness in kula valuables are also found. For example, the whiteness attributed to a woman in her first pregnancy and to all newly-born babies again symbolises newness and cleanliness in that they are uncontaminated by history. A woman becomes part of history through her biological productivity. At one level, this is a woman's prime social value. Until she has given birth for the first time, a woman has no real social history. With her first offspring, she begins her social history, from which generations later she will be recalled as an index to *dala* (subclan) solidarity [see also Weiner, 1976]. Therefore, she is made white, symbolically representing her newness and subsequent entry into the generation of her history. She is symbolically clean and uncontaminated because she has not yet produced objects of distraction, contention, diversion and competition. A baby is likewise white when it is born. By definition, it has no history

244

and is, therefore, innocent of the impurities generated by historical growth.

Black in the colour symbolism of vaiguwa refers to impurity. The undesirable vaiguwa are black (kobwaubwau). The original *Spondylus* shell from which the discs were formed is considered impure. Something in its development had gone wrong; it was 'sick'. Emotionally, black or any of the darker hues are ugly, diseased, and dangerous. Disease is caused by black blood that is allowed to stay within the body. Bloodletting is practised extensively to release and dissipate this dangerous blood. People with particularly black skins are said to be ugly and undesirable as partners. A widowed person is painted black and kept black until the ceremonial cleansing. Until then, he/she is closely associated with death. These people are considered ugly, undesirable, and dirty. The ceremony performed at the end of this particular stage in mourning cleanses the body, makes it 'white', clean, desirable and new.

In the classification of shell valuables, red is the colour associated with the highest ranking and most desirable pieces. Although the redness of the mwari and the redness of the vaiguwa are measurements of quite different criteria at one level, the overall consensus is that all shell valuables should be red, symbolising sexual desire. Mwari are described as male and vaiguwa as female. When a successful path is operating, the *vaga* (opening transaction/attractor) and the *kudu* (closing transaction/attracted) are described as married. During their marriage the redness (high rank) of one is continually attracting the redness (high rank) of the other, and between them, they are attracting others into their path. When the marriage is broken, it is conceptually attributed to one of them being attracted to *another's* redness. Culturally, red is used as a colour of attraction and symbolises sexual desire. Young, unmarried women who are sexually available wear very short red skirts to attract partners. Red may be symbolically advertising their willingness to form sexual liaisons. Married women, except at certain ceremonial occasions where attractiveness is condoned, wear only drab coloured skirts at knee length. A red skirt would not be worn by a married woman unless she were making a non-verbal statement concerning a willingness to redirect her sexual favours. At the cleansing ceremony, where the black mourning pigments are washed off her, a widow is given a new red skirt to symbolise her regained freedom to participate in the competition for sexual partners (see Tambiah, 1968, for further discussion on Trobriand colour symbolism).

Summary

It is necessary in competitive exchange to have an explicit value system

Shirley F. Campbell

for the articles exchanged. In the classification of kula valuables, a value system is defined by qualitative criteria. Kula shells are not inherently valuable, but have value attached to them according to aesthetically determined criteria. Principles on which shells are classified are weight, dimension, colour, age, and tactile qualities. Generally speaking, it appears that the classifying system operates at two levels. At one level in the classification of mwari, parameters of weight, dimension, and touch feed *Conus* shells into categories at the lower end of the scale. Because these parameters are relatively fixed in *Conidae*, other criteria are brought into play as a means of allowing mwari to move between categories. At this level, criteria for classification are colour and age. In the classification of vaiguwa, this system is turned on its head. At one level, the principle of colour is used to fix *Spondylus*-shell discs into categories defining rank. Colour is a natural and relatively fixed state in *Spondylus* shells. To allow vaiguwa to move between categories, human influenced qualities of dimension and touch are used. In this way, we have certain qualities initially fixing new shells into lower ranks of the classification system, and other qualities operating as movement indices between categories. Because the physical qualities of *Conus* and *Spondylus* shells are structurally different, principles for fixing status at one level and for movement at another level in the classification of mwari are turned around in the classification of vaiguwa.

In the classification system of shell valuables, mwari and vaiguwa are able to attain rank according to qualities defining age and history. This system not only stimulates competition between men, but also helps to define the rank that individual men in competition can attain.

Notes

1 The material presented in this paper was collected during fieldwork on Vakuta Island (one of the Trobriand Islands) between September 1976 and January 1978, and is, therefore, primarily indicative of the Vakutan point of view.

   Fieldwork in the Trobriand Islands was supported by an Australian National University Scholarship and Research Grant. I gratefully acknowledge Geoffrey Mosuwadoga and the Papua New Guinea Public Museum and Art Gallery for sponsoring my research in Papua New Guinea and offering assistance during my stay there. My thanks to Professor Anthony Forge and Dr Michael Young for invaluable suggestions and advice; to Jörg Schmeisser for drawing Figures, 1, 2, and 3, and to Dr Paul Ratcliffe and Ms Pearl Campbell for editorial comments.

   I am indebted to the Kula communities of Vakuta, Kitava and Dobu, and especially to Kunabu of Vakuta and Antonio of Kavataria for giving their knowledge and insight.

2 On Vakuta Island, the term vaiguwa has replaced the term *soulava* which was documented by Malinowski in 1922 as referring to the kula shell necklace. As vaiguwa is today the more common word used in the above reference, it will be used exclusively in this paper.

3 On Vakuta Island, I learned and spoke the Vakutan dialect. In this paper, the Vakutan rather than any of the Kiriwinan dialects is used.

4 Malinowski states that mwari are made from *Conus millepunctatus* of the *Conidae* family (1922:502). From informants' comments, however, it seems likely that there are in fact several varieties of the *Conidae* family used. I, therefore, take the more general term as adequate referent to the family of shells used in mwari construction.

5 According to Malinowski (and others following him), the mwari was female and the vaiguwa the male partner. The shape of the shell valuables would seem to reinforce this supposition. However, it is interesting to note that information from Vakuta and the lagoon area of Kiriwina points to the opposite being the case. The reasons given for this by informants are firstly, the mwari is generally worn by men and the vaiguwa by women. Secondly, the relative ease or otherwise in the exchange of valuables reflects everyday relationships between men and women. For example, obtaining a mwari was likened to the day-to-day distribution of betel nut between men; whereas obtaining the vaiguwa was likened to the far more difficult procedures in soliciting sex from women. It was found to be easier to obtain mwari from Kitava than vaiguwa from Dobu.

6 The word pwala would seem to be related to the words puwala or puwana, referring to male testicles. Puwala is also an alternative term for the *Ovula ovum* shell attached to the u'una end of vaiguwa (see p. 234 and Figure 3).

7 Although it is apparent from the specific choice of words that vaiguwa refers to plant terminology, with references to 'trunk', 'roots', and 'top growth', at one level these may metaphorically be recalling the human body; for example, the 'roots' or anchoring feet, the 'trunk' or main body including legs, and the 'top growth', which in other contexts is associated with the upper body where mind and emotion are located.

8 *Spondylus* has been the accepted classification of shell used in making vaiguwa. The accuracy of this classification, however, has recently come under question. John Liep has made the initial query, and an analysis of shell previously thought to be *Spondylus* shows that it is *Chama*. Nevertheless, until further evidence is available, I shall continue to use the convention of *Spondylus* in classifying shell used for making vaiguwa.

9 At this stage, I am uncertain as to the reason why my data is different to that of Malinowski. It is not for me to say, in preference for my own data, whether Malinowski's description of the kula is wrong, or that he was misinformed. Indeed, it may well be the case that because of the time-span between Malinowski's work on the Trobriands and my own, the discrepancy in certain facts concerning the kula is a result of historical phenomena. Another possible cause for the apparent disparity may relate to the fact that Malinowski worked primarily from Omarakana, while I had the vantage point of Vakuta.

10 This statement was made to me by a Dobuan and agreed to by others, while we were discussing the rank of a particular mwari in my possession.
11 Although Vakutans note Muyuwa (Woodlark Island) as the source of white shell strings, Fred Damon, a recent fieldworker on Woodlark, rejects the notion that an industry exists there.

10   Kula on Kitava*

GIANCARLO M. G. SCODITTI
with
JERRY W. LEACH

Introduction

Kitava is an elevated coral island with a central plateau about 150 metres above sea level. The island lies about 25 kilometres east of Kiriwina and Vakuta in the Trobriands, about 70 kilometres west of the Marshall Bennetts, and 150 kilometres west of Woodlark, which is called Muyuwa. The last population census in 1971 recorded 1,372 inhabitants, giving a population density of 61 per square kilometre (158 per square mile) and a density relative to arable land of 114 per square kilometre (292 per square mile). Virtually the entire population lives and gardens on the fertile plateau. The southwestern perimeter of the island is a defunct European coconut plantation used sporadically now for indigenous copra production. The remaining littoral is primary lowland rain forest and occasional beach. Kitavans call their language Nowau, the name of the southernmost beach from which they believe the island was first peopled.

Kitavans are almost all subsistence gardeners, growing principally the yam (*Dioscorea esculenta* and *alata*) and small quantities of sweet potato, taro, tapioca, banana, and coconut. Their methods of cultivation are essentially those described by Malinowski in *Coral Gardens and their Magic*, though their tools are now the steel axe, the machete, the metal adze, and the metal or wooden digging-stick. One major village of the island has abandoned garden magic due to mission influence. All men fish but seafood is eaten rarely, associated mainly with ceremonial occasions. Kitavans keep small numbers of pigs, dogs, and chickens. They earn cash from copra and from migrant labour but, unlike Kiriwinans, very little from carvings. Their per capita income in the mid-1970s was roughly 2 Kina (USA $3) per year.

Kitava is divided into three regions: Kumwagea, Lalela, and Okabulula. The southwest region is one large village (*varu*) called Kumwagea, containing five hamlets (*katupusura*) and associated garden lands, in

249

which 22% of the island's population live. Kumwageans think of themselves as emigrants from Vakuta Island in the Trobriands and their dialect resembles Vakutan closely. They also consider themselves the most 'modern' village on Kitava as they received the first Methodist (now United) mission station on the island in 1901 and now have a primary school, aid post, and cooperative store. The village was redesigned European-style in the 1960s into two linear rows of semi-traditional houses with a path-street down the middle.

The southeast region Lalela has 35% of the population in three villages called Lalela, Lalekaiwa, and Toraigasi. The former is linear and modelled on Kumwagea whereas the latter two are circular in design as described in Malinowski's writings (1932: 8–9 and figure 1). The people of Lalela region consider themselves the autochthons of Kitava but place their ultimate origins in the Marshall Bennetts. Their dialect is still quite similar to that of Iwa, Digumenu, Kweiwata, and Gawa. All three regions of Kitava have a strong tendency towards endogamy.

Okabulula, the north, contains 43% of the population, living in a series of small circular hamlets. The people claim dual origins from Woodlark and the Omarakana area of northern Kiriwina (Malinowski 1935 vol. 1:2 and *passim*) and their dialect does have resemblances to the speech of both areas. The principal tension among the three regions concerns the land boundary between Okabulula and Lalela. Several wars (*kabilia*) were fought over this issue in the 1970s.

The descent system of Kitava is quite similar to that of Kiriwina as reported in Malinowski's *Sexual Life of Savages*. There are four totemic matrilineal clans (*kumila*) and numerous matrilineages (*dara*), some of which are land-holding and some of which are not. There is little evidence of any virgin birth belief (Malinowski 1932; E. Leach 1966) in contemporary society and it is likely that this was previously a metaphorical ideology only. Kitavan mortuary ceremonies are roughly like those of Kiriwina (Weiner 1976:61–120). However, they do not now and probably never did practice the *soi* ceremony (contra Malinowski 1922:489) in which large quantities of *kula* valuables, dammed up by a death, were released to partners in all directions.[1] Traditional religious and magical beliefs largely persist though the island is nominally all Methodist. Kitavan souls (*baloma*) go to Tuma, the Trobriand island of the dead, later to be reincarnated. Garden and kula magic have disappeared or become very secretive in Kumwagea because of the exhortations of indigenous pastors there.

Kitavan kinship categories and roles are *mutatis mutandis* the same as those of Kiriwina (Malinowski 1932:433–51 and *passim*). Marriage is usually virilocal, but uxorilocal residence is not infrequent. Post-marital

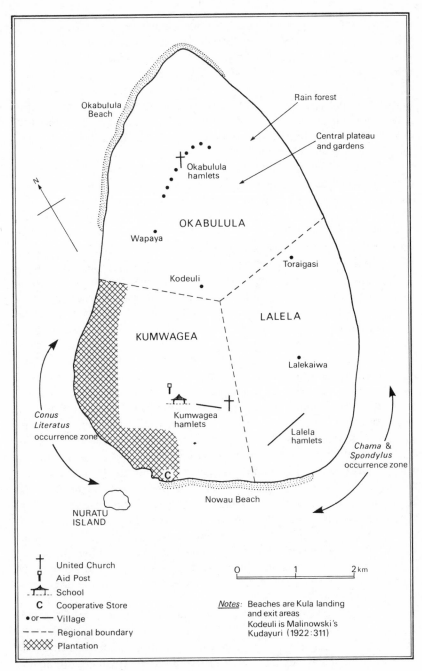

Okabulula
Beach

Rain forest

Central plateau
and gardens

Okabulula
hamlets

N

OKABULULA

Wapaya

Toraigasi

Kodeuli

LALELA

KUMWAGEA

Lalekaiwa

*Conus
Literatus*
occurrence zone

Kumwagea
hamlets

Lalela
hamlets

Chama &
Spondylus
occurrence zone

C

NURATU
ISLAND

Nowau Beach

0   1   2 km

<u>Notes</u>: Beaches are Kula landing
and exit areas
Kodeuli is Malinowski's
Kudayuri (1922:311)

Map 1. Kitava Island.

251

residence tends to be near the father or maternal uncle of the groom. Polygyny (*vilayawa*) was formerly common for leaders (*tokarewaga*) but now only one hamlet leader has two wives. Pre-mortem inheritance tends to be cognatic except for land while post-mortem transmission is largely matrilineal. Kitavans live in nuclear families averaging 2–4 children per married couple. Houses are of traditional materials, with occasional iron roofs, built in pre-colonial ground-level A-frame design (Malinowski 1922: Plates XXV and LXII) or raised style (1922: Plate LVI) or raised long-front Fijian-style houses, much larger than earlier types, which were introduced in the 1920s. Most households have simple yamhouses (*bwema*) which store garden produce in the roof. There are on the whole island only five display yamhouses (*bwemaveka* or *liku*), owned by hamlet leaders, as made famous in Malinowski's Trobriand ethnographies (1935 vol. 1:240–72). The giving of harvest prestations in yams is still an important ceremonial transaction of life-long significance between men and, oversimply put, the women of their matrilineage plus their husbands.

Kitavans have a more egalitarian political structure than Kiriwina. They do not rank their matrilineages into chiefly (*guyau*) and commoner (*tokai*) categories (Malinowski 1922:62–70). There is no leadership position, formal or informal, for Kitava as a whole or for its clans (contra Seligmann 1910:671). The regions are 'led' in a largely informal sense by the leaders of the most pre-eminent or largest hamlets or villages. Regional leadership is more pronounced in external affairs, such as war or kula, than in internal matters. Internally there are primus-inter-pares leaders in gardening, dancing, carving, fighting, magic, church affairs, school matters, and cooperative-store activities. These men tend to be hamlet leaders or those of experience in modern institutions. Kitavan hamlet leadership is less prominent in everyday affairs and not based in control over land as is hamlet managership described by Weiner for Kiriwina (1976:38–44 and 68–9). The famous Trobriand term guyau (Malinowski 1922:62–70), meaning village chief, is rarely ever heard on Kitava. No Kitavan leader has the privileges of self-decoration of Kiriwinan chiefs as partially outlined by Weiner (1976:237–8). Two hamlet leaders of Kumwagea and Okabulula have seen fit to paint their houses as chiefs, though this is criticised on Kitava as a recent and pretentious imitation of Kiriwina. Powerful men inevitably have a reputation for sorcery (*bwagau*).

Malinowski never visited Kitava during his research though he met Kitavans on Kiriwina (1922:479 and Chapter XX). He presented an overly homogeneous picture of cultural variation in the northeastern kula area, basically seeing it as a projection of Kiriwina, as indicated below:

For the natives of the Eastern islands, from Kitava to Woodlark, have the same social organisation and the same culture as the Trobrianders, and speak the same language with dialectical differences only (1922:478).

A government census of Malinowski's day (1916) recorded 908 inhabitants of Kitava, indicating a population increase of more than 50% since his work six decades ago. The research reported here was carried out over twenty months between 1973 and 1976 and was the first fieldwork of more than a few days ever conducted on the island.

Kula participation

In the mid-1970s, there were 181 men and one woman from Kitava in the kula. This represents about 90% of the adult men of the island.

Those outside the kula but resident on Kitava, roughly about twenty, an unknown number being away for work or training, were considered social marginals (*tonagowa*) by their fellows. None were physically abnormal or psychologically defective. They were, however, characteristically introverted. They tended to be poor gardeners and withdrawn in village activities. Several had no command of magic of any type. Two were obviously less intelligent than the norm and several were sexually promiscuous though married. The non-kula men were considered socially unworthy people. None were leaders in any social context. They were often the brunt of jokes, even to their faces, being ridiculed for unacceptable personal attire, ignorance of social customs, dirtiness, inability in mixing betelnut to a proper state of redness, and poverty of speech. Such men seemed to have failed to please their seniors who could have brought them into the kula, to have been thought bad bets by overseas kula transactors, or to have lost their fathers early in life.

Only one elderly Kitavan was 'retired' from the kula, principally because of frailty and cancerous mouth sores making his speech almost unintelligible. Most men try to remain in the kula until death whatever the hardship. This is admired socially. Such men become doyens of the kula. As they become less active transactionally, they serve increasingly as teachers of the young men learning about the system. They also gradually give away their shells, kula paths (*keda*), and partners (*soyu-* or *karitau*) to junior associates, whether relatives or not.

Most men enter the kula around the time of their first marriage, usually within a year before or after the event. However, men do not get their first kula shells as a marriage gift from their new affines or their own kinsmen. Marriage therefore roughly times entrance into the kula by loosely marking the passage to adult status, but weddings in themselves do not open kula careers.

253

Giancarlo Scoditti

Kula careers are usually opened by the receiving of a promise (*biga katotila*) of a first shell from a senior man of Kitava, though men of one's peer group or overseas kinsmen or friends may also serve to bring in new transactors. During the period between the promise and the delivery of the shell, usually several months, the behaviour of the junior man should express generosity of service and pleasantness of personality towards the senior. There is no obligatory prestation during the promissory period or after the receipt of the valuable. Any gift or service given must studiously avoid the obvious connotation of reciprocation or repayment for the shell.

The handing over of the promised valuable is always private. This usually means the event occurs inside the house of the senior man and is unobserved by others, even though the public outside may understand the nature of the meeting. Such occasions are normally at dawn, when the village is vacated, or at night after everyone is asleep. There is no necessary ritual speech or phrase said by either party at the transfer. Often there is little or no reference made to the shell at all, the junior having been informed about it in earlier meetings. Kula magic is never transmitted during these events. The giver and receiver chew betelnut together, the senior preparing the mixture and sharing it with his junior protégé. The meetings end with the departure of the visitor with the shell hidden in his arm-basket.

The receiving of the shell does not in itself put the new man in the kula. The crucial symbolic boundary for entrance is the first transaction with a partner which must be part of a collective expedition either to or from Kitava. Going off alone or receiving a new partner alone would attract derision. Usually a newly-acquired shell is linked to a kula path and to established partners to the east and west of Kitava. A young entrant is told in detail of the partnerships and expected to follow them as he is seen as 'taking the place' of the senior man who brings him in. If the path were broken at the outset, the new transactor would lose reputation and possibly his potential career. He would also risk losing access to the kula magic which his patron would normally teach him some years later. Young married men in the kula seldom have any magic at all. This last gift is held back by seniors until very late in life, one of the underlying reasons for the conservatism of junior kula participants who are normally very mindful of etiquette, paths, and partners. In mid-career, with magic and early reputation secure, the breaking of paths and the manipulation of partners and shells to personal advantage become a more realistic possibility.

There are essentially two types of 'first kula partnership'. The first type, the strong form, occurs when a Kitavan is brought into the kula by someone from another island, effectively forging a new link in a kula path. This kind of partnership is spoken of metaphorically as like a 'first love'. It should remain unblemished throughout the lives of both men, being the most honest, generous, and hospitable of their kula relationships. The tie created is said to be more open than any other, even that with one's brother or father. When one has multiple partners on an island, one always goes first to and usually stays with a first partner. When approaching death, a man may give the kula link with his first partner to his own son or sororal nephew, attempting to maintain the tie beyond his death. This transition, though a mark of respect, means the loss of the quality of strong-form first partnership. If the son or nephew is not agreeable, the still active partner may refuse the younger man, staying with the original tie until death whatever the risk or cost. A first partner mourns through ritual wailing (Weiner 1967:64–7) the death of his co-eval, though he does not undertake the affinal obligations of shaving the head or blackening the body (Malinowski 1932:130–9) nor does he contribute to the deceased's mortuary ceremonies. The weak form of first partnership occurs when one Kitavan, usually a senior, gives a shell and its path to another Kitavan, normally a man of his own region. The neophyte may or may not know his new partners on other islands. The deeply personal quality of the strong-form first partnership is not likely in this case. Deceit and path-breaking may occur later in the weak-form first kula relationship, especially after the death of the Kitavan patron. Entrance into the kula by the weak form of the first partnership is far more frequent than by the strong form.

There is one Kitavan woman in the kula. She is one of the three strongest flying witches (*diu* or *siwasiwa*) on the island, all of whom are women. The kula woman entered the system upon the death of her mother who was also a flying witch and a kula transactor. All of the contemporary woman's partners, three to the west and four to the east, are men. The woman herself, however, never sails or leaves Kitava. Her father acts for her in external transactions, while he himself is also in the kula in his own right. Even when the woman's partners visit Kitava, they transact with her father but only in her presence. She remains the decision-maker over the path of the shells, even on other islands when her father acts on her instructions. The kula woman claims to have transacted about 300 armshells (*mwari*) and 300 necklaces (*veiguwa*) in her kula career. If so, and others do not dispute the assertion, she would be one of the two most active Kitavans in the kula. She is considered very powerful in kula, but not necessarily in other social activities, and is believed to have killed many famous kula men on Kitava and around the entire ring. Her partners are said invariably to give her their best shells, to

Giancarlo Scoditti

transact quickly and without resistance, and never to have tricked or broken a path with her.

Altogether ten Kitavan women and a number of girls are considered flying witches. They inherit their power from their mothers but it becomes much more intense as they become elderly. They are dangerous to women and men, especially the latter (Malinowski 1922:237–66; 1932: 38–40). Witches attack young women who are beautiful or who have handsome lovers or children. They also defend their locality against other flying witches. They are said to have fiery faces, long canine teeth, and snakes for hair. Their mode of attack is by blood-sucking or strangulation. Witches are a danger to men of any age who are good gardeners or own numerous pigs. Men with good harvests or large litters give preventive gifts as indemnity. Flying witches are at their most dangerous, however, in relation to men's kula activities. They attack when new canoes are being built in the village, when the men are away on expeditions, when the partners of Kitava men come to the island, and when there is a famous shell, especially a necklace, around. The flying-witch belief complex seems, in part, to express the jealousy of women, and male projections of female jealousy, over the freedom of men in the kula.

Overseas exchange

With only recent minor exceptions, all Kitavan kula transactions involve overseas partnerships. There is almost no inter- or intra-regional kula on Kitava itself. Kitavan men say that internal kula would vitiate the meaning of the exchange system by keeping men unknowledgable of foreign areas, by failing to test them against the rigours of sailing, and by leaving them to tied to the skirts of their womenfolk. The redistribution of material resources among islands is not given as a *raison d'être* of kula in the 1970s.

The three regions of Kitava (see p. 249) act separately from each other in kula though the regions do not always act *en masse* for particular expeditions. More often than not, only a portion of the kula men of a region sail outwards together in search of shells, others staying home for purposes of work, for lack of gifts available to overseas partners, because of ill-prepared canoes, or embarrassing complexities arising from earlier exchanges. Before an expedition, Kitavans send out a reconnaissance canoe to check (*katubayasa*) the whereabouts and volume of shells being sought, as well as the plans of their hosts. This practice is also used by expeditions intending to come to Kitava. It is not, however, invariably necessary as sufficient information may pass by means of inter-island trawlers, the movement of school children, or visits to the government stations and hospitals in order to allow a decision to be made. Reconnoitring is nevertheless wise as it gives notice to hosts of an imminent visit, allowing them to marshal their resources and seek out shells quickly if necessary. Kitavans are canoe conservatives with regard to kula. While happily travelling by trawler for other purposes, they disparage such on the kula and denigrate the Kiriwinans, Vakutans, and Dobuans who often mount their expeditions by modern vessels.[2] Trawler kula is said to eliminate knowledge of the sea, to curtail freedom of movement, and to be unmasculine. Such passage sometimes costs money which the Kitavans seldom have.

There are eighty men of the Okabulula region of northern Kitava in the kula. Their western ties are with the eastern coast of northern Kiriwina, depicted as centring on Omarakana village (Malinowski 1922:479), and with the Marshall Bennetts, Madau Island, and the north coast of Woodlark in the east. Except for the Marshall Bennett Islands, the northern and southern regions of Kitava have separate non-overlapping kula paths (*contra* Malinowski 1922:Ch. XX). In the mid-1970s Okabulula had eleven kula canoes (*tadobu*) of the western kula type (Malinowski 1922: 141–5 and Plate XL), not the Gawan type (*nagega*) as mentioned in *Argonauts* (1922:496), though Malinowski was not in error in his day. Kitavans changed canoe styles in the last sixty years because the technological knowledge was brought by immigrating Vakutans, because the western style is cheaper in labour and materials, and because the new type is faster. Malinowski recorded 'about twelve' Kitavan kula canoes (1922:122). Today there are twenty-seven overall.

Okabululans usually sail as small expeditions of three canoes, roughly twenty-five or so men, every other year to northern Kiriwina. They go in search of necklaces of which they might collectively return with five or ten. There is little chance that each participant will receive a shell on these occasions. Normally very few armshells are carried on these journeys and those usually for the completion of a transaction promised when the northern Kiriwinans were previously on Kitava. Armshells are not used for solicitation or simultaneous exchange on these occasions. Okabululans carry only a small volume of material resources to northern Kiriwina, principally betelnut, mats, piglets, sandalwood oil (Malinowski's aromatic resin called *sayaku* used as scented body paint; 1932:250, 255), coconut-fibre skirts, small baskets, and body ornaments (*diginagoma*) made from the crowns of the *Conus literatus* shell. Ebony clubs, walking sticks, and lime spatulae as well as cowrie shells have more or less dropped out of the exchanges (1922:481). These goods are given as gifts, implicitly solicitory, to kula partners. They are not used for bartering (*gimwali*) purposes with non-partners, another change from

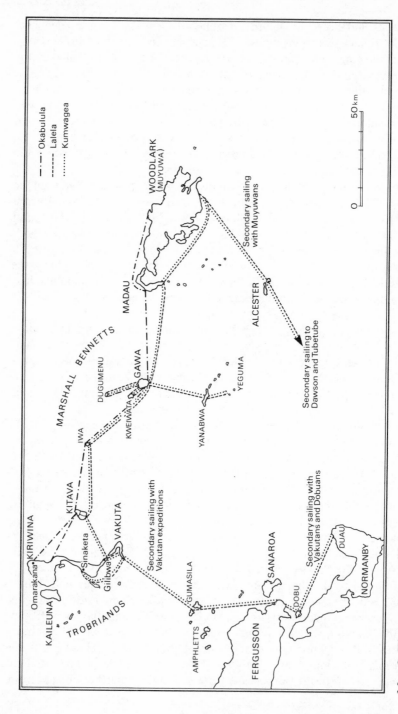

Map 2. Kitavan kula routes.

Malinowski's day (1922:481). While the Okabululans are still on Kiriwi-na, their partners give them return prestations mainly of tobacco but also, to a much lesser degree, betelnut, piglets, canoe-lashing vines, cassowary or cockatoo feathers, and red banana-fibre skirts (1922:480). Secondary trade or purchase of commodities (gimwali) does take place on these expeditions, but it is now largely monetised and takes the form of transactions in trade stores wherein the Kitavans seek cloth, rice, sugar, machetes, metal pots, kerosene, batteries, biscuits, matches, and tobacco. Men are embarrassed somewhat about this trade on kula, saying it is forced upon them by the demands of the women back home. Okabulu-lans visit northern Kiriwina more frequently than the Kiriwinans come to Kitava and access to the trade stores is one of the major propelling mechanisms behind the differential frequency of kula trips. There is one cooperative store on Kitava but it is frequently nearly empty.

Northern Kiriwinans visit the Okabulula region roughly once every three years, sailing *en masse*, about 150–200 strong, sometimes by canoe but more often by government trawler (J. Leach 1978:69 and 200–1). An expedition could roughly expect to acquire about 250 armshells while on Kitava. The largest number of armshells acquired by one man in recent times is eleven. Kiriwinans carry as solicitory presentations tobacco, betel-nut, money, cloth, canoe-lashing creeper, turtle-shell earrings, and small European commodities. Almost all transactions are with partners so there is no indigenous barter or purchase at all in this link of the kula. The northern Kiriwinans are much more open to the use of European commodities in solicitation because they have much more access to them at home. They are willing to use money in solicitation, meaning sums up to 5 Kina (USA $7) or so, whereas the Kitavans would rarely, if ever, do the same in reverse. Mussel shells have dropped out of these exchanges with the easy availability of knives and as well combs, lime pots, and plaited fern are no longer used transactionally (Malinowski 1922: 480).

The volume and value of solicitory gifts going from Kiriwina to Okabu-lula is considerably greater than that which is returned. The Kitavans say they are very important to the northern Kiriwinans and hence do not have to give as much. They also explain that the ethos of kula is generosity and that it is right that the wealthy should transfer goods to the poor. How-ever, it must be said northern Kiriwinans outnumber their Okabululan partners by about two and a half times. They also apparently receive considerably more armshells than they give necklaces.

In their eastern relationships, Okabululans see their primary ties with Madau Island and northern Woodlark. Sailing, however, by small ex-pedition of about three canoes or large sojourn of about ten, is not direct to these areas but via Iwa and Kweiwata-Gawa in the Marshall Bennetts. These are principally stopping points where there are few kula partnerships and only a little trade. At Iwa, Okabululans barter yams and betel-nut, usually for chickens. The chickens are a sore point with the Kitavans as the Iwans are said to be overly mercenary in seeking money for them as often as possible. Iwans, incidentally, have the least access to cash of any kula island in the northern sector of the ring. The Okabululans usually stop only a day at Iwa, sleeping on the beach due to physical difficulty of access to the villages and their great fear of the notorious flying witches of the island. The northern Kitavans sail onward to Gawa, another stopping point, where they have a few partners and do minimal trading. They then carry on to Madau Island,[3] especially the villages of Boagis, Mwadau, Kuduweta, and Moniveyova, followed by Kaulay, Dikwayas, and Kulumadau on northern Woodlark (see map p. 311 for location).

Okabululans have numerous kula partners on these two islands, even more than with Kiriwina. The usual pattern is for a small expedition of some twenty-five men to visit a select few of these villages in search of armshells, of which they might return with five to twenty-five depending on availability. These trips are fairly frequent, some going out though not always successfully reaching their destination every year. The northern Kitavans take tobacco, betelnut, piglets, Kiriwinan skirts, and mats as solicitory gifts. Yams and coconuts which fill their canoes are there for personal consumption en route, during which they will also fish. The Madauans and Muyuwans give as counter presentations clay pots, traditional combs, sandalwood oil, obsidian, piglets, betelnut, minor amounts of ebony, mats, tobacco and magic. Formerly this was a principal link for passing green Woodlark andesite[3a] westward for stone tools, but this ceased generations ago (Malinowski 1922:481) and is not known about by young Okabululan kula men as very little of the stone exists on Kitava now. There is no barter with non-kula partners in the Woodlark area and only a small volume of trade-store purchasing as most of the stores are outside the target areas. The men of the northern Woodlark area travel to Okabulula less frequently, by canoe or trawler, usually in two separate groups as Madau Islanders or northern Muyuwans. Their solicitory gifts are those which they exchange on Okabululan visits, only the quantities are larger and money is sometimes used. Despite the high status of their western (Kiriwinan) kula partners, Okabululans actually prefer their eastern ties. They say that eastward kula sailing is more exciting and dangerous, that personal ties are closer there because of their origins in the area, and that they acquire more wealth from those links. Okabululans justify the imbalance in their favour by arguing that, as autochthons of the region, they deserve some of its resources and by noting that the Madauans and Muyuwans are wealthier overall.

There are sixty-five men of the southeastern region of Kitava, Lalela, in the kula. Their western ties are with Vakuta Island and south Kiriwina, especially Gilibwa village, and their eastern partnerships with the Marshall Bennetts, southern Madau and Woodlark villages, Yanabwa, and Yeguma. Lalelans had eight kula canoes in the mid-1970s. They usually sail *en bloc* both westwards and eastwards, going outwards in either direction about once every two or three years. The focus of western partnerships is Vakuta where every Lalelan kula transactor has a partner. Some five to ten men have partners in Gilibwa and in the Sinaketa area of south Kiriwina. It is linkages with men of high rank in Sinaketa that are especially sought. A full expedition to the Vakuta area could expect to bring back fifteen to twenty-five necklaces under normal circumstances. Lalelan solicitory gifts are essentially the same as those of the Okabululans in northern Kiriwina (see p. 257). Vakutans return betelnut, piglets (1–4 months old), canoe-lashing vine, tobacco, and clay pots (*kuria* or *valata*). Only the large and medium-sized pots are acquired now, the small ones having dropped from circulation due to the availability of metal pots. There is only a very small amount of barter or monetary purchase (gimwali) between Lalelans and Vakutans. Most resources for transaction are given to partners and buying takes place in the Vakuta cooperative trade store. Roughly ten Lalelans claim direct partnerships in the Amphletts and on north Fergusson. However, they sail southward only as a part of a larger Vakutan expedition, never on their own. It is probable that they are travelling with a Vakutan partner on an arranged plan to make a double transaction, i.e. passing a promised necklace immediately through the Vakutan onwards to his Kitavan link. Vakutans come to Kitava by canoe or trawler on small expeditions but sail by canoe alone on large expeditions of 100 or more participants. They normally visit the two southern Kitavan regions simultaneously, acquiring about twenty-five to sixty armshells from each area. Vakutans solicit with the range of resources mentioned above, but also including tobacco and money.[4] Presentations are to kula partners in southern Kitava and there is little or no barter or purchase.

Lalelans exchange eastward with the Marshall Bennetts, with the southern villages of Madau Island and the northwestern villages of Woodlark Island (see map p. 311 for location), and with Yanabwa and Yeguma to the south of Gawa. There are, in fact, two sailing routes outwards from southern Kitava. They both have Iwa as first stop and Kweiwata–Gawa as second. An expedition would never sail to Iwa and then return home except under very abnormal circumstances. However, it might return from Gawa without further easterly or southerly sailing. The factors that count most in deciding to continue or return are the time already expended on the journey, the weather encountered and expected, the valuables by then acquired, and the state of impending activities on Kitava, especially gardening. If continuing, the expedition could sail to Boagis Village on Madau and onwards to southern Woodlark. Alternatively, it could go south to Yanabwa and Yeguma. The Woodlark route is the primary one because of the volume and value of presentations that can be expected from the larger population there. The southerly route is taken usually in search of famous shells thought to be in the area, but is far less frequently chosen. On occasions, an expedition may split and go both directions from Gawa at once.

When Lalelans sail to Iwa, they carry small yams (*teitu*) and large ones (*kuvi*), tobacco, betelnut, cloth, piglets, machetes, and bananas. By far the most important exchange resources are the yams as Iwa is deficient in its supply. Tobacco is probably second in value. Roughly two-thirds of the resources taken on expedition and intended for exchange stay in Iwa, the remaining islands being wealthier in yams. Iwa is generally considered the biggest drain on Kitavan resources of any community in the kula east or west. There is no barter or purchase with Iwans. Resources are given to actual or potential partners in solicitation of armshells. The gifts are reciprocated by small quantities of uncarved ebony. Lalelans do not see this island as a bounteous source of armshells, despite its being a primary stop for them. The best region for shells is considered southern Madau and Woodlark Islands. The Kitavans think of Iwa as the most dangerous of the eastward and westward islands, principally because of the quantity and especially lethal quality of the flying witches there. Some Lalelans actually refuse to sleep in Iwan houses or hamlets, even those of their partners, because of this fear. The overall pattern of unbalanced resource transfer applies on reciprocal journeys. Iwans, who travel in group expeditions of five to seven canoes of some sixty or so participants, usually arrive on south Kitava with empty canoes and require feeding during their stay on the island. Conversely, unlike the Lalela–Vakuta link, the Lalela–Marshall Bennett route requires the eastward kula voyagers to take most of their own food, normally yams and coconuts though they also expect to fish, during their 4–8 week sojourns. If there is a balancing mechanism in Iwan–Lalelan relations, it may well be magic. Most Kitavan magic is said to come from the east, especially the Marshall Bennetts and Woodlark. Iwa was also formerly an entrepot for Muyuwan andesite passing westward for stone tools and valuables (Malinowski 1922:481). Iwans carry on one type of exchange with Lalela which is very important to the kula yet carried on outside its context. All the island's overseas canoes (tadobu) are from that region, due apparently to the excellence of the wood and of the workmanship of the area. In the mid-1970s two such canoes were purchased for one middle-sized, medium-value armshell (mwari) each. The transactions were not between kula partners and the rate of exchange was considered exceptionally low by Kitavans, who saw a canoe as requiring four or so such shells for adequate compensation.

Lalelans give the same range of items to Gawans and Kweiwatans as to Iwans (see p. 262) but in considerably lesser volume. They receive ebony, mats, obsidian, and betelnut in return. Gawa is considered a good source of armshells, in the east second only to southern Woodlark. Exchange with Gawa is seen as relatively balanced. On Woodlark Lalelans tend to arrive with depleted resources and to depend more on small gifts, the passage of significant political and economic information, and perspicacious kula speech in the solicitation of valuables. The Lalelans receive, while visiting Woodlark and hosting the Muyuwans at home, large clay pots (*kuria*), ebony, mats, obsidian, sandalwood oil, ·magic, songs and dances, but almost no European commodities other than tobacco. The transfer of resources on aggregate clearly favours the Kitavans, explained by them as deservedly so because of the land and material wealth of the Muyuwans. Lalelans voyage eastwards roughly about once a year and return with forty to sixty armshells, usually taking no necklaces with them when they go. The men of the Marshall Bennetts plus occasional other islanders take about thirty or thirty-five necklaces from Lalela more or less annually.

There are thirty-six men and one woman of the southwestern region of Kitava, Kumwagea, in the kula. They have the same kula routes westward and eastward as the Lalelans and the pattern of resource transfer is also very similar. Kumwageans claim 114 westerly kula partnerships, including two anomalous ones between a schoolteacher and a medical orderly and two Okabululans, and 118 easterly partnerships. The average man therefore has about three firm kula ties in either direction and this can be taken as the modal figure for Kitavans as a whole. Only two Kumwageans had a single partner on either side while, at the top end of the scale, one man had six partners in each direction. Despite the appearance given in the aggregate numbers, a considerable number of Kumwagea transactors, twenty-three to be exact, did not have the same number of partners on either side. A common pattern is to have three on one side and four on the other, but one man was linked to four Vakutan–Gilibwan partners while having only one to the east on Iwa. Yet another claimed three to the west and south but six spread over all the relevant eastern islands. Concerning concentration of partnerships, about half those to the west and south were with men of Vakuta–Gilibwa. To the east 58% were in the Marshall Bennetts, 24% on Madau and Woodlark, and 18% on Yanabwa and Yeguma. A full Kumwagean expedition to Vakuta–Gilibwa could expect to return with twenty-five to thirty-five necklaces in an average year whereas a trip to the east would normally bring back thirty-five to forty-five armshells. These figures more or less pertain for onward circulation when Vakutans or easterners arrive on Kitava for reciprocal visits. All Kitavans recognise that there are more armshells in the kula than necklaces, that armshells are easier to solicit and acquire, that they are usually the first shells given over to others to begin their kula careers, and that they have more internal uses in other Kitavan transactions. There is no emic explanation of why the imbalance in numbers of shells exists. Nor is there any explanation why the armshells have become unpaired since Malinowski's day (1922:386 and 503–4) or the longest necklaces shortened (1922: frontispiece and 472–3).

Kumwageans and Lalelans exchange with the same communities to the west and east, yet they never sail as a single expedition. Nevertheless, their sailing on voyages of any size is nearly simultaneous. An expedition from one region will be followed by a concomitant trailing expedition from the other, usually only a few hours or at most a day behind. On arrival, the two groups beach their canoes, sleep, eat, and circulate in the villages separately, though contiguously and with a constant eye on each other. A prominent feature of this community competitiveness in situ is the intensification of kula solicitation by presentation and speech with which it is associated. Rivals from different regions engage in verbal deflation of their counterparts, either privately or publicly, including even face-to-face insults. The usual ploys are criticism of the opposition for lack of winsomeness and generosity, dishonesty, ignorance of kula lore, and lack of skill in everyday capabilities, the metaphor which is the ability to mix betelnut properly. Serious quarrels sometimes erupt, though this is not common, but physical fighting is culturally unaccept-able and not known in this context. It is interesting that the balance of resource flow, excluding armshells and necklaces, is different for southern and northern Kitava. The northerners are net gainers in their westerly and easterly relationships. Both southern communities regard them-selves, by contrast, as net losers *vis-à-vis* Vakuta to the west and Iwa to the east, though further eastward their balance evens up and with Wood-lark is considered favourable.

From the Kitavan point of view, there is not a great deal of resource flow between islands outside the context of kula. In terms of traditional goods, the principal extra-kula link is between Iwa and Kitava. The Iwans get their large canoes from southern Kitava, but also make numerous

ann\
Iwar
Besi(
others. *There is little reciprocation normally, the*

giving *ir vital port-of-call position to the full.* are
five a *from Gawans and Yegumans but seldom* tobacco,
though *o to Vakuta for mortuary exchanges* roughly that
entirel *ies of goods. Kitavans send betwee* store from 1912 to
tinned f *ear to the Kiriwinan trade* des fitfully, depending on the
order of *e small because transac* sa copra. In the mid-1970s, the store
1966 in a *mmodities sought* time. There was, for example, no cargo
their own *ts, and machet*
in-flow o *ts, and* delivered to it in 1974 or 1976 and no trade with passing trawlers.

Without a doubt, the Kitavans regard the circulation of valuables as the central focus of the kula (Malinowski 1922:509–16). They point out that kula continues whether resource transfer is high or low, that it is possible to acquire shells and partners without other material resources at all, and that nothing they receive from subsidiary kula transactions is essential to their everyday lives, though several things add qualitatively to their standard of living. Kitavans do not see trade (gimwali) as intrinsically linked to and a function of the kula (Uberoi 1962:140). Trade in this sense is seen contemporaneously as an innovation on kula expeditions which has taken place within living memory, though the actor's view here is short-term and analytically circumscribed.

Internal uses of valuables

There are no internal kula exchanges on Kitava,[5] with the exception of the Kumwagea schoolteacher and his brother who have partners in the northern region. These relationships began in the 1970s and are the only remembered instances of internal kula partnerships. They are dis- approved by other Kitavans as improper and ignorant, leading to no knowledge of sailing and little of other islands and leaving such men too tied to their wives and womenfolk.

Kula armshells and necklaces do, however, have social usages in Kitavan transactions, though these are conceptually outside the kula (sometimes *kura*) system. The two most important extra-kula exchanges involving the shells are in marriage and in canoe presentations. In mar- riage gifts, the father of the groom, if he has valuables at the appropriate time, would be expected to give a necklace to the father or mother's tur.

tobacc

master-t

owner. It

as is often

highest qua

were the appropriate p.

edge and complete skill of the

brother of the bride. Such a necklace would be of medium
the scaling of shells,[6] not normally a famous one. The
the girl would reciprocate in yams and then be free to
back into the exchange system by giving it to the pa
giver, by passing it to a partner of his own, or by
ionship. In canoe presentations, the owner of a ca
supplies the builders and carvers with yam
throughout the construction process.
receives one armshell of medium
der is also an expert (tokabitam
n a set of armshells woul
carver explained
as they sy

The other minor ways in which kula shells pa...
are as payments to sorcerers and flying witches, as payment...
acquisition of sorcery and kula magic, or as gifts to master carvers for
teaching a neophyte. Kula shells do not enter into land transactions,
mortuary ceremonies, or contemporary peacemaking after warfare
(Seligmann 1910:665–8). Kula shells which move in internal exchanges
may be held by the receiver for months or even years, used in other
non-kula ways, or put back into the system. They do not become personal
possessions forever outside the kula. The expectation is that all shells
eventually return to inter-island circulation. Sale of kula shells is unheard
of on Kitava itself though other areas, particularly Kiriwina and secondarily Vakuta, are known, disparagingly, for the practice.[7] Nevertheless,
Kitavans do sometimes give shells conceptual monetary equivalents. In
the mid-1970s, the smallest armshells were valued at about 7 Kina (USA
$10) and the largest and finest at about 135 Kina (USA $190). A small
unfinished cone shell which would have become a low-quality armshell
was sold to a European for 5 Kina (USA $7) in 1976. Similar information
on necklaces was not collected.

Kula shells are displayed on Kitava in two contexts. The first is as a
collective presentation on the landing beach on the return of a voyage.
The second is during harvest dancing (*milamala*) when the necklaces are
worn mostly by the daughters of kula men. A man with no daughter
would see that his son or niece would wear his newly-acquired ornament.
All necklaces are displayed on these occasions, not just the best, even if
one girl wears five or six at once. Armshells, by contrast, are rarely seen
at harvest dancing, but, if so, usually on the son of a kula man who is not
yet himself a transactor. Men are in general much less willing to display
their armshells than their necklaces, in public or in private, while on

266

Kitava. In place of armshells, one sees on male dancers a circular minor valuable (*diginagoma*; see Malinowski 1932: Plate 75) which is made from the crown of the *Conus literatus* shell. These ornaments are mostly manufactured on Kitava though a very few come from the Marshall Bennetts. They are exclusively male property and most men own one which they keep throughout adolescence and adulthood. The objects are principally decorative though they may occasionally take on exchange functions in kula solicitation or as temporary armshell-surrogates while waiting for a proper armshell to be available, any luxury gift in return being proper ultimate reciprocation. The diginagoma is, unlike the kula armshell (Malinowski 1922:503), made entirely by one man, usually the finder. The objects are not sold monetarily but are associated with the value of about 3 Kina (USA $4). Elderly men often pass these ornaments down to their sons and junior kinsmen as they come of dancing age.

These cone-shell ornaments were formerly made in imitation of a valuable of great historical, but not contemporary, significance in the kula, the near-circular boar's tusk (*doga*). These were described by Malinowski (1922:357) but unrecorded photographically (see Seligmann 1910:517–19 and Finsch 1887:Tafel VI and notes). There are between ten and thirty boar's tusks left on Kitava, owned by men as private heirlooms and worn in dancing or on kula expeditions. The oldest Kitavans claim to remember a time when the tusks were circulating valuables like armshells. They say the tusks, never voluminous in number, were traded out of the kula through the perfidy of the southerners in the ring. The ceremonial tusks were always very time-consuming and expensive to produce through pig husbandry and no one now attempts to grow them in the nearly circular form. The tusks can still be armshell-substitutes but this is very rarely done. They are conceptualised at a monetary value of 5 Kina (USA $7), though never sold.

Another minor valuable is the lime spatula (Malinowski 1922:358) made of whalebone or human shinbone. About ten to fifteen of these remain on Kitava, owned by senior leaders. They are usually passed down patrilaterally from father to son to grandson or received as very rare gifts from kula partners. Bone spatulae are not remembered as ever having been circulatory valuables. Spatulae as kula gifts are not solicitory nor do they create specific obligations for a counter-presentation. They are given only from one prestigious transactor to another as a sign of their special relationship. Such spatulae are often considered extremely personal objects, especially those of human bone which are the most common. Sale is said to be unthinkable though their monetary equivalent is put at about 20 Kina (USA $28).

Another minor valuable is the double-rowed *Spondylus* belt (*wakala*) of broad discs. These were not discussed in the *Argonauts*, except for the process of manufacture (1922:366–75 and Plate LII), though they existed as important insignia of rank (1922:Plate LXV) and as exchange objects. Kitavans say that these belts formerly circulated, like necklaces, in a clockwise direction and were transacted between leaders of different areas. The ornament, especially important in adult harvest dancing and in adornment of the deceased in mortuary rites, dropped out of kula altogether after World War II. Now only the leaders of Kumwagea and Okabulula keep one as heirlooms. They are no longer used for display or decoration. Their monetary equivalent is placed at about 45 Kina (USA $63).

The green andesite[3a] axeblades (*beku*), so prominent in Weiner's recent analysis of Kiriwina (1976:179–83 and *passim*), are small (less than 20 cm long), few in number (less than ten), and transactionally almost functionless on Kitava. They are kept mainly as heirlooms. They are known by elderly Kitavans as important gifts in kula in the past. Kiriwinans are said to have accumulated the best ones over the years.

Symbolism in kula

Kula expeditions are at one level symbolic representations of the life cycle and behaviour of a butterfly. Butterflies are considered the most beautiful of animals near to man, ensconced land creatures which transform themselves through their own inner power into a free and soaring form, breaking the fetters of their land-based existence and winning favour in nature simply through their attractiveness.

Expeditions begin with exit from the home village, single file and silent to the beach for the departure of the canoes. The row of men is the caterpillar, many-legged, a unity of multiple similar sections propelled peristaltically in one direction. The chrysalis stage is on the beach at the junction of land, sea, and sky. The men huddle quietly before the launching of the canoes, some occasionally washing in the shallow sea though long since clean during preparations in the village. This unusual languid period changes with the excited noisy launching and the unfurling of the sail. Symbolically, the canoe is polysemic, but its sail is unmistakeably like a butterfly's wing (Malinowski 1922:Plates XL and XLVIII). The canoe prowboard (*lagimu*) also includes a level of structure drawn from the butterfly imagery, principally the eyes in the centre and wing-flanges of the double-sided splashboard (Scoditti 1977:213). The whole splashboard 'may even be read as a head bowed over the chest of a body taking wing or jumping into the air' (Scoditti 1977:221), though the canoe is thusly by no means only a butterfly. Skilful sailing is itself said to be like flying over the surface of the sea, especially felt in the buoyant lift over the crests of the waves. Malinowski recorded numerous examples of butterfly and flying metaphors in kula magic (1922:130–2, 340–1 and 249–5 and 428–63 *passim*) and, of course, in the famous myth of the flying canoe of Kudayuri (1922:311–21), which, incidentally, is no longer extant in toto on Kitava, having died with its owner in the 1960s. The landing of the expedition on the host island sees the second form of the chrysalis as the men bathe and adorn themselves in the shallows and on the beach in preparation for the ornamented single-file march of the caterpillar into the host village. The cycle reverses itself at the departure of the expedition for home.

Kula dress tends to be conservative, a reversion to traditional attire even among men who have abandoned it. Older men still wear the high prestige areca-palm pubic covering (*yobuwa*), usually one freshly made. Younger men wear the same or a newly cleaned, or preferably bought, red lap-lap. The body is cleaned in the sea and oiled with coconut so as to shine. Shininess is a perceptual quality of deep kula significance. At one level, bodies should be a reflecting medium or mirror. Metaphorically, partners should see themselves in each other, an expression of the narcissism in kula ideology. At another level, the body should be radiant like the sun to attract the attention of potential and actual partners. The sun imagery is augmented by the use of bright yellow pollen sprinkled over the torso. Shininess of body is especially expected of young men as it is understood they lack 'shininess' of speech. The emphasis reverses for elderly exchangers with more importance attached to brilliant discourse than appearance. 'Shininess' of aroma also applies to kula dress and grooming. Sandalwood oil is applied to shoulders and chin as an attractant and to increase the self-confidence of the wearer. Other odoriferous and visual stimulants are wild mint (*Ocymum basilicum*), worn tucked under upper-arm bands, and frangipani crowns or necklaces. Another visual attractant is the red hibiscus worn in the hair and red facepaint (*dova*), made from betelnut, put on the lips and on the cheeks in circular daubs. Black and white facepaint, prominent in many other contexts, is not used in kula. Red is the quintessential personal kula colour, more meaningful in that social context than any other. Redness stands in many contrast-sets – for the inner excitement of the transactor against the socially-prescribed calmness of his exterior being, for the extra-dimensional movement outward from the 'flat' background of every day life in home and village, for the self moved forward into a new plane of extroversion and assertiveness, for the extra-normal social closeness of kula friendships against a background of 'colder' normal relationships, and for the colour of, for Kitavans, the mythological founder of the kula,

Giancarlo Scoditti

Monikiniki (Malinowski 1922:201, 311, 348, 420, and 441), an androgynous being whose historical icon is a bright red snake (*mwata*) found on the island.

Kula speech between actual or potential partners is a *parole* syndrome for a single social context and has special phonological, syntactical, and semantic characteristics. It begins after greeting and chewing betelnut together (or eating) and may last for hours, ceasing immediately after the transferal of a shell. There are four unusual phonological properties of ceremonial kula speech. It is faster than everyday discourse and higher in pitch by several half-tones. The intonation pattern employs elongated breath groups like chanting or reciting magical spells. Words are truncated by dropping final and sometimes penultimate syllables and in addition juxtaposed terms are elided. In general, there is acoustical condensation and intensification which sounds halfway between everyday speech and magic. Speed is, of course, a common attribute of a wide range of kula symbols (Malinowski 1922:130–2, 137–9, 215–16, 392–463). Syntactically, normal word order and the future tense of verbs tends to be avoided. In kula ideology, the present is ideally a structural repetition of the past. Past-present are to the future as predictability is to unpredictability. Avoidance of the future tense is to put into ritual abeyance any reminder of the sometime chicanery, self-interest, and uncertainty in kula transactions. Semantically, archaic words, especially from Woodlark and from Dobu–Duau, are prominent and new borrowings in everyday speech from English, Motuan, or Pidgin are entirely eliminated. Interestingly, the archaicisms are seen to emanate from the origin zones of the two types of kula valuables, armshells being understood to come from Woodlark and necklaces from Dobu–Duau. Some archaic terms are unclear in meaning even to their users. Flattery is crucial in kula solicitation. A shell holder is complimented very personally in his speech, appearance, smell, intelligence, honesty and propriety in kula behaviour. By contrast, shell seekers denigrate their competitors. Such speech has a gamelike quality. Though seeker and competitor may be from the same village, such kula criticism is not ideally the basis of hostility on return home. The reciprocation of kula ridicule occurs only on expeditions, present or future, and should be by cultural convention sealed off from significance in everyday life. A prominent feature of ceremonial kula speech is the verbal closure of the kula circle by recitation of paths, partners, and shell histories of full shell traverses. Verbal closure conceptually contrasts with the social impossibility of men themselves sailing around the kula ring. One of the underlying structural dynamics of the kula is the paradox of attempting to close and complete this impossible circle.

The term in Nowau for circle is *kakokobonu* (sometimes *kakokabonu*), sometimes used to conceptualise the kula as a system. Another Kitavan expression is 'the kula is like the red snake asleep' (*kula makara mwata bougwa i masisi*), referring to its coiled position. There are multiple correspondences between the concepts of kula and of circularity. Firstly, the exchange system is ideally thought of as closed chain of partners, lack of closure implying one's untrustworthiness, absence of prestige, and general incapability in the eyes of other transactors. Secondly, the kula is ideally a circle of many-stranded shell paths around which the valuables, in theory, predictably circulate. The circle of paths is, however, said to have a weak perimeter in the south where leakage of valuables, especially armshells, occurs. Thirdly, the kula is thought of as a chain of islands and villages through which resources move. The valuables may complete the circle but men and other material resources are ensconced sectorially in only a part of the circumference. Fourthly, the kula circle stands for the coiling of the mythological snake-being Monikiniki (see p. 270). This representation appears in harvest dancing formations which always move in an anti-clockwise direction ↻ , as armshells do and boar's tusks did around the kula ring. Fifthly, the circle appears in red facepaint on the cheeks of kula transactors on expedition and, incidentally, only in that social context. Sixthly, the armshells with their circularity are considered a better metaphor of the kula than necklaces. Armshells are, of course, permanently closed whereas necklaces are thought of as linear in their proper state but also as capable of openness or closure, hence representing the actual, less-than-idea nature of the real kula. Finally, in kula ideology, the circle stands for complete knowledge of the cosmos, realisable but never actually attained by men, given that only they have the capability of knowing the world through travel, diving under the sea, exploring the terrestrial underworld of caves, climbing mountains, and acquiring astronomical and ornithological information. Women, by contrast, as relatively immobile creatures of the land surface, have little chance of this hypothetical state of knowledge which is one of the ultimate goals of kula men.

The gender symbolism of kula shells (Malinowski 1922:356) is relatively insignificant to Kitavans. Information on the topic never came forward spontaneously but could be elicited by questioning. The Kumwageans saw the armshells metaphorically as male and the necklaces as female. The reason given was that the armshells represented the ideal state of complete knowledge attainable only by men. Ipso facto, necklaces, as a residual converse, must be female. It is, however, also clear that armshells have much greater non-kula usage on Kitava and are also much more dominant sociolinguistically. Interestingly, Lalelans reverse the gender identification of the shells, maintaining the Malinowskian schema (1922:356). The *raison d'être* seems to be that necklaces represent cumulative knowledge, prestige, and wealth as acquired by men over a kula career, whereas armshells represent, by contrast, static non-expanding value.

The matrilineality of Kitava is *mutatis mutandis* substantially the same as that of Kiriwina as reported in the cumulative writings of Malinowski, Powell, and Weiner. Kitavan men see kula in tendential opposition to matrilineality and to women, who stand metonymically in their minds for the pressures of everyday social control. Kula is a domain of activity in which men are at their freest, temporarily relatively unfettered by the constraints inherent in the everyday balance of power between the sexes. Men are less influenced by women in their handling and disposal of kula shells than they are in the possession and transmission of any other kind of property. Kin-linked kula succession tends to be patrilateral. Transmission of shells, partners, and paths, by no means a kin-bound process, has a tendency to be from father to son to grandson or from grandfather to grandson when it is. Men say their true personality can only be expressed in kula, all other social contexts being more constrained and distantiated. Their behaviour is observably more extroverted on the kula, especially on overseas expeditions. Kula is said to make men more sophisticated, to allow them to use their intelligence more openly than any other occasion, and to make them physically stronger. Interestingly, their dietary balance changes markedly in favour of protein-rich fish while on expedition. The souls of kula men are said to be more active as a result of participation in the exchanges. More exactly, they dream and daydream more. Kula men see their ceremonial exchange activity as their best potential avenue for immortality. Ordinary men, whether in the kula or not, carry their names with them to the spiritual underworld after death. Famous kula men, however, leave their names behind linked to prominent shells. The souls of these men go unnamed into a perpetual existence of a spiritual overworld, their transition to which is marked by thunderstorms and lightning. Such souls of the overworld never return through reincarnation or during the annual post-harvest ceremonies as is common for other spirits (Malinowski 1954:149–274). Kula on Kitava is the principal domain of expansion of the male self otherwise embedded in a matrilineal social organisation.

Notes

* Scoditti is the principal author of this paper but the editorial contribution of J. Leach both in the text and the footnotes has been very substantial.
1 Campbell, in critique of an earlier draft of this paper, writes: 'Kitavans and Vakutans practise what is known as *bora bora*, which in effect does dam up kula valuables to some extent. When we went to Kitava in June 1977, there was a *bora bora* on for a dead woman. Because of the sex of the deceased, the "hold-up" was not as serious as people said it would be were the deceased male. Nevertheless, certain exchanges and preliminary counselling had to occur before kula could proceed.' Scoditti notes that there is a ritual taboo on kula exchanges after a death on Kitava. This is often honoured in the breach. If functional, and it seldom is effectively, it tends to freeze shells in place on Kitava rather than allowing a continuing accumulation over time.
2 Campbell writes: 'It is funny that the Kitavans complain about the Vakutans using trawlers for kula expeditions. Vakutans complained bitterly about Kiriwinans, Dobuans, and to a lesser extent Kitavans using government trawlers.' Scoditti saw two small expeditions by government and mission trawler from Vakuta. Leach saw a large Vakutan canoe fleet on Kitava in July 1973.
3 Damon, in critique, writes: 'I doubt very much that Kitavans sail on to MUYUW (Woodlark) and to the particular places mentioned. . . It may be the case that these different folks have relationships going to these places, but I doubt that they frequently sail there and exchange on anything like a regular basis. In my two years, one or two boats from Iwa came to Woodlark, and none from anywhere west of there. Moreover, these voyages were made to check things out down the line on somebody's relationship, but not to carry out specific exchanges. Similarly, some MUYUW may sail as far as Kitava or even Kiriwina, but this is primarily to check out specific connections and not to make exchanges. If a few exchanges do occur, these are relatively insignificant articles, thought to be bad – evidence of a breakdown somewhere in-between, not part of a regularised *ked* (kula path).'
3a See note at p. 26.
4 Campbell writes: 'To my knowledge, Vakutans do not use money in solicitation of kula valuables.' Scoditti notes that tobacco is the most common medium of solicitation and that his citing of money is based on observation.
5 Scoditti did not inquire about and did not hear the indigenous term *kitom* while on Kitava. He believes it possible that the concept may not exist there as the islanders are not internal exchangers or the introducers of new Kula shells into the system.
6 See the papers by Munn and Campbell herein for material on the ranking of shells. The Kitavan lexical set is closer to Gawa (cf. Munn p. 302, Figure 1) though the armshell category *buruburu* is not used and the necklace categories *bagiyeru* and *bagitorobu* (cf. Campbell p. 242, Table 2) are kinds of *soulava*.
7 Campbell writes: 'Again it is rather amusing that the Kitavans accuse the Vakutans of selling valuables. I heard it the other way around, of course.'

PART III

Northeastern kula area

11   Gawan kula: spatiotemporal control and the symbolism of influence

NANCY D. MUNN

I. Introduction

This study is a preliminary analysis of Gawan *kula*[1] as a system of action. My aim is to examine kula (Rougwaw, *kura*) as a mode of action through which, over time, an actor concentrates into himself symbols of influence or control that are sedimentations and icons of the acts which produce them. Kula is viewed both as a system which constructs a particular inter-island form of Gawan sociocultural space and time, and as a medium through which the actor gains a certain control over this spacetime (the spacetime of kula which he, in interaction with others, produces). Enmeshing himself in this system of action, he develops his own sociopolitical value in its terms.[2]

All Gawan men have the option to enter into kula; while kula is not the most fundamental procedure for gaining community standing, it is nevertheless crucial. I suggest it is the field of action specialized to the creation of the *symbolism* of influence: it constitutes a specialized sphere of operations for exercising multiple acts of influence (persuasion and strategic control); through long-term successful engagement in these acts a man creates the symbolic figuration of himself as a leader, or man of influence (*guyaw*, also *tasayesa*, a man of wealth; *takurakura*, a man successful in kula) to whom others should 'listen' (*rega*) or to whose requests and exhortations they may be influenced to 'agree' (*tagwara, kabikawra*).

Since kula involves Gawans in managing the circulation of shells – in acts of acquiring armshells (*mwari*) and necklaces (*veiguwa*) and transmitting them to persons on other islands – spatiotemporal control in Kula is centered in control over motion (mobility and stasis of shells). On the one hand, this control constitutes the form and medium of the sociopolitical process of influence and influence-building; on the other hand, these acts of influence are the effective cause or social dynamic that puts shells into motion, thus creating what I later define as the structural level of kula spacetime (the level formed through shell circulation). I outline my analysis of kula action below; notions of spacetime and value are explained subsequently.

In kula a man continually acts to obtain the consent of others to give him shells. This consent is metaphorically formulated in Gawan terms as 'moving the mind' of the partner (see Part II). The receipt of a desired shell, for which he has exercised persuasion, signifies the receipt of an element of control which refers, on the one hand, to successfully completed control over the action of another (a man's success in making another release a shell to him): on the other, to control over the onward passage of the shell which will make him the focus of the persuasive acts of others. Furthermore, possession of a given shell may have significance for a man's potential effectiveness in persuading partners to give other shells at a later time, since any significant transaction has some generalizing carry-over to future transactions.

In this sense, each act of successful acquisition of a named shell (not all shells are named, see Fig. 1) produces for the recipient an element of influence 'embedded' in the shell, or in his possession of it; this influence, as we shall see, is coded in the Gawan concept of *butu* (fame). As I show later, butu translates the actor's control over the movement of a shell into a symbolic value attribute of actor identity; butu itself, analyzed in Gawan terms, can be understood as a form of motion, an icon of the process which produced it.

The control embedded in possession of a shell includes not simply Ego's ability to get others to act in ways that carry out his own will, but also his capacity for becoming the focus of the attempts of others to get him to act as *they* wish. This latter capacity is an equally important component of Ego's influence, since kula articulates the influence-building acts of a nexus of individuals; it is only at the level of this articulation that it becomes possible for the acts of a single individual to be regularly reproduced over time. Put otherwise, only on this 'social' level can kula as a system of action be reproduced in (and through) the actions of individuals.

The kula career of any given actor consists of his ongoing reproduction of basic acts of influence (acts of control over the movement of shells). Through the successful long-term performance of these acts he builds up his fame, so that a kula career is ideally developmental: the most successful senior men have concentrated into themselves a maximal control over motion which makes it possible for them to kula in a different way than young men in the early stages of their kula careers (see Part IV).

A condition of making one's fame is the construction of 'strong paths' (*keda; keda matuwa* or *tawutora*). A path is a specific sequence of partners on other islands; at any given time a man may be a member of more than one path. Kula shells may arrive on a path, or are obtained from partners or non-partners in off-path transactions and later put on a path or used to make new paths.

A path of partners is the sedimentation of motion (the path of a shell): it is made and maintained only through shell circulation (see Part IV). By developing strong paths a man can increase his control over this circulation so as to extend his influence across inter-island space (as for example, through 'long distance' arrangements by which desired shells are shunted onto one of his paths).

We can thus distinguish two sorts of focal symbols of a man's development of control in kula: fame and 'strong paths'. The latter defines a man's control in terms of the structure of kula relationships within which he embeds himself. The path relates specifically to the continuative or reproductive level of kula referred to above, and is crucial to the construction of a developmental kula career; moreover, the path is the basic mode of coordinating the influence-building acts of individuals which enables a 'continuous' shell circulation in kula. The 'strong path' and 'fame' can be described respectively as social and individual symbols of self that condense Ego's control over motion, and which he himself produces through long-term engagement in kula.[3]

Kula spacetime. The anthropology of exchange is frequently concerned with time in connection with the economics and politics of long-term debt (e.g., Lévi-Strauss, 1969; Sahlins, 1972; Strathern, 1971). In the present study, however, I regard kula as itself a spatiotemporal structure and process through which islanders create a mode of inter-island spacetime. My account presupposes a particular view of sociocultural spacetime (and of action systems). Drawing in part on phenomenological perspectives, I regard spacetime as being constituted through experience-forming processes, i.e., in Heidegger's (1962:78 passim) terms through 'being in the world'. A given, socioculturally-defined action system such as kula formulates a particular way of 'being in the world'; the internal structures of the system provide processual forms in terms of which experience is constructed. These forms are, as it were, 'spun out' by actors in the course of activities undertaken as part of (and in terms of) the action system, so that certain objective structures of the social world, and the specific forms of subjective experience are coordinately 'produced'.

The processual form of such a system (its abstract relational form as a process) consists of spatiotemporal relations – specifically, the particular modalities of these relations (involving formulations of such aspects as succession, duration, distancing, directionality, etc.) which characterize

Nancy D. Munn

and govern the system. For example, when we refer to the creation of a long-term circulation (successive relocation) of kula shells from island to island; or the formation of a directional patterning of a binary set of opposed sequences (the opposed direction in which each shell moves), we are summing up certain aspects of the spatiotemporal structure of kula.

However, kula does not merely constitute a particular spatiotemporal form. What is crucial is that through this form (and in its terms) an ongoing spatiotemporal manifold is constructed in the experience of the islanders. By this I mean that the action system involves the means of generating a continuum in which the ongoing present (spatiotemporal field) is experienced as continually surpassing itself, engaging the future; and the past is continually being engaged within the present which surpasses it. I refer to this process – in which expectation and past reference (and coordinately, different spatial references) are regularly being formed within the present – as one of spatiotemporal synthesis. The basic means by which kula actors synthesize spacetime through engaging in kula operations will be explained shortly.

I am arguing therefore, that sociocultural action systems (or the activities through which they become operative) do not simply go on *in* or *through* time and space, but that they form (structure) and constitute (create) the spacetime manifold in which they 'go on'. Actors must 'make' this manifold, thus concretely producing their own spacetime. It follows from this view that sociocultural spacetime is not homogeneous or 'singular'; rather, to adapt a statement of Roman Jakobson's (quoted in Holenstein, 1976:31), 'each system in movement possesses its own time [-space]'. Different action systems in the same society can construct different spacetime formations: for example, the community and inter-island spacetime which Gawans construct through their cyclic community entertainments (*kayasa*) is different from that of kula, although these two systems articulate with each other. The unified spacetime of a community is a result of totalizing processes (e.g., the mutual adjustment and impingement of different action systems, the employment of generalized value symbols and principles emerging from and/or governing the relations of different structures, etc.). These modes of totalizing are, however, outside the purvue of this account.

Turning now to the spatiotemporal form of kula, I suggest that kula duration and 'successiveness' are constructed essentially through motion which emerges on different levels of process. I distinguish these levels as ecological and structural spacetime, adopting Evans-Pritchard's (1942: 94ff.) labelling, but adjusting his notions to my own framework. The ecological level is seen here as the lower level of the spatiotemporal

280

system: i.e., it is a condition of, and is incorporated into the higher structural level. The relation between the two levels can be epitomized as follows: the ecological spacetime of kula is constituted by the travels of men to 'move' shells; the structural level by the travels ('paths') of shells to form relations ('paths') between men. In the present paper I deal with *the structural level only*, since it is this level that is generated by basic kula acts of persuasion and strategy. I shall comment briefly, however, on the ecological level.

The framework of ecological spacetime is formed out of the pattern of kula voyagings; for the inhabitants of any given island or kula community it consists of travel to locales in opposed kula directions and the travel of others to their own islands. The kula phasing of major reciprocal voyagings is contingent upon both 'natural' (e.g., the winds) and social factors. On this level, spatiotemporal synthesis is formed through the constitution and adjustment of expectations regarding visits from islanders in the opposed kula directions, and the plans for travel to these islands; people must wait for the arrival of shells on the islands of immediate partners, and in general, concern themselves with events affecting shell locations. Previous journeys affect future travels to and from islands in different directions. For instance, if Gawans have not gone to Iwa and Kitava for necklaces between November and April of a given year (travelling in the periods of favorable winds), they cannot expect a major kula visit from Muyuwans in subsequent months, the latter having heard that there are no necklace accumulations on Gawa. Past and future are thus engaged within the present. As I have pointed out elsewhere (Munn, 1972): 'the timing of [kula] exchange is built up in terms of an interconnected chain of temporal adjustments, for the planning of . . . sailings from one's own [island] . . . must take account of events [on the island] . . . of immediate partners, and these in turn are related to kula events in the ring as a whole'. In this way, an inter-island, ecological spacetime is constructed.

Turning now to the structural level, I distinguish two dimensions: the duration formed through shell circulation, and that formed out of the *exchange* which articulates the two directional sequences of shell circulation. The former can be reckoned in terms of the speed with which shells are transacted (how long they are held by a partner; how swiftly they can be obtained, etc.). I discuss this duration in terms of the Gawan qualitative symbolism of relative slowness (*mwawutu*) or 'tightness/difficulty' (*kasay*) and speed (*nanaakwa*) or 'looseness/easiness' (*pwapwasa*) in the transmission of shells. Rather than being an abstract, quantitative reckoning, this symbolism is itself the condensed node of a level of bodily or activity spacetime that intersects both ecological and structural levels (for example, on the ecological level, the speed of canoe travel is an important aspect of canoe symbolism). On the structural level, this notion of speed expresses the relative control of actors over shells and over each other, thus conveying the subjective significance of duration, or the spacetime reckoned. Indeed, speed (-slowness) should be seen as a value symbolism of spatiotemporal reckoning which defines the relation of shells in given transactions to actors' control capacities (cf. below, on value).

The same symbolism may refer to the dimension of exchange: here it specifies the speed with which an opening gift (*vaga*)[4] of one shell category is 'bitten' (*geda*), 'pierced' (*besa*) or 'married' (*vay*) by a matching shell (*gulugwalu; kudu*, 'tooth') of opposing category. This duration is that of an imbalance or debt: the period during which Ego has transmitted an opening gift, and not yet received a matching return.

The creation of debt is the basic means through which exchange spacetime is synthesized in kula: 'a non-actual but possible future [is brought into] the present' (Sherover, 1971:272) through the *initiation of debt*, and the past is bound within the present through the *closing of debt*. The spatial aspect of this synthesis can be seen in the fact that the opening shell from one direction creates anticipation of a return shell from the opposite direction; further, ego's receipt of a shell at say a Muyuw village at a given time implies his acquisition of a return shell at say, an Iwan village at some later time (most exchanges being spatiotemporally distanced). Conversely, the return shell 'binds' a reference to the opposite direction of the first shell (and the opposite kula locality of the latter's receipt) within its own directional locus.

The dynamic underlying this synthesis is a fundamental Gawan value principle which also motivates Gawan activities outside of kula: namely, the requirement of equalizing summed up in the English loan word 'squaring' (*skwera*, general Gawan term, *mapu*) which Gawans frequently use in this connection. 'Squaring' requires that an unmatched shell must (eventually) be matched by another shell of opposite type defined as its equal according to the kula set of value standards for shells (Fig. 1). Squaring also operates in kula contexts other than those of opening and closing gifts (for example, Gawans speak of squaring a partner's illicit diversion of a shell from their common path by later diverting another shell to repay the original diversion, etc.). While other types of equalizing in kula are optional (in contrast to the necessary equalizing of the opening gift), they can operate similarly to synthesize spacetime.

Once a shell is matched, it is necessary to create a new imbalance in order to keep shells moving along a path (i.e., for transactions to be reproduced). As Sahlins (1972:222) has pointed out: 'the exchange that is . . . unequivocally equal . . . cancels debt and thus opens the possibility of contracting out'. The other pole of equalizing is therefore renewal of inequalities through new opening gifts, or through exchanging opening gifts of opposite category shells (which need not be equal, see Part III). This dynamic generates the ongoing resynthesis of kula (exchange) spacetime.

Considered with respect to the actor, this resynthesizing (carried out through repeated acts of influence) constitutes the ongoing kula career. As a man pursues this career, he must not only balance debt, but in order to keep his paths active, regularly renew debt – i.e., continually resynthesize his own kula spacetime. This process of renewal is necessary in order to 'climb' (*mwena*), or become a guyaw. The value dynamic underlying debt renewal is, implicitly, that of hierarchy ('climbing').

Value. Whereas spacetime relations define the form of the action system as a process (and the terms in which the spacetime manifold is produced by actors), value may be said to define the process as a *felt* ordering of differential relations or significances.[5] From this point of view, it is essentially through value that action/process passes into the subjective feeling world of the actors: value at once 'makes sense' out of action and gives it 'necessariness' from the subject's perspective. Value is thus produced by/in the process (as an aspect of it), and is a dynamic motivating its production. For example, as I have suggested, equalizing motivates the synthesis of exchange spacetime: an opening gift is 'felt' as an imbalance which must eventually be rectified; but, obviously, equality is also produced by the matching of the initial valuable with its return. Similarly, the value of hierarchy or superordination is a basic dynamic of debt renewal, but hierarchy is also produced in the process.

An actor produces *his own* value in kula by the degree to which he gains mastery over kula spacetime, thus defining his relation to the process so that he himself becomes a term in the system of relative significances. To the extent that the actor can concentrate the process into himself, he can eventually produce himself as a guyaw; but whatever his level of achievement, it is because he defines his own relative worth through engaging in kula, that the actor does not simply produce the system, but also produces himself.

As the 'ready-to-hand' media through which men act (and the structural level of kula spacetime is formed), kula shells also become defined as value terms in the system of significances. Although men appear to be the agents in defining shell value, in fact, without shells, men cannot define their own value; in this respect, shells and men are reciprocally agents of each other's value definition. This interaction is the ground of the 'mingling' (Mauss, 1968:184) or symbolic interchange of qualities between men and things.

Nancy D. Munn

A critical feature of kula shells in their function as agents of human value definition is that, in contrast to men, they are classified into explicit categories of relative worth (which I call value standards,[6] see Fig. 1), based on the possession of certain 'qualisigns' (Peirce, 1955:101ff.) of value. As I argue in concluding, the Gawan classification of shells is implicitly a classification of men which encodes the developmental character (the incremental control of spacetime) of the successful kula career. The model depicts a hierarchy of increasing worth as the value-outcome of successful long-term participation in circulation through which both shells (as circulating media) and men (as managers of shell circulation) come to condense their circulatory power within themselves and valorize each other.

II. Persuasion as motion

In order to engage in kula a man must gain the 'agreement' of other men to give him shells. In this section I examine the model of persuasion repetitively expressed in Gawan kula magic (*mega*).

The central aim of kula spells is to 'move' ego's partner to give desired shells quickly (*nanaakwa*). The partner's physical motion or/and the movement of shells signify that his mind is being 'moved' (*tovira*, turned); conversely, moving his mind signifies that both his body and the shells are being put into motion.

On Gawa the notion that one cannot know another person's mind (*gera bi-takines*, we cannot see) is an epistemological premise underlying sociopolitical relationship (cf. Weiner, 1976:217; Damon, 1978:75). The aim of controlling the partner's mind – collapsing his will into that of the ritualist's through the latter's own action – should be understood in this context.

This control is conveyed through images of swift motion. In many spells the ritualist constitutes the partner's and his own 'motion' in a parallel or inter-connected manner. Motion then becomes the form of the relation between the Gawan and his partner that gives them the semblance of mutuality. Such apparent 'mutuality' or 'mechanical solidarity' is the essence of successful persuasion. To paraphrase Parsons (1963:51): in exerting this kind of control, one attempts to establish a 'we' in the sense that parties have views in common 'by virtue of which they stand together'. Here, the common view to be established is the mutuality of the Gawan's and his kula partner's desires in the movement of shells. The persuasive act may be understood as the capacity of the actor to affect the mind of the partner by making the latter's will (desires) correspond to his own.

Gawan kula: spatiotemporal control and the symbolism of influence

Many kula spells are concerned with the beautification of the ritualist through washing in the sea and decoration. In one spell, the ritualist going into the swelling waves gains 'another appearance' (*kweitara magi-ra*) he is *migirew* (shining, pure). My informant explained that the partner, seeing this appearance, is sympathetic (*karinuwara*): i.e., moved to give shells.

In another washing spell, the ritualist slaps his body with a slippery fish, thus acquiring a brilliance and mobile lightweightness (*gagaabala*) which make him so attractive that the partner gives swiftly. A similar spell features a fish (equated with the desired shells) which leaps and turns (tovira) towards the Gawan. Since kula shells themselves are ideally glowing (see Part V), the Gawan's ability to move them is, in effect, being identified with his ability to form himself in terms of their ideal qualities, or to become beautiful like the shells. The Gawan attempts to pre-form the partner's intentions (–actions) by giving mobile (–beautifying) qualities to his own body (prefiguring, as it were, his acquisition of the shells as an attribute of himself); these mobile qualities induce a corresponding, reciprocal motion in the partner so that he divests himself of the beautifying shells.

The condensation of these elements within a single 'image-act' such as the 'fish-leaping/slapping' occurs in other spells where 'turning towards' is explicitly a movement of the partner's mind. In one spell aimed at moving the partner's wife (who in turn will influence her husband) a red parrot flying south and north (a characteristic spell image conveying the spanning of space) is equivalent to the fish image. The parrot's beauty lies in its red color, which along with its call, expresses happiness. Its movement conveys both the swift flight of the necklaces towards the ritualist (they will 'go and come out (*sakapu*) to you'), and the happiness of the partner's wife to see the Gawan. Since the bird is the necklaces moving in the Gawan's direction, it probably condenses the Gawan's happiness and perhaps also his beautification (although my informant did not state these points explicitly).

The same spell refers to two ancestral sisters, the Rama Dobu, with whom the partner's wife is equated. The Rama Dobu came to Dobu from Kweawata, north of Gawa. The older sister now sits on Dobu 'looking away from' Gawa (and Kweawata); the younger sister however, having been more sympathetic towards their brother on Kweawata, sits looking *towards* this region. The older sister is *Kura Dobu*,[7] the 'tight/hard' or 'slow' way of playing kula while the younger is *Kura Masima*, the 'soft/easy' or 'fast' kula.

The Gawan ritualist attempts to make the older sister turn around towards him (*i-katovira nano-ra*, he turns her mind), and be sympathetic like the younger: he attempts to transform the 'slow-tight' into the 'fast-easy'. The red parrot flying back and forth and calling out her mind turn, or *is* this turning. Since the Rama Dobu are equated with the partner's wife, the latter's mind is being transformed, and her 'refusal' (*kayusa*) changed to happy affirmation of the Gawan's desires (the movement of the shells). The birds in motion (necklaces coming to the Gawan) embody the Gawan's effectiveness in moving the wife (or Rama Dobu); in effect, they embody the 'mutuality' of the two, the unitary form of the relation between their individual interests. It is as if they are 'of like mind'.

A third type of spell uses the imagery of the earth tremor (also connected with thunder) to signify the loosening of the shells. In one example, the Gawan prepares his possessions for a kula trip, putting into his mat bespelled betel nut for his partner. This preparation (*katabayasa*) is an earth tremor; the partner's betel chewing signifies that he is 'going out of his mind' to give shells to the Gawan, and so will speedily produce them. The earth-tremor is both the partner's trembling happiness, and (along with thunder), the Gawan's influential speech and fame; 'Not my speech, my speech earth tremor; not my fame, my fame thunder.' 'Earth tremor–thunder' condenses the Gawan's motion (his sailing preparations, his speech and fame); the loosening of valuables, and the partner's motion.

In sum, the spells depict obtaining the partner's agreement as the construction of a particular kind of spacetime in which motion (a swift traversal of space – for example, the leaping fish, the parrot's flight) defines the form of the relationship between the partner and the ritualist. The image of commonality rather than divergence is created through the rhetorical 'translation' of the will of each into a synthetic image of mobility. Since this 'translation' is made through the will or act of the persuader, it is as if *he* moves the shells rather than their possessor (his partner). Although persuasive power in obtaining shells is regularly represented as the capacity to produce swift movement, we shall see later that the capacity to *slow down* the movement of shells also defines a mode of control.

The Concept of Fame. When a man receives a named kula shell of note (especially vaga but also gulugwalu), it is his butu (fame); Gawans say that his butu 'climbs' (*i-mwena*) or 'goes all around' (*taavin*, tovira). One Gawan complained in public meeting that the 'name' (*yaga-ra*) of one of his northern Muyuw partners had 'gone around' as the result of the vaga necklace the Gawan had given him, but that he himself had not received any *vaga* armshell from his partner. This spread of a man's name is his butu (cf. Malinowski's 1935, v. 2:273, translation of butu as 'to spread'). It derives from his receipt and possession of a shell and not from the act of onward transmission, thus reflecting a man's capacity to 'move' his partners to accede to his own will.

Gawans describe fame by saying that 'one's name travels around' (*i-taavin*) or 'turns around' (tovira). One man said: a man might go northwest to Iwa and Kitava, and his name will tovira because he received necklaces at these places – i.e., it will turn back southeastward reaching the Muyuw people who hear about his achievement. In this example, the name returns in the direction from which the Gawan has come (and towards which the necklace will go), travelling apart from the Gawan himself. The point is that fame goes in the direction from which shells of the opposite category will come. Men in this direction may use this knowledge in arranging future transactions. In the hyperbolic imagery of one kula spell, southerners hearing of a Gawan's receipt of a necklace rushed to set sail northward to Muyuw (presumably to obtain the necklace).

We find a similar theme in Fame chants (*butu-ra*) which Gawan women compose in praise of individual kin and affines who have given them necklaces to wear.[8]

One chant speaks of 'my fame, *muridogu* [middle standard] armshell . . . in my hand [the sailors] see.' The recipient's 'fame' (his armshell) is put in the boat; a kula man in Alotau (on the mainland) hears of him. Another chant tells how a man's 'fame' (an armshell he has obtained) will later go and be matched by a necklace on Dobu.

A shell-recipient's fame is here envisaged as translating his motive power from control over his immediate partner (in shell acquisition) into control over a wider kula spacetime involving men in the opposite kula direction, who in turn will be influenced to move shells to him because of his current power to move a shell from his partner. Put in another way, fame appears as a capacity to synthesize kula spacetime through creating a potentiality for future acquisitions of a shell from the opposite direction (as well as through enabling men in the opposed kula directions to arrange *their* future acquisitions).

While the travels of a man's name extend him spatiotemporally beyond himself (i.e., beyond his physical person) this extension also entails a 'rising' in esteem, connected with the concept of the guyaw. 'When you are given a kula shell, your name is spoken; people come to know your name. You climb (*ku-mwena*).' As another man put it: '[I am a] guyaw, they [other islanders] speak my name.' Conversely, with loss of esteem one 'falls': *i-busi butu-ra*, 'his fame falls', contrasts with *butu-ra ira wanakayo*, 'his fame goes on high'.

Fame can be seen as the inter-island circulation of a man's 'self' in the form of his good name. Butu translates the material shell and its motion into a personalized attribute of the actor (his esteemed name or value). Indeed, Gawan metaphors link fame to beautifying body decoration. For instance, in one kula spell aimed at spreading a man's fame, head-feathers worn by male dancers are a metaphor for the kula necklace 'decoration' (*bubera*) of the guyaw: 'his feather, guyaw, sound spreads echoing, the Raramani people know'. Here, fame is the knowledge or 'noising abroad' (*buragara*) of a man's bodily beautification (his persuasive power, since 'beauty', as we have seen, condenses a man's capacity to move his partner to give him a shell). Indeed, if we consider that kula shells are body-decor, and that the feather headdress materially extends the person (cf. Munn, 1977:49ff.), then fame is a further expansion of beauty *beyond* the physical person in the inter-island world. In this sense, fame decorates the guyaw.

In conclusion, we may suggest that butu is an icon of the action which produced it. Just as a man moves or 'turns around' the mind of his partner to obtain shells (*ikatatovira nanora*) so also his own name moves or travels around (*itovira yagara*) because he received a shell. Moreover, since butu involves the interested responsiveness of other islanders to the recipient, it entails, in effect, a 'turning of the minds' of more distant others to him. Butu generalizes the immediate control exerted in a transaction: as a product sedimented from this control (and an icon of it) it is also detachable from the fixed locus of the act – an acquired aspect of social identity that can operate as a component of a man's influence in later transactions.

Although I have spoken of butu in terms of the single transaction, it is the continual passing of kula shells through a man's hands that actually yields guyaw standing; a kula guyaw has *singay butu*, 'much fame'. The basic unit of the individual's butu 'production' (like that of shell 'production') is, however, the single transaction. It would seem on this basis that butu, as a generalized symbol, would be cumulative. 'Cumulation' cannot be understood, however, in any numerical or clearly ranked sense. Nevertheless, the general level of a man's butu is conveyed in some respects by the shell standard he can typically acquire at different stages of his kula career (see Part IV).

III. Persuasion and strategic control

In this section, I examine modes of persuasion and strategy as the dynamic through which the multiple connectivities of kula spacetime (and its control) are constituted by actors. I also develop further the sense in which structural duration (speed/slowness of shell movement, exchange) may be seen as an aspect of influence processes and a 'measure' of actor control.

Persuasive mechanisms in a given kula transaction derive both from generalized components of influence sedimented out of previous influence-creating transactions, and from immediate mechanisms for influencing the partner.[9] For example, kula fame, or the strength of partnerships (the latter deriving from past transactions with the individuals involved, see Part IV) may be understood as generalized elements implicit within the control a man can exert in any given transaction. Hospitality in food (*skwaiobwa*), or aid in obtaining a pig when requested (*kerasi*), also function as critical sources of generalized influence with immediate partners.

Hospitality (and related aid) is distinguished, however, from *pokala*; the latter is a gift of hard goods (e.g., cloth, money, mats, low-standard kula shells) and other non-edible items; pokala in the more specific sense is aimed at the acquisition of particular shells, and circumscribed in time, but in a more general sense is part of an ongoing process like hospitality. Pokala may also refer to shell transactions aimed at obtaining a shell (*rogita*).

While the explicit purpose of pokala in the specific sense is persuasion, hospitality, in contrast, is the ongoing base of the relationship between a man and his immediate partners without which a man cannot build path partnerships; hospitality continues as long as the partnership, irrespective of whether shells are 'thrown' between the men in a given kula year. As one man said: a Gawan can throw a shell to a partner one year and then not throw valuables for a time, but he will still eat at that man's home. Men stress that the *wowura* (base) of kula is hospitality in food (and pigs).

In the breach, a failure in hospitality or related forms of aid can negatively affect a man's persuasiveness in a particular kula transaction.

A man of Gawa (*A*) went to a northern Muyuw partner (*B*) for a pig to help him meet obligations at the finale of the Gawan dance entertainment. *B* was unable to supply the pig; partly for this reason, *A* denied *B* a necklace when the latter visited the Gawan dance. *B* responded to the Gawan partner's refusal in a speech to Gawans assembled at the dance, saying that he would now have to return home without kula. When armshells later come to his village, his armshells won't be 'made'; only *his* house (among all the others) will be empty of necklaces. 'I might lack armshells because there is no "bait" (*mwaaku*) to make [them].' Referring to *A*'s previous gift of a vaga necklace (part of an ongoing transaction), he pointed out: 'truthfully, your "child" [*natumu*, i.e., the result of your necklace, the armshell or armshells, that may come back to you] is now there [in the south]; later I might "harvest"; [but] the Boagis people will go to the Raramani, and will tell them "that man has nothing".'[10]

The Gawan's refusal of a shell to the Muyuwan is treated by the latter as implicating a train of consequences on their mutual path. Obviously, the Muyuwan is pressing his own interests, but his rhetoric points, nevertheless, to significant assumptions of a kind similar to those we have already seen in connection with butu: shells are themselves media of persuasion – their presence 'baits' shells of the opposite category. The Muyuwan asserts that without a necklace he cannot obtain further armshells for himself or his Gawan partner, since his own persuasiveness with the southerners will be weakened. Obtaining a shell points to and entrains future capacities to obtain other shells of the opposite category; the Muyuwan chides his partner for the loss of these positive potentialities, suggesting the Gawan's own future control capacities may be limited by his current attempt to limit those of the *Muyuwan* (by refusing him a shell).

The case highlights certain aspects of the way in which kula creates an ongoing spatiotemporal manifold. The future is constituted in immediate events on Gawa which are treated as having a potential 'ripple-effect' in the inter-island world. These effects (actualized on other islands) in turn can be expected to 'ripple back' and later affect events on Gawa (or the Gawan's kula – for instance, what he acquires when he visits Muyuw). We have to imagine the complex overlapping, multiplicity and ramification of such linkages at any given moment in order to grasp something of the densely objectified spacetime formed in the islanders' experience through kula.

The intrinsic persuasiveness of kula shells may be further illustrated by the fact that the use of pokala to acquire specific shells is ordinarily restricted to opening gifts. Although it is possible to ask a return pokala if a partner has asked pokala for a vaga (see below), one does not usually expect to pokala for a gulugwalu because, in effect, persuasion has already been activated through the medium of the other shell for which it is being exchanged. Indication of the capacity to provide a return for a given shell is, moreover, a major means of convincing another man that he should release a desired shell. Finally, providing a shell to close a long-outstanding debt can also be used to persuade a partner to release another desired shell as vaga (see the case of MANUTASOPI below).

Gawans do not expect to pokala for all vaga. Pokala with partners for vaga armshells is not regarded as a regular procedure, whereas pokala (of non-kula goods) for vaga necklaces is considered more usual, especially with men who are only casual, occasional partners (*pilidada*). One man expressed these differences between armshells and necklaces very strongly, saying that a vaga necklace can be obtained if you have a return shell, or if you pokala, but armshells can be obtained without either.[11] Consistent with this attitude is the fact that the *pro forma* performance of kula magic and adherence to certain food restrictions are significant in the northern trips for necklaces, but not the trips to Muyuw for armshells.

Gawans always explain this differentiation of necklaces and armshells by saying that necklaces are difficult to move (tight) and travel slowly; frequently, one may have to sail more than once to obtain a much desired (vaga) shell. Armshells, however, are 'loose' and travel more swiftly. Pressed to rationalize this asymmetry, informants explain that armshells are male (*tawaw*) and necklaces are female (*viray*). Women must be persuaded through gifts in order to obtain their agreement to sexual relations: they are 'tight' and it takes a long time to gain their consent.

Men, on the other hand, are mobile (for example, they are the main overseas travellers; and men 'go to meet women', not vice versa): armshells are therefore male.[12]

Differences in Gawan expectancies regarding speed of movement of the two types of shells point to an implicit value distinction: considered in terms of 'persuasion value' (or the relative control that must be exerted by actors to obtain shells) an element of hierarchy in the relation between the two shell categories ambiguates the stereotype of equal exchange (necklaces have higher persuasion value) but does not affect the explicit exchange value of shells.

While I cannot further examine this problem here, I would note merely that it is part of a wider differential evaluation of the northwestern and southeastern kula sectors (cf. note 7), which yields asymmetries in the bipolar directional model of inter-island space: the northwest sector is felt to be 'slower' than the southeast – shells move more slowly and (on this view) participants play a slower game. Nevertheless, when it comes to the persuasive use of shell transactions to obtain high-standard shells both armshells and necklaces appear equally 'tight' and their acquisition requires persuasive manipulation of shells of the opposite category (cf. the MANUTASOPI case below).

Once a man has obtained a shell, the degree of strategic control he can exercise is variable. For example, a gulugwalu coming on one path should automatically continue on that path, so that, as we have seen, the recipient does not have to pokala; by the same token the recipient's decision-making powers are limited by the path relationship. Nevertheless, a man may on occasion choose to divert (-ili) a gulugwalu onto another path, an act considered reprehensible 'theft' (*veiraw*), but not uncommon in kula strategy, expecially in the play of senior men.

From the perspective of the shell-holder (rather than the would-be recipient), pokala is a means of controlling the onward movement of a shell; the holder may determine whether pokala is required or not, as well as the type of pokala. One man described the following strategy:

Supposing a Gawan receives a high-standard armshell as vaga, and an Iwan partner wants it. The Gawan might decide to give the Iwan a 'smaller' (lower standard) shell instead. To obtain the large shell the Iwan must find a match for the smaller. The small gift makes it impossible for him to speak about the larger armshell which he really wants: 'It has closed his throat' (*boisakavini kayora*) because he is now in debt for the smaller shell. The necklace he later brings to match it is his pokala (or rogita) for the large armshell.

At this point, the Gawan might decide to release the large shell, or instead, require a second pokala like the first. His decision may be predicated on his desire for further pokala, or/and on the fact that the partner does not yet have assurance of a necklace equivalent to the desired shell. Demonstration of the capacity to

Nancy D. Munn

return an equivalent necklace is apparently the clincher, obtaining agreement to release the armshell. The pokala transactions are thus a kind of holding action until the partner has had time to make arrangements for a match, or/and for the Gawan to see if the partner can indeed locate one.

The partner may have to match three smaller shells before he can gain possession of the larger one. However, once the Iwan receives the latter, he can, if he wishes, reverse the control strategy by asking a return pokala of the three smaller armshells from the Gawan. If the latter fails in this, the Iwan might divert the large necklace onto another path, so that the Gawan would not obtain the promised return for his armshell. (In this case pokala is being asked for a gulugwalu.)

Should the Gawan decide at the end of the Iwan's pokala not to release the large armshell, he must give a few 'small' armshells to the Iwan to 'square' the latter's pokala of necklaces. This substitution is required in order to insure that he himself does not 'fall' but 'climbs'. If he should decide on this course of action, he 'quiets the body' (*bimategu wawora*) of the large armshell, and it stays on Gawa. 'It "lies down" unmatched' (*imasisi sabwamu*).

In this type of transaction, strategic control by the possessor of the desired shell *slows up* its movement. Initially, the Gawan exerts control over his partner by 'closing his throat' with a substitute shell. The subsequent transaction is a special form of a widely-used type called *i-kavagesa*, 'they make vaga' (not a pokala transaction), in which two partners decide to transact shells of unequal value. The larger shell 'climbs' (i-mwena) over the smaller one. One partner sends the smaller vaga along the path to locate an equivalent; the other finds a match for the higher standard vaga. The latter is more likely to stay in the hands of the immediate recipient until a return is located; it may also take longer to find its return, the smaller shell being more readily matched. The match for each, however, is eventually transacted between the partners.

In this transaction the initial, but not usually coincident, exchange involves two vaga. Since each vaga contains the potentiality for another shell (a gulugwalu) the partners create debt and delay closure.[13] Rather than simply denying shells because they are unequal, they (and the path) are involved in an ongoing transaction (important in keeping paths alive, see Part IV).

While the vaga transaction is a mutually supportive agreement (in which the partners are, in effect, of 'like mind'), the pokala case is not. The Iwan must first carry out the Gawan's will in order to gain the latter's consent to release the desired shell. This kind of persuasion illustrates especially well the parallelism of kula and non-kula political action: if a young man wishes to gain favors from an older man he must 'agree to work for' and 'listen to' him, to follow his wishes; the younger's worthiness is thus tested. Accession to the senior Gawan's wishes in turn becomes the means whereby the junior persuades the former to 'agree' to give him the desired favors.

Similarly, in this pokala, the Gawan 'closes' the partner's 'throat' through the substitute shell; in effect, the Iwan has to 'listen' to the Gawan. Bringing the return shell for the substitute, he has successfully carried out the Gawan partner's will, and shown as well his capacity for moving a shell from partners in the appropriate path direction. This substitution regulates the speed of movement of the large shell, and also exerts control over the Iwan partner. The possessor of the large shell can 'stretch' the time it stays on Gawa (thus exerting spatiotemporal control). If he wishes to be especially 'tight' he might 'quiet the body' of the shell, making it stay on Gawa without a match despite his partner's efforts. In such a case, the partner's persuasiveness fails – the Gawan and the shell remain 'unmoved'; but his pokala must be 'squared', unless the Gawan is willing to let his own status fall. The principle of equalizing limits the control the Gawan has over his partner in this transaction.

Equalizing also operates if the partner successfully persuades the Gawan to release the shell. Then, if he wishes, he can legitimately ask for a return pokala to 'square' his own pokala, thus asserting equality of control. If the partner fails to obtain pokala from his Gawan partner, he can equalize his own control by diverting the promised match, reassigning its spatial trajectory. Thus further delays in the matching of the original shell can be introduced. The initial request for pokala carries the potentiality of this further delay (the possibility that a future, reciprocal pokala might be required should the shell finally be released). We can see here the generative effect of the requirement of equalizing any imbalance in extending the duration of a transaction.

While the magic of persuasion expresses the ideal of the successful persuader in terms of speed – the point being to move shells rather than keep them – the type of control that can be exerted by a man once he receives a shell may involve delaying motion or slowing it up. He can make the shell 'lie down', retaining possession until release becomes judicious. The capacity to move a shell can be translated into the capacity to slow it down, or more generally, to regulate the timing of its onward passage. Maximal control of this kind is the prerogative of senior kula men. Significantly, only relatively senior men should perform major kula magic: through seniority one comes to incorporate both speed (magic) and slowness – i.e., maximal control over motion, or duration (see further, Part IV).

I turn now to a second example of the interplay of strategic control and persuasion deriving from the complex history of a kula competition. I give a *simplified abstract* here.[14]

Nancy D. Munn

In 1974, the long illness of a Gawan man (*A*) was ascribed to a kula transaction. It was thought certain other men on Gawa could have been angered by *A*'s acquisition of MANUTASOPI, an armshell of highest grade, and caused his illness through witchery. Furthermore, a special arrangement with *A*'s Kitavan partner (*C*) resulted in MANUTASOPI going directly from Boagis to Kitava, bypassing Muyuw and Gawa. Thus Gawans had further cause to be aggrieved.

Part of the background of this case is as follows. A Boagis man (*B*) had four paths through different Gawan partners on which there were outstanding debts. *B* let it be known that whoever wanted MANUTASOPI, his kitomu, should match one of these previous vaga. *C* of Kitava was on a path to *B* which led through *D* of Gawa; *C* wanted MANUTASOPI but was angry at *D*, one reason being the latter's connivance in handling the armshell KOKWA. KOKWA was a double armshell (cf. Malinowski, 1922:504) which *D* acquired from *B* of Boagis to match a double necklace *C* had previously given to him (and which he had sent on to Boagis). Instead of giving the double KOKWA to *C*, the Gawan split it, diverting part to another Kitavan partner, and giving only one part to *C*.

The (now divided) KOKWA then travelled another path of *C*'s which included *D* of Gawa, but not the Boagis partner. Its match in a later transaction, SINUBEITA, came to *C*. *B* of Boagis wanted SINUBEITA. *C* used it both to pay back *D*'s diversion of part of KOKWA, and to obtain MANUTASOPI. He diverted SINUBEITA along a *new* path going through *A* of Gawa to Boagis. This shell apparently compensated *B* for the diversion of part of KOKWA, since he had no return for the armshell's second segment. In this sense, SINUBEITA was a return to *B* for the latter shell.[15] Diverted onto his path, SINUBEITA became his vaga.

A of Gawa was in good position with the Boagis partner. Sometime earlier, he had obtained a necklace which went to *B* for the long-term debt of an armshell KUWABU, transacted on an old path, some of whose members had died or retired. *A* of Gawa and *B* replaced these men on their respective islands. This path, however, had fallen into disuse until revived in part by *A*'s payment for KUWABU. In closing this *debt*, *A* apparently strengthened his chances for obtaining MANUTASOPI. (Although it is not clear that this debt was paid explicitly to obtain MANUTASOPI, it may have been so. At any rate, it helped *B* reduce his long-term debts.)

The old path of *A*'s did not originally include *C* but *C* saw that certain Iwan and Kitavan partners on it were in conflict; going to *A* with SINUBEITA, he suggested these men be removed and he (*C*) and another Iwan be substituted. *A* and *C* would take SINUBEITA to *B* in order to obtain MANUTASOPI on this path. *C* thus gained a second path to *B* of Boagis enabling him to obtain the desired shell without going through *D* of Gawa.

Finally, *A* and *C* went to Boagis together and obtained MANUTASOPI. The offer of SINUBEITA clinched the deal, making *B* agree to release MANUTASOPI. MANUTASOPI would now be on a path it had regularly travelled in the past, serving to square another old debt on this path.

In this example, controls exerted by different men through manipulating MANUTASOPI, KOKWA and SINUBEITA are complexly intertwined. With MANUTASOPI in his possession, *B* of Boagis attempts to obtain returns for outstanding debts. His strategy puts men on his paths through

Gawa and northward in competition for MANUTASOPI. Further spatio-temporal control (e.g., calling in past debts; affecting the actions of distant partners) is thus exerted through controlling the onward passage of a shell.

One can see how the fact that one's name goes around the islands as the current possessor of a renowned shell is translatable into additional controls. The motion of butu which condenses the actor's initial control over motion (persuasion of a partner to release the shell) can itself be 'unpacked' into further controls exerted by the recipient over other partners (and shells) on the onward route.

Furthermore, the Boagis man's strategy is linked to the strategies of other partners, and to the surfacing of the dense nexus of past kula relations between them (and between him and them) within the context of the MANUTASOPI transaction. Thus *C*, a key actor in the situation, establishes himself on *A*'s path through Gawa, displacing partners on his own island and Iwa (and apparently using SINUBEITA as a persuasive device). By this means he opens up relations to *B* through *A* of Gawa. This new spatial control allows him to obtain MANUTASOPI without *D* of Gawa with whom he is on bad terms. Furthermore, he uses SINUBEITA to persuade *A* to allow MANUTASOPI to bypass (*kalipoy*) Gawa; together *C* and *A* also manage a bypass of Muyuw. *C* thus obtains the shell more swiftly than he could have otherwise.

C's maneuvering is connected with the previous ill-will between him and *D* of Gawa (derived in part from *D*'s handling of KOKWA). The elaborate network of past transactions and their residue in attitudes towards partners are caught up as formative factors in present trans-actions. As Burns (1958:138–9) has put it: 'when we act, we deal with a situation set up for us by the actions of others and ourselves in the past, and the result is another situation in which we and the others will have to act further . . . [The] mark of . . . [a single act's] effectiveness depends on what the next act is. The end of a single act, that is, is not reached until the completion of the "next", and in some sense, it is never reached.' In this sense, kula constitutes a cumulative, mythico-historical process in which a nexus of past events (multiple transactions and their effects) are 'car-ried' in the ongoing present of any single transaction and operate to affect the future.

IV. The kula path, the 'continuative' structure of kula, and the kula career

In order to enter into kula on a long-term basis a man must become a partner on an already extant kula path or he must 'make' (*i-vaga*) a new path of partners for himself. A path is initiated (*silamaw*) only through putting a shell into motion – i.e., by a transaction. A completed path forms a circle in that, *i-parat*: it meets or 'comes together'. At any given time, a path may be incomplete, since a shell (or shells) which makes the path may have travelled only so far. Although not all shells involve path-transactions (see Part I), only the path forms inter-personal relationship in a way that gives a single transaction potential for continuity. The 'closed' or maximally connected spacetime of the completed path models this potential as an unending cycling.

Gawans treat the making and strengthening of paths as central factors in building kula fame because of this spatiotemporal potential. As one man put it: when a man exchanges a shell with a non-partner, each individual can take the shell he receives as his *vaga* [to transact as he pleases]; the transaction ends with one equivalent (usually immediate) exchange. But when a man 'throws' (*leva*) shells in a path or potential path transaction, the matter does not end (*gera ikosi*: it is not finished).

Men could decide to continue a non-path transaction by using the shells as vaga to build a common path. Shells then acquire a potential for yielding additional, later transactions between the pair. Ego and Alter can continue their connection only by becoming enmeshed in 'tertiary' relations external to them as a unit; these relations then form the ground of the binary relation (cf. Simmel, 1950:145). This spatiotemporal expansion (in which the ground of each binary relation lies outside itself) forms a path.

A path itself can remain viable only if new vaga are given (technically but not always from the partner providing the gulugwalu) once a shell is matched,[16] or/and if other vaga are already circulating on the path. Receipt of a vaga marks a partner's esteem and interest in maintaining the path, and is critical to path continuance. The use of vaga (debt-formation) is the key to the reproducibility of a kula path and the ongoing resynthesis of the spacetime it entails. We have already seen some ways in which vaga serve to extend kula transactions and their operation will shortly be sketched further.

It follows from the basing of kula reproducibility in path construction that a man who does not build paths cannot engage in the long-term renown-building process of kula. A man of substance in kula has more than one such path, at least three complete paths being common. As one man said: 'those who have paths get kula [shells]'.

Although the completed path defines the morphology of a perpetually reproducible circulation, it is not a static, permanent set of partnerships; the reproducibility of one's kula transactions on that path is not assured. Paths that are not activated by a more or less regular passage of shells can fall into disuse, and 'disappear' (*i-tamwaw*). Such paths may sometimes be renewed by arrangements to move shells along them once again (cf. the MANUTASOPI case above). Paths may also disappear when a deceased member is not replaced: such a breach short-circuits the movement of shells, debt payment, and the initiation of new transactions. Moreover, part of a path membership may be changed if some individuals on it are felt to have become unreliable. Finally, a man may also make new paths throughout his kula career.

A path of partners does not, therefore, hold together apart from the movement (or presence) of shells on it. The path of relatively stable partnerships can be understood as the sedimentation of a process of motion – the circulation of shells over time.

Old paths valued for their 'strength' (matuw, 'mature', tawutora, 'strong') are tested partnerships, the sedimentation of multiple transactions, attesting the capacity of one's kula to be reproduced. Just as shells of high standard are considered 'old' (*kweiboga*), so also old paths are highly valued, and usually connected with more senior men. Like butu, the path is a symbolic extension of the actor formed through the motion of shells he has transacted (and an icon of the circulation process), but unlike butu, it extends a man through a specific structure of linking and linked 'others' rather than simply through the motion of his name. As a man becomes embedded in older paths so this structure by which he can as it were 'reach' outwards beyond his own island becomes a more stabilized aspect of his own identity.

A youth begins in kula by making his own paths and/or by inheriting ready-made paths primarily from a senior *dala* kinsman. He may establish a hospitality relation with an older man on another island as the base for a kula partnership but he may also initiate partnerships with youths of his peer group. His first shell may be acquired from a senior dala kinsman whom he has aided, or from his father.

Most younger men in their twenties have not yet inherited paths because their seniors are still living and have not retired from kula. Young men are 'still making their paths'.

(1) *A* in his mid-twenties, received an armshell from *B*, a 'mother's brother' for whom he works. *B* obtained it from Yaraba. *A* gave his vaga to an Iwan who 'made a path', giving the shell onward. A necklace was returned for this armshell, but the Yaraba partner did not give *B* (and *A*) any new vaga.[17] *A* looked for another partner, dropping the Yaraba-Gawa segment. He found a northern Muyuwan partner who, *A* says, is *taw bwein* (a good man); from him *A* obtained a small armshell.

(2) *C*, in his early twenties, worked for *D*, his own mother's brother. *D* instructed him to kula with a particular Iwan, because in the past this man's senior matri-

Nancy D. Munn

lineal kinsman had been a partner of *D*'s own dala mother's brother. *D* wanted his nephew to form this partnership so as to reactivate an old path (*si-kebokura*: their traditional kula; *si-keda tamoya*: the elders' path) which had disappeared when these two men died. He gave his nephew a small armshell to start his own path with the Iwan. *C* says that when the return comes he will offer it to *D*, who may well say to him 'You throw it yourself.' If so, *C* will give it to an older northern Muyuw man with whom he has a hospitality relation, and who originally gave the armshell to *D*. [Thus *C* would make his own path.]

Both cases illustrate initial stages in the construction of kula paths, suggesting the emphasis on developing relations with a potential for confidence. The Gawan interest in reviving old paths is illustrated in the second case, where the younger man is encouraged to pick up the lapsed path of two partners in the grandparental generation, an arrangement we may infer is attractive partly because of the new partnership's capacity to draw on some of the strength built up in an old path.

The strength of a path is connected with the quality of social relationship or 'confidence' it contains. The description 'taw bwein' (a good man) referred to above, is a standard idea conveying trustworthiness. The 'good man' 'cares for' (*i-yamata*) your shells, waiting for you to come for them, and not yielding to the persuasiveness of others. He does not divert shells, but 'watches well over the path'.

One man explained that his good kula relations were due to his own reliability.[18] If he asks, he will receive shells; on Iwa they send his necklace down to the beach [a sign of good relations – the man does not have to go to his partner's home to receive the shell, as is more usual]. *They treat him this way because he does not divert valuables.* Some others will wait and wait. These men do not have good relations with their partners [by implication, they receive shells more slowly].

The state of a man's path relations is thus a generalized component of his control in any given kula act. The 'good' man ideally receives shells 'swiftly' just as he gave shells 'swiftly' (not diverting them from the path). Trustworthiness is sedimented from acts of 'likemindedness' or mutuality (cf. Part II)[19] joining partners in 'swift' reciprocal giving over time. Such relations are critical to path maintenance. A man continually monitors his partner's reliability, and even a section of a relatively old, strong path may be changed due to difficulties with particular partners (cf. the MANUTASOPI case, above).

My informant from the previous commentary changed a section of an old path because the original Iwan partner diverted a gulugwalu, and failed to match certain armshells travelling this path.

A southern Gabuin partner on the same path received the armshell MWA-SIYATAPAISIYO. He told path members (who transmitted the information to Gawa) to obtain the necklace TABUWABU to match MWASIYATAPAISIYO. My

298

informant arranged with another Iwan (not his now-suspect partner) to get TABUWABU. MWASIYATAPAISIYO then travelled by this new northern route to Vakuta, the Gawan having substituted the men through whom TABUWABU came, on the Iwa–Kitava–Vakuta section of this path.

In this case, the Gawan reconstructed the 'weakened' (*gweya*) section of his path by offering MWASIYATAPAISIYO for TABUWABU. The Gabuin partner made a 'long-distance' arrangement to obtain TABUWABU from outside his and the Gawan's path; this arrangement also insured that TABUWABU would not be diverted, and strengthened the path.

As I have suggested, path strength or reproductive potential also requires the regular playing of vaga. A man may attempt to demonstrate and increase this strength by the following type of move:

Supposing one throws an armshell that 'lies down two years [considered a little slow].[20] We wait, no necklace [comes].' You then may take two large vaga armshells to your Iwan partner. Later one may receive two or three vaga necklaces because partners on this path (especially from Vakuta to Dobu) see by this act the strength of one's path. This move makes the necklaces 'stand up' (*tokaya*).

This type of vaga transaction is associated especially with more senior players, but we have already considered similar widely used moves in which partners transact vaga. Moreover, lengthy transactions involving more than one vaga linked to an initial vaga are favoured in kura Dobu[7] (see note 13). Since these vaga temporize through creating mutual debt, they keep the path from 'disappearing' and through them the men strengthen their relations.

Vaga transactions are also especially associated with old paths, and with increasing seniority in kula.

On a strong (old) path where one plays *kura Dobu*, one should not talk about gulugwalu with one's partner, because if two shells 'pierce' each other the transaction is finished. The basic idea of kura Dobu, however, is that 'it doesn't finish'. Even when a shell is the gulugwalu for another, it is bad manners to speak of this explicitly: to do so is to '*nanaakwa*' (i.e., to express the relationship in terms of speedy closure). On a young path, however, you may speak of gulugwalu for you are making your path. Then as you grow older the path 'slows down' (*i-mwawutu*); it becomes an old man (*i-tamumoya*). (Elsewhere this informant equated 'slowness' with 'becomes guyaw', 'great fame' and kura Dobu – tight Kula.) Just as a man *bi-kaitukwa* (may go with a staff) as he grows old, so also armshells and necklaces go more slowly in the kula of older men. [This alludes to the Gawan stereotype of an old person moving slowly, leaning on a staff.] When an old man [with strong paths] dies, his shells are put on his arms [in the house of mourning where the body lies in state]; then they will be taken away by the younger men of the dala who will make them go fast again.

The notion of closure contradicts the ideal model of the old path. It is as

299

Nancy D. Munn

if by speaking about gulugwalu with a long-time partner, a man expresses a lack of confidence in the path and the relation: trust should, as it were, transcend the need for reaffirmation, and one should not speak of speedy closure where continuity is the ideal. In point of fact, men are concerned with obtaining gulugwalu for their vaga, and are angered if partners unduly delay or divert returns. The goal of kura Dobu, however, transcends the value of equalizing, since it is focused in the reproductivity of the path, the value of debt or continuity, through which the path itself is reproduced.

But the concept of slow playing is ambiguous. On the one hand, slow playing with vaga as a cooperative act between partners can keep a path viable, thus increasing the sum of confidence in it. On the other hand, being a slow player can involve 'coming' partners: holding onto valuables until one can develop a maximizing strategy that may include playing partners off against each other; and it may involve both diversion, and more specialized trickery. In this respect, the slow player is the antithesis of 'taw bwein,' the reliable man.

As a man grows older (more influential) he can play a 'tight' game (he holds valuables tightly, *kasay i-yosi*). My informant contrasts the 'good' (bwein, i.e. fast) flow of his own kula with that of older men, remarking in another context that he and other less senior men would be afraid to kula so tightly. He exemplifies this tight playing:
A., a Yaraba man, received REIKUDUMUDUMU, a necklace of the highest grade, which was to match TUWIDAMA, an armshell held by *A*'s older partner on Yeguma (*B*). The latter held both TUWIDAMA and KUBURUBURU, two (highest grade) armshells. 'He held them tightly' (i.e., for a long time). Instead of giving his Yaraba partner the pre-arranged match TUWIDAMA he gave him KUBUR-UBURU as vaga, and he gave *C* on Gawa (his partner on another path) the armshell TUWIDAMA to match WOYIRESI in *C*'s possession. [The path with *C* was older than that with the Yeguma partner, and *C* is exceptionally prestigious.] Since *C* received the diverted valuable, he '*i-guyaw* (climbed). [The recipient of a diversion makes an element of fame for himself.] REIKUDUMUDUMU became a vaga rather than a gulugwalu, travelling from *A* to *B* and south. *A* was not angry because he could expect a new match for REIKUDUMUDUMU from *B* [and in the meantime the two had exchanged vaga]. If *B* later returns the promised match for REIKUDUMUDUMU, all will be well. But if the new gulugwalu is diverted, *A* will be angry. 'This is the way old men play. It is kura Dobu.'

In this form of tight playing (in which 'slow' implies the attempt to regulate the overall speed and trajectory of shell motion in one's own terms), the Yeguma man managed to support both paths: he maintained reasonable relations with his Yaraba partner through the Yaga transaction in which he kept this path open, and also muted his partner's anger at the diversion of a gulugwalu; coordinately, he satisfied the prestigious long-term partner on his old path by giving him the diverted shell (which the latter apparently preferred to KUBURUBURU, and which, as a diversion, was the Gawan's 'coup'). An astute combination of *diversion and kavagesa transactions* satisfied partners *on more than one path*. In other words, *B* of Yeguma both utilizes and maintains his position as the fulcrum of more than one path of kula circulation, or as the *relation between these two sets of relations*. This level of spatiotemporal control (control of the relational structuring *between* one's paths) requires a balancing act in which, in effect, one must learn 'how to win by cheating without being disqualified' (Bailey, 1970:6).

In this respect, the role of diversion is particularly important. As noted earlier, diversion of gulugwalu is regarded by Gawan informants as theft; this attitude may also, however, be applied to path vaga even though diversion of the latter can be expected in kula playing. Actually, diversion is implicated in the path system, since it is one of the means of making new paths. Possession of more than one path also points to the probability of further diversions from one established path to another, as men become subject to the interests and persuasiveness of more than one set of partners. Thus one middle-aged man attempted to defend the fact that he still had only one path by saying that a man with more than one, is tempted to divert shells.[21]

In fact, men of substance in kula have to develop some capacity to balance operations: diversions from one path must later be replaced in order to assuage cheated partners and keep the path from disappearing, or to keep themselves from being dropped from the path. At any given time, the diversion may strengthen relations with one partner (or path) while temporarily weakening it with another, but over time a man must make good to the cheated partner if he wants to maintain his path position. He may 'rob Peter to pay Paul' but eventually he must 'pay back Peter', thus maintaining the overall strength of his paths (cf. also, Fortune, 1963:217). This procedure involves a man in temporizing that includes both legitimate and illegitimate procedures as the means of manipulating his paths as an *interconnected system of relations* rather than operating each as a separate cycle of its own.

Although all men of standing in kula engage to some extent in these procedures, their intensification becomes possible in the play of senior men whose generalized influence (sedimented into strong, old paths and great renown from the long-term circulation of shells through their hands) makes it possible for them to maximize this more complex level of spatiotemporal control. In short, in this type of kula a man has concentrated sufficient control into himself (as symbolized by his social extension of self in old paths, and his individual extension in fame) to be able to

Nancy D. Munn

engage in 'deep play' (Geertz, 1973:143): he can take excessive chances with partnerships both to express and to maximize his own position as a node of power in the system.

V. Conclusion: the value standards of shells as a model of the kula career

Turning now to the value symbolism of the shells, I suggest that the schematic ordering of shells into standards can be seen as an indigenous model of the kula career, and of the basic value principle of equalizing and its reproduction through the renewal of imbalances (inequalities).

Gawans distinguish three basic, named standards with some subordinate or intervening grades (Fig. 1). Each shell category has its stereotypically equal standard of the opposite category, represented on the horizontal axis of the diagram. Within the classificatory terms of the set, this relation models the value principle of equalizing, coding in categorical form the spatiotemporal synthesis of the unitary exchange in which the directional movement of one type of shell implicates the further movement of an equal and opposite shell from the opposite direction at another time. Conversely, the diagram's vertical axis depicts the ranking of low to high ('small' to 'large') standards. Shells of 'larger' standards 'climb' (mwena) over shells of 'smaller' standards which 'fall' (busi). I argue that this ranking encodes the long-term hierarchizing process, or continual resynthesis of spacetime through which men define their own value in the system.

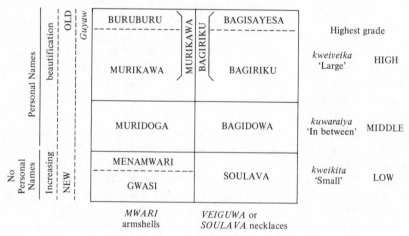

Figure 1. Gawan value standards and grades of shell.

302

Thus we find a sterotypic correlation between shell ranking and the successful kula career in which a man also 'climbs' and becomes a renowned guyaw: the set of value standards can be seen as like an 'age grading' code. This grading is conveyed both in Gawan correlations between shell standards a man typically acquires in different stages of his kula career, and in their attribution of differential properties or qualisigns of value to the shells as one moves from lower to higher standards.

Shells of the *gwasi–soulava* standard have no names; as one man remarked, they have no fame and no path. Gwasi can arrive in numbers, or individually, but they are not remembered because of their namelessness: they 'disappear'. As one man put it, a man would be 'ashamed' to give a proper name to these shells because another man would see that they were 'small'. The size of shells refers to the diameter of the armshell's 'mouth' (*wado-ra*), and to the length of the string of soulava in the case of the necklaces. According to the stereotypic value model, the low-standard shells are too small to slide up the arm; low standard necklaces are said to extend only from the elbow to the finger tips.[22]

Qualities of color, texture and decor, along with size combine to define the beauty of shells (cf. Campbell, this volume). Shells of low standard are regarded as the least attractive. Armshells have a minimal decoration of *yavig* (*Ovulus ovularum*) shells attached to their base (less than 7 or 8 shells). Low-standard necklaces may lack a *gineuba* (pearl shell attachment); the shells are larger in diameter, than those of the higher standards, lacking the evenness and glowing smoothness (*girigiri*) of the highest standard. The former are also thought of as 'red' while the latter are 'light' or 'white' in color.

Age is an important value criterion. Low-standard shells are regarded as relatively recent entries into kula (*kweivaw*, or *yedavaw*, recently ground), while high standard shells are said to be kweiboga (old, from the past). Color and glow may also connote relative age. *Murikaw* armshells ideally have brown striations called 'rainbow' (*ureri*) which are taken as indications of age. Discussing a particular necklace, some men explained that it was only a *bagidowa* because it was not very old; its lack of age was signified by the dark redness of the shells. Rubbing his hand down the necklace, one man explained that as shells get lighter and more glowing (i.e. older) they gain in value.

High standard shells may also be described as 'guyaw.' Moreover, as one senior informant indicated, a man of kula eminence may receive gwasi–soulava only from non-partners. These low-standard shells can start a new path, but do not travel on old paths.

Young men begin their kula careers with low-standard shells, working their way into the middle and high standards. All men stress that younger men may obtain high standard shells only if they inherit old paths, for these shells 'come out' only on the *old* paths. Furthermore, shells of the highest grade (*buruburu* and *bagisayesa*) are obtainable only by men of the highest kula standing – guyaw – described in age-grading terms as tamumoya (old men). Conversely, the acquisition of one of these shells can initiate a man's entry into high standing.

These latter shells are limited in number.[23] Men of substance in kula strive to obtain each of these shells at least once during their career, and others know whether they have achieved this or not. One man suggested that at that time only one Gawan had great fame because he had obtained all these shells; three other notables had obtained at least one of them. Just as there are a limited number of shells of the highest grade, so also there are a limited number of guyaw of high eminence. Scarcity applies to both media and men.

There is thus a general correlation between the beauty, notability and age of shells, and the seniority and fame of transacters. Significantly, the stereotypic equation of age with beauty reverses the Gawan life-cycle stereotype which connects age with ugliness, while emphasizing the bodily beauty of youths (Munn, 1977; cf. also Weiner, 1976 chapter 5). The successful kula guyaw is reconstituted by this reversal in terms of the 'beauty' of maximal spatiotemporal control (maximal fame) as expressed in his capacity to acquire the most famous, 'oldest' kula shells.

It is as if both shells and men are seen as starting their "careers" without renown or memorability; as the transactions in which they participate multiply, they become increasingly famous and 'beautiful', concentrating into themselves the continuous reproduction of their circulation and exchange (the shells) or the circulation of shells through their hands (the men). The hierarchy of shell standards can be seen as condensing the overall value structure of the spatio-temporal exchange process; as such, it serves to define the relation of persons and shells (as coordinately, value products and agents of each others' value definition) to the process, or system of action as a whole.

Notes

1 Fourteen months were spent on Gawa (The Marshall Bennetts), 1973–4; May–July 1975. I am grateful to the National Science Foundation for supporting both trips (NSF grant no. SOC 73–09141 AO1).

In 1979–81 I conducted further research on Gawan kula (NSF grant 78–41A) and I have made some minor adjustments to the text based on this later work. Otherwise the paper is based on the earlier field study and was written prior to the more recent research.

Gawan kula: spatiotemporal control and the symbolism of influence

Gawa is an uplifted coral island of some 445 people (in 1973–4; in 1979–80 my census showed 532 people). Gawans have a yam and taro subsistence base, and are professional canoe builders, trading their seagoing vessels southward for kula armshells and other goods (Munn, 1977). The Gawan language, Rougwaw, belongs to the 'Kilivila' group (Lithgow, 1976).

Gawans reside in small hamlets and hamlet clusters laid out across the top of the island. Descent groupings are matrilineal, each dala (Malinowski's 'sub-clan') having an informal leader (guyaw), usually its senior man. Each dala and its leader is ideologically the equal of the others. Dala are aggregated into four general categories (*kumila*, Malinowski's 'clan'). Gawans also recognize certain major community functionaries: these are men thought to possess the most powerful gardening magic and witch-killing (-curing) magic in the community; as well as the leader of the dala owning the Gawan dance entertainment. Individuals filling these roles are all dala leaders, and tend on the whole to be prominent in kula.

With some exceptions (e.g., retired men; unmarried men of no standing), all adult Gawan men kula. (Unlike their Yanaban and Muyuwan neighbors, Gawan women do not kula.) Gawans trade directly with Iwa and Kitava for necklaces (some paths go to Kitava *through* Iwa, but many go directly to Kitava); they do not ordinarily kula with Kweawata, with whom they compete. Armshells are received from two main southern routes: via Yanaba (Rougwaw, *Yaraba*) Yegum, and via northern Muyuw (primarily through Kawuray, Dikwayas, Kuropwan, Kawuway and Muniveyov).

2 My notion of action has been influenced in part by Marxian and phenomeno-logical traditions in which the actor is seen as producing himself through his work or activity. Sartre's (1960:63ff.) concept of the 'project', for example, and his view of static wholes as 'the congealed reproduction of the generating act' (1976:63) have been suggestive to me in conceptualizing aspects of kula.

3 The notion that kula involves the production of self-related symbols specifi-cally through the production of famous 'names' is discussed from a different perspective by Damon (1978) in his analysis of Muyuwan kula.

4 A vaga is a shell unencumbered by debt which produces debt. A man's sources include shells acquired from non-partners or partners that are not on an established path; "opening gifts" on an established path; shells diverted (pili) from another path (such shells entail a new return whatever their status on the previous path). An important source of vaga are *kitomu*: shells received in payment for restricted types of non-kula services or items, and considered personal possessions. Gawans derive kitomu primarily from their canoe trade. When a man's kitomu travels a kula path, the return shell becomes his kitomu and vaga. *Kitomu* thus continually produce new returns for him (as well as attracting additional shells to his paths). Although kitomu can be used to illustrate my present argument, I do not examine them here (but see Munn, 1977). It should be remarked, however, that since a man incurs no debt for this type of vaga, kitomu create 'breaks' in the cycle of indebtedness necessary if a transaction is to begin and end with someone. Although (as this volume shows) kitomu exist throughout the 'ring', they are not the only type of shell that can function in this way; Gawans also distinguish *kunayireyira* which, although differently generated, function much like kitomu. Unlike Muyuwans

(Damon, this volume) Gawans do not typically regard all shells as *someone's* kitomu.

5 My definition of value was stimulated by Terence Turner's (n.d.) adaptation of the Saussurian concept of value in a recent, important study.

6 Gawans have no cover term for the value categories. The term 'standard' was used in conversation with me by the Dobuan captain of a government vessel in the kula area in 1972, prior to my Gawan fieldwork.

7 *Kura Dobu* refers to the kind of kula thought to be played especially by the peoples from Vakuta to Dobu (but more generally from Kitava onward), and can also refer to 'tighter' playing in general (cf. Malinowski, 1922:94, 360). *Kura Masima* is the easier kula of islands to Gawa's south sometimes including Gawa, or a swifter game. One man called all path exchanges kura Dobu, contrasting them with swiftly completed non-path exchanges (kura Masima).

8 Women decorate only with the necklaces; men may wear both types of shells.

9 I do not consider persuasion mechanisms at the level of performance, but speech (both style and content) is critical. On impression management see Guidieri, 1973.

10 The reference here is to vaga rather than gulugwalu. Vaga transactions are discussed later.

11 In my current data (1979–80) the incidence of pokala of non-kula goods for particular shells of either category does not appear high; and men frequently explain that they do not pokala with partners of long standing or with potential (new) partners who are kin (of own dala or kumila), see note 1.

12 The sex ascription is consistent with the marriage–sexual model of kula exchange which I do not discuss here. Inter-island variation in the sex of each shell type apparently occurs or/and has occurred in the past: Malinowski (1922:356) states that the armshells are female and necklaces male; my Dobuan informant (see Note 6) insisted on the same ascription. Muyuw (Damon, 1978:85f.), and Vakuta (Campbell, this volume) reverse the ascription, like Gawa (and to my knowledge, Iwa). Scarcity may be a factor in the relative tightness of necklaces (kula conference discussion, 1978), as some of my (1979) informants are aware. Another indigenous explanation is historical. One man, like some others, regarded necklaces as prior to both pig tusks and armshells in kula, explaining that when tusks were later exchanged for necklaces the former had to be brought to the necklaces (the tusk 'went to meet its wife'). This implicit connection of higher value with age (here, historical priority in kula) parallels the explicit connection between them in the hierarchy of shell standards (see below Part V).

13 In one instance, a man estimated about four years between the initial arrangement and matching of the larger shell. More complex long-term transactions often occur in which an initial vaga of fairly high standard is followed by a smaller vaga of opposite category called the *kurarera* of the larger one. This and a second kurarera are both matched and finally the initial debt is closed with the *katuwupa* (i.e. match) of the first large vaga. My (1979–80) data suggests that such debts can sometimes extend over twenty years or more.

14 My summary relies primarily on the detailed discussion of this transaction with one well-informed man, but it is also based on explanations by another, and a public speech by one of the principals in the case. The case also appears in

Damon (1978:92f.), illustrating the apparently catastrophic effect of the bypass of Muyuw on the Boagis partner.

15 My informant's account of the use of SINUBEITA as a return for KOKWA'S second segment involves some contradictions; I state what seems to be the basic implication of his remarks.

16 Kitomu (see Note 4) are the exception, since they are continually vaga for Ego, and can be continued on the same path at his discretion.

17 I do not know why in this case, the new vaga was expected from the *recipient* of the gulugwalu rather than its donor; it may be that the onus was on the *senior* Gawan's partner to continue the path.

18 The remaining case examples in this section derive from a single informant, but the general implications involve characteristic features of kula emerging in other data.

19 I am indebted to Terence Turner for drawing my attention to the connection between trust and the notion of 'likemindedness' or mutuality developed in Part II.

20 One year is 'good'; two years a 'little tight'; three years 'tight'; four years and up is 'bad'.

21 Although membership on more than one path yields greater access to shells than membership on one path only, it would seem that an indefinite increase of the number of active paths would also (among other problems) strain good relations with previous partners, because it would increase competition for shells. Expansion in the number of a man's paths has contradictory dimensions I do not discuss further here.

22 A distinction must be drawn between the value model and qualisigns of value, on the one hand, and the instantiation of these values in the classification of particular shells. For example, men recognize that high-standard necklaces are often short, because they have been cut up as they travel around the islands, and are used to make necklets (on Gawa, these are given to women to wear). One man also cited a particular armshell of high standard which he said cannot go up beyond the elbow (although failure to meet the size criterion is certainly much rarer in the case of armshells than necklaces). Similarly, a new shell of exceptional beauty can be placed in the highest standard (although not in the highest grade until it has some age). However, whether or not higher-standard shells are actually older (and low standard shells relatively new), the model connects high value with age. This connection appears, nevertheless, to reflect possibilities built into the qualisign system which enable *some* shells to 'climb' into the higher categories as they age (cf. Campbell, this volume). Most of my Gawan informants (1979–80) recognize that such changes can take place. These views contrast with those of Muyuwans who regard a shell's standard as fixed (see Damon, 1978:86f). In the present paper, however, I am concerned with the value model itself rather than these problems of its instantiation.

23 I have record of some twenty shells of this grade but there are additional shells approximating this grade for which informants' evaluations are more variable. Furthermore, some men equate the terms *Bagisayesa* and *Burubura* with *Bagiriku* and *Murikaw* respectively, not treating them as a grade of shells within the high standard. These men say that *Bagisayesa* refers to a Bagiriku

307

Nancy D. Munn

in the speaker's possession, rather than one by a man on another island. Such shells make the recipient *tasayesa* (a man of wealth) and hence the label. Whether the highest grade is labelled or not there is a small number of shells within the high standard that informants regularly rate over others.

12 What moves the kula: opening and closing gifts on Woodlark Island

FREDERICK H. DAMON[1]

Malinowski states that in the *kula* 'opening' and 'return' gifts are different in 'name, nature, and time', but that they must be 'equivalent' (Malinowski, 1922:352–3). Why? This question and the implications to be drawn from its answer is the subject of this paper. It will become evident that the principles governing the exchange of wine in cheap French restaurants have little if anything to do with the differences between opening and return gifts in the kula. However insightful the principles of reciprocity may be for apparently uninstitutionalized aspects of men in society, the kula is clearly a vast institution that is understood and operated, on Woodlark Island at least, by a different set of principles. To grasp the 'laws of motion' of these principles is the purpose of this paper.

It is convenient to think of Woodlark society as being dominated by three different social formations. One is the kula (*kun*), in reference to which Woodlark people think of themselves as part of a large system, one which includes directly or indirectly nearly the whole of Milne Bay Province. Another may be termed Woodlark kinship, meaning by this the entire set of institutions and ideas indigenously separated from the kula. Finally there is the encroaching western system. A reasonably complete picture of Woodlark must deal with each of these formations, the contradictions within each and between each. In this paper I deal extensively only with the major contradiction in the kula. But since Woodlark has received little ethnographic attention beyond the cursory notes in Malinowski (1961, 1967, Vol. I), Seligmann (1910), I outline here first Woodlark geography and kinship, and second the island's recent history.

An overview

Muyuw

The best description of Woodlark Island is that provided recently by Ollier and Pain (1978). The island is formed about a volcanic and mountainous core. Mt Kabat is the highest volcanic cone, at about 700 ft above sea level in the center of the island. Two mountain ranges rise to the south of Kabat, the highest upwards of about 1,300 ft and generically called Sulouga. Coral foundations almost completely encircle the mountainous center of the island but these formations seem to have been subjected to secondary geological movements. The coral platform appears to rise out of the water on the northern side of the island while it sinks on the southern side. Consequently while there are steep cliffs as much as two hundred feet high on the northern side of the island, and no reefs, there is a gradual slope downwards towards the south, and reefs extend off the southern shoreline as much as five miles. The general shape of the island is thus rectangular with the long sides just over forty miles in length, more or less east to west, and the narrow sides about eighteen miles in width north to south. The north/south slope of the island seems to be repeated in miniature in three places on the island, two in the far west forming the peninsula-like extension of Woodlark, Muadau Island, and in the far southeastern end of the island. Two relatively large river systems rise in the central part of the island and flow to the east. Consequently the interior of the eastern half of the island is rather swampy, broken here and there by stands of sago and betel nut. The western half of the island, excluding the Mwadau peninsula, is dense jungle broken only by two lakes from which one small river runs to the south.

Compared to the islands to the west, from Gaw to the Trobriands, Woodlark's population is sparse (1850 est. 2,200; 1910 est. 800; 1971 est. 1,700). Perhaps in consequence the vast majority of the island remains dominated by climax forest. But it is the belief of Woodlark people that the island's soil is far inferior than that of the islands to the west. Thus while Woodlark people grow most of the same kinds of crops as the people to the west, yams, taro, sweet potatoes, bananas, etc., they believe that from a quantitative point of view they do less well than their neighbors. Soil differences, and thus expected success in gardening, also, however, are thought to vary on the island itself. In general people claim that western conditions are better than eastern conditions for crops. However, social aspects of production greatly influence the recognized ecological factors, and presently most people in the east are more productive in the indigenous system than those in the west.

Map 1 shows the major divisions of Woodlark society and the location of present-day villages.

The indigenous term for Woodlark Island and culture is M U Y U W. As a place name this term is understood according to a kind of segmentary logic. At the highest level 'M U Y U W' denotes the major landmass, Budibud (Laughlan Islands), some forty-five miles to the southeast of

Woodlark, Nasikwabw (Alcester Island), and Yemga (Egum Island), but not Yalab (Yanaba Island). Included in this major category are the three outer groups just mentioned and three divisions in the main area, from east to west, Muyuw, Wamwan, and Nayem. From a linguistic point of view minor dialect differences distinguish these areas. But people in Budibud have their own language, according to informants, and some of the people whose function is to sail to the south speak the Misima language as their native language, although they also speak MUYUW. Below the second level of segmentary opposition there is no consistent way in which place names are organized. For example, eastern MUYUW, Muyuw, is further divided into three divisions which are in turn divided up into smaller segments while in central and western MUYUW beneath the main headings there are only 'villages'.

The concept that is subject to MUYUW's kind of segmentary logic is *ven* (Compare Trobriand *vela*), which may be translated as 'Community'.

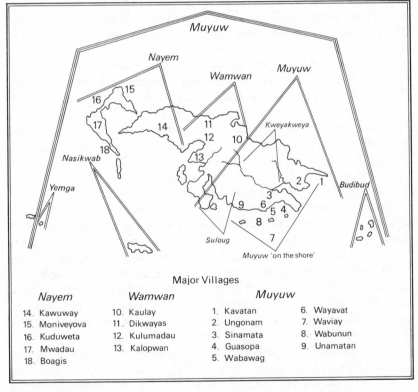

Map 1. Muyuw: segmentary organization of the concept 'community'.

Frederick H. Damon

This is moreover a complex notion and I have so far only described one of the paradigms by which it is used. In this context it is, however, important to understand that the concept *ven*, community, is like a 'scene' for social action, not an agent or agency of that action.

The Trobriand distinction between matrilineal clan, *kumila*, and sub-clan, *dala*, is found in MUYUW, *kum/dal*. Clans are conceived to contain subclans. But these two categories are also thought to function in different ways. MUYUW clans ideally depict proper marriage relationships, the symmetrical 'conveyance' of men and women between one clan and another over time. In MUYUW's model of how these clans operate there are four such clans, the same four as in the Trobriands. There are, however, a total of eight clans. Clan representatives are not distributed over the MUYUW landscape according to any paradigmatic construct, rather according to the working out of less inclusive principles, in short the society's history. Clans are synthetically related to one another but subclans, although contained in specific clans, are thought of individually. The focus of the concept subclan is on a brother/sister relationship. In subclan origin-myths usually a brother/sister pair come out of the ground together at some specific location. This location is conceived to be the property of the subclan, but this is a kind of 'false' property, the top of a mountain or a swamp, for example. In fact brothers and sisters must be separated from one another, this separation leading to the totality of what constitutes 'marriage' or 'kinship' in MUYUW. Marriage in MUYUW is consciously orientated about a cyclic notion, the beginning of a given cycle being the separation of a brother and sister, the end coming with a set of rituals following the deaths of the children of a given marriage. Other rituals mark various stages of this process. But the marriage ends when the disjunction created by the brother/sister separation is bridged by the 'replacement' of the gender-defined productiveness of the brother and sister. This replacement is actually the purpose of the MUYUW kinship system. Furthermore it is a kind of 'conversion' so that finally subclans hold 'true' property, land, sago and betel-nut orchards, pigs, and certain kinds of kula valuables, all obtained from the real loss of male and female productivity by marriage. Unlike either clans or communities, subclans may then gain, or lose, real property. But in so far as MUYUW kinship is concerned the agents of its action are male and female identities, the agency marriage. Clans and subclans are ideological constructs which depict, contain, or realise the results of this action.

Although MUYUW subclans may differentiate themselves by acquiring or losing real property, they are not, unlike Trobriand subclans, related to one another hierarchically. In MUYUW there is no formal political or symbolic hierarchy, no 'center'. I have described elsewhere

(Damon, n.d.) what I believe to be the analogical equivalent to Trobriand hierarchy in MUYUW.

The major difference between MUYUW and Trobriand society is then the absence of hierarchy in the former place and its presence in the latter. Other differences accompany, I believe, this one. First, the famous Trobriand brother/sister exchanges, called *urigubu* by Malinowski (but see Weiner, 1976:40) are present but significantly reduced in importance in MUYUW. In eastern and central MUYUW these prestations are made with taro, they are only occasional, and they are never elaborated into public rituals. In western MUYUW they are made with yams, and are annual events, I was told, but they likewise are not ritual or semi-ritual events. Second, there is no ideal marriage pattern in MUYUW like the Trobriand 'rule' for patrilateral cross-cousin marriage. MUYUW believe that people from Gaw west to the Trobriands marry their cross-cousins, but then consciously deny practice of the custom themselves. In fact, MUYUW kinship terminology is identical to that in the Trobriands with the exception of the cross-cousin term (*nubie–*: FZD=MBD).

MUYUW/Woodlark History[2]

The high points of Woodlark history are these: In 1812 Budibud was named the Laughlab Islands and probably first discovered by Europeans. There was probably some contact between Europeans and MUYUW between 1812 and 1835–6, but only in 1836 was the island named after the British whaler 'Woodlark'. From 1847 to 1852 French Marist missionaries tried to make a mission on the southeast corner of the island, but in 1852 they were replaced by members of the Milan Foreign Mission Society, a few of whom were killed by MUYUW before they all left in 1856. For a decade following 1880 a lone German trader lived on Budibud where he organized copra production and constituted a continuing source of European goods. The development of coconut plantations on Woodlark, predominantly by Europeans, followed the German's lead with some intensity until about 1930. In 1890 William MacGregor arrived on Woodlark, representing 'government', the purpose of which was to apprehend and hang the murderers of two Europeans. One of the 'murderers' was hung and this event is of considerable symbolic importance to present-day MUYUW. In 1895 gold was discovered on Woodlark, leading to a rapid influx of Europeans and a continuing interest in the island's mineral potential. After a decade or so several larger concerns controlled most of the mining activity. In 1920 the government station, which had located on the island because of the gold rush, moved to Misima, the location of the

Frederick H. Damon

next gold rush. The last gold mine closed with the advent of World War
II. With the start of the Pacific War all Europeans were evacuated from
the island, but American forces constructed an airstrip on the southeast
corner of the island and used this place as a staging center for the battle of
Guadalcanal. As many as 10,000 American troops were on the island for
parts of 1942 and 1943. Shortly after the war Mr Donald Neate Sr, who
had first come to Woodlark about 1920, returned to the island to re-start
some of the gold works and develop a larger business concern. In the
mid-1950s this concern was transformed into Kulumadau Enterprises, by
the senior Neate's son and his wife, Mr and Mrs Donald B. Neate Jr. The
company's foundation was made more secure by shifting it to a lumber
mill although the Neates continued to do some trading for copra, *Trochus*
shells, and alligator hides. In 1962 the Neates saw to it that the old World
War II airstrip was re-opened, and a government Patrol Post was located
nearby, at Guasopa. By the early 1970s, although there was a government school at Guasopa, a Catholic-sponsored school in the center of the
island at Kulumadau, and everyone was nominally a member of the
United Church, the Neates were the dominant European influence on the
island. They owned and operated three trade-stores, had successfully
talked some people in central and western MUYUW into carving ebony
for export, and were continuing a modest program of expansion in
their lumber concern. About half of Neates' regular employees were
MUYUW people, most of the rest from elsewhere in Milne Bay. But the
relationship between MUYUW people and the Neates was at best ambiguous, and in 1978 some MUYUW people, apparently with government
assistance, bought out the Neate's concern; the Neates have left the
island (Lithgow, D., personal communication).

The continuing transformation of MUYUW into Woodlark Island
over the last 170 years or so does not seem to have been a pleasant
experience. Between roughly 1850 and 1910 the island may have lost
two-thirds of its population, mostly to Western diseases, it seems, but the
indigenous explanation is sorcery. By approximately 1870 the stone
quarries at Suloug seem to have stopped functioning, and by about 1920
a set of inland villages in eastern MUYUW had virtually collapsed.
These villages were, among other things, carvers of various wooden tools
and middle-sized outriggers. With the demise of these villages individuals
elsewhere took over their economic functions, but a form of interdepend-
ency was destroyed in fact, if not yet in ideal. This in fact is an important
theme running throughout the colonial experience. Budibud is entirely
planted in coconuts – this is why the German trader settled there in the
1880s – and is to serve as a source of coconuts, pigs fed off the coconuts,
and skirts, produced from coconut fronds, for the rest of MUYUW.

314

These things were and are to some extent traded to MUYUW, which had, traditionally, no coconuts, for various kinds of food, mostly sago, of which Budibud had little. But with European plantations begun on Woodlark, and forced government plantings beginning in the 1920s, this interdependence has been altered somewhat. Corresponding to the actual transformation of the indigenous system is the ideology, coming down from government people and the educated MUYUW youths, of 'self-sufficiency', a condition which is apparently supposed to come about by everyone getting involved in the world copra-market. European intrusion is located on other levels as well. Beginning in the 1920s the government and missions began open interference in some MUYUW rituals; the loss of one of these MUYUW still resent. Also under the colonial umbrella, but largely if not completely independent of direct government action, certain ritual forms belonging to peoples on the southern side of the kula ring have been forced on MUYUW. They resent this too.

There is evidence that between 1900 and 1920, after a period of considerable disruption, new MUYUW power-constellations had formed under the colonial system. MUYUW themselves note that the present-day composition of most villages is completely different than what it was in the 'old times'. This does not mean that they believe that in the past everything was perfect or unchanging, but rather that they recognize the present being in part defined by social forms not of their own making. By 1972, however, the generation that had formed the first synthesis under the colonial regime was all dead, and a newer generation of leaders were struggling to reconsolidate these now old positions, or generate new ones. As the remainder of this paper should make clear, much of this action necessarily follows from the internal organization of the kula. But it should be noted that added to the ambiguities of the period during my own fieldwork was some considerable confusion as to what 'Independence' and 'Papua New Guinea' meant.

The kula

Introduction

The main concern of this paper is to explicate the distinction between 'opening' gift and 'return' gift in the kula. These are Malinowski's terms (1961:98, 352–7), translations of the Trobriand *vaga* and *yotile*. In MUYUW identical concepts figure prominently in the kula, but the terms are somewhat different. For vaga, MUYUW say '-*vag*'; for yotile, they say '-*gulugwal*'.[3] The identity of a kula valuable as a vag or gulugwal

315

Frederick H. Damon

is independent of its identity as a *mwal* ('armshell') or *veigun* ('necklace'), but if a vag is a mwal its gulugwal must be a veigun, and vice versa.

Malinowski notes two general themes with regard to the opening and return gift, one stressed, the other unstressed. First he notes that the two prestations are different in 'name, nature, and time'. By name he merely refers to the vag/gulugwal (MUYUW) distinction. By time he notes that the two exchanges are not simultaneous, vags coming necessarily before gulugwals. Most important however is how these differ in nature. The central point Malinowski focuses on is the distinction between vags as 'spontaneous' and gulugwals as 'obligatory'.[4] Whatever else Malinowski may have meant by this spontaneous/obligatory opposition, the following is most important: once a vag is given over a gulugwal must be returned. In MUYUW, for example, no matter what has preceded the giving of a vag no non-owner of an article may take it without first having it formally presented, ideally, in a manner already well-outlined by Malinowski – the dominant/submissive pattern between the giver and the receiver respectively. The same is not true of a gulugwal. A gulugwal is owed to some specific person, and if he does not receive it he may take it (although this would be bad etiquette). Claims on vags are different from claims on gulugwals.

The second point Malinowski notes about the vag/gulugwal opposition, but does not stress, is that a gulugwal must be 'equivalent' to a vag. This is important. As is known kula valuables are ranked, and a gulugwal must be equivalent to a vag *vis-à-vis* this ranking system. MUYUW told me that what determines a valuable's rank is its size, not the process of circulation. A big mwal is generally one which has a large diameter while a large veigun is one whose individual pieces are uniformly small in diameter and uniformily red in color. Unless a veigun has become extremely short, length is not recognized as a significant feature. MUYUW recognize three major categories of each kind of valuable, *mwalikaw*, *mwalibut*, and *mwal*, for mwals from most to least valuable, and *bagilikw*, *bagido'u*, and *soulava*, for veiguns. Although MUYUW do not seem to have any other major categories they do distinguish variations within any category. Thus while there may be about fifty or so mwalikaws and bagilikws, I found considerable consensus on the top twenty or so of each of the articles in these top classes.[5] Thus it is not the case that, for example, a high-ranking mwalikaw could have a low-ranking bagilikw as its gulugwal. Such an exchange MUYUW would classify as 'uneven' (*ikayal*), and the two articles could not therefore be paired as vag and gulugwal.

What I examine in this paper is the double aspect of the relationship

316

between vags and gulugwals. While on the one hand they must be equivalent, on the other there is some kind of asymmetry between them. Clearly the dynamics of the kula result from the contradiction between these two principles. As exchange theory would have it, these dynamics would be explained either by the fact that a gulugwal has less value because it is the second gift, or because there must be some uncertainty about equivalence. In either case one should disambiguate the situation by returning two gifts instead of one. Both of these reasons however are incorrect. One reason why they are incorrect is that just as there are two aspects to the vag/gulugwal distinction so are there two aspects to the way every kula valuable is understood. On the one hand every kula valuable is either a mwal or veigun while on the other every kula valuable, MUYUW claim, is also a *kitoum*.[6] Because of the critical significance of the concept kitoum one is forced, I believe, to deal with the kula not in terms of exchange theory but rather with a production theory of society.

MUYUW and the kula: an overview

Before dealing directly with the significance of the vag/gulugwal distinction it is first necessary to properly contextualize the kula on MUYUW.

MUYUW kula to 'produce' a 'person's' 'name'. Just as it is said that the purpose of the capitalist system is the production of 'commodities', so it is the case that the kula produces a person's name. The category I translate by 'person' is *gamag*. It is the agent of kula action and its quantitative dimensions are the result of the kula. It may be either male or female.

MUYUW claim that according to a person's success, or failure, in the kula he or she does, or does not, age. I do not believe that this representation results merely from the accurate perception that older people are generally the most successful in the kula. The point MUYUW are making here is conceptual, not perceptual. The kula is conceived to lead to old age, a greater accumulation of lived time. When questioned on this point MUYUW proved the assertion by pointing to the differences between an older and younger brother in Boagis village. The older brother was less successful in the kula than the younger man, but the younger brother has lost most of his hair, his teeth, and he looks withered. Although the youngest, he is by virtue of his experience in the kula the oldest. Conversely, the older brother has most of his hair, all of his teeth, and is physically much stronger. Although the oldest, by virtue of his relative lack of success in the kula, he is the youngest. The thing that the kula produces represents, more or less, social time.[7]

Although everybody in MUYUW participates in the kula in theory, the

317

institution functions to differentiate one person from another. Consequently there are some people who kula little and others who for all practical purposes do not kula at all, at least during certain stages of their lives. The result of the kula then is a skyline of differentiated persons, some of whom have 'high' names while others have 'low' or no names at all. If one adopts MUYUW's way of looking at other places and itself but begins at some distant point in the ring, say Dobu, then three MUYUW names stand out, are 'seen', above all others: Molotaw in the one-village island from Yemga (Egum); Takumboub from Boagis; and Lobess from Waviay, a post-World-War-II offshoot of Nasikwabw (Alcester Island). These are the three most successful persons in the kula on MUYUW at the present (1975). Their names are the highest because they have circulated around the kula ring more than other names by means of the exchange of mwals and veiguns. However, as one moves closer to MUYUW other names come into view. In the west several more emerge from Boagis, and one, Meskolos, appears from the two-house village of Kuduweta. In central MUYUW the name Aygeol stands out from Dikwayas, but this name remains overshadowed by Aygeol's deceased father (Vawous) and older brother (Mikdulan). In eastern MUYUW Aisi, from Wabunun, and Kabilu'a, from Wabawag, come quickly into view. As one comes closer to MUYUW many more names emerge. Usually just one or two stand out from any village, but in some places, namely Wabunun, five or more may appear relatively quickly.

The purpose: to make a person's name go high, to make it seen. And the agent: a person. These two features of the kula immediately distinguish it from what I call MUYUW kinship. MUYUW kinship is retrospectively oriented to replace what was expended in the past *vis-à-vis* a given marriage, and its agents are gender-specific.

A person builds a name by combining together, in the context of specific communities, work and certain spheres of exchange. I now briefly describe each of these notions, 'community', 'work', and 'sphere of exchange'. The first two are closely allied.

Earlier I noted that the MUYUW concept ven is understood as a 'scene' for social action with a kind of segmentary logic separating and combining different vens, communities. In the context of the kula the notion remains that of a scene for action, but it also refers as much to a kind of organic as mechanical solidarity. Different communities do different kinds of 'work', and this is how they are differentiated. The word I translate by 'work' is *wotet*, and this is a general or abstract concept. Thus Yemga (Egum), Boagis, Nasikwabw (Alcester), and Waviay have as their primary work sailing whereas the rest of MUYUW, relative to these places, garden. Before it ceased producing stone materials, Suloug's work was producing axes and knives which it exchanged with other places for their work. Although European forms of work, and especially the activities sponsored by the Neates, did not leave this MUYUW formation untouched, I believe that the wage labor and piece work started by them was as much absorbed into this traditional scheme as it served to begin transforming it. Because of the Neates in central MUYUW people from Gaw expect to receive from people in central MUYUW money, tobacco, flour, and cloth just as formerly, and to a lesser extent now, they expected to receive from them sago, sleeping mats, clay pots and armshells. People in central MUYUW do not 'work' clay pots in the sense that they produce them, but they do receive them from other people in MUYUW who get them from their original producers, people whom MUYUW call LOLOMON people on the southern side of the kula Ring. In the context of 'community' and 'work' getting kula valuables is perceived to be work, a given place's work depending upon context. Thus eastern MUYUW people tell people from central MUYUW that they 'work' mwals while central MUYUW people 'work' veiguns. But, relative to LOLOMON, south of MUYUW, eastern MUYUW people work veiguns while LOLOMON people work mwals.

It is from the articulation of different spheres of exchange that links are forged between different communities, their work, and the production of a person's name. 'Sphere of exchange' is an accurate translation of the MUYUW term *ked*. Weiner (1976) has translated the similar Trobriand term, *keda*, by 'road', and I will use either 'sphere of exchange' or 'road' here although 'way' is more evocative of the different MUYUW uses of this important term. I discuss the interaction between different roads using the familiar distinction 'conveyance' and 'conversion' (e.g. Bohannan, 1955).

There are many different spheres of exchange in MUYUW and these are rather explicitly ranked. Some of the more important, and their relative rankings, are listed here:

Highest: mwal/veigun
              pig/pig
              food/boat work
              clay pots/sleeping mats
              yam seeds/taro seeds
Lowest: betel nut/betel pepper

This list indicates that for a given mwal a veigun must be returned, and for a given pig another (of like size and sex) must be returned, etc. Also, however, it indicates that the mwal/veigun road is more important, and, more or less, contains more 'value', than the, for example, betel nut/betel pepper road. This list however is by no means exhaustive. It does not depict the most important articles which move between MUYUW and Gaw, excepting kula valuables, and it does not adequately portray the exchange relationships between Budibud and MUYUW. Mwals and veiguns hardly ever pass between Budibud and MUYUW and there is, presumably therefore, a significant difference in the way conveyances are conducted. Without going into all of the details, between Budibud and MUYUW debts are for the most part canceled rather quickly, whereas this is not at all the case within the rest of MUYUW, and between MUYUW and other places. But between MUYUW and Budibud most exchanges are conducted for the purpose of conveyance while within MUYUW and between MUYUW and other places most conveyances are designed to lead to conversions, and ultimately the production of a person's name.[8] A name is realized through the conveyance of mwals and veiguns.

Although the issue is too complex to treat in detail here, it is important to realize that the structure of exchange on the kula road is different than the others. The form of exchange in the kula is triadic whereas it is dyadic on subsidiary roads. A mwal or veigun must go to some third person (MUYUW: -mul), and this movement to or through a third person is an important aspect of the 'finishing' process of the kula as a productive activity. Lower-level valuables need not go to some third person. This does not mean, however, that, a pig will not go from A to B to C to D, for this often happens. But this procedure involves no more than the concatenation of a set of dyadic exchanges, and A has no control over the pig that C gave to D. If what was exchanged along this line was a kula valuable however, then A would have some control over C or the article D now holds.

Rates of exchange exist, sometimes loosely defined, for every road. Mwals and veiguns exchange against one another vis-à-vis the ranking principles I have already noted. Pigs exchange for the same size and sex. The main gardening villages must garden enough so that sailing villages can devote similar amounts of time to sailing. One clay pot is exchanged for one standard-sized sleeping mat. A large packet of betel pepper should receive several hundred betel nuts. But these exchanges are not called gimwal (cf. Trobriand gimwali), a term which roughly denotes two owners exchanging complementary use-values. Instead these exchanges – excluding the exchange of kula valuables – are called siwayoubs. This word is probably cognate to the Trobriand wawoyla, which Malinowski (1922:353–4) translates as 'wooing'. In MUYUW one makes a siwayoub to make another person have the same 'mind', 'intentions' (nano-) as oneself. If I give someone a pig as a siwayoub that person later owes me a pig of the same size and sex, but what I really want, and what I give the pig for, is a kula valuable. If I do not receive the kula valuable, eventually, then I give no more pigs even if the first is paid back.

In summary, lower-level roads are initiated to gain access to the kula as a road. While in form they are conveyances, in function they are conversions. But recall that kula valuables are ranked. Let us note the implications of this.

First, initiating a relationship with a pig means a more serious commitment than initiating or maintaining it with just food or betel nut. Therefore one expects larger kula valuables coming against pigs than against food or betel nut. Second, giving an extra amount of some particular thing also calls for larger rather than smaller kula valuables. A specific example will make this point clear. Up to the mid-1960s there were numerous small kula relationships[9] between Boagis in western MUYUW and Wabunun in eastern MUYUW. Accompanying the exchange of small kula valuables was a continuous flow of food, often sago, from Wabunun to Boagis. About 1965 a Wabunun elder decided to try to convert some of these small relationships into larger ones. Hence he organized Wabunun to overwhelm Boagis with food and pig at the next opportunity, a certain ritual. The conversion worked. Wabunun got two large kula valuables which were designed to be the initial articles on two large relationships, roads.

A further point may be drawn from this specific example. The dynamics of the relationship between Wabunun and Boagis are not best understood as like a 'potlatch', even on the subsidiary spheres of food and pig. For obvious geographical reasons Boagis, as a sailing village, gets most of its support from the gardening villages directly to its north (Mwadau, Kuduweta, Moniveyova). Wabunun then was not competing with Boagis, rather with these other villages. What it succeeded in doing is giving more food and pig to Boagis than these other villages. Hence the effect of the exchange was not so much to 'put Boagis down', but to partially exclude other villages from Boagis' kula.

From the discussion to this point it may be appreciated that there are two aspects to the conveyance and conversion processes outlined so far. Both are intimately related to each other, yet they are distinct. One deals with the qualitative relationships engendered by exchange: there are different roads for different things and each has conveyance rules more or less well formed. The other relates to the quantitative dimension of the things on each road and the relationships between different roads. In the long run, the greater the magnitude of the things given on subsidiary roads the greater the magnitude of the kula valuables exchanged on the kula road.

One reason for emphasizing the qualitative and quantitative coupling of principles in MUYUW conveyance and conversion processes is that in some cases these two 'realities' are separated rather than combined. They are combined in the procedure MUYUW call siwayoub, but they are separated in the precedure MUYUW call a *pok*.[10] Whereas a siwayoub is given to make a relationship, the end specifically a kula relationship, a pok is given to get a specific kula valuable. In a siwayoub one gives to tie two persons together. In a pok one gives something – anything, from indigenous to European goods – to force somebody to give over a specific kula valuable. Generally speaking, the things given in a pok do not have to be given back, but this is tricky. For if the things given in a pok become too large in value – the highest I have heard about involves upwards of A\$ 200 – then the recipient of the pok may be forced to give up his mwal or veigun as a kitoum, not just as a mwal or veigun. This remains true whether or not the article was its holder's kitoum in the first place. Too large a debt can change the definition of a kula valuable from that of either a mwal or veigun to that of a kitoum.

Let me elaborate on this crucial point. If a pok is small then there need be no formal attempt to return it. A kula valuable will be given according to normal conveyance rules and something of a kula relationship may result. But if the pok is large then its recipient will have to try to return it. This may be done by following normal conveyance rules, the results of which may be a substantial kula relationship. Often, however, the pok recipient must pay back the pok by giving up his kula valuable as a kitoum. If this should happen then the person who receives the kitoum takes it as a return on the pok and need not return a mwal or veigun, whatever the case may be. He has gotten a kitoum, not a vag, not an 'opening gift', and therefore he need not return a gulugwal, a 'closing gift'. The person who gave up the kitoum, if it was not his kitoum, must still return a gulugwal to the person who first gave him the article as a vag. This may be difficult, and poks are therefore perceived to be dangerous. Poks tend to separate people from their mwals or veiguns, not unite them on a ked, a road.

To summarize: 'persons' kula to produce their names. These persons are located in specific 'communities', and different communities have different 'work'. The relationship between person, community, and work is articulated by different 'roads'. Lower-level roads should feed into the highest road, the kula. While these smaller roads interrelate different persons in contiguous communities, the kula ties together numerous different local connections, binary in form, into a more complex association which is triadic. The greater the value of things circulating on subsidiary roads the greater the value of the articles circulating on the corresponding kula road. Although qualitative and quantitative aspects of the conveyance/conversion process are sometimes combined, in one specific transaction they are separated. In this kind of transaction an owner of a mwal or veigun may be forced to give up that article not as an mwal or veigun, but as a kitoum. That a given kula valuable may be a mwal, or veigun, and a kitoum, is extremely important to understand. As we shall see, a kitoum is what is 'resident in', to use Mauss' phrase, a mwal and veigun.

The double aspect of production: 1 – kitoums

With the foregoing as background I now begin the explanation of our major problem: the nature of the relationship between vags, opening gifts, and gulugwals, return gifts.

From Malinowski's text it was noted that there are two dimensions to the exchange of these two articles. First, they must be equivalent. Second, there is some asymmetry between them. I begin with the question of equivalency, the point of departure for the concept kitoum.

I closed the previous section by pointing out that a mwal or veigun may be transformed into a kitoum. Let us look at this more closely. On first encounter MUYUW speak of kitoums as if they were just another kind of kula valuable. Thus there are mwals, veiguns, and kitoums, and one does some kinds of things with the first two, and other things with the kitoum. Functionally the differences between these articles coalesce around the distinction between conveyance and conversion. One produces a name by the exchange of mwals and veiguns in accordance with the conveyance rules already described. Kitoums are used however in what appears to be a set of very direct conversions. Pok has already been so described. Another involves the large outrigger canoes (*anagegs*) usually produced on just Gaw and Kweywata. These canoes are sent to MUYUW and then often exchanged further to the south. Whoever finally holds the canoe owes the original producers a bunch of kitoums. Although other things are exchanged in the context of a canoe transfer MUYUW claim that the kitoums are the real payment. The standard 'price' is five kitoums, but this varies at least with the size of the boat. A small one may bring only three or four, while a large one may bring six or seven, according to MUYUW. Kitoums are also used to pay off pig debts. Should a recipient of a pig be unable to make a return on that pig then the giver may ask for the debt to be cleared by a kitoum. The number of kitoums owed per pig varies with the size of the kitoums and the pig, but generally only large pigs lead to debts which have to be paid off in kitoums. In my experience the persons involved in such an affair determine the equivalency rates themselves, but I was told that if the creditor asks for

Frederick H. Damon

only one or two kitoums this means he or she wants large ones. This kind of a transaction is called a *soug*, but this term is not confined to pig/kitoum conversions. If two kula partners run up big debts then some third person may try to take over the position, road, of one of them by paying off some or all of the debts of the other with his own kitoums. These kitoums go as gulugwals on the road, for some or all of the outstanding debts, but the giver loses them as kitoums, while he gains the road. This transaction too is called a soug.

Kitoums are also used to pay off certain debts engendered by the MUYUW 'kinship' system. I noted earlier that the MUYUW kinship system is different in structure from the kula, but one of the most important ways these two systems intersect relates to the way kitoums move back and forth between each. Hence a brief but incomplete discussion of this process here is important. If, and only if, a man takes a woman out of her village to be his wife – which he should do to be a 'male' – then upon her death he owes her group, usually her brother or his children, one or more kitoums. These kitoums are said to 'replace' the 'work' the woman gave to the man while the two were married. This transaction is called a *po'un*. Should a man not have any kitoums to offer his wife's people, he will likely offer a pig, or pigs, sago or betel-nut orchards, or gardening land. Kitoums, however, are what MUYUW want. Note that, as in the case of a pok and other transactions involving kitoums, the kitoums given over as a po'un do not have to be returned. A kitoum is given to 'replace' past work. It does not engender a relationship. When the kitoum is given the relationship is over.[11]

Such, in any case, seem to be the differences between mwals and veiguns on the one hand, and kitoums on the other. The former two are used in conveyances while the latter one is used in conversions. This impression is reinforced by the fact that only a few of the kula articles any individual handles or sees are either his or her kitoums, or the kitoums of people he or she knows. Upon further inquiry however, MUYUW note that every kula valuable is somebody's kitoum. Underlying the existence of every kula valuable as a mwal or veigun is its existence as a kitoum. The concept, 'kitoum' allows for the commensurability of mwals and veiguns, and other things, and persons. This is why a mwal or veigun may be pressed into a kitoum by the transaction called a pok. What we must now do is examine how kitoums enter the process of circulation as mwals and veiguns.

When one gives a mwal or veigun to a partner (*veiyou-*), and the article is also one's kitoum, then the stress in the exchange is somewhat different than if the article is just a mwal, or veigun. Informants discussed such exchanges in very conservative terms: one is extremely careful about to whom the article is given, and under what conditions it is given. In short, the article is given so that something will come back for it immediately. The emphasis is not on the relationship generated by the exchange of a mwal or veigun, but rather on getting a return for one's kitoum as soon as possible. Informants picture mwals and veiguns as moving continuously in two circles around the kula Ring. Ideally as one matures and expands one's kula those two rather abstract circles, one for mwals, the other for veiguns, will become realised in terms of specific named persons, and in the largest relationships ('Big Roads'), the circles do sometimes close. But the model for kitoums is different. Over time the model does not change. One repetitively exchanges one kitoum, which may be a mwal, for another, which must then be a veigun.

Using the opposition vag/gulugwal let me review these points using the hypothetical set of people, A–B–C–D–E–n . . . A. With this set 'C' has two people whom he calls 'partners' (veiyou-) B and D. A, E and n are called by C 'partners of partners' (-mul). When C gives a kitoum/mwal to D it is a vag. This pattern moreover is recursive along the line of people. D's partners are C and E, his partners of partners are A, B, and n. But the kitoum/mwal/vag that C gave to D is just D's mwal/vag. When the gulugwal for that vag, a veigun, comes back, it will be a gulugwal for everybody but C. It will not be a gulugwal for C, it will rather be a kitoum, and therefore something which C can throw as a vag, in the other direction, to B. D has no choice but to give the gulugwal/veigun to C, because the valuable is his kitoum/vag/veigun. A finality at one level, a kitoum is a potentiality at another: the cycle can start over in the other direction.

This point in the circulation process of the kula is crucial. Having a mwal that is a kitoum replaced by a veigun, which is now the kitoum, 'reproduces' (Balibar, 1970) one's position in the kula. This is, however, a conservative moment in the movement of articles. Although a kitoum returns to its owner as a vag, it does not, according to M U Y U W, change in 'value'. Let us look at this notion of 'reproduction' a bit more carefully.

Getting a return on a kitoum actually represents two related but slightly different aspects of what I call reproduction. First, the returned kitoum may now begin a new cycle in the kula unencumbered by past revolutions. For example, when I 'throw' a vag/mwal/kitoum, the veigun I get back is a vag, and I may do with it as I please. At the same time the mwal I first threw must travel on the road of the veigun I now have until it comes to the person who owned that veigun as a kitoum. Then it may move as a vag. This aspect of the circulation logic of the kula suggests that a kula valuable can not increase in value merely by being circulated. Mwals and veiguns move as such until they are reclaimed as kitoums

Frederick H. Damon

whence their past routes may be forgotten and they may start over again.[12] The second aspect to this notion of reproduction is just as important as the first. By the fact that a person can claim a return on a kitoum he or she has demonstrated an ability to manipulate successfully other and lower roads without getting encumbered in debts to the extent that a kitoum must be relinquished. Of course periodically kitoums are 'lost' due to the transactions listed earlier, but a key to many peoples' success in the kula is accumulating enough kitoums so that smaller ones may be devoted to necessary conversions while the larger ones are held onto for the purpose of building one's kula roads, and then name.

A couple of specific examples will help illustrate some of the points I have been making here:

Dibolel and Ogis, elder and younger brother respectively, are two young, ambitious, and relatively successful men in the kula. Although both live in Wabunun, in eastern MUYUW, Ogis organizes most of his kula as if he lived in Waviay, a sailing village across the lagoon from Wabunun. Often these two men work together on the same roads, Ogis working the relationship to the south in Lolomon, Dibolel working to the north and west in MUYUW.

For reasons which are mostly fortuitous, Dibolel has five or so kitoums, a lot by MUYUW standards. What Dibolel finds particularly convenient about this situation is that he can give his kitoums to his younger brother so that he, Ogis, can take them south and only 'throw' them when he knows exactly what is going to come back for them. In two ways this is more advantageous than what is afforded most people in MUYUW. First, in giving his kitoums to Ogis, Dibolel is not just giving them to another 'person', a 'partner', he is also giving them to a 'younger brother'. This is almost like not giving them away at all since Ogis himself is, currently, slated to inherit these valuables. But second, Dibolel, represented by Ogis, retains nearly complete control over his kitoums nearly a hundred miles to the south, in Lolomon.

Dibolel's use of his kitoums is classic, extremely conservative, but not untypically so. Older, more experienced, and more successful people, however, do use their kitoums in a slightly more daring fashion. Some of these procedures are outlined in the next section so I need not review them here. However, the use elders make of their kitoums only follows from the fact that they already are fairly secure about the people with whom they are dealing. If and when things do break down then the kitoums may be called in, no matter who is holding them, and where they are.

Let us note another case, one which is considerably more complicated. Ostensibly it involves an informal meeting between two men, Aisi from Wabunun, and his major partner to the west and north, Kalipwal, from Dikwayas. The meeting was held one night in January 1975, and it lasted all night. Two or three years earlier Aisi had given all (about 10) but one of his mwals to Kalipwal, the one he did not give called 'Nimov', and very large. Kalipwal had wanted Nimov very badly, but as the situation was very complicated Aisi sent Nimov directly west to the island of Iw, rather than through first central M U Y U W and then Gaw. This considerably upset Kalipwal (and others), and the 1975 meeting, initiated by Kalipwal, was an attempt at reconciliation. Some background information is relevant here, information which is common knowledge to probably everyone in M U Y U W forty to forty-five years old or older: Kalipwal is a sister's son of probably the most successful man in the kula in Mu Y U W in the twentieth century, Vawous. By the time of his death (*c.* 1950), Vawous controlled two of the three largest kula roads going into M U Y U W and had smaller relationships into every village on the island. For his death Vawous had arranged that his roads and his kitoums be divided between his sister's son and his own sons; Kalipwal got the roads, but Vawous' own sons got his kitoums. This created a paradox. Most large relationships are built out of kitoums, but now the kitoums were separated from the roads. This paradox was realized with regard to Vawous' old connections to Wabunun since Wabunun, and one road in particular, was the strongest connection to the south. Hence in the twenty-five years since Vawous' death two men, one on the basis of the road, the other on the basis of the kitoums, were trying to deal with one position in Wabunun. (This is why the mwal, 'Nimov', went around Dikwayas.)

To return to the January 1975 meeting; Kalipwal had come to Aisi to try to convince him how much he, Aisi, needed Kalipwal. With Aisi owning three very large kitoums, however, Kalipwal was not in a very good bargaining position, and towards dawn Aisi nonchalantly asked Kalipwal how many kitoums he had. Although infuriated, Kalipwal did not answer this question, and he did not have to. Aisi, and everyone else in M U Y U W, already knew the answer: None. The question was posed to tell Kalipwal that he was by and large dependent on Aisi for the big valuables he got, and not the other way around.

The point here is not difficult to grasp. The vast majority of valuables Aisi and Kalipwal have exchanged with one another, will exchange with one another, and the majority of the valuables that their predecessors exchanged, were not their kitoums. However, given the absolute control they do have over their kitoums, these few articles become significant power sources, pivots, for other valuables. Ultimately owning a kitoum fixes a person's position in the kula.

To conclude this section: vags, opening gifts, and gulugwals, return gifts, must be equivalent because in the final analysis they are somebody's kitoum. At a certain level of abstraction the kula ring consists of individual owners of kitoums exchanging these articles back and forth. This 'simple circulation' merely reproduces one's position in the kula.

2 – The circulation of mwals and veiguns

There is a 'disjunction' between the circulation of kitoums and the circulation of armshells and necklaces. Kitoums are used in direct conver-

Frederick H. Damon

sions such that a given agent is formally separated from his kitoum. Conversions for mwals and veiguns are always indirect *vis-à-vis* siwayoubs, and agents remain in control of their articles. When kitoums enter the kula road for the production of names they do not circulate in the same way as mwals and veiguns. When X receives a return for a kitoum, that article is not a gulugwal, it is a kitoum, and again may be thrown as a vag.

The 'disjunction' between the circulation of kitoums and the circulation of mwals and veiguns situates the contradiction between a vag and a gulugwal. A gulugwal must be equivalent to a vag in terms of size because in the final analysis it constitutes somebody's kitoum. Kitoums are the underlying explanation for the conveyance rules of the kula. From another perspective vags and gulugwals are not equivalent, and it is tempting to say that gulugwals have less 'value' than *vags*. Hence Malinowski's description of the two transactions in terms of 'spontaneous' and 'obligatory'. Let us look at this more carefully.

Giving a kula valuable as a vag to somebody is tantamount to making a relationship, making two people veiyou- to one another. MUYUW most often describe the result of this transaction by the English work 'book'.[13] The use of this word is based on their experience of seeing transactions in European trade-stores. When you go into a store and get something without paying for it, the storekeeper writes the price of the article taken down in a book. Later, of course, one must pay for the article. MUYUW believe that it is not good to have a 'book' in the context of the trade-stores, that ultimately in the European sector one should be all paid off. However, when they use the term 'book' in the context of the Kula it is a good thing because it means that an ongoing relationship exists between the people so related. In this context a gulugwal has the appearance of having less 'value' than a vag because it ends the relationship. 'Value' of course is not really the issue. 'Value' relates to the quantitative dimensions of kula valuable. In this context a vag and a gulugwal must be equivalent. But from the qualitative point of view, the relationships created by the exchange of 'value', they are different. A vag makes a relationship, but a gulugwal ends a relationship.

The notions I have just tried to describe are borne out clearly in the way MUYUW classify different kinds of kula actions. Four terms describe two oppositions. In the first opposition 'trading' is opposed to ked, or road. When MUYUW use the European word 'trading' to describe kula action they have in mind trade-store activity where the purpose is buying one thing with another, some article for money, such that when completed the relationship is over. In short after a vag is given a gulugwal is returned immediately, and nothing else. Sometimes this activity is likened to 'whoring'; one gives a woman a dime, has intercourse with her, and then the relationship is over. In this context ked or road is said to be 'like a marriage' (*magina ivay*). In a 'road' the relationship should last until death, like a marriage, and more vags should be given than gulugwals.

The second opposition distinguishes 'little ways' from 'big ways' (cf. footnote 9). The point is that actors perceive themselves to be related to one another over longer periods of time, even though in a 'little way' a second vag is generally not given before a first is paid off.

We are now at the point to see why it is that the kula involves expanding tendencies. To be successful in the kula one must create relationships. To keep a relationship one must be able to counter the equivalence, conveyance, rules by which the kula articles circulate. The requirements of a road contradict those of the exchange of equivalents. The result of this contradiction is either that individual kula relationships collapse, or they expand.

There are numerous informal and formal ways by which people deal with this contradiction. The weakest involves merely declaring that one article is not equivalent to another. If it is an obvious fact that, for example, a given mwal is larger than a given veigun, then there is no problem. The articles continue to move as vags. Each then will have to find its equivalent, and in the meantime the relationship continues. If it is not obvious that the two articles are 'uneven' then the two parties to the transaction may just declare them to be so. But if this is an opening move in a relationship then the individuals involved will realize that they are 'fudging', that they are laying claims to a certain 'strength' which is not yet proved.

A more desirable response is to return two articles for one, one a gulugwal, and the other a vag. The rationale for this procedure was explained to me specifically in the context of kitoums, so let us describe it from that perspective. If one merely returns a gulugwal this article will travel back to the point of departure of the vag as a kitoum. When the owner of the kitoum receives it, he has gotten only what he owns, what he had to get. This therefore indicates that the people that handled his kitoum were not strong enough to build anything with it. Hence he will feel little commitment to pursue that road again. If, however, he gets a return on his kitoum, the gulugwal, and also another article, a new vag, then he will know that somewhere down that road somebody is 'working'. Hence he will try to build that specific relationship. Note that 'schismogenesis' does not explain the logic of this procedure. Some person began by throwing his kitoum as a vag. When he gets back a return on a kitoum and another vag, he has moved from throwing one vag to a state wherein he can now throw two (in the other direction). Since this is what a

Frederick H. Damon

person needs to build his 'name', this is a good tactic for developing a relationship. Exchange theory *per se* does not explain this maneuver, but 'ownership' does.

There are, however, some problems in this maneuver. Let us say that B has received an article from A, and B knows that A is strong. Therfore B wants to develop a significant relationship with A. The problem B faces is how to get two, or more, valuables from C or a number of Cs. If B can get several valuables from one C then there is no difficulty in this situation. But if B has to get several articles from several different Cs, then problems arise. For B may have to tell two or three people, different Cs, that he is building a relationship, a significant one, with each of them, when in fact he only desires to do so with one person. In this context then, one C is clearly being used for the benefit of another C. This situation is by no means rare: people often say that the only way to get ahead in the kula is to lie.

Let us continue the case: B now has several valuables from different Cs. He gives these to A and A realizes that B is 'strong'. A will then do his best to return to B not only the gulugwal(s), but new vags. It is at this point that B will likely run into trouble with some C. For one C will only get a gulugwal while another will get a gulugwal and a vag(s). The first will then undoubtedly call B a liar, and avoid kula relationships with him again. This C may claim, for example, that only because of his article did B get a new vag, and hence he should get that vag, not the other C. In any case, situations like this are legion, and they lead to near endless frustration and ambiguity in the kula.

Let us summarize this case: The expansive tendency of the kula leads to arrangements like this:

$$
\begin{array}{l}
---C \\
1.\ A---B \\
---c
\end{array}
$$

This arrangement is ambiguous and alienating, and should be replaced by:

$$
2.\ A---B---C
$$

which, if the relationship does mature, will probably lead to the repetition of 1, only further down the line:

$$
\begin{array}{l}
---D \\
2.\ (1)\ A---B---C \\
---d
\end{array}
$$

In my experience this procedure is occasioned by middle-sized kula

330

valuables passing between people, or some people, who are usually young but ambitious. In theory at least this kind of kula action may lead into 'big ways'. But when larger kula valuables come into play in still incompletely formed roads a different tactic is used to force more vags into circulation. Rather than the more or less informal maneuver just noted, one of these is highly formalized, and named – *vakanis naman*.[14] It goes something like this. Some person, A, gives a number of kula valuables – whether mwals or veiguns is immaterial – to B. No specific C is in mind. Of these valuables at least one is very large, a member of the highest of the three classes of kula articles (mwalikaw and bagilikw) the others much smaller, maybe not even named. The smaller articles are to be used as 'pawns' for the largest. In this setting B will expect a number of Cs to come in pursuit of his big article. Moreover they are likely to approach him with very big articles of their own. When I have seen this procedure enacted, or when people have discussed instances of it, the valuables that C brings to B are large, but not large enough for B's armshell. For example, B's valuable may be on the upper end of the highest kula classes while C's may be on the lower end of the same class. In any case C will throw his article hoping to get B's article. Instead B throws him, quickly, a small article.

C's intention in this maneuver is to get B's large article. B's however, is to keep his article, attract as many others as possible, and not alienate any potential C. Hence he throws the small article to keep C thinking he still has a relationship, and hence a chance at getting the large article. B however does have to worry about the possibility of C taking back his large article once he realizes that he is being put off. Should this happen, then B will take back his own small article. There is a point to emphasize here. In situations like this, no C ever likes what is being done to him. He is coming to B with the best thing he has to offer and is told it is not good enough, and that for all practical purposes B is waiting for somebody else. In short this tactic is only really advantageous for A and B. If they play the relationship correctly they begin with one big vag and several small ones, but get in return several fairly large articles to throw as vags in the other direction. Moving in the direction of B to A to n . . . this procedure helps consolidate a road – the number of vags moving on the line increases. Moving in the other direction, however, the emphasis is different. It is on the quantitative aspects of the articles involved rather than the qualitative relationship created by the exchange of the articles. C comes away from such encounters having lost his big article and having gotten a little one in return.

Sometimes B may get a big article from A but no small ones. If possible B may then try to get other small articles from some other A. This in fact

Frederick H. Damon

happened in relation to the fifth largest mwal that came into MUYUW in
1971–2, and it will be useful to review what happened:

The *mwal* is named Dayay, and was given to a man in eastern MUYUW whom I will
call O. O wanted the article to go to a man in a central MUYUW village, whom I
call K. For reasons which I will not explain here, K could not come to get the
article, but another of O's partners, D, did get two veiguns of considerable size
with which he thought he could get Dayay. O heard that D was coming for Dayay
with two veiguns about a week before he arrived. He then went to two other men,
W_1 and W_2 (two brothers), who had small Kula relations with O. He asked for and
got two mwals from these men after explaining to them why he wanted the
valuables. There was in fact something of a kula relationship which connected W_1,
W_2, O, and D, but the two Ws knew that O was using them to protect Dayay and
not trying to build up their road. When D arrived O did not even let him finish his
talk ('invocation') before he hauled out the two mwals and defined them as
returns for the veiguns, coming on their 'old road'. D was 'put off' by this
maneuver, but he did return to his village with two mwals at a time when few were
to be found anywhere. O saved Dayay for K, and W_1 and W_2 had two veiguns,
and, more importantly, an opportunity to use O in the same way he had used
them.

This case is slightly different from the normal one where the idiom
vakanis naman is used. The person who gave O Dayay was not well
enough organized to set him up with smaller articles to protect Dayay.
But O was well enough organized to get assistance from elsewhere.
Dayay was saved for (potentially) bigger things, and O kept his relationship with D intact if a bit strained. Hence the case is like that outlined
above since 'A' and 'B' succeeded in cutting the intentions of some 'C'
while accumulating vags as opposed to paying them off with gulugwals.

The practices just reviewed accumulate vags for one, two, or perhaps
more persons to the detriment of some other person, or the outstanding
relationships between any B and C. There is however another procedure
which is not designed to divide people over the quantitative dimensions
of specific articles, but rather unite them qualitatively by the accumulation of vags along a whole line of people. This procedure is in many
respects rather simple conceptually, but it is difficult to manage in actual
practice. Where the preceding practice may involve only a few minutes,
months or years of interaction, this next one tends to get extended over
very long time periods. Five years is probably a minimum – roughly one
revolution of a wave of articles – but I know of one which has lasted for
thirty years and may last many more. This transaction is difficult then
because it involves a whole set of people agreeing on the same thing over
an extended time period, a period which may extend beyond the lives of
some of the people in the set-up.

As a set of activities this procedure is not named. What is named are the individual transactions of which it is composed. The tactic involves one vag being exchanged for two vags and a gulugwal. For example, A gives an article to B. I will call this V_1. B and C then agree that the first article given back to B is the initial vag's *tavnayiel*, the indigenous term, which I will call V_2. C then comes up with another article called *busebuw* (after *sebuw*, which denotes affinal prestations), V_3. The final article from C to B is called the *anakatupw*, which means 'its cut-off', and this is the gulugwal for V_1. What has happened here is that A and B begin by throwing one vag and get to throw two back in the other direction. When C throws the gulugwal for V_1, A and B are still related to him *vis-à-vis* V_2 and V_3. Of course each of these articles must be returned, but it is doubtful that the gulugwal for V_3 will have been returned before this whole series has been set up again *vis-à-vis* some other article. And it must be understood that this is precisely what people want: permanent debt within which new debts, vags, are continually being made.

I have outlined the tavnayiel–busebuw–anakatupw series in terms of three persons A, B, and C. This was for convenience only. With the larger articles, the only ones that ever really get bound up in this system, as much as half of the kula rings – geographically speaking – may have to come to terms about how this set will be organized before the first vag is thrown. This is why the larger kula valuables tend to move so slowly. It is not uncommon to hear of specific large valuables that have remained in the same place for five, ten, or fifteen years (articles which are often the holder's kitoums), the reasons for which should be clearly understood. For if one mishandles a big kula valuable one may only get back a gulugwal, but if the article is correctly handled one may get back three big ones for it. When it is realized that most really successful people in the kula do not get to handle really large valuables until they are maybe forty-five or fifty years of age, and that one of these series may take fifteen years to work through, how one of these schemes fits into the experience of one's life may be readily appreciated. Some people told me that in the past men were murdered over arrangements like these; other people told me they still are (by magic).

In the context of this formal series, V_1–V_2–V_3–gulugwal, other informal exchanges occur, most of which are implicitly tied to the movement of this series. Thus to keep V_2, V_3 and the gulugwal moving back to B and then A, these two agents may have to keep giving other valuables to C, and the rest of the people down the line. These articles are not part of the formal series, but they do condition to some extent its existence. In any case the net effect is again that more *vags* are being piled up on one another: the road expands. This is not 'simple circulation'.

Frederick H. Damon

The effect

'Opening' and 'return' gifts have to be equivalent in terms of rank or value, but the former makes a relationship while the latter ends it. And ending a relationship is decidely not what MUYUW want. To counter the rules of the kula from one perspective MUYUW operate it from another, or try to. They try to increase the number of vags, as opposed to gulug-wals, flowing on a given road. But to counter the contradiction between vags and gulugwals means that the entire set of supporting relationships tying a particular 'community' to the kula must also expand, become more intense. There is a direct relationship between the size of one's name, the goal of the kula, the numbers and sizes of the kula valuables an individual handles, and the amount of work generated within a particular community. The kula leads to exceptional performances.

Exceptional in several ways: first, I mean merely the amount of work certain individuals do. In the sailing villages along MUYUW's southern side (Waviay, Nasikwabw, Boagis, and Yemga), the more successful or ambitious people sail more than others (and raise or acquire more pigs than others). In the gardening villages on the mainland successful men and women have larger gardens than the others. A unit of the MUYUW garden may be used to outline the order of differences in this respect. These units are about eighty feet (plus or minus twenty feet) in length and about 160 feet in width. Given good conditions (climatic among others), important or ambitious people will plant about four of these units where-as the average is about one. Important people of course are also more careful about what they do with their resources than others, and this is seen most clearly with those people who participate in 'European' work. Those people who get money for some of their work and who are more successful in the kula are careful to turn a substantial portion of their money into the kula, either directly, or indirectly through European goods. Not surprisingly those people who only do some kind of piece work, making copra, carving ebony, etc., rather than wage labor in the lumber-mill, seem to be more successful at this than others. The first person the Neates got into ebony carving, for example, has achieved considerable success for himself in the kula, but he has also been careful to avoid becoming dependent upon carving. As the Neates have said, this man 'has put every last penny he ever earned into the kula'. Meskolos, the elder in the two-house community of Kuduweta in western MUYUW is another interesting example. Meskolos is generally regarded as the best gardener east of Kitava, and he clearly produces more food than any other individual on the island. He also, with the assistance of his son, produces a fair bit of copra. Unlike some others, however, he has avoided

334

getting trapped in petty commodity-production. He only produces copra when the prices are high and when the nuts are falling fast. Even in these conditions he is careful to alternate his copra production with gardening. Consequently Meskolos treats his partners sumptuously. But if he does not get what he wants in the kula, his partners feel it. In early 1974 Takumboub, one of Meskolos' main partners in Boagis, refused to give him a large mwal, 'Mantasop', so Meskolos cut off his food supply. Takumboub and his wife fled Boagis for Suloug, his wife's father's residence, where they ate coconuts and sago.

First, then, the contradiction between vags and gulugwals results in individuals, specific 'persons', working far harder than most others. But second, and probably more important, this contradiction results in significantly different 'forms of cooperation'.[15] I outline this facet of the kula in terms of a dichotomy between developing extra kula relationships as opposed to developing extra support for lower-level roads.

People who have big kula relationships tend to develop numerous other roads, some potentially significant in terms of the numbers and sizes of kula valuables flowing on them, others not significant from this point of view at all. In fact MUYUW say that there are only three big roads in the whole kula, although they know that there are several others which approach these three in size and numerous ones even smaller.[16] Some of these 'little roads' are not really for the purpose of the kula, rather for accumulating other things. But most of these little roads descend from important persons. More importantly, the more relationships a person has, however small, the more people he or she may have to draw on if a number of kula valuables are all of a sudden needed on some big road. The actual example I gave with regard to the practice called vakanis naman illustrates this point. O needed a couple of mwals to protect another, and he got these by means of an older and less significant relationship. Many situations like this seem to arise for important people in the kula, and they are in good condition if they do not need to get out of them by making some transaction basically zero-sum. In short, important people tend to work numerous small kula roads most of which in the long run will lead nowhere by themselves, but they afford important sources of kula valuables in crisis or quasi-crisis situations. To form these relationships agents must have command of resources for lower-level roads.

Let us now note lower-level support relationships, and first of all those having to do with affinity. First, most people who do well in the kula do not really become successful until they are forty of fifty years of age. Often this is because most of the articles they will have received before this time will have been taken over by some proximate generation affine. If, for example, X gets an article by virtue of some lower-level conversion, but X's wife's father wants it, there is little that X can do to prevent this person from taking it. In contexts like this the normal asymmetry between a giver and receiver of a kula valuable is dominated by the asymmetry deriving from affinity. X, in this case, will still be owed a gulugwal, but he will have lost the opportunity to make his own road. (Because of this penetration of the kula by MUYUW 'kinship' some men refrain from getting married until certain aspects of their kula are more or less well developed.) In short, affinal relationships often constitute kula resources for elders, and not a few people do not get seriously into the kula until these affines are dead.

Affinity of course can often be turned into an advantage. Meskolos' son is married to the daughter of the biggest man in Moniveyova village. Kampeyn, a big man in Boagis, recently married a woman from Budibud, his reason being that now he has an instant tie into the Budibud pig 'bank' which he can draw on for his kula. Sometime between the late 1930s and the mid-1940s Lobess, one of the biggest men in MUYUW, dropped one woman to marry the daughter of his main partner. While I was in MUYUW Lobess' chief competitor, Molotaw, from Yemga, tried, but failed, to marry his son to a woman of a specific village to cement a kula relationship there for decades to come.

For the contemporary MUYUW scene, however, more important than constructing affinal relationships to serve the direct needs of the Kula is the construction of 'groups' (*bod*). These 'groups' are rather loose associations of 'persons' (gamags). With whom people actually work and live is determined by these associations, but, as I say, they are rather loose. A given person may be a member of more than one group, and he or she may shift from one group to another over time.

These 'groups' are made by some individual feeding or otherwise supporting some other and usually junior person. Relationships of affinity or consanguinity are, by and large, irrelevant to these formations. What is relevant is that some person has publicly supported another, and because of this the latter works for the former. Not surprisingly successful people in the kula tend to have larger such groups than other people. And although it involves a lot of work to get one of these groups going, and to maintain it, once these formations are in operation they afford individuals a great deal of support.

MUYUW 'kinship' and MUYUW 'groups' are different *forms* of association. In the context of the kula there is a tendency to develop the latter to a considerable degree, and sometimes in such a manner that the former is significantly altered. For example, MUYUW do not practice cross-cousin marriage: they say: 'We marry without reason.' However there is one village, Wabunun, which has instituted something akin to a cross-cousin marriage rule. Between 1920 and 1930 the elders of this village decided that the best way to preserve the community's position in the kula was to effectively make cross-cousins marry. It is important, however, to note precisely what this meant and means to the members of Wabunun. For although the village takes a good bit of criticism from other M U Y U W for marrying like Trobrianders, what they in fact have done is not set up a cross-cousin marriage rule but rather forced 'persons' of the same place to marry one another. By marrying their 'persons' together, by keeping the 'group' to a significant extent endogamous, persons who have the same standards of work are kept in the group and do not leave it by marriages to outsiders.

And Wabunun's standards of work are far higher than those of other places. Earlier I noted that big men across the island produce larger gardens than other people. Generally speaking, four units of the size specified represent what a big man will be working under optimum conditions. Lesser folks will produce significantly less food. But in Wabunun four units are about what average persons do, and the big men may have two or three times that number.

The kula is the reason for Wabunun's working standards, and its apparent shift in M U Y U W kinship norms. By about 1920 the village had become the strongest in eastern M U Y U W in the kula, and by the means of one big road. Since then its ethic has formed about this particular road, and under the guidance of a set of brothers who, based on comparative M U Y U W 'political' action, performed brilliantly. What is distinctive about their performance is the way they concentrated all their efforts on just this one road, while they encouraged other Wabunun people to create their own roads. In other words they created a group of people aimed at building and sustaining primarily one large relationship, but rather than also controlling smaller roads themselves they encouraged their supporters to develop and expand their own kula. This is why, as I noted when I introduced the kula, about five rather than one, two or three names are 'seen' in Wabunun.

There is a direct logical relationship between the focus of this paper, the contradiction between a vag and a gulugwal, and Wabunun's particular position in the kula. Because of the stated contradiction a kula relationship must expand. For these relationships to expand more labor must be mobilized. Comparatively speaking, Wabunun has been more successful in mobilizing labor than other villages and, consequently, it does better in the kula than most other areas. But Wabunun's particular solution to the requirements of the kula is only one of a number of possible solutions, and whatever they are they must work themselves out through time. In this regard while what I have called a 'group' is now

337

Frederick H. Damon

more important that other ways of organizing lots of labor, this is true
only because of Wabunun's recent and specific achievement. Between
roughly 1900 and 1960 Dikwayas, under Vawous and his eldest son,
Mikdulan, probably controlled more of the kula going in and out of
MUYUW than Wabunun ever did and will. But this was obtained at
considerable expense. Vawous did not spread his success throughout the
Dikwayas population. Rather he seems to have corralled as much as he
could under his own direct control not giving anything to anyone else
until his eldest son came of age. One way he accomplished this was by
allowing the colonial administration to believe he was a 'paramount chief'
on the supposed Trobriand model (there is no formal notion of hierarchy
in MUYUW like that in the Trobriands), and he died insisting that he
owned all of the land upon which Dikwayas is built, all of the land its
members garden on, and all of the sago and betel swamps its members
traditionally exploit. His two youngest sons still believe this. But other
Dikwayas people do not. And this contradiction periodically leads to
bitter disputes. Twenty-five or more years ago, for example, Dikwayas
was a big village. Now, while upwards of 150 people claim that they are
Dikwayas people, some of these people live in Moniveyova, in western
MUYUW; others live in shacks on the outskirts of the Neate's work-area
at Kulumadau; still others live at Dikwayas' landing a mile below the
village; and finally several more just live in their gardens. What was a big
village twenty-five years ago now looks like a ghost town. But it is not just
the timbers of Dikwayas houses that are rotting. I was told that if
somebody in Dikwayas catches fish or wild pig these things are usually
eaten in the bush or at night in the village. And if in the village, the
rubbish from the meal is thrown behind someone else's house so that
those people are assumed to have eaten without sharing (and therefore
subject to sorcery).

We end this section then with the kula firmly couched in the pragmatics
of MUYUW social life, specifically Wabunun and Dikwayas. These two
communities represent to some extent polar positions on a continuum of
possibilities for organizing or re-organizing MUYUW existence to meet
the expanding dynamics of the kula. Both however must be understood in
historical terms, the logic of that history ultimately defined by the requirements of the kula. But on one end of that continuum Vawous'
success in alienating most of Dikwayas has resulted in a literal scattering
of people and the rotting timbers of forgotten houses. In Wabunun the
tactic was different. Similar kinds of resources were mobilized but this
was accomplished in such a way that although much of Wabunun's labor
went and goes into one big road, numerous other people also have the
possibility of drawing on that labor pool. In Wabunun the notion of

'community' has been transformed from that of 'scene' to that of 'agent', the twisting of M U Y U W kinship norms an aspect of that transformation. Although one man, Aisi, formally controls the three major kitoums in the village, the people consider those kitoums to be the 'community' kitoums, and not Aisi's, or even his subclan's.

Conclusion

My major concern has been to describe the logic, and the implications of the logic, behind the distinction vag/gulugwal, 'opening gift' and 'return gift'. Rather than reviewing the main lines of the argument I conclude instead by raising some broader comparative issues.

M U Y U W believe that the kula, and in particular those aspects of the kula discussed in this paper, transcends the particularities of the individuated island cultures that exist in the kula ring. In so far as the kula is concerned everybody who participates in it is, so to speak, a member of the same group. However right or wrong they are about this, it is certainly correct that 'exchange' in the kula does not exist only at the boundaries of the 'tribal group'. It would be therefore incorrect to say of kula valuables, as Godelier says of Baruya salt (1977:151), that they circulate as 'commodities' outside of M U Y U W but as 'gifts' inside. Moreover, to the extent that one uses Marx's *Capital* for purposes of ethnographic comparison, what is analogous to Marx's 'commodity' is not a kitoum, mwals, or veiguns, or even pigs, boats, clay pots or food, but rather one's name. Using Marx's categories the kula is much more like a system designed to produce 'exchange value' than 'use value'. Its goal is not the reproduction of the individual's place in the group, but his transformation. And as is evident in Wabunun's case, much more eventually is at stake than an individual's name.

Given this point one may wish to ask about the utility of the notion of 'capital' for describing what happens in the kula. This term, of course, involves one in considerable, if standard, problems of comparison and translation, problems which begin with the varying uses of the term in our own society. Douglas (1967), for example, understands by 'capital' primarily a 'thing', and writes that the major difference between modern societies and those in which there is some kind of 'primitive commerce' is that in the latter 'the productive energies are not directed in any very notable sense to the long-term accumulation of real capital goods' (1967: 126). Godelier, paraphrasing Marx, offers a more sociological, even anthropological, definition: 'In its essence, capital is not a thing but a relation between men realized by means of the exchange of things. It is a social fact . . . Capital presupposes the existence of certain social rela-

Frederick H. Damon

tions, and it is within this social structure that material things become capital' (1972:286).

Taking Godelier's comments as a point of departure consider briefly kitoums. First, kitoums are made by some person or persons, they do not come swimming out of the water by themselves. Second, if not originally produced by the owner a kitoum is acquired by a direct transfer of labor, embodied in a pig or canoe. Third, keeping a kitoum presupposes that the owner relates to other agents such that, relatively speaking, he is not in debt to them. Fourth, although on one level the circulation of kitoums does not lead to the possession of more kitoums, on another level having a kitoum to circulate often does lead to the giving and receiving of more mwals and veiguns, those things one uses directly to produce names. Finally note how kitoums are 'inherited'. If owners of kitoums are asked from whom they received these articles they first respond by listing some father, mother's brother, etc. However, on further inquiry one discovers that such relationships as these are not the crucial component of the transference. What is crucial is that the recipient was a 'person' (gamag) of the giver. He had worked with the owner, and the article was given as the ultimate return for that work.[17] Two points should be noted here. First, before the elder dies the youth is essentially the elder's productive resource. Second, by that relationship the youth eventually receives a thing, a kitoum, which is thought to represent the labor he had earlier given the elder. By virtue of the youth's capacity to generate value for the elder he has acquired his own value in the kitoum. In short, people are capital.

Notes

1 Research on Woodlark Island was conducted between early July 1973 and early August 1975, supported in part by a National Science Foundation Grant (GS–39631), and a National Institute of Mental Health Fellowship (F 01 MH57337–01). The core of this chapter is a revision of Chapter 5 of my Ph.D. dissertation (Damon, 1978). Many things are owed Professor Martin G. Silverman for initiating me into the theoretical framework which pervades this work; to Mr Chris Gregory who, since July, 1978, has been a valuable critic; and to many M U Y U W people who carefully explained to me why they were not just 'exchanging'. If my debt to Sahlins' penetrating rereading of *The Gift* (1972: Chapter 4) is not obvious in the text I proclaim them here.

2 My understanding of M U Y U W's history is largely dependent upon the works of Affleck (1971); Laracy (1970); and Nelson (1976). Nelson visited Woodlark in 1974 and I learned much from him at the time. Affleck is currently doing graduate work in History concerning Woodlark's early missionary experience, and much about the island in the nineteenth century will be learned from his work.

3 Vag, as 'opening gift', is probably related to the verb, vag, which means 'make' or 'produce', but I did not investigate this correspondence in the field. These words may both have a possessive prefix. Possession in MUYUW is important, and resembles that in Dobu (Fortune, 1963:65–8). I reserve for another publication extended treatment of MUYUW possession classes and concepts.

4 Mauss (1954:93, footnote 25) implicitly criticizes Malinowski's use of the word 'spontaneous', and he is right to do so. 'Opening gifts' are forced by other prestations (cf. Mauss (1950:178, footnote 1)).

5 In this volume Munn and Campbell discuss how kula valuables are ranked on Gaw and Vakuta respectively. Although Vakutans seem to introduce more formal distinctions than do MUYUW, in most respects the principles for ranking seem to be quite similar. The major difference is my assertion that, in MUYUW, rank does not result from the process of circulation. I may note that two veiguns that MUYUW consistently ranked in the top twelve in the whole kula had not, as of August, 1973, completed one circuit around the kula ring. The issue involved here is important and remains unresolved.

That large-diameter mwals are higher than small-diameter mwals, and that, conversely, small diameter veiguns, with evenly colored pieces, are higher than large-diameter veiguns, is to be explained, I think, by the simple fact that more labor goes into producing each of the higher kind than the smaller kind. The opposition between the two is apparent, not real.

6 The concepts 'mwal' and 'veigun' are in one possession class while the concept 'kitoum' is in another. See footnote 3.

7 To explore the utility of Marx's labor-time theory of 'value' in the kula I believe that one should begin with this association between time and the thing that is being produced. Not dealing with indigenous notions of time and what is produced seems to me to be the major problem in Godelier's otherwise admirable article on Baruya salt money (1977).

8 Most of these conveyances are of course doubly or triply motivated. For example, one exchanges pigs to exchange kula valuables, but most of those pigs are used in MUYUW mortuary ceremonies.

9 These are called *palaysio*, based on the word *pal* (see Trobriand *pari*). The purpose of these relationships is generally the acquisition of something other than the kula from some other place. Thus these relationships are ways of converting 'down'. The smaller kula valuables that tend to travel on these relationships also tend to be passed through numerous people in any given village – so as to collect more work. Large kula valuables moving on 'big roads' (*ked avakein*) tend to pass from one village to another, or one kula community to another (e.g. Muyuw/Wamwan) with few people directly participating in the exchange.

10 See the Trobriand, *pokala*. In MUYUW the concept pok is used only in the context of the kula.

11 In describing the functional differences between kitoums, and mwals and veiguns, I have also described, in part, how kitoums are obtained. Also, however, kitoums are obtained by finding *Conus* shells and turning them into mwals. Kula valuables generally, in MUYUW, get named as they are held by their first owner and maker. The names refer to this person, although exactly

Frederick H. Damon

how this is so is usually forgotten or not known for most valuables. During my two years in MUYUW eight *Conus* shells were found in Wabunun, six large enough to be turned into mwals. All were middle-sized valuables, and named. I doubt that many more mwals were found in MUYUW during this period, but I know of two others. Five new veiguns were introduced into the kula ring from MUYUW, all having come there directly from Rossel Island. Two were considered to be of the highest class (bagilikw), and one ('Damun'), was though to be exceptionally high.

12 The question of 'rank', 'size', or 'value' should not be confused with how well a valuable is known. It of course takes some time before a new article is well known. But an article does not become valuable because it is well known, it becomes well known because it is 'big'.

13 The indigenous term for 'book' is *kwalavag*, which, however, I never heard in use, and learned only by asking early in my fieldwork. Consequently I neglected to investigate the relationship between this probable agglutination, *kwa-la-vag* and the various meanings of the word 'vag'.

14 On vakanis naman: *Va-* and *ka-* are causitive constructions, the first meaning 'to make a hole in' something, the second meaning more generally 'to cause'; *-nis* is a verb meaning 'to shred or tear'. *Nama-n* means 'his hand', and in the example given refers to 'C'.

15 This term is from Terray (1972), but note that I do not equate a 'form of cooperation' with a 'mode of production'.

16 The three 'big roads' according to MUYUW run, in part, from (1) Gaboyin (Dawson Island)–Yemba–Yalab–Iw . . .; (2) from the south to Boagis–Kuduweta–Gaw . . .; (3) from the south to Waviay–Wabunun–Dikwayas–Gaw. From events described in this paper it should be clear that at least two of these, (2) and (3) are unstable. The same is true of (1); until approximately 1925 thus road went from Yemga to Guasopa in eastern MUYUW rather than into Yalaba, and during my research period there was a concerted effort to get it back along this earlier route. In any case most of the high names noted earlier in this article (p. 318) were produced on one of these three roads.

17 In a not so curious way the concept 'kitoum' enjoins the contradictions between MUYUW and the colonial system. When Neate's employees quit his lumber-mill they often feel cheated because they did not receive something tantamount to a kitoum. Here they are not discounting their wages, only indicating that their wages are only designed, in their view, to sustain them, not pay them for what they have given the Neates.

PART IV

Southern kula area

13 Kula traders and lineage members: the structure of village and kula exchange on Normanby Island[1]

CARL EUGENE THUNE

Introduction

Like other inter-cultural trade systems, the *kula* can be seen either as a formal system in and of itself or as grounded in, conditioned by, and existing in terms of local needs, it being but one of the strategies through which these local needs may be satisfied. From this perspective we can consider the differing relative weights kula traders attach to achievement within these two dimensions of the kula. At one end of such a continuum is a central concern with accomplishment within the inter-island dimension of the kula such as Malinowski described in his account of the Trobriand kula (1922). At the other end is a central focus on the uses and consequences of kula trade for localized interests such as is perhaps best to be seen in the kula as practiced by the traders of northeast Normanby Island.

Though the majority of the adults of northeast Normanby trade kula valuables, the northeast Normanby kula is not a major preoccupation in their lives. At the same time northeast Normanby has a somewhat marginal role in the kula ring, participating in the kula but not apparently being essential to it. In many respects this diffuse, invisible quality of the northeast Normanby kula is the result of the specific way it is tied to and grounded within a local village world of exchange strategies and transactions between affinally related matrilineages which most surely are central to Normanby society.

Northeast Normanby Island

Like the other d'Entrecasteaux islands, Normanby Island displays considerable cultural and linguistic diversity (Lithgow, 1976; Roheim, 1946; Williams, 1931) which in large measure coincides with the cultural and social distinctions made by the Normanby people themselves. One such relatively discrete linguistic and cultural unit is that primarily composed

345

of Loboda and Kwanaula villages which are located on the northern tip of eastern Normanby in the general area of Cape Pierson. The majority of the approximately 750 people of Duau[2] (as this area was traditionally known) speak a single language, though several dialects of it are to be found, each of which is localized in a single hamlet-cluster.

Duau people sharply distinguish themselves from people of other Normanby villages, stressing their own relative linguistic homogeneity, their traditional participation in the kula ring which was unique among Normanby villages, and their close relationship to the people of Dobu and East Fergusson. At the same time they stress their distant, anonymous, and frequently hostile relationships with other nearer Normanby people whom they traditionally fought, ate, and consequently still avoid.

In its general outlines Fortune's description of Dobu, Sanaroa, and Tewara, and Roheim's descriptions of Normanby hold true for Duau (Fortune, 1963: Roheim, 1946, 1948, 1950a, 1950b, 1954, 1957). Duau

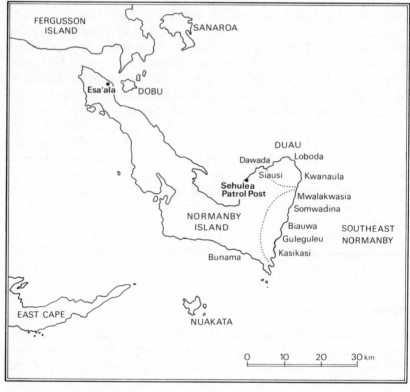

Map 1. Normanby Island.

people are subsistence swidden agriculturalists, though today having a small monetary income derived from copra production and occasional governmental or plantation labor. Government, missionary, and school influences though present and generally (if superficially) accepted, have not really altered the traditional structure of society beyond eliminating warfare and rendering inter-village contact less dangerous and less difficult.

On Normanby as in the Dobu-speaking region, the *susu* (the minimal matrilineage), is the most important social unit, with marital bonds rather tenuously linking different susu. The basic day-to-day social unit is the susu-owned hamlet (*kasa*) in which reside some of the members of the owning susu along with their spouses, children, and other relatives. Kasa are small, rarely containing more than twenty residents. Whereas kasa are the important unit for informal, day-to-day activities, the susu is the unit for maritally-based or mortuary-related exchange activities.

Hamlet clusters are composed of geographically adjacent kasa, containing between seventy-five and 175 people. Villages in turn are largely governmentally-defined units composed of several hamlet clusters which are associated primarily as a result of their geographical propinquity rather than their cultural or linguistic homogeneity or historical relationship. Though having an unstable, accidental quality and no general organizational structure, these units provide a convenient unit for certain informal, non-matrilineally-based, larger-scale activities such as kula expeditions or government work-projects which require a greater number of people than a susu or kasa and its affines can normally provide.

Traditionally more important was the district composed of a number of villages or hamlet clusters, the people of which shared a common language, culture, and body of traditions. Such districts as Duau are roughly equivalent to the unit to which Malinowski refers when he speaks of a kula district.[3]

To the southeast of Normanby is the district Duau people term Kainawali (literally, 'Ware speech'), composed of a variety of small islands including those of the Calvados and Engineer Groups, Dawson Island, Tubetube, Ware, Nuakata, and Basilaki. Most of these islands are small and low, having little heavy bush and largely unproductive soil. Hence a good deal of the Kainawali people's food must be acquired through the trade of such things as Ware manufactured clay pots (*walata*) and other locally-manufactured goods or dried fish or shellfish. These are brought in trading expeditions to East Cape and the more productive high islands such as Normanby where they are exchanged for yams and other tubers. During the former more-leisurely kula expeditions between Duau and

Carl Eugene Thune

Kainawali this trade was an important accessory to kula activities (cf. Seligmann, 1910; Belshaw, 1955; Malinowski, 1961).

However, Kainawali traders also traditionally traded with Normanby Island hamlets not involved in the *kula* and, even when trading with kula villages, there was probably considerable informal barter (*gimane*) which took place outside the bounds of formal trade partnerships. Partly for this reason, Kainawali has been a prime mover in bringing about the expansion of the kula ring through the incorporation of traditionally non-trading communities into it, primarily by developing kula partnerships from pre-existing non-kula trade relationships. Today because of changes in the kula and because of the availability of tradestore-purchased European goods in Kanawali itself, the Kainawali food shortage is less severe. As a result, the trade of kula valuables and foodstuffs have become largely independent of one another.

Modes of transaction

In Duau there are four relatively distinct spheres within which goods, including kula valuables, may move. First, they may be 'shared' between members of the same localized susu as one person uses or receives goods ostensibly belonging to a susu mate. In such a case no payment is made and no real transaction is said to have occurred. Such unaccounted sharing includes a vast number of externally invisible movements of minor goods and mundane food which occur on a day-to-day basis. And it includes movements of feast-quality pigs, yams, and other goods which occur as a susu prepares for an inter-susu feast. Valuables for example may be 'given' by one susu mate to another if the latter person requires them for some transaction with his or her spouse's susu mates (*haihai*).[4] In such a case the susu acts as a single unit which gives a valuable to the haihai of one of its members.

However, valuables whose major if not sole role lies within the kula may also be 'shared' in this way, as when, for example, one of a pair of siblings conducts kula trade with Dobu and the other with southeast Normanby or Kainawali. Children 'inheriting' valuables from their mother or 'mother's brother' (*waha*-) before her or his death are also said to have received them through their elders' sharing with them.

A second form of transaction typically occurs when goods are exchanged between a susu and its *kwabu*-[4], moving from the susu as a whole through one of its members to that person's spouse and thence on to that person's spouse's susu which itself acts as a second and opposed unit. Such exchanges are the primary means whereby relationships between susu are established, demarcated, reinforced, and eventually, with the

348

last mortuary payment, terminated. And, it is through participating in such relationships that individuals actively and deliberately establish who they are within the village world, just as it is by sharing valuables and other goods with susu mates that they establish themselves as central figures within their own susu. These marriage and mortuary exchanges are the high points of Duau social life, far overshadowing all other social events including those related to the kula.

In many respects exchange less unites the two maritally-related susu than establishes a total and complete differentiation between them which in no way may be bridged. Such affinal exchanges are carefully accounted, recorded, and ideally balanced. Duau people themselves stress that marriage within one's susu is bad because the inter-susu exchange which should accompany any marriage either cannot occur, in which case the marital pair remain like siblings to one another or can occur only at the expense of permanently splitting the ideally indivisible susu (cf. Fortune, 1963).

Though affinally-based exchange is the most common form of intra-village transactional activity, in recent years it has been used as a model for the construction of similar transactional events between unrelated susu. Housewarming parties (*wali*) originally introduced by early missionaries are only one such event in which two unrelated susu exchange distributions of food and other goods which are accounted and balanced.

A third form of transaction is that termed gimane which may roughly be glossed as 'barter', 'purchase', or 'sale'. Gimane occurs between social strangers and normally is precluded between those having an even putatively consanguineal or affinal relation. Quite unlike sharing, exchange, and kula trade, gimane takes place between individuals as discrete individuals involved in a single impersonal transaction. Because both sides of the transaction occur simultaneously no temporary transactional imbalance obtains. Hence gimane transactions carry within themselves no requirement for a continuation of the relationship in the future. Self-interest and the search for personal advantage govern the transaction as goods move as mere material objects rather than as objects which may be used to develop a permanent relationship between the two traders.

Gimane, especially of goods for money, is socially irrelevant and not altogether respectable, particularly when conducted using prestige goods such as valuables, high-quality yams, or pigs. Goods exchanged in gimane transactions should be truly owned by the seller unlike the prestige-goods to which the holder's susu mates have secondary rights. Hence it is no accident that the most frequent occasion for gimane is with outsiders: teachers, government representatives, the plantation owner at Dawada plantation, or buyers at the Alotau and Samarai markets.

Carl Eugene Thune

Comprising a fourth sphere, is the kula trade of valuables, ideally between traditional trade partners (*muli*) whose relationship partakes qualities of both sharing and exchange, consanguinity and affinity. Between muli, as within the susu, food is shared, things may be taken without asking, and a certain almost consanguineal solidarity between those so linked is to be found. But, as with the affinal relationship, that which is received should be precisely repaid, resulting in a certain tension, ambivalence, and even hostility between muli.

However, within the broad context of kula trade, valuables may move between muli, or even between anonymous people of different districts in what are recognized as *gimane* transactions. This gimane of valuables may be either delayed or simultaneous, between permanent muli or between anonymous strangers desiring no permanent relationship. In this latter form it may depart rather far from the classic form of kula trade as for example when Egom people sail directly accross the ring to trade necklaces for armshells with Duau people whom they have never met before.

There is no way to speak of the kula as such in the Loboda language. No single word specifically refers to or describes it and it alone. The kula is not even an unnamed discrete institution in Duau in any recognizable sense.

The verb -*kune* which would be used to describe kula-type activities also describes affinally-based exchange-activities, most of which are of more immediate and dramatic importance in Duau than is the kula. At the same time -kune would not be used to describe gimane transactions of kula valuables.

Kune, when used in its noun form, can describe various items which are given to affinally-related susu in the course of a variety of mortuary or marriage-based transactions. Of these, by far the most important are the larger yams which are required for any formal distribution. Pork is optional, though it should be present at any more important event. It is kune of this kind which a susu must have if it is to discharge its responsibilities to its own members and its kwabu-.[5]

One specialized use of the term kune is to refer to the valuables which may be distributed on such occasions but which also are used as a highly restricted form of compensation, 'payment', or 'acknowledgement' for certain exceptional things for which lesser items, no matter how numerous, are inadequate. These valuables are similar to and generally identical to the valuables circulating in the kula which are also referred to as kune.

As a result, there is a continual movement of kune, including kune valuables, within Duau. Though it is possible for a susu to get by without giving kune valuables on such occasions, if a person has hopes for a position as a major figure in local inter-susu activities or intra-susu affairs, he or she must have access to kune valuables to define his or her susu's inter-susu relationships.

The most common kune valuables are *bagi* ('necklaces') and *mwali* ('armshells'), though other kune valuables include *mwahu* (a noseplug), *gadiwana* (a Spondylus *sapisapi*-bead-covered belt), *palelesalu* (an over-sized, greenstone axeblade), *giniuba* (a large pearl shell), and *dona* (a Spondylus-shell-bead necklace with a curved pig's tusk 'pendant'). Palelesalu and gadiwana, though rare, still circulate in the kula ring in the same way as do mwali, being exchanged for bagi. The other kune are exchanged within Duau in a way similar to their exchange within Normanby Island villages not traditionally a part of the kula ring.

What is common to all kune, whether used solely within the district, within the kula, or within both realms, is their ability to move in formal transactions. All valuables are kune because even if they are merely being held as permanent heirlooms, they eventually may move back into the kula and/or the village exchange spheres. Yams, pork, and other goods are termed kune once they actually begin moving in the local sphere.

Historical background of the Normanby kula

Originally on Normanby only Loboda and Kwanaula village people participated in the kula. Sailing counter-clockwise around the ring they went to the small islands of Kainawali in search of bagi. Kainawali is of major importance to the kula because it is there that the kula ring adjoins the non-kula districts in the southeastern Massim in which bagi are manufactured. It is there too that the kula ring is in contact with the axehead-trading system of the southern Massim (in Belshaw's (1955) terms, the kune ring) to which palelesalu originating in Muluwa and traded counter-clockwise around the ring are given in exchange for bagi.

Because the people of these southeastern islands value both palelesalu and bagi there is a real concern that important bagi may reach this area in the course of kula trade and not be returned, thus being permanently lost to the kula ring. Indeed, some suggest that a successful Normanby Island kula trader must have sufficient trading skill and personal magnetism to assure that bagi are not diverted by Kainawali traders from the kula ring in this way.

A second strategic aim of Normanby traders when dealing with part-ners in Kainawali is the acquisition of bagi not previously traded within the kula through exchange or gimane of palelesalu, pigs, or more informally, money. Because a palelesalu is worth a doubled bagi such as is usually traded in Kainawali, rather than a single bagi as is now normally used in kula ring transactions[6] Normanby traders are in a position to profit considerably as new doubled bagi which may be divided and traded separately enter the kula ring in exchange for single palelesalu.

Today direct kula trade between Duau and Kainawali traders has largely ceased because the people of the villages of southeastern Normanby (Biauwa, Somwadina, and Guleguleu and, to a lesser extent, of Mwalakwasia, Kaisikasi, and Bunama) have adopted the kula and have constituted themselves as a new kula district trading counter-clockwise with Kainawali and clockwise with Dobu and Duau. In the past, people of this area lived in the mountainous interior of southeastern Normanby with little contact with coastal people. Broadly they had a culture resembling that of other villages of interior Normanby such as Me'udana (cf. Schlesier, 1970). However, in the past forty years they have moved to the coast and have 'purchased' sailing canoes from the Kainawali people.

No one in Duau is quite sure how or why these people began to participate in the kula. One suggestion is that they received valuables as parts of marriage-exchange prestations when they married people of the Kainawali area. Bagi received from Kainawali in this way could then be passed on to Duau people in exchange for mwali.

Whether this is indeed the origin of these people's participation in the kula is unclear. It is the Duau people's own suggestion and makes sense in terms of the way valuables are exchanged within the district along affinal lines, moving out and then possibly back into the kula again in the process.

For Duau the development of southeast Normanby as an independent district has resulted in the end of the former sailing expeditions to Kainawali, as people now individually make the eight-to-ten-hour trip on foot to southeast Normanby, perhaps spending but one night before returning home. These kula exchanges are an individual matter between the two muli involved, in some respects resembling the 'internal kula' which Malinowski (1922:464–77) described between different areas within the Trobriands. They are undramatic and not formally or publically structured, having little of the excitement characteristic of the expeditions to Dobu which are normally organized on a collective basis. Little accessory exchange of food or manufactured goods accompanies this trade and none of the collective organization of expeditions to Dobu nor the collective feasting and distribution of valuables upon the voyagers' return is to be found.

Loboda and Kwanaula people have always sailed west to Dobu and adjacent districts of East Fergusson in search of mwali. In the past considerable accessory trade of foodstuffs and manufactured goods accompanied this trade.

From Dobu came certain varieties of yams and bananas, axe blades originating in Woodlark, obsidian, and more exotic goods such as Amphlett clay pots and Trobriand 'grass skirts' and lime pots. Much of this exchange apparently consisted of delayed, informal gifts between established muli rather than barter (gimane) between relative strangers, though this, too, occurred.

Formally trade with Dobu has not changed since the beginning of contact, though today Duau people usually travel to Dobu and East Fergusson in diesel-powered boats as they no longer own inter-island sailing canoes. Most commonly the people of a village or hamlet cluster charter such a boat for a collective expedition though individually some seek passage on some one of the frequent boats traveling between the Dobu and East Fergusson area and Duau.

Given the expense of boat charters, today younger men organize expeditions to Dobu rather than the older men who, as successful traders, would have organized expeditions of sailing canoes in the past. Only younger traders are sufficiently knowledgeable about the 'European' sphere to enable them to charter a boat and are at the same time sufficiently energetic and skilled at mobilizing their fellow villagers to produce copra on the relatively large scale necessary to raise the minimum of 40 Kina (USA $56 in 1977) to pay the charter. At the same time, the press of work related to cash-cropping, government and local school mandated projects, and local mission-based or -sponsored undertakings has drastically reduced the time available for kula trading, making the large-scale expeditions of the past a virtual impossibility (cf. Berde, 1974).

In part as a result, the role of the kula in village organization has been undercut as the older more important and traditionally more influential traders, who possess the knowledge necessary for proper kula organization and practice, must share the role of central organizer with young men who are not especially knowledgeable about or skilled in proper kula trade. Though the younger men's success in local village organization has found a new expression in kula organization, their lack of detailed traditional knowledge largely precludes their consolidating their position.

In the contemporary kula at least thirty people must be packed into a single twenty-five- to thirty-foot boat for expeditions to Dobu, leaving little room for any but the most essential personal effects, food for the trip, and magical paraphernalia. Hence, no gifts of food for the traders' Dobu muli are carried, and, when the boat returns, very little in the way

353

of gifts from their muli are brought back to Duau. Again the changes in the kula reflect an increasing detachment of the kula from the local sphere (except insofar as it provides a potential source of valuables for local use), for former gift exchanges with muli involved susu mates, kasa residents, and affines in support of a central trader in a way which today rarely occurs.

Today many of the people of Dawada and Siausi Villages, the two villages immediately adjacent to Loboda, participate in the kula on the same basis as do Duau people.[7] Traditionally these people lived in the interior of the island, had little contact with coastal Duau people, and apparently did not participate in the kula. After the end of inter-village warfare Dawada Village and some Siausi susu moved to the coast and Dawada and Siausi people began to adopt various facets of coastal Duau culture, including the kula. They acquired valuables naturally through intermarriage with traders of traditional trading areas. With the cessation of warfare and consequent decline of inter-village isolation, Duau people argue such villages would naturally inter-marry, acquire valuables, and begin kula trade with their former enemies, there being a sort of natural florescence of the kula to accompany the predictable development of inter-village affinal relationships.

Elsewhere on Normanby a few isolated individuals are involved in kula trade, although for them it is a purely individual participation, not being conditioned by the close articulation of kula activities and village exchange activities such as is found in Duau and to some extent in southeast Normanby. Bagi and mwali are occasionally held even by Normanby people who are not clearly involved in the kula at all, being exchanged along affinal lines or perhaps merely being held in a semi-permanent fashion as personal heirlooms. The kula trade of *kitoma* valuables (see below) is optional and these, especially in villages not directly a part of the kula ring, are frequently privately held for many years by such individuals before possibly being returned to the kula ring.

Despite its participation, Duau has probably always been marginal to the kula. In the past, many Dobu and East Fergusson traders sailed directly to Kainawali without stopping in Duau, or if they did stop, their visit was only a short stop on a more distant voyage to Kainawali. Even today with the development of the southeast Normanby district, many Dobu traders continue to sail directly to Kainawali, or if they stop in Normanby, stop only in the villages of southeast Normanby muli. Though such bypassing of Duau by Dobu traders is resented by Normanby people who feel their district should be an integral link in the chain of kula districts, there is little they can do about it.

What is left of both branches of the kula is not just the streamlined kula shorn of accompanying exchange and barter of non-valuables which Lauer describes for the Amphletts (1970a), but a kula trade of valuables by increasingly discrete individuals acting largely independently of one-another. Nevertheless this is but a development of one dimension of the kula which has always been present, in no way representing an altogether new development.

Kitoma and Kunedawesi kune

All bagi, mwali, gadiwana, and palelesalu belong to either one of two general classes, kitoma and *kunedawesi*, which differ solely by the rules governing exchange of valuables belonging to them. Kitoma valuables are valuables which are property of the holder who is an owner (*toniwaga* or *toni gwegwe*) in the same sense that a person is an owner of a canoe or a pig. He or she has the right to exchange or gimane the owned kune valuable for anything else, money, a pig, another valuable, or land, or to give it in a marriage, mortuary, or other village exchange as well as to use it in kula transactions. In fact, kitoma kune frequently leave the kula ring to be given in affinal, intra-district exchange transactions to people who subsequently will return them to the kula by trading them with their own muli. Kitoma kune may also be purchased for money and received for unusual services rendered and subsequently used for local affinal or kula exchange.

In contrast, kunedawesi valuables are 'pure' kula valuables existing solely to be traded within the kula ring. They are never actually owned by the holder who only momentarily possesses them before passing them on in a delayed-exchange transaction for some other, also kunedawesi, valuable. Hence the holder never has full rights to dispose of them as he or she wishes. To do so would be to give away or gimane something to which the holder does not have full rights and ultimately to defraud the muli to whom it is owed and to whom the holder is in debt. Hence no matter how pressing the need, kunedawesi kune should not be withdrawn from the kula for use in local-exchange transactions.

However, even kitoma valuables along with the things which normally occasion their exchange (e.g. land, spouses, pigs) are important not because of their individual utility but because they may be used to establish, confirm, or clarify relationships with other susu. In other words, kitoma valuables differ from kunedawesi valuables in their greater convertibility, a convertibility which allows them to be converted into relationships between susu.

Kitoma valuables may be exchanged within the kula ring, kitoma bagi like kunedawesi bagi moving clockwise around the ring in exchange for

355

Carl Eugene Thune

kitoma mwali which, like kunedawesi mwali, move counter-clockwise. However, though the trade of more valuable kitoma kune tends to approximate the delayed exchange of kunedawesi kune, the trade of less valuable kitoma kune is less formalized and is open to negotiation on the part of the individuals involved in any specific transaction. One may, for example, formally exchange kitoma kune with a permanent muli or trade them in a gimane-type transaction with a permanent muli or a relative stranger within the broad context of the kula or even entirely outside it as one's needs and interests require.

At times people complain that the gimane of kitoma kune is not entirely appropriate, reflecting a narrow and shortsighted interest in the valuables themselves rather than in the long-term relationships which they may mark. However, as long as kunedawesi kune are not traded in gimane transactions, gimane of kune within the context of the kula is not really wrong.

Kitoma valuables may be traded in the kula or not, as the current holder desires. There are always a number of people who hold kitoma valuables which are no longer traded in the kula, whether because they are too old to travel, because they have become uninterested in trading them, or because they are afraid of the always present danger of not being 'repaid' by their muli. Eventually even these valuables will be returned to the kula and affinal exchange system, either when they are bequeathed by their current holder to some younger person or when they are given to another susu as a part of a prestation made at a local village feast.

Because kunedawesi kune are never owned, a recipient of such a valuable is automatically in debt to the muli from whom it came. When it is passed on to his or her other muli, that person becomes indebted in turn to him or her. With the movement of kune in the opposite direction, the direction of indebtedness with respect to each partner reverses as the central person is now in debt to the second muli and the holder of a debt from the first. From the perspective of any given trader his or her status is one of continual oscillation from debt to credit with respect to each muli, never returning to a final balance. Hence there is a structural requirement that the trade partnership continue.

In contrast, the owner of a kitoma kune holds a debt from the muli to whom it was given which may be cancelled at the moment a kune is received in repayment. Hence after each pair of kitoma transactions the traders are in a position to sever the partnership.

It is possible, however, for traders to trade unowned kitoma kune. Such traders receive a valuable from a muli who does have ownership rights to it, thus becoming in debt to him or her. It can then be passed on to an opposite muli who in turn becomes indebted to the central trader.

356

With the movement of a valuable in the opposite direction the two debts are wiped out and a transactional balance in both directions is recovered. At that point there is no structural pressure for the partnership to continue.

A number of traders are in this position, hoping through astute trading eventually to acquire kune of their own. Others are temporarily placed in this position as they must withdraw their owned kune from the kula ring for use within the local sphere.

Though in therory kitoma valuables may never be exchanged for kunedawesi valuables, in fact such transactions do occur. In such an event, the kitoma valuable changes its category and becomes a kunedawesi valuable at the same time that the kunedawesi valuable becomes a kitoma valuable. However, only the classes to which the respective valuables belong change; their names and relative value remain unaltered.

In a real way, the central arena for kitoma valuables is the local affinally-defined sphere, for it is in service to local needs and ambitions that they are traded in the kula. Any person exchanging kitoma valuables within the kula must do so in a way which will not prejudice their ability to participate in these local transactions. Hence the rule allowing kunedawesi kune traded for kitoma kune to shift categories ensures that the locally-oriented trader who temporarily invests kitoma kune in the kula ring will always receive a kitoma kune which may be returned once again to the local affinal exchange sphere.

When Duau people exchange kitoma valuables within the kula ring it is always in hopes of increasing the number of kune to which they have full ownership rights. In many respects then, the successful kula exchange of kitoma kune has the effect of allowing the trader to increasingly dominate his or her own susu's exchange-activities.

Because kunedawesi valuables and very important kitoma valuables have no direct role within the village,[8] traders who concentrate on their exchange do not necessarily have this kind of domination of their susu's locally-based affairs. It is the younger and middle-aged traders, those who trade less important kitoma valuables and few if any kunedawesi valuables, who acquire influence within the district as a result of their kula trading activities. These people are in their physically most productive period of life, being most directly in a position to mobilize the labor and energies of susu mates and affines in service to their interests. At the same time, they are the people most capable of producing the yams and pigs on the scale which is required for maritally-based exchange activities. Older traders, if they are successful in the kula, concentrate more and more on valuables which move primarily if not wholly within the kula ring, gradually relinquishing their direct influence within the local sphere to younger, less important traders who deal in kitoma valuables.

The mechanics of kula trade

When properly traded in the kula, a valuable follows a specific, known *keda* ('path') consisting of the various muli through whom it should pass as it moves around the kula ring before eventually returning to Duau. At the same time that one inherits a valuable after its previous holder's death or withdrawal from active participation in the kula, one inherits the keda and the muli with whom the previous holder traded. Thus, in a real way, what is inherited is not so much the valuable itself but the exchange position on the keda and the exchange partnerships linked with it. This inheritance includes any existing 'debts' or 'credits' associated with the position.

Kitoma kune which are passed between affinally-related susu in the course of village exchanges are not accompanied by their keda in this way. Rather the recipient incorporates such received kune into his or her pre-existing kula-trade relationships, uses it on a keda constructed between new muli, trades it informally in gimane transactions, or merely holds it without trading it.[9] This, in fact, is one of the most common ways in which younger people enter the kula for the first time. Indeed, except for the most valuable kitoma kune which move solely within the kula, kitoma kune are not permanently tied to a keda, this being the counterpart of the fact that they are individually owned by people who may trade them as they wish. At the same time it is a function of the fact that those trading kitoma valuables will eventually have to return a valuable to the affinally-related susu from which it came. Hence kitoma trade is frequently temporary and must be timed to articulate with local requirements for feast repayments.

When describing the keda Duau people speak in formal, ideal, and abstract terms as if each trader had only two immediate muli, one in each direction. Hence, each keda would consist of a non-branching chain of positions, one in each district, which form a closed circle. In this idealization, the kune which any particular person holds will return to him or her again and again each time it completes the circuit of the kula ring.

Some people describe specific susu as hereditarily associated with specific keda and with the valuables which travel along them. Using the formal, circular model to describe the keda, they suggest that the susu has traditionally held the trading position through which these valuables pass when they reach Duau, as the position itself, the trading partnerships with which it is linked, and valuables themselves are inherited within it.

In fact, children do inherit valuables from their fathers and both fathers and children stress the importance and desirability of this form of inheritance,[10] at least in the concrete instances in which they are involved. However, the high divorce rate and the commonly resultant estrangement of fathers from their children has had the effect of rendering inheritance along more or less strictly susu lines much more common than the public discussion would indicate. Finally, there is some tendency for the most important valuables, be they kitoma or kunedawesi, which are most clearly tied to a keda, to be inherited within the susu, with only the less important valuables being bequeathed by fathers to their children.

It is uncommon, though possible, for a person to inherit valuables and the respective keda with which they are associated from two different people. Such might be the case if a person received valuables from two different members of his or her susu, or perhaps if he or she received one valuable from his or her father and another from a member of his or her own susu. In fact, one might even inherit two valuables associated with different keda from the same person.

In any case, when a person holds positions on two different keda, the two keda and the respective valuables associated with them should be kept separate. Thus bagi coming from a muli on one keda should not be given to an opposite muli on a different keda.

Note that this interpretation of the keda precludes any competition between traders of the same district since each would occupy a position on his or her own unique, closed, non-branching, circular keda, allowing him or her access only to valuables which move along it and never to those moving along any other keda. Hence, the kind of strategic switching of valuables between keda favored by the major Trobriand traders should be altogether precluded for it, along with competition between traders of the same district to acquire valuables from the same muli, is impossible.[11]

This ideal model and its relatively close relation to reality also suggests Duau people are in a relatively powerless position as they seek to influence their muli's kula activities to advance their own interests. And it suggests the Duau relative lack of knowledge of the details of kula trade in adjacent districts has its basis not only in the marginality of Duau to the ring but in the absence of local power which could turn such knowledge to the local trader's advantage.

Finally, it suggests that simultaneous gimane of kula valuables is a more reasonable strategy for Duau kula traders to pursue than is formal delayed exchange which requires greater control over and consequent trust of one's muli. Indeed some younger less important traders explicitly say they gimane in the kula out of recognition of their weakness and in hope of eventually building a major kula position centering on trade of

359

kunedawesi kune which carries within it sufficient power and moral authority to ensure proper repayment by their muli.

In actual fact, Duau kula partnerships, particularly those of younger traders involved in the trade of kitoma valuables, are unstable, frequently breaking down amidst cries of fraud and theft. Perhaps at some level the permanent partnership is the ideal but for many traders the acquisition of valuables by any means is of more immediate importance than is the maintenance of a long-term kula partnership.

Nevertheless, despite the fragility of trade partnerships, whenever Duau people engage in the exchange on a delayed basis there is the assumption that there will be a long-term balanced reciprocity. Failure to repay what was received quickly results in malicious gossip and loss of status. However, in no sense does it enhance the status of the trader who gave without being repaid, nor is this in any sense the goal of the transaction. If both sides repay what was received, exchange can continue and the relationship validated by it can be maintained. With default by either party further exchange is precluded, the relationship is broken off, and everyone loses.

Indeed, traders should not seek to advance themselves at their muli's expense (though in reality this seems to frequently happen). Rather, they, with other muli on their keda, should try by collectively supporting one another as a group to increase the number and the quality of valuables available to them. They, as a group, rather than they as discrete individuals, should and then will acquire the fame which their successful trade brings.

In general, kitoma valuables are less securely bound to a keda, being 'owned' by the current holder rather than temporarily held by traders who will shortly pass them on. Hence, even when they primarily move in the kula, they may be shifted from keda to keda or from the kula to the local exchange sphere with relatively little criticism. In this, Duau trade of kitoma kune resembles the Trobriand competitive trade of valuables more clearly than does the trade of kunedawesi valuables which might seem to be the ideal kula valuable.

In contrast to the Trobriand kula, the kula in Duau is a basically democratic institution with, for example, all Loboda susu but one engaged in kula trade, at least to the degree of holding one valuable and occasionally trading with it.[12] However, most people never hold more than a single valuable at a time. Certainly a Loboda Village expedition to Dobu would result in most people acquiring only one valuable apiece with perhaps one or two of the group of thirty receiving two. Given the vagaries of kula trade and village exchange, at any given time the majority of traders would not actually have any kune valuables in their possession.

Though Duau people speak with respect of successful kula traders of the past who accumulated or had control over numerous valuables, and though today they seek success and fame in their kula transactions abroad and in their exchange of yams and organization of feasts at home, they are, in fact, radically egalitarian. This is merely the counterpart of their democratic view of exchange and their formal rejection of competition. Success in any way beyond the average arouses hostility, malicious gossip, active non-cooperation on the part of relatives and, frequently, death from envious *barahu* ('sorcerers') or *welabana* ('witches').

If anything, the changes of the Duau kula of the last fifty years have led to an even closer approximation to this ideal of egalitarianism than was formerly the case. Today there are no really major figures who dominate Northeast Normanby society and the Duau kula in the way that some men of substance (*esa'esa*) did in the past (cf. Roheim, 1950a). Perhaps part of the reason for their disappearance is to be found in the disappearance of geographically-based positions of power and authority such as those related to warfare.[13] Indeed, as traditionally legitimized and achieved positions of power independent of susu status have disappeared, social status grounded within the susu and susu interrelationships has become more visible and more important.

In other words, status derived from the trade of kitoma valuables because they can be used to establish and validate locally-based intersusu position and relationship is now more important and socially necessary than is status derived from kunedawesi trade which transcends local susu, kasa, and even district boundaries. Hence it is probably more necessary than in the past to have access to some kitoma kune valuables which frequently are either acquired from or invested in the kula. This may, in part, explain the democratization of kune, particularly kitoma kune, ownership and kula participation.

The structure of village exchange

Local affinally-defined exchange activities are midway between the permanent, formal, delayed kula exchange of kunedawesi kune and the free, negotiated, simultaneous exchange of kitoma kune. This fact reflects the long-term relationship which should exist between maritally-related susu but allows a transactional balance to be established between the two susu when the deaths of the members of the linking marital couple requires the susus' affinal relationship to be severed.

All affinal exchange activities come in balancing pairs. At the end of the second, the two susu should be in the same relative transactional position with respect to one another as that from which they

Carl Eugene Thune

began. Though balanced, because each susu ultimately began in debt to the other (since each 'received' a spouse from the other), each pair requires the existence of the next and a continuation of the relationship.

Should the original recipients be unable to match what was given, there is considerable grumbling and complaint on the part of the original feast-givers. However the original sponsoring susu does not gain status at the expense of the original recipients. Those who acquire fame from such affinal transactions do so as co-members of a dyad which has successfully exchanged with one-another rather than as discrete individuals. In this emphasis on the cooperative mutual attainment of status, the affinal feast is reminiscent of the ideal form of kula trade.

Structurally all feasts between affinally-related susu are identical. However, their increasingly large scale means later feasts such as the *kabimasula* are more complex but also more explicitly and rigidly reflective of an underlying ideal structure.

Kabimasula literally means 'to place food', 'to place yams', or 'to make or fill a *masula*'. Masula can refer either to yams, to food generically, or metaphorically, to the large cylindrical display rack which is filled with high-quality large yams which make up the bulk of the kabimasula prestation. In addition to the large yams, betel nuts, sugar cane, pigs, cooked food, baskets, money, trade-store goods, and possibly valuables may be given. The bulk of these are provided by the kwabu- and children of susu mates (*labalaba*)[14] of the sponsoring susu. Generally the receiving susu will distribute a good deal of this kabimasula prestation to their own labalaba and kwabu-.

Simultaneously at the kabimasula the recipient susu supported by their kwabu- present an only somewhat smaller quantity of small yams, *mona* ('pudding'), cooked food, possibly valuables, and other goods to the first susu as a *maisa* for the kabimasula they received. Maisa can mean 'payment' or 'price' particularly in gimane-type transactions in which it should be of value identical to that of the goods received. Maisa can also refer to a kitoma kune received in the kula in exchange for a kitoma kune simultaneously or previously given. However, in affinally-based feasts the maisa is in no sense a transactionally balanced prestation, for the kabimasula can only be repaid by a second kabamasula or structurally similar cognate feast.[15]

Indeed, the maisa is not only quantitatively less than what is received but of a wholly different, lower order. Occasionally valuables are given as a maisa but, like other forms of maisa, they have more of the quality of acknowledgement gifts than that of a true balancing payment. Most of the maisa is passed on by the sponsoring susu to their supporting

362

kwabu- and labalaba in acknowledgment of their help in gathering the kabimasula prestation.

The succession of mortuary feasts, culminating in the *bwabwali* feast releasing the survivors from their mourning obligations (cf. Fortune, 1963:194–6), is a culmination of this search for transactional balance between the two susu. During the bwabwali the surviving spouse, father in the case of a deceased child, or child in the case of a deceased father, along with their susu mates, are not only freed from further mourning, but are compensated with a large prestation of yams and other goods for their privations. At the same time, they present to the survivors the bwabwali prestations, a massive quantity of yams, valuables, and other goods in compensation for their loss of their susu mate.

It is this use of valuables to compensate surviving susu mates which is the most important and most frequent but also most unpredictable occasion for movement of valuables within the village. Though it is not obligatory in the case of children or unimportant people, it is expected, and its absence reflects badly upon the paternally and formerly affinally-related susu of the deceased. The giving of valuables is a mark of the humility by the giving susu in the face of their former affines, an acceptance of responsibility for the death, and a tangible expression of the honor of the deceased and his or her susu.

Bwabwali necessarily come in pairs though the delay between the two deaths may be many years. Like the kabimasula, the affair essentially deals with transactional statuses between susu rather than individuals which must be ultimately balanced, though the second balancing bwabwali may only occur many years after the first.

All subsequent mortuary feasts are based, not on the transactional position of any two susu with respect to one another, but on the position of the susu of the deceased with respect to a generalized and collective social universe. *Sagali* and a number of cognate mortuary feasts collectively honour all susu mates who have died since the last sagali. However, unlike affinally-based mortuary feasts, the recipients of kune (in this context principally pork and yams) which is distributed at the sagali are essentially individuals or representatives of territorial units not specifically situated within a matrilineal field. Sagali attract people from a number of villages and even other islands, many of whom come out of curiosity and hope for excitement rather than as a result of any special relation to the sponsoring susu.[16] Hence, the exchange is largely unaccounted. The assumption is always that whatever is given to a person, susu, village, or district will be returned when the recipients give a sagali, but this is not of particular strategic concern.

Affinally-based exchanges have a four-party structure rather than a

Carl Eugene Thune

two-party structure such as is typical of kula transactions. In addition to the two central susu which formally exchange goods, there must be the two outside susu, one of which ultimately gives the majority of these goods to the sponsoring susu and the other of which ultimately receives the bulk of the goods received by the formal recipients.

The two-party structure of kula exchange is a reflection of the fact that kula trade requires only donors and recipients, neither of which need be structurally located with respect to their susu, kwabu-, or other muli. In contrast to this two-party structure, most visible in the gimane of kula valuables, affinal exchanges, by requiring the two exterior susu, necessarily locates the transaction within the matrilineal world.

Sagali in turn typify a different structure for they are three-party events in which the third, recipient, party is of a generalized, non-matrilineally defined collectivity. Though the sponsoring susu's kwabu- are an independent party, they support the sponsoring susu against the generalized recipients. As with all three-sided events, the aim is to honor the deceased and his or her susu rather than to transact with affines.

Sagali-type feasts, because they are generalized and non-transactional, are directed toward geographical rather than matrilineal units. Hence to a degree they free the principal organizer from the bonds of his matrilineal situation and offer the possibility of an inter-district fame similar to that offered by the kula trade of kunedawesi valuables. And, because they are fully independent of affinal relationships it is not surprising that kula valuables play no role within them.

Kitoma and the translation of value

Kula, village exchange, and gimane include gimane in the external monetary sphere, are three relatively distinct and discrete formal transactional spheres between which most goods cannot formally and directly move. Kitoma valuables alone possess the ability to 'translate' (cf. Steiner, 1954) value formally and publicly from one sphere to another and it is really they alone which can do this.

It is this ability which accounts for the centrality of kitoma kune to the Duau social world. And yet, it is also this ability which accounts for the apparent marginality of the most formal kula activities, for it prevents the kula from being a unique realm in which a unique, locally-important value and status may be acquired. Instead, it is simply one more sphere, along with that defined by gimane, including gimane with the proceeds derived from cash-cropping and certain other village activities, in which value may be generated primarily to be translated back into local affinal relationships.

364

Obviously this does not eliminate the kula as an important sphere. However it does explain the reason that gimane, or at least informal kula exchange of kitoma kune, is the most common form of kula transaction especially among younger people who are primarily interested in village-based, matrilineally-located status. It also suggests that despite the position of Duau in the kula, Duau use of kune within the kula is essentially similar to the use of kune or kune-like objects in areas of Normanby not traditionally a part of the kula, where what little exchange of valuables which occurs within the broad context of the kula is only by gimane.

In a sense those exchanging kitoma valuables and deeply involved in four-party transactions strive to locate themselves ever more clearly and powerfully within a web relating their susu to other affinally-related susu. For them the locus of action lies between susu and hence the fact that their kula trade of kitoma valuables may depart considerably from the formal ideal is of no concern. Indeed, for them the real danger is that they might be sucked into the formal kula in a way which, even if it did not result in the loss of their kune, would at least remove them and their valuables from the local sphere, yielding only a marginally useful inter-district status at the expense of considerable time, travel, hosting of ever-hungry visitors, and exposure to envious fellow villagers. Successful formal kula has its advantages such as the frequently mentioned hospitality which a trader may find in other districts, but it, unless it can actually provide owned kitoma valuables usable at home, offers very little useful to traders seeing themselves as primarily modest susu members living in a matrilineal world.

The few kunedawesi traders by contrast neglect this dimension of their social identity, instead developing simultaneously a unique relation to a distant muli, a status specifically within the formally-delimited sphere of the kula, and a status as member and representative of their own susu to a generalized universe. This is much the same generalized focus as that of those involved in constructing sagali and other generalized three-party feasts and it should not be surprising that sagali sponsors are frequently kunedawesi traders.

The former major Duau kula traders who focused on the exchange of kunedawesi or highly-valued kitoma kune represent a florescence of one dimension of the kula and a temporary suppression of the ethic of egalitarianism. But this florescence is of just one dimension, only temporary and necessarily unstable, for even it must ultimately be grounded in a matrilineally-based, affinally-defined universe. Today the matrilineal, egalitarian dimension of Duau culture has largely overshadowed such individualistic personal strivings.

This form of the kula is less dramatic than a primarily outward-looking

Carl Eugene Thune

overseas kula by traders in search of inter-island fame, less easy to romanticize into a tale of argonauts and sailing fleets, but very much more in tune with the egalitarian world of Duau, centrally structured around the susu and its tentative attempts to found affinal relationships with other susu. Perhaps it is indeed hierarchy and strivings for status which dominate the Trobriand kula and its relation to Trobriand society, but it is an egalitarianism only temporarily broken by individualistic achievement of a wide-ranging personal status which defines the nature of the present-day Duau kula.

Notes

1 Fieldwork providing the material on which this paper is based was conducted in Loboda Village on Normanby Island, Milne Bay Province, Papua New Guinea, from December 1975 to April 1977. It was supported by a NIMH Predoctoral Fellowship, Number 1 F31 MOH5340.

2 Loboda Village people indicate that the term Duau was originally restricted by Normanby people to this district of the Island (cf. Williams, 1931:175; Roheim, 1946:212–13). In recent years it has been used, particularly by people elsewhere in the Massim and by government personnel, to refer to the eastern half of Normanby Island if not to the whole island. Here I shall restrict it to its original usage.

3 The kasa is roughly equivalent to Fortune's 'village'. The units I term the hamlet cluster and the village are approximately what he terms the 'locality' (cf. Fortune, 1963:1–21).

4 Haihai are an individual's spouse's susu mates. Kwabu- is a more general term referring to the susu mates of the spouse of any one of one's own susu mates.

5 See note 4.

6 In the kula ring until recently mwali were exchanged in pairs and bagi were exchanged as doubled lengths of *Spondylus* shell beads. Some time ago these paired valuables were divided, thus effectively doubling the number of valuables available, though doubled *bagi* are still the standard unit of trade in Kainawali.

Northeast Normanby people indicate this division of valuables was necessitated by the increase in the number of traders seeking valuables as villages previously not a part of the kula ring were incorporated into it. At least in Loboda it would seem that the shortage of valuables which lead to their division was also caused by wider, more democratic participation in the kula.

An additional cause of the shortage of valuables is a 'leakage' of valuables as they leave the area where they were traditionally traded and enter into other exchange systems, or as bagi are taken by Massim people going to school or for work elsewhere in Papua New Guinea. Bagi are also frequently removed from the system as they are cut to produce the short necklaces (*magamaga*) which young people like to wear and which fathers like to give to their children.

These latter two factors appear to have produced a considerable imbalance in the number of bagi and mwali within in the kula ring.

7 In part for this reason Duau is increasingly being used to refer to Siausi and Dawada as well as Loboda and Kwanaula villages.

8 Very valuable kitoma kune are generally not removed from the kula to be used in local exchange-activities for they would normally be owed or promised to a muli. While it is true that a trader giving a valuable in the local sphere can expect a valuable in return at some subsequent point from the susu to which he gave it, the delay between giving and receiving is frequently long and unpredictable. The trader may in any case be doubtful about the recipient's ability to return a valuable of value equivalent to that given. As a valuable received in a local repayment transaction would either be given directly to the holder's muli or given to an opposite muli (so it could be changed from bagi to mwali, or vice versa, as is necessary) before being returned to the original expectant muli, receiving a significantly less valuable valuable would make repayment within the kula impossible.

There is no rule that in local transactions bagi must be repaid with mwali or vice versa. In fact the majority of valuables exchanged within the village are mwali, though this varies some depending on the season of the yearly exchange cycle. Presumably this reflects the excess of mwali over bagi in the kula ring and the withdrawal of mwali from the kula ring for use within the district provides one mechanism for redress of this imbalance.

9 In longer perspective the donor of a kitoma valuable to an affine could hope subsequently to receive a valuable from the same affines which might then be put back into the kula to move along the same keda as that from which the original came. However, the fact that people generally try to use kune not owned or promised to a muli along with the unpredictable and often long delayed occurrence of feasts repaying earlier feasts given means that this in fact occurs less frequently than might at first appear.

Not surprisingly, removal of valuables from the kula to use in pressing local affairs is a cause of considerable disruption of kula trade and the source of many disputes between muli. Older traders stress that a successful trader must be willing to endure long and unexpected delays in receiving owed kune because muli are frequently forced temporarily to remove valuables from the ring, even at the detriment of their own kula trade. The fearful and insecure trader who has difficulty dealing with the delays caused by his muli's local demands frequently severely damages his or her trade by provoking disputes with his or her muli when patience would have resulted in eventual repayment of the expected valuables.

10 There is always a certain ambiguity in what seems to be inheritance of kune by children from their fathers, for such inheritance is between affinally- or formerly affinally-related susu rather than within a single susu, as is the case of kune inherited from one's 'mother' or 'mother's brother' (*waha-*). Hence, it is frequently treated as if it were a part of a formal exchange between two affinally-related units rather than an informal movement of goods within an essential solidary and undivided nuclear family. In any case, fathers seeking mates to circumvent pressure of their susu mates to keep valuables within their susu frequently exploit this ambiguity by perpetuating the fiction that the

giving of kune to their children represents a formal exchange and hence is allowable while in fact making an essentially outright gift of kune to their children which need not be repaid.

11 Northeast Normanby people know that valuables shift between keda elsewhere in the kula ring, particularly in the northern portion and in Kainawali, areas over which they have little control and for the most part about which they have little direct knowledge. However, to the extent that they can exert influence over trade in adjacent districts of the kula ring, they attempt to assure that valuables remain on the proper keda.

12 This one non-participating susu actually has several kune which for various reasons are not traded in the kula. They are nevertheless available for use in local, affinally-based exchange.

13 Government-sponsored positions based on geographical units such as those of village councillor are irrelevant to traditional activities, both local and inter-island.

14 Labalaba are approximately the individuals Fortune terms 'boundary men' (Fortune, 1963: 14–17 *et passim*). In Duau however the term covers all of the children of a susu's male members, irrespective of whether their fathers are alive or dead.

15 Normally kabimasula are given in pairs like most other affinal exchanges. However, occasionally a person will give a kabimasula to another person to whom he or she is in debt for reasons which require a formal repayment. A migrant lacking his or her own gardening land might repay a susu allowing him use of their gardening land by presenting a kabimasula to them. Such a payment need only be made a single time, for after it the sponsor of the feast receives *de facto* rights to continue to make use of the recipient's garden land.

16 Because major sagali may bring together people of a variety of islands, they may be the occasion of kula transactions, negotiations, and discussions. However no valuables are formally presented by the sponsoring susu because, given the orientation of the sagali to honour a specific susu as a discrete entity, there is no transactional opposite to which they could be presented nor from which they could be received.

14 Kune on Tubetube and in the Bwanabwana region of the southern Massim[1]

~~~~~~

MARTHA MACINTYRE

Tubetube, westernmost island of the Engineer Group, is a small volcanic island about four miles long and one to two miles across. It consists of three hills with the highest rising to just over 600 feet. Sandy beaches often less than 100 yards wide fringe the whole island and here are situated all the villages. These are backed by a rocky slope which rises steeply behind the clusters of houses. The population, at present numbering 140, has been declining since the period of early contact with Europeans when several epidemics swept the island. Recently people have moved to other islands in the Engineer Group, such as Koyagaugau (pop. 54) and Naluwaluwali (see map p. 372).

Most of the fourteen hamlets consist of two households, usually comprised of two generations of the same *susu* or matriline. As copra has long been the only cash crop grown on Tubetube, every available piece of flat land is now thickly planted with coconuts. Tubetube was the first place where copra production was established in the late 1890s when the Dobuan mission sent Mr J. T. Field to the island (cf. *Annual Report* 1898–9). For most people now on Tubetube, copra represents the only source of income as all the people are basically subsistence gardeners, growing yams, sweet potatoes, bananas, taro, paw-paw, pineapples and a variety of tree cabbage in their gardens. These gardens, formerly situated on land now occupied by coconut groves, are now located exclusively on inland slopes and though most are within one mile of the village, access often involves a steep and rocky climb. Fish is eaten almost every day. Men, women and children dive or fish with a line from small outrigger canoes on the reefs surrounding the island. Some men who fish with long lines and nets sell their catch to the Co-operative Fishing Company at Samarai. They also dive for bêche-de-mer, Trochus shells, and other pearl-shells which are sold to traders.

As the island has no rivers, all fresh water has to be obtained from

369

wells. Only one village does not have a well. Tubetube is subject to severe droughts which seriously affect gardens and oblige the people to trade for yams, usually with villages on Duau. Women produce clay pots specifically for this purpose.

Tubetube is known throughout the region for its pottery and, until about thirty years ago, the trade flourished with islands to the east and west. Pots are still regularly traded with the people of Duau and Dobu but are never exchanged for cash. In recent years the people of Ware have become the major producers of pottery in the region, selling their pots at Alotau and as far east as Sudest and Misima. Ware and Tubetube pottery are stylistically similar, but the clay of Tubetube is coarser, with more impurities, which makes it more difficult to work. As a result the Tubetube pots are noticeably thicker, lacking the sheen on the exterior surface that distinguishes the fine Ware pots. These finer Ware pots are preferred for feasting. Most women on Tubetube are potters and younger women continue to learn from them. Despite a decline in the pottery trade, the craft continues to flourish and is a focus for social prestige among women.

Tubetube was the second island in the region to be converted to Christianity by the Methodist Mission set up at Dobu. J. T. Field, a devout man who came as the mission carpenter with Bromilow, felt that he had been 'called' by God to convert the notorious cannibals in this region, and so chose Tubetube after hearing tales of their bloody raids on Duau. He arrived in 1892, bringing several Samoan and Fijian assistants who established a village on the southeastern tip of the island. Mr Field and the Samoans are the subject of many stories concerning the transformation of Tubetube society. Prior to their arrival (and for some twenty years after) the men of Tubetube were feared throughout the south as raiders and cannibals. The early Annual Reports include several references to their activities. For example, in 1887, Romilly reported a raid by ten men on a mainland village where all but one child were killed. However, by 1889, the Magistrate F. P. Winter felt able to state that 'the natives of the Engineer Group were at one time a terror to neighbouring islands owing to their murderous raids . . . apparently some time after the Protectorate was established, they ceased these raids and from that time onwards have been quiet, well-behaved natives'. (*Annual Report*, 1897). The men of Tubetube continued to fight with their traditional enemies on Duau and Panaeati, and their last major raid, involving the massacre of a whole island population in the Calvados Chain, occurred as late as 1911.

Today most people are Christians and the mission heavily influences all aspects of social life. The pastor is the acknowledged leader of the community. He is a direct descendant of the chiefly (*guyau*) family on Tubetube and is also the most important *kune* (*kula*) trader on the island.

In the past one family was acknowledged as hereditary guyau and people are still conscious of the rights this position inferred, such as the wearing of boar's tusk necklaces (*dona*) at feasts and the right to rattle one's lime-stick when getting lime from a pot. The pastor's prestige is grounded in a traditional leadership-role, with his skill as an orator, his extensive knowledge of traditional customs, and most particularly his great skill in kune, in many respects more important than his position as pastor.

These two aspects of Tubetubeans' history – their prowess as warrior and their missionary role in the area – are the major themes in stories and legends of the past and in their conception of their distinctiveness with respect to other, nearby islands. The people of Tubetube see the island as the most important place for kune and attribute this to their previous dominance in war. They also maintain that kune changed with the spread of Christianity, as networks began to extend between islands that had formerly been enemies and the powers of the warrior guyau were reduced. As a result, kune was democratized and within twenty years many more men were involved. Women too were then able to become kune traders.

Contemporary Kune

Tubetube, and other islands in this area where the Tubetube language is spoken, maintain an important position in the network of exchanges in the Massim, involving armshells (*mwali*) and necklaces (*bagi*). They all refer to themselves as Bwanabwana people. Bwanabwana consists of eight inhabited islands: Tubetube (Slade), Naluwaluwali (Skelton), Kwalaiwa (Watts), Tewatewa (Hummock), Koyagaugau (Dawson), Anagusa (Bentley), Kitai, and Ware. These people intermarry and often have gardens on more than one island. Ware is the only island of the group that does not have direct links to the kula of the northern Massim.

The Tubetube term for a kula path is *kamwasa* meaning 'path, road or way'. There are three major routes to the northeast, all of which pass through Koyagaugau and onwards to Egom, Nasikwabu (Alcester), and Murua. To the northwest, the links are with Duau and Dobu. At least two men have kamwasa which bypass Kitava, Vakuta and the Trobriand Islands. In one case, the valuables go from Tubetube to Koyagaugau to Egom to Gawa to Iwa to Dobu and then back to Tubetube. The other route is from Tubetube to Murua to Gawa to Iwa and then on to Dobu before returning to Tubetube.

Men and women in the Bwanabwana region have trade partners (*muli*) on other islands and 'internal' exchanges often involve prominent Tubetube or Koyagaugau kune traders acting as agents for their Bwanabwana

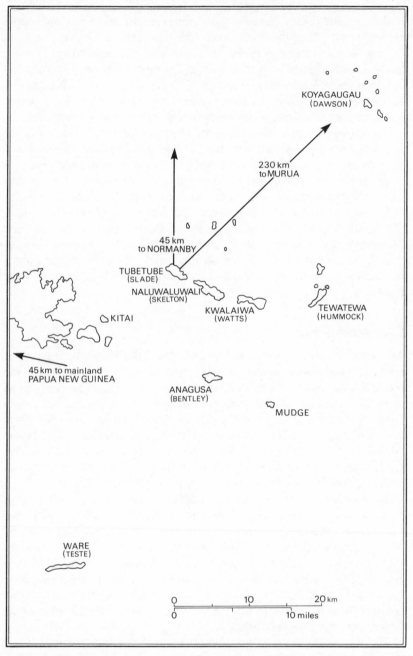

Map 1. Bwanabwana region (called Kainawari on Normanby and
Loloman on Woodlark).

partners. The types of exchanges vary but they all come under the term *leau*, a virtual synonym of kune. This includes all exchanges of mwali (symbolically female) and bagi (symbolically male) and usually refers to those exchanges which occur in the context of purchasing a pig. Sometimes other valuables such as stone axeblades (*palelesalu*) and *Spondylus* shell belts (*wakisowa sapisapi*). At present someone acquiring a stone axeblade is more likely to use it in a direct exchange (*gimwala*) with someone from Sudest or Panaeati where these items are traded for bagi. In this way a person can acquire a new *kitomwa* (personal kula-shell free of extant obligation to other traders) and use it for kune.

The population of each island in the Bwanabwana Group is small, the largest being Kwalaiwa with about 200 people. Although most families have at least one valuable, and a few young men are involved in kune in a minor way, the number of people recognized as prominent kune traders is small when compared with some of the islands in the northern part of the ring. On Tubetube there are six men who kune, on Koyagaugau five men, on Naluwaluwali two men, on Kwalaiwa three men, on Anagusa two men, on Kitai one woman, and on Tewatewa there are three men and one woman. All major transactions in kune between the Bwanabwana region and other islands follow the kamwasa of these twenty-three people. In terms of actual voyages, most trading is done by the men of Tubetube and Koyagaugau who take the valuables belonging to their internal Bwanabwana partners. At present Tubetube's involvement is seen to be decreasing when compared with the recent past. This decrease is attributed to the declining population and to the fact that there are fewer young men to take over. As a result kune has become more concentrated, with many valuables passing through few hands. It is also generally recognized that Koyagaugau is gaining prominence in kune, a development which is associated with the migration of one of Tubetube's major kune traders about twenty years ago. More men on Duau have recently established themselves as kune traders with partners on Tubetube and Koyagaugau to the south and Fergusson and Dobu to the north.

Kula has been so reified in anthropology, and to some extent is apparently differentiated conceptually from other exchanges in the Northern Massim, that it is hard to avoid questions which presume a system that is exclusive of other exchanges. The people of this area, however, do not think of kune in terms of an exclusive exchange of valuables and are apt to bring into their explanations all sorts of details relating to pigs, land acquisition, and the purchase of canoes. In these terms then, it would appear that the Bwanabwana region is where the 'kula ring' is subjected to serious disruption. For each kune trader the kune of mwali and bagi between partners as a means of acquiring regards more kitomwa through the expeditious use of those items in circulation which a trader can claim as his or her own. Kune is one way of gaining wealth and prestige which can then be used in a variety of ways within one's own community. Tubetube men believe that every mwali or bagi in circulation is somebody's kitomwa. They also believe that the people in this region can claim more mwali than any of the other islands involved, and that the Muruans own most of the bagi. It did not surprise them that many people in the North did not think that kune items could be claimed as kitomwa because how were they to know precisely who they belonged to. The only certainty is that the Boyowans (Trobrianders) did not own as many as the people of Tubetube.

A Bwanabwana man may kune simply with mwali and bagi or he may integrate the exchange of valuables (maintaining the flow in the correct direction) with the acquisition of a pig or a canoe. For example, one Tubetube man described the purchase of a canoe thus:

I went to my partner on Murua [Woodlark] and asked him for a canoe. On this trip I threw him a *mwalikau* [armshell of highest-rank category] as *logita* [opening or sustaining gift in kula relationship; same as *vaga* and *basi* in northern kula area]. One year later I returned with a canoe full of yams and pots, the meat of four pigs, and two high-ranking armshells. He took these as his kitomwa [personal kula shells free of extant obligation to other transactors]. The next year when the canoe was almost finished, I returned with two more armshells, two live pigs, and some yams and pots. That then was enough. I returned a couple of months later with enough men to sail back both canoes [the one brought and the one purchased]. I collected the canoe and my partner gave me the necklace which was the return for my first armshell given as logita.

This type of exchange can be a way of opening a kune partnership. Men on Koyagaugau still get their canoes from Murua in this way and the term used is kune. In the past Tubetube men would kune canoes from Murua, Gawa or Boagisa and then exchange them with Dobuans. As canoes last many years, such exchanges are comparatively rare; however, the kune or leau of pigs occurs frequently.

In the past, exchanges followed patterns still practised in the northern kula area, but today almost all exchanges are direct and without delay. The term for opening gift (called basi or vaga elsewhere) is logita. This is sometimes distinguished by a prefix indicating small or large. Almost all exchanges are direct and reciprocated on the same day. The partner (muli) arrives and 'throws' his bagi or mwali. He then negotiates for a particular valuable by chewing betel nut and partaking of numerous meals prepared for him by his Tubetube partner's wife until he receives the item he came for. Only occasionally does he return empty-handed. This method of exchange is called *wamali*, which means spear. The change to wamali exchange is associated with the decline in actual kune voyages and with the fact that Tubetube has no kune canoes. However, the Koyagaugau traders who still use canoes maintain that much of their kune is of the wamali type, too.

Pokala (solicitation of valuables) is practised in two forms. Firstly, if a man wants his partner to divert a valuable which he knows is destined for another kamwasa, he may feast this partner with a pig or some other food. The second way is to negotiate a feast by allowing the partner to set the terms of the pokala. In this way the person possessing the desired valuable can either refuse or set the terms of the pokala very high so that his partner is then forced to return home and attempt to raise the pokala demanded by calling upon his own relatives to give him yams, betel nut, pigs and pots. If he can then fulfil the terms of the negotiated pokala, his partner will divert the item. The first type of pokala is done in hope, the second with certainty of reward.

Kune on Tubetube cannot really be understood without some explanation of the various uses of kitomwa. As elsewhere in the Massim, kitomwa are those valuables which are the personal property of an individual or occasionally a whole village. In the Bwanabwana region they are essential for all exchanges involving the transfer of rights over land and for use as compensation in cases of injury or death. There are five major exchanges involving kitomwa: mortuary payments (*lowalowa*,) competitive feasting between susu and patriline for rights over land (*ligaliga*), marriage exchanges (*kasole*), exchange of pigs or canoes (kune/leau) and compensation payments (*pwaoli*).

Lowalowa involves the giving of kitomwa to the senior member of a susu at the funeral of a man or woman who held rights over particular gardens or coconut plantations. The lowalowa secures those rights for some member or members of the younger generation and is paid by an in-law, i.e. someone outside of the dead person's susu, on behalf of his children. For example, if a woman dies, her daughter's husband will lowalowa her brothers or sisters on behalf of his children, stating the particular land which he is securing with the kitomwa presented. It is therefore a way of specifying inheritance.

Ligaliga is an exchange which follows the funeral. It often takes place a long time later and usually consists of two feasts. The first is offered to the dead man's susu by members of his patriline in order to win the rights over his gardens or coconut plantations. If the susu does not want to relinquish these rights, then they must offer a counter-feast and present more kitomwa to the patriline. Sometimes there is no reciprocation. In most cases the land in question is not in current use or is land which the father had given to his children to work during his lifetime. Sometimes

375

the ligaliga is offered while the man is still alive. Recently, a man on Naluwaluwali feasted his father and father's brother for land which they held but had not used for many years. The man called upon his brothers and sisters to give pigs, yams and rice. At the feast formal speeches were made when the kitomwa were offered. These were offered firstly by the son when laying claim to the particular land and then by the father when yielding the land to his son. This form of ligaliga is not reciprocated.

Marriage exchanges formerly involved kitomwa, but now these are only given on request on Tubetube with the family specifying the type of valuable they want. On Koyagaugau all kasole require at least one kitomwa from each side. There are a series of other exchanges in marriage. The first two involve prestations of food such as yams, rice, sugar and pork and in addition, usually, tobacco. The next exchange is termed *gamwa kabi* (opening work) when the families of the bride and groom work for a whole day on their in-law's garden or coconut plantation. The final exchange called *muli kan* (the food which comes from behind) consists of large quantities of yams. Kitomwa are only exchanged in the first prestations.

Kune or leau for pigs may be initiated by a pokala in which the owner of the pig sets a price. Until very recently all pigs were exchanged for kitomwa and the breeding and fattening of pigs represented the main way of accumulating new kitomwa. Now some pigs can be bought for money. When kitomwa are used, then the seller asks for either mwali or bagi. The buying and selling of pigs is one way in which kune valuables 'leak' out of the system in Tubetube as a person may wish to buy a large pig for ligaliga and use a kitomwa which has been circulating and is expected to move on from Tubetube to a kune partner. On the other hand it is a means of getting mwali or bagi from other islands (Ware in particular) and then putting them in the kune by 'throwing' them to an established partner on Dobu or Murua.

Kitomwa are required for all compensation payments relating to injury or death. The term for all types of compensation using kitomwa is pwaoli. In the pre-colonial period the payment of pwaoli as appeasement constituted the major use of kitomwa as it involved the exchange of up to four hundred items. The items followed the same directions as kune. The Tubetube people see this as being explained simply by the fact that at that time all mwali came from Boyowa (Kiriwina) while the Muruans were the only people who were the allies of Rossel and Sudest so that they controlled the manufacture and distribution of bagi. Tubetube and Koyagaugau informants often repeat the phrase 'baguna kune io kalea silatoyawa' which translates literally as 'in the beginning kune and war went together' but is probably best understood as meaning that the origins of *kune* are in the alliances for war. It is also said that pwaoli and kune do the same work and this is why the guyau show contempt when they throw mwali or bagi because they are saying 'I could kill you but as you are my ally, I will not. Just remember that you are the weaker in fighting.'

This story explains the idea of war and kune going together and it also offers the Tubetube version of how the kula ring was formed:

Tokunu's first kune voyage

This is how kune began for us. There was an old man called Tokunu on Panamoti. That old man used to sit on the point which is on the Muruan side of Panamoti. One evening he was sitting on that rocky point making string for his nets from pandanus. As he was gazing at the sky, he noticed some birds who were flying in the direction of Nasikwabu. They flew high over Nasikwabu and disappeared beyond Bilawakwabu, a village on that island. He could not see this, though. He had just noticed that every evening the birds flew in that direction. So, that evening as he sat working his pandanus, he said to himself, 'Each night those birds are flying somewhere.' He realized that there must be land over there. He went back to his village and ordered the men there to cut down a tree and make a canoe. [The Panamoti word for this type of canoe we on Tubetube call *kewalalowa* is *kenanakela*. These are the canoes for kune.] So they set to, cut down the tree and worked solidly until it was completed. They then put on the side planking and they caulked it.

Before this time Panamoti had no gardens. They grew no yams and their only foods were shellfish, fish and coconuts. If they wanted food, they came down to Tubetube because they were our friends and our allies in war. This Panamoti man said, 'Tommorrow we must prepare for a journey. We are going to Tubetube, so we must look for shellfish. 'However', he continued, 'tomorrow I will not take anybody from any other village. Only my sister's sons may come with me because the trip is dangerous, and we may face a battle and we may die.' [This is to stress the dangers of the journey and refers to the leader's responsibility for any deaths which might occur. If they were men of another susu, he would have to give kitomwa as pwaoli, or compensation.]

At this stage none of his men knew of his plan nor of his observation that each evening birds flew and disappeared over the horizon. They did not know that he had really decided to follow them. So, when they had finished the canoe, they went and found shellfish and dried them on a platform. When they had finished the next day, he said, 'Launch the canoe!' They set off. He said, 'We are going to Tubetube' They then set sail past the point and then he said, 'Change direction.' They turned the canoe towards Murua. Night fell and dawn broke. In the morning light Nasikwabu appeared before them. They sailed up and pulled into the shore. As they did this, a Nasikwabu man saw them and so he got his men together and they assembled with their spears, their shields and with all their weapons. They decided that they would go down to the canoe and kill Tokunu and all his men. But their leader said, 'Keep calm. I will speak to them first.' So he called out, 'Hey! Where are you from?' They answered, 'We are from Panamoti.' Then the Nasikwabu man said to his men on the beach, 'Enough, we speak the same language.' Thus they put down their weapons.

Tokunu put a mwali in a basket. That mwali was called *Ode*. He went up to them with Ode in the basket and threw the Nasikwabu man that mwali. Then, the Nasikwabu man threw Tokunu bagi. When they had exchanged all their valuables according to the way guyau do, Tokunu as a final gesture took the decoration on the front of the canoe [*kimuluwa*], pulled it out and threw the Nasikwabu man that as well.

When it was all over, they launched the canoe, set sail and went back to Panamoti with all their baskets of *bagi*. Then they went down to Tubetube with these baskets of *bagi*, and the Tubetube men took the *bagi* and went to Dobu, their ally to the East and so the circle was made. It all began with that canoe voyage. When we Tubetube men took the *bagi* to Dobu, we brought back *mwali*. That is the essence of *kune*. Tubetube is the centre of *kune* here because we were the fiercest warriors and our only allies were Panamoti and Dobu.

The traditional enemies of the Bwanabwana people were mainly in the East and the North. They had to pay mwali in appeasement and in order to retrieve the skulls of those relatives who were brought back and eaten. Most of these mwali went directly to the guyau. Thus his descendants explain their predominance in terms of the inheritance of mwali paid to the guyau for pwaoli

The term pwaoli also refers to the payment given to a susu who bury another islander on their land. If a person dies a long way from home and has to be buried, then his susu offers kitomwa to those who buried him. Formerly, and today in secret because of regulations about disinterment, the skull is then dug up and sent back to the relatives.

All kitomwa may be circulated in kune, and their owners have no compunction about their removal for other uses. In practice, however, they tend to keep certain ones in circulation because of their fame and because of their capacity to draw other valuables.

The only time these famous kune valuables will be removed from circulation is for the purpose of displaying them at a large mortuary feast for the ancestors of a particular susu. This is called a *soi*. All the kitomwa owned by that susu are gathered in so that, during the soi, they may be set up on a *tanalele* (a pole usually put up on the beach to show the spoils of a successful kune voyage). This is simply a display of the wealth and prestige of the susu and no kitomwa are exchanged in a soi. Afterwards, however, the partners of those men who took their kitomwa out of the kune, who have come for the soi, negotiate kune transactions. Soi and kune are therefore viewed as linked because there is usually a resurgence of kune trading immediately after a soi. It is then that those valuables which have been 'dammed up' during the lengthy preparation for the feast are released into the system.

Note

1 This paper was written, *at the insistence of the editors,* after one month's fieldwork on Tubetube. The reason was to fill out in brief form some of the major remaining gaps in the anthropology of the whole kula area. Any errors are subject to correction in future publications by Ms. Macintyre. The paper was written on Tubetube without access to library sources. The author was, however, the Bibliographer to the Kula Conference in 1977–9. Ms. Macintyre wishes to thank her principal informant Fred Boita of Tubetube for his invaluable contribution to this paper.

PART V

D'Entrecasteaux fringing area

15 The theme of the resentful hero: stasis and mobility in Goodenough mythology[1]

⋗⋗⋗

MICHAEL W. YOUNG

I propose to pursue the theme of the essential duplicity of exchange activities on Goodenough: the ambivalence and ambiguity of giving and receiving things of value as expressed in some of the permutations of local mythology. I can only select a few of the more important myths for consideration, however, and I do not have space to indulge in labyrinthine exegesis. I take as my point of departure the tale which Malinowski refers to as 'the most noteworthy of all the Kula myths' (1922:307): Kasabwaybwayreta (or in Fortune's spelling, Kasabwaibwaileta). The six published versions of this myth do not differ greatly.[2] Reo Fortune's version from Tewara is the most detailed and discursive, and because it follows the rhythms of the vernacular it conveys a canonical air. Briefly, it tells of an ugly, sore-covered hero who, helped by his mother, sails to Boyowa and wins a coveted necklace by shedding his skin to reveal an irresistible beauty. His defeated rivals (the hero's brothers, sons or cross-cousins, according to the version) are furious when his grandson tells them he has found the valuable hidden inside an ulcer on Kasabwaib-waileta's head. They conspire to maroon him on a sandbank. The versions show more variability in the second half of the myth, though most concur on the hero's ascent to the sky, his marriage there, and subsequent descent to Tewara by a tree. After being reunited with his mother the hero 'punishes' the people by turning them into birds. In Malinowski's version he transforms into an 'evil spirit', showing 'how bitter he feels towards humanity' (ibid:325); in Fortune's version he decorates himself, laments, and dives into the sea to emerge at Woodlark, thereby abandoning his own people.

Neither Kasabwaibwaileta's name nor his story are known on Goodenough, although on the few occasions that I recited it there myself it excited some interest. My listeners clearly found it evocative. From a Goodenough Islander's point of view (though he perhaps would not articulate it quite this way), Kasabwaibwaileta is a composite figure, an

383

amalgam of several local heroes. Likewise, his story is evocative because it is a conflation or a hodge-podge of scenes, acts and events – some patently identical, others concealed by inversion – which belong severally to different Goodenough myths. If we put aside the presupposition that Kasabwaibwaileta is 'about' the kula rather than anything else, then we can partly decompose it and illuminate its themes afresh by viewing them from the standpoint of their Goodenough analogues.

For example, on hearing the Kasabwaibwaileta story one of my Bwaidoka friends was moved to remark on its similarity to Matabawe, the tale of a snake-hero, a source of wealth, who is insulted and abandons his people by diving for Muyuwa.[3]

M1

A woman gave birth to a snake which she kept hidden in a cave. As the snake grew, so did the cave. She took it a pot of food each evening and in exchange her son Matabawe gave her one of its teeth. These tusks were fashioned into pendants [*matabile*] and the village became wealthy. One day the woman took a small child to the cave. It screamed in terror when it saw an ugly 'grandfather' and spilled broth all over him. Matabawe was affronted. He blamed his mother for bringing the child, and declared that he was going to abandon them. That night he left his cave, dived through the reef (you can still see the passage he took), and swam to Muyuwa taking all the wealth with him.

Now this myth could serve as a rationale for Goodenough's exclusion from the kula: their impoverishment following some act of 'original sin' which breached the contract of a precarious exchange. But my friend knew nothing of the kula (or *kune*) and he seized only upon the following similarity between Kasabwaibwaileta and Matabawe: a snake-man or man-snake who hoards valuables and abandons mankind in resentment.

A Kalauna audience to whom I told Kasabwaibwaileta's story sought an immediate linguistic identification with a local hero called Hudiboyaboyaleta. Their names are only coincidentally similar, however, for Hudiboyaboyaleta means 'Overripe Bananas' and (according to Roheim, 1950a.:188) Kasabwaibwaileta means 'Sores Everywhere'. But they have much in common, being successful men who hide 'valuables' in their hair which are discovered by grandchildren while delousing their heads.

M2

Hudiboyaboyaleta or Ulewoka ['Bitter Anus'] magically grows food and conceals it in a knot in his hair. He does not appear to need to eat. His granddaughters enjoy delousing him because his lice are fat and sweet. But he always warns them not to touch the bundle in his hair. One day he falls asleep and the girls' curiosity gets the better of them. They open Hudiboyaboyaleta's bundle and the food, a rich abundance of it, gushes forth. The old man wakes up and berates them. He explains his secret of abstinence and teaches them the magic of prosperity to avert famine. Then he leaves them and sinks down into a pool forever.

Notwithstanding this hero's beneficial role in providing his heirs with the magic of prosperity he is an ambivalent figure; there is a rock in Kalauna named after him which is said to 'disappear' sometimes – an event which causes famine.

This myth is one of the four which, in Kalauna, are associated with the performance of *manumanua* (which literally means 'staying in the house'). This is a communal ritual, performed by the 'guardians of the village' whenever famine threatens. It is believed to work by reducing appetite, dispelling hunger and thereby inducing people to eat less. It is also said to 'anchor' the food and 'send away' or 'banish' a quasi-personified famine.

Turning to another of the manumanua myths we meet another character who hoards food. His name is Kuyakwokula ('Hard Stone' or basalt) or Manukubuku ('Grandfather Bird', which is remarkable for clamping its beak shut with a loud snap).

M3
Kuyakwokula takes his three grandsons on a canoe voyage to the Amphletts. They have plenty of provisions aboard, but at each halt he denies the young men food and drink, promising each time that he will permit them to eat at the next place. Eventually they return home, the young men weak from starvation and thirst. The youngest brother – namesake of his grandfather – cuts off his head in fury. The head sinks into the sea, the elements are disturbed, but the eldest brother (and heir) calms them with his magic. Later the two elder brothers, who are afraid of their violent younger brother, abandon him by tricking him into founding a village elsewhere.

In this myth, also a charter for the magic of abstention, the voyage the men embark upon is a kind of anti-*manuamadumadu*. They take a new canoe but (contrary to custom) take their own food with them instead of soliciting it as gifts from other villages. The voyage is self-contained and seemingly purposeless, for the men initiate no exchanges. As a lesson in *lokona* (purposeful food-abstention), however, the voyage incites the resentment of the hungry brothers against the stone-hearted grandfather. The relevance of this myth and the previous one to the theme of manumanua can be grasped by interpreting them as attempts to resolve the contraries: retention (or failure to ingest) versus expulsion (or failure to be restrained). The dogma of manumanua declares that sitting still is efficacious.

A third manumanua myth gives charter to the ownership and use of coconut magic. The hero is Tomoudi or Ulefifiyo ('Waggle-Bottom') which, incidentally, was the name of the eldest brother in the previous myth.

M4

Tomoudi is a good provider [i.e. unlike the over-retentive grandfather]. He grows abundant gardens and fishes every day. When he arrives at the beach he takes off his head and sets it down, then he lies in the water until several large fish have swum into his stomach. Then he stands up and disgorges these on the beach. He replaces his head and sets aside the fish for his kin and affines. Then he catches himself some sprats with a handnet. One day his wife decides to spy on him as she and the whole village suffer stomach pains every time they eat Tomoudi's fish. She observes his routine and is appalled at his novel and disgusting way of catching fish. She petulantly kicks his head into the sea and it sinks. When Tomoudi staggers ashore and cannot find his head he berates his wife for killing him. He expires on the beach telling her how to instruct their two sons. The sons bury him according to the magical procedures he gave, and in time the first coconuts grow from his body. The sons discover that their father's inheritance is a rich one ['the nuts are like our father's head', they say], for they exchange coconuts for shell valuables with visitors from far and wide.

I leave it to some imaginative structuralist to propose a formula which might aptly summarize the role of the hero's head in all of these myths. There is no cult of the head in Goodenough, nor were its people ever headhunters. Clearly, however, we are dealing with permutations which suggest that the head – in its curious uses of concealment and releasing – is a source of wealth and prosperity. In the next myth, however, it is the heroine's body which hoards, then inadvertently releases, an abundance of wealth.

M5

Vineuma ['Mute Woman'] is the grandmother of the bird hero Kiwiwiole. She is immobile like a stone, with sealed orifices. Her daughter Neyalueya ['Praying Mantis'] is swept downriver and over the sea to Muyuwa by a flashflood. She is found by a Muyuwan man who hides her in his house as his second wife. Her presence is detected by his first wife who sees urine leaking through the floor. [We may note in passing that Roheim's version of Kasabwaibwaileta from Gomwa in Fergusson (ibid:185) tells how the hero, cast into the sky and secretly married, is hidden and discovered in precisely the same way.] Neyalueya teaches the Muyuwans how to plant taro and perform manumanua to preserve it when it is harvested. [Some versions of the story say that Muyuwa had no food at all, and that the people licked stones.] She gives birth to a son she calls Kiwiwiole ['Mangrove Bird']. One day, when he is a grown boy, Kiwiwiole is playing with his half-brother when he accidentally spears his arm. [The game they are playing is the same as that played by Kasabwaibwaileta's children-in-the-sky in Fortune's version. There the spear thrown at a rolling section of banana tree stem accidentally opens a shell in Pleiades's armband, and when Kasabwaibwaileta lifts it up he sees his village below (ibid:220–1).] For Kiwiwiole, the arm-spearing incident is fateful in a similar way, for it also leads to his return 'home', though away from rather than to his mother. Kiwiwiole and his mother are insulted when the angry co-wife berates them for hurting her child; she calls Kiwiwiole a homeless drifter who floats on flotsam. His mother laments and secretly turns Kiwiwiole into a bird by sewing feathers onto him while he sleeps. When he awakens she teaches him to fly and directs him to Goodenough to visit her kin. He returns with samples of all her crops, which she plants. Later she sends him back for good, building him a canoe of sugar cane and filling it with all the varieties of food valuables. He poles across the sea to Goodenough but disobeys her instruction not to turn around before he has beached the craft. The vessel overturns and all the food is lost: it sinks to the bottom of an estuary where it turns into stone [cf. Malinowski 1935(I):70]. Kiwiwiole climbs up the river to his mother's village and finds his stone-like grandmother Vineuma. He feels sorry for her and plans to open her eyes, mouth, anus and vagina. He wraps a small snake (noted for its sluggish disposition) in a bundle of leaves and places it by her. When she feels the snake coiling over her she tries to scream in fright. All her sealed orifices burst open and [like the moment when Kuyakwokula's head is tossed into the sea, and Hudiboyaboyaleta's hair is let down] there is a cataclysmic release. Like the other heroes she is resentful at this act of a grandchild, and after teaching him all her magic she sinks down into a pool forever. Some versions of the tale have her visiting several places first in a kula-like enterprise to acquire wealth [in the form of shell valuables] for Kiwiwiole.

There are so many permutations of Kasabwaibwaileta in this complex myth that the effect is kaleidoscopic. He is 'fragmented' into at least three characters: grandmother, mother and son (or should we say, rather, that he is a conflation of them?). For argument's sake let me compare and contrast him with Neyalueya:

Kasabwaibwaileta	Neyalueya
Ugly snake-man	Beautiful insect-woman
Voyages by sea to Boyowa	Washed by sea to Muyuwa
(Voluntary quest)	(Involuntary fate)
Wins valuable by magic	Makes garden by magic
Marooned	?
(Involuntary fate)	
Marries in the sky	Marries in Muyuwa
Hidden in house and is	Hidden in house and is
discovered	discovered
Child spears 'armband'	Child spears arm
Descends to own village	Sends child to own village
with child's help	(1) by air (2) by sea
Turns kin (and mother)	Turns son into bird
into birds	

These by no means exhaust the parallels, direct or inverted, and perhaps we should ask how Neyalueya came to be swept downstream – since there is an intuitive analogy here with Kasabwaibwaileta's fate in being marooned by his resentful kin. In only one version of Kiwiwiole/Neyalueya/Vineuma is it clearly explained – and the answer is perfectly opposite and almost predictable. What would a beautiful girl be resented for? Her success in attracting lovers. So here is the perfect inversion of Kasabwaibwaileta's situation. Neyalueya, goes the story, had a sister Kasifwaifwa ('Skinny Praying Mantis') who was jealous of her pretty elder sister. Every night boys would come to court them and every morning Kasifwaifwa would ask her sister what courting gifts she had been given. The answer was always the same: the best betel nut and finest quality shell valuables. Kasifwaifwa, however, is given only the most inferior betel nut and the crudest of ornaments. So when they are about to cross a flooded river one day and Neyalueya is hesitating before her leap (the way a praying mantis does), her jealous sister gives her the fatal nudge which sends her swirling downstream and over the sea to Muyuwa. Thus, if Kasabwaibwaileta is the kula hero who is marooned by jealous kinsmen for winning wealth through beauty, then Neyalueya is the manumanua heroine who is banished by a jealous sister for the same reason.

I shall digress a moment and comment upon the contextual significance of the set of four stories which give charter to the rites of manumanua. I have described the ritual briefly elsewhere (Young, 1971:174–7). The community is enjoined to silence and immobility while the two or three magicians sing their spells, recite their myths, and manipulate leaves, stones and other paraphernalia. The body symbolism involved, in conjunction with the 'stilling' spells and the repeated conjuring of stony heroes, is manifestly an attempt to 'anchor' the food. And here, of course, there is a direct parallel with the *vilamalia* ritual of Kiriwina, which is also replete with imagery of hard, immoveable stones (*binabina*) (Malinowski, 1935 (I):219; 476), and storehouses which are likened to 'well-laden canoes', 'firmly moored and anchored' (ibid:249). 'My village is anchored, like an immoveable stone is my village', runs one spell (ibid (II):233).Manumanua in Kalauna, like vilamalia in Oburaku, is 'a magic which can be performed at times of hunger, sickness or disaster'; and it 'bars the way of hunger into home and village', by 'closing the road' (ibid (I):237). It is said, in Kalauna also, 'to turn the village' in times of hunger (ibid). Moreover, the manumanua spells 'express the desire to make the food strong, tough, resisting all forces of decay and consumption' (ibid: 224). The myths give some clue as to how this is thought to be achieved.

I cannot adduce all the evidence here to support the following interpretation, for I have given highly compressed versions of each myth. But it can be said that each myth plays variations on the basic opposition fundamental to *manumanua* ideology: that is, stasis and continence versus mobility and unrestraint. The stony heroes and heroines, it will be recalled, are activated by mobile, restless heroes (usually designated as 'grandchildren') who have bird or insect names. Now in Goodenough Islanders' experience food has a distressing habit of periodically disappearing in famine; hence the attempt of manumanua to 'bring it back' and anchor it. To be immobilized food must be imparted with the static properties of stone; it must be petrified – though in the process stone may be reciprocally mobilized: thus the disconcertingly active stones and mountains of Goodenough mythology. What manumanua is believed to accomplish can be expressed by a chiasmus:

Mediating between the states of stillness and movement are acts of 'turning' or 'revolving' (*vilana*, which has many semantic correspondences to the colloquial English uses of 'turning'). The myths are also replete with 'turning' imagery: from Tomoudi's turning body and the turning weather when heads roll and bodies burst asunder, to Kiwiwiole's food which turns into stone when his canoe turns over, a result of disobeying his mother's instruction not to turn around too soon. 'Turning' is the means of converting stasis into mobility and vice versa. Magicians physically turn stones in yam magic (to anchor the tubers in the garden), in pregnancy rites (to turn the child), and in *bakibaki* sorcery to expel people from the village by turning the centre stone of the sitting platform which is believed to anchor them there. Fancifully, one might observe that the turning point of Kiwiwiole's story occurs during the game of rolling banana stems (called *o'o*, a splendidly gestural utterance), when his fate is made to turn on his resentment at being insulted.[4]

In the deeply-rooted opposition between stasis (which is generally auspicious and has connotations of safety), and mobility (which is generally inauspicious and has connotations of risk), we can glimpse Goodenough Islanders' attitude towards wandering from place to place in *manuamadumadu* (which I need hardly point out is an antonym of *manumanua*). There is, one might say, a metaphysical underpinning to their anxieties about wandering.[5] There is an aura of mystical danger about it because it flouts the moral philosophy of sitting still; to wander is somehow to invite the disaster of famine. I overstate the case, of course, for not all men see their place as in the home; but it is true that the manumanua magicians, the owners of the myths, should set an example to their fellows by staying quietly at home and avoiding all frivolous peregrinations. This being so, when Goodenough men do undertake manuaumadumadu it is with an acute sense of quest. As Roheim suggests (ibid:200), the motivation is partly bravado and the necessity to confront their deepest fears.

On a mundane level, of course, all the peoples of the area appreciate that visiting exchange of whatever kind cannot take place without secure stocks of food at home.[6] *Malia* ('abundance' in both Kiriwina and Goodenough) is a prerequisite for wandering, and this being so the expeditions become a vivid demonstration, and even a celebration, of malia. Thus in the Goodenough view, manumanua effects the stasis which makes the mobility of manuamadumadu feasible. Finally, we may note the existence of comparable imagery in the Trobriands: the anchoring and mooring of garden magic and vilamalia contrast with the cataclysmic imagery of thunder and earthshaking so characteristic of kula magic (e.g. Malinowski, 1922:341). Such symbolism (not to mention the perils of leaping stones and flying witches) is associated with the 'releasing' of kula valuables, just as the upheavals of Goodenough mythology are associated with the release of pent-up food wealth – and, one might add, the simultaneous transmission of its magical control to an heir.

Let me return now to the mythology itself, to consider another flawed hero with a stigmatized body-image: Kawafolafola, whose name means 'Pierced Neck'. He is afflicted with a hole in his throat and consequently has difficulty in eating. There are innumerable versions of his story, not all of which are mutually consistent, but I will give a generalized account of one set of them. His kinship with Kasabwaibwaileta will be quite evident.

M6

Kawafolafola's grandchildren laugh at him because whenever he eats the food falls through the hole in his throat. He is resentful and decides to punish them. He equips a canoe and takes the boys on a voyage, then maroons them on a desert isle. They survive by finding a hole in the coral and living on fish and coconuts. Later Kawafolafola returns for them, but they trick him in turn [sometimes by the same ruse of muddy water which Kasabwaibwaileta's kinsmen use], and they sail away in his canoe. In some versions they cut off his head first, in others they leave him to be devoured by demons. Jenness and Ballantyne (1928:83–104) published a version in which Kawafolafola is reconstituted and brought back to life by his daughter, the children's mother; but in his own resentment at being abandoned he 'sends away' all the food and betel nut, leaving Goodenough destitute.

So far as I know, there is no magical knowledge associated with this or any of the other 'marooning' versions of Kawafolafola, so they might be said to have folktale rather than real myth status. The same is probably true of many other versions, although in some of them the hero does rain magic to create a deluge which floods the world (hence his identification with the biblical Noah in some parts of Goodenough).[7] In yet other versions he meets the sexually voracious Wanuwanu women encountered by Kasabwaibwaileta in two of Roheim's versions.[8] But perhaps the most important version of Kawafolafola known to Kalauna people is one which gives charter to a system of yam-growing magic. This is owned by one of the most influential descent lines and is used to structure the yam-growing cycle of the whole community. The myth which legitimates it will be seen to play upon many of the themes we have met in previous stories.

M7

A woman gives birth to two yams and two human sons. When they grow up the mother teaches her sons (Kawafolafola and Wameya) how to plant and tend their 'brothers'. They both become yam-growing experts, but they compete and quarrel over their prowess. Kawafolafola is the more boastful and arrogant though Wameya is ostensibly the better gardener. Wameya resentfully makes a flood which carries his house, containing himself and his family, across the sea to Fergusson Island. He settles beneath Mt Oyatabu, while Kawafolafola remains beneath Mt Oyamadawa'a on Goodenough. Wameya had also taken all the soil away, so Kawafolafola plants in vain. He promises a pig to any bird who can fly to Oyatabu and retrieve the soil. After several large birds have tried and failed, a tiny bird called Kikifolu succeeds. He brings back a bundle of soil which the rain spreads over the island again. Later Kawafolafola decides to equip a canoe and visit his brother. Wameya shames him by giving him massive meals and an abundance of food (Oyatabu yams included) to return with. Later Wameya repays the visit, only to catch Kawafolafola by surprise with his rain magic, and he gets a rather sparing and indifferent reception. The two brothers part again having insulted one another in complementary ways which are supposed to reflect upon the respective yam-growing customs of Fergusson and Goodenough.

This long and complex myth is an extended commentary upon the relationship which Goodenough men have with their quasi-human yams, and the complications for sibling relationships which a shared inheritance of yam magic brings. The myth may be said to investigate the similarities within the natural difference between men and yams on the one hand, and the differences within the natural similarity between brothers on the other hand. Its relevance for us here, however, is that large yams (*kuvi*) are to most Goodenough men what kula valuables are to most Trobriand men; the passion, perils, magic and sorcery which go into their acquisition, hoarding and exchange are every bit as compelling for them.

There is one other ungiving, ambiguous hero of Kawafolafola's stature in Goodenough mythology: Honoyeta, whose story gives charter to the most terrible sun magic. He is neither a great hoarder nor a great provider like many of the other heroes; rather, he scorns to give and to receive and

Michael W. Young

(like Jean-Paul Sartre's Saint) would renounce himself to the point of wishing upon the world the ultimate, destructive potlatch.

M8

Honoyeta is ostensibly an old man with an ugly, wrinkled skin. His two young wives feed and tend him, and they periodically go to the beach for shellfish. As soon as they have gone, the senile Honoyeta doffs his skin and emerges as a shining, beautiful young man. He takes his fish spear and descends to the beach, where he encounters his wives and courts them in the guise of a handsome stranger. He gives them fish, then hurries back home to don his aged skin. His wives return and cook for him, lying about how they acquired the fish. Eventually, by noticing that the betel nuts the stranger at the beach gives them are from their own trees, the wives grow suspicious. One of them stays behind to spy on him while the other makes her accustomed visit to the beach. Seeing her husband's game, the first wife destroys his skin while he is gone. He returns and discovers what has happened. He is angry and resentful, refuses to eat, and in the morning abandons them. He goes from village to village in search of death, in a kind of parody of manuamadumadu, challenging people to give him massive prestations of food by his beauteous appearance – but then rejecting it and moving on. At last he comes to Yabiliva where he insults a man by insisting that the child he carries is his brother and not his son [i.e. by conflating the generations]. The man calls for assistance and the villagers try to spear Honoyeta. But they cannot kill him. At length he instructs them to club him with a special wood and he falls. They cut him into pieces and prepare to cook him. But his body remains raw. His flesh continues to speak and he gives explicit instructions for his burial. The villagers carry his remains over the mountain to Galuwata and bury him in a stone tomb. He continues to address them until his tomb is completely sealed, saying that when magic moves his bones there will be drought and famine, and when his bones are stilled there will be prosperity. Honoyeta's spirit becomes the sun, and all those who had touched his body die.

The dozen or so versions of this myth that I possess are remarkably consistent and show none of the extreme variability of Kawafolafola. Some narrators give the myth a cargo-cult flavour by using it to 'explain' the poverty of Papuans (just as they do with the myths of Matabawe and Kawafolafola). They read the attempt to kill and eat the hero as a kind of original sin, and would see him as a sacrificial hero by identifying him with Jesus.[9] But while the Primal Father theme is irresistible, it should be stressed that Honoyeta denies himself as sacrament to the 'sons' who kill him and would eat his body. There is no solace of sacramental cult, no atonement of eucharist. Other versions are content to suggest that Honoyeta was somehow responsible for the origin of death, and that the world was forever impoverished by his fate. And to bring this survey of Goodenough mythology full circle (so that the serpent bites its tail, so to speak), let me mention that one narrator of the story of Matabawe – the snake who took away all the wealth – declared that Matabawe returned to

Goodenough, changed into an old man, acquired two wives and called himself Honoyeta, the snake-man.

The majority of the myths I have mentioned appear to explore, through the permutation of a limited number of themes, the ambivalence and fragility of various modes of exchange, all of which must be mediated by deception. Stigmatized heroes and heroines offer, win, hoard or reject wealth, evoking jealousy leading to their abandonment, or, their secrets having been discovered, leading to their resentful rejection of 'mankind'. If there is a single contradiction at the heart of them which in their various ways the myths attempt to pose and resolve, it is something like this: food is good to eat (and valuables are good to keep), but it is good *not* to eat food (and good *not* to keep valuables). The paradox seems both to vitalize and vitiate Goodenough society, with its covert competition and its obsession with sorcery. It shapes the value system, colours the ethos, and charges the political action. And in the felt ambivalence between private hoarding (which may be publicly sanctioned) and public magnanimity (which may be privately denigrated), there is the deepest fear which no one will name: the horror of greed.

I have hardly begun the task of analysing the myths adequately here, but I hope to have evoked some sense of the kula myth of Kasabwaibwaileta as a contingent creation in a continuum of transformations. In the context of the Goodenough myths I have presented, this kula myth speaks to the same problems of wealth – its acquisition and inheritance, its dearth or abundance – in egalitarian societies so prone to paying themselves (in Mauss's phrase) in the false coin of their dreams, whether that coinage be shell valuables or long yams.

Notes

1 This paper was written partly to complement my other contribution to the symposium: *Ceremonial Visiting in Goodenough Island* see pp. 395–410. It will be more intelligible, therefore, if it is read as a sequel to that chapter. I have analysed the myths which appear below in greater detail in a forthcoming monograph on the biographies of several Kalauna magicians, tentatively titled *Manumanua: Living myth in Kalauna.*
2 Malinowski, 1922:322–4; Fortune, 1963 (1932): 216–20; Roheim, 1950a:184–91. In addition to the four versions he collected on Fergusson and Normanby, Roheim presents summaries of the versions by Malinowski and Fortune. Ms Shirley Campbell recorded short versions of the myth from Vakuta and Tewara in 1977 and I am grateful to her for showing them to me. They substantiate the other versions in most details.
3 In Goodenough, Muyuwa refers to the undifferentiated northern Massim.

4 Cf. Fortune's observation that the magic of the kula in Dobu is directed to Kasabwaibwaileta in an attempt to get him to 'turn around' and assist the aim of the magician (1963:229).

5 Roheim (1950a:198–201) discusses the ontogenetic basis of these anxieties from a psychoanalytical viewpoint (e.g. 'wandering is aggression against the mother'). Given his premises much of what he says for Duau is illuminating for Goodenough also.

6 Malinowski notes that the overseas kula expeditions must be postponed until the crops are ready, and obviously cannot take place if they fail (1935 (i):53).

7 The tale of his building the ark resembles the story of the Flying Canoe from Kitava (Malinowski, 1922:311–16) in which the people are sceptical about the purpose of a landlocked canoe. In one of the versions of Kiwiwiole the same device occurs: people refuse to help because the canoe is too far from the sea.

8 See Roheim 1950a:188. Roheim quotes his Dobuan informants as saying that Wanwanuine is the Land of Women. Goodenough lore has it that the women are called Wanuwanu and their island Kwedina, which is located between Goodenough and the Trobriands. They abandoned their husbands for not providing meat! See also Malinowski, 1929:422ff. on Kaytalugi.

9 Interestingly, one of Shirley Campbell's narrators (from Tewara) commented that Kasabwaibwaileta was Jesus's son who came to that part of the world 'to make it safe'.

16 Ceremonial visiting in Goodenough Island[1]

MICHAEL W. YOUNG

In this chapter I hope to shed some light on the *kula* by presenting comparative material on visiting ceremonial gift exchange in Goodenough Island. While these forms of exchange are pale and parochial shadows of the kula, I regard them as analogous institutions. They have somewhat similar economic and political functions, and they involve reciprocal visiting between communities to solicit things of value. Moreover, the gifts solicited are referred to as *niune*, a term which is cognate to *kune*, the Dobuan and Duau name for the kula. To my knowledge, however, none of the districts or political communities on Goodenough ever participated in the kula ring. Traders from Kavataria, Kaileuna and the Amphlett Islands visited northern and eastern Goodenough, but they did not appear to conduct formal kula.[2]

All major exchanges on Goodenough involve the principle of niune. That is, any exchange with political import which occurs at the inter-clan or inter-community levels is structured by a rule which requires the recipients of the prestation to pass it on to their exchange partners. From ego's point of view, *niuneku* (i.e. 'my niune') means: 'a gift given to me which I cannot consume or use myself'.

Suppose I, a man of Kalauna, wish to raise my standing at home by challenging my traditional enemy (*nibai*) in another village to a competitive exchange of food (*abutu*). I send my internal exchange partner (*fofofo*) to ask my enemy for food and pigs. If they accept the challenge both our villages will compete to give the most. The men of my patrilineal group are designated 'initiators' (*inuba*), and we will be helped by our hereditary exchange partners (fofofo), whom we call 'those who eat our niune'. We will also be helped by other members of our village community (*tabotabo*). All the food given to us inuba by our enemy is our niune, and when the contest is over we must pass it on to our fofofo. They distribute it among themselves and among the residual group of tabotabo. Then, because they cannot let us go hungry, they will compensate

395

Michael W. Young

us with food and pigs of their own. Later, if my fofofo wants to make abutu to their enemy in turn, my group will act as their fofofo and we will receive their niune to distribute and consume.[3]

The constitutional rules here outlined for abutu also apply to the conduct of all forms of political exchange on Goodenough (though I should note that in their application there are innumerable local idiosyncrasies). Let me now catalogue the major forms of such exchange, indicating very briefly their chief characteristics.

1. Festivals (*lumiami*, literally 'to stay and stay'). These are delayed exchange entertainments lasting a year or longer which culminate in sumptuary give-aways. The clans of a village, assisted by their respective *fofofo* partners, take turns in sponsoring festivals. For the duration of their festival the sponsors (inuba) are accorded temporary rank as 'chiefs' (*kaiwabu*). Within a village or a geographical area comprising several villages, the festivals form an interlocking cycle in time by virtue of debts incurred by those who received niune gifts from the sponsors. The festival cycle is therefore self-perpetuating as clans seek to pay back their pig and food debts, and, by making fresh prestations, establish themselves as creditors.

2. Competitive food exchanges (abutu, literally 'food fame'). These are simultaneous exchanges at either clan or village levels, in which both sides pit their resources against one another in the attempt to 'win' by giving more food than can be repaid (cf. the analogous harvest contest of *buritila'ulo* in Kiriwina, Malinowski 1935:181–7). There are effectively two types of abutu: intravillage ones which are intended to settle quarrels and redress delicts (particularly wife-stealing) within the community, and intervillage ones with traditional enemies, which have some of the formal panoply of warfare. Through the complex network of niune debts and reciprocities involved, abutu may be linked in series over a period of time but they cannot form perpetual cycles like festivals. Debts incurred in abutu cannot be repaid via a festival (and vice versa), a rule which insulates one mode of exchange from the other.

3. Visiting exchanges (*manuamadumadu*, literally 'house hurrying'). These involve planned expeditions to near or distant villages to solicit niune. The distinction between manuamadumadu and intervillage abutu, in which an enemy is challenged to present one with a massive food prestation, is not absolute. What may begin as an innocent manuamadumadu expedition in search of modest prestations, can escalate into an abutu with massive commitment of resources. The impulse to shame visitors by giving them more food than they bargained for is a difficult one for Goodenough Islanders to resist.[4]

For the remainder of this chapter I shall discuss two principal forms of manuamadumadu: the sea-borne variety found in Bwaidoka and other coastal communities, and the overland version which is found throughout the island but which I shall describe for the hill village of Kalauna. First, one more key term must be mentioned: that which refers to hereditary exchange partners and protectors in other villages. These are called *tolama* (or *solama*), the people with whom one has hospitable and mutually supportive relations, whose ancestors allegedly saved the life of an ancestor of one's own, and who are the appropriate people to visit for the purpose of soliciting gifts. I have outlined the ideology of tolama relations elsewhere (Young 1971:50; and Young 1977:131–3).

Wakaefuefu in Bwaidoka

In the coastal communities of Goodenough the custom of ceremonial visiting for the purpose of soliciting gifts (*efu*) is associated particularly with the launching of new canoes. This practice probably extends throughout the Massim, though the only descriptive accounts are Malinowski's for Kiriwina (1922:Chap. VI) and Chowning's for the Molima of southern Fergusson (1960). On Goodenough it occurred most commonly along the relatively densely settled eastern coastline, from Belebele to Wagifa, and hinged particularly on the canoe-building centre of Bwaidoka in Mud Bay. By means of *wakaefuefu* the barrier of Moresby Strait was overcome, enabling the extension of a trade partnership network to the major canoe-building districts of western Fergusson (Fatavi or Kalokalo, Milaveya or Kukuya, and Molima), and thereby facilitating the distribution of shell valuables and other goods throughout the area. A detailed understanding of traditional activities in this sphere is now irretrievable; Diamond Jenness, the Oxford-trained anthropologist, failed to take the same fieldwork opportunities in the northern D'Entrecasteaux which Malinowski was to embrace in the Trobriands only four years later. In what follows I outline the institution of wakaefuefu as I found it in Bwaidoka in 1967, alluding where relevant to informants' accounts of past practices.

Jenness and Ballantyne (1920:185–8) provide a brief description of canoe manufacture and sailing in Wagifa and Mud Bay (i.e. the communities of modern Bwaidoka), and I will not cover the same ground here. One or two observations are necessary, however. Sea-going canoes of the sturdy *masawa* type were never constructed on Goodenough; the largest seen by Jenness was a Wagifan *waka* which carried 13 men (*ibid*: 36). I have also seen two or three of similar size in Wagifa and in Moratau on the west coast, which trades sporadically with the mainland; but it is rare indeed to find a canoe in eastern Goodenough nowadays which can seat a crew of more than eight. Bwaidoka, the largest canoe-building centre after Wagifa, has ceased to produce waka altogether. (Waka are canoes with built-up planking; all canoes without planking, by definition smaller, are called *ayebu*). In 1973 the four villages which constitute the census ward of Bwaidoka (with a combined population of more than 1,200), could boast between eighty and ninety canoes in good repair. But more than half of these were merely one- or two-man vessels, and only a dozen could accommodate a crew of more than five. Clearly, then, most Bwaidokan canoes can be used for nothing more adventurous than fishing or commuting across the placid waters of Mud Bay. Some of the larger ones have ventured as far afield as Kalokalo, Yamalele or Mapamoiwa on western Fergusson, usually on trading trips. (During a local famine in February 1972, for example, a flotilla of canoes from Bwaidoka made the rather arduous voyage to Yamalele and Fagalulu – a distance of some 25km – where hungry men bartered plates, utensils, clothes, and even heirloom shell valuables for bundles of sago.)

In Molima (Chowning 1960) it was the practice for a hamlet leader to construct a canoe as a memorial for a dead man, and to use the gifts solicited for it to provision a mortuary feast. This was not done in Bwaidoka, though not surprisingly, big-men found an expression of their local influence and renown in sponsoring the construction of a canoe, and the ownership of a modest-sized one even today is the mark of a leader's status. Canoe manufacture remains a uniquely specialist activity, the expertise for which belongs to one or two descent lines in each Bwaidoka village. No more than a score of men have the requisite knowledge to make any but the smallest canoes, and only five or six know how to lash the larger ones properly. Traditionally, the technical skills of lashing were governed by taboos and reinforced by magical incantations which invoked the assistance of ancestral spirits to make the lashings strong and supple, and to impart lightness, speed and flexibility to the vessel. Even today, after eighty years of heavy missionization, some restrictions (sexual and dietary) are still observed by the old experts who lash the outrigger to a canoe's hull. Women are still forbidden to approach or sit upon a new canoe, lest their skirts contaminate it and jeopardize its inaugural voyages. The experts perform little if any magic nowadays, however, even on the larger canoes.

Feasting and celebrations sponsored by the owner or *toniwaka* accompanied the launching of a new canoe. It then embarked upon a maiden voyage with a crew of young unmarried men and the toniwaka himself, seated on the outrigger platform with the ostentatious dignity of a *kaiwabu* (see Young 1971:248ff.). Bwaidoka elders claim that their fathers circumnavigated Goodenough in their new plank canoes, as well as venturing almost as far as Dobuan territory to the east. The last two waka to be built in Bwaidoka, shortly after the Second World War, were taken as far as Molima on one trip and Basima (northeast Fergusson) on another, both places being well beyond the reach of tolama ties. There were said to be few open hostilities on such expeditions, though the reception they received was not always friendly. The visitors would always pause before approaching a village, wash and adorn themselves with paint and simple decorations, and sing spells to 'soften' the hearts or minds of their potential hosts (cf. Jenness and Ballantyne 1920:161). Gingerly approaching a strange village, the canoe would draw into the shallows, allowing the toniwaka to step ashore alone, spitting prophylactic ginger at his feet before announcing himself: 'Don't be afraid of us. I am Lauwafa of Bwaidoka. We have not come for war. We have come for efu gifts for our canoe.' Even if no one was willing to come forward and befriend them (*vetubuiyana*) by the ceremonial exchange of betel nut, some seemingly reluctant offerings might still be forthcoming: a dog or pig thrown down on the beach, and a few shell valuables draped disdainfully over the canoe prow. The visitors would accept without demur whatever was given, invite a return visit, and paddle on to the next village. Friendly districts, where true tolama of the toniwaka lived, promised more relaxed encounters. Hosts and visitors would chew betel together, exchange gossip, and share cooked food provided by the hosts. The treachery of tolama was always a possibility; but my informants recalled no case when Bwaidokans had been attacked on such voyages, at least since the end of the Bwaidokan wars with Kukuya about the turn of the century (see Young 1977). Such expeditions lasted a week or more and the itinerary – partly planned and partly adventitious – might encompass a score of foreign villages; though I suspect this would only have been the case if there were two or more canoes making the voyage. The canoes returned home when they had been given as much food as they could carry.

The distribution of the spoils followed from the basic principle that everything he had been given was the canoe owner's niune and therefore prohibited to him: hence he was obliged to pass the gifts on. Ideally everything went to his fofofo. Some of the pigs, raw food and valuables would repay previous debts owing to his fofofo, others would establish the toniwaka as the creditor. Later, of course, when his fofofo had built a new canoe and sought gifts in the same manner, the toniwaka could expect all his niune to be reciprocated. Meanwhile, when the distant tolama and foreign villages made their return visits, the toniwaka indebted to them would call on his fofofo to assist in paying them back. Insofar as this system of reciprocal visiting had impetus it was analogous to the festival cycle. The canoe-visiting 'system', of course, was founded on a more precarious form of reciprocity, and was subject to greater vagaries of whim and weather. Whereas the festival cycle was linked to the growth period of pigs, the canoe-visiting cycle of any fofofo partnership must have been geared to the life-span of their canoes – some six years in the case of the best timbers used for hulls. I have no data to confirm that this notional 'system' of delayed exchange ever took on more than an ephemeral existence, however, and it would be unduly credulous to assume that it could work smoothly in the uncertain conditions which preceded European contact any more than in the changing conditions which followed it.

Having presented a broad outline of the traditional institution I now turn to its modern version. The reduced scale of canoes nowadays entails a reduction of scale in practically everything else: expenditure of time, labour and economic resources, as well as the curtailment of ceremonial and magical accompaniments, shorter voyages and a commitment of less passionate interest in them. Most of the adventure and all of the danger has gone from wakaefuefu, and the pragmatism of the younger generation is almost baffled by what drove the old men to sail so far for pigs and valuables which they could have obtained closer to home with far less trouble. 'It was their idea', the younger Bwaidokans shrug. 'They did it for their pride and adventure. Now we go to different places, too, but by European boats.' Shell valuables, the fruits of successful voyages in the past, have now been almost wholly replaced in the internal exchange economy by cash and trade items of European manufacture (utensils, clothes, etc.), and it is these things which young men bring home today from their working trips abroad. But the practice of wakaefuefu still flourishes in a minor way, and although the social sphere of its operation has contracted, the flow of raw vegetable food through its agency is probably greater now than ever before.

During the months of my first visit to Bwaidoka (May–July 1967) more than a dozen new canoes were launched and sent visiting for efu. This was an exceptional year. An unusually good yam harvest had provided the security and wherewithal for a frantic season of wakaefuefu. The whole of Mud Bay became involved in reciprocal visiting, though the stimulus came from the four villages of Bwaidoka (Kabune, Melala, Ukuna and Banada), where all but one or two of the canoes were built. The canoes ranged in size from three-man (nothing smaller is ever sent visiting), to one which seated a crew of seven.

The launching of a new canoe is still something of an event. The day it is completed and freshly painted (nowadays with trade dyes and manganese from old torch-batteries), the toniwaka provides a feast for all those who have in any way helped in its construction. The same night he also sponsors a celebration in his hamlet, and there is singing and dancing until dawn. As dawn breaks several young men push the canoe to the water's edge and launch it to the mournful clamour of conch-shell trumpets. The composition of the crew will have been decided beforehand by the toniwaka; generally speaking, they are his own sons, sisters' sons, and the sons of the canoe builder or any other young men who have a special claim to the privilege of taking the new canoe on its maiden voyage. They are adorned from the night's entertainments; and they jump aboard and ply their freshly painted paddles. If there is another new canoe in the vicinity other young men will fetch it to race the newly launched one. For several minutes at sunrise both canoes race parallel to the shore, until the watchers visually certify one as the swifter. On its return to the owner's hamlet children pelt the new canoe with food rubbish until the sea is littered (cf. Chowning 1960:34). The owner hopes his canoe will be showered with food likewise when it 'asks' for efu. The crew then departs for the first visit, paddling away with flourishing strokes which splash the water high in the air behind them (cf. Malinowski 1922:342).

Whether or not they are expected at their destination the crew are greeted with reserve and even ignored for a time. (On one maiden voyage I accompanied, the man we were heading for hurriedly picked up a bush-knife as we approached, so that he could be 'working' and pretended to ignore us for several minutes.) If the crewsmen are very youthful and their canoe insignificant in size, they may have to shuffle awkwardly on the perimeter of the hamlet for hours, waiting to be noticed by the host and invited to chew betel with him. Most visits nowadays are made to tolama, to whom a friendly message will have been sent the night before, warning of the impending visit. No warning is given of the rarer visits to traditional enemies (nibai), however, for the toniwaka's intention is to embarrass them by catching them unawares without efu to give, thereby enabling him to disparage them for having 'no food'. The visiting crew wait while the host and his helpers fetch food from their stores or nearby gardens. They re-appear in ones and twos, bringing yams, taro, bunches of betel nut and banana plants complete with leaves. They dump them noisily in front of the visitors, shouting defiantly and taunting them about their ability to pay back quickly. A couple of chickens, a dog or even a cat may be given nowadays, but only rarely a pig.

Meanwhile, the toniwaka waits at home for the canoe's return. Toniwaka do not accompany their new canoes nowadays; they say that they would be 'ashamed' and that they would not be given any efu if they did.

401

This convention seems to have developed as the size of canoes diminished. Characteristic dissembling is also involved, however, for the toniwaka may well travel by another vessel and join his new canoe at its destination, especially when this is his traditional enemy's hamlet. But he will not board his own canoe or be seen to ride on it, as if to preserve the fiction that it is the canoe itself which 'asks' for efu.

When the laden canoe returns the toniwaka makes an inventory of the gifts, then sends them on to his fofofo, who distributes them in his hamlet. Alternatively, the first canoe-load of gifts may be sent to the builder as further payment for his services; in this case it is the fruits of the second voyage which the fofofo receives. Only if there is a third voyage (and fewer than half the canoes I observed bothered to go visiting a third time), do the toniwaka's own group receive anything. On this occasion, the gift may be divided three ways: one portion to the canoe-builder, another to the fofofo, and the remainder to the toniwaka's own hamlet, though he, of course, will abstain from any of this food himself.

Return visits by the erstwhile hosts may be made within a week, a month, a year or even longer. They do not need new canoes to recover their debts; they may borrow one or come on foot. They can expect to receive the same kind and roughly the same quantity of foodstuffs that they gave – with the little extra that the donor's pride dictates. If the visitors are traditional enemies, the repayment will be given aggressively and the 'little extra' may become threateningly large, thereby escalating the transaction to the threshold of abutu.

The politics of wakaefuefu is an intricate matter for which I have insufficient space to explain fully here. Generally speaking, similar considerations of strategy (for giving and receiving prestations) to those I have described for abutu and festivals in Kalauna apply to the politics of canoe-visiting (Young 1971). It is innately competitive, though diffidence would disguise this fact. The ultimate objective of a toniwaka is to maximize his prestige as a food-producer at the expense of the reputations of his rivals, but almost as much energy is expended in concealing this objective. Wherever food flows in any quantity on Goodenough, there are fertile grounds for disputation, and when quarrels surface then so does naked politicking. Inevitably, disputes arise over the conduct of wakaefuefu.

One major row and innumerable minor ones blew up in Bwaidoka during June and July 1967. The largest one almost embroiled the whole of the community – all four villages – in an abutu contest. Responding to a request for efu from a Melala canoe, the men of the hill settlements of Ukuna poured down to the coast in a body, painted for war and wielding gigantic yams. There had been three canoe visits to Ukuna that week already, and the hill villagers (who possessed no canoes themselves) became exasperated with the constant soliciting for food gifts. Hence, on the seemingly innocent visit of yet another new canoe, they responded with collective resentment. The startled crew, on being greeted with the aggressive offer of tons of raw food, hurried back to Melala to fetch their toniwaka and a number of other Melala leaders. The arguments lasted for hours and abutu seemed inevitable as more and more hamlets took sides. Eventually, Bwaidoka's strong man – the President of the Goodenough Island Local Government Council – called a moratorium until the following day. He was adamantly opposed to abutu, seeing it as a threat to the harmony of his community and an obstacle to the measured economic development of his ward. (He opposed it on 'religious' grounds, too, and supported the Methodist Mission's decree that 'fighting with food' was a wicked waste of God's provender and a temptation to violence.) The following day he mobilized majority opinion behind him when he brought a token of his own massive food resources to the meeting and offered it to the hot-headed Ukuna men. Realizing that they would be resoundingly defeated in abutu if they had to take on the President's village (Banada) as well as Melala and part of Kabuna, they backed down and accepted the principle that wakaefuefu was to be conducted only in a friendly spirit with the exchange of measured equivalences. It is significant that most of the oratory that day was concerned to deny that wakaefuefu was in any way competitive.

Numerous minor disputes that season also concerned escalations, mis-calculations in the size of efu, mistimings of visits (such that, for example, a host would be nonplussed to be visited by two new canoes at the same time), and return visits which were made too promptly and thus smacked of unfriendly spite or undue greed. In brief, it was all too clear that the wakaefuefu visits hither and thither across Mud Bay were quite uncoor-dinated, so that clashes of interest frequently occurred. When a hamlet had been approached by a new canoe for the third or fourth time in almost as many days, the tempers of the hosts became frayed, and they gave efu with the petulance and antagonism normally reserved for en-emies. To my knowledge, however, there were no outright refusals during this period, although some of the efu prestations were pathetically small ('just coconuts', as the disgruntled toniwaka complained). Those who gave small efu were usually shamed by being given a much larger return when they repaid the visit. Thus, the obligation to give generously, whatever immediate hardship it might entail, was still being sanctioned by the force of traditional values.

In this respect, a significant difference emerges between the wakaefuefu of the past and those of today. Besides being more spectacular, the former were more leisurely voyages, taking longer, ranging further and acquiring larger and more varied efu gifts from more distant sources. A corollary of the distances involved was that ample time was available to repay. Moreover, the distance between a toniwaka's village and the other places he visited was such that shame was a weak sanction. The delayed exchange of pigs and valuables proved to be more or less insulated from other, purely local events, and the transactions took place between virtual strangers: here today, gone tomorrow and forgotten for many months. Nowadays, on the other hand, the areal scope of visiting has severely contracted; efu consists of foodstuffs only and the transactions are beset by aggravating competitive strains. There is the competition to give as between traditional enemies, and the competition to receive as between the various toniwaka. Since the communities of Mud Bay are in close and continuous interaction, modern wakaefuefu brings in its wake all the problematics of shaming, competitive giving, and a tempting escalation towards the controlled violence of abutu. Befitting the relatively puny size of the canoes now constructed in Bwaidoka, wakaefuefu is nowadays thoroughly insular, and more pettily competitive than it is heroic. Finally, wakaefuefu is more than ever before an end in itself for the actors. Though unlike the *tasasoria* and *kabigidoya* of Kiriwina it never was a dress-rehearsal for, nor provisioning prelude to, an even grander enterprise.

Manuamadumadu in Kalauna

Situated almost an hour's climb from the coast, Kalauna has little to do with the sea and most men cannot even paddle a canoe, let alone build one. Lacking canoes, their gift-soliciting expeditions are made on foot. If nothing else, this enables much larger parties to travel, including women and children. To meet one of these is to be reminded of a straggling medieval army on the move complete with camp followers.

Manuamadumadu (*manua* – 'house', figuratively 'home' and hence 'village'; *madu* – to run, hurry, rush) denotes 'to rush from place to place'. An expedition is initiated by a leader who is usually a man of standing in the village. Notwithstanding the fairly *ad hoc* recruitment of a manuamadumadu party, it is internally differentiated on the same lines as the participant groups in a festival or *abutu* contest. Thus, it always consists of three categories of persons: the leader and his agnates up to clan level (inuba), their permanent internal exchange partners (fofofo), and the rest – the residual category of tabotabo. Women and children who accompany the party are designated accordingly: married women belong to their husband's group (at least for the purpose of the expedition), while children belong to their father's. The inuba are the formal recipients of the niune, but it is the fofofo who are responsible for distributing it among themselves and among the tabotabo. Such distributions are guided by an ethic of fair-sharing; it would cause bitterness and invite sorcery attacks if the fofofo allocated themselves the prime cuts of pork and the choicest baskets of vegetable foods. 'The tabotabo were also drenched by the rain and scorched by the sun', it is said. That is, having shared the discomforts and dangers of the expedition they are therefore equally entitled to its rewards. For their part, members of the tabotabo category reciprocate by helping the fofofo provision the inuba's compensatory gift of *kamoabi* (literally, 'to clasp the stomach').

One can see that these rules compel the widest distribution of the food and any other goods received on the expedition. There are other similarities of pattern to abutu and festivals. The leaders of a manuamadumadu may be refered to as kaiwabu. When the party enters a village the fofofo should lead the way; the kaiwabu should follow quietly and sit aloofly to one side, allowing their fofofo to do all the talking while they chew betel and appear unconcerned in the proceedings. Under no circumstances must they eat in public. If they are to be given shelter for the night by tolama, the kaiwabu will eat sparingly in the privacy of a house after dark. They may break the usual rule of silent self-effacement, however, by joining the rest of the party in dancing and singing if these are part of the planned agenda to entertain their hosts. This brings me to the rationale for undertaking manuamadumadu.

The commonest explanation is summed up in the term *vebiyala* (or *lubiyala*), which can be glossed 'to show off something'. *Biyala* is the name of the fluted, dried pandanus leaf streamer or 'flag' which is used throughout the Massim. Biyala can be used to decorate anything from a canoe, a drum or a house to a large yam (cf. Malinowski 1922:216; 407, for the significance of *bisila* streamers in Kiriwina). Vebiyala, then, refers to anything which is being 'celebrated' by being shown off: a new feather headdress, drum, limepot, comb, or even a new pair of shorts. Occasions on which such things are formally shown off are also referred to as vebiyala (see Young 1971:238–9). This custom gives scope for minor cultural innovations by putting a premium on the new gimmick or fashion. But besides its inaugural use, there is another idea behind the display of a new object or fashion, and this has to do with securing public acknowledgement of its ownership. In the case of certain things celebrated as vebiyala, this amounts to acquiring 'patents' for them. Thus a new design on a house or headdress is patented by the act of receiving gifts for it. Henceforth, if anyone copies that design without the permission of the owners the latter can demand compensation (traditionally in

405

Michael W. Young

the form of shell valuables); a claim which would be backed by those who had given gifts for the recognition of the patent. Once entitlement is secured, the design, song, dance or whatever, becomes the custom (*dewa*) of the patrilineage which owns it and is thenceforth part of the heritable, accumulated property of that group. Obviously, however, only certain things can be carried to other villages and shown off in this way: drums, decorations and apparel, and various performing arts.

The largest manuamadumadu in living memory in Kalauna took place about 1959. It was sponsored by Didiala, a big-man of Lulauvile, the 'food-bringing' clan which claims – like Tabalu in Kiriwina – special rank by virtue of its control of crop and weather magic (see Young 1971:62–4). The Lulauvile leaders had recently averted a famine by a performance of manumanua ritual (*ibid*:174–7). Didiala's aim as a 'guardian of the crops' was to tour the island and 'inspect' the state of revived prosperity – though needless to say, Lulauvile's tenuous hegemony in Kalauna is not acknowledged anywhere else. But there was another excuse for going to 'dance around the island', as Didiala refered to his manuamadumadu: his sons had brought back a couple of foreign drums from their working trips to Port Moresby. They had purchased them – one a Rigo and the other a Mekeo drum – for their new 'sounds', which they wanted to introduce to Goodenough Island along with the songs, dances and decorations which went with them. Didiala's intention was to patent them for his group and use them to 'ask for food' (*au'a veveola*). Accordingly, a large group of men, women and children (amounting to about half the community) visited almost a dozen districts in as many days, walking as far as Utalo on the western side of the island before returning by the same route. Sickness struck the party during the first week and many returned home, fearful of sorcery. Even Didiala was stricken in Utalo, which induced him to lead the remnants of his expedition back home. The sickness was blamed on the envy of one of the other Lulauvile leaders, who had allegedly doctored the feather in his hair with sorcery. As it bobbed in the breeze it spread the contagion. The expedition was nonetheless a modest success. The party had been given several pigs, a great deal of raw food, mats, pots and other utilitarian goods. These were all Didiala's (and his clan segment's) niune, and they were distributed by his fofofo among themselves and other members of the expedition.

I should note in passing that unlike the overseas kula expedition, manuamadumadu is constitutionally designed, as it were, to minimize internal competition between members of the party. Away from home, the kula canoes compete with one another for valuables, and on each canoe it is every man for himself (e.g. see Fortune 1963:210). The Kalauna manuamadumadu party, on the other hand, has an organic

406

solidarity and singleness of purpose owing to the basic rule of niune and the threefold status composition of the party. Jealousies may arise within the inuba, however, and one leader may resent the prestige accruing to another; hence, as we have seen, the attribution of misfortunes to a sorcerer of the inuba group. But his motive was believed to be sabotage, the spiteful disruption of the enterprise – not the desire to win gifts for himself. Niune is a hedge against avarice; one gets it only to give it to others.

I could give several other examples of manuamadumadu: ones undertaken for more frivolous reasons; ones undertaken to brave the ceremonial hostility of a village under mourning taboos (cf. Malinowski 1922: 346–7 and Fortune 1963:198); ones which returned with a paucity of niune and ones which provoked the fervour of abutu. But the systemic aspects of manuamadumadu gift exchange should by now be fairly clear. Unlike festivals which interlock through the complex network of debts and credits which they sustain, manuamadumadu expeditions have only minimal long-term economic significance. Ideally, the festival cycle is open-ended and never-ending, for the claims of reciprocity are forever being reversed and renewed. In reality, the cycle may falter and lie fallow for long periods, but it can always be revived by the promptings of creditors and fofofo, and when a festival is under way the boost to local production is immense. Manuamadumadu, on the other hand, involves a one-to-one balanced exchange, delayed rather than simultaneous, which when completed cancels the relationship established by the initiating expedition. Cycles, circuits, long-term reciprocities provisioned by surpluses created by forward planning, are not thereby generated. Once niune has been repaid the transient political alliance formed through the initial prestation lapses, and it is unlikely to be renewed for many years, if only because the communities are victims of the lethargy of distance.

The ethos of 'asking for food'

In conclusion, I wish to comment generally upon gift exchange-behaviour in Goodenough. Malinowski recorded, somewhat inadequately, the 'customary behaviour' of kula transactors, noting that, for example:

The etiquette of the transaction requires that the gift should be given in an off-hand, abrupt, almost angry manner, and received with equivalent nochalance [*sic*] and disdain (1922:352).

He then adduced elementary psychological universals to account for the 'reluctance' to receive and the 'histrionic anger' of the donor, both of which he saw as exaggerated, but nonetheless direct, expressions of

Michael W. Young

'natural human' sentiments. He thereby missed the opportunity of viewing them as ceremonial, even symbolic, expressions of complex political
relations; and had he grasped their importance as *styles* of giving and
receiving, he might have remarked upon the singular importance of
deception, masking of intention, dissimulation and other forms of (in
Mauss' phrase) 'social pretence'.

In Goodenough, as in Kiriwina, there are 'customary behaviours'
associated with the conduct of gift exchange, and although I cannot deal
with them here in any detail, to omit them altogether would be to miss
much of the action. For illustration, I will focus on the soliciting behaviour for niune I have had cause to mention frequently throughout the
chapter, namely 'asking for food' (au'a veveola).

First of all it is obvious that Goodenough Islanders do not 'ask for food'
unless they have a surplus on hand. Hungry people in these societies do
not solicit food, and to ask for it ceremonially is a declaration of confidence in one's ability to repay it with interest. Second, it is also obvious
that to 'ask for food' has aggressive overtones, most of all when traditional enemies are being challenged to an abutu contest. Despite the
folk-model analogy, 'asking for food' is a rather different proposition
from asking for a fight, though we must remark upon the similarities. The
'aggressors' simulate a war-party in dress, paint and demeanour when
they visit another village to ask for food. Hornbill feathers, for example,
which men wear in their hair, signify that the wearers have hostile intent
and are prepared for battle – in this case a fight with food. The feathers
are said to 'ask for food' themselves; they are signs with performative
force. There are other martial parallels in the preparatory magic commonly used. In the past, war magic was made to alter the state of
consciousness of the warriors: to make them courageous, reckless and
'fighting mad'. Other magic was used to alter the states of mind of the
enemy: to make them timid, fearful and weak. Today, analogous spells
are sung to strengthen the resolve of the party asking for abutu, to enable
them to 'talk hard', persuasively and irresistably, thereby 'forcing' the
enemy to be reckless and lavish in giving. Reciprocally, other spells are
designed to alter the mood of the enemy, to make them receptive to the
challengers' request (cf. Malinowski's account of kula magic, especially
the 'magic of persuasion', 1922:347–9). In addition to these psychological
or affective coercive magical techniques (the efficacy of which appears to
derive from belief in them), there are rhetorical stratagems. The man
who is asking for food in an enemy village must be prepared to woo by
flattery, wheedle, bluff, plead, beg, incite, and even weep with anguish.
He can try virtually any trick of persuasion except direct insult, for it is the
conventional prerogative of the hosts to abuse their visitors. Not being on

408

home ground, the visitor would be risking violence to himself and his party if his rhetoric carried him too far into calumny and invective. He must observe a certain tact, therefore, in inciting some anger but not too much. Nor can he outrightly *demand* food, for it naturally lies within the power of the enemy to refuse it where no obligations are due (i.e. where there are no previous debts, and where there is the absence of a delict for which abutu can be sought as a redress). As we have seen, a tactic commonly employed by the challenging party is to make a demand by proxy, as in the sign of the hornbill feather. Other kinds of objects (a spear, a skull, a stone) can be displayed or presented to the enemy; they mutely ask for food like the vebiyala objects shown off in manuamadu-madu. In one case I witnessed, a miniature model of a food-container was silently presented by the challenging fofofo to his opposite number. As it happened, the latter refused to accept it, signifying his refusal to engage in abutu. Much of the rhetorical discussion on this occasion was about the model itself, which metonymically stood for the niune which one side hoped to receive and the other was determined not to give. Functionally, of course, such displacement in discourse enables the parties to keep cooler heads and to exercise their tact strategically. But it is also charac-teristic of the more general practice of dissimulation, and is figurative of the very ethos of power relations in Kalauna.

In comprehending gift-giving behaviour, one has to read between the signs. There are interpretative problems of bodily signs, for example, which have conventional significations yet may be negotiable like the rest. *Sefaiya*, the stylized war-prance performed by an 'angry' donor who wields his yam as if it were a weapon (.Young 1971:198), is appropriate to certain situations and between certain parties. It fits the situation of food-potlatching and surrogate warfare in which yams are indeed weapons; but it is an expression and not a cause of it. Being a conven-tional simulacrum of an agonistic mood (described by clenching teeth, a rigid neck, trembling arms etc.), it can be as ironic, as feigned, as theatric-al – or as 'real' – as the performer wishes. Like the wink or the slammed door, its 'meaning' is not at all self-evident, and everything depends upon the intention of the actor and the context of his performance.

The consciously assumed masks and dissimulations which would dis-guise not only self-interest but the source of power, present problems of interpretation even for those living intimately under their sway. Any Kalauna man who took at face value the speech and acts of others would soon be a baffled loser. Under such conditions of pretence, the standard-ized emotions (anger, shame, resentment, sympathy, etc.) which are said to be expressed by gifts of food cannot be taken literally, for emotions, too, can be negotiated, framed and displayed. All this being so, it is quite appropriate – one could almost say 'it follows' – that messages should be externalized, made factual, objective, and hence less ambiguous, as when natural or manufactured objects are made to 'ask for' on behalf of their human manipulators. And having projected their projects into inanimate things which mediate, which 'ask for' the food of an enemy, for instance, the manipulators appear to believe that they have increased the force of their message, made irresistable and univocal, a coercive energy in itself – like a magic spell. At the same time, being externalized in an object, the request absorbs responsibility from its manipulators. This deflection removes some of the onus in the case of an unsatisfactory response.

Goodenough culture appears to encourage a regress of masking and mediation. The gift of niune mediates between strangers or enemies; but they only engage through the mediation of their respective exchange partners (fofofo), who for their part dissemble by employing mediating objects which 'ask' on their behalf. Meanwhile, the principals, the kaiwabu, stay out of sight or sit stonily silent, affecting total uninvolvement. One wonders if this deviousness and evasion are symptoms of some terror of violence? Hardly; but one cannot resist the reflection that for a people who once killed and ate one another with a fair degree of regularity, the present-day insulations against direct, hostile confrontation are impressively reinforced.

Notes

1 Field-trips to Goodenough in 1966–8 and 1977 were sponsored by the Australian National University, and in 1973 by the S.S.R.C. and the Smuts Memorial Fund of Cambridge University.
2 See Jenness & Ballantyne 1920:34–6, for a summary of Goodenough trading relations with neighbouring areas in the past, and for some speculations on the 'comparative isolation' of the northern D'Entrecasteaux.
3 A detailed account of competitive food exchange in Kalauna is presented in Young 1971.
4 In many parts of Goodenough, all or any of these three major forms of exchange may be linked with mortuary exchanges also, but I cannot dwell on this aspect here.

17 Wealth and exchange among the Molima of Fergusson Island

ANN CHOWNING

Introduction

In 1957, when I first visited the Molima (Morima) of the south coast of
Fergusson Island,[1] they numbered around 1,400, living in small hamlets
scattered from the seashore up into the foothills of the mountains that
separate them from their closest relatives, the inhabitants of Salakahadi
(or 'Ebadidi) in the central plain of the island. They had been pacified and
converted to Christianity in the 1920s; only the oldest had tasted human
flesh. Salakahadi had been somewhat more conservative. Molima and
Salakahadi are very similar linguistically, and these two regard themselves as sharing several culture traits that distinguish them from their
neighbours, such as the participation of women in warfare and their
principal mortuary ritual, the *dayo*. The languages belong to the same
sub-group of Austronesian as those to the east, usually grouped together
as Dobuan, and are much less closely related to the languages spoken to
the west, in Kukuya and on Goodenough (see Lithgow 1976:458–61).
Nevertheless, there is little justification for Jenness and Ballantyne's
statement (1920:135) that Molima 'belongs culturally to the southern
D'Entrecasteaux', in contrast with their western neighbours, the Kukuya.
Although the Molima lack the peculiar Goodenough traits of 'agnatic
ideology, a puritanical attitude towards sex, absence of belief in female
witches and relatively undeveloped trade relations' (Young 1971:6), they
also lack some of the best-known Dobuan traits, as described in Fortune
1932, including matrilineality (but see Chowning 1962), male sorcerers,
and participation in the *kula*. Certainly the Molima seem to resemble
societies in the western part of Fergusson as much as those in the east –
not surprisingly, given that in the period prior to the imposition of
Australian rule, friendly relations with speakers of Dobuan dialects
extended no farther than the small population called Nade, immediately
to the east of Molima. Other Dobuan speakers were met only in cannibal-

411

istic raids, though the close linguistic resemblances between Molima and Dobuan suggest that this permanent state of hostility was relatively recent.

With pacification, the situation altered completely; the Dobuan dialect learned by the first missionaries is used in schools as well as church (formerly Methodist, now United Church), and the Molima lexicon has been greatly affected by Dobuan. Nevertheless, it must be remembered that Molima words often differ somewhat in meaning from their cognates in Dobuan, and still more from their cognates in other Massim languages. Where these differences seem likely to cause confusion, they will be noted.

In many ways, Molima attitudes towards wealth, and uses of it, fit into general Massim patterns. The overwhelming importance of mortuary ceremonies, though new to Goodenough (Young 1971:232), is amply attested for other regions. Many of the objects involved in exchange are similar or identical, though the Molima seem to have lacked ceremonial axe-blades while valuing enemy carcasses. Nor is the Molima association between wealth and prestige or leadership as distinctive as it might seem at first glance; the association holds through most of the Massim as in most of the rest of Melanesia. A few apparently peculiar features of Molima culture may well occur elsewhere in the Massim, but because they have not been reported, and because they may help account for the differences between the Molima and some better-known Massim socieities, they will be mentioned here. The first is an absence of unilinear descent groups, coupled with a preference for marrying a fairly close consanguineal kinsman (no closer than second or, in some families,[2] third cousins). A result is to mute the rivalry between descent groups (which in Molima are cognatic) and affines that is so conspicuous elsewhere; in Molima, each of a pair of brothers may act on opposing sides in affinal exchanges, being equally related to both spouses. (For fuller information, see Chowning 1962.)

A second distinction is the absence of male sorcery, in the narrow sense of malevolent magic designed to injure or kill another. (Protective spells which punish thieves are performed publicly and considered legitimate.) Malevolent magic does exist, to bring bad luck to traders or attract pigs to a garden, so that the successful man is threatened by envy, but not to the extent of fearing for his life (contrast Young 1971:111–12). In Molima, killing is performed by female witches, while men are curers, but witches usually choose their victims for other reasons than envy (see Chowning 1959). Access to positions of leadership is not uncontrolled, however; the position should be hereditary, and a would-be leader who tries to make his name without having been trained by a father, uncle, or grandfather is subjected to ridicule and is unlikely to gain much of a following.

Finally, in contrast to the common pattern elsewhere in the Massim, most exchanges of valuables are of like against like, with an emphasis on exact matching, whether the objects are armshells or a witch's victim who is chosen because he is the same size as the shade of the corpse which another witch had given her to eat. Exchanges of identical valuables are found elsewhere in Melanesia (see, e.g., Chowning 1974:158), but in this particular region they seem noteworthy. Competitiveness, with the aim of enhancing one's reputation and embarrassing recipients, is expressed in prestations of vegetable food and pork, but even here an ultimate settling of all debts is the idea. Opportunities for obtaining scarce goods do exist, to be exploited by the needy and the ambitious, but most of them are so enmeshed in the ceremonial exchanges that they will be discussed together.

The category of valuables

Property in Molima falls into a number of separate but occasionally overlapping categories. Although the discussion will focus on the items that may be called valuables, these can only be understood in relation to certain other goods and categories, particularly gardening land, vegetable foods, pigs, trading canoes, and small objects of everyday use. In its broadest sense the term *gwegwe*, 'things', encompasses all of these except land. More narrowly, however, it designates valuables, so that a person speaks of his portable wealth (that is, excluding pigs, fruit trees, land, and magical knowledge) as his gwegwe. (The term is probably cognate with Sabarl *gogomwai*.) In what follows, gwegwe will always have this latter meaning. A special verb, *pela*, is used for the giving of gwegwe in any transaction.

The type valuable, the most important and most common, always implied when no particular one is specified, is the armshell (*kiwali*). Large armshells are grouped in a special sub-category of prime valuables, *gwegwe matana*, together with long fine necklaces (*soulawa*), curved pig's tusks (*dona*), and the imitations made from the base of a Conus shell (*dona kao*). The principal remaining valuables, in addition to smaller armshells and shorter and cruder necklaces, are large Amphlett pots (*nukuna*), of a size used only for feasts; ornamental belts, especially those covered with rows of shell discs (*sapisapi*; the belts are called *kaipesi* or *kai pwesi*); decorated pearlshell pendants (*kalibwaga*); and bunches of cassowary feathers (*me'utu*). Minor components of the category are feathered headdresses and hair ornaments worn by dancers and warriors,

413

and lesser jewelry such as shell noseplugs and women's armbands. Smaller pots, used for everyday cooking or for taro pudding, are not included. Although all of the gwegwe are useful at least as ornaments, a number of other esteemed possessions do not seem to have been included; they may be bought, but do not figure in the transactions, such as marriage payments and compensation, which characterize gwegwe. Examples of excluded objects, all of which may be prized heirlooms, are weapons, which include finely carved clubs; a variety of decorative lime spatulae; drums; and the large lime pots carried by Big Men. When we compare the list with that of objects used in the kula region, the outstanding omission is the ornamental axe-blade. I never heard such a thing mentioned nor did I see anything of the sort among the wealth of leading *kaiwabu*[3], either that shown to me personally or that displayed at funerals. Decorated utilitarian axes, now with steel blades, may be carried as a badge by the sponsor of a major ceremony, but if non-utilitarian blades ever reached Molima, they do not seem to have become important.

All kiwali, soulawa, and nukuna have personal names. Names of the first two are attached to them when the Molima receive them, whereas the recipient of a large pot obtained through trade gives it a name of his choice which then remains with it. The meaning may be lost as the pot passes to new owners, as seems to be the usual case with names of kiwali and soulawa. I was told that other gwegwe do not have names, but in the spell that is sung as male dancers are adorned, the name of a specific dona is mentioned repeatedly, and it may be that dona were inadvertently omitted from the list. Personal names are also attached to canoes – always to the plank canoes used in overseas trade, and sometimes to simple dugouts as well. In some but not all cases, the name refers to the dead person to be commemorated by the canoe. The same is true, perhaps invariably, of the names given to the large limepots carried by Big Men as a badge of distinction. As far as I know, these are the only possessions to be named apart from domestic animals. I suspect that the names given canoes and limepots express different attitudes from those given gwegwe. The former, as sometimes happens with the name of a pig, honours the owner, referring to his situation and activities, especially in achieving renown. By contrast, the names given gwegwe single them out not just as members of a category set apart from those that include ordinary cooking pots and everyday jewelry, but mark them as individuals with identity separate from that of individual owners. Nowadays the name is often written in pencil on an armshell or scratched onto one of its pearlshell dangles.

I did not hear any suggestion that kiwali and soulawa are personified or assigned gender (nor did I ask). Armshells are worn equally often by men and women; soulawa only by women, and dona and dona kao by men. Both of these last two are badges of a Big Man, and not ordinarily worn by others. At major dances, however, each of the three male dancers who perform together displays a single mounted dona clenched between his teeth (though a white cowrie shell ornament may be substituted). The only other evidence of sexual association with gwegwe is a myth about a man who marries a star-woman whose eyelashes and skirt strands are composed of soulawa. Before ornaments are donned by dancers or traders, spells are recited over them as part of the whole complex of attraction magic, which at dances is directed both towards donors of food and members of the opposite sex. In theory, only male dancers, who are the visitors, should be practising magic, but many of the same spells are used for both sexes.

Obtaining gwegwe

Of the valuables, a substantial number are (or were) obtained by trade, but some were made locally. In the past, the Molima collected Conus shells in their own waters and manufactured armshells, while obtaining some from outsiders. They still collect and sell the whole shells to other Massim peoples, but say that now all their armshells originate in the Trobriands. I neglected to ask how local armshells differed from the Trobriand ones, as they were said to do. The kiwali now in use differ from at least some kula armshells in always being large enough to be worn, and in being adorned with beads, bits of pearlshell, and pandanus strips, rather than with *Ovum ovulum* shells.

Dona are thought by the Molima, along with the Kukuya and Nade (Duduwega 1975:25), to be the tusks of a mythical giant serpent who lived in a local cave and gave them to people who brought him offerings of food. I do not know whether dona kao and kalibwaga were manufactured locally, but suspect that the latter at least was, since I can find no mention of similar objects being used elsewhere. These usually circular pendants, decorated along the edges with beads, are worn (by female dancers) strung at the end of a soulawa. All of the disc-shaped beads, from soulawa to sapisapi, which are used to decorate many objects, come from outside Molima, although the Salakahadi people decorate woven armbands with large white discs (*kadakada*) which they manufacture from Nautilus shells given them by the Molima. In return, the Molima get from Salakahadi the black wild banana seeds (*botoboto* which are important decorative items throughout the Massim.

The remaining gwegwe were obtained from farther afield. Prior to pacification, major trading extended only in two directions, to the south and west. Nade, Salakahadi, and Kukuya were all part of the system of ceremonial exchange, but of these, only the Kukuya also served as a major source of trade items. No new goods came from Nade; the exchanges only involved food. As has just been noted, a few minor coastal and bush items passed between Molima and Salakahadi, and there were others, such as tortoiseshell earrings, coconuts, and saltwater-fish from Molima, and game and freshwater-fish from Salakahadi. None of these items was classed as gwegwe, and all were given in transactions phrased as gifts. Gwegwe passed between Molima and Salakahadi only in the form of mortuary payments (see below).

Formal exchange, including trade, is called 'une, a word cognate with Dobuan 'une or *kune*, and almost certainly with kula. The Molima distinguish the kula, with which they are now familiar, as '*une-tete*.) As a verb, 'une also refers to the distribution of food at mortuary feasts. Transactions are divided into sale or barter, *gimwane* or *samu*, in which the price is paid at once, and gift, *oboboma*, in which the return is delayed, often for years. Additionally, there are separate verbs for prestations of pigs and dogs, of raw yams, of gwegwe, and of minor items such as betelnut.

In the sense of trade, 'une includes both what Young calls ceremonial visiting and purchasing expeditions. Both bring back a similar range of goods, but the technique of obtaining these is quite different. Traditionally, the Molima undertook major expeditions in two directions – to the Wamira region of the New Guinea mainland, and to the west: Kukuya, Wagifa, and Goodenough. Kukuya is adjacent to Molima and can be reached on foot, so that transactions are not limited to periods of calm. Of the overseas trips, that to Wamira was the most hazardous. From New Guinea the Molima imported pots, cassowary feathers, and fibre belts; in exchange they gave obsidian from local sites, scented leaves from the bush, sago which they manufactured, and soulawa obtained by trade from the west. The Molima desire for pots reflects the value placed on boiled food; roast food is reserved for snacks, mourning, and taboos associated with the performance of magic. Although most of the pots that reached Molima were made in the Amphletts, the straight-sided New Guinea type was valued for the manufacture of taro pudding, *mona*, which is more easily stirred if there is no inturned rim. Mona is an essential ingredient for feasts and is also used for offerings to spirits. The cassowary feathers, tied into duster-like bundles, are sometimes worn as adornment and are always flourished in the hands during the more elaborate dances. Furthermore, curers use them to summon back bewitched bundles of personal leavings, which can then be disenchanted. The feathers were also included in the warrior's headdress. But the purpose of the voyage was not simply to obtain useful goods. As with the voyages to the west, the leader gained considerable prestige from making the trip; only a few men possessed the magical and practical expertise needed for manufacturing the canoe and completing the voyage, and these experts were said to have been the principal Big Men, kaiwabu,[3] within Molima. They were also the leaders in the trips to the west.

Most of the trips to Kukuya and to Wagifa were ceremonial, in contrast to the barter that was conducted with the comparative strangers of Goodenough itself. Much of Goodenough lay outside the area within which visiting was comparatively safe; within this century, Goodenough men attacked and ate members of a Molima trading expedition who had been their erstwhile trade partners (*gumagi*, a term that within Molima also means 'friend'). Ceremonial visiting differs from barter in that the travellers take nothing with them except their new or refurbished canoes. They are given foodstuffs, particularly yams, bananas, and live pigs, but also a variety both of utilitarian goods, such as small cooking pots and wooden dishes, and of valuables, notably armshells, dona, and soulawa. (For a more detailed account, see Chowning 1960).) Of these, only the food and perhaps the dona were of local origin; the remaining goods were obtained by the Kukuya directly or indirectly from the Amphletts, and many of them seem to have originated in the Trobriands.

In Goodenough, the Molima received the same objects, but by purchase. Above all, they sought pots, both nukuna and small ones, but might also buy dogs and pigs. Small pots were purchased for sago, often packed with dried fish; kiwali were more likely to be offered for large pots and pigs.

Stone for some axe blades was dug from the ground in Molima. In 1958 I saw a small blade, of the type still being used for manufacturing sago, given by a Kukuya man to a Molima visitor; Jenness and Ballantyne say (1920:35) that the Kukuya supplied 'stone adzes' of unstated origin to the mainland of New Guinea. If stones found within Molima were ever traded, I did not record the fact.

It will be noted that armshells moved in both directions as, less obviously, did pigs and dogs. The reason is twofold. First, as noted above,[4] armshells were manufactured in Molima as well as outside. Second, then as now, Molima–Kukuya relations depend on a precise matching of armshell against armshell. When a new Molima canoe visits Kukuya, several men are likely to receive armshells, which they cannot use or pass on until an equivalent has been found to give to the donor when he makes a return visit. The armshells are measured against each other to demonstrate their equivalence when the return, the 'cooked' payment, is made. (New debts are 'raw'.) Although trade partners are generally considered trustworthy, tales of unpaid debts involving loss of an armshell are common, and young men sometimes condemn their trustees for having wasted the patrimony of the former by unwise attempts to increase their own prestige by dispensing armshells. Nevertheless, it is interesting that the Molima regard their own system as less likely to result in loss than the kula.

In ceremonial visiting, many useful and valued goods are acquired, but except when they are the repayment of something previously given the host, the identity of these is totally unpredictable. How much is given depends to a great extent on the expedition leader's reputation as a kaiwabu (as well, he considers, as the magic performed by himself and the other members of the expedition and the taboos observed by those who remain behind in the village). In the speeches that accompany the gift-giving, the donors make much of the status of the recipient and rather more of their own, in being so generous. However successful ceremonial visiting may be, the same person may find it worthwhile to bring the same canoe back to the same region in order to obtain particular objects, such as more pots, by barter. The economic advantage of the Molima over some of their neighbours results from the higher rainfall, which allows more taro to be raised to supplement the more seasonal yams, and the sago swamps. Although Molima has in the past suffered droughts so bad that children were sold (to be eaten) in exchange for vegetables (cf. Jenness and Ballantyne 1920:32), it escaped the food shortages that afflicted other parts of the D'Entrecasteaux in 1957–8 (Young 1971:171–2). Furthermore, in the past, Molima was less dependent on external trade than were many other parts of the Massim; only stone axe-blades (probably)[5] and pots had to be obtained from outside the area. In view of what has been said about trade in pigs and dogs, it is worth mentioning that these, under the label of ne'une cannot be eaten by the trader lest his trade magic be invalidated, and were passed on to others.[6] All other objects could be kept, many being dispensed to the traders' female relatives, 'the women he looks after', who had observed onerous taboos during his absence. But so long as they had kiwali and dona, internal exchange could proceed satisfactorily without foreign valuables such as soulawa. Apart from pots, utilitarian objects manufactured abroad were also not essential; although the Molima admire the workmanship of Trobriand wooden bowls and lime spatulas, they carve adequate ones of their own. Undoubtedly a major motive for continuing overseas trade was the opportunity it offered a kaiwabu, actual or aspiring, to acquire or increase his personal prestige. The most esteemed kaiwabu was the successful trader, whose feats demanded such daring that he was typically the war leader as well ('une-savia ana kaiwabu'). When it was too difficult or dangerous to travel beyond Fergusson Island, the links with Kukuya maintained by delayed exchange made it possible to obtain exotic goods locally, since the Kukuya had access to a considerably wider range of foreign traders than did the Molima (see Jenness and Ballantyne 1920: 34–5). The particular link between ceremonial visiting and mortuary feasts will be discussed further below.

The uses of valuables

Gwegwe serve a wide variety of functions, the most mundane of which are to pay for other goods and services, and to provide compensation for an offence. Minor services, or those rendered to close kin, are repaid with food, usually including a pot of mona; participants in work bees, such as yam planting, are rewarded in the same way. An example of such a minor service is manufacture of a kiwali, the shell itself being supplied by the future owner. But major services such as carving end-boards for a canoe, or curing someone who lives at a distance, are paid for with gwegwe. As a duty to the community, its kaiwabu should personally hire and pay the weather magician who relieves a drought. Between close kin, major services such as continually providing game and fish for an elderly person may be paid for by passing on magical knowledge, but this should not go to outsiders, who would be compensated for the same services with gwegwe.

Payments in gwegwe made at marriage confer rights over the woman and, to a limited degree, over her children. It is said that if no gwegwe matana, usually a large armshell, has been paid for a women, her brothers can interfere when her husband beats her, but after that he 'bosses' her. Unless a marriage follows a formal engagement, which involves not only the payment of preliminary gwegwe but an extended period of bride-service, the handing over of valuables may be delayed for many years, and if the groom agrees to permanent uxorilocal residence, may be dispensed with altogether. But if gwegwe are not given during the life of the marriage, they should be paid when one of the spouses dies (see below). On the whole, the payment of gwegwe in marriage assumes less importance than the constant exchange of foodstuffs, *po'ala*,[7] between the families of the bride and the groom. It is considered improper for the parents of the couple to be directly involved in payments surrounding their marriage; they neither receive gwegwe nor consume po'ala. Some other kinsman of each spouse, occasionally a woman, assumes the re-sponsibility for 'bossing' the marriage. This is the one occasion on which Molima try to outdo and shame each other; the po'ala is delivered with much ostentation and semi-joking aggressiveness. The same foods – large

419

fish, turtles, wild game, and raw vegetables – are offered on each side, and the idea is for contributions to be balanced by the time the exchanges end with the death of one spouse. Unsettled debts, which also include the contributions of affines to mortuary ceremonies, sponsored by the deceased should be settled after he dies (see below).

In adopting a child, gwegwe are paid to the parents or parent, and the same is done when one parent wants to assume full rights over the child of a divorce. The adopter, however, expects to receive a share of any gwegwe paid at the child's marriage or funeral.

A major category of payments in gwegwe is called *guba*, which in some contexts can be translated as compensation. This includes the payments made to the close kin of each victim when blood feuds are settled. A person who kills another by accident or drives another to suicide can sometimes avert vengeance by paying guba. The term also applies to the payment given by a man to the wife he divorces, and the fine paid by a detected adulterer or thief, as well as to the compensation owed an affine in whose presence one breaks wind. Most commonly, however, the term is applied to two types of payments made at funerals. First, if an important person dies, his kin from other villages come to attack his co-residents, tacitly accusing them of neglect at the very least. The attack can be stopped or warded off if someone manages to slip armshells onto the arms of the attackers. These need not be repaid in any way; they are simply said to relieve the feelings of the bereaved. By contrast, the gwegwe given to less aggressive mourners who come from a distance, which are also called guba, obligate them to make a mortuary feast (*bwabwale*) for the dead at some later time.

At a funeral, gwegwe have other functions as well. First, if the dead person was married, the final payments are made at this time, the amount depending on how much has been given before. If a man had paid little for his wife, a large number of gwegwe should be handed over to her kin at the funeral. The husband's family puts the valuables on the body, and the wife's removes them. In the case of a dead man, the wife's family hangs gwegwe in front of the corpse while it is displayed to the mourners, and after the burial, designates them for members of the husband's family. Here the amount given depends on the state of indebtedness as regards both gwegwe and po'ala, though it seems to be general practice, though not always the expressed idea, for the man's side to pay more for a marriage than the women's.

Some of the gwegwe displayed at a funeral serve still different functions. Of those belonging to the dead person, some may either be buried with him or destroyed by his heirs as a sign of grief. At several funerals, I was told that the armshells on the corpse would be buried, but they were always removed; I did, however, see a dona kao worn by a kaiwabu buried with him, along with paper money and his carved cane, and paper money destroyed at another funeral. Also, a wealthy person, or a member of a wealthy family, even a small child, is singled out by having large amounts of gwegwe draped over and around the body. This action has an additional purpose. Beautiful in themselves, the gwegwe also beautify the wearer, helping restore him to his most glorious appearance during life. He is also bathed and shaved, rubbed with scented oil especially prepared, and painted with decorative designs. Ideally the accompanying spells for a man should include the love magic with which he won his wife. The result is to bring the onlookers to a full appreciation of what they have lost, increasing their grief but also leaving a fond memory of how the person looked at his best – an attitude hardly unfamiliar to Westerners. Malinowski (1922:512–13) lists various reasons why Trobrianders bring valuables to a dying person, some of which might apply here; that the Molima feel joy simply at the sight of gwegwe is indicated by their being briefly lent to a widow as she is released from the last of mourning, so that they can add to her pleasure. But the Molima do not assume that the spirit of the dead man is present while he is being adorned; on the contrary, it is ritually dispatched to the land of the dead, usually Lotuma, the Trobriand Tuma,[8] before the weeping begins 'lest tears flood the path' (to the embarking place at the western end of Fergusson). It is feared that a ghost who remains around the village would cause mischief.

Finally, the dirge sung by women who dance flourishing possessions of the deceased refers to him as a trader (*to'une*). The dirge is the same for everyone, containing as it does references to overseas voyages which are equated with the trip to Lotuma. At the funeral of a kaiwabu, however, specific trade magic songs are also sung by the men adorning him, and the possessions flourished are gwegwe rather then any memento of the dead, as at other funerals.

Mortuary ceremonies and exchanges

Very occasionally a death passes almost without notice, as when an old woman without close kin was discovered dead in her garden hut and simply buried. But in most cases death touches off a complex series of observances which are essentially the same regardless of the age and sex of the corpse. Nevertheless, a married man who is also a father tends to receive the fullest treatment (with special elaboration if he was a kaiwabu). I shall take such a case as the example, noting where variations may occur.

When the death becomes known, or is imminent, the knowledgeable kin collect to unravel their various connections to the dead man, so that they themselves can be divided into the two major categories of workers, *geyawuna*, and mourners, *valevaleta*. The basic distinction is that the principal link to geyawuna is through a woman; they are primarily the persons called *ova* (MB, ZC) during life. (If the corpse is a woman, however, her children would mourn her, just as she would mourn them, and the principal geyawuna are her ZC.) In many other Massim societies, the geyawuna, often called by a cognate term, are specifically members of the dead person's matrilineage, but in Molima the category does not normally include members of the dead person's generation, and does include, for example, the MF. (See Chowning 1962.) Although geyawuna can act as valevaleta, deciding to mourn for reasons to be described below, the opposite behaviour is not approved, and can be dangerous. A woman who does not mourn when she should is suspected of being a witch, and contact with close personal possessions of the dead, for anyone other than the geyawuna, is likely to make them sicken and die. If there is doubt about the category, a person should behave as valevaleta. Nevertheless, the closest kin of any description may help the geyawuna tend the body before the burial.

The specific duties of the geyawuna include helping the residents of the village adorn and set up the body for viewing, and preparing food and betelnut for mourners. A geyawuna then sends the soul of the dead person off, and formal mourning begins (though the closest kin are allowed to weep before this). The geyawuna tend the corpse, waving away flies and flexing the limbs; adorn it much more fully in preparation for burial; dig the grave; carry out various graveside rites such as passing on the dead person's names and checking for the cause of death; and bury it. Meanwhile most of the valevaleta remain behind, weeping and singing dirges. Contact with the corpse, and with the bones encountered in clearing out what are usually communal graves, is regarded as somewhat dangerous, and the geyawuna have to cleanse themselves carefully afterwards. They do not, however, observe the food taboos and other restrictions on ordinary activity which are imposed on the valevaleta. Throughout all the ceremonies that follow the burial, the geyawuna receive food from the valevaleta and in return lift taboos from the latter.

The property of the dead person is divided up at the funeral. Gardening land goes directly to his descendants (but see below). So do the gwegwe, which belong to his children. They also inherit an overseas canoe, but only after making a feast for the geyawuna, who can use it until then. Small fishing canoes, like all other close personal property, are in the category of *lulube*, to be taken by the geyawuna or destroyed (along with the house in which the person died). The geyawuna give the widow a minimum of cooking and eating equipment, and also provide her with food during the mourning period. The contents of her dead husband's garden and yamhouse are particularly taboo to her, and are not eaten by her children, but may be used by them for the mortuary feasts. For some years, until a special feast is made for the geyawuna, the children may not eat from any trees planted by the dead man; if the trees stand in the village in which he is buried, the taboo is permanent. Pigs are inherited by the children, who may share with the geyawuna; they are likely to use these pigs for mortuary feasts, but need not do so.

At the funeral, the sequence of mortuary feasts is decided. The most usual is the triple set called bwabwale. Mission pressure has eliminated the full mourning costume and lengthy incarceration for the surviving spouse, but otherwise bwabwale remain unchanged. At the first feast, the geyawuna are fed, remove from the valevaleta the taboo on eating any food but roasted vegetables, and, in the past, put on the valevaleta, the mourning costume the latter had prepared for themselves. At the second feast, everyone but the widow is released from mourning, and the third is for her release. She can remarry but should not return to her family until and unless a *sagali* (see below) is made. Much of the payment for her remarriage goes to the family of her former spouse.

An ambitious man sponsoring a bwabwale tends to make it large enough so that he can feed additional guests who are neither geyawuna nor valevaleta. If he is wealthy, he may also have to deal with the remote kinsman, possibly a member of the geyawuna, who decides to undertake the most arduous mourning with the aim of being paid in gwegwe, fruit trees, or garden land. If not adequately paid he may simply claim the goods, most unanswerably if he practiced the extreme form of mourning of the past, cutting off a finger joint. Furthermore, if bwabwale are not repaid within the descent group that jointly owns gardening land, the defaulter may be barred from his portion; the rights depend on carrying out this particular duty. That is, if A and B are 'brothers' and A made a bwabwale when B died, B's son must make one when A dies or lose the land rights that he shares with B's son.

Failing such a debt, putting on bwabwale is considered fairly onerous, not to be undertaken unless various kin agree to make the effort of providing all the feasts. (The geyawuna give them very small feasts in return for each one.) If no bwabwale is made, there are other ways of feeding the geyawuna and having the taboos lifted within a short time, the precise techniques varying from family to family. On the other hand, a would-be kaiwabu is not satisfied with the bwabwale, but will undertake a major mortuary ceremony, a sagali. There are various types of sagali, from the simplest, the *kwelipisali*, with no singing or dancing, to the most complex, the dayo. Any of these would only be sponsored by an actual or incipient kaiwabu, who enhances his own reputation while ostensibly honouring a dead kinsman, of either sex and any age. The type of sagali which depends on collecting foodstuffs by taking a new canoe on ceremonial visits to other communities has been described elsewhere (Chowning 1960). In the past, only a few men from coastal villages had the necessary expertise to be canoe-makers; most kaiwabu made other kinds of sagali.

The sponsor is called *tonisagali* or *tonibutu*, but the former term may also be applied to his co-residents. A sagali involves the co-operation of many people; often spoken of as a village affair, it may involve affines who shift residence to help. But on the whole, it operates as a type of po'ala, a series of exchanges between the village of the sponsor and those of his affines. The sponsor holds one feast to announce his plans, and another to allocate garden plots and to farm out pigs. When the pigs and the yams are mature, nightly dances begin, attended by the affines, who are fed and given quantities of raw food. In turn, they will bring decorated baskets of yams to fill the enormous yam-rack which is a feature of any sagali, being partly filled by the sponsor and his helpers, the close kin of the dead person. The delivery of yams by the affines gives them an opptunity for aggressive joking, both verbal and physical; it ends with a careful counting of the yams contributed by each side, with the difference noted as po'ala debt. Dancing follows: at a dayo, a complex dance by the women of the sponsor's group, followed by one or more, each with drummers and three male dancers, from the affines. Other sagali have similar male dancers but lack the complex female dance. At the end, cut-up pork and yams are distributed (with care not to return a group's own offerings) to the affines, especially the dancers; to the geyawuna; and to other guests. Putting on a successful sagali, which attracts so many yams that everyone is satisfied but some yams are 'left to rot', is the only way to become a true kaiwabu. Men who sponsor po'ala and bwabwale, but nothing more, are said to be just 'kaiwabu of the village', with a purely local reputation.

It might be thought that a tonisagali needs only ambition, hard work, one or two sows, and a knowledge of the etiquette of feasts and exchanges to achieve success. But if he does not also possess gwegwe, he can never take the first steps that would persuade many people to co-operate with him and work for him. When he is seen to be willing and able to excel in paying for marriages, exchanging goods with foreign visitors, dispensing guba and a variety of minor gifts such as the gwegwe given a woman at her first pregnancy, he has shown that those who help him put on the sagali are likely to receive their reward. The inheritance system gives the eldest son of a kaiwabu a great advantage, even if his father has not specifically singled him out as his replacement. Along with the requisite knowledge, much of which is magical, he receives control of gwegwe, pigs, and perhaps a trading canoe, and if he is old enough, can launch his real career with the arrangements made at his father's funeral.

Recent changes and the kula

In the period following pacification, the Molima and their neighbours extended trade more widely. Some Molima sailed directly to the Amphletts, and a few men even learned enough there to make pots of local clay when they returned home. Jobs in the pearling industry and visits by ship enabled men to acquire some Trobriand artifacts on the spot; soulawa are specifically mentioned. At the same time, the Molima stopped making canoes strong enough to reach New Guinea, but because the Kukuya kept up the New Guinea trade, and canoes from New Guinea came to the D'Entrecasteaux with greater frequency, pots and cassowary feathers from the mainland were still available.

The most interesting new development was trade with Dobuan speakers. Initially the Molima simply paid a variety of goods – canoes, pots, kiwali, and soulawa – for pigs. By the 1950s, however, the easternmost Molima census division, Fayayana (Paiaina), had been drawn into an extension of the kula.[9] I saw one transaction in 1958, with the Dobuans coming from the hills behind Bwaioa, and in 1975 was told that Fayayana was still the only part of Molima participating. The Molima are said to have agreed to Dobuan urgings on the grounds that the kula is an additional way of achieving status as a kaiwabu.[10] The Molima participants wear a special narrow jointed shell armband (*nima-pasapasa*), which they regard as a mark of a kaiwabu who is in the kula. As has been mentioned, most Molima say that the chances of losing one's valuables are too great in the kula, and they also deplore the inconvenience of having to obtain different kinds of valuables in different places. But some of the abstainers engage in other transactions which may feed into the kula; for example, one man said that he had sent a kiwali to Rogea with a friend, and expected to get a soulawa in return.

At the transaction which I saw, the Molima gave only kaipwesi, necklaces, and neck pendants, including not only dona but crescentic ornaments of tortoiseshell and pearlshell which were unfamiliar to me. Dangling over the shelter in which these were examined was an armshell too small to be worn, decorated with *Ovum ovulum* shells, unlike the usual Molima kiwali. The soulawa were examined with great care, felt and rolled between the hands; some strands were much more uniform than others. Their names were mentioned; one at least had it scratched onto a dangle. In the first transactions, phrased in Molima as *maisa*, 'payment', a woman carried a soulawa to the recipient. At the end, the women gave pots and skirts, described as oboboma, to the visitors; I was told that they expected in time to receive plaited mats and metal pots and dishes in return.

By 1975, other external ceremonial exchanges had greatly declined. With the building of a wharf in the 1960s, Molima had become much easier to reach by ship, and cash crops more worthwhile; the Local Government Council acquired its own ship shortly after my departure in 1975.[11] A trade store beside the wharf supplied a variety of goods; clay pots were almost never used for cooking everyday meals. Nukuna were still needed for feasts, but with a little borrowing, the local supply seemed adequate. Ceremonial visits had lost their practical functions, and almost no new large plank canoes were being built. The carving of end-boards seemed to have ceased; most canoes had plain wooden rectangles nailed to the ends. They were used to carry loads of food to sell at the government station at Mapamoiwa, but presumably trade magic played no part in these transactions. The new desire for cash was hardly unexpected; by this period, a man could hardly maintain his reputation without being able to buy a variety of manufactured goods and pay for an education for his children.

Nevertheless, the mortuary ceremonies and observances, and the affinal exchanges, continued virtually as before. Wreaths of chicken feathers often replaced the old feather headdress, and female dancers sometimes wore necklaces of plastic flowers, but the activities were traditional, and so were the reasons for holding them. As the Molima continue to marry outsiders and to spend increasing amounts of time travelling and working away from home, the old methods of gaining prestige, of ratifying marriages, and of honouring the dead may change radically, but two conservative forces exist: the recent acclaim given to traditional Molima dancing, especially the dayo, by outsiders, and the involvement of surrounding Massim societies in very similar sorts of activities. Unlike many people in Papua New Guinea, the Molima are not surrounded by people who look down on their way of life. The present trend to substitute cash for kiwali in payments will probably continue, but the reason may well be a high valuation of gwegwe, and a reluctance to part with them too readily, rather than depreciation.

Notes

1 Fieldwork in 1957–8 was financed by a National Science Foundation Post-doctoral Fellowship, and a brief return visit in 1974–5 was supported by a research grant from the University of Papua New Guinea.

2 The word 'family' is used by the Molima to translate *boda*, a term which includes various kinds of cognatic kin groups, from ego's personal kindred to the descendents of a single individual. See Chowning 1962.

3 In contrast to Goodenough practice (Young 1971:76), *kaiwabu* (Big Man) in Molima designates a permanent position. See also Seligman 1910:744.

4 In what follows, the present tense will be used for situations still obtaining in 1957–8, and the past for those that changed after pacification.

5 Molima supplies from stones equated with thunderbolts were presumably scanty.

6 Molima attitudes and terminology are a transformation and partial inversion of those on Goodenough. In Molima, as in Dobu, *nibai* means cross-cousin rather than enemy, and although the FZS has rights over the MBS, who tends to turn over to the FZS pigs received in trade as well as catches of large game, the FZS often uses the gift for the donor's *po'ala* (Chowning 1962:97). Often the cross-cousins are on the same side in other exchanges. When a pot of food is given to someone with the statement, 'Your ne'une', it simply means that the donor received it in trade; the recipient can and does eat it. Cf. Young 1971:69–74.

7 In Molima, po'ala refers only to exchanges of food between affines.

8 The Molima have three lands of the dead, the others being Bwebweso on Normanby and a place in the interior of Fergusson. Village location and history tend to affect ideas about where the dead go, but in the songs and spells at one funeral, I heard all three mentioned.

9 The second word in the Molima term for the kula, 'une-tete', may derive from a verb meaning 'to walk along a ridge, branch, log bridge'. A Molima informant familiar with the northern part of the kula described armshells and necklaces as 'fighting', while a Dobuan simply illustrated the process with a circling motion of his hands.

10 The Molima equate kaiwabu with the Dobuan *esaesa*, defined as 'wealthy man' (Grant, 1953:70).

11 In 1958, problems of transport along the rugged Molima coast made copra production something of a waste of time. The wharf has made a great difference, and a number of new cash crops are now being grown.

1 Master carver, village leader, and kula transactor Narubutau using a steel-tipped adze to make a prowboard in Yalumgwa village in northeastern Kiriwina. 1974. Photo J. Leach.

2 Pandanus sail under construction in Okaiboma village in northern Kiriwina. 1972. Photo J. Leach.

3 Government trawler carrying a contingent of kula men from northern
Kiriwina to Kitava. Trawler kula alters the timing and pace of
expeditions. 1973. Photo J. Leach.

4 Two Woodlark Islanders with kula necklaces returning from
exchanges on Kitava and shopping on Kiriwina. They will reconnoitre
the islands west of Woodlark on the way home. 1973. Photo J. Leach.

5 The famous mwari Nanoula. This shell was mentioned by Malinowski in 1922 (p. 504). At the time of my fieldwork it was kula'd to the Vakuta district. Its fame continues to accumulate. Photo S. Campbell.

6 Armshell of unique form, recently discovered buried on Nuratu Island near Kitava and now circulating in the kula. The full cone is used; there is a slit below the crown; wave-like engravings and red paint are on the surface. Possibly an earlier kula valuable. Photo J. Leach.

7 Roboti of Giribwa village, who succeeded in acquiring Nanoula, shown here wearing Nanoula (armshell) and the necklace Kasanai, given to Roboti by a Dobuan in an attempt to lure Nanoula. Photo S. Campbell.

8 Vakutan men discussing their hard-won acquisition of armshells. They are returning from Kitava and have stopped on a beach to rest before finishing their journey. Photo S. Campbell.

9 A man brings ashore betel after one of the frequent casual trips Gawans make to northern Woodlark. On such trips a few armshells are also generally acquired, though the trips are not specifically kula voyages. Photo N. Munn.

10 Prow of a Gawan canoe beached on northern Kiriwina. 1973. Photo J. Leach.

11 Group of Kiriwinan kula-men enter single-file and silent into the street-structured village of Kumwagea on Kitava. 1973. Photo J. Leach.

12 Counting the valuables. After the *bagi*, axeblades and ceremonial limesticks are presented, those who 'eat the feast' line them up on a mat or on women's skirts (also presented) and count them publicly. Grass Island village. October 1978. Photo M. Lepowsky.

13 Grass Islanders demonstrate *bagi*-making techniques. The *bagi* shells are visible behind the wood and bush-cord rotary drill. The rough necklace will later be ground on a grindstone. Grass Island village. October 1978. Photo M. Lepowsky.

14 Men on Rossel display two very long *bagi* necklaces made there. Photo S. Berde.

15 These Yelans discuss the distribution of food to the contributors of kö in a bridewealth instalment. The kö discs are strung together in a 'rope'. The contributors of valuables in these payments are rewarded with food in proportion to the degree of their involvement. Photo J. Liep.

16 On Yela, the standard unit of ndap payment is a set of ten (ndapti). At the redistribution after a pig-feast, associates of the pig-owner here get one ndapti and two kö each. The ndap are of progressing rank from left to right in each row. Photo J. Liep.

PART VI

Southeastern Massim area

18 The impact of colonialism on the economy of Panaeati[1]

STUART BERDE

This paper examines the system of exchange of the Panaeati, an island people located in the Louisiade Archipelago in southeast Papua New Guinea. First, I discuss the early times when the islanders raided their neighbors. Next, I discuss the period of time after pacification when the Wesleyan missionaries were the strongest outside influence on the Panaeati. Finally, I discuss the contemporary era when the islanders have had to accommodate their system of exchange to the requirements of the local government council. Throughout the paper I refer to the *kula* and compare it to the system of exchange on Panaeati.

Located approximately 200 miles from the eastern tip of the mainland, Panaeati is a coral-filled island built on the remains of an ancient volcanic range. The island is five miles long and three miles across at its widest point. The population is about 1,000 people. The most outstanding resource of the island is a thick forest where a hardwood species grows which is excellent for building canoes. In the Louisiade Archipelago, these trees (*Callophyllum inophylum*) are found only on Panaeati and the people have taken advantage of this fact to become expert canoe-builders and traders.

The Panaeati divide their history into three historical periods and canoe trading has been conducted somewhat differently in each of the periods. In the first era, the era of raiding, the islanders were afraid to trade their canoes to outsiders because these enemies would use the canoes to raid Panaeati. Therefore, the Panaeati traded canoes only to their allies. In the second era, when the British Government brought peace to the region in the late 1880s, the extent of canoe trading increased to include all of the islanders in the Louisiade Archipelago. Finally, when the Australian Administration introduced a system of local government councils in the Archipelago in the middle 1950s, the pattern of trading changed again. The government encouraged the islanders to stay home and work on community projects instead of sailing and trading. As a

431

result, the Panaeati began to limit the amount of time that they spent away from their home. I now examine the Panaeati economy in more detail, beginning with the economy in the era of raiding, which I call the early times.

In the early times, there were three major residential divisions on Panaeati which often raided each other. The raids were led by fighting leaders called *asiara*, men who were known for their courage and their ability to withstand pain. Each division had several fighting leaders. Their power and strength came from magic, given to them by special female 'witches' called *misinana*. Besides the witches, other women played a special role in fighting, for they could stop violence by waving the outer layer of their grass skirts.

Hostility was a major factor which restricted the amount of produce which a married couple obtained from their gardens in the early times because a couple could not easily obtain labor cooperation from others. Women have always done most of the garden work on Panaeati. For protection in the early times, the women were accompanied to the gardens by their husbands. The usual pattern was for a married couple to plant one garden each year. These single gardens were separated by areas of bush. The produce from one garden supported the subsistence as well as the ceremonial requirements of a couple. However, planting one garden presented a problem to the early Panaeati.

The problem was that a couple could not tell whether they would have a successful harvest each year. The uncertainty came from the fact that they had to plant their garden in one type of soil and they had no way of knowing whether that specific type of soil would respond well to the amount of moisture which accumulated during the year. There are four types of soil on Panaeati and each varies in drainage quality. People tried to plant in soils which *usually* drained well because this was the requirement for growing yams, the most important crop. However, with an erratic annual rainfall, people could never be sure whether they had made the correct choice of soil. The only way to improve the gardening situation would have been to plant several gardens annually in different types of soil, taking advantage of all the possibilities. This is what people do today, but in earlier times poor mobility and poor labor cooperation forced people to plant only one garden.

Along with poor mobility and poor labor cooperation, gardeners in the early times were also limited by stone axes. These axes were imported from Woodlark Island and they served as ceremonial valuables as well as utility items for clearing gardens and building fences.

While people at times did cooperate with each other when they cleared new gardens, informants stated that couples could not count on this help, causing them to rely mostly on their own labor. One aspect of gardening where cooperation has always been critical is repairing fences which have been damaged by wild pigs. If the fences are not repaired quickly an entire garden can be lost to the pigs. In the early times, disasters such as these were common.

After the gardens were cleared and burned in September, people planted their yams in October. The yams matured in April, supplying the islanders with produce to give to canoe workers and to people attending mortuary ceremonies.

The period of time just before the yams apppeared was a 'hungry period', called *hoalu*. To help them during the hoalu today the Panaeati import sago from the richer islands such as Misima, Motorina and Sudest. However, people could not have done this so easily in the early times because it was unsafe to visit foreign villages and trade. The early Panaeati did utilize their own limited sago supply during the hoalu and they also planted taro and sweet potatoes early so they would be mature during the hoalu months. Wild fruits and nuts also provided relief during the hungry period.

Poor labor cooperation and the problems of walking safely to the gardens limited the harvests of the entire population. The men on Panaeati who were exceptionally active in the system of exchange, the 'big men' (*guiau* [*guyau*]), thus faced the same agricultural problems as the rest of the people. The guiau, however, had more food to distribute because they were polygamous. In exchange for advice and trade items, the families of the wives of the guiau gave them garden produce. By distributing this food and by lending valuables and pigs, the *guiau* controlled the system of exchange in the early times.

Some of the extra food which the guiau accumulated was distributed to men who built canoes for the guiau. Building canoes was difficult for men with only one spouse because they could not so easily accumulate surplus food and people would not work unless food was provided. Canoes have always been associated with the generosity of the builders. Builders in the past and today are required by custom to distribute pork at the larger canoe-work parties. Most of the canoes in the early times were built for the in-laws of the builders because the Panaeati were hesitant to give canoes to outsiders who could use them to raid Panaeati.

While all trade in the early times was affected by fear of physical attack and fear of sorcery, the Panaeati were not isolated. While they were fairly self-sufficient in garden and marine resources, occasionally they imported food and betel ingredients. These trading ties with outsiders were also important for establishing allies who joined together to raid mutual enemies.

Raiding and trading went together in the early times. Big men wanted to obtain the skulls of foreign victims who were members of the same clans as the deceased who were close to the big men. When someone was killed in a raid the big men asked friends to obtain skulls as recompense. In exchange for the skulls, the big men gave pigs, axeblades, wooden bowls, food and a variety of other items. After the exchange, the skulls were shattered and the pieces were swept away, symbolizing the end of the big men's grief.

The fear and suspicion which dominated trade and all activities in the early times ended with the arrival of British Government under the direction of Sir William MacGregor in the late 1880s and with the subsequent arrival of the Wesleyan missionaries under the direction of the Reverend William Bromilow in 1891. When they recount their history, the Panaeati group these two events together, wrongly crediting the missionaries with pacification. While it is difficult for us today to separate the impact of the government personnel from the impact of the missionaries on the economy of the Panaeati, it is safe to say that the arrival of the government forces brought about a condition of peace which had a great impact on the economy, and the arrival of the missionaries furthered the same process. These changes occurred in the system of gardening and in the extent of trading and ceremonialism.

After pacification, safe mobility and cooperation made it easier for people to work more gardens per household. If a garden in one soil-type failed, then one in another soil-type might be successful. The pattern of gardening changed with the improvements in labor cooperation. Instead of couples making isolated gardens, they gardened together in large fenced-in blocks in which each couple had a separate garden. The advantage of this pattern was that people shared the responsibility for clearing and repairing the fences.

The new pattern improved the security of the harvest for all people. For monogamous couples, the impact of these changes was that they, along with the guiau and their wives, had food to give to canoe workers and to people attending mortuary ceremonies. Hence pacification allowed more people to participate actively in the system of exchange and obtain public recognition for their efforts than was the case in the early times.[2]

The food security was also improved by the introduction of new crops, brought to Panaeati by the Polynesian teachers who accompanied the white ministers. These crops were helpful supplements during the hoalu period of the year when food was in short supply. Similar introductions have been reported for the Trobriand islands and for other parts of Melanesia.[3]

The impact of colonialism on the economy of Panaeati

During the early years of pacification, steel tools began to replace stone ones, making clearing bush and building garden fences much easier. With steel tools and with better cooperation, people quickly repaired their fences and saved their gardens from wild pigs.

The increase in food that resulted from the improvements in agriculture on Panaeati had the effect of increasing the frequency and size of public gatherings, such as canoe work parties and mortuary ceremonies. This increase symbolizes the early colonial era (which they call 'the mission period' (*topwololo ana sauga*)) for the Panaeati. It was a period of time when men sailed to other islands to attend ceremonies and to trade. On these trips, some men married local women. Because in-laws have always been required by custom to continuously exchange goods, marriages led to interfamily alliances. This was a great improvement from the situation in the early times when people had few contacts on other islands and were afraid to visit most foreign villages. Today, the Panaeati refer to the mission period as a time when family ties spread throughout the region. When they visited their in-laws, the early Panaeati also met new friends with whom they traded. One man from the pottery-producing island of Brooker, near Panaeati, told me the following story about how he met a new trade friend.

Robert sailed to Sudest and was looking for things for his *soi* ('mortuary ceremony'). He landed at Griffen Point, Sudest Island with three canoes filled with one hundred pots. He had heard of Daniel but had not met him yet. He went up to the house of Daniel and told him that there were pots available. He gave Daniel all of the pots, which were distributed among Daniel's people. Daniel left with a large pig and plenty of sago . . . During the war years, Brooker invaded Sudest and took a girl back with them. This girl was raised on Brooker and gave birth to a male child. Robert is the son of this man while Daniel is the sister's son of the original (abducted) girl. When the two of them (Daniel and Robert) began to talk to each other, Robert told him that they had this relationship in common. Thus in exchanges between the two of them, they never mention the return.

The traditional trade items, such as pigs, axeblades and wooden bowls from Misima Island, remained important after pacification. The red shell necklaces, called *bagi* by the Panaeati and famous for their part in the kula exchanges increased in importance after pacification. Before this period of time bagi trading was mostly done by the Rossel and the Sudest, who live in the eastern end of the Louisiade Archipelago, and only a few bagi were traded westward to Panaeati. My informants' statement that only a few bagi were traded out of the Rossel and Sudest region in early times has an important implication for our understanding of the historical dimension of the kula.

Malinowski states that the necklaces used in the kula were from the

435

Sudest and Rossel area, not from Sinaketa in the Trobriands.[4] However, he was describing the situation as he saw it after European contact, not the precolonial situation. If my informants' statements are correct, we must assume that most of the bagi circulated in the kula in the early times were bagi from Sinaketa. Malinowski recorded the result of the introduction of bagi from the eastern end of the Louisiade Archipelago in colonial times. The increase in the amount of bagi in the kula was due to two factors: First, European traders paid Rossel and Sudest craftsmen to manufacture bagi for trade with the local people, increasing the total amount of bagi. Second, peaceful trade relations allowed more people in the Louisiade Archipelago to trade bagi westward to the Wari who passed the bagi to the kula participants. The introduction of more bagi together with safe travel conditions had the effect of allowing more people than ever before to take part in trading in the Louisiade Archipelago. This must also have been the case in the active kula region. However, Malinowski does not mention an increase in participation in the kula after pacification.[5]

Malinowski was not theoretically prepared to include history in his account of the kula. As a result, he presented an idealized pattern, leaving out certain historical details, such as the introduction of large numbers of valuables. He was nostalgic for a period untouched by European contact. Part of this nostalgia came from the fact that Malinowski's close friend the Chief of Omarakana was losing his strong position to the Chief of Sinaketa who was closer to the European source of bagi. It is fair to hypothesize that the kula positions of the Chief of Omarakana and the Chief of Sinaketa increased after pacification because the introduction of more bagi made it possible for more of their men to take part in the exchanges. The position of the Chief of Omarakana subsequently decreased from the competition from the Sinekata who were able to obtain even more bagi because they were pearlers and the traders gave the bagi in exchange for the pearls.[6]

The islands in the Louisiade Archipelago never exchanged bagi among themselves according to the rules of the kula. During the mission era (and today) the Panaeati and their neighbors borrowed bagi to give to someone as part of mortuary exchanges or as part of canoe exchanges. A debt of a bagi can be cleared by presenting a bagi of equal size and color-quality. It can also be cleared by giving the lender a pig or an axeblade. Unlike the kula participants, these islanders do not exchange bagi for armshells (*mwali*). However, the islanders in the Louisiade Archipelago did give bagi and mwali to kula traders who have come into the region looking for these items since pacification.[7] The peoples of the Louisiade present the items to these outsiders according to the local trading rules.

The impact of colonialism on the economy of Panaeati

The Panaeati told me that when they gave mwali to Woodlark visitors they did not know what the Woodlark did with them when they returned to their homes. One man from Brooker Island told me: 'We just do not know how to work with the mwali.'

Despite the fact that the Panaeati trade mwali to the Woodlark and also trade bagi to the Wari and the Tubetube, living east of Panaeati, the Panaeati do not consider themselves part of the kula trading system. The important point to them is that they have always exchanged valuables according to a different system of rules than the system used by the kula peoples.

The rules of trading which the Panaeati past and present know best involve trading canoes for pigs, valuables and food. The items they receive in exchange for the canoes are distributed at mortuary ceremonies.

Looking for trade partners with whom they could begin protracted arrangements involving the exchange of canoes for goods, the Panaeati employed a pattern of trading which began in early times and continues today, in which they obtained pigs, garden food and valuables from the future recipients of the canoes before the canoes were presented. While they told their trade partners that the edible goods were to be used to feed the people who would build the canoes, the Panaeati used these goods for other purposes, delaying the completion of the canoes until they obtained more goods, either from the recipients or from someone else. This pattern worked particularly well in transactions with people living far enough away from Panaeati to be unable to press them for delivery of the canoes. Referring to this practice, Sir Hubert Murray, Administrator of Papua, remarked that 'commercial probity had so far advanced among the customers of the canoe-builders that long terms used, even in the old days of the territory, to be arranged for payment'.[8]

Canoe building in the past and today is a test of the ability of young men to distribute food to others. Their first canoes are made for the families of their wives and they are referred to as 'in-law canoes' (*muliwagana*). While they may make subsequent canoes for their in-laws, they also build canoes for trade friends with whom they have a better chance of receiving early presentations, and with whom they have a better chance of receiving more goods for the completed canoes. When the missionaries arrived in Panaeati, the islanders were actively exporting their canoes.

The Methodist missionaries and Sir William MacGregor, the first Administrator of British New Guinea, chose Panaeati for a new mission station because of the canoe-building and trading fame of the people.[9] The missionaries wanted to use the island as a base from which to spread their work to the rest of the region and they must have perceived that the trading ties between the Panaeati and the other islanders would be useful for this purpose. According to the record, the Panaeati at first were not too interested in the teachings of the early missionaries. In describing their response to his efforts at changing some of their ways, the historian Hank Nelson quotes Brother Samuel Fellows, whom Bromilow placed on Panaeati:

They are as proud as the proudest Pharisee that ever lived, and as mean. This, with their inherent tendency to lying and deception makes it an easy matter for them to deceive themselves with the idea that they are an exceptionally good sort of people, with whom it would be difficult to find serious fault.[10]

While he found his work difficult in the early months, Nelson notes that by 1893 Fellows was encouraged as:

children went to school, congregations paid closer attention during services, the hymn, 'Pull for the Shore' promised to be a great favourite, and some young people were repeating the Lord's Prayer before going to bed at night. Soon after Fellows left the Louisiades in 1893, the propriety of the Panaeati sailing their canoes on Sunday when on long voyages had become an important question for both the islanders and the missionaries.[11]

The missionaries had an extensive impact on the economy of the Panaeati. I already noted that they introduced several foods which were very useful during the hungry period of the year. Christian etiquette also had its effects on the behavioral style of trading and exchange.

The Panaeati borrowed certain activities such as sitting together and eating food from spread banana leaves from the Polynesian mission teachers. The islanders also added hymn singing to their traditional mourning activities. Today people sing all night for the deceased and receive small items from the family of the deceased. Finally, Christian etiquette had an effect on the manner in which the traders borrowed goods from each other. One man told me how he went to his trade friend on a different island in order to request a pig. The man from Panaeati included the word 'please' in his request because he had learned that this was the proper way to ask for something. The trade friend was so grateful for a new term, as words have magical power, that he gave the requestor a pig and told him that he did not have to present a return pig.

It is difficult to know whether or not the early missionaries were critical of the great amount of time that the Panaeati traders stayed away from their homes trading and attending ceremonies. We can assume that to a certain extent the missionaries recognized that the increased communication from visiting and trading helped to spread Christianity as the Panaeati traders came into contact with more people and discussed the activities of the missionaries on Panaeati. In the Panaeati version of their history, the missionaries and not the government personnel were responsible for peace and the consequent increase in trade. The islanders feel that the increased amount of goods and the introduction of Christianity together brought a new prosperity to their region.

Besides manufacturing canoes, the Panaeati also manufactured pottery. These two items secured for the Panaeati a strong trading position. The Brooker also were very active traders during the mission period because they manufactured pots for trade. The Brooker and the Panaeati were intermarried and because of this fact the Panaeati allowed the Brooker to cut timber which the Brooker hauled to their homes where they completed their own canoes for trade. The Brooker were experimenting with a design modified from the traditional sailing canoe for which the Panaeati were famous.[12] The new canoes, called *sailau*, were successful because they were fast and could be easily tacked. Finding advantages to the new type of canoe, the Panaeati also began to make them during the 1930s. They constructed three types of canoes then: the traditional model, the traditional model with the addition of a new rigging, and the sailau.

Canoe traders during the period of time when the missionaries were the strongest influence in the region (from 1891 to the middle 1950s) had as much time as they needed to complete trade arrangements when they visited partners on different islands. This is because during the mission years, unlike today, the Panaeati were not pressured to stay home and complete civic responsibilities. In the past, the islanders were only required to maintain the mission station and to work on the missionaries' gardens two days a week as well as fish on Saturdays for food for the Sabbath when no work was allowed. While this might seem like a busy schedule, it cannot compare with the intensity of the schedule since the government council system was introduced by the Australian Administration in the middle 1950s.

Since the 1950s, the Panaeati and their close neighbor Pana Pom Pom have been represented at the Louisiade Local Government Council by two councillors. Besides these, there are six census-ward committeemen who manage the island's business. The councillors and the committeemen hold weekly planning meetings to discuss the important civic work of the island. Along with the weekly meetings, every morning Monday through Friday, each committee man calls his neighbors together to plan the work for the day. The Panaeati schedule private activities, such as gardening and canoe building, along with public activities, such as working in the cooperative store and on the primary school grounds into a five day working week. Mondays are usually free for private activities. The cooperative store manager dispatches work on

Stuart Berde

Tuesdays. On Wednesdays, people usually maintain the gardens of the missionaries and work at the mission station. Thursdays are usually free unless there is a special activity for which the people have to prepare. The busiest day of the week is Friday because it is devoted to public works, such as maintaining the island path, the government school and the medical aid post.

Scheduling has its benefits and its drawbacks, according to the Panaeati. Its benefits are the tighter control which it gives people over gardening. Its drawbacks are the restrictions it places on inter-island trading and feasting. The scheduling system benefits the system of gardening because it allows for tight organization of the labor pool for certain emergency occasions. An example of this occurred during my stay on Panaeati when the committee men coordinated an effort to plant the gardens of the entire population after the planting had been dangerously delayed because the people had gone to a ceremony instead of planting.

Today, when a man wishes to sail to another island he tells the committeeman when he will return. While the committeemen do not give orders, their word is honored and people comply. The committeemen discourage people from staying away from Panaeati for long periods of time. In support of the argument posed by some informants that such tight scheduling has hurt trading. I found that pottery trading and feasting for food has been decreased since the 1950s to a point where very few Panaeati women made pots in 1970 and 1971. I also found that mortuary ceremonies were shorter than they were in the mission period.

The busy schedule also had the effect, according to informants, of eliminating the true big men from the society. This is because men today do not have the time to amass the goods that big men need to keep up their prestige. For example, the Panaeati love to eat pork and big men must obtain pigs to feed the community. Men on Panaeati obtain pigs as well as other goods either through exchanges for canoes or through borrowing goods, usually one at a time. While scheduling has not affected the overall amount of goods that canoe traders receive, it has affected the overall amount that borrowers receive. Canoe traders obtain early presentations while the canoes are being made plus large final presentations when the canoes are transferred to their new owners. Scheduling has caused builders and their recipients to coordinate their plans so builders will not have to wait long periods of time (as their elders were required to do during the mission years) while their trade partners obtain items to present for the canoes. Coordination is often accomplished by the two parties sending each other letters so that the recipients of the canoes will be prepared with their offerings when the builders arrive.

Borrowers of goods have a more difficult time than canoe traders because borrowers can only promise to return equivalent items in the future. These promises are less compelling than promising canoes. As a result, borrowers spend a lot of time searching for trade partners who will lend them items and then the borrowers must wait for their trade partners to actually produce the items. They must wait because the partners must in turn borrow items to give to the original borrowers. The inability to spend the amount of time necessary has made it impossible for strong men to become true big men today.

Despite the nostalgia for the role of the big man and for the freedom of the mission years, Panaeati canoe builders are continuing the traditions of their elders by building and trading canoes. Like their elders, the Panaeati build canoes in order to obtain goods to sponsor mortuary ceremonies. By sponsoring these ceremonies, men obtain residential land rights and, in the process, honor their ancestors. Thus the Panaeati are motivated to participate in inter-island trade because of the rewards of their inter-island system of exchange. This connection between the external system of exchange and the internal system of exchange is the most important feature of the Panaeati economy.

I suggest that the connection between the two systems of exchange can help us understand why people participate in the kula. In her analysis of the internal system of exchange on the Trobriands, Weiner states that the Trobrianders need valuables of all kinds in order to fulfill exchange obligations in their own communities. One important type of valuable is the stone axeblade, called *beku*. The Trobrianders like the Panaeati present these axeblades to their in-laws.[13] Weiner further notes that some shell necklaces and armshells which are obtained on the kula trips are used in the internal system of exchange in the Trobriands. These valuables, called *kitoma*, are not yet part of the formal overseas kula, but the Trobrianders return home and present them to their neighbors in exchange for the rights to use land.[14] The importance of these valuables in the internal system of exchange cannot be overemphasized. In fact, Weiner sees the kula as the mechanism for obtaining valuables for the internal system:

Men need valuables for the marriages of their sons, brothers, and sisters' sons and men need valuables when a death occurs. If the *kula* is the most expedient road to find wealth objects *for one's own use* (my emphasis), then I suggest that the search for valuables remains a driving force behind the *kula* exchange of an armshell or a necklace.[15]

Her view balances that of Malinowski, who stressed the circulation of kula valuables throughout the region at the expense of clarifying how the valuables were used in the communities of the traders. Stressing the internal system of exchange broadens our understanding of the motivation of traders, for we see that traders have two reasons to participate in the kula: they participate because they want to obtain valuables which they will pass on to their partners on other islands, and they participate because they want to obtain valuables which they present to people within their own communities. What are the rewards in the internal systems of exchange which supply part of the motivation for traders to visit other islands?

When Panaeati men sponsor mortuary ceremonies in their internal exchange system they remember the care and love which the fathers of the deceased gave to the deceased when they were young.[16] The land rights which men obtain when they sponsor these ceremonies symbolize the love between fathers and children. Like the Panaeati, the Trobrianders participate in exchanges in order to obtain rights to the land of the fathers.[17] In both societies, land has important symbolic value because of its connections to the ancestors, and in both societies fatherhood is honored.

Fathers are nurturing figures both in Trobriand and in Panaeati families. For example, impregnation by the father is necessary for the formation of the Trobriand child and the child is said to resemble the father through impregnation and through gifts of food.[18] The Panaeati are especially grateful to the fathers for the gifts of garden food which they gave the children when they were young.

I contend that the love between fathers and children in their own belief system is one of the reasons why the Panaeati have so enthusiastically embraced Christianity. The love between fathers and children represents a common ground between the islanders and Christianity. The common ground is generosity.

Christianity has become the idiom through which traders discuss exchange. A man or a woman who does not distribute food generously or who does not lend pigs and valuables is said to not understand 'Christian generosity' (*mololu*). The big men and their wives who lived during the mission era were the ideal generous Christians, because they regularly gave food to their neighbors, and people always went to them for advice.

Today the Panaeati, like their elders who were described by the Rev. Fellows, still do not work or conduct ceremonies on the Sabbath. Their enthusiasm for Christianity, however, has not dampened their enthusiasm for their traditional system of exchange. Men still build canoes and sponsor mortuary ceremonies and women still garden with great pride. It remains to be seen, however, whether people will be able to participate in these activities when the government council system increasingly makes demands on their time.

Notes

1 This research was funded by the National Science Foundation and the University of Pennsylvania Museum. The research was conducted from January 1970 to September 1971.
2 Similar responses to pacification are reported in A. Strathern, *The Rope of Moka* (Cambridge, England, 1971), p. 54 and M. Young, *Fighting with Food: Leadership, Values, and Social Control in a Massim Society*, (Cambridge, 1971), p. 223.
3 For the Trobriand Islands see L. W. Austen, 'Culture Change in Kiriwina', *Oceania*, 16 (1945) pp. 15–60. For other parts of Melanesia see H. C. Brookfield and D. Hart, *Melanesia: A Geographical Interpretation of an Island World*, (London, 1971), pp. 84–5.
4 B. Malinowski, *Argonauts of the Western Pacific*, (New York, 1922), p. 507.
5 Strathern notes that more Melpa people took part in exchanges after the introduction of Shells by the Europeans.
6 Malinowski, p. 468. The Chief of Omarakana was also weakened because the missionaries and the Administration kept him from acquiring more wives. Malinowski, p. 464–5.
7 The islanders from Woodlark (or Murua) have not come to Panaeati for some time. While they invited the Panaeati to visit them, the Panaeati are afraid of the long journey. A party from Yegum Island, near Woodlark, annually visits the north coast of Misima Island for trade.
8 J. H. P. Murray, *Papua or British New Guinea*, (London, 1912), p. 143.
9 W. E. Bromilow, *Twenty Years among Primitive Papuans*, (London, 1929), p. 171.
10 H. Nelson, *Black White and Gold*, (Canberra, 1976), p. 35.
11 Ibid., p. 36.
12 The new canoe had a canvas gaff-rigged sail instead of an oval one which was made from pandanus leaves. Rather than follow the traditional design with the mast forward, the mast now was in the center and the bow and stern were interchangeable. The new canoe was fastened with copper nails instead of lashings.
13 A. B. Weiner, *Women of Value, Men of Renown: New Perspectives in Trobriand Exchange*, (Austin, Texas, 1976), pp. 182–3.
14 Ibid., p. 181.
15 Ibid.
16 Male and female deceased are both honored by mortuary ceremonies. Men present three feasts in which pigs are killed. The final feast is called a soi and is common in the Southern Massim. Women present yams in honor of the dead. For these efforts, men receive residence land rights and women receive garden land rights. For a complete description of the mortuary and land-right complex see S. Berde, 'The Impact of Christianity on a Melanesian Economy', in *Research in Economic Anthropology*, vol. 2 169–187.
17 Weiner, p. 152.
18 Ibid., p. 123, where she cites Malinowski, *The Sexual Life of Savages in North-Western Melanesia*, (New York, 1929), pp. 204–9, 208).

19 Syndromes of ceremonial exchange in the eastern Calvados: the view from Sabarl Island

DEBBORA BATTAGLIA

The Calvados Chain is a string of coral, metaphoric and volcanic islands within the Louisiade Archipelago, south east of mainland Papua New Guinea.[1] Scattered along the Chain are approximately 2,250 people in beachfront hamlets or villages, the largest with a population of 220.[2] For administrative purposes, the area is divided into western and eastern islands, corresponding to categories of 'lower' and 'upper' in local usage.

This is an introduction to patterns of exchange, and in particular the primary types of ceremonial exchange, in eastern Calvados society. The most important of these is *segaiya*: a series of mortuary feasts featuring public, inter-clan exchanges of symbolic objects, luxuries and food. Segaiya transactions are approached as ritual gestures of equivalence – i.e. they are conducted in the spirit of balanced reciprocity – and stand in contrast to the other major type of collective exchange, known as *leau*. Traditionally, leau involves incremental transactions between trading partners, the object of which is status-gaining for an individual and his place. Today, however, leau is almost exclusively about canoe purchases and these are infrequent. Its rules are easily mastered in comparison to segaiya and, in the eastern Calvados, completely lacking in mystique.

The ethnographic sketch which follows is background for understanding the ethos which delineates these two very different exchange syndromes.

Overview of the Calvados Chain

Two languages are spoken within the Chain: Saisai (also called Nimowa) in the 'upper' or eastern islands and Misima in the 'lower' or western islands (see Map 1). Saisai speakers can further be divided into the Sabarl dialect group (people of Sabarl, Panabarli and Nigahau) and the Nimowa dialect group (people of Nimowa, Yeina, Dadahai, Wanim, Panatinani

446

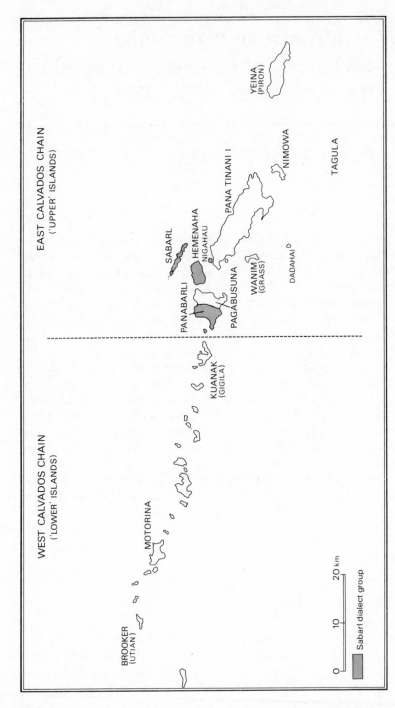

WEST CALVADOS CHAIN
('LOWER' ISLANDS)

EAST CALVADOS CHAIN
('UPPER' ISLANDS)

BROOKER
(UTIAN)

MOTORINA

KUANAK
(GIGILA)

PANABARLI

PAGABUSUNA

SABARL

HEMENAHA
NIGAHAU

WANIM
(GRASS)

DADAHAI

PANA TINANI I

NIMOWA

TAGULA

YEINA
(PIRON)

0   10   20 km

Sabarl dialect group

Map 1. The Calvados Chain.

and Panabusuna). Misima is the lingua franca of the Chain and English is used in the local schools.

Mission territories correspond to the basic divisons: in the west the Methodists; in the east the Roman Catholic Mission of the Sacred Heart, established on Nimowa in 1947. Government activities have had little or no effect on daily village routine compared to that of the missions, which are associated with education, with access to money and with regular and emergency medical aid (in that order). Generally speaking, there is less mission and government permeation the further west one moves along the Chain.[3]

Throughout the Calvados Chain a subsistence economy prevails, based on swidden agriculture, lagoon fishing and sago-making. Harvesting takes place in the southeasterly season, June through October – a time when ocean currents are relatively slow and the tides are lowest. Thus as beaches appear to 'grow', people mark the growth of garden produce, while at the same time schools of large fish are sited more frequently near the reefs. The favourable weather and abundance of food in turn allow for an upsurge of inter-island voyaging in connection with trading and feasting – the latter contributing pork and store-bought rice as well as greater quantities of fish to the staple diet of yams and supplementary tubers, sago and coconut. However, malnutrition and anaemia are nonetheless prevalent.

Contrasting with harvest-time is the long, lean northwesterly season following the November doldrums. During this time food is limited to gleanings from old gardens and a few mid-season sweet potatoes (not considered 'real' food), small fish and crustaceans, bush fruits, and of course sago. Also, high northwesterly winds and strong currents not only prevent people from net-fishing, but sometimes separate them from gardens, sago and even fresh water. This simple fact of environment has contributed to a distinctive *Weltanschauung* and ecological orientation in Calvados Chain people – a world view embodied in the concept of '*taval*'.[4] Loosely translated, taval means 'island'; but more accurately an isolated place deficient in the basic supports for human life, both physical and social.

'Islanders' share the notion – perceived as a common hardship and a common challenge – that inhabiting a taval sets them apart from people of Rossel, Misima, Tagula or the mainland, i.e. from those who inhabit 'lands' (*hiyeba*) sufficiently large and endowed to meet the needs of the people who live there. Welded, then, to a person's identity as an islander is a sense of being separated from subsistence goods and valuables alike; needs which can only be met by venturing out from home. These adventures thread people onto a trade relationship network in a process likened to the lacing of shell beads 'taval-style' (viz. upright in a row but not touching) along the edge of a ceremonial valuable.

Sabarl Island

Sabarl (or Sabara) Island in the eastern Calvados is regarded as the most taval of any in the Chain. It has no topsoil to speak of, no fresh water and no sago. For almost everything they need, the Sabarl must sail two miles to the island of Hemenaha where they have exclusive land rights, or to the mosquito-infested northern side of Panatinani.

Yet despite rather dramatic deficiencies, Sabarl has the largest total population (420) in the Calvados Chain as well as the largest village. The reasons for this are encoded in the taval ethos and in particular the cultural ambivalence towards natural hardships. For although Sabarl is known as a 'hard place', which on the one hand is a source of pride for those who live there, its comforts and beauty and the security of its numbers are likewise deeply appreciated. The white, unobstructed beaches of Sabarl offer refuge from the mangrove swamps, crocodiles and snakes of Hemenaha and Panatinani, and Sabarl is virtually free from sandflies and malaria-bearing mosquitos. Historically too, Sabarl sink-holes and limestone caves were once used as strongholds against raids for valuables by neighbouring islands and by warriors from the western Chain, who were often joined by Engineer Group and Panaeati canoes in raiding the eastern Chain and Tagula – who in turn raided each other.

Sabarl social organization

The domestic family is the most salient social and economic unit in every day Sabarl life. As a rule, households are virilocal and on Sabarl virtually all are monogamous, although polygamy was once a prerequisite of male political power.

Garden land is owned by either sex and descends bilaterally; residence land by a woman only if she is exceptionally 'strong'. A 'strong woman' (*yova suwot* – lit.: 'woman true') is one who produces food beyond what her children require; a feast-sponsor and expert in ceremonial exchange. Her male counterpart (*tologugui*) likewise excels in managing land and symbolic valuables. However, unlike females, whose political careers usually begin after marriage, males are introduced into political life during childhood and in general male leaders are more experienced, striking higher profiles within the political arena.

Notwithstanding, the strong position of women is a salient characteristic of Sabarl social organization. Divisions of labour within the island microcosm are distinguished by the fact of women frequently doing 'men's work' – i.e. what the Sabarl and their neighbours would classify as such. Unlike women of neighbouring 'lands' who seldom (if ever) navigate sailing canoes and rarely invade the domain of deep-sea space traditionally associated with men's activities, all-women Sabarl crews frequently sail beyond the reef *en route* to 'masculine' jobs such as sago-making, as well as to their gardens. A Tagula woman making sago with her 'sisters' would be told she was working 'Sabarl style' (*sabsabarl*). Less frequently, Sabarl women accompany husbands and children or clan-mates in search of valuables or supplementary food, or to negotiate canoe purchases. These off-island voyages, and the knowledge that women can (if necessary) navigate on their own, make Sabarl people as a whole 'better sailors than the Panaeati' in the eyes of Sabarl men.

On occasions of collective exchange, the matrilineage rather than the individual household or individual village is the significant corporate unit, and all claims to political power as well as public statements of allegiance articulate on this level of organization. However, matrilineal units are viewed as embodiments of clan on such occasions. Since most exchange feasts are responses to deaths and often demand shows of support by people representing three separate clans (the deceased's, his father's and that of his spouse) with members living in various villages on various islands, several island communities can become involved. A host's ability to tap this non-corporate network of blood relations, affines and offspring for subsistence goods and valuables is the measure of his or her political strength. Thus the dynamics of clanship generate intra-island communi-ties, which are typically distinguished by language, ritual vocabulary and clusters of close kin.

On Sabarl, there are three primary exogamous clans – Guau, Maho and Manilobu – members of which can be found throughout the Louisiade Archipelago. However, there is one important factor which crosscuts the community-making effect of clanship: namely, the 'power of place'. This is expressed as rules of inheritance which select against heirs residing off-island, or even outside of the home village, by requiring that claims to valuables or land be validated by repeated use resulting in tangible feedback into one's place of origin. 'Feedback' here must also be understood in a cosmographic sense as a process of honouring and insuring the tutelage of local ancestors, whose graves anchor their memories as well as their supernatural services to their earthly vicinities.

Past patterns of trade

Before pacification, Sabarl subsistence trade tended to stay within the dialect group. During the lean months, yams could be obtained from Tagula in exchange for sago and high-quality Sabarl lime, but the risk of sorcery and ambush was high. Betelnut and pigs were acquired in the same way, though usually from Yeina, Kimuta or Misima,[5] due to origin ties there. Ceremonial wooden dishes were also found at Misima and Kimuta where they were traded for lime, sago and lower-order valuables (e.g. small stone axe-blades). Other luxuries came very sporadically. Mailu traders travelling 'up' the Chain every two or three years sought cone shells (*Conus literatus*), cleaned and roughly cut, in exchange for tobacco and the black banana pods used in shell necklaces. Clay pots manufactured by arch-enemies at Panaeati, Brooker and Motorina were rare in the eastern Chain (where people used giant clam shells for cooking vessels) and most were acquired in local waters as booty from captured canoes. The first planksided outrigger on Sabarl was a Panaeati canoe taken in battle around 1920. However, since the western Chain islands faced frequent shortages of sago and lime, a few partnerships were established with Sabarl and the sago-rich eastern Chain even before pacification. Often the trade was initiated by women of Brooker or Motorina, who could navigate in enemy waters without men aboard and thus without fear of attack. As we shall see, valuables were sometimes exchanged at the same time.

Nonetheless the 'hunger for valuables', an integral part of the taval ethos, alone sufficed to draw war canoes to Sabarl where famed leaders ruled over all the Sabarl-speaking islands from communal treasure-houses during the first three decades of the century. Since human sacrifices were required for each such house, there was occasional raiding for victims, usually between Chain islands and Sudest.

Historically, then – i.e., within living memory – ceremonial exchanges involving valuables were largely conducted within dialect groups, whereas exchanges between dialect groups (e.g. between Sabarl and Nimowa speakers) were nominally for food and luxuries which were not considered motivations for raiding. Valuables were *exchanged* outside of the dialect group only sporadically by exceptional people under stressful conditions, since traditionally more honour was attached to seizing them.

Overall, the risks attending all types of exchange overwhelmed the proscription against combining different categories of trade within one trip. Consequently, unless a person was overtly political and/or viewed the dangers of frequent voyaging as a challenge, sailing for valuables often included, as it does today for related reasons, some subsistence trade and vice versa.

Upon this culturescape, interaction with Europeans was meanwhile developing roots. In a 1932 patrol-report[6] there is mention of Panawina people 'selling' copra to a Panawina trade store, probably in exchange for money, metal tools, tobacco, cloth, and other European luxuries. Sabarl men were crewing on government vessels and serving as village constables at the same time.

Then, between 1942 and 1947, a double-edged pacification by state and church fast changed the trade situation. When in the wake of cargo-cult violence many of the able-bodied men in the Chain suddenly disappeared into mainland jails, the women and old men themselves repaired houses, nets and canoes and sailed to gardens or in search of supplementary subsistence items and luxuries.[7] By the time the men returned – an average of five years later – traditional enmities were blurred by the common experience. And although marriage between 'upper' and 'lower' Chain islands never occurred as a result, within ten years of the Catholic Mission opening its school on Nimowa, inter-marriage within the eastern islands (and including Tagula) which had formerly regarded each other warily, if not with open hostility, had increased by about 30%.

Patterns of trade today

Today, the old inter-island wariness continues to surface as sorcery and poisoning accusations which do inhibit the forming of new trade relationships although they enforce existing ones. Also, the process of decentralizing mission schools, which began in the eastern Calvados ten years ago, has had the effect of re-establishing a trend towards marriages within dialect groups. Since pacification, however, subsistence and luxury trade is more freely conducted with Sudest and across east/west Calvados Chain boundaries. Panaeati (primarily) and Brooker (secondarily) are now established sources of deep-sea canoes. Pots from Brooker and Motorina are easily obtained for sago[8] and from Panaeati for money. Pigs can still be acquired cheaply at Sudest, either by traditional exchanges of yams, valuables and sago or – without contradiction and increasingly – by using money.[9]

Although Nigahau and Panawina produce copra regularly, diving for Trochus and bêche-de-mer have replaced copra as a means of obtaining money for taxes and school-fees on Sabarl. Unless traders are in the area on behalf of Misima trade stores, these products are taken by canoe to European-owned stores on Nivani (near Misima) or Panawina, or to the locally-owned Tagula trade store where purchase price per pound is, however, low. It is said to be a mother's responsibility to find school-fees for her children, which she usually does by bringing lime on consignment to the trade stores or by sending it to Misima[10] with the Sabarl-based government councillor. Lime-exchanges for money are still sporadic and unreliable although as solicitory gifts for acquiring valuables, lime is felt to be highly effective. Of the European luxuries, only tobacco, rice and tin plates have entered the sphere of ceremonial exchange as hospitality-essentials. Money has become an acceptable substitute only for lower-order valuables.

Valuables

Three major types of valuable were circulated in the Calvados, as they are today – namely, stone axe-blades, shell necklaces and mushroom-shaped lime spatulas. These have always been individually owned and operated without restriction to one sphere of exchange or another. However, supplies and patterns of distribution appear to have changed considerably over time. For this paper, I shall be looking at the three major symbolic valuables in greater detail than edible valuables (pigs and uncooked yams) or 'bulk wealth' (clay pots, tin dishes, pandanus mats and fibre skirts).

The standard of ceremonial exchange valuables throughout the Calvados Chain is the greenstone (laminated ignimbrite) axe blade or *tobwatobwa*. This is believed to be a natural object unshaped by man, something which always has been and always will be in circulation somewhere. Suau and Murua are often mentioned as places of origin, but people speculate freely on the subject. It is said that Misima, called 'Giam' or 'axe-blade' by people in the eastern Chain, is the centre for axe blades now, and that the people of Misima obtain their blades from Siloga on Murua or from Duau where they lie in estuaries, growing as shells grow.

What is commonly agreed is: (1) that stone axe blades are not appreciated in their places of origin – largely non-sago-growing areas to the northwest – and are popular in the eastern Calvados because of associations with tools formerly used in sago-making, and (2) that the blades first came to this area via trade and wartime contact with Brooker and Panaeati people who themselves acquired the blades elsewhere in exchange for shell necklaces; the necklaces moving 'down' the Chain and northwest, axe blades coming 'up' the Chain and southeast. There exists at least an ideal exchange ratio of shell necklace (one) for axe blades (several), emerging at certain times and in certain contexts as a requirement of the proper opening or resolution of a ritual sequence (e.g. leau exchanges – see pp. 460ff.). An ideal 'same type' exchange, which is more frequent than an axe-blade exchanged for another type of valuable, involves the exact matching of blades (*patapatal*) according to length and thickness, any increment taking the form of an additional valuable and not of a better-quality match. Size and thickness are equally important criteria for judging blade-quality, above colour or streakiness. For example, among stone axe-blades only very thin types (*poposisi* or *pepa ston*) can be used to pay a sorcerer assassin.

Axe-blades are stored in personal boxes in a private area of the house along with other precious things (e.g. money, prayerbooks, magical substances, books of magic spells). One small blade, called *hiyesagi* or *tobwatobwa gongon* ('axe-blade calling') in theory remains there at all times to 'attract' other blades. This supposed ability to draw blades – and in other contexts to self-reproduce – is unique among valuables. Also, unlike the way in which other valuables are commonly solicited by magic aimed at 'greasing' a trading partner, axe-blades can be asked to come direct from the ancestors. However a direct request of this sort is a matter for experts, and only those who know protective spells, usually influential men and exceptionally strong women, venture to the graves of their ancestors in order to perform the magic. Likewise, there is restricted ownership of the magic used to urge tiny 'mother' and 'father' axe-blades to procreate other axe-blades during mortuary ceremonies. In fact, a blade lying on its own on such an occasion, without markings or specially carved handle, is said to have been 'called' rather than donated by a living person.

During an exchange, axe-blades are temporarily inserted into wooden handles, marked with lime paste and thus displayed in the form of an implement of power capable of 'hitting' (i.e. of matching and thereby cancelling out) other valuables. The handle is a prop: on one level a kind of personal signature and on another a traditional visual theme in the conglomerate display of wealth. Slung over the shoulder as a person leaves for the scene of exchange, it is merely a sign that he carries with him the true substance of wealth, the blade, intending to trade it away. In this sense, the handle serves the purpose of wind chimes on a shell necklace (see pp. 234–6) – heralding the arrival of the valuable and the decision of its owner to participate in exchange.

A second major valuable is the mollusc shell necklace or *bak*. The production of shell necklaces take place mainly on Rossel Island, and it appears that those in the eastern Calvados were manufactured only at Rossel, Misima and Murua during the last half of the nineteenth century. Experiments in production elsewhere began shortly after World War II, i.e. in the early days of pacification. However, the work was then and remains today sporadic and project-oriented rather than geared to steady production, and the workmanship is mediocre.

The red-rimmed mollusc shells (*sapsap*) are found along the reefs. Shell distribution is thought to be thin around the Chain islands, becom-

Debbora Battaglia

Sample axe-blade increments[11]

Terms	Dimensions	Quantities
tobwatobwa 'axe-blade'	fingertip–wrist	1 *tobwatobwa*
kabole lamlamwana 'sago leaves'	fingertip–50mm above wrist	2 *tobwatobwa*
kabole 'sago'	fingertip–50 mm above *kabole lamlamwana*; usually thick	5 *tobwatobwa*
poposisi/pepa ston 'paper stone'	same as above but very thin	10 *tobwatobwa*

ing denser around Tagula and abundant around Rossel. Dead mollusc shells or the white part of live ones are used for the white discs which flank black banana pods (*gudugudu*) at the ends and centre of the strand. It is said that the three pods per necklace are important in that they divide the strand into an 'away' and a 'return' side, inhibiting the tendency of shells to stray from home. Discs made from plastic or rubber hosing are currently acceptable in everyday choker-type necklaces (*samwakupwa*) but black pods are sought even for these.

A full-size necklace is specifically marked for ritual or ceremonial use by the attachment of a helmet-shell pendant (*talimwadau*) or 'head'. The

Sample shell-necklace increments

(a) Thickness, colour-based

bolovagela	Necklace with claws from the Black-breasted Buzzard (*Hamirostra melanosterna*) or *manak* attached at the 'clasp' end and in the middle of each side.
kaukaubagi	Light-coloured (orange); thick.
bak hawana	
bak yalumoi	Slightly redder than above; slightly thinner.
bakmurlua (Murua)	Slightly redder than above; slightly thinner.
bagilugu (Engineer Group)	Small, thin, dark red discs.
Kakalavina	Large, thin, dark red discs.

(b) Length-based

bak	Long necklace (at least 1 metre per side).
yalumoi	3/4 length: 'Murua style'.
tinai	One side, white at ends, named after large intestine. One side of *bak* or *yalumoi*.
samwakupwa	Short; half *tinai*.

Sample lime-spatula increments

hiyenga	A two-dimensional lime spatula made of tortoise shell. Crescent width = approx. 150mm. Length = approx. 300 mm. These mushroom-shape spatulas are ornately carved. Lime powder is pressed into etched lines and shell discs are knotted and threaded through holes along the edge of the crescent-shaped section so that the discs stand upright in a row. This type of threading is called taval ('island'). Black-lip shell pendants (*kepu*) dangle from the ends of the crescent.
gogomwaneni	Two-dimensional lime spatula of painted wood with one side bak (see p. 17) threaded on. Crescent width = shoulder joint to shoulder joint. Iconographically same as Hiyenga.
gobaela	Same as above with two sides of bak threaded on. Crescent width = outside shoulder to outside shoulder.

'head' renders the necklace unwearable and fully activates it symbolically – e.g. a necklace without its pendant could not be used to commission sorcery.[12] The pendant also enhances the value of the necklace, primarily determined by the quantity of shell discs, by adding more discs (a) in the form of two strands connecting the pendant to the necklace (b) in the form of the pendant's 'crown' (*sivi painan*) and (c) in the form of a chiming shell fringe (*salusalu*) which dangles from the pendant's rim. I will mention in passing the third type of valuable, the mushroom-shaped lime spatula (*gobaela* or *hiyenga*) which is sought merely as a support for the mollusc shell discs attached to it. The number of shells determines the value of the object.

Trade partners

Trade partners are called *tutuila* which is the general word for kin as well as the word for harbours, connoting off-island ties in the context of the search for valuables as well as for food. In acquiring tutuila, clan affiliation is a factor in the sense that the 'best' partners are thought to be the members of one's father's clan (*hetamtamana*). A person's first partner is traditionally arranged by his father along these lines during childhood, although members of a persons's mother's clan (i.e. his own clan-mates) are the first to be tapped for subsistence items.

Men commonly have women trade partners and vice versa. In other words, women are not merely surrogate men in relation to exchange. In the case of a strong family, brothers and sisters may act as one tutuila unit, receiving partners and pooling hospitality items in the house of the eldest sibling (provided he lives in the home village) once the father and/or mother have retired from active political life. Siblings may also sail together in search of wealth or subsistence items, accompanied by the older male children of the sibling unit. Likewise a husband and wife are apt to share partners, particularly once their children are grown and the woman is freer to travel about by canoe. However, if a couple is 'strong', i.e. if both husband and wife sponsor exchange feasts on their own, they generally have partners individually as well. In this case they sometimes speak for one another in trade transactions, but the responsibility for the outcome lies with the true partner. It is expected that once she has married and fully entered the sphere of adult activities represented by in-law obligations, even an unambitious woman will have responsibility for at least one partner. In this context it is interesting to note a few statistics relative to Soter, the most powerful man in the Sabarl dialect group. Of his 64 partners in ceremonial trade, over 20% are women. Only 5% of these entered into the partnership while single compared to Soter's 50%. Two were the widows of partners – one of whom has remarried but maintains ties with Soter exclusive of her husband.

The ideal starting point for a political exchange relationship is a person's paternal cross-cousin (*nubaiu*), with whom a ritual feeding relationship may already exist – in theory at least since birth. This particular paternal cousin is called 'my father' (*tamau*) regardless of whether he is male or female. His 'father' will call him 'my child' (*natu*) rather than 'my cross-cousin'.

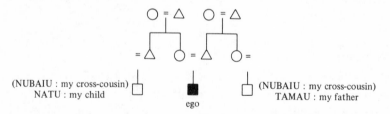

(NUBAIU : my cross-cousin)
NATU : my child

ego

(NUBAIU : my cross-cousin)
TAMAU : my father

The gift of a valuable from a 'child' to his 'father' often marks the entrance of the 'child' into the realm of ritualised exchange. This usually occurs at puberty for a boy and at marriage or childbirth for a woman. A person's ritual guardian may or may not develop into the one special partner referred to as *lotolomo* ('person sought'): i.e. the person one 'goes to last' in search of valuables since he can always be trusted to put other exchange obligations aside. However, in the subsistence sphere, a ritual guardian acts in an analogous way as a foster parent.

The search for valuables

Sailing in search of valuables (*lolobutu*) and sailing in search of subsistence or luxury items (*hahalau*) are classified as separate, incompatible activities by the Sabarl. For example, when opening an exchange discussion with '*alobutu*' ('I search for wealth'), one should not on the same visit attempt to barter. Nonetheless those who seldom engage in political exchange and have only one or two trade partners often do mix objectives. As mentioned earlier, a politically ambitious person is likely to pay attention to formalities.

It is always difficult to request and even more difficult to request valuables. Indebtedness (*vaga* = debt) is considered burdensome but necessary and one of a child's first lessons is in requesting things he will not directly repay, namely things for his parents. A 'clever' person is one who incurs more debts than he repays – planning and acting aggressively. Moreover, this confident behaviour is a sign of having earned or inherited magic for protection against sorcery attempts by jealous rivals. Men are thought to die before women because they leave home in search of valuables earlier in life.

Lobutu magic

Charms used as magic for non-subsistence asking take the form of ancestral relics preserved in scented coconut oil. Women are rarely contestants for the *lobutu* charms of their fathers or mothers' brothers – the inheritance of which causes raging disputes and sorcery threats. One source of the feuding is that in lobutu magic (as in certain other magical procedures) potency is thought to reside in the magical substance (*hepwiye*) more than in magical words (*ngengaiya*). Thus, because the power of an ancestral relic is intrinsic to the relic rather than imparted by means of words, a lobutu relic in oil is valuable even if the accompanying spell died with the previous owner. In short, the efficacy of the magic is not critically impaired by the absence of a spell: although spells help to 'guide' the magic, there are secondary sensory carriers to do this (e.g. scents and appearances). Rather, of primary importance is the way lobutu oil, when applied to the lips, 'greases' ordinary words and makes them captivating and persuasive. The magical lobutu substance, as an outgrowth or extension of person (usually human hair, teeth or fingernails), exhibits a process of reaching out to another, which is its root significance. Of course, ancestral sanction graces the operation – emanating from a gravesite on the residential property of the owner of the relic; exerting draw on people and wealth to the place of origin.

Debbora Battaglia

Any requests for hair or other relics should be made as a person is dying, and his granting the request is one sign that he expects to die shortly. After his death, hair that can be pulled out easily is accepted in the same spirit. This mitigates rivalry somewhat, but points up the importance of the oil which embalms the relic and the association of potency with oil which has been 'aged', i.e. with the process and not merely the fact of it having been in contact with the relic. In short, there is a difference between 'old' and 'nouveau' magic. The oil is a symbolic distillation of ancestor.

For a woman to inherit a lobutu magic, usually her husband's, is unusual but not impossible – particularly if there are no strong contenders in the village where she and her husband have lived and if she has demonstrated an active interest in exchange during her husband's lifetime.

Notably, there is no magic for subsistence asking apart from the magic directed at a person's own garden and ancestors to make asking unnecessary. In other words, subsistence sailing is itself a sign of inadequacy. This accounts for much of the reluctance to undertake it, in contrast to the challenge-meeting attitude towards sailing for valuables and, as argued earlier, indicates an exchange hierarchy which by nature of the separate mental sets defining it, can without contradiction, accommodate different types of exchanges within, say, one journey, since these are operating from completely separate evaluative premises. It might even be said that sailing for valuables is a face-saving *response* to the shame of subsistence sailing and that the circuitry of the taval world-view is here essentially constituted. With this idea forward, the question of what bearing it has on specific ceremonial exchanges can be addressed.

Exchange syndromes: leau and segaiya

What follows is an introduction to the two main types of collective exchange, and to the idea that more important for understanding them than tracking objects, mapping the resulting sequences, and packaging it all under what is presumed to be the local label (e.g. segaiya or leau) is a procedure which examines each type of exchange as a transactional syndrome, the name for which is regarded as a symbol of the ethos which substantially generates and sustains the exchange. Using this approach, transactions – more than in form – can be compared in substance, both within and between cultures.

Segaiya

The word 'segaiya' is used in three separate ways. Firstly it is the generic term for any exchange feast governed by the principle of equivalence,

458

and constitutes in this sense a major transactional syndrome which includes for the most part commemorative feasts. Secondly 'segaiya' is a gloss for the most important in the set of commemorative feasts, also called the feast of Sago Pudding (or Moni). Thirdly, it is the name for the gifts of uncooked food and/or valuables which a person periodically presents to the particular cross-cousin he calls my 'father' (see p. 456). The following discussion concerns 'segaiya' as a generic term, in which sense it is considered the essential value-upholding phenomenon in eastern Calvados society today.

Understanding segaiya begins with understanding the reciprocal nature of feeding relationships, and for a Sabarl person the lessons begin not when somebody dies but at the beginning of his own life in the village. The lessons which specifically relate to segaiya are expressed in terms of clanship: a person learning about his position as a member of his mother's clan in relation to his father's clan and later, to that of his spouse.

As discussed earlier, each person is assigned a ritual guardian who calls him 'my child'. Periodically, and especially when a 'child' is ill, the ritual guardian presents him with cooked food, young coconut and valuables in a symbolic gesture of nurture. These gifts from a 'mother' or 'father' to his 'child' are called 'bones' (*titiwa*) in reference to the double obligation of guardianship: during life to maintain the very core of the 'child's' physical strength and provide food if his real father should die, and at death to attend to his remains and prepare him for the journey to the afterworld. The latter is the most binding commitment. Without a proper entrance into afterworld society, a person's spirit is thought to be adrift and perishable, becoming inaccessible to petitions from the living for help or tutelage.

In exchange for his duties, the ritual guardian can expect to inherit a good deal from his 'child', and throughout his life the 'child' feels indebted to his guardian for the burden he has accepted. Thus at some point, the 'child' begins to pay tribute to his guardian's generosity. Such gifts from a 'child' to his ritual guardian are called segaiya. They are given to remind the 'father' or 'mother' that the relationship is not taken lightly and will bear fruit some day at the 'child's' commemorative feast. Assembling the gifts also trains the 'child' in the intricacies of obtaining 'help' from relatives and friends. If segaiya gifts are given frequently enough, there is a good chance the 'father' or 'mother' will relinquish some of his inheritance rights to the 'child's' surviving brothers, sisters, nieces, nephews, or spouse; i.e. those who have helped the 'child' supply segaiya gifts to the guardian.

One effect of this arrangement is that the bulk of an inheritance is kept from descending exclusively through either the child's mother's clan (represented by his own brothers, sisters and sisters' children) or his father's maternal clan (represented by his ritual guardian) or that of his spouse (including his own children if the spouse is a woman). Also the collective activities of the mother's matrilineage during segaiya establish the right to claim land.

Consider the interaction of these three primary units – mother's, father's and spouse's clans – in the following (highly condensed) outline of segaiya exchanges. What emerges from the table is a large-scale act of balancing debts by means of gestures which for the most part[13] act out and resolve the oppositional relationship between the focal group (M) related by blood and their affines (F and S). The object is a total cancellation of debt between these groups and the equal re-distribution of property (primarily valuables and land) among the clans.

Segaiya, then, commemorates not the dead but the life-support networks damaged by a death in the community. The ceremonies are about surviving: a net-mending of sorts and a reformation, in stages, of food links. Last but not least, its rituals are the only means of decontaminating in the spiritual sense people and places exposed to death pollution.

Leau

Consider the following description of a typical traditional leau:

Yankok is a big man at Nigahau and he has one shell necklace (bak). I see this and ask Nigahau people to leau this bak. When Nigahau brings the bak to Sabarl their canoe stops in front of my house. Yankok and some of his friends bring the bak and hang it outside of the house – it doesn't matter where. It is a sign that this is leau business inside. Then I take ten axe-blades (tobwatobwa) out to their canoe. After this the men who have been waiting in the canoe come inside my house. Inside there is a 'path' made of mats and on it are maybe thirty axe-blades in their handles. The Nigahau people stay three or four days. We cook for them, we make sago cakes and pudding and kill a pig. They return home with the axe-blades. Then two or three years later, I receive word that they are ready to 'call back the leau' (*leau gongon pahavina*). My 'brothers' and I go to Nigahau with nothing in our hands. They cook for us and give me forty tobwatobwa plus four. Then I either give them one bak as *golase* (closing gift) or it is my turn to look for more tobwatobwa and so it goes on. If I die before the leau is closed with a bak and I still owe my partner leau, my son will give him two axe-blades to claim (*posela*) my debt or what is owed to me. Then later he can open leau with this man for himself.

Leau exchanges were, in the past, an important means of communicating political power. This communication took the form of a multi-level challenge – a function of the unequal and incremental nature of the exchange. First, there was the challenge to leadership within the dialect

	SEGAIYA GESTURES				SEGAIYA COUNTER-GESTURES	
I	*Solu* ('Appeasement')					
(a)	S/F	wailing service →	M		(repayment = V (a)) ←	
(b)	F	ritual service →	M		(repayment = IV (d)) ←	
(c)	F	cooking service →	M	F	cooked food ←	M
II	*Hoiyalayala* ('Call and Response')					
(a)	S/F	edible valuables →	M		(repayment = (b)) ←	
(b)	F	ritual service →	M		(repayment = IV (d)) ←	
(c)	F	food-getting →	M	F	cooked food ←	M
III	*Hanlekeleke* ('Repealing the food Taboo')					
(a)	S	symbolic valuables →	M	S	ritual service ←	M
(b)	M	edible valuables →	F	M	ritual service ←	F
(c)	F	ritual service →	S/M	F	money; valuables ←	S/M
(d)	F	cooking service →	M	F	cooked food ←	M
IV	*Moni* ('Sago pudding')					
(a)	S	edible valuables →	F/M	S	edible valuables ←	F/M
(b)	F	ritual service →	S/M	F	ritual and cooked food ←	S/M
(c)	S	symbolic valuables →	F	S	ritual service ←	F
(d)		(see I(b))		(F	symbolic valuables	M)
V	*Vetantan* ('For Those Crying')					
(a)		(see I (a))		(S/F	cooked food	M)
(b)		(see II (a))		(S/F	edible valuables	M)
VI	*Gebyuwas* ('Burn to clean')					
(a)	S/F	edible valuables →	M	S/F	edible valuables ←	M
(b)	M	ritual service; cooked food →	S/F	M	ritual service ←	SF

M = mother's clan: esp. sister's son of deceased
F = father's clan: esp. ritual guardian of deceased
S = surviving spouse's clan: esp. widow/er of deceased.

group, which subsumed a challenge to spiritual powers (e.g. magic for calling valuables) and by extension to the power of an opponent's ancestors. Between dialect groups and island communities the implicit challenge was to raid for the large quantities of valuables amassed – i.e. *leau* had the effect of luring enemy canoes into familiar waters.

The extent to which leau actually drew neighbouring dialect groups and communities into trade relationships can only be surmised. There is one case of people of Sabarl feeding valuables into the western Calvados which were later used to leau with Misima. This occurred in the early decades of the century and terminated just prior to World War II with the death of the link character, a Motorina woman named Labayoni. Labayoni together with children and clan sister, would sail her fleet of deep-sea canoes, on trading voyages into the eastern Calvados enemy territory. Apart from trading away Brooker and Motorina clay pots for eastern Chain sago and garden produce, she would accumulate objects with which to leau with a Misima trading partner (probably another 'strong woman' living near Balimatana) in time for the Misima partner to kula with visitors from Murua.

It was in Sabarl's interest to cooperate with Labayoni. Through her could be obtained 'murua style' (*bak murlua*) shell necklaces at a time when Rossel beads were rarely seen due to enmity with Tagula, as well as stone axe-blades from further up the Chain. It is also said that small and large kula armshells would find their way down the Chain where they were kept as curiosities, and may even have gone to Mailu traders. Labayoni also used her considerable clout to recruit or restrain warriors from the Engineer Group in the interest of economic cooperation she was either seeking or denied. Interestingly, a Yeine woman named Sam, who died of old age in 1970 and who likewise made leau her 'business', operated in much the same way – i.e. by bribing the leaders of enemy groups (esp. Sudest and Panaeati) to stop fighting in the interest of trade.

It is important that Labayoni's trading-partners in the Chain did not leau large quantities of valuables to her, but fed one or two items (mainly axe-blades) into the stream with no concern as to what they were giving *vis-à-vis* the type of object they would receive. On Sabarl (population about 300 during these times) only three men of various clans took part in the trading. It should be noted that these three acted as trade and military advisors to the only Sabarl leader ever to develop direct links with the kula, which he did in the early 1920s while patrolling as a coxswain aboard a government trawler in the northern Massim area.[14]

Today, there are many discrepancies in the use of the term leau and these reveal something important about leau as a syndrome of exchange.[15] Stuart Berde's informants, primarily Panaeati people and a few Wanim (Grass) Islanders, use leau to mean the combining of different types of valuables into multiples of five (1974:279). However, throughout the eastern Calvados I was told that leau denotes the large-scale and incremental asymmetry of the transactions and would never be used, as Berde suggests, for the act or art of combining valuables on other occasions where the object is to make a public gesture of matching exactly or cancelling out one like category of item with another. Since, as I have shown, this process of cancelling debt is the keynote of segaiya exchanges, it may be that leau suggests a scenario so completely different in terms of motivation that to think in terms of similarities is not only foolish but offensive.

Leau, segaiya and the taval world-view

Leau is thought of as a decision on the part of an individual to engage in status-gaining for himself and for his 'place' (island/village/neighbourhood). As such it is essentially an extroverted gesture which, as Belshaw points out *vis-à-vis* kune and kula exchanges (1955:30) indicates value placed on expanding social networks. Originally, it was also indicated that the person in whose name the leau was transacted had more than accepted the risk of sorcery which in Calvados society accompanies any grand gesture; he had in fact issued a challenge based upon his own knowledge of (or reputation for knowing) protective magic.

Segaiya on the other hand is a kin-oriented *response* to death in the community and to the triumph of sorcery which most deaths are thought to represent. As such, segaiya is essentially an inward-looking, defensive activity carried on in the name of the dead person in the tone of appeasement. Segaiya discourages expansion, e.g. by discouraging permanent residential moves away from the segaiya community – and stresses instead regrouping. This is expressed in the local idiom: (1) as the homing of valuables at segaiya time: there is marked pressure on the eldest lineage heir to keep major valuables in the village (as well as in the lineage) regardless of whether he or she lives there, and (2) as the homing of lineage members to physically establish claims to residential and garden land. In short, status-gaining is an effect or reward and not a reason for segaiya exchanges – an important difference relative to leau. 'Because this is leau', I was told, 'mother' and 'father' axe-blades were not placed inside a mat to procreate more blades as they were for segaiya. In other words, leau and segaiya operate differently: leau as an accounting of human accomplishment; segaiya (like garden magic) as an unpredictable and intrinsically inadequate response to human limitations and to problems of regeneration.

Debbora Battaglia

Yet it is segaiya which dominates the realm of political exchange today. Addressed as it is to both subsistence and non-subsistence matters, i.e. to the facts of 'island' life, natural and cultural, segaiya is seen as a pivotal means of working out the taval predicament and it is viewed and valued as the representation of the burden of taval isolation, despite its western classification as 'internal' or intra-community, exchange.

It is the merging of internal and external realms of exchange – partly a function of unrestricted individual ownership of valuables, partly an historical accident – which differentiates the profile of eastern Calvados exchange from that of kula areas to the north. And it is not unrelated that in kula areas, predominantly non-sago regions, axe-blades are regarded as secondary wealth items while in the far south they epitomize exchange. The movement of property in the form of pre- and post-mortem descent, governed by the syndrome of segaiya and closely tied to attitudes towards nurture, today generates the essential framework for obtaining objects with which to connect with other islands and to systematically control the taval predicament as neither raiding nor leau ever could. This movement, I was told, 'looks like tobwatobwa'.

This is not the place to discuss symbolism. But in a significant way, valuables and segaiya performances alike conceptualize as artifacts rules for a whole way of life and not merely for one exchange event or personal objective. Understanding this, the continuing value of the segaiya syndrome over others in this area can likewise be appreciated.

Notes

1 Fieldwork on Sabarl Island 1976–77 was financed by the following sources, which I gratefully acknowledge: Esperanza Trust (Royal Anthropological Institute), the Smuts Memorial Fund, the Wyse Fund, the Crowther-Beynon Fund, the Clothworkers' Union (Girton College) and the Anthony Wilkin Fund.
2 1976 census.
3 However, Tagula (Yamba, Sudest, or Taguna) remains a local bastion of sorcery and traditional beliefs which has a traditionalizing influence on Chain people.
4 'Taval' (Misima language) = *'saisai'* (Saisai langauge). The former is more commonly used on Sabarl.
5 Specifically, the Misima villages of Ebora, Liak, Ewena and Mumuga are mentioned in connection with third and fourth generation ancestors.
6 Ivan Champion, A.R.M./Misima: Patrol Report 1931–2, 4 May 1932.
7 Peaceful trade relations were probably already consolidating during the decade before, since in 1942 a Brooker canoe sought refuge on Sabarl from the ships of the ANGAU government's punitive expedition. At that time, the

shooting death of a young Brooker woman by a government officer outraged Sabarl residents.

8 One medium pot equals 5 double bundles.

9 For example 1 large pig equals 20 kina (Sudest) = 40 kina (Piron) = 80 kina (Misima).

10 One large bundle = 40 toya; medium 20 = 30; small = 10.

11 All sample typologies are typical rather than exhaustive or necessarily consistent categories.

12 It is probable that the helmet-shell pendants were first manufactured on eastern Tagula and later adopted by Misima people as a replacement for polished coconut-shell pendants commonly associated (through myth and children's stories) with human heads. In view of the importance of the 'head' of a bak, it is interesting to note Stuart Berde's comments on the exchange of human skulls (*baloma leau*; 1974:50–5) in pre-pacification times and his speculation that skull transactions and the partnerships developed through them were models for expanded political exchange after pacification. I never obtained detailed information on skull exchanges in the eastern Calvados, although they did occur. However, it is still widely believed that sorcerers exchange the dead bodies of their clan-mates; authorizing the killings to repay debts of human 'pig' incurred at inter-island spirit feasts. In these exchanges heads are said to feature prominently.

13 Members of M publically allign with S or F only when acting as in-laws themselves, i.e. in their supportive roles.

14 R. M. Vivian, A.R.M./Misima: Patrol Report No. 7, 1929–30 – 4 June 1930; Patrol Report 1921–2 – 21 June 1922.

15 Belshaw (1955) notes that *pan leau* in the Ware language means 'trade partner' in commercial exchanges as well as in the ceremonial exchanges known as *kune*. Indeed, traditional leau as described earlier somewhat resembles a type of exchange between Ware and Misima which Belshaw calls kune type I. He states that leau is a 'straight link between Ware and Misima, possibly with Sudest sometimes brought in' (1955:27). I never found a Calvados or Tagula (Sudest) person who had heard of the activities Belshaw refers to as kune I and II. However, in kune as in traditional leau, the sequence of exchange is asymmetrical and in both types, shell necklaces seem to signify a pact to exchange. Leau, of course, is incremental whereas kune as Belshaw describes it results in equivalent exchange, and in this sense Belshaw's kune type II is more like contemporary leau, involving canoe-purchases (cf. Berde 1974). Significantly this indicates a shift away from leau as challenge, and consequently away from its power to establish authority.

20 Sudest Island and the Louisiade Archipelago in Massim Exchange

MARIA LEPOWSKY

Introduction

Sudest is the largest island in the Louisiade Archipelago, the group of islands which separates the Solomon Sea from the Coral Sea.[1] Lying about 200 miles southeast of the mainland of Papua New Guinea, it is encircled by an enormous lagoon, one of the world's richest fishing grounds, which stretches all the way back to Ware Island, forty miles from the mainland, and connects with the main barrier reef following the south coast of Papua New Guinea. This lagoon ends on the eastern side of Sudest. The neighbouring island of Rossel, only twenty miles to the northeast and the last land until the Western Solomons, 250 miles distant, is isolated from Sudest by a deep-sea passage notorious for its high seas and winds and its tricky currents.

Sudest Island consists of one major mountain range running the fifty-mile length of the narrow island, but only about 2,075 people live on the island. No whites reside on Sudest. Formerly, the entire population lived in tiny hamlets in the interior of the island in sites chosen for ease of defence against the raids of both other Sudest people and of islanders from as far away as the Engineer Group. They also lived inland because the central mountain range has fine fertile soil for gardens on its slopes, and water sources which are reliable year-round. By contrast, the soil along the coast is frequently too gravelly or too swampy, the smaller coastal streams may go dry toward the end of the southeast tradewind season, and the larger rivers turn into salty estuaries near their mouths which may extend up to a mile or even two miles inland.

In 1943, the wartime military administration (ANGAU) ordered the people of Sudest to settle in designated village sites along the coast. This was in response to a series of 'cargo-cult' inspired murders and other incidents of violence and raiding which occurred in the neighboring Calvados Chain Islands after the evacuation of the civilian colonial government personnel from the region and after the populace had been ordered to send a number of men to Milne Bay to labor for the Allied soldiers. Since that time about half the Sudest people have lived in coastal villages, frequently walking several miles to reach their gardens, while the others have settled in tiny hamlets in the interior. The true name of Sudest Island is Vanatinai, which means, 'Place of my Mother', or 'Motherland'. The islanders speak an Austronesian language, as do all the people of Milne Bay Province except for their close neighbors, the Rossel Islanders. But, there are at least three major dialects on Sudest, and the people of Western Point (or Boboghagha) Village have their own separate language. Other dialects of Sudest, which originated in now-deserted parts of the island, are now spoken only by older people. All dialects – but not Western Point language – are mutually intelligible. This dialectical diversity is one indication of the length of time which Sudest has been inhabited. By contrast, the Misima language is spoken from Misima Island itself to Panaeati and the Deboyne Lagoon Islands and in the West Calvados Islands as far as Kuanak Island, fifty miles southeast of Misima, with only minor local pronunciation differences. Between the Misima language area and Sudest live 1,200 East Calvados Chain Islanders who speak their own language, frequently called Saisai or Nimowa.

The Sudest belong to twelve exogamous matrilineal clans. Each clan has a series of linked totems consisting of one or several birds, a snake, one or several fish or marine animals, a tree, and a type of bush cord or vine. One of the bird totems is most commonly used to identify a clan, and a stranger is immediately asked: 'What is your bird?' Although clan names and languages vary, the set of totem birds identifying various clans is much the same throughout Milne Bay Province, and a first-time visitor to Sudest from elsewhere in the province may thus determine who his or her clanmates are, the people who would be most likely to offer him or her hospitality and to enter into exchange relationships with the stranger. These are also the people whom custom dictates should not be taken as sexual partners.

Sudest is rich in sago swamps, and sago is the primary dietary staple as well as a major export item. The abundance of sago also means that the island supports a large number of domestic pigs, which are fed sago pith and household scraps. The islanders are well aware that one of the main reasons that people from the Calvados Chain, Panaeati, Misima and even distant Ware Island yearly mount long overseas sailing expeditions to Sudest is to obtain pigs for ceremonial use.

The Sudest cultivate yams, sweet potato, tapioca (manioc), taro, banana, pumpkin, pineapple, papaya, and other crops. Their neighbors seventy miles to the northwest, the much more heavily missionized Misimans, say that Sudest people are poor gardeners who do not plant enough and who are always off on trading voyages instead of working in the gardens. But many Sudest gardens provide the food surplus which is essential for hosting the memorial feasts which are central to ceremonial life, and baskets of yams and other of the less perishable kinds of produce are commonly given to overseas visitors as part of a set of exchanges. It is true though that gardens on the densely-populated island of Misima seem to be more intensively worked. Misimans fence their gardens to protect them from marauding bush and village pigs, and they stake their yams to produce larger tubers. Unfenced Sudest gardens are frequently laid waste by pigs, and Sudest yams are unstaked, the inhabitants relying for good harvests far more upon elaborate systems of yam and other garden magic than do the Misimans.

The abundance of good garden land, water, and sago stands on Sudest contrasts sharply with the situation in the Calvados Chain Islands which begin a few miles northwest of Sudest. Except for Joannet (Panatinani) and Panawina, the Calvados Chain Islands are all small, infertile, and drought-prone. Their inhabitants are more oriented to the sea than are Sudest or Misima Islanders. They own more sailing and paddling canoes and spend more time fishing. Many of them sail frequently to Sudest or Misima in order to barter. The people of drought-ridden Brooker (Utian) Island in the West Calvados regularly sail to Misima to trade various types and sizes of Brooker-Island-made clay cooking pots for bundles of sago and baskets of yams. They also trade their pots for the large Misima carved wooden platters which are much in demand on Sudest and which may be traded there for the sago which is more available on Sudest than on Misima. Whole Brooker families sail every year after the yam harvest to Sudest and set up house as guests of a Sudest trade friend for several weeks while their hosts make sago for them. A standard clay cooking pot, measuring about fifteen inches in diameter, is exchanged for five double bundles of sago on Sudest. When the Sudest sail to Brooker, they can buy a pot for only one bundle of sago. But this long voyage, even though it is within the lagoon, is arduous and time-consuming, and despite the Sudest population of 2,075, there are only about seventeen sailing canoes on the island. By contrast, there are 200 people on Grass (Wanim) Island, ten miles northwest of Sudest in the East Calvados Chain, and they own eleven sailing canoes. The Grass Islanders are trade specialists. As its almost universally-used English name indicates, the island is grassy and infertile, and its water sources sometimes go dry, forcing the populace to sail several miles across to Joannet (Panatinani) Island to fetch water and to make most of their gardens. But the only village on Grass Island is

469

Maria Lepowsky

situated on a narrow strait through which almost all the sailing canoes and European boats bound for Sudest Island must pass. Frequently Brooker and Motorina Islanders, anxious to trade Brooker clay pots for sago, will sail only as far as Grass Island, where the inhabitants will trade them three double-bundles of Sudest sago for a pot and save them the longer trip to Sudest. The Grass Islanders both sail the pots to Sudest to barter on their multi-purpose trading trips and give them to visiting Sudest people and other islanders as part of exchanges involving ceremonial valuables.

The Grass Islanders and other East Calvados people, such as the Panabari and Nigaho villagers, occasionally sail to Misima, which has a large population and poor fishing resources, to barter baskets of smoked clam in the villages for baskets of yams and other produce – at a rate of one to one – and to obtain the wild pandanus sleeping mats and large carved wooden platters in use throughout the archipelago. The food is consumed at home, but extra mats are sometimes given as farewell gifts to trade friends or important guests at feasts, and the platters frequently are given as partial payment for Sudest pigs.

Canoe exchanges

Grass Islanders and their relatives at Panabari Village on Panawina Island also contract for and buy Panaeati Island sailing canoes (*sailau*), use them for about a year and then sell them at a profit to Sudest people, making deliveries to the Sudest villages and saving the Sudest the time and trouble of dealing with the distant Panaeatians. Panaeati has a virtual monopoly on making the intricately-carved, canvas-sail single-outrigger canoes, although in a recent consumer rebellion sparked by a disinclination to pay the high Panaeati prices, the villagers at Hebwaun (Bwailahine) on Joannet (Panatinani) Island several years ago began building their own sailau, using Panaeati designs. A few Sudest men used to make the old style of sailing canoe with an oval pandanus sail which was used throughout the region until the 1950s. But the Panaeati specialization in canoe-building is reflected by a Sudest myth in which Rodyo, the creator spirit, instructs another spirit named Bwaileva to build the first canoe, which is named Madai or Lolwalowan. Bwaileva then sails Madai from Sudest to Panaeati at Rodyo's command and tells the Panaeati people that henceforth their work will be making sailing canoes and that they will use the canoes to exchange for garden produce, sago, pigs, and ceremonial valuables from the Sudest and other islanders.

Sailing canoes are still bought primarily with traditional valuables, although money is becoming more important as Panaeati builders rely

470

more on trade-store food to feed their laborers. The canvas sails must also be purchased with money, and they may cost K60–K150 (U.S. $85–210). For a big sailau, a Grass Islander might give ten large pigs, five long shell necklaces (*bagi*), fifteen greenstone axeblades (*tobotobo*), 200 double-bundles of sago, and many dozens of pots of cooked garden produce and baskets of uncooked produce, plus the amount of cash needed to reimburse the builder for feeding his laborers, frequently K50–K200, and to purchase the sail. The number of bagi needed for sailau purchase is said to have inflated in the last twenty years due to the large number of bagi being manufactured nowadays and in circulation in the archipelago. In the old days, one bagi for each prow of the canoe was standard, and older builders still ask only two or three, but 'new people' demand five to seven bagi.

A Grass Islander might use the sailau for a season for trading voyages and more prosaic trips to the garden or to visit relatives, maintaining it well, and then resell it on Sudest or nearby islands for about twelve pigs, six bagi, twenty tobotobo, 300–400 double-bundles of sago, large quantities of cooked and uncooked produce, and the same amount of cash as the purchase price. Some Sudest people buy canoes directly from Panaeati. Sailau are bought on the 'installment plan', with advance payments of pigs, sago and produce theoretically used by the builder to feed the Panaeati laborers. Starting in about August or September, after the yam harvest and the clearing and planting of new yam gardens, and until December, canoes full of Panaeati families are frequent visitors to the villages of the East Calvados and Sudest, seeking further payments of pigs, food, and ceremonial valuables on canoes already under construction and soliciting new orders. They bring Panaeati-made clay cooking pots as gifts to their buyers: these pots are expertly made, but Panaeati clay is widely agreed to be inferior to that of Brooker, and Panaeati pots are considered much less durable. Brooker and Panaeati are the only two islands in the Louisiade Archipelago where pots are manufactured.

The common practice is for the buyer to take possession of the canoe, normally by buying a sail at a trade store (at Badia, Sudest Island or at Nivani Island) and sailing to Panaeati with an extra crew on board to sail the new one home after half of the purchase price has been completed. Canoe-purchase is called *leau*, or *reau* on Sudest. The payment of valuables in a canoe purchase is made by placing the requisite bagi or tobotobo on the deck of a visiting Panaeati sailau, while the Panaeatians watch stoically from the canoe.

Although relations between Sudest and East Calvados people and Panaeatians are seemingly cordial, the canoe buyers complain that Panaeatians are frequently guilty of sharp practices such as promising a canoe to one party, collecting pigs, food and valuables from him and then selling the completed canoe to someone else. The aggrieved would-be buyer may never see his goods again, and he suspects that they have been used to fulfill ritual obligations at Panaeati memorial feasts (*hagali*). People say the buyer has no recourse in this situation, and the several days' sailing necessary to reach Panaeati may protect the builders from the wrath of buyers who may not have ready access to a sailing canoe in which to make the trip.

Canoe purchases commonly take about five years to complete. A well-cared-for sailau will last seven to ten years; I once travelled in one which was twenty years old. Most sailau change hands several times in their lifetimes.

The dug-out, single-outrigger paddling canoes are much quicker and easier to make than the large sailau with their built-up planked sides, and paddling canoes are built on all the islands in the archipelago. A strong paddling canoe may be commissioned from a local expert. In one case, a Sudest man recently purchased a new one from a trade friend at Sabara Island in the East Calvados for one bagi, five tobotobo, one large pig, and sixty bundles of sago.

Exchange routes of the Louisiade Archipelago

Favored with an abundance of sago, produce from their gardens, pigs, fish, and shellfish, the Sudest Islanders need not travel to trade for food as many of the Calvados Chain peoples must do. Most Sudest exchange trips are made in search of ceremonial valuables which are necessary for discharging ritual obligations at memorial feasts for the dead and numerous other occasions. The nature of these valuables and their many uses on Sudest are discussed in a later section. Particularly after the yam harvest and the clearing and planting of the new year's yam gardens, the Sudest travel to the other villages on their own island – by foot over the mountains and through the swamps, by paddling canoe and by sailing canoe – in quest of bagi necklaces, greenstone axeblades (tobotobo), the shell valuables called *daveri*, and ceremonial limesticks called *wonamo jilevia* and *ghenagá*. These journeys are called *ghiva* or *robutu*. The term ghiva is also commonly used as a verb describing the process of formally requesting valuables.

An outsider observer is immediately struck by the fact that women go on ghiva expeditions, unlike in the *kula* exchange area to the northwest, where women are forbidden on exchange voyages. In fact, women sometimes lead expeditions on Sudest and overseas. There are big women as well as big men on Sudest and in the Calvados Chain Islands. A big man or woman on Sudest is called a *gia*, which literally means 'giver', and the power and prestige of the *giagia* arise because they consistently strive to obtain more ceremonial valuables and other exchange commodities, give more valuables away to exchange partners, host more feasts, and give away more valuables and goods at ceremonial occasions hosted by others than the minimum which Sudest custom requires of every adult.

It is the big men and big women of Sudest who, with their families, are likely to travel overseas to *ghiva*. Their most common destinations are the islands of the East Calvados Chain, especially Panaman, Dedehai, Grass, Joannet and Nimowa Islands. The Sudest obtain ceremonial valuables, pigs, Brooker Island clay cooking pots and other items from these islanders for use at home. They are also frequent guests at the East Calvados feasts, whose ceremonial sequence and whose customs vary significantly from those of the Sudest, bringing ceremonial valuables, pigs, sago, garden produce and betelnut from Sudest to present to their exchange partners for use at the feasts. The East Calvados Islanders also attend Sudest feasts, bringing their anxiously awaited return contributions.

The Sudest sail the Calvados Chain all the way to Brooker Island, stopping to ghiva at all the islands en route. Less often they leave the lagoon to cross to Panaeati or Misima in quest of bagi or tobotobo. East Calvados and Sudest exchange partners sometimes sail together on these longer trips in one or more sailing canoes.

The Sudest occasionally sail across the treacherous channel to Rossel Island. They say that the isolated Rossel Islanders are hungry for certain imports and that the favourable exchange rates make the dangerous trip worthwhile. The Rossels will give a large pig with tusks in exchange for four Brooker Island clay pots. The Sudest bring tobotobo originating on the Suau Coast, Duau (Normanby) Island, and Murua (Woodlark) Islands to Rossel, as well as the ceremonial limesticks of wood called ghenagá and those of tortoise-shell called wonamo jilevia, which are made on Sudest, and the conch-shell pendants for bagi, called *bubugera*, also manufactured on Sudest. The Rossel Islanders even import bagi from Sudest, although they produce more bagi for export than any other region in the Massim area. This is how bagi from Murua and other distant islands come to circulate on Rossel. The Sudest shell currency called daveri is virtually identical with the Rossel currency called *ndap*, and the Rossel import daveri from Sudest. The Sudest also occasionally bring Misima carved wooden platters and pigs. The scarlet lories and green parrots which are numerous on Sudest are prized on Rossel as marks of status, for they are kept by the wives of big men. The Sudest say that the Rossel will give a fine bagi in exchange for a green parrot.

Maria Lepowsky

The Rossel Islanders export bagi and *savisavi*, a necklace of large discs of bagi shell sewn together flat instead of cylindrically. Many of their ndap are given in exchange to the Sudest. One of the most coveted items from Rossel is the rare type of fine long axeblade called a *giarova*, which literally means 'give – Rossel Island'. Giarova come from a stream below Mt Goywo, near Jinjo Village. Sudest visitors may also be given pigs, baskets of taro, the finely-made small round betelnut baskets for which the Rossel are famous, and sandalwood bark (*ome*), which only grows on Rossel and which is highly valued on both islands as a powerful magical aid and medicine.

Nowadays, there are only a few sailing canoes left on Rossel, but in earlier times the Rossel Islanders used to sail to Sudest regularly on exchange voyages, particularly to East Point (Seghe) Village, with whose inhabitants they were heavily intermarried. They also attended Sudest feasts and brought goods to aid their affines and other exchange partners. Nowadays, some Rossel people visit Sudest for exchange purposes by means of mission or government trawlers or else in one of the European-style motor vessels built on Rossel Island. The Sudest say they used to sail to Rossel more frequently a generation ago than at present, circumnavigating the island and sometimes leaving their canoes anchored at coastal settlements such as Abeleti and walking into the interior to visit exchange partners residing there.

It is rare for any other islanders besides the Sudest to visit Rossel, although a big man from Nigaho Island in the East Calvados Chain was planning an expedition to Damenu Village on the west side of Rossel in February of 1979 to claim a fine bagi owed to him by a Rossel exchange partner.

I was startled to hear that Grass Islanders who have sailed to Ware, Tubetube, Bwasilaki, Samarai and Duau (Normanby) have never been to Rossel Island. The Grass people and other Louisiade Islanders occasionally sail to Duau to obtain light-weight logs for use as canoe outriggers. They also look for tobotobo at Duau, the Suau Coast, the islands near Samarai and the Engineer Group Islands, bringing *Conus* shells, bagi, and sago with them. They return with yams, black face-paint, and a scented bark used in healing magic called *keminana* from Duau, and clay cooking pots from Ware Island.

Ware is the southern nexus of the kula ring. It is also one of the main points at which valuables from the Louisiade Archipelago flow into the kula area and articles originating in the kula region, especially axeblades, enter the Louisiade. Misima and Panaeati Islands in the northern portion of the Louisiade are actually part of the kula, traditionally sailing to Murua for bagi later passed to exchange partners at Ware and in the

Engineer Group, who provided them with the armshells which Louisiade Islanders either call *mwasowaru*, as in the Ware language, or *mwali* as in Muruan. But local informants say that Misima and Panaeati were frequently by-passed in kula exchanges even in earlier times, with the Muruans exchanging directly with partners from the Engineer Islands and Ware. Nowadays, the Misimans very rarely sail to Murua, although the Muruans come to Misima in some years, bringing their own bagi (*bag Murua*) and stone axeblades, and looking for Louisiade *bagi* and pigs. There seems to be very little kula exchange at Misima, although I was told there that 'the old people who always stay in the house still have a few mwali'. There are regular sailing voyages between Panaeati and Murua, *via* Waramata and Egum Islands, and there are still some marriage ties between the two distant islands. Panaeati informants say that today bagi and mwali may be exchanged in either direction from Panaeati, unlike in the classical kula. The Muruans commonly bring bagi, stone axeblades, mwali, and clay cooking pots to Panaeati, seeking to exchange them for pigs, Louisiade bagi and *Conus* shells, the raw material of the mwali armshells. Since *Conus* shells are found in abundance in the lagoon around Sudest, the Sudest and East Calvados people commonly bring *Conus* shells to give as 'gifts' to Panaeati exchange partners, who pass them in quantity to the Muruans in exchange for bagi and stone axeblades. One Panaeati man told me that in the old days, Panaeati big men used to wear mwali at important feasts (hagali).

At the present time it is the indefatigable traders of Ware who are the main conduit between the kula region and the Louisiade. The Ware Islanders visit Sudest, the Calvados Chain, and Panaeati almost every year in sailing canoes and small European-style cutters they have built themselves. They mainly bring stone axeblades from the Suau coast, Duau, and Murua and their own clay cooking pots. In exchange, they may receive bagi, pigs, bundles of sago and gifts of *Conus* shells. Sudest people say that the trade link with Ware is ancient, and a major Sudest clan traces its origin to Ware. But an early European visitor met a Ware man living at Rehua on the south coast of Sudest in the 1880s who said he had been adopted as a child after the Sudest had killed and eaten the adults in his party (Wawn 1893). I met a young Ware man living at Dedehai Island in the East Calvados with his 'namesake', an old Sudest man – from Rehua – who had visited Ware and named his exchange partner's infant after himself twenty years ago. Two years ago, the younger man remained behind to live with his aged namesake while the rest of the Ware party sailed home again from Sudest. A mixed group of Sudest and East Calvados people planned, in December 1978, to bring pigs and sago to an upcoming large feast on Ware to aid their exchange partners and to return the young Ware man to his home.

This young man had sailed twice from Ware to Murua *via* the Engineer and Alcester Islands. He said they brought stone axeblades, clay pots, and mwasowaru shells to Murua, receiving bagi, Muruan stone axeblades, pigs, and even money in exchange. He had also travelled to Duau, Dobu, and Fergusson Islands with expeditions bringing *both* mwasowaru and bagi, plus clay pots, and receiving armshells, bagi, stone axeblades, pigs, and baskets of yams, plus some money. As at Panaeati, there nowadays seems to be a decay of the traditional kula pattern of exchanging necklaces clockwise and armshells counterclockwise, although this informant stressed that bagi are never taken from Ware to Murua 'because there are too many bagi at Murua'.

The Ware are the principal agents in moving bagi manufactured at Rossel, Sudest and the East Calvados Islands into the D'Entrecasteaux Archipelago. They also manufacture finished armshells from *Conus* shells obtained in the Louisiade, trading them not only to the D'Entrecasteaux but to Murua and even to the Mailu and the Motu of Central Province, who covet the armshells for use in brideprice exchange and who pay cash to the Ware people.

The Mailu too are annual visitors to Sudest and the East Calvados Islands. They sail their long, double-hulled canoes 350 miles to the Louisiade on the northwest wind in about March, live on their canoes anchored off local villages, and dive for *Conus* shell, hoping to sail home when the southeast wind begins to blow in early May. Until the 1950s, they used to be accompanied annually on this expedition by Motu-speakers from Hanuabada and the other villages in the Port Moresby area. The Mailu give 'gifts' of tobacco, trade-store plates and cloth or black wild banana seed (*boribori* or *gudugudu*) which is used in the Louisiade for stringing on bagi necklaces but which does not grow there. In return, the Mailu may make their own sago and help themselves to coconuts. The local islanders also occasionally give them *Conus* shells or sell the shells for a small amount of money.

The nature of exchange

There is no clear-cut regional pattern of valuable exchange in the Sudest Island region as there is in the kula trading areas to the northwest where, traditionally at least, necklaces always move clockwise and armshells counterclockwise. The Sudest and their neighbors mount expeditions in quest of ceremonial valuables, pigs, sago, garden produce and household goods when ceremonial obligations – at home or to overseas exchange partners – to contribute valuables at an occasion such as a memorial feast force them to seek these goods. Even though it is true that the Rossel–Sudest–East Calvados bagi-manufacturing area exports enormous quantities of bagi to islands throughout the Massim by means of traditional exchange links, it also imports rare and valued kinds of bagi made elsewhere, such as 'bag Murua' from Woodlark Island. Greenstone axeblades from Duau and Murua Islands and the Suau Coast are the main items which the Sudest-area people seek from their exchange partners to the northwest. But even the Ware Islanders, who are renowned for their ability to offer these same axeblades to the Louisiade people, will sail to Sudest and the East Calvados in hopes of locating the rare giarova, the greenstone axeblades from Rossel Island, which the Ware are said to prize highly. When the Woodlark people sail to Panaeati, they bring clay cooking pots as gifts, even though the Panaeati make and export their own pots. Visitors to Ware bring Ware pots back home to Sudest and the East Calvados, even though the route to and from Ware always involves a stop at Brooker Island, a closer, abundant source of good-quality clay pots. The Sudest export many pigs to distant islands but routinely ask exchange partners on other Louisiade islands to provide pigs as contributions to upcoming Sudest feasts.

The Sudest call an exchange partner '*lo boda*', which literally means 'my person' or 'my kinsperson'. Partners are frequently no relation to each other, but many exchanges are made with kinspeople, members of one's father's clan, and affines. The partners may be of either sex, and many women are active in exchange, leaving their children, households and gardens behind and walking, paddling, or sailing with other interested people to distant villages to seek valuables or to attend a feast and offer contributions to the host.

Sometimes an exchange is concluded on one occasion, as, for example, when a pig is carried off by visitors after the owner has been given a long bagi and perhaps a greenstone axeblade or two. But it is more common for one partner to visit the other and request a valuable or pig with the understanding that the debt (*yoghani*) will be repaid whenever the second partner needs her/his valuable or pig for some ritual occasion and travels to the home of the first to seek repayment (*ghodege*). This system rests upon partners' trust of each other's willingness and ability to repay. Often a visitor travels to a Sudest village from a distant island in search of a pig or a *bagi* owed him or her from an earlier occasion and is forced to live for days or weeks with the partner's family while the partner sets off on his or her own expedition to nearby villages and islands in order to locate the desired item. Some people take advantage of their partners. I met one old Nigaho Island woman after her third unsuccessful one hundred mile round trip voyage by sailing canoe to Rehua on Sudest Island to recover the replacements of two long bagi she herself had made and given to a Sudest exchange partner several years earlier. Traditionally, her only recourse would have been either persuading her allies to raid her partner's village or to practice sorcery or witchcraft against him, but her young nieces and nephews planned to report him to the government officer in charge at Tagula Station, Sudest, in hopes of frightening him into paying his debt.

Occasionally, wealthy and important people practice a formal kind of exchange called reau on Sudest, and leau in the Misima and East Calvados languages, terms which are more commonly applied to the purchase of a Panaeati Island sailing canoe, which is quite a different procedure. Rossel Islanders too know how to reau. The requestor visits his or her exchange partner and presents a fine valuable, a reau, such as a long bagi or greenstone axeblade. The partner then responds by a presentation (*gaugau*) of a large quantity of valuables, such as twenty or thirty axeblades or ceremonial limesticks or daveri (shell currency). Later on the same visit, the requestor is also given a final valuable, or *gorasa*, which might be a bagi, an axeblade, or a single extra daveri. The roles of the partners will normally be reversed the following year or when they next meet.

The magic of exchange

The Sudest and their neighbors believe that all success in obtaining valuables is due to magic, for no one really wants to part with the desired objects. Before setting out on an important quest the leader of an expedition usually prepares the magically-enhanced scented coconut oil called *bunama*. Bunama is occasionally referred to as 'the food of tobo-tobo'. Grated coconut is boiled in a special clay cooking pot which has never been used to boil food. Magically powerful scented roots, bark or leaves are added to the pot, followed by a relic of a dead kinsperson such as a tooth, a fingernail, a fragment of skull or bone, or a lock of hair. Then a magical spell is recited over the contents. People who are requesting valuables wash themselves carefully before entering a village and then apply this bunama to their bodies. They also wear their newest and most attractive garments and may decorate themselves with flowers and scented leaves tucked into their hair and armlets. A few big men put on the *Trochus* shell armlets which are a mark of high status after performing special magic over them. The visitors' aim is to overwhelm their hosts with their beauty, to make the hosts dizzy and trembling with desire so that they 'change their hearts' and hurry to give away valuables with which they never intended to part. The relationship between exchange partners, who are frequently of the same sex, is explicitly likened to that between lovers.

Some Sudest expedition leaders follow a more stringent set of magical rules. All members of the party purge their stomachs by drinking salt water, which is also said to 'make their voices hot' (persuasive). They may eat only ginger and coconut which has been roasted on the fire, the same dietary proscriptions followed by a would-be sorcerer. Women and girls are blinded with desire by the bright skin of youths accompanying the party, even though the bunama has not been applied to anyone's body and is merely being carried along. But the expedition members are forbidden to indulge in sexual dalliance. If they have failed to obtain valuables, their leader may decide during the trip to instruct the youths to seduce the local women in order to change the luck of the party, but any unauthorized sexual adventures would cause the bunama to dry and begin to stink.

Members of the visiting party are normally treated as honored guests, being served the finest food available by the host and family and eating and sleeping in solitary splendor in the best part of the house. It is poor etiquette to discuss the purpose of the visit until after breakfast the next morning. Then, the expedition leader hands the bunama bottle, which is in a basket tied onto a pandanus sleeping mat, to a particularly handsome youth in the visiting party, who sits on the ground in front of the host's house with the bundle on his lap. The leader stands near him and, completing spells meant to enhance the potency of his words, begins a loud ritual speech called *tara* designed to persuade members of the host hamlet to give an abundance of valuables to the visitors. The local villagers gradually assemble to listen and then disappear into their houses to produce their valuables, which they hand to their personal exchange partners in the visiting party. In late 1978, about twenty men and women from Rehua on the south coast of Sudest walked to most of the villages on Sudest to make this formal tara challenge. They were given valuables by most households in every village they visited. This custom seems to be peculiar to Sudest and to be less common nowadays than in earlier times.

The practice of waiting until the visitors' departure before requesting or presenting valuables holds for almost all exchange situations. Sudest and East Calvados people say the Ware Islanders have a slightly different custom: they carry their valuables down and place them on the visiting canoes, just before the visitors depart the island.

Some Sudest Islanders know certain magical procedures which enable them to find bagi and greenstone axeblades buried in the ground under trees or in secret locations in the bush. They appeal through magic to the spirits of dead ancestors, who aid them by revealing the locations of valuables through dreams sent to the living. The valuables themselves are said to have been 'planted in the ground' in earliest times by Rodyo, the Sudest creator spirit. Other important Sudest people possess the powerful magic which causes special small greenstone axeblades, tiny daveri (shell currency) and certain individual pieces of bagi literally to 'give birth' to many larger valuables while locked in the magician's private storage box. I was told of one old man whose floor collapsed under the weight of the new valuables he produced through this kind of magic.

The primary ingredient in any form of magic for obtaining valuables on Sudest is the relic of a dead ancestor, the tooth or piece of bone or hair called a *muramura*. It is best obtained just after death, with the survivor verbally asking the corpse's permission to take the relic and pleading for the spirit's future aid in finding valuables. This aid is conceived of as part of an exchange between the dead and the living. The valuables with which a corpse is decorated are removed just before burial, but their essence travels with the spirit to its new home on Mt Rion. The valuables the spirit later helps the living to find are seen as a repayment of these burial decorations.

Ancestors are also called upon for protection against the jealous sorcery of others. Anyone who dares to be successful in exchange activities is risking his or her life, for someone is always waiting to humble those proud of their wealth and reputation by inflicting sickness and death on them and their families. Most illnesses are routinely attributed to the envy of some powerful sorcerer. One old man told me how a rival made magic to cause a sudden wind to capsize his sailing canoe. He and his party nearly drowned, and his precious metal box full of valuables tore loose from its lashings and sank to the bottom of the sea. But no important person would become prominent in exchange without the security of being adept at sorcery and counter-sorcery.

Travellers must beware too of the witches which haunt the sea, particularly at night, when they send their spirits out to cut off the lips of sailors with a pearlshell so that they will 'talk like dogs' and be unable to find their way home.

Malevolent supernatural creatures called *sirava* or *silava* on Sudest and *silapa* on Misima infest the lagoons and rivers of the Louisiade. Their true form is said to be that of a giant octopus which tries to overturn canoes and boats in order to drown their passengers. Sirava masquerade as fish, stones, and even logs floating on the sea. They are only found in certain specific locations, and travellers must observe taboos which vary with each sirava in order to pass their domains, the most common being a ban on conversation until the dangerous area is safely cleared.

Memorial feasts and exchange

Sudest Islanders must prepare a series of feasts, called *zagaya* or *thagaya*, to commemorate the death of each individual. All kinspeople, as well as the affines of the deceased and his or her kin, plus anyone who is under obligation to any of these people, must organize contributions of cooked and uncooked produce, sago, pigs, and ceremonial valuables for these events. They begin with the burial and move through the feasts called jivia ('break') *velaloga* ('for walking'), *ghanrakerake* ('food goes out') and *mwaguvajo*, over the course of between three and twenty or more years, depending upon the wealth and the number of exchange partners of the kinspeople and their helpers. In-laws are expected to contribute substantially with the knowledge that following a death in their own lineage, the flow of goods will be reversed. In-law contributions are called *muli*.

One individual is selected to be the host and organizer of each ritual event. He or she is called 'the owner of the feast' (*zagaya tanuwagai*) and is normally a close relative of the deceased, such as a child, a parent, or maternal uncle, or else is close kin of a surviving spouse. Women can and do host feasts: the main requirement for zagaya tanuwagai is that he or she have enough prestige and enough exchange partners to mobilize sufficient quantities of the goods necessary to discharge group obligations to the dead. The feasts themselves feature the formal presentations of contributions of food, pig, and valuables to the host, who then with his or her helpers oversees the feeding of the guests, who may number many hundreds at large zagaya. All-night traditional drumming, singing, and dancing is finally followed by the ritual draping of seated mourners, whose skin is blackened with burnt coconut husk, with ceremonial valuables and by the ritual transfer of these valuables to a designated person.

The recipient is normally a patrilateral cross-cousin of the deceased who was chosen during the latter's infancy or childhood by his or her father from among his kin to stand in a special exchange and heir relationship to the child. The person is called *tau*, which is a reciprocal term. A tau may be of either sex, and every Sudest person has one. Tau frequently call each other 'my father' (*ramagu*) and 'my child', even if the tau is female, and tau relationships represent a series of patrilateral links in an otherwise strongly matrilineal area. The 'father' will have a tau and heir chosen from among his or her *own* patrilateral kinsfolk. A good tau is supposed to contribute food, pigs, ceremonial valuables and trade-store goods upon request without as strong an expectation of return of equivalent items when needed as from normal exchange partners, for when the 'child' dies, the tau is supposed to be given all of the valuables collected at the last memorial feast. He or she is then said to 'eat the feast' (*ighan zagaya*), or to 'eat the fruit' (*ighan ghunoi*) of the deceased. The tau and his or her helpers then must lead the mourners to a stream or to the sea, wash off the black mourning pigment, oil their bodies with coconut oil, cut and dress their hair, cut the long mourning skirts of women and dress them in new, knee-length festive coconut-leaf skirts (and dress male mourners in new clothes), paint their faces, decorate them with shell necklaces (bagi), and put flowers and magically-enhanced scented leaves in the erstwhile mourners' hair and fern-fibre armlets. Then the tau leads the newly-resplendent principal mourners, particularly a surviving spouse, to dance publicly in the village center for the first time since the death years earlier. Afterwards, all mourning obligations of surviving spouses and other affines, who bear the brunt of mourning restrictions rather than the deceased's close matrilineal kin, are lifted. If the zagaya honored a dead father – or one of his kinspeople – his children (who are *not* his kin) may for the first time since the death eat pig, coconut, sago or garden produce belonging to the father's clan.

If the tau dies before his or her 'child', which frequently happens, a new one is chosen from among the father's kin. Some people contribute much more to their tau during their lifetime than others. Frequently on Sudest, a powerful kinsperson of the deceased will make it publicly known that he or she expects to 'eat the feast' as compensation for a lifetime of aiding the dead person in finding the pigs and ceremonial valuables which were necessary to fulfill the latter's own ritual obligations. Open defiance of such a demand is very rare, because anyone who angers such a powerful individual is believed to be risking being killed by sorcery. Frequently there are several claimants to the 'fruit' of the memorial feasts, and the other surviving kin and affines must attempt to placate all parties, often by deciding that the flow of valuables will go to different people at each of the series of required feasts, or by searching for extra valuables to be presented to several people at a big zagaya.

The demands of the memorial feast sequence affect the lives of every Sudest adult. At any given time, almost every household will be related by blood or marriage to someone who has died fairly recently and whose feasts have not yet been completed. Each person knows then that he or she will be expected to contribute garden vegetables, sago, pigs, or ceremonial valuables to some upcoming ritual event, and it is necessary to produce or to borrow these items beforehand to uphold one's good name. The demands of the feast system insure that Sudest people grow more food, make more sago and raise more pigs than they would if they only had to satisfy basic subsistence needs.

Big feasts normally occur a few months after the yam harvest, which is in July, and the clearing and planting of the new year's yam gardens. First the organizer must decide that there is enough garden produce, including expected contributions from other kin and from affines, to feed all the invited guests for up to several weeks, for it takes that long for the guests to assemble from distant islands and villages. Then the hosts will make sago for the feast, they and their helpers spending several weeks to produce up to 2,000 double-bundles of sago. Meanwhile, all the people of the deceased's lineage and their spouses' close kin must search the Sudest villages and the villages of more distant islands for the necessary ceremonial valuables.

Ceremonial valuables

The most important would-be contributors must try to find the reddish ceremonial shell necklaces called bagi. Bagi are manufactured, using a wood-and-string hand-operated pump drill and a grinding stone, on Rossel Island, in the East Calvados Islands such as Grass, Panawina, Joannet, Dedehai, Panaman and Nimowa, and, more rarely nowadays, on Sudest, where only the inhabitants of Western Point (Boboghagha) Village still regularly make bagi, for the Western people are culturally closer to the East Calvados Islanders than they are to the other Sudest villagers. Men do most of the arduous diving for the shell, but many East Calvados women are expert bagi-makers. Bagi are also occasionally made further northwest along the Calvados Chain: once when paddling off Western Point, Sudest, we met two Panaumara Island men diving in the lagoon for bagi shell, and I have seen unusual bright orange bagi which was manufactured at Bagaman Island, the distinctively orange bagi shell also being found off Motorina Island, which seems to have been a more important bagi-manufacturing center in the past. During the nineteenth century, the trade links between Murua (Woodlark Island) and the Louisiade Archipelago seem to have been more important than they are nowadays, and many *bag Murua*, as they are called, were in circulation in the Louisiade. I saw several of the pinkish-purple bag Murua change hands at Sudest and East Calvados feasts in late 1978. Another type of bagi used more often in the past is called *yarumoi*. It too is pinkish-purple in color, and some people say they are made on Murua, while others say they were made long ago on Sudest; Sudest people also used to manufacture or trade for bagi-decorated woven belts called *kaipwesa*, but at present, there is only one left on the island. I have also been shown a long, narrow dark brown piece of polished hardwood perforated along the rim with small holes. This is called *jeja*, which means

483

dolphin, and my informants insisted that this object literally is a dolphin's tooth (*jeja ninie*). The perforations are for stringing bagi along the outside, and jeje so decorated were formerly used as ceremonial valuables.

There were several other types of bagi formerly in circulation said to be from 'down there', meaning the kula region, which were acquired *via* Ware or Misima–Panaeati and may well have been made at Murua. *Gugua* resembled bag Murua but were thicker, *bore* were white bagi, and *gari* were very small in diameter and red. Made closer to home were *elagherova* (literally, 'large one from Rossel Island'), a wide bagi made at Rossel and no longer circulated at Sudest feasts. Dalepa were white *bagi* made on Sudest.

In the nineteenth century, the Sudest also exchanged *sibom*, bagi-rimmed bone limesticks made from the wing or leg bones of a big black bird called *taradi* (cassowary?) which lives on the Papua New Guinea mainland. I was told early European traders used to bring sibom to Sudest to barter for gold. They are no longer in use.

The people of the Louisiade had very little contact with whites, except for occasional visits from whalers and later traders, until gold was discovered on Sudest in 1888. Suddenly, there were hundreds of white miners on the island. Only a few trade-store owners remained a few years later, the miners having moved on, buying gold the Sudest themselves had learned to mine in exchange for European foods, black stick tobacco, metal knives and axes and strangely, Rossel-Island-style bagi. One storekeeper in particular, a widow named Mrs Mahoney, discovered about 1900 that Sudest people were more likely to bother panning for gold if she offered bagi for sale. So she imported Rossel Island men to dive for the shell, which is even more abundant in the lagoon off Sudest than it is off Rossel, where there is more demand for it, and to manufacture bagi. Some Sudest people say that this was the first time that bagi were made on Sudest. They say that previously there was very little (some say none) of the red Rossel bagi, which they now call *bagi moli*, or 'true bagi', in circulation on Sudest, and that it was only in the 1890s, following the cessation of most fighting due to the intervention of Europeans, that Rossel Islanders visited their sometime allies and sometime enemies, the Sudest, bringing their bagi as a peace offering and exciting much desire for them among the Sudest. In any case, the skill of bagi-making spread during the first half of this century all over Sudest and the East Calvados Islands, although by the present time, the Sudest seem to have lost interest in this tedious and exacting process more rapidly than the East Calvados, or Saisai, people, who remain prolific bagi-makers, perhaps because they are more generally oriented to maritime activities (i.e., diving for the shells, which may take months) and because their islands are more ecologically marginal, forcing them to rely more heavily on trade and exchange even to obtain food. A standard ceremonial bagi consisting of two four-foot long strands or 'sides' tied together with a conical 'head' of a conch shell decorated with bagi, black wild banana seed, and pearlshell pendants – the 'head' is formally called a bubugera – can be exchanged for a large pig. Bubugera are manufactured on Sudest and traded to all the islands between Misima and Panaeati and Rossel. One 'side' of a bagi (without the heavy bubugera) is frequently worn at feasts as a necklace, particularly by women. Very short bagi which just loop around the neck are called *samakupo*, and many people wear them daily for decoration. A few of the longest, reddest, thinnest, oldest and most remarkable bagi are named, and their histories may be traced.

Another bagi-decorated valuable used on Sudest is an oversized, carved wooden ceremonial limestick with a mushroom-like shape called a ghenagá, *ghena* being the Sudest word for an ordinary limestick. These too are traded throughout the Louisiade Archipelago, but there do not seem to be many in circulation on Sudest. They are not essential ceremonially, as other valuables may be substituted for them.

More common and also manufactured on Sudest are the smaller, exquisitely-carved tortoise-shell limesticks called wonamo jilevia (literally, 'tortoise-shell'). These are made only on Sudest, but again are traded throughout the archipelago. They too have their rims decorated with flat discs of bagi sewn through tiny holes. Sudest men (women do not seem to carve either ghenagá or wonamo jilevia) make the limesticks and then wait until they obtain a bagi necklace through the exchange system, then take it apart and stitch it to the limestick to create a new valuable. Wonamo jilevia and ghenagá are said to be equivalent in value to a large stone axeblade.

The Sudest also use large gourds (for the powdered lime used in betelnut chewing) ceremonially. Their ornamental stoppers of fern fibre feature one long boar's tusk springing from the top and are sometimes decorated with bagi. These ceremonial gourds, called *ghumu tinai*, or 'the mother of the lime', are not normally ritually transferred at feasts, as are other valuables, but the Sudest consider their presence in the baskets of the feast host and his or her helpers to be an essential sign of wealth to set off the ceremonial limesticks which are in fact transferred to the person who 'eats the feast'.

Perhaps the most essential ceremonial valuables on Sudest are the greenstone (ignimbrite) axeblades called tobotobo. There are many thousands of them in circulation. The majority are the smaller blades called *tawai, gozara, malomalo,* or *bwam,* which measure from fingertip to wrist on an adult. Before the midnineteenth century, when European iron axes first reached the region, bwam were essential for practical use as axeheads, especially for clearing the rain forest to create new garden land and for chopping down sago palms. They were also used as weapons. Sudest people say that five bwam equal one very long axeblade, just as European money has different denominations. The long blades, which are frequently a foot in length and may stretch from fingertip to elbow, are called *giazagu*. They are occasionally called *palelesalu*, especially in the East Calvados, which seems to be a term borrowed from the Ware language. The Sudest say that bwam, giazagu, and intermediate sizes of blade called *kasabwaibwaileta* and *giazagu damwadamwai* (or 'leaves') come from 'down there'. When more closely questioned, they say that 'down there' may mean Ware Island, Duau (Normanby) Island, Loloman or Dawin on the Suau Coast on the Papua New Guinea mainland, or Murua (Woodlark) Island, more specifically Siloga, a name they know refers to the site on Murua where axeblades are found. They say that all of these locations except for Ware Island are the places where the axeblades originate. Sudest believe that tobotobo are not shaped by human beings but that they 'grow in the streams like shells in the sea' in these favored locations. Ware Island is the nearest source for these tobotobo. The Ware traders obtain the blades from Suau, Duau, and Murua by offering mwasowaru (mwali) armshells or bagi, both likely obtained in the Louisiade Archipelago, as well as their own clay cooking pots. They then may sail as far as the Calvados Chain or Sudest to exchange the tobotobo, their pots and a few other items such as face paint from Duau for more bagi, pigs, bundles of sago and oddly, even for the rare kind of long tobotobo called a giarova. Giarova originate on Rossel, again supposedly just growing in the streams, this time in a secret location in the interior above Jinjo Village near Mt Goywo. Giarova are exceptionally long and thin blades which are dark green and do not have the white striations which are prized in some giazagu, particularly those from Suau. Ware visitors are said especially to covet them.

The only tobotobo which come from Sudest itself are three-inch long, thick, crudely-chipped triangular greenish blades called *roguigu*, or 'one which calls'. I was told these have been on Sudest 'since the world was made', and that Rodyo, the Sudest creator spirit who lives on Mt Rion, the island's highest peak, 'planted them in the soil' long ago. I doubt if these ever were functional axeblades. People said children in the old days occasionally used them as toys, but today they are treasured as magical aids, for a person who knows the right magic is said to be able to make them literally give birth to large tobotobo like giazagu and giarova. They are also said to 'call' other valuables to join them.

Tobotobo are displayed at memorial feasts and in other situations where they are ritually transferred wedged into large, ornately-carved, 7-shaped wooden handles called *enima* or *yenima*. They traditionally have the stylized head of a bush fowl (*mankweli*) carved at the top of the acute angle. Enima are completely non-functional as handles, and a person must carefully keep one hand on the axeblade and the other on the handle, or the blade will fall out during a ritual presentation, which often happens. Especially skilled Sudest (and some East Calvados) men carve the enima for their own use or to trade, and they are sometimes used as far away as Misima. The Sudest people count the number of the unwieldy enima being carried to a feast or away from a village to find out the number of tobotobo which particular individuals intend to contribute to a feast or have obtained on a trading venture. The tobotobo themselves are sometimes called *enima ghunoi*, or 'the fruit of the enima'.

The small, ancient-looking orange shell-pieces called daveri were probably even more important on Sudest as ceremonial valuables hundreds of years ago than they are today. There are many thousands of them on the island. The term daveri and tobotobo are both frequently used to refer generically to all types of valuables. Most Sudest daveri are two to three inches long, and they are kept in tiny woven coconut-leaf pouches. Daveri are the same as the ndap shell currency of nearby Rossel Island, with the longer Sudest daveri looking identical to lower-denomination Rossel ndap. Many inch-long true Rossel ndap circulate on Sudest (without coconut pouches) for they are a popular item of exchange. Sudest treat the smaller, bright orange Rossel ndap as equivalent in value to the longer, deep orange Sudest daveri. Length and redness are desirable in daveri. Their use as valuables exchanged at memorial feasts has spread from Sudest to the nearby East Calvados Islands only in the last twenty years. Sudest believe that all daveri are literally the excreta of a mythical snake which used to live on the island (see below) and they were not made by human beings, even though they still sometimes find the unshaped daveri shells in their natural form when diving in the lagoon.

One last ceremonial valuable is also used even today as a spoon and a vegetable peeler. It is called *gile*, and it is a polished and shaped pearl-shell. Particularly large and fine ones are called *ginuba*: Sudest say ginuba are only found if a person appeals through magic to a dead kinsperson, whose ghost may then consent to reveal the specific location of the ginuba in the lagoon waters to the sleeper in a dream. Gile are essential in the memorial feast called *jivia*, or 'break', where the kinspeople of the deceased are ritually fed by mourning in-laws with specially-prepared sago using a gile.

487

Maria Lepowsky

People aspiring to host feasts must also accumulate many other items of wealth by requesting them from exchange partners. They include such manufactured goods as Brooker Island clay cooking pots, Misima carved wooden platters, wild pandanus sleeping mats, wooden hair combs, garden and betelnut baskets, fern-fibre armlets, and decorative women's coconut-leaf skirts. All these will be ritually transferred to the person who 'eats the feast'. Objects such as clay pots, mats, and decorative betelnut baskets, as well as metal trade-store plates, cups, cutlery and fabric, are also necessary as gifts for drummers, singers and dancers, who perform all night during the feast and as farewell gifts to important guests who have come to contribute valuables to help the host. The trade-store goods and sometimes such items as bags of rice, tea-boxes, bales of sugar, and blocks of trade-tobacco may also be obtained by using traditional methods of requesting goods of exchange partners for use at an up-coming feast, just as baskets of garden produce or bundles of sago are requested.

Other uses of ceremonial valuables

On Sudest, the act of travelling to someone's home to request ceremonial valuables and other goods is called ghiva. The most common stimulus for a ghiva expedition is an upcoming memorial feast to which one is obliged to contribute, but there are many other occasions when valuables are necessary. These include land-purchases, canoe-purchase and canoe 'rental', brideprice payments to house builders, payments to sorcerers (contract killings), dispute settlements or compensation payments, payments to mourners, love gifts, and payments at the ritual hair-cutting of the first-born boy and girl in each sibling set. In earlier times, valuables such as *yarumoi* (bagi), tobotobo and daveri were used to form a war alliance, to pay war-allies for their services, to bribe would-be attackers and to make peace.

The purchase of several acres of good garden land might require about thirty tobotobo, several fine bagi, ten daveri, various other valuables, many baskets of produce, and dozens of bundles of sago. The process of paying this off frequently takes many years. Canoe-purchase is discussed earlier. When 'chartering' a sailing canoe (sailau) and crew in order to ghiva for one day, it is customary to present the owner with a clay pot full of garden produce boiled in coconut cream. For a longer period, for example two weeks, a large pig or a bagi would be appropriate.

Brideprice is called *vazavó*. It normally consists of one bagi and two large or ten small tobotobo. The groom's family must then present the family of the bride with baskets of garden produce.

A housebuilder is paid bagi, tobotobo and pigs, and he and his crew are fed while they work.

I was repeatedly told that one daveri is enough to pay a sorcerer to kill someone, and I was once shown a daveri that was supposed to have turned bright red from the victim's blood after being so used. But most people thought that a sorcerer would want at least one bagi and five tobotobo. Sudest is notorious for its virulent sorcery, and some individuals are said by local people and government officials to extort valuables from people who are afraid that if they refuse the 'request', they or their families will fall sick and die.

Compensation payments are called *sasi*. A bagi might be given to settle a serious quarrel or an insult. A few years ago, a man was coming to visit a Sudest village when the inhabitants laughed at him for his shining bald head. Deeply offended, he submerged himself to the neck in the stream at the village boundary and refused to come into the village until he was given a bagi as *sasi*. In another story, a man died and his clan sister from the other side of Sudest came to mourn. So intense was her grief, they told me, that she remained just outside the settlement tearing her hair and crying wildly. She too refused to come into the house until one of his family gave her sasi, in this case a tobotobo. The idea of compensation in the latter case probably relates to the belief that some individual was said to have worked sorcery on the dead man, although in this case it was not a member of the immediate family.

The Sudest have a custom called *buwa*, where the first time a man or boy is discovered to have spent the night inside a house with an unmarried woman or girl, the woman's family presents a small basket to the man filled with items such as daveri, gile, fabric, trade-store plates and cutlery, money, and sometimes even bagi or tobotobo. The man is not supposed to take these things, but to add an equivalent amount of valuables to the basket and return it to the woman's family, after which he may sleep with her without further payment for as long as is mutually agreeable. These items are distributed among her kinsfolk and do not go to her.

It is also customary for men to give love gifts (*mwadai*) to their paramours. As one young girl explained: 'If you sleep with young boys, they might give you some tobacco or money, but if you sleep with big men [giagia] they will give you bagi and tobotobo.'

After a first-born child is about six months old, its mother's kin make a small feast and present the father with one long bagi and one giazagu. The baby's hair is then ritually cut for the first time. This ceremony is supposed to be held for the first boy and the first girl born to a couple.

Maria Lepowsky

The mythology of exchange

The Sudest say that Rodyo, the creator spirit, gave all ceremonial valuables to them 'when the world was born'. Rodyo, who is sometimes also called Loi, caused the world to be born by thinking of it. Himself a member of Magho clan, he created all places, the sun, the moon, the sea, and all people, assigning them to the various clans and appointing their totems. Nowadays Sudest people are more interested in recounting the following story than they are the original creation myth:

The peace of the community of spirit beings who live to this day on Mt Rion, the highest peak on Sudest, was long ago disturbed by one of their number called Alagh [or Ghalagh]. Rodyo found himself unable to sleep, so he banished Alagh from the island. Alagh sailed away 'to the land of Europeans' with Egogona, one of his two wives, in a European-style boat built by Bwaileva, Rodyo's carpenter. With him he took all the noisy objects belonging to Europeans which Rodyo found objectionable: engines, hammers and nails, horses, cattle, chickens and ducks, and all the other implements of Europeans, including their money. That is why the Sudest use ceremonial valuables and traditional artifacts, and Europeans use money and have a completely different set of material possessions.

The unspoken corollary to the above story is of course that if only the right magic is used, Alagh may one day sail his boat Buliliti back to Sudest full of the European cargo which he took away so long ago.

The daveri is said to be the original and most important valuable on Sudest, in some contradiction to the story of Rodyo's assigning the Sudest people all of their valuables at once. The following tale of the introduction of daveri to Sudest is the most widely-told myth on the island today:

Long ago, there was a snake [mwata] living on Goodenough Island.[2] One day it decided to leave – one version holds that the snake was angry over some slight given it by the Goodenough people, another that it was a 'Satan snake' which had murdered someone and was driven off, and a third that it found Goodenough Island too noisy because of the constant sound of drumming and decided to seek out a new home where there were no drums. The snake departed, sleeping the first night at Sanoroa Island, and then it went to Eyaus on the south coast of Misima Island. It continued to the south coast of Sudest Island and travelled up the large river called Ghekiwidighe, creating its present snake-like bends. The snake found shelter in a cave called Egheterighea on the north side of the island, just underneath the mountain known as Tuage. There it was discovered by an old woman, who fed it secretly. Every morning she would bring it a big plate of moni [sago and green-coconut pudding], and every morning the snake would in gratitude give her a piece of its excrement. The snake's excrement [mwata re] was daveri.

The old woman had two grandsons who worked hard to make sago and who were puzzled as to why their bundles of sago kept disappearing [in another version there are thirty youths making sago]. The grandsons decided to spy on the old

490

woman. They followed her to the cave and saw her give the snake moni and receive daveri in exchange. Furious, they drove the snake away from the cave with sticks of *maje* and *zhuwe* [two trees which bear edible nuts]. It fled to the mangrove-lined shore at a place called Egotú. Just before it left Sudest Island, it turned back to the old woman and begged her to fetch its sandalwood bark [ome] which it had forgotten in its haste. The snake then dove into the sea using the ome as its 'boat' and as protection for its belly. The snake was actually a person afflicted with leprosy [*raibok*]. It was attacked on one side by a swordfish and on the other by a shark, for they were attracted by the smell of its sores. As the snake dodged its two adversaries, it created the S-shaped passage in the reef which is still called Snake Passage even by Europeans. The snake reached Piron [Yeina] Island safely. But when it looked back, it could still see the mountain of Tuage on Sudest. Determined not to stop until it had left behind even the sight of the mountain where it had known unhappiness, it continued to Rossel Island. It went up the large river called Kwejinewe near Saman Village on the south coast. But the way up the river was blocked by two crocodiles with their noses close together. The snake said a magical spell:

Pijo pajo kambajo yonavodu.
Nyi wala du ['You close your eyes'].

The crocodiles closed their eyes and the snake slipped past. The crocodiles then blamed each other for letting it through, and they fought, cutting each other into little pieces. The snake reached the river's headwaters. It is still there today, and anyone who knows the right magic may go there and see the snake in its true human form.

A young woman from Goodenough Island living temporarily on Sudest told me a similar story from Goodenough:

There was a 'special snake' which used to live on a pile of flat stones which was the traditional meeting place in one Goodenough village. One woman fed it, going there alone each day. After her two sons had grown up, she took them with her one day, cautioning them not to frighten the snake. But when they saw it, they shouted in fear, and the snake left, going to Sudest and Rossel Islands. It took with it all the fish and valuable shells, and this is why the waters around Goodenough are so poor, while those of Sudest and Rossel are very rich.

The Goodenough version states explicitly that the snake is the bringer of valuables and that its being carelessly frightened away resulted in impoverishment of the seas, the source of both food and of shell for making valuables. The Goodenough people are said to be still hoping for the snake to return with all the valuables it once took away. When it left, I was told it created off-shore oil deposits with its belly, a source of wealth being explored a few years ago by an American company.

On Sudest, the snake left its excrement behind in the form of daveri – a striking corroboration of the classical Freudian equation of money with excrement. But when it was driven away, the snake took its sandalwood

491

with it. Sandalwood grows only on Rossel and not on Sudest. It is highly valued on both islands for its magical and medicinal power, and nowadays, it is imported from Rossel by the Sudest.

I was also told that there is a mountain on Goodenough near the snake's original home called Tuage, the same name still borne by the peak under which the snake is said to have sheltered on Sudest. It is tempting to speculate that the whole snake-myth represents an otherwise forgotten early migration from Goodenough to Sudest and Rossel, or at least an early exchange voyage!

On both Sudest and Rossel, many of the spirits believed to inhabit the mountain peaks and other locations are said to be human in shape but to assume the form of a snake at will. Village sorcerers are also said to be able to turn themselves temporarily into snakes.

There are no origin myths about tobotobo on Sudest. But, there is a story known today only to a few old people of three spirits which are said to be the 'owners' (*tanuagaji*) of all tobotobo. The first is named Maoni, and he lives on top of the mountain called Rubi, which is near the eastern tip of the island. A second spirit, also called Maoni, lives on top of Mt Ima, above Araida Village on the north coast. Both of them are said to be 'in charge of' all tobotobo from Murua, Duau, Suau and Ware, the region normally referred to as 'down there'. The third spirit is named Basidi. It used to live at Etubuda, a place on the shore near Western Point, Sudest, but it migrated long ago to the top of Mt Ngwo (Mt Rossel), the tallest peak on Rossel Island. Basidi is in charge of giarova, the axeblades which come from Rossel.

No one was able to tell me how or why these beings are the 'owners of tobotobo', although a few people probably know how to appeal to them magically for aid in obtaining valuables. Most Sudest had never heard of Maoni or Basidi, although there is an expression, '*Ighoa maon*', which means 'He/she has ceremonial valuables.' But this is not a frequently-used term. People usually call ceremonial valuables *kune* or *ghune*, words which are very likely borrowed from the language of Ware Island, where kune refers to the exchange relations called kula in the Trobriand Islands.

There are no Sudest myths concerning the origin of bagi, but a few people had heard the following Rossel-Island story which I also was told when I visited that island:

Once an old woman and her granddaughter lived at Yongga Bay on the north coast of Rossel Island. The girl would come down to the shore every day to fetch seawater for salting food. One day she saw a small snake. She hit it repeatedly to try and kill it. Instead, it grew larger and ate her. When her grandmother came to look for her, the snake said, 'Your granddaughter hit me and tried to kill me, so I ate her. But here is something as brideprice for her.' It gave the old woman a bagi. That is how Yongga Bay came to be the first place where bagi was made.

Just as in the daveri origin-myth, a supernatural being in the form of a snake presents an old woman with the first piece of shell currency as part of an exchange and as compensation. Yongga Bay is even today renowned for the manufacture of fine red bagi.

When I first came to the Louisiade Archipelago, I met a Misima man who said he had at his home village the oldest and most famous bagi in the whole kula region. Its name was *Kumakala Kedakeda*, which he translated as 'the track of the monitor lizard'. This bagi had been circulated on every island between Kiriwina and Rossel, he said, and he himself had obtained it from an old man at Pantava Village on Sudest in 1969. He was keeping it because its renown 'called' other valuables to him, although he admitted he had been criticized for removing it from circulation for so long and was warned that he was exposing himself to grave danger of sorcery.

I realized that this bagi bore virtually the same name as the one which was won by the mythical hero Kasabwaybwayreta in Malinowski's (1922: 322–4) and Fortune's (1936:216–20) versions of a kula tale from Kiriwina and Tewara respectively. Later, I found a published Misima version of the same myth (Peter 1976). The Misima tale is much like the other two: a hero, here named Mwasiana Kulikuli, is afflicted with scabies (*kulikuli*). He travels to Murua Island with five canoes of men in quest of a fine bagi called Kumakala Kedakeda. By slipping off his diseased skin and charming the owner and his wife with a special betelnut, he wins the coveted bagi. But on the way home, he is left on an island called Laulauwana by his jealous compatriots. He follows a star into the sky, marries, and eventually climbs back down to earth onto his own special betelnut tree by using Kumakala Kedakeda as a ladder. He finally hosts a big feast at which the magnificent bagi is displayed.

My own requests to informants on Sudest and the East Calvados Islands to recount 'the story of Kumakala Kedakeda' produced quite a different tale. I was repeatedly told that this was a story from Ware Island either learned on Ware or from Ware visitors on exchange voyages. This long story begins with the entire population of an island (identified by some informants as Misima) migrating to Ware in fear of three dangerous supernatural animals, a pig named Boyogaragara, an octopus and an eagle. One woman is left behind on the island because she is afflicted with scabies. She has intercourse with a white heron (the totem bird of an important clan) and gives birth to the hero, Mankaputaitai. He grows up, and his mother instructs him to kill each of the beasts, which he is able to do. He sends a magical sign in the form of a toy canoe to Ware, and all the people return home. When they come to thank Mankaputaitai for killing their enemies, he becomes angry and goes to lie under a tall pandanus tree. His uncles take three young girls one after the other to offer them in marriage to him. Mankaputaitai says, 'I want only one thing. Give me the bagi called Kumakala Kedakeda.' So they bring it and hang it over a branch of the pandanus tree, and it is so long that its conch-shell pendant (bubugera) touches the sand. Then Mankaputaitai marries all three of the girls and provides a big pig and plenty of food for everyone to eat at his marriage feast.

The payment of a fine bagi to the triumphant warrior is congruent with the early custom of giving tribute in the form of cermonial valuables to a distinguished fighter. But Mankaputaitai is angry with the people for having abandoned his mother to her fate because of her scabies and thus will not be placated until he is given the very longest, finest bagi and all three of the girls as compensation (sasi). It is curious that the motif of the hero abandoned because of a repellent skin disease who triumphs later continues to be associated with the story of Kumakala Kedakeda in all of these versions, although here it is Mankaputaitai's mother and magical ally who is afflicted with scabies. It is also intriguing that in the important Sudest myth of the snake who brings wealth in the form of daveri but who is insulted and driven away, the hero is said to suffer from the running sores of leprosy. As in the Trobriand Islands, the Louisiade peoples strive to make themselves more beautiful through physical and magical means in order to be successful in obtaining valuables. The moral here might be that it is unwise to mistreat a would-be exchange partner who is physically repellent and who seems to be offering a worthless item in exchange for hospitality, because one may lose an opportunity for great wealth. Chasing away the mythical snake from Sudest is widely agreed to have been a big mistake.

Exchange and cultural change

Before the coming of the Europeans, trade and exchange relations in the Louisiade Archipelago were frequently disrupted by war. Even peoples with a long-standing trade relationship might become adversaries. The Sudest say that in the old days, the Brooker Islanders used to sail to Sudest to trade their clay cooking pots for bundles of sago just at they do nowadays but that these same Brooker Islanders would occasionally raid the coasts of Sudest, killing and kidnapping the inhabitants and plundering villages and gardens of food and valuables. Oral tradition indicates that the total volume of trade was considerably less in the last century than it is today: the Sudest and Calvados Chain Islanders owned fewer sailing canoes than at present, and the safety and potential benefit of an exchange voyage were affected by what seems to have been a constantly changing pattern of alliances and enmities between island peoples. Several informants pointed out that on the larger islands of Sudest and Misima, it was neighboring groups within each island who were most often at war with each other and that each small local group negotiated its own agreements to trade with islanders from overseas. Sometimes they even invited distant trading partners to join them in battle against neighboring enemies on the home island and rewarded their allies with ceremonial valuables. It is striking that the peoples whom the Sudest say most frequently raided their island in earlier times – the Brooker, Sabara, and Engineer Group Islanders – all lived on small islands which are especially prone to drought and crop-failure and where even nowadays there is not always sufficient food at home to support the whole population.

But despite the early hazards of warfare, the network of interisland trade and exchange routes seems to have been as extensive as it is today, even if the total number of trips made and the volume of goods exchanged were much lower. Peaceful exchange voyages represent a more efficient and less risky way of obtaining desired items, such as garden produce, sago, pigs, clay pots, stone axeblades and ceremonial valuables, than raiding, and maintaining trade relations between islands which produce a variety of specialized and desired commodities leads to a higher standard of living for all parties.

Early uses of ceremonial valuables and patterns of alliance and enmity which affected exchange may be seen in the story of Dulubia, which is widely known on Sudest and the East Calvados. Dulubia was the leader of the last war party from the Engineer Group Islands to invade the Louisiade, an event which took place about 1910, a full twenty years after the white goldminers had left Sudest Island.

Dulubia and his followers used to sail every year from their home on Kwaraywa Island in the Engineer Group to Sudest, Grass and other Louisiade islands to kill and eat the inhabitants and plunder their villages. One year, when the Grass Islanders heard that Dulubia's party had already landed at Kuanak Island in the East Calvados, whose people were Dulubia's allies, they sent a message to a champion Sudest fighter named Kalinga, proposing a formal war alliance by the traditional method of giving him a shell necklace (a gugua) wrapped in a package with cracked-open *saido* nuts. Kalinga visited Grass Island to discuss strategy with his new allies and returned home. Dulubia and his people sailed past Grass Island, throwing spears at the islanders on the beach and spearing one man through the hand. They continued to the south coast of

495

Sudest, anchoring near the present-day village of Madawa. The Sudest led the foreigners to inland Sine Village where Kalinga lived, for Dulubia and Kalinga had long been friends and probably exchange partners, even addressing each other as 'my namesake', a mark of a close relationship.

The unsuspecting Dulubia sat and talked in his own language with Kalinga while five whole betelnut trees were cut to give him as a present and food was prepared. Kalinga told Dulubia to call all of his people into the village to eat. Kalinga's mother took off her outer skirt and handed it to her son, the signal to attack. Kalinga produced a European axe buried in the ground where he sat. Dulubia said, 'My namesake, what are you doing with me?' Kalinga replied, 'I am killing you because you attacked Grass Island.' After their leader was slain, the Kwaraywa people fled in all directions. Dulubia's wife removed her skirt so that a pursuer could not seize it. Kalinga grabbed her arm and told her not to be afraid, for the Sudest only planned to kill Dulubia.

Seeking vengeance, the Kwaraywa people attacked the Sudest village of Helahau, where their new leader Iwaraya, Dulubia's wife's brother, was killed when he was hit on the head by a stone. His younger brother led the rest of the party by sea to nearby Sapelahau Village, where two Sudest men on shore frightened off the attackers by holding two sticks as if they were shotguns. The Kwaraywa next went to Mamanila Village on Panawina Island in the East Calvados, massacring the Mamanila people, who had been so intent on distributing and eating a large, freshly-cooked turtle that they did not see the enemy canoes approaching. The Kwaraywa continued to nearby Panaumara (Palakelu) Island. The Panaumara fled up into a big tree in which they had built a house to use during enemy raids. The Kwaraywa set fire to the tree. When it was about to fall, the Panaumara threw down a shell necklace (gugua) to stop the fighting. The Kwaraywa put out the fire with seawater and sailed home.

Meanwhile, Dulubia's body had already been eaten by the Sudest. Kalinga and his people took Dulubia's head to Grass Island, where it was roasted in a stone oven. The Sudest decorated the head with facepaint, scented resin, flowers and leaves and presented it formally to the Grass Islanders. The Grass people ate it, each person consuming a mouthful of Dulubia's brain. Then the Grass Islanders presented their Sudest ally Kalinga with about 100 valuables, mainly greenstone axeblades and yarumoi and gugua shell necklaces, and killed a pig for the Sudest to eat. Dulubia's skull was placed in a shallow cave behind the village, where it remained until only a few years ago, when an old Grass Island woman, angry because the skull was being used as a magical aid by sorcerers, hurled it into the sea.

The custom of ritually decorating and presenting the head of a slain enemy and the accompanying cannibal feast were called *ghanmagha-maghada*. Normally the body was cooked separately in clay cooking pots specially decorated with ornamental leaf-pendants and strings of white cowrie-shells. These pots were always broken after the feast. In the days before pacification, the principal occasions at which shell necklaces, greenstone axeblades and other valuables changed hands in the Sudest–East Calvados area were these feasts, when one group would present its allies with the decorated head, literally called the 'skull' (*kinore*), of a mutual enemy in exchange for ceremonial valuables. The Misima-area peoples seem also to have practised exchanges involving skulls, for several Misima informants mentioned that 'the old people used to use skulls instead of bagi', acquiring the skull of an enemy from an exchange partner, then ritually shattering it to 'clear' all mourning taboos resulting from the death of a kinsperson.

One East Calvados informant from Joannet Island said that in early times, an individual's death meant the surviving spouse's family had to kill someone and present the body of the homicide to the kinspeople of the deceased, who held a feast at which the body was eaten. He said that nowadays pigs are substituted as the obligatory contribution of the spouse's family. The implication seems to be that the survivor is held responsible for the spouse's death through sorcery and that the homicide is compensation. Fortune (1963) reports a similar custom on early Dobu Island.

Sudest people stress that before pacification, they did not hold the elaborate series of feasts in memory of deceased kin and affines which is 'traditional' nowadays. They say that the constant threat of warfare inhibited the long exchange voyages, the production of food surpluses, and the gathering of the large groups of people from many places which are necessary in order to hold a big feast (zagaya). One big man respected for his knowledge of Sudest history told me that in fact the custom of making zagaya in order to 'clear' the death of a relative through the presentation of pigs, food, and ceremonial valuables was an ancient one practiced on Sudest in earliest times, although the number of valuables exchanged then was far less than it is today. He said that later an increase in warfare and raiding disrupted this ceremonial complex so that in the generations immediately prior to white control of the region, there were no zagaya held at all, and cannibal feasts were the main occasions at which ceremonial valuables changed hands.

Another Sudest ceremony which has ended with the advent of the colonial era is called *ghembena*. It used to take place when a powerful big man had chosen his successor. Representatives of all the communities on

Sudest, but no one from off the island, would bring pieces of the shell currency called daveri, and these were ceremonially placed in a line on the young man's thigh as symbols of allegiance. This old custom suggests that even in the chaotic early days when many local Sudest groups were intermittently warring on each other, there was some degree of pan-Sudest political cohesion.

Although warfare and raiding in the Louisiade Archipelago did not cease completely until about 1943, the relatively peaceful conditions in the early part of this century resulted in the revival of the zagaya ceremonial complex on Sudest and, the Sudest claim, the gradual adoption of many of their feasting customs by their neighbors in the East Calvados Islands, who generally trace their origins to Misima Island. More Panaeati sailing canoes were exported into the area, and more exchange voyages were made within the Louisiade Archipelago as well as to Ware, Samarai, the Engineer, and D'Entrecasteaux Islands, facilitating the flow of a far greater volume of ceremonial valuables, food and useful household articles throughout the southern Massim region. The production of bagi necklaces increased on Rossel Island and the manufacture of bagi became common on Sudest and especially on certain of the smaller East Calvados Islands, which were not always able to produce enough food to support their own populations. The Grass and the Brooker Islanders increased their dependence upon trade and exchange, becoming almost full-time trade specialists.

European metal axes were introduced into the Louisiade in the mid-nineteenth century, but the demand for greenstone axeblades of all sizes increased during the colonial period. As Sudest-area big men and big women vied with each other to demonstrate superior generosity and wealth by hosting increasingly lavish feasts and by giving more valuables to exchange partners, the number of bagi, greenstone axeblades and other valuables considered necessary to make a proper showing at a feast became inflated. While two to five ceremonial valuables were considered to be a sufficient number to present in order to 'clear' mourning taboos at the pre-colonial, earliest feasts, the transfer of forty or more valuables is not uncommon even today at Sudest–East Calvados memorial feasts.

The expansion of the feasting complex and of ceremonial exchange activities seems to have reached a peak in the period just before World War II. The first missionaries came to live in the Sudest region in 1947, and both the early Australian Roman Catholics and the Misiman (and Tongan) United Church Mission workers were quick to condemn the 'pagan' excesses of the exchange and feasting activities for taking up so much time and energy, for in those days, large Sudest feasts frequently lasted for a month or more, and there are many feasts every year on the island.

From the 1950s to the present day, the influence of government representatives and their directives has increasingly been felt in the Sudest area. Members of both the earlier colonial and the present-day independent administration have tended to agree that the Sudest and their neighbors would benefit from curtailing their feasting and their 'sail-about' and spending more time earning money to pay their council taxes and their childrens' school fees by working copra, diving for *Trochus* and blacklip pearlshell, and so on.

The Louisiade Local Government Council, which included the Sudest region until late 1978, decreed that feasts were only to take place in the month of December, with November understood to be a month of preparation for them in which exchange-related journeys might take place. These regulations are almost completely ignored by the Sudest–East Calvados peoples, whose feasts still take place from September to as late as April.

The newly-formed Yeleyamba Local Government Council took office in January of 1979. Comprising the islands of Rossel, Sudest, and the East Calvados, the Council is said to be named for 'the ancient trade link' between Rossel and Sudest, as 'Yele' means Rossel and 'Yamba' means Sudest in the Rossel-Island language.

The young, mission-educated members of the new council say that the Sudest–East Calvados peoples waste too much time on feasting and traditional exchange trips. Many of the councillors participate actively in these affairs, and no one proposes abolishing feasting or trading. Everyone from the area seems to take pride in the strength and vigor of traditional customs, a pride which is common throughout Papua New Guinea in the period since independence. But many young councillors advocate further restrictions on the length of time allotted to feasting and exchange trips, the number of feasts permitted, and the number of valuables contributed at feasts, some suggesting that people work for cash and present money instead of valuables at feasts rather than spending so much time walking and sailing long distances in quest of ceremonial valuables which they are not sure of obtaining successfully. So far, these ideas have met with marked resistance on the part of the older generation.

Conclusions

The data from Sudest Island and the Louisiade Archipelago show clearly that 'traditional' exchange activities have undergone many changes since

Maria Lepowsky

the earliest remembered times. Even prior to the intervention of whites, exchange was affected by changing ceremonial requirements and a seeming increase in warfare prior to the colonial period, perhaps due to a rise in local population beyond the subsistence capacities of the smaller islands in the Calvados Chain and the Engineer Group. Pacification stimulated trade, exchange and the zagaya ceremonial complex, despite white disapproval of these activities.

Even today, the elaborate exchange networks insure a higher standard of living in the Louisiade. Exchange promotes regional economic specializations based upon ecological constraints and resources and impels the production of surpluses of garden produce, sago, pigs, pots, other household items and ceremonial valuables. Exchange voyages remain the most efficient means of redistributing the surpluses throughout the islands. They also increase and regulate the social contacts of the small isolated groups who inhabit the archipelago, providing an incentive to continued peaceful relations. The movement of people during exchange trips and visits to memorial feasts enlarges each individual's social world, and many marriages trace their origins to such voyages and feasts, especially important in a region of small communities where there are few potential marriage-partners available without violation of the local rules of incest.

Exchange voyages also facilitate the flow of ideas and the diffusion of custom. Informants repeatedly trace myths, magical spells, dancing and singing styles, and feasting customs to visitors on exchange expeditions.

Exchange activities in the Sudest area are an avenue to potential wealth, prestige, and power open to any woman as well as to any man who chooses to exceed the minimal demands of custom in obtaining valuables. This contrasts sharply with the situation in the kula ring to the northwest, where women are expressly forbidden to go on kula voyages and to compete for valuables with men.[3]

In the Louisiade, there is no distinct separation of 'internal' exchange within one community and the 'external' overseas exchange. Visitors from distant islands bring valuables to contribute to purely local feasts and participate in local ritual, and a visitor may not succeed in taking a valuable home until it has changed hands several times more to satisfy the demands of local custom.

Malinowski (1961:86) wrote that 'the kula is not done under stress of any need, since its main aim is to exchange articles which are of no practical use'. This statement does not hold true for exchange activities in the Louisiade Archipelago. Here the ceremonial valuables which change hands have a distinctly 'practical use': they are an essential form of currency, and they must be obtained by all adults in order to satisfy the

500

demands of custom in a wide variety of situations, including memorial feasts, brideprice payments, land, house- and canoe-purchase, dispute settlements and compensation payments. It is the presence of an upcoming social obligation such as an impending feast which inititates most Louisiade exchange voyages. Perhaps even on Kiriwina, the kula articles have a 'practical use' as forms of currency essential for discharging ceremonial obligations, and kula voyages are more closely tied to the internal demands of local ceremonial exchange than Malinowski describes.

Notes

1 Research on Sudest Island from January 1978 to February 1979 was funded by United States National Science Foundation Dissertation Research Grant Number SOC 75–01878 and by the Chancellor's Patent Fund and the Department of Anthropology of the University of California at Berkeley. Their financial support is gratefully acknowledged.
2 The snake was a female being named Bambagho whose home on Goodenough (Mwalatau) was near a creek in the kune grass called Yome.
3 Cf. Fortune (1963) and Malinowski (1922) however recent research indicates that women do participate in kula exchanges on Tubetube (Macintyre, personal communication) and Kitava (Scoditti, this volume p. 255).

21 Ranked exchange in Yela (Rossel Island)

JOHN LIEP

The riddle of Rossel Island

During a two months' ethnographic survey in the island of Yela in 1921 W. E. Armstrong discovered the role of shell valuables in local exchanges. The shells have become known as the 'Rossel Island money' and have received much attention by economic anthropologists. It is a strange and extremely complicated system of valuables, and Armstrong's record is remarkably extensive for the period of its publication. But the renown of the 'Rossel Island money' is also due to the explicitly theoretical approach taken by Armstrong.

He regarded the Yela shells as a monetary system, and he constructed what is maybe the first model in social anthropology to account for the functioning of the system. On the basis of what he saw as the fundamental elements of the system he presented his explanation, as 'the simplest and most pleasing solution of the majority of the facts' (Armstrong 1928:64). The model presumes that the taking of interest is the key principle of Yela exchange, to a degree that compound interest even enters into the relationship of value between the monetary units. However several features of the exchange system, as reported by Armstrong, were inconsistent with his interpretation. These contradictions have become the cause of much argument about the 'Rossel Island money'.

The present analysis is based on eighteen months of fieldwork in Yela from late 1971 to 1973. My main purpose was to investigate the modern exchange system and, possibly, clear up some of the confusion.[1, 2]

The case of the Yela valuables calls for discussion on two different levels. First, there is the question of the empirical facts, as far as they can be established. This involves comment on Armstrong's ethnography and his original interpretation. Another question is the various secondary interpretations and models of the 'Rossel Island money' put forward by other scholars. A discussion of these contributions involves wider issues

John Liep

about the nature of 'primitive money' and ceremonial economics. These problems will be taken up elsewhere.

In this paper I shall be concerned mainly with establishing the facts of Yela exchange. I shall present a condensed account of the valuables and important forms of exchange, which, I hope, will clear up the most obscure points of the existing ethnography. I shall argue that Armstrong's analysis was based on a misinterpretation of the basic forms of exchange of the Yela valuables. What he perceived as instances of interest taking were in fact specific procedures in a system of gift exchange. Armstrong saw the Yela economy as a commodity economy and therefore interpreted such features as the working of money capital. Having arrived at this inadequate conception of the system he elicited statements from his informants, which I find are questionable.

Armstrong's model

I shall briefly summarize the main features of the system, as Armstrong saw them, and the outline of his model.

In Yela valuables were involved in a range of transactions, from payments for baskets and limepots to pigs and wives. There were two kinds of 'shell money': *ndap* and *kö*.[3] Most payments involved both kinds. The working of the kö system although remains rather obscure in Armstrong's description and his model only concerns the ndap.

The ndap were divided in a large number of classes of increasing rank, which Armstrong refers to as 'values'. He listed twenty-two main 'values' and numbered them from No. 1 to No. 22. (1928:61).

According to Armstrong's opinion the stock of ndap was extremely limited and virtually constant. He estimated the number of ndap to about 1,000 (in a population of 1,500). Especially the higher 'values' were very scarce. Armstrong reports eighty-one shells in the eight upper classes (1928:62–3).

The classes of shells were ranked according to value, but there was no common unit of value. There was no way to express the value of a shell of a given class as a number of units of any other class. Thus, a No. 14 was more valuable than a No. 13 but there was no direct way to state how much.

Specific goods and services were associated with specific classes of ndap, so that for a specific transaction (e.g. the payment of a canoe) a shell of a specific class was required.

As there was a great shortage of ndap shells it was not likely that a man would possess the shell required for any specific transaction he became involved in. He could not pay with a shell of higher value, for no change

504

could be given on any shell (1928:65). Accordingly a good deal of lending and borrowing had to take place.

Armstrong reports a principle of increment in connection with credit operations. A man could acquire a shell of a higher value from another man by handing over to him a shell of a lower value: 'There is a term *ma* which is used to describe the relation of a value to the value below, and the natives clearly recognize the principle that a given value may be acquired by lending its *ma* for a short period of time' (1928:65). For Armstrong this clearly meant that interest was being charged on loans, and he stated the principle formally, thus: 'if any coin in No. n be lent for a certain short interval of time, the recipient of the loan will have to repay the loan by a No. $(n+1)$' (1928:63). So if a No. 4 was lent, a No. 5 must be repaid, etc. Armstrong states that for a longer interval of time the borrower would have to repay a No. $(n+2)$, and so on: 'With regard to loans for longer periods, my informants gave me examples of a No. n becoming a No. $(n+2)$, a No. $(n+3)$, and so on' (1928:65).

To explain the systematic interrelationship of value between the classes of ndap (which was of course the condition for the system to be regarded as a standard of exchange value), Armstrong based his model on the principle of interest. If a shell of a class n after a certain period of time was repaid with a shell of class No. $(n+1)$, and after a second period with a shell of class No. $(n+2)$, then the value of a shell of class No. 22 could be expressed as the value of a shell of class No. 1 plus compound interest for 21 periods of time. Or, put in another way: 'a wife could be said to cost a year, a basket of taro a week, and so on' (1928:64).

Thus 'any commodity or service may be more or less directly priced in terms of' the ndap shells, which function as a genuine monetary system facilitating the 'trafficking in pigs and concubines, in canoes and wives' (Armstrong 1924:423).

The specific features of the system would force any person to engage in frequent borrowing, and of course to lend what he had. A certain class of people, the *ndeb*, had specialized in monetary dealings. Armstrong compared these men with a 'London bill broker'. Their occupation was to act as middlemen by arranging loans. They earned a profit by enforcing a speedy repayment of loans due to them, and lengthening the time of repayment of their own debts (Armstrong 1928:66).

We now come to the features, which are inconsistent with the model. (It must be stressed that Armstrong was quite frank in reporting the shortcomings of his interpretation and the evidence that contradicted his model.)

As we approach the upper classes of ndap the amount of shells in each class becomes extremely limited. Thus, there were only twenty shells in the important class, which Armstrong numbered eighteen. These shells were involved as the principal ndap in payments for canoes, pigs and wives (1928:88, 93). Loans of shells in this class, and the ones below it, frequently had to be made. Their repayment with interest would demand the use of shells of classes above No. 18. But the shells in these classes were more scarce yet. (Armstrong notes only ten shells in each of the classes 19, 20 and 21 (1928:62)). In any case no debt exceeding the limit of No. 22 could be repaid. It is clear that Armstrong's model does not work with respect to the high ndap 'values'.

These high-rank ndap (from No. 18 and above) were also peculiar in another respect. They were regarded as sacred and handled with reverence (1928:68). The circumstances of their circulation and ownership are not clear in Armstrong's description. They were possessed by 'chiefs', 'though continually lent by the latter to their subjects' (1928:66). Other informants held that the shells in the classes from No. 19 and above had passed out of circulation and remained in the possession of 'important chiefs' (1928:68). Surprisingly No. 18 shells could be borrowed for a short time without the debt increasing. Shells in this class were not, as a rule, repaid by a coin of higher value. How strange that Armstrong's informants insisted that the same principle of increment operated throughout the system: 'that a No. 17 becomes a No. 18, a No. 18 a No. 19, and so on – in just the same way as with the lower values' (*ibid.*).

Armstrong describes another procedure in transactions of high 'value' shells. This had to do with the transfer of lower 'value' shells in connection with the long-term loan of a high-rank shell. If ndap were concerned the amount of lower 'value' ndap associated with the high-rank shell was called the *döndap* of that shell (1928:72). Armstrong interpreted the feature of the döndap as an alternative way of paying interest. As he understood the procedure the döndap increased with the length of the loan of the principal. One or several instalments of interest could be paid, and at the end of the period the original high-rank shell was returned.

Armstrong supplies constructed examples ('obtained by questioning one or two informants') of this method of interest payment for different classes of shells and loans of different periods (1928:73–4). But the examples are not altogether consistent.[4]

Although Armstrong's general model of the value interrelations throughout the classes of ndap is invalidated, this alternative way of paying interest seems to enable the system to work in practice. Interest on loans of the 'values' below No. 18 would then be paid by the first procedure (repayment by a single higher 'value' shell), and interest on loans of the high 'values' – from No. 18 and above – by the second procedure (repayment of the original shell plus a döndap of lower 'value' shells).

Such are the main facts, as Armstrong stated them. The whole of the argument has centred around these data and their interpretation. Now follows my own account of the Yela valuables and their exchange. On the way I shall refer back to Armstrong's description for comment and criticism.

The Yela exchange system

Yela was situated in the extreme periphery of the Massim trading system. Yet its role in the system was important. It was once one of the main places of manufacture of the shell necklaces exchanged in the *kula*. Necklaces of red shell discs were the only export article from the island. They are to some extent still made and traded westward to the Massim. Several kinds of these necklaces are used in internal exchanges in Yela. The shell used for the red discs is the *Chama (pacifica) imbricata*. Kö are made from the same shell. Ndap are made from the shell of various *Spondylus* species.[5] The habitats of the two genera overlap. It seems that the richest fishing grounds for both kinds were formerly considered sacred, tabooed places. These areas could only be approached by applying certain magic formulas. Such knowledge is highly private and local property. It tends to be in the possession of influential big men. It is therefore most likely that the shell resources and the production of shell valuables were formerly controlled by big men in the coastal localities (cf. 1928:60).

Chama necklaces were traded to Sudest Island against such goods as clay pots and carved wooden bowls. But also valuables were imported via Sudest. The most important were the ceremonial axe-blades of Muyuw (Woodlark) greenstone, common throughout the Massim.

It is my opinion that socio-political control in Yela formerly was connected to the control over trade relations to Sudest. The rigid system of exchange in Yela was dominated by the minority of men who possessed the scarce high-rank ndap. It seems probable that their position was based on the control over the import of foreign goods and valuables from Sudest. This control would have been in the hands of big men of the coastal areas, but no single locality seems to have been able to wield a complete monopoly. There was probably competition about relative dominance between leaders of different areas. The pronounced hierarchization of the ndap and kö systems could be seen as an effect of such processes, where rivalry about status-distinctions was reflected in increased differentiation of shell ranks. It is a possibility that at least some of the ndap of high rank were not of Yela origin, but were acquired from Sudest.[6]

A complex exchange economy had evolved in Yela. The different kinds of valuables were employed in various combinations in a wide range of social prestations and payments for goods and services. They entered into bridewealth, mortuary prestations, homicide payments often associated with cannibalism) and payments for houses, canoes, fishing nets, pigs and garden crops.

The payments were characteristically composite and ranked, involving graduated participation by contributors. That is, they were usually composed of two or more kinds of valuables; a range of valuables of different rank was involved, and the prominence of the contributors could be gauged from the number and rank of the valuables they contributed. High-rank payments, such as bridewealth, payments for victims of cannibalism or for status goods (such as pigs, houses or canoes) demanded the transference of one or more ndap of superior rank. These were, and are, very scarce. There are, as Armstrong notes, only twenty shells of the category *chaamandü* (his No. 18), which is still the principal ndap in bridewealth and other major payments.

The rarity of the high-rank shells reflects a controlled exchange system, where a minority of big men directed the circulation of prerogatives of rank and the regulation of social relations through marriage. Armstrong mentions 'chiefs' – *lemi* – but is uncertain about their position (1928: 185ff.). They were obviously powerful big men in control of wealth.

The establishment of the colonial regime severely endangered the indigenous controlled economy. Pacification was effected during the first decade of this century and European traders and planters became active on the island. Homicide and cannibalism were outlawed. The result was that the hegemony of the big men was broken. Opportunities to acquire new status goods became open to young men through plantation work. Communications with Sudest and access to indigenous trade-goods from there became easier with the establishment of European boat traffic between the islands. The production and export of shell necklaces was to a large degree taken over by the traders (cf. Bell in Armstrong 1928:227).

Under these circumstances the controlled exchange of the upper ranks of ndap became unmanageable, and the big men reacted by taking them out of circulation. They became permanent possession of their holders and only transferable through inheritance. But the big men insisted that the big ndap were still required, albeit on a nominal basis, for the proper performance of prestations. Thus the payment of a pig demands the transfer of a chaamandü ndap, but only for a night. The next day it is returned to its owner, and is replaced by a number of lower-ranking ndap.

This explains Armstrong's statement that 'chiefs' owned the big shells, but continually lent them to their subjects. At the time of his fieldwork the upper ndap ranks had already become stationary. The process took place about the time of the First World War.

Today valuables (ndap, kö, stone blades, necklaces), in varying combinations, are still essential for mortuary payments and bridewealth. They also circulate in payments for houses, canoes and pigs, for food and garden crops, as well as for some forms of labour. Cash has entered into some payments, but the big men have wisely banned cash from the most important social payments – the mortuary payments and bridewealth.

Valuables are, however, not means of commodity exchange. There is no open market for products like houses and canoes, or for foodstuffs. The majority of houses and canoes are self-produced. Contributions of vegetable food to pig feasts are remunerated by a small share of the payment for the pig. But in everyday life food is transferred by means of kinship reciprocity without the intervention of payment. Transactions of garden crops usually concern the transfer of seedlings to a man who wants to expand his own food production. Exchange of craft goods is sporadic. Only the meat of domesticated pigs is rarely distributed without payment.

It is thus obvious that the Yela economy is not a market economy.

The ndap system

Ndap are single pieces of *Spondylus* shell. The form is often oval or triangular, and a hole has been drilled at one end. The colour varies from white, over yellow and orange, to red. The lower-rank categories are mainly known by their colour pattern, while the scarce higher-rank ndap are known individually, and the appearance of the shells in a high-rank category need not be similar. They tend, though, to be smaller and of a more delicate patina.

The Yela may conceptualize a scale of ranking by naming a series of ndap categories from high to low. This gives an indication of the relative rank of categories. But it does not mean that ndap categories correspond to a linear and finite series of ranks. Actually, two categories may have the same rank, or may overlap in ranking. Again, the individual shells in a ndap category are not necessarily of a uniform single value – some are 'more big', some 'more small'.

Any numbering system of ndap categories is therefore misleading because it implies that the numbered sequence represents a linear order of classes interrelated through a uniform principle of value.

I will therefore avoid the use of numbers, when referring to categories or rank levels. When I in the following explain principles of exchange I will use letter symbols (*l, m, n,* . . etc.), and when I supply examples I will use the Yela name of categories. In my list (Table 1) I have included the categories that were frequently quoted in conversations with informants about exchanges.[7]

The list is by no means exhaustive. There are altogether some forty different categories of ndap (cf. Armstrong 1924:423). Many of them are ancient low-rank categories, which are still used, together with more common ones, in transfers of 'small ndap'. Others are subcategories of medium-rank ndap.

On the basis of a survey of ndap in a village of 160 people I estimate the total number of ndap in Yela to be about 15–20,000. By far the major part of these are 'small ndap' (from mdbono to chaamö). (The total population of the island was about 2,500 in 1973). This figure is much higher than Armstrong's estimate of a 1,000 ndap in 1921. I suspect that Armstrong underestimated the amount of ndap. On the other hand it is likely that large amounts of lower-rank ndap were produced in the years following his visit. I have mentioned that the ndap exchanges had been drastically reorganized a few years before Armstrong arrived. The big men had decided that all ndap with an individual name should become stationary. This involved all categories down to tangwolündo. Shells of the categories from chaamandü to tangwolündo are now only nominally transferred in payments. After a short time they are returned to their owners, and replaced with an amount of lower-rank ndap. This procedure must have increased the demand for ndap of low rank considerably.

The following divisions of ndap ranks can then be distinguished, according to their position in relation to the circulation process. From the highest rank down to tangwolündo all ndap are withdrawn from open circulation. They are transferred by inheritance, usually from father to son. They are all individually named, are regarded as ancient, and believed to have been made by the gods. The shells from tangwolündo up to chaamandü are still formally involved in ceremonial exchanges, but return to their owners again. Shells from ranks above chaamandü are now only used as security for chaamandü shells or high rank kö (except shells of the highest rank, kuchem, which has not been used for any purpose in living memory). Shells in ranks from teputündbo and down are still freely circulating. A number of these categories are still produced.

The scale of ndap ranks does, in some way, provide a measure of the social value of things exchanged in Yela. If it is said that the chaamandü is

Table 1. *List of main ndap categories*

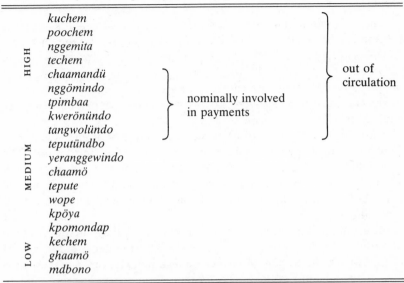

HIGH	*kuchem* *poochem* *nggemita* *techem* *chaamandü* *nggömindo* *tpimbaa* *kwerönündo* *tangwolündo*	nominally involved in payments	out of circulation
MEDIUM	*teputündbo* *yeranggewindo* *chaamö* *tepute* *wope* *kpöya*		
LOW	*kpomondap* *kechem* *ghaamö* *mdbono*		

the 'pay' for a pig this does not mean that the price of the pig is a chaamandü. Actually the chaamandü is only transferred for a night. The next morning a collection of lower-rank ndap is substituted. But the scale of the substitute payment, the number and rank of the lower-rank shells, is determined in relation to the initial ndap involved. The chaamandü is the 'master' of the payment.

I have stressed that the shells in Yela are not media in the commodity exchange of a developed market. Relationships of exchange-value between the shell categories have not been established. It is not possible to reduce the value of a high-ranking shell to a sum of any standard unit of value. The composition of a major payment demands a combination of a range of shell ranks, which come together by contributions from many people. The payment necessitates the involvement of men in possession of shells at different levels of the rank hierarchy. The structure of social differentiation is a dominant factor in the conduct of exchange. This works against a valorization that would level all shell categories to be measurable by a common, uniform standard of value.

It is therefore no wonder that exchange-values in terms of cash exist only for the lower ndap categories – up to chaamö, which is said to equal a shilling (10 *toea* or 14 cents). Above this category informants' estimates of the cash value of ndap shells become exceedingly vague.

John Liep

The kö system

The ndap is the dominating of the two systems of ndap and kö. This is reflected in the fact that the classification of ndap structures the kö system as well. The higher-rank categories of kö are referred to by means of ndap categories. From kuchem down to yeranggewindo each main category of ndap has its corresponding category of kö.

The classification of low-rank kö does not follow that of ndap. They are covered by the terms *tpyapökö* and *perekö*.[8]

A kö unit is a set of ten discs of shell on a string of dried banana-leaf. Categorization depends on the diameter of the discs in the unit. The wider the discs, the higher the rank. The diameter varies from about 12 mm for the lowest-ranking category, to about 40 mm for *kuchem u kö*. A limited amount of kö, except the highest ranking category of kuchem, are still made in Yela.

My estimate of the number of kö, based on my village survey, is a total of about 2,000 kö on the island. Armstrong estimated 800 kö in 1921 (1928:70). The discrepancy between our estimates is not so great as in the case of ndap. High-rank kö have not become stationary. The replacement of high-rank shells with large amounts of low-rank shells has therefore not become a regular and frequent procedure of kö exchange, as in the case of ndap. The demand for low-rank kö would therefore not have increased in proportion to that of ndap.

Armstrong notes that kö are regarded as women's wealth, but that this is probably a fiction (1928:69). Informants told me that kö were formerly used only by women. Probably the 'femaleness' of the kö is rather a reflection of the circumstance that kö exchanges are harder to operate than ndap. Exchanges of ndap were much simplified when the big ndap went out of circulation. High-level kö exchange does, on the other hand, still occur, but is complicated to carry through. This would correspond to the categorization of kula armshells and necklaces. The kind that is scarcest and therefore more 'heavy' in exchange is regarded as female (cf. Campbell, Munn, and Weiner in this volume and J. Leach 1981).

The rules of exchange of kö are based on the same principle as those of ndap. So the study of contemporary kö exchange may provide valuable clues to how ndap exchange was performed before the system 'froze' at the top.

Organization of payments

The mortuary payments consist mainly in a payment of ndap, stone blades and necklaces to the deceased's sub-clan from the spouse's subclan. Another, similar but smaller, payment is from the deceased's sub-clan to the deceased's father's sub-clan (descent is matrilineal). The organization of the mortuary payments differs from that of all other payments. They do not, therefore, serve well as a base for outlining the main principles of exchange, and I will leave them out of further discussion here.

All other major payments involve the presentation of a high-rank ndap, and its subsequent withdrawal and substitution by one or more lower-rank ndap. A standard unit of such payments is the *ndaptii.*

A ndaptii (tii=line) is a set of usually ten ndap covering a range of ranks from medium- to low-ranking categories. The value of a ndaptii depends on how far up the rank scale the set goes, and how many ndap of good rank are included. A low-value ndaptii consists only of inferior shells (from kpöya/wope and down); a valuable one is led by a teputündbo or yeranggewindo and contains other ndap of good rank too.

There is also a section consisting of a number of kö, which often are strung together to form a long 'rope'. The kö payment covers a range of ranks from high rank to low. The principal kö is usually of the rank corresponding to the rank of the initial big ndap involved in the same payment. Subsequent kö on the rope are of lesser rank, down to low-rank kö. The rope will thus taper from the width of the first kö down to the width of the last.

One or two of the kö are mobilized in a way which I am going to explain more fully below. This mobilization mechanism is one of the essential procedures of Yela exchange. It involves one or more auxiliary prestations supporting the principal one. In a stepwise chain of transactions the person who gives away a valuable receives an inferior one from another person. This may be done with ndap, kö or even money. If the payment is not for pig, only one step in rank (two subtransactions) is involved. A kö of somewhat inferior rank is provided for the donors of the leading kö.

The pig feast

The pig feast plays an important part in Armstrong's discussion of exchange (1928:80–3, 88–92). It involves the most complicated of all transactions. I shall therefore discuss it in greater detail.

There is usually only one pig at a feast, but the beast has been fattened to great size (150–225 kg). The pig is divided into eight main parts.[9]

There are thus eight possible part-transactions. The original owner of the pig will receive the payment for the main part – the middle back – and usually for one or two other parts. The remaining parts he will give to

John Liep

kinsmen, affines, people who have helped to feed the pig, or a local big man.

For each part there is an 'owner' and an 'eater': the man who sponsors the payment of the part. On the 'owner's' side there are a number of people who are going to have a share of the payment, when the 'owner' redistributes it. On the 'eater's' side a large number of people contribute ndap and kö at the day of the feast. They may be kinsmen, exchange-friends or just 'village people' (ordinary people, not of big man status).

Around each part a separate procedure of payment evolves: the more elaborate, the larger the part. The following is a description of the ideal scheme.

For each part there is a ndap presented to the 'owner' who keeps it for the night of the feast. The rank of this ndap varies from a chaamandü for the middle back down to, say, a yeranggewindo for a leg. After the presentation of the shell the part is handed over to the 'eater', who supervises the distribution of the meat. This initial ndap has been mobilized in the way described above. For the better parts this mobilization takes place through several intermediary transfers of lower-rank ndap. The procedure is quite complicated, and I can not enter on a lengthy description here. All the contributors in the chain receive slices of pork and vegetable food at the feast, in proportion to their contribution.

The day after the feast the initial ndap is withdrawn and the 'owner' instead receives an amount of lower-rank ndap. The highest-ranking shell of these will be one of those, which were involved at a lower step in the mobilization of the initial ndap. It is regarded as the principal substitute of the initial higher-rank ndap. The rest are ndap collected at the distribution of the part at the feast.

All these ndap together are considered a replacement for the initial big ndap. The number of ndap in the replacement has some relation to the rank of the initial ndap. But the relative proportion of ndap, kö and cash in the payment for a part influences the amounts of each. If there are more kö in a payment, the number of ndap will generally be lower. And if cash is included, the number of both kö and ndap will decrease. Again, the actual size of the part influences the size of the payment. So there is no direct correspondence in value between the initial ndap and its replacement.

A section of kö is also paid for each part. One or more of these (those of highest rank) are mobilized stepwise. There may be up to ten kö mobilized, through several steps, for the main part, and maybe only one or two, in one step only, for a leg. Again each participant receives meat in

514

proportion to his contribution. In addition to the better kö, mobilized in this way, are given other, lower-rank kö collected at the distribution of the part. Nowadays the kö are only strung to form a rope for the main part. The kö section is handed over to the pig-'owner' with the ndap section the day after the feast.

Some of the high-rank kö paid for the larger parts of the pig are later withdrawn. This may take place weeks or months after the feast. Such kö return to their owners. The persons on the pig-'owner's' side, who received these kö, will instead receive the next kö in the chain of mobilization of the initial kö.

There may also be cash paid for some of the parts. It may be coins collected, with ndap and kö, at the distribution of meat. But also money may be mobilized according to the procedure described. This is always in a single step, doubling up the amount in cash. A person is given a one- or two-kina note, and he then contributes two or four kina which are transferred to the 'owner' of the part.

In all the cases where the process of mobilization takes place the valuable that starts the chain, the low-rank ndap or kö or the kina note, comes from the side of the 'owner' of the part. Thus the chain of mobilization is in fact a cycle, where a solicitory valuable is 'invested', and a bigger return comes back to the same person. The 'owner' of a part will usually himself 'invest' one ndap (the one involved in mobilizing the initial ndap), one kö (the one involved in mobilizing the highest rank kö) and one of the kina notes that are being doubled. Other people 'invest' the remainder of the solicitory kö and kina. In addition to the return on their solicitory kö the 'co-investors' get a share of the small kö and ndap in the payment.

These people are, like those to whom the principal pig-'owner' gives parts of the pig, a mixed category of kin and other persons to whom the 'owner' of the part is obliged. Besides those that have provided solicitory valuables other people get a share at the redistribution of the payment. Most of these have taken part in the preparations for the feast. The principal pig-'owner' has specifically engaged two or three men to work preparing the feast. They build one or more sheds to house the guests, a storehouse for food, a lean-to for the dancers, and they make a large amount of sago. The workers are also paid out of the payment for the part.

The formal scheme, which I have presented here, is often not strictly followed nowadays. Some parts at a feast may be transacted according to the full ritual. Others may be quite unceremoniously paid with a mixture of low-rank ndap, kö and cash.

John Liep

Procedures of exchange

Modes of circulation: security

The major prestations (except the mortuary payments) involve both ndap and kö. Many contributors participate on the sponsor's side to raise the payment, and many people share in its redistribution on the side of the recipient. A considerable amount of shells, ranging from high rank to low, must be released to take part in the prestation.

The mode of circulation varies according to the rank of the valuables concerned. Low-rank ndap and kö are lent and contributed informally. There are no further conditions attached to the gift than an expectation of future reciprocation from the borrower, or the sponsor of the payment. Preferably the return gift should include an increment – that is, the valuable returned should be of slightly higher rank than the previous gift. The transfer from the side of the sponsor to the side of the recipient of a payment is therefore also a quite uncomplicated transaction and can be regarded as a straightforward alienation of the shells.

In the case of higher-rank valuables the mode of circulation is much more restricted. We have already seen that higher-rank ndap do not really circulate at all, but only take part on a nominal basis in prestations. They must return to their owners again. Higher-rank kö do circulate, but their exchange is surrounded by limitations. The circulation of high-rank kö often involves complicated cycles with subsidiary prestations before the exchange is finally closed.

We shall now take a closer look at the principles involved in the exchange of high-rank ndap and kö.

The basic principle operating in high-order exchange is that any transfer of a shell involves another shell of different rank taking its place.

A relatively simple way to get access to high-rank valuables for those who already possess valuables of the same rank-order is by the giving of *security*. Valuables used as security are *tiindap, tiikö*, etc. (*tii*=line; here an operation at about the same rank-level). Security is usually given to elicit valuables from people who are not directly involved as supporters of a prestation. When shells are lent against security there is usually a firm agreement that the valuable only participates in the prestation on a temporary basis. When it is given back to its owner the security is returned.

The security for kö of high rank is usually a kö of lower rank together with a necklace or ceremonial axe-blade to make up for the difference in value between the kö. For big ndap the security is usually another ndap of somewhat higher rank than the one borrowed (cf. Armstrong 1928:67).

516

Complementary ranks: pledge

When people accept a more heavy engagement as supporters of a prestation they release their valuable against a lower-rank pledge – a *ngmaa* (of
the same kind of valuable). This is an essential element of Yela exchange.

As will appear from the following discussion the feature of the ngmaa is
similar to the *basi* in the kula. Basi are gifts of lower-rank kula valuables
connected to the exchange of higher-rank kula valuables. A basi may
either be given to solicit a big kula valuable or, in default of an equivalent
countergift, to put off the partner for some time (Fortune 1932:234;
Malinowski 1922:355–6. See also Campbell's contribution to this
volume). The ngmaa is also related to the *pek*, or initiatory gifts, in the
Moka (Strathern 1971:97).

Corresponding to this practice of giving pledge is a notion of complementarity between rank-levels in both the ndap and kö systems. Lower-
level ranks are seen as steps leading to, or retreats from, higher-level
ranks.

This notion of complementarity between rank levels is expressed by the
terms *ngmaa* and *nuö*. Thus if m and n are two complementary shell ranks
and $m<n$, m is the *ngmaa* of n and n is the *nuö* of m. Nuö means point
(e.g. the point of a spear). Nuö also has the connotation of a debt or
obligation. The term ngmaa[10] means 'dodge': e.g. at mortuary feasts
aggrieved guests sometimes throw objects, like pieces of banana stem or
firewood, after men of the deceased's village. These people dodge
(ngmaa) the missiles by leaping aside or jumping. Formerly they used to
throw spears: the ngmaa is a way of dodging a point – the nuö.

There are no strict rules that prescribe the appropriate ngmaa for each
category of ndap and kö. In actual exchange this is open to consideration.
Much of the discussion in the circle of elders assembled, when a payment
is composed, is concerned with deliberations about the 'proper' rank of
the ngmaas for the big shells.

The table below is an approximate guideline to ngmaa–nuö relationships for ndap.

In the process of raising shells for a prestation the concept of complementary ranks is applied in the following way.

A person who lets his valuable support a prestation receives a lower
rank pledge, the *ngmaa* of his original shell.

In the diagram, A releases the shell of rank m from B by the deposit
with B of a shell of rank l.

$$A \qquad B$$
$$\xleftarrow{\quad m \quad}$$
$$\xrightarrow{\quad l \quad}$$

Table 2. ngmaa–nuö *relationships for* ndap

		poochem
chaamandü	is *ngmaa* for	*nggemita*
		techem
tpimbaa ⎫ *kwerönündo* ⎭	are *ngmaa* for	*chaamandü*
kwerönündo ⎫ *tangwolündo* ⎭	are *ngmaa* for	*nggömindo*
teputündbo	is *ngmaa* for	⎰ *tpimbaa* ⎱ *kwerönündo*
yeranggewindo	is *ngmaa* for	*tangwolündo*
*tepute**	is *ngmaa* for	*teputündbo*
chaamö	is *ngmaa* for	*yeranggewindo*
kpomondap	is *ngmaa* for	*chaamö*

*tepute overlaps in rank with chaamö

The transaction may be arranged and the ngmaa given some time before the feast. But the transaction is effected in public at the feast. B has now staked his shell in the exchange system. It has passed out of his direct control. B does this on the expectation of future reciprocity. He has not relinquished his claim to possession at rank-level m. And he has not risked the full worth of his shell. He holds the ngmaa, one or more steps lower in the hierarchy. The ngmaa is his pledge or guarantee. It is B's evidence that he contributed the nuö of rank m, and it represents his claim to regain the nuö. He may under some circumstances go to A and present the ngmaa, demanding the return of his shell. If A is able to procure the original shell B has no further claim. If this is not possible A should give B a shell of slightly higher rank, if A is 'a good man'.

Informants express contradictory opinions about the firmness of B's claim and A's obligation. Seen from the point of A the ngmaa is a dodge, which enables him to keep B 'floating' for an indefinite period. How long a time will pass before B gets his return, if ever, depends on the personal relation between the two, on their overall exchange ledger, and on their persistence in the game of exchange.

Alternatively B may attempt to 'let the ngmaa grow itself'. If he is approached by another man, C, who seeks a shell of rank l for payment, B may give him the ngmaa and demand the return of a better shell.[11] C must agree to repay a shell of somewhat higher rank, say of rank x, where $l<x<m$. By successive transactions of this kind the shell of rank x may be turned into one of rank y and again into one of rank z, where $z = m$, or maybe even $z>m$.

In the instance, we have been discussing, only two persons were concerned. But the procedure may also involve a number of people who become participants in a chain of mobilization. This is the way big shells are released in the pig feast. The following example concerns the chain of mobilization for a high rank kö.

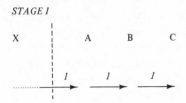

STAGE I

In the diagram X is one of the 'co-investors' on the pig-'owners' side. He has provided one of the solicitory kö, which the pig-'owner' collects and presents to the pig-'eater'. A is a supporter of the pig-'eater'. A is given the particular shell, stemming from X, to 'work'. A passes the shell on to another person, B, and he passes it on to C. (There are alternative ways to 'work' a kö, but this one is the simplest.)

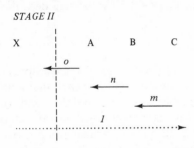

STAGE II

C is the first person to 'raise the stake'. He keeps the solicitory kö of rank *l* and gives a kö of rank *m* to B. B again raises the level by keeping the kö of rank *m* and giving one of rank *n* to A. A finally raises the level to *o* and keeps the kö of rank *n*. *o* is the big kö, which is transferred to the pig-'owner's' side at the feast. *m* and *n* are only involved in the mobilization of *o*. In each step the lower-ranking kö is the ngmaa of the higher-ranking.

The distribution of pork at the feast is supervised by the pig-'eater'. He will give the appropriate number of slices of pork to A, who will pass the meat over to the subsidiary supporters, B and C, according to their level of participation.

We are now able to judge Armstrong's statement that compound interest is the key element of the exchange system. Armstrong was working under the assumption that exchange in Yela was conducted along principles similar to those of a capitalist economy. There was hardly any theory of gift exchange at the time of his fieldwork.

He discovered that a man could obtain a shell from another by 'lending' him its ngmaa – clearly an instance of incremental return. The concept of interest immediately suggested itself. So the item of information was transposed into 'the principle that a given value may be acquired by lending its ma for a short period of time' (see p. 505). The actual operation was turned into its opposite. When Armstrong was told about sequences where 'a No. 17 becomes a No. 18, and a No. 18 a No. 19' (see p. 506) this, by the same line of reasoning, became the working of compound interest on the loan of a single shell.

It is clear that Armstrong's interpretation of Yela exchange was based on a misunderstanding of the notion of the ngmaa and of the mobilization chain. It is true that in the process of 'letting the ngmaa grow itself' there is an increment on the return on a loan. But the aim is to retrieve the loss of a valuable once possessed. It is true as well that people expect that the reciprocation of contributions should be generous. (They also complain about the tricks and stinginess of the big men.) But this is far from the systematic principle of interest-taking which Armstrong describes.

Complementary ranks: substitution

There is another connection where the notion of ngmaa appears in a somewhat different sense. This is the case where a shell that a man has received in a payment must return to its owner, and the recipient must accept an inferior *substitution*. This is always done with the stationary higher-rank ndap, which only enter nominally in prestations. But also big kö are often only temporarily involved in prestations. The big kö are scarce. It is often not possible to arrange a payment where all the owners of the series of higher-rank kö are willing to support the prestation, to the extent that they will release their kö for an indefinite period and wait until they can somehow be recompensed by the sponsor. Therefore the chains of mobilization are sometimes partly 'de-escalized'.

Let us assume that this was the case in the example discussed above. X received the kö of rank o at the feast, but already at that time he was notified that it would have to go back at a later date and would be substituted with the ngmaa.

X holds the big kö for some weeks, or months. Then it is returned to A, and X instead receives the next kö in the chain – that of rank n, which came from B. X now holds the ngmaa of the initial kö. He may have some claim to a kö of the rank to which he holds the ngmaa, but my evidence is contradictory as regards the strength of such a claim.

STAGE III

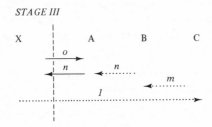

In the case of big ndap the substitution cannot be of the immediately complementary lower-level rank. It cannot be the direct ngmaa of, say, the chaamandü. It must be several steps further removed in the hierarchy, because the ranks above are out of free circulation. For instance, the ngmaa of the chaamandü is a tpimbaa or kwerönündo, but the substitute given to the recipient of a payment, instead of the chaamandü, would be a teputündbo or yeranggewindo. In a loose sense the substitute is still said to be the ngmaa of the initial shell, but the more precise term is kaape ('hold-half'). In this case the recipient has no valid claim to the big shell, which the inferior shell substitutes for, or to any shell among the ranks of ndap which are now stationary.

Replacement payments

As I stated earlier neither ndap nor kö are reducible to a common standard of value. But in a circumspect way they may be compared and a kind of exchange is possible. Exchange of ndap and kö is called *ndöndap* and *ndokö* (*ndo* = dead; nullifying any further claim).

If some medium-rank ndap is due to a man, and a repayment is going to be made, he may prefer to get ndöndap instead of a single shell. The payment should consist of some ndaptii headed by the ngmaa of the original shell. (In practice the leading shell of the ndöndap is often more than one step down in the hierarchy from the original.) In this case the ndöndap is a true compensation to the person who once before owned the ndap.

In other cases the ndöndap is rather a substitution. This is the case when it goes instead of the big stationary ndap that people cannot obtain any more. The collection of ndap transferred to a pig-'owner' or house builder, when the chaamandü has been withdrawn, is regarded as the ndöndap of the chaamandü. The form of the payment is the same – a ndap of medium rank, which is the kaape of the initial ndap, and some ndaptii the number and value of which depends on the rank of the original shell. Like other Yela payments the ndöndap is a hierarchically structured

John Liep

payment. It is headed by a lower rank associate of the ndap being replaced, and ndap below this level are included in numbers inversely proportional to their rank level. The diagram shows the ndöndap as a segment of the total ndap hierarchy.

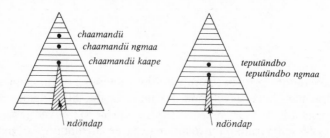

A ndokö is composed similarly to a ndöndap, but consists of both kö and ndap. Ndokö payments seem relatively large compared to ndöndap payments. The explanation is probably that whereas most *ndöndap* represent a substitution *instead of* a big shell, ndokö are payments which truly compensate for the alienation of a shell.

Apart from the cases where the ndöndap substitutes for one of the ndap which are out of circulation, these replacement payments are not common. They come about by collection of contributions like other payments.

We can now see that also Armstrong's interpretation of the ndöndap/ ndokö procedure must be rejected.

Armstrong presumably came across the procedure of ndöndap when he had already formed the opinion that interest-taking was a central feature of the 'monetary' system. His principle of interest-payment by means of progresively higher-rank shells already faced some difficulties, when applied to high-rank shell-debts. It is in this connection that he first refers to a second procedure of interest payment. This information 'was given by an informant, when I pressed him to follow up the consequences of an initial minor debt' (Armstrong 1928:67). At this point of his investigation the procedure of ndöndap had to fit into an already established interpretation of the exchange system.

The structure of the payment Armstrong describes is identical to the replacement payment discussed above – even to the detail that the ndöndap consists of ndap only, while the ndokö consists of both ndap and kö (1928:71–2). The difference is that Armstrong interprets the procedure as interest paid on the loan of a shell. He holds that the payment due increases with the length of time of the loan and appends a number of constructed examples, which show this feature of increment. My informants could make no sense of these examples. But they recognized

522

Armstrong's picture of an 'interest payment' (1928: pl. XXIa) as a payment of ndokö, the replacement payment they still perform.[12]

I must therefore come to the conclusion that Armstrong thoroughly misunderstood the function of ndo, and that his examples were fictions supplied by informants, who did not understand what he was aiming at.

Thus the cornerstones of Armstrong's explanation of the Yela exchange system were founded on misapprehensions. What he took for forms of interest-taking were in one instance cycles of unbalanced exchange, in the other circumscribed forms of conversion.

The role of the ndeb, Armstrong's professional money-lenders, must now be seen in another light. The major prestations demanded that many shell-possessors had to be approached and complex loans arranged. A *ndaapi* (my spelling – literally 'money-man') was a man who was known to be especially skillful in manipulating the credit operations necessary for raising payments. This is an aspect of big man behaviour common elsewhere in Melanesia.

Conclusion

The preceding argument amounts to a rather devastating critique of Armstrong's work. I hope to have documented that his analysis went wrong because he tried to force his observations into a frame they did not fit: that of western finance-capitalism.

I would, none the less, like to end up by paying homage to his memory. In the short time available for his inquiries he collected a surprisingly detailed material. Actually there is a mass of evidence in his chapters on exchange which by far surpasses what Malinowski presents in the whole of *Argonauts*. His investigation was guided by a keen theoretical mind. And, although this led him to the wrong conclusions, it guided his search into essential aspects of the exchange system.

In so far as I have succeeded in unravelling some of the complexities of exchange in Yela it is to no small extent due to the continuous challenge I experienced in the field from his remarkable account of the 'Rossel Island money'.

Notes

1 Fieldwork in Rossel Island 1971–3 was financed by grants from the Danish Social Science Research Council and from the Australian National University, which are hereby gratefully acknowledged.
2 In early 1971 the island was visited by Stuart Berde who, for one week, made inquiries into Yela exchange. Berde has presented an alternative model of the

John Liep

system (1973). His evidence partly supplements and partly contradicts Armstrong's. Berde's interesting notes have stimulated my own conception of the Yela valuables. I find, however, that much of his material is defective and his interpretation of the system inadequate. This is understandable considering the very short duration of his stay in Yela. A satisfactory discussion of Berde's account requires an examination of the data in detail. For lack of space I have therefore decided to publish my comments on Berde's paper elsewhere.

3 In his 1924 article Armstrong uses the spelling *dap* and *kö*, and in the monograph from 1928 ndap and kö. The correct spelling is ndap and kö.

4 Thus, the 'interest' worked out for a No. 18 for 2–3 months comes to 25 döndap (low-value ndap), and for one year to 80 döndap. But for the lower-rank class of No. 15 'interest' for the same period amounts to 40 döndap and 100 döndap!

5 Armstrong, as well as Malinowski, believed that necklaces were made from *Spondylus*. (Armstrong 1928:59; Malinowski 1922:86) He meant that the kö were probably made from a giant clam. (*ibid.*) On the identification of shells used for valuables see my note in *The Kula: A Bibliography* (Macintyre 1983:85–6).

6 Armstrong mentions the existence of ndap in Sudest, and the import to Yela of shells for the manufacture of ndap of low rank. But these imported ndap were regarded as 'imitations', he states (1928:60). Also today some ndap of western import are looked upon as inferior. This devaluation of imported ndap may however be a result of the expanded communication after European pacification. I know of a high-rank ndap (of the important category of chaamandü), which originally came from Sudest.

7 I quote Armstrong's list of ndap (1928:61) for comparison.

11. Yelengwinjinindo	22. Kwojuma
10. Yelengwindo	21. Pwojuma
9. Tiama	20. Gimida
8. Tebudongwo	19. Tejema
7. Tebuda	18. Työmundi
6. Uabe	17. Bwelejumgwanagu
5. Kwaia	16. Gumindo
4. Pwomondap	15. Yananindo
3. Kejim	14. Pimba
2. Gamö	13. Kwarunundo
1. Dondwo	12. Tangwolondo

Differences in spelling are due to the very difficult Yela phonology. Any list of ndap categories is a selection. Different informants may include more or less categories. I have omitted a few, which appear in Armstrong's list. His Nos. 15 and 17 are rare and infrequently used, and his No. 11 is a subcategory of his No. 10. He put his No. 8 (teputündbo) in a wrong position on the rank-scale.

8 kö means 'punt pole'. Thus *chaamandü u kö* is 'chaamandü his pole'; the chaamandü being compared to a canoe. The higher-rank kö may also be referred to as *kökna* (e.g. *chaamandü kökna*). Kna is 'thick end' or 'trunk'. (cf. Armstrong who writes *kagnö* (1928:69)).

Tpyapö means 'tell'. The exchange of these lower-rank kö is less restricted than that of high-rank kö. They move more around and 'tell the story' of the big kö. *Pere* means 'pull'. This refers to the use of these low rank kö as solicitary gifts (see p. 519).

9 According to Armstrong there are ten parts. Each part is paid with a single ndap, the ten shells comprising a series of adjacent 'values' from No. 18 to No. 9. (1928:79–80, 90) It is possible that the rules for cutting up and paying of pig have changed. My informants, however, asserted that pigs are cut up today as they were before. It would also be curious to pay ndap of different rank for parts of the same size, such as the legs.

10 ngmaa is of course the same word as Armstrong's ma.

11 No security or ngmaa is given for B's ngmaa in this case.

12 Armstrong uses *dogo* as a general term for these 'interest-payments' (1928: 71). This is a mishearing of *ndokö*. A feast where 'interest' is paid he calls *dogo momo*. This is actually *ndokö mumu* – the occasion of paying ndokö (*mumu* means 'look'). This comes from the fact that the only 'interest-paying feast' Armstrong saw was a payment of ndokö (1928:74–5).

PART VII

Conclusion

22 The kula: an alternative view

‣‣‣

EDMUND LEACH

The Conference from which most of the papers in this volume are derived took place in my house and was funded by grants for which I was the principal applicant. So although the editing of this volume has been primarily the work of Jerry Leach I must certainly acknowledge some responsibility for what is now published. The conference was, unquestionably, an outstanding success. It has already generated a large body of supplementary fieldwork, some facets of which are partly reported here (e.g. papers by Macintyre and Lepowsky), as well as a further Kula Conference held at the University of Virginia in the summer of 1981.

The main purpose of the Cambridge Conference was to bring the Malinowski–Fortune ethnography up to date and to bring together in one place all the major specialists in this particular branch of ethnographic enquiry, but also, as Jerry Leach's Introduction makes clear, we hoped to stimulate further debate about the general nature of the *kula* and other kula-type institutions considered as a species of exchange. On this latter issue my own view as an outsider differs substantially from that of some of the insiders. One important 'insider' view is that which Jerry Leach has outlined in his Introduction which indicates the main themes around which the theoretical debate has been focussed ever since the days of Malinowski. In order to provide some meat for a dialectical argument I shall develop in this Conclusion a somewhat different viewpoint, leaving the reader to evaluate the merits of the two contrasted styles of analysis.

As now arranged, the various papers in this volume are grouped by geographical region and not by theme. For those readers, and they may well be the majority, who are primarily interested in extending their knowledge of the ethnographic facts, this is probably the best arrangement, although I myself feel that the resulting partitions serve to inhibit comparative discussion. So I shall ignore the details of particular papers, some of which I find extremely interesting, and concern myself only with very general topics of the sort that were raised in the Introduction.

529

Edmund Leach

Jerry Leach there suggested that the papers in this volume would help to answer two kinds of question. (1) What goes on in kula transactions, especially in those parts of the kula area not observed at first hand by Malinowski? (2) Why do kula transactions take place at all? I cannot really agree with this.

Certainly these contributions add very greatly to our ethnographic knowledge but, in that respect, it seems to me that their main effect is to demonstrate that the kula as observed by Malinowski (and he himself recorded a number of significant variations) was part of a huge spectrum of possible ways of doing more or less the same kind of thing. The papers presented here exhibit some of those possibilities but they do not show that there is anything fundamentally similar about the institutions thus described. In place of Malinowski's confident, but quite unjustified, assertion that the kula is 'an exchange of an entirely novel type' (1922: 511) we are left with the feeling that, while the various systems which the inhabitants of the Massim area and their anthropological interrogators lump together under the label kula have a vague family resemblance, there is probably no single feature which is common to them all. If this is so then it is a very important discovery but it implies that, after a fashion, we end up knowing less than we did before!

As for Jerry Leach's second conundrum: Why does the kula take place? Why does it go on? I entirely agree that this is a question which has cropped up repeatedly in the earlier literature of the kula and is implicit, or explicit, in many of the present contributions, but I do not myself believe that this is the kind of question on which anthropologists should focus their attention. The 'why' questions posed by ethnography are always unanswerable.

If I observe a pair of competent chess players and notice that every now and again there is an exchange of pawns, white for black, or perhaps a white bishop for a black knight, it is not sensible to ask: 'Why does that happen?' It is simply that that is the way the game is played, each party making a different assessment about the probabilities of the future development of the game. And if you say: 'But why is chess played like that?', the only possible answer is historical: the modern game of chess evolved a long time ago out of other somewhat chess-like games, not because it was specially efficient for any particular purpose but because people found it was fun to play. Nowadays great chess players gain international renown but that is not why they play chess!

But having established the rules of the game, chess players built up a tradition, or rather a great variety of traditions, about how to start the game, how to pursue it, and how to bring it to an end. I do not find that it makes any sense to ask a chess player why he opened with a Queen's

Gambit rather than a Ruy Lopez and it does not seem to me that it makes any sense to ask why the various Massim islanders play the game of kula as they do and keep on inventing new variations.

Nevertheless, there are other kinds of question, which Jerry Leach does not raise in his Introduction but which are implicit in some of the contributions to this book, which do seem to me to be worth asking. Essentially, I would suggest that what the reader needs to think about is not: 'Why do people kula?' but rather 'What are the consequences of the fact that people kula?'. 'What difference does it make?'

Jerry Leach emphasises the fact that existing theories do not explain why, say, the Trobrianders are in the kula and the people of Goodenough Island are not. That seems to me to be an historical question which we can never hope to answer. On the other hand, a careful consideration of the new evidence should allow us to identify which particular differences between Trobriand and Goodenough culture (which are in many ways very similar) tie in with the fact that Trobriand men engage in kula and Goodenough men do not. And from the viewpoint of any kind of functionalist anthropology this would be very interesting.

This brings me to another aspect of the Introduction which I want to contest. Jerry Leach recognises, indeed he emphasises, that the kula overall is a much more varied set of institutions than Malinowski had supposed, but, in the end, he returns to the idea that the defining principle of the kula, the really essential feature on which he bases his demographic count of participants [see pp. 16–19], is what he calls the 'opposite flow rule' [*bagi* clockwise; *mwali* counter-clockwise] and he implies that there is something mysterious about this which needs to be 'explained'. This is certainly one of the matters which most puzzled Malinowski and which has continued to puzzle many subsequent authors. But, from a structuralist viewpoint, I find this particular issue relatively straightforward.

All possible forms of exchange are either symmetrical: 'an eye for an eye', 'a glass of beer for a glass of beer', or asymmetrical: 'a loaf of bread for a coin', 'a gift in kind for a service rendered', 'deference on one side, patronage on the other'. The combination of these two possibilities, the relations between relations: equality–inequality, similarity–difference, continuity–discontinuity, '+/− *versus* '0', constitutes the 'atom of coding', the fundamental type of a 'distinctive feature' in every imaginable form of communication system from the level of molecular biology upwards.

In the present context the relevant point is that the 'opposite flow rule' cannot possibly have any meaning *in itself*. It acquires any meaning that it possesses only because of its context. And in that context it is always, either implicitly or explicitly, both *contrasted with* its contrary – 'reciprocal exchange of like objects' – and *likened to* other forms of asymmetrical exchange. For example, if we consider only the evidence provided by Malinowski (1922, 1935(1)) then it would appear that in Malinowski's day the asymmetry of kula prestations on Kiriwina was structurally similar to the asymmetry of the annual harvest gift of yams (*urigubu*), which moved in the direction from a man to his sister's husband, and was reciprocated in the opposite direction by gifts of kula-type valuables, either after a short interval by the custom called *likula bwayma* (1935(1):189) or after a long delay, by mortuary gifts.

On the other hand, these asymmetrical exchanges were contrasted with the symmetrical exchange of harvest yams between members of the same matrilineage (see 1935(1):Index refs. to *kovisi*).

But in other islands this structural parallel would not apply, so the 'opposite flow rule' would carry different overtones for kula participants. For example, Malinowski (1935(1):295) records that on Vakuta the rules of the game for the urigubu harvest gift of yams were reversed. The exchange was initiated by the gift of a kula-type valuable from the sister's husband to the sister's brother.

One would like to know how this contrast ties in with: (a) differences between Kiriwinan and Vakutan political structures and (b) fine details in the difference between kula-exchange practice on Kiriwina and on Vakuta. We should not assume, as Malinowski and most of the contributors to this volume tend to assume, that a synthetic totality THE KULA can be pieced together from components derived from reports from different islands, even when, as in the Kiriwina–Vakuta case, the islands are immediately adjacent.

But in addition to this contrast between symmetrical and asymmetrical exchanges, there is also the contrast between exchanges which are expressive of permanent relationships (social indebtedness, persisting jural rights and obligations) and exchanges which have the effect of cancelling out a previously existing 'debt', of either an economic or a legal kind. When I pay the baker a coin for my loaf of bread that is the end of the matter; the transaction is asymmetrical but complete. There is no residual debt. But the relationship between kula partners is one of permanent indebtedness just as it is between 'wife giver'/'wife receiver' lineages in societies which practise 'Kachin-type marriage'.

I find it surprising that Melanesian specialists have not given more attention to the generality of such coding principles. As is well known, Lévi-Strauss's *Les Structures élémentaires de la parenté* (1949) is an elaborate exercise constructed around the theme of the basic contrast between symmetrical and asymmetrical exchange. Although his theory is very general, Lévi-Strauss pays relatively little attention to the exchange of perishable commodities and concerns himself almost entirely with the exchange of women, either for other women (restricted exchange – prototypically Australian marriage systems) or for bridewealth goods which are seen as temporary surrogates for other women (generalised exchange – prototypically the North Burma Kachin).

Although the Trobriand kula, as described by Malinowski, has nearly all the characteristics which Lévi-Strauss (mistakenly) considers to be typical of exchange systems of this latter kind, the kula is only given a passing mention in a footnote (Lévi-Strauss 1949:316 n.2; 1969:259 n.2). Only three subsequent authors [Kelly (1968), Ekeh (1974), Damon (1980)] seem to have appreciated the broad similarity between features of Malinowski's model of the kula and Lévi-Strauss's 'generalised exchange', and it is only in the third of these papers, which has been published since the Cambridge kula conference took place, that the crucial issues are really brought out. I strongly recommend readers of this volume to study Damon's 1980 paper.

I want now to raise a related but rather different issue. If I were to criticise Damon's paper I would complain that, like almost everyone else who writes about this topic, he concerns himself too much with the kula as a 'thing-in-itself', that is, as a phenomenon which exists independently of the various island cultures with which it is associated and as something of which the social or economic utility has to be 'explained', instead of as a residue of history which is used and manipulated in many different ways in different parts of the Massim area.

The assumption that the kula can be treated as a 'thing-in-itself' derives from Malinowski's model of a 'kula ring'. Almost all the contributors to this volume (including Damon for part of the time) not only assume that the 'ring' really exists but that this existence is somehow crucially relevant for our understanding of kula operations. This seems to me to be a fallacy. Belief in the existence of a 'kula ring' by participant actors is primarily the expression of a model of asymmetrical exchange; whether the 'ring' 'really exists' or not is for the most part irrelevant.

Some readers will find this a strange proposition. After all a variety of authors have produced maps of the 'kula ring' and the present volume contains a carefully revised updated version. This lastest map is unquestionably by far the most reliable record to date of the region within which kula-type transactions are known to take place. Moreover, in his 1980 paper Damon has been able to demonstrate that certain high-ranking kula valuables do indeed move around a circular path just as Malinowski said and that, in this respect, they obey the circulation rules which Lévi-Strauss and his Dutch predecessors spelled out, both for asym-

533

Edmund Leach

metrical marriage exchanges of the matrilateral cross-cousin marriage type and for 'circulating connubium' in general. Nevertheless, I would insist that the 'kula ring' concept contains a large component of fiction.[1]

The concept of *kitoum* (*kitoma*) was first introduced into the literature of the kula by Weiner (1976:129) but was greatly elaborated by a number of contributions to the Cambridge Conference discussions (see p. 24) and has subsequently been given extensive consideration in Damon's 1980 paper. Kitoum exchanges clearly form an integral part of 'the kula system', in so far as there is such a thing, but their principle of operation is of quite a different kind from the 'opposite flow rule' transactions which Malinowski and his successors have isolated as 'typical' of kula operations. This 'discovery' is of fundamental importance for all theorising about the kula.

Kitoum exchanges are not of the symmetrical ('restricted exchange') type in any simple sense; they do not ordinarily involve the immediate exchange of a kula-type valuable for an exactly similar valuable, but that broadly is the ideology. Initially a kitoum is a kula valuable taken out of the one-way-flow cycle by the temporary 'owner' in order to settle a private debt of a non-kula type. Such debt settlement will involve short-run asymmetrical exchanges. However, if, in the course of further private transactions, the individual concerned acquires a kula-type valuable which is acceptable as the exact equivalent of the one which he previously removed from its 'proper' course, he is entitled to feed this newly acquired valuable back into the kula system along the same 'path' which he previously interrupted.

The relevant point is that the kitoum cycle, from start to finish, is of limited geographical range and, overall, of the symmetrical type. It corresponds at least in some respects to the 'restricted exchange' of Lévi-Strauss's typology though it has the added characteristic that it leaves no residual debt (or relationship) between the parties concerned. In this respect kitoum (as described by Damon) is complementary to the more familiar type of kula transaction described by Malinowski which has the contrary characteristic found in all 'generalised exchange' systems by which all the participants in the system are continuously in debt to their 'partners' on either side. But that does not imply circularity!

Let me elaborate that last point even though it is already implicit in Damon (1980), just as it is explicit in my various criticisms of Lévi-Strauss (1949) and the Dutch 'circulating connubium' literature. Any individual participant in a generalised exchange system is ordinarily only aware of what goes on in his or her immediate vicinity. For example, as a Kachin male I know that I am expected to find a wife for my son among OUR *mayu ni*, the affines on my mother's side, and that my daughter should find a husband among OUR *dama ni*, the affines on my father's sister's husband (sister's husband) side. Likewise I know that our mayu ni will be seeking to marry off their sons to girls from THEIR mayu ni while our dama ni will be seeking to marry off their daughters to boys from THEIR dama ni, and so on. However, whatever mythology may present as an ideal model, I do not usually know more than that.

On the other hand, if I want to explain such a system to others who are unfamiliar with the immediate facts, I will always do so in terms of a model. And since models must be tidy and without loose ends, the chain of affinal links will be made to come back on itself as in a circle. The mayu ni of the mayu ni of the mayu ni are represented as identical to the dama ni of the dama ni. But that is a manner of speaking; I do not, in ordinary circumstances, *know* what actually happens, and, in ordinary circumstances, it doesn't really matter.

And so it is with the kula. In Kiriwina or Muyuw or wherever the same identifiable valuable turns up from time to time travelling in the same direction as before. To explain this observed fact one must have a model which asserts that such objects have travelled along the circumference of a circle at each point of which the owner-for-the-time-being has adhered to the same rule of asymmetrical, 'opposite flow rule', exchange.

The model explains the facts as I actually know them; moreover, as Jerry Leach and Damon have both shown, modern developments in communication make it possible for enthusiastic players of the kula game to check up on the actual movements of particular, much-sought-for, items. It is also true that when an identifiable valuable eventually returns to its point of departure it has certainly travelled on some kind of 'circuitous' (if not 'circular') path. But all sorts of things may have happened to it on the way and the ring path is in no way fundamental to the 'real' system.

Damon's view seems to be that through the device of kitoum exchanges the kula valuables acquire the characteristics of 'capital' in a straightforward economic sense; they contain a store of value which can be converted into other things. This gives a utilitarian twist to the whole business of the kula which is otherwise missing. I accept that this is a valid interpretation of his own contemporary Muyuw data, but it is not an explanation of THE KULA, considered as a Massim-wide thing-in-itself.

At the present time, throughout the capitalist world, financiers of varying degrees of respectability have taken to treating highly valued works of art as 'capital' which provides a hedge against monetary inflation. But this undoubted fact does not 'explain' how post-impressionist painters, in late nineteenth-century France, came to paint as they did, nor does it explain why a painting by Cézanne is likely to be valued by art

Edmund Leach

historians (and also of course by speculative financiers!) at many times the worth of some other painting of similar date and similar subject matter associated with a less renowned 'name'. Artistic value and art-trade value are not the same thing, though it seems to be implicit in Damon's 'Marxist' analysis that the latter somehow 'explains' the former. It certainly seems to be the case that renowned kula valuables are stores of value of several different kinds, but we do not learn anything about the nature of their value as ritual objects (i.e. 'works of art') by noting that, in special circumstances, this value can be converted into commodity value of a more commercial sort.

The force of all these remarks is to urge the Melanesian specialists who are active in this field to be more functionalist in a Malinowskian sense. There is no such thing as THE KULA. It is rather that in the geographical zone which has come to be regarded as the kula area there is a certain general similarity about the ways in which non-utilitarian 'valuables', consisting of such things as armshells, shell necklaces, boars' tusks, stone adze-blades and the like are 'traded around'. In the process of such 'trading', individual items may sometimes acquire 'economic value' of a straightforward sort. But this is not always the case. A variety of different kinds of 'value' are involved in the total complex of exchange relation-ships that are to be observed. The nearest approach to a 'common' scheme of values in the whole set is that originally perceived by Mauss: social relationships entail 'prestations' – *obligatory* gift giving. Any net-work of social relations is a structure of indebtedness. The value that attaches to a kula valuable at any point in its wanderings is the value of the debt relationship which it has most recently served to express.

Malinowski and Mauss believed that the 'symbolic value' embedded in these valuables and expressed in their exchange was wholly distinct from 'economic (utilitarian) value'. Firth has been critical of that position right from the start. In 1957, while giving Malinowski due credit for recognis-ing 'that existence in primitve economic systems of what others have later referred to as different circuits or spheres of exchange', he implied that Malinowski tended to exaggerate the degree to which these different spheres were really separate.

Malinowski gave the impression that the exchange of kula valuables was an end in itself, an almost mechanical routine in which the rewards were emotional rather than economic or political. My 'chess-game analogy' has similar though less mechanical implications. The whole point of a game is that the precise outcome is unpredictable. But for Firth there is a market in kula valuables and the basic problem is to discover how the values that prevail in that market are determined. It seems to me that there is a confusion here.

536

What I am arguing is that there are many varieties of kula. The kula 'game' is played in different ways in different parts of the map even though the 'pieces' with which it is played are, for the most part, the same. In each part of the map a distinction needs to be drawn between the 'value' of a kula valuable considered as a piece in the kula game, and the 'value' of identically the same object when it is utilised in a non-kula form of exchange. In different parts of the map the degree of separation between these two types of 'value' varies; moreover in different parts of the map there are different social mechanisms for bringing about a temporary of permanent transformation of one type of value into the other. These variations need to be stressed not glossed over.

What Damon tells us about the switch from *mwal/veigun* (kula) valuation to *kitoum* valuation for the Muyuw case is fascinating but it cannot be generalised. In other parts of the system the game is played differently.

And in the same vein I would emphasise that authors and readers should not be taken in by the deceptive conservatism of some of the ethnography. At the Cambridge Conference we were shown dozens of splendid colour-slides made within the last few years which could have provided perfect illustrations for Malinowski's *Argonauts*. But that does not mean that the institution of which these slides were a pictorial record was identical to the institution observed by Malinowski in 1917. As Jerry Leach has noted (p. 12) at least one of the armshells now circulating in the kula was quite recently discovered in the course of excavation. But the fact that archaeology indicates that kula-type armshells and necklaces have been around in the Massim for nearly 2000 years need not imply that any institution functionally related to any of the present-day systems of kula-syle exchange existed in the remote past.

Even the recent past is open to doubt. There is little historical material in this volume, a deficiency which will hopefully be made good in the proceedings of the University of Virginia Conference, but there are already clear indications that the appearance of continuity between what Malinowski observed and what the present contributors have observed is deceptive. Malinowski himself was almost certainly deceived about the historical depth of what he was describing.

Almost the first printed description of the Trobriand Islands is that which appears in Finsch (1888b:205–10). It could be that Finsch was misinformed, but he was particularly interested in the possibilities open to European traders and thus took special note of existing forms of inter-island trading as they were reported to him. It is therefore with surprise that one now reads the very positive statement that, while Kiriwina was visited for purposes of trade by the inhabitants of Normanby, Welle, and Woodlark, the Trobrianders themselves made no

Edmund Leach

overseas voyages because their 'canoes which lack sails are unsuitable for journeys on the open sea'. This does not seem at all likely to be true but it is perfectly possible. Kiriwina may have been drawn into the cycle of kula exchanges, not just relatively late, but very late indeed. I am not myself urging that this was in fact the case, but I believe that the sum of relevant ethnographic facts has been very much more fluid over time than has commonly been supposed.

On that sceptical note I will end. There are hopeful indications that the Cambridge Conference marked a new beginning rather than the conclusion of a long-ago anthropological story. What is now needed is much greater attention to local variations and to the way the local variations, both in the past and in the present, have been fitted into the local social system considered as a more or less self-contained totality. The kula as a glorious thing-in-itself has now become important for aspiring Massim Area politicians but, among anthropologists, it may have seen its day as 'an exchange of an entirely novel type'.

And when we come to look at the kula, not so much as a single institution but as a theme and variations, we may well end up by deciding that the most interesting variations are not those northern examples which have been so intensively studied by Malinowski and his successors, but the 'anomalous' cases from the fringe areas to the south and south-east, some of which are tentatively described for the first time in this volume. So I repeat once more: we know less today about kula-style exchange than Malinowski thought he knew in 1922. But that comment is in no sense a denigration either of the work of Malinowski or of the various Trobriand area specialists who have contributed to this volume. The real value of this symposium is that it gives some indication of the extent of our continuing ignorance in the three related fields of ethnography, history and theoretical understanding. Nevertheless it marks a giant leap forward from where we all stood less than ten years ago.

[1] Notice for example that J. Leach's fully updated map of the Kula Ring at pp 20–1 puts Misima and islands to the south *outside* the ring but that Ike Gawan opposition Kura Doba/Kura Masima (p. 306 note 7) implies a much less restrictive usage.

538

Bibliography

Adams, R. 1975. *Energy and Structure: A Theory of Social Power*. Austin: University of Texas Press.

1978. 'Man, energy and anthropology: I can feel the heat, but where's the light?', *American Anthropologist*, 80: 297–309.

Affleck, D. 1971. *Murua or Woodlark Island: A study of European–Muruan Contact to 1942*. Canberra: Unpublished B.A. Honours Thesis at Australian National University.

Annual Report on British New Guinea. 1893–4. Brisbane: Government Printer.

Armstrong, W. E. 1924. 'Rossel Island money', *The Economic Journal*, 34: 423–9.

1928. *Rossel Island*, Cambridge: Cambridge University Press.

Austen, L. 1939. 'The Seasonal Calendar of Kiriwina, Trobriand Islands', *Oceania*, IX, 3:237–53.

1945. 'Cultural Changes in Kiriwina', *Oceania*, 16: 15–60.

Bailey, F. 1970. *Strategems and Spoils*. Oxford: Basil Blackwell.

Balibar, E. 1970. 'On Reproduction'. In *Reading Capital* by Louis Althusser and Etienne Balibar. Translated from the French by Ben Brewster. London: New Left Books pp. 254–308.

Barton, F. 1904. 'Report on Central Division'. *Annual Report for British New Guinea 1902–3*.

1910. 'The Annual Trading Expedition to the Papuan Gulf'. In C. G. Seligmann's *The Melanesians of British New Guinea*, Cambridge: Cambridge University Press.

Belshaw, C. S. 1950. 'Changes in Heirloom Jewellery in the Central Solomons', *Oceania*, vol. 20: 169–84.

1955. *In Search of Wealth*. American Anthropological Association, Memoir no. 80, vol. 57: no. 1, part 2.

1965. *Traditional Exchange and Modern Markets*, Englewood Cliffs, N.J.: Prentice-Hall.

Berde, S. J. 1973. 'Contemporary notes on Rossel Island valuables', *Journal of the Polynesian Society*, 82: 188–205.

1974. *Melanesians as Methodists: economy and marriage on a Papua New Guinea island*. University of Pennsylvania: Ph.D. dissertation, University Microfilm 74–22808.

1979. 'The Impact of Christianity on a Melanesian Economy' in *Research in Economic Anthropology: A Research Annual* [Ed: G. Dalton] Vol. 2: 169–87.

Blau, P. M. 1964. *Exchange and Power in Social Life* New York: Wiley.

Boas, F. 1966. *Kwakiutl Ethnography* (H. Codere, ed.), Chicago: University of Chicago Press.

Bohannan, P. 1955. 'Some principles of exchange and investment among the Tiv', *American Anthropologist*, 57: 60–70.

1959. 'The impact of Money on an African Subsistence Economy', *Journal of Economic History*, Vol. 19, No. 4: 491–503.

Bohannan, P. and L. 1968. *Tiv Economy*, Evanston, Ill.: Northwestern University Press.

Bourdieu, Pierre. 1977. *Outline of a Theory of Practice*, Cambridge: Cambridge University Press.

Bromilow, W. 1929. *Twenty Years among Primitive Papuans*, London.

Brookfield, H. C. with Hart D., 1971. *Melanesia: a geographical interpretation of an island world*, London: Methuen.

Brunton, R. 1975. 'Why do the Trobriands have chiefs?', *Man*, n.s., vol. 10, no. 4: 544–58.

Burns, T. 1958. 'The Forms of Conduct', *American Journal of Sociology*, 64: 137–51.

Callen, J. S. 1976. 'Settlement patterns in pre-war Siwai: an application of central place theory to a horticultural society', *Solomon Island Studies in Human Biogeography*, no. 5, Chicago: Field Museum of Natural History.

Campbell, S. 1978. 'Restricted access to knowledge in Vakuta', *Canberra Anthropology*, vol. 1, 3: 1–11.

Capell, A. 1969. *A Survey of New Guinea Languages*, Sydney: Sydney University Press.

Carter, F. W. 1969. 'An analysis of the Medieval Serbian oecumene: a theoretical approach', *Geografista Annaler*, 51B: 39–56.

Cassady, Jr. R. 1974. *Exchange by Private Treaty*, Austin: University of Texas Bureau of Business Research.

Champion, I. (A.R.M./Misima). 1932. *Patrol Reports 1931–32*.

Chowning, A. 1959. 'Witchcraft among the Molima of Fergusson Island', *Philadelphia Anthropological Society Bulletin*.

1960. 'Canoe Making among the Molima of Fergusson Island', *Expedition: Bulletin of the University Museum Pennsylvania*, vol.3 (1): 32–9.

1962. 'Cognatic Kin Groups among the Molima of Fergusson Island', *Ethnology*, vol. I: 92–101.

1974. 'Disputing in Two West New Britain Societies'. In *Contention and Dispute* (A. L. Epstein, ed.). Canberra: The Australian National University Press.

Codrington, R. H. 1891. *The Melanesians: Studies in their Anthropology and Folklore*, Oxford, Clarendon Press.

Connell, J. 1977. 'The Bougainville connection: changes in the economic context of shell money production in Malaita', *Oceania*, vol. 48. no. 2: 81–101.

Coote, W. 1883. *The Western Pacific*, London.

Dalton, G. 1965. 'Primitive Money', *American Anthropologist*, Vol. 67 44–65.

Damon, F. n.d. 'The Past and the Present: an Interpretation of Woodlark Island Trenches and Megalithic Structures'. Unpublished paper.

1978. *Modes of Production and the Circulation of Value on the Other Side of the Kula Ring*. Princeton University Ph.D. dissertation.

1980. 'The Kula and generalised exchange: considering some unconsidered aspects of *The Elementary Structures of Kinship*', *Man* 2: 267–92.

Douglas, M. 1967. 'Primitive Rationing: a Study in Controlled Exchange'. In *Themes in Economic Anthropology* (R. Firth, ed.). London/New York: Tavistock: 119–47.

Dudwega, D. K. 1975. 'Traditions of Nade Village', *Oral History*, vol. III: 2–34.

Dutton, T. 1978. 'Language and trade in central and south-east Papua', *Mankind*, 11: 341–53.

Egloff, B. J. 1971. *Collingwood Bay and the Trobriand Islands in recent prehistory*. Canberra: The Australia National University Ph.D. dissertation.

1972. 'The sepulchral pottery of Nuamata Island, Papua', *Archaeology and Physical Anthropology in Oceania*, 7: 145–63.

1978. 'The Kula before Malinowski: a changing configuration', *Mankind*, 11: 429–35.

Einzig, P. 1949. *Primitive Money in its Ethnological, Historical and Economic Aspects*, New York.

Ekeh, P. 1974. *Social Exchange Theory*, London: Heinemann Educational.

Epstein, T. S. 1968. *Capitalism, Primitve and Modern*, Canberra: The Australian National University Press.

Evans–Pritchard, E. 1942. *The Nuer*, Oxford: Oxford University Press.

1951. *Social Anthropology*, London: Cohen and West.

Feil, D. 1978a. *Holders of the Way: Exchange Partnerships in an Enga Tee Community*. ANU Ph.D. dissertation.

1978b. 'Women and men in the Enga Tee', *American Ethnologist*, 5(2): 263–79.

Fellows, S. 1973. Papers of Rev. Samuel Benjamin Fellows 1883–1900. Pacific Manuscripts Bureau, Microfilm 601. The Australian National University.

Fink, R. 1965. 'The Esa'ala-Losuia Open Electorate'. In D. Bettison *et al.* (ed.). *The Papua New Guinea Elections 1964*. Canberra: The Australian National University Press.

Finsch, O. 1887. 'Abnorme Eberhauer, Pretiosen im Schmuck der Sudsee-Volker'. *Mittheilungen der Anthropologischen Gesellschaft in Wien*. Redacteur Franz Heger, XVII. Band, Wien.

1888a. *Ethnologische Atlas*. Leipzig: F. Hirt und Sohn.

1888b. *Samoafahrten*. Leipzig: F. Hirt and Sohn.

Firth, R. 1936. *We, The Tikopia*. London: George Allen and Unwin, Ltd.

1939. *Primitive Polynesian Economy*, London: Routledge and Kegan Paul.

1951. *Elements of Social Organization*. London: Watts and Co.

1952. 'Notes on the Social Structure of some South-Eastern New Guinea Communities. Part I, Mailu', *Man*, 52: 99.

1957. 'The Place of Malinowski in the History of Economic Anthropology'. In *Man and Culture* (R. Firth, ed.). London: Routledge and Kegan Paul: 209–28.

1967. (ed.) *Themes in Economic Anthropology*. ASA Monograph No. 6. London: Tavistock.

1973. *Symbols: Public and Private*. London: Allen and Unwin.

1975. 'Seligmann's Contribution to Oceanic Anthropology', *Oceania*, 45: 272–82.

Forge, A. 1972. 'The Golden Fleece', *Man*, vol. 7(4):527–40.

Fortune, R. 1932. *Sorcerers of Dobu*, London: Routledge and Kegan Paul. Revised edition 1963. New York: E. P. Dutton and Co., Inc.

Gathercole, P. 1978. '*Hau, Mauri*, and *utu*: a re-examination', *Mankind* 11 (3): 334–40. Special issue on *Trade and Exchange in Oceania and Australia*. J. Specht and J. P. White (ed.).

Geertz, C. 1973. *The Interpretation of Cultures*, New York: Basic Books.

Gell, A. 1975. *Metamorphosis of the Cassowaries: Umeda Society, Language and Ritual*, London: Athlone Press.

Godelier, M. 1972. *Rationality and Irrationality in Economics*, translated from the French by Brian Pearce. New York: Monthly Review Press.

1977. *Perspectives in Marxist Anthropology*, translated from the French by Robert Brain. Cambridge: Cambridge University Press.

Gostin, O., W. Tomasetti, and M. W. Young, 1971. 'Personalities versus Policies'. In Epstein, A. L. *et. al* (ed.) *The Politics of Dependence: Papua New Guinea 1968*. Canberra: ANU Press.

Grant, R. 1953. *A School Dictionary in the Dobu Language*, East Cape, Papua New Guinea: Methodist Mission Press.

Groves, M. 1960. 'Motu Pottery', *Journal of the Polynesian Society*, 69: 3–32.

Guidieri, R. 1973. 'Il Kula: ovvero della truffa. Una reinterpretazione dei pratiche simboliche dell isol trobriand', *Rassegna italiana de Sociologia*, Anno XIV, no. 4.

Hage, P. 1977. 'Centrality in the Kula Ring', *Journal of the Polynesian Society*, 86: 27–36.

Haggett, P. 1967. 'Network models in geography'. In *Models in Geography* (R. J. Chorley and P. Haggett, eds.): 609–68.

Harding, T. 1967. *Voyagers of the Vitiaz Straits*, Seattle: University of Washington Press.

Harris, M. 1969. *The Rise of Anthropological Theory*, London: Routledge and Kegan Paul.

Heidegger, M. 1962. *Being and Time*, translated by J. Macquarrie and E. Robinson. New York: Harper and Row.

Herskovits, M. 1940. *The Economic Life of Primitive Peoples*, New York: Alfred A. Knopf.

Hinton, A. 1972. *Shells of New Guinea and the Central Indo-Pacific*, Australia: Jacaranda Press.

Holenstein, E. 1970. *Roman Jakobson's Approach to Language*, Bloomington: Indiana University Press.

Irwin, G. 1974. 'The emergence of a central place in coastal Papuan pre-history: a theoretical approach', *Mankind*, 9: 268–72.

1977. *The Emergence of Mailu as a central place in the prehistory of coastal Papua*. Canberra: the Australian National University: Ph.D. dissertation.

1978a. 'The development of Mailu as a specialized trading and manufacturing centre in Papuan prehistory: the causes and the implications', *Mankind*, 11: 406–15.

1978b. 'Pots and entrepots: a study of settlement, trade and the development of economic specialization in Papuan prehistory', *World Archaeology*, 9: 299–319.

Jenness, D. and A. Ballantyne. 1920. *The Northern D'Entrecasteaux*, Oxford: Clarendon Press.

1928. *Language, Mythology and Songs of Bwaidoga*, New Plymouth, New Zealand: Avery and Sons.

Kapferer, B. 1976. 'Introduction: transactional models reconsidered'. In *Transactions and Meaning: Directions in the Anthropology of Exchange and Symbolic Behaviour*, (B. Kapferer, ed.). Philadelphia: Institute for the Study of Human Issues.

Kaplan, S. 1976. 'Ethnological and biogeographical significance of pottery sherds from Nissan Island, Papua New Guinea', *Fieldiana Anthropology*, 66: 35–89.

Kasaipwalova, J. and U. Beier. 1978. *Yaulabuta: an historical poem from the Trobriand Islands*, Port Moresby: Institute of Papua New Guinea Studies.

Kelly, R. 1968. 'L'échange généralisé à Dobu', *l'Homme*, 8:54–6.

Key, C. 1968. 'Pottery manufacture in the Wanigela area of Collingwood Bay, Papua', *Archaeology and Physical Anthropology in Oceania*, 6: 653–7.

Labouret, H. 1953. 'L'Echange et le Commerce dans les Archipels du Pacifique et en Afrique Tropicale'. In *L'Histoire du Commerce*. (J. Lacour-Gavet, ed.) Livre i, Tome iii.

Laracy, H. 1970, 'Xavier Montrouzier: a Missionary in Melanesia'. In *Pacific Island Portraits*. (J. W. Davidson and D. Starr, eds). Canberra.

Lauer, P. K. 1970a. 'Amphlett Island Pottery Trade and the Kula', *Mankind*, 7:165–76.

1970b. 'Sailing with the Amphlett Islanders', *Journal of the Polynesian Society*, vol. 79, no. 4: 381–98.

1971. 'Changing patterns of pottery trade to the Trobriand Islands', *World Archaeology*, vol. 3. no. 2: 197–209.

1974. *Pottery traditions in the D'Entrecasteaux Islands of Papua*, Occasional Papers in Anthropology, no. 3. University of Queensland.

1976. *Field Notes from the D'Entrecasteaux and Trobriand Islands of Papua*, Occasional Papers in Anthropology, no. 7. University of Queensland.

Lawton, R. 1968. 'The Class Systems of Kiriwina'. Unpublished paper.

Leach, E. 1958. 'Concerning Trobriand Clans and the Kinship Category *Tabu*'. In *The Developmental Cycle in Domestic Groups*. (J. Goody, ed.). Cambridge: Cambridge University Press.

1966. 'Virgin Birth', *Proceedings of the Royal Anthropological Institute*: 39–49. London.

1978. 'The Kula in its historical context'. Unpublished paper for Kula and Massim Exchange Conference.

Leach, J. 1975. *Trobriand Cricket: an ingenious response to colonialism*. Documentary film produced by Government of Papua New Guinea.

1976. 'The 1972 Elections in the Kula Open'. In *Prelude to Self-Government*. (D. Stone, ed.). Canberra: The Australian National University Press.

Bibliography

1978. *The Kabisawali Movement in the Trobriand Islands*. Cambridge University: Ph.D. dissertation.

(in press). 'The Conflict underlying the Kabisawali Movement in the Trobriand Islands'. In *Micro-nationalism in Melanesia*. (R. May, ed.)

1981. 'Imdeduya: a Kula folktale from Kiriwina', *Bikmaus: Journal of Papua New Guinea Affairs, Ideas, and the Arts*.

LeClair, E. and Schneider, H. 1968. *Economic Anthropology*, New York: Holt, Rinehart, and Winston.

Lee, D. 1949. 'Being and Value in Primitive Society', *Journal of Philosophy*, Vol. XLVI: 401–15.

Lenoir, R. 1924. 'Les Expéditions maritimes, Institution sociale en Mélanésie Occidentale', *L'Anthropologie*, Tome 34: 387–410.

Lévi-Strauss, C. 1949 *Les Structures élémentaires de la parenté*, Paris: PUF
1969. *The Elementary Structures of Kinship*. London: Eyre and Spottiswoode.

Liep, J. 1978. 'Exchange and Social Reproduction in the Kula Region'. Unpublished paper for Kula and Massim Exchange Conference.
1983. 'A Note on Shells and Kula Valuables'. In Macintyre, M. 1983, pp. 85–6.

Lithgow, D. 1976. 'Milne Bay'. In *Austronesian Languages, New Guinea Area Languages and Language Study*. (S. A. Wurm, ed.), vol. 2. Department of Linguistics. Canberra: The Australian National University.
1978. 'Present Trends in Kula at Dobu'. Unpublished paper for Kula and Massim Exchange Conference.

Lounsbury, R. 1965. 'Another View of the Trobriand Kinship Categories', *American Anthropologist* 67, 5, Part 2.

Macintyre, M. 1983. *The Kula: a Bibliography*, Cambridge: Cambridge University Press.

Mackay, R. D. 1971. 'An Historic Engraved Shell from the Trobriand Islands–Milne Bay District', in *Records of the Papua & New Guinea Public Museum and Art Gallery*, Vol. 1, No.1.

Malinowski, B. 1915. 'The Natives of Mailu: preliminary results of Robert Mond research work in British New Guinea' *Transactions of the Royal Society of South Australia*, 39: 494–706.
1918. 'Fishing in the Trobriand Islands', *Man*, vol. XVIII, no. 53: 87–92.
1920a. 'Kula: the circulating exchange of valuables in the archipelagoes of eastern New Guinea', *Man*, XX, no. 51: 97–105.
1920b. 'Classificatory Particles in the Language of Kiriwina'. In *Bulletin, School of Oriental and African Studies*, vol. I, part 4: 33–78.
1921. 'The Primitive Economics of the Trobriand Islanders', *The Economic Journal*, vol. XXXI.
1922. *Argonauts of the Western Pacific*. London: Routledge and Kegan Paul. Reprinted with identical pagination 1961 by E. P. Dutton and Co. and 1978 by Routledge and Kegan Paul.
1926. *Crime and Custom in Savage Society*. London: Routledge and Kegan Paul.
1927. *Sex and Repression in Savage Society*, London: Routledge and Kegan Paul.
1929 (1932). *Sexual Life of Savages*. London: Routledge and Kegan Paul.

Revised edition issued in 1932 as *Sexual Life of Savages in North-Western Melanesia* (third edition). Reprinted 1968.

1935. *Coral Gardens and their Magic*, vols. I and II. London: Allen and Unwin, New York: American Book Company and by London: Routledge and Kegan Paul. Reprinted 1965 with same pagination and new introduction by Indiana University Press.

1948. 'Myth in Primitive Psychology' and 'Baloma: The Spirits of the Dead in the Trobriand Islands'. In *Magic, Science and Religion and Other Essays*, Glencoe Ill.: The Free Press. Reprinted in 1954 by New York: Doubleday Anchor.

1967. *A Diary in the Strict Sense of the Term*. London: Routledge and Kegan Paul.

Marx, K. 1867. *Das Kapital: Kritik der politischen Oekonomie* Vol. I; Vol. III (1894). Cited here from the Russian 'official' translation *Captial* Vols I & III Moscow: Progress Publishers.

Mauss, M. 1954. *The Gift*. London: Cohen & West. I. Cunnison's translation of Mauss's *Essai sur le Don* 1925. Reprinted 1974 Routledge and Kegan Paul.

1950. 'Essai sur le don'. In *Sociologie et Anthropologie*. Paris: Presses Universitaires de France, pp. 145–279.

Meggitt, M. 1972. 'System and Subsystem: the te exchange cycle among the Mae Enga'. In *Human Ecology*, 1 (2): 111–24.

1974. 'Pigs are our hearts! The Te exchange cycle among the Mae Enga of New Guinea', *Oceania*, vol. 44, no. 3: 165–203.

Montague, S. 1974. *The Trobriand Society*. University of Chicago: Unpublished Ph.D. dissertation.

1978 'Church Government and Western Ways in a Trobriand Village'. Unpublished paper for Kula and Massim Exchange Conference.

Moreton, M. H. 1905. 'Resident Magistrate's Report: South-eastern Division'. *Annual Report for British New Guinea 1904–5*.

Munn, N. 1972. 'Symbolic Time in the Trobriands of Malinowski's Era: an Essay on the Anthropology of Time'. Unpublished paper.

1977. 'The spatiotemporal transformation of Gawa canoes'. *Journal de la Société des Oceanistes*, Tome 33 (mars-juin), 54–55: 39–53.

Murray, J. 1912. *Papua or British New Guinea*. London.

Nelson, H. 1976. 'Woodlark Island'. In *Black, White and Gold: Goldmining in New Guinea, 1878–1930*. Canberra: The Australian National University Press.

Ollier, C. and Pain, C. 1978. 'Geomorphology and Tectonics of Woodlark Island, Papua New Guinea', *Zeitschift für Geomorphologie*, vol. 22: 1.20.

Parsons, T. 1963. 'On the Concept of Influence', *Public Opinion Quarterly*, 27: 37–67.

Peirce, C. 1955. *Philosophical Writings of Peirce*, New York: Dover.

Peter, Olive. 1976. 'The Myths of Misima', *Oral History*, 4 (2): 16–52. Port Moresby: Institute of Papua New Guinea Studies.

Pitts, P. 1965. 'A graph theoretical approach to historical geography', *Professional Geographer*, 17: 15–20.

Polanyi, K. 1957. 'The Economy as Instituted Process'. In Polanyi, K., C. W. Arensberg, and H. W. Pearson (ed.) *Trade and Market in the Early Empires*. New York: Free Press.

Bibliography

Powell, H. 1956. *An Analysis of Present Day Social Structure in the Trobriand Islands*. University of London: Ph.D. dissertation.

1960. 'Competitive Leadership in Trobriand Political Organisation', *Journal of the Royal Anthropological Institute*, 90: 118–48.

1965. Review of Uberol (1962) in *Man*, 65: 97–9.

1969. 'Territory, hierarchy and kinship in Kiriwina'. *Man* (N.S.), 4: 580–604.

1978. 'The Kula in Trobriand Politics or Why did some of the Kiriwinans have semi-hereditary Big Men but apparently not hereditary chiefs?'. Unpublished paper for Kula and Massim Exchange Conference.

Quiggin, A. 1949. *A Survey of Primitive Money*. London: Methuen.

Rappaport, R. 1967. *Pigs for the Ancestors*, New Haven, Conn., Yale University Press.

Rathje, W. 1978. 'Melanesian and Australian exchange systems: a view from Mesoamerica', *Mankind*, 11: 165–74.

Reid, J., Schiffer, M. and Rathje, W. 1975. 'Behavioural Archaeology: four strategies', *American Anthropologist*, 77: 864–9.

Rivers, W. 1926. 'Trade, Warfare, and Slavery'. In *Psychology and Ethnology* (Elliot Smith, G., ed.). London: Kegan Paul, Trench, Trubner, and Co.

Roheim, G. 1946. 'Yoboaine, a war god of Normanby Island', *Oceania*, vol. 16 no. 3: 211–23 and no. 4: 319–36.

1948. 'Witches of Normanby Island', *Oceania*, vol. 18, no. 4: 279–308.

1950a. *Psychoanalysis and Anthropology*, New York: International Universities Press.

1950b. 'Totemism in Normanby Island, Territory of New Guinea', *Mankind*, vol. 4, no. 5: 189–95.

1954. 'Cannibalism in Duau, Normanby Island, d'Entrecasteaux Group, Territory of Papua', *Mankind*, vol. 4, no. 2: 487–95.

1957. 'Death and Mourning Ceremonies at Normanby Island', *Man*, vol. 37: 49–50.

Rye, O. 1976. 'Keeping your temper under control: materials and the manufacture of Papuan pottery', *Archaeology and Physical Anthropology in Oceania*, 11: 106–37.

Sahlins, M. 1965. 'On the sociology of primitive exchange'. In *The Relevance of Models for Social Anthropology*. (M. Banton, ed.). ASA Monographs No 1, London: Tavistock.

1972. *Stone Age Economics*, Chicago: Aldine-Atherton.

Salerio, C. 1862. 'D. Carlo Salerio über die Inseln im Osten von Neu-Guinea'. Notes and map of Salerio for 1852–5 period on Woodlark, published by A. Petermann in *Mittheilungen aus Justus Perthes Geographischen Anstalt über Wichtige neue Erforschungen auf dem Gesammtgebiete der Geographie*: 341–4.

Sartre, J. 1960. *Critique de la raison dialectique (précédé de Question de méthode)*. Paris: Gallimard. Translated by A. Sheridan-Smith, 1976, London: New Left Books and Atlantic Highlands: Humanities.

Saussure, F. de 1966. *Course In General Linguistics*, New York: McGraw-Hill.

Saville, W. 1926. *In Unknown New Guinea*. London: Seeley, Service and Co.

Schapera, I. 1955. 'The Sin of Cain'. *Journal of the Royal Anthropological Institute*, 85: 33–43.

Schlesier, E. 1970. *Me'udana: Sudost Neuguinea.* Braaunschweig: Albert Limbach Verlag.

Scoditti, G. 1977. 'A Kula Prowboard: an iconological interpretation', *L'Uomo*, vol. II, no. 2, Ottobre: 198–232.

Seligmann, C. 1901. 'A Type of Canoe Ornament with Magical Significance from South-eastern New Guinea', *Man*, 16.

1910. *Melanesians of British New Guinea*, Cambridge: Cambridge University Press.

Seligmann, C. and Strong, W. M. 1906. 'Anthropogeographical investigations in British New Guinea', *The Geographical Journal*, vol. XXVII, no. 3.

Sherover, C. 1971. *Heidegger, Kant and Time*, Bloomington: Indiana University Press.

Silas, Ellis. 1926. *A Primitive Arcadia: Being the Impressions of an Artist in Papua*, London: T. Fisher Unwin.

Simmel, G. 1950. *The Sociology of Georg Simmel*, translated and edited by K. Wolff. Glencoe, Ill. and London: The Free Press.

Smith, A. 1776. *An Inquiry into the Nature and Causes of the Wealth of Nations.* London: Dent. Reprinted 1970.

Sraffa, P. 1960. *Production of Commodities by Means of Commodities*, Cambridge: Cambridge University Press.

Stanner, W. 1933. 'Ceremonial Economics of the Mulluk-Mulluk and Madngella Tribes of the Daly River, Northern Australia: a Preliminary Paper', *Oceania*, 4:156–75, 458–71.

Steiner, F. 1954. 'Notes on Comparative Economics', *British Journal of Sociology*, vol. 5: 118–29.

Strathern, A. 1969. 'Finance and Production: Two Strategies in New Guinea Highlands Exchange Systems', *Oceania*, vol. 40, no. 1: 42–67.

1971. *The Rope of Moka: Big Men and Ceremonial Exchange in Mount Hagen*, Cambridge: Cambridge University Press.

1972. *One Father, One Blood: Descent and Group Structure among Melpa People*, Canberra: Australian National University Press.

1975. 'By toil or by guile? The uses of coils and crescents by Tolai and Hagen big-men', *Journal de la société des Océanistes*, vol. 31, no. 49: 363–78.

1979–80. 'The "red box" money cult in Mt. Hagen 1968–71', *Oceania*, vol. 50, no. 2: 88–102, 161–75.

Strathern, M. 1972. *Women in Between: Female Roles in a Male World, Mount Hagen, New Guinea*, London: Seminar Press.

1975. *No Money on our Skins: Hagen Migrants in Port Moresby*, Canberra: Australian National University Press.

Tambiah, S. 1968. 'The Magical Power of Words', *Man*, (n.s.) vol. 3: 175–208.

Terray, E. 1972. *Marxism and 'Primitive' Societies*, translated from the French by Mary Klopper. New York: Monthly Review Press.

Terrell, J. 1976. 'Island biogeography and man in Melanesia', *Archaeology and Physical Anthropology in Oceania*, 11: 1–17.

Thomassin, Fr. 1853. Letter to mission journal written October 12, 1851. *Annals of the Propagation of the Faith*, vol. XIV:292–8. Note: Original letter and journal were in French with different volume and pagination numbers.

Bibliography

Turner, T. n.d. 'Anthropology and the Politics of Indigenous Peoples' Struggles' Unpublished M.S. (To be published in *Cambridge Anthropology*).
Uberoi, J. P. Singh 1962. *Politics of the Kula Ring*. Manchester: Manchester University Press.
Vivian, R. (A.R.M./Misima). 1922. *Patrol Report* 1921–2: 21 June 1922. 1930. *Patrol Report* 1929–30, no. 7: 4 June 1930.
Warnotte, D. 1927. *Les Origines Sociologiques de l'Obligation Contractuelle*. Brussels.
Watson, L. 1956. 'Trobriand Island clans and chiefs', *Man*, 56: 164.
Wawn, W. 1893. *South Sea Islanders and the Queensland Labour Trade, 1875–1891*. London.
Weiner, A. 1976. *Women of Value, Men of Renown: New perspectives in Trobriand Exchange*. Austin: University of Texas Press.
  1977. 'Trobriand descent: female/male domains', *Ethos*, 5: 54–70.
  1978. 'The reproductive model in Trobriand society', *Mankind*, 11(3): 175–86. In special issue of Oceania on *Trade and Exchange in Oceania and Australia* (J. Specht and J. P. White (eds.)).
  1979. 'Trobriand kinship from another view: the reproductive power of women and men', *Man* 14 (1):
  1980a. 'Reproduction: a replacement for reciprocity', *American Ethnologist* 7 (1): 71–85.
  1980b. 'Stability in banana leaves: colonization and women in Kiriwina, Trobriand Islands.' in M. Etienne and E. Leacock (eds.) *Women and History: Studies in the Colonization of Precapitalist Societies*, New York: J. F. Bergin.
  n.d.a. 'Private thoughts and public speech: the ritualization of social interaction.' Paper for 1979 AAA Meetings.
  n.d.b. 'Women, wealth, and political hierarchy: a reproductive view of the sex division of labor'. Paper for 1980 Wenner-Gren Symposium No. 85 on the Sex Division of Labor, Development, and Women's Status.
  1982: 'Plus précieux que l'or: relations et échanges entres hommes dans les sociétés d'Océanie', *Annales*, 1982.
Williams, F. 1931. 'Bwara Awana houses on Normanby Island', *Man*, vol. 31: 174–8.
  1936. *Papuans of the Trans-Fly*. Oxford: Clarendon Press.
Young, M. 1971. *Fighting with Food: Leadership, Values and Social Control in a Massim Society*. Cambridge: Cambridge University Press.
  1977. 'Doctor Bromilow and the Bwaidoka wars', *Journal of Pacific History*, vol. 12 (3–5): 130–53.

Index

Index

butterfly: symbolism of caterpillar, chrysalis, and, in start of kula expedition, 268, reversed on arrival, 269

butu (bitu), see fame

buzzard, black-breasted (*Hamirostra melanosterna*): claws of, attached to shell necklaces, 454

bwabwali, mortuary feasts: Duau, 363; Molima, 423, 424

Bwaidoka, coastal canoe-building village, Goodenough, 397
wakaefuefu in, 397–404

Bwanabwana district (Kainawari, Lolomon), islands where Tubetube language is spoken, 347, 371, 372, 373

Bwaiowa, south-east Fergusson I., 2, 18

bwibwi, seeds used to decorate kula valuables (tinkle against each other), 234, 236

Callen, J. S., 45

Callophyllum inophyllum, tree affording good timber for canoes, found only in Paneati, 431, 439

Calvados chain of islands, Louisiade, 347, 445–8
canoes in, now and formerly, 495
languages in, 445–6, 468
raid by Tubetube on (1911), 370
shell necklaces made in, 23, 484–5
trading contacts of, 468, 473, 476

Campbell, S. F., 17, 88, 102, 109, 147, 161, 163, 170, 201–27, 229–48, 273, 303, 306, 393, 512, 517; (1978), 226

cannibalism, former: in Dobu, 187, Fergusson I., 411, 412, Normanby I., 346, Sudest, 496, 497, and Tubetube, 370
Molima children sold for, in famine, 418

canoe-building: ceremonial visiting in connection with, Goodenough, 377, and Molima, 398
fun-and-games aspect of, 204
in Kudayuri myth, 181–2, 184
places specializing in, 71; Brooker (sailau), 439, 451; Gawa, 308, 323, 374; Goodenough (small), 397–8, 400–1; Iwa, 262–3; Kweawata, 323; Paneati, 431, 441, (sailau) 439, 470–2; Siassi traders, 75–6
rewards for: Goodenough, 402; Paneati, 433, 440, 471, 472

Sudest myth about beginning of, 470

timber for: Paneati, 431, 439; light-weight logs for outriggers, Duau, 474

in Trobriards, in two stages, with ceremonies at launching, 188–9

canoe lashings (creepers); as kula gifts, 259, 261
magic in connection with: in canoe building, 190, 192, 194, 200, 398; in Kudayuri myth, 180, 185, 186

canoe magic: as attempt to convey to canoe the attributes of flying witches, 200
in building, 188, 189, 190–1
as dala property, can be used against rivals, 199
for protection at sea, 144–5, 196
relation of, to Kudayuri myth, 191–2

canoes: butterfly symbolism in decoration and sailing of, 268–9
change of type of, Kitava, 257
decoration of, 188
deep-sea (*masawa*), 188
dugouts with single outriggers (Louisiade), 472
flying, Kudayuri myth of, 180–2, 269, 394; interpretation of, 182–7
inheritance of, Molima, 422
as male property, 181, (themselves female) 188, 191; women forbidden to approach a new, 187, 398
new design of, with canvas sail (*sailau*), 439, 443
numbers of, on kula expeditions, 92–3
rental for hiring, Sudest, 488
washing of newly made, 190, 200
women crews for some, Sabarl, 449,450
wrecked, thought to turn man-eaters, 172, 194, 196

Capell, A., 19

capital: people as, in kula, 339–40
'Rossel Island money' seen as, by Armstrong, 504

capitalist commodity exchange, *see* commodity exchange

cargo-cult violence, 451, 467

Carter, F. W., 32

carving: of ebony for export, organized by Europeans, 314, 334
gifts of kula valuables to masters of, 266
in Kulupasa, Kiriwina, 134
schools of, 227

cash: amount earned from Europeans, Kitava, 249

Index

Index

Gregory, C., 103–17

Groves, M., 67

Guasopa village, Woodlark, formerly in kula, 342

Guidieri, R., 306

gulugwal, gulugwalu, kula return gift for vaga: in Gawa, 290, 292, 296, 299, 300; diversion of, to a different pathway, 291, 298, 301
  in Woodlark: contradictory relation between vag and, 315–17, 325, 328, 337; as someone's kitoum, 327

Gumilababa, highest-ranking village in Kuboma district, Kiriwina, 31
  chief of, 134, 135
  in connectivity analysis, 35, 44

guyau, guiau, Panaeati: Big Man with extra food to distribute, active in exchanges, 433, 434; disappearing in modern conditions, 440–1

guyaw, Gawa: kula operator with fame, 283, 287, 288; associated with high-standard shell valuables, 304, and with slow movement of valuables, 299; term also used for high-standard shell valuables, 303

guyaw, Kiriwina: villages and subclans of recognized rank, 30–1, 39

guyaw, Tubetube: hereditary chief, 370–1

gwasi, low-ranking armshells, Gawa, 302, 303

gwegwe (Fergusson I., Molima), portable wealth, *gwegwe matana,* prime valuables, 413
  payments made in, in compensation, 420, at funerals, 420–1, 424, at marriages, 419–20, in reward for major services, 419

Hage, P., 5, 6, 54, 58

Hagen, Mount (Melpa), district in New Guinea Highlands: moka exchange system in, 73, 74–5, 82, 87; entry into, 77–8

Haggett, P., 32

haircutting, ritual, of first-born boy or girl: valuables for, Sudest, 488, 489

hamlet (*kasa*), social unit, Normanby I., owned by matrilineage group, 347

Harding, T., 54, 73, 76

Harris, M., 4, 6

Hart, D., 16, 54, 57, 58, 71, 443

harvest contest, Kiriwina, 396

harvest dancing, Kitava: wearing and display of kula necklaces at, 266

healing magic, 474

health services, 15

Heidegger, M., 279

helmet shells, as pendants on shell necklaces, enhancing their value (Calvados), 24, 451–2, 465

Hemenaba I., Calvados Chain, 448

hero, myths of resentful, Goodenough, 383–93

Herskovitz, M., 41

hiri system of long-distance trade, between Port Moresby and Gulf of Papua, trading Motu pottery for sago, 9, 67

history, in ranking of kula valuables, 241, 244

hoarding, of tambu shell in Tolai exchange system, 75, 82

Holenstein, E., 280

Honoyeta myth, Goodenough, 391–2

hornbill feathers, signifying hostile intent, worn in 'asking for food' ceremonies, Goodenough, 408

hospitality, in food and pigs, in kula partnerships, 289, 297; example of failure in, 289–90

housebuilders, rewards for, 488, 489, 508, 509

housewarming parties (*wali*), with exchanges between unrelated matrilineages, Duau, 349

human sacrifice, required for chiefs' treasure houses, Sabarl and neighbouring islands, 450

hungry period (*hoalu*), before yam harvest, 433
  new crops for, 434, 438
  yams obtained by Calvados from Sudest during, in exchange for sago, 450

immortality, for a man's name, obtained by linking it to a high-ranking kula valuable; souls of such men go to spiritual overworld, 12, 204–5, 272

incest taboos, 174

incest myth, 197

inheritance: of kula valuables, keda, and partners, Duau, 358, 359, 367–8
  'power of place' in, Sabarl (selection against heirs residing off-island), 449
  of status of Big Man, Molima, 424–5
  of various types of property, Molima, 422

interest: principle of, in moka system and lower levels of kula, 113
  taking of, assumed in Armstrong's

558

Index

Index

Index